INTEGRATING CURRICULAR AND CO-CURRICULAR ENDEAVORS TO ENHANCE STUDENT OUTCOMES

INTEGRATING CURRICULAR AND CO-CURRICULAR ENDEAVORS TO ENHANCE STUDENT OUTCOMES

EDITED BY

LAURA A. WANKEL
Northeastern University, Boston, MA, USA

CHARLES WANKEL
St. John's University, New York, NY, USA

IN COLLABORATION WITH

JORDAN LAROSE
QUINCY GREENHECK

United Kingdom – North America – Japan
India – Malaysia – China

Emerald Group Publishing Limited
Howard House, Wagon Lane, Bingley BD16 1WA, UK

First edition 2016

British Library Cataloguing in Publication Data
A catalogue record for this book is available from the British Library

ISBN: 978-1-78635-064-0

ISOQAR certified
Management System,
awarded to Emerald
for adherence to
Environmental
standard
ISO 14001:2004.

Certificate Number 1985
ISO 14001

INVESTOR IN PEOPLE

Contents

PART III: INTEGRATING INTERNATIONAL LEARNING INTO CURRICULA

PART IV: LEARNING FROM PEERS

PART V: LEVERAGING CO-CURRICULAR ENDEAVORS

List of Contributors

Anne Bradley	Bay of Plenty Polytechnic, Tauranga, New Zealand
Michael Cohen	Deakin University, Burwood, Australia
Stephanie L. Colbry	Cabrini College, Radnor, PA, USA
Aram deKoven	University of Wisconsin, Eau Claire, WI, USA
Stan M. Dura	Western Governors University, Eugene, OR, USA
Dawn M. Francis	Cabrini College, Radnor, PA, USA
Cath Fraser	Bay of Plenty Polytechnic, Tauranga, New Zealand
Ryan Fuller	University of Arkansas at Little Rock, Little Rock, AR, USA
Arthur Gibb	U.S. Naval Academy, Annapolis, MD, USA
William F. Heinrich	Michigan State University, East Lansing, MI, USA
Wesley S. Huey	U.S. Naval Academy, Annapolis, MD, USA
Selena Kohel	Cottey College, Nevada, MO, USA
Janet L. Kottke	California State University, San Bernardino, CA, USA
Dandrielle Lewis	University of Wisconsin, Eau Claire, WI, USA
Philippe Mairesse	Université de la Sorbonne, Paris, France
Kristen McIntyre	University of Arkansas at Little Rock, Little Rock, AR, USA
Richard L. Miller	Texas A&M University – Kingsville, Kingsville, TX, USA

Kevin Moore	University of Tampa, Tampa, FL, USA
Kevin M. Mullaney	U.S. Naval Academy, Annapolis, MD, USA
Andrea North-Samardzic	Deakin University, Burwood, Australia
Deborah A. Olson	University of La Verne, La Verne, CA, USA
David Owen	University of Bedfordshire, Luton, United Kingdom
Elly Philpott	University of Bedfordshire, Luton, United Kingdom
Peter Richardson	Bay of Plenty Polytechnic, Tauranga, New Zealand
Jennifer E. Rivera	Michigan State University, East Lansing, MI, USA
Kenneth S. Shultz	California State University, San Bernardino, CA, USA
Gemma Smyth	University of Windsor, Windsor, Canada
Emma Stenström	Stockholm School of Economics, Stockholm, Sweden
Joseph J. Thomas	U.S. Naval Academy, Annapolis, MD, USA
Charles Wankel	St. John's University, New York, NY, USA
Laura A. Wankel	Northeastern University, Boston, MA, USA
Rebecca J. White	University of Tampa, Tampa, FL, USA

About the Authors

Anne Bradley is a Senior Academic Staff Member at Bay of Plenty Polytechnic in the School of Business delivering first and second year papers on the New Zealand Diploma in Business, with a research interest in collaborative and flexible work and learning environments. Anne's career began in the tourism industry which led to her first teaching role 18 years ago and has since been involved in curriculum development, teacher education, and business studies both in New Zealand and the United Kingdom.

Michael Cohen is a Senior Lecturer in Finance at Deakin University where he teaches insurance, risk management, and leadership. He has previously occupied positions at Victoria University and in South Africa and the United Kingdom. His current research interests are in management education, implicit theories of leadership, investment assets of retirees, and risk reduction.

Stephanie L. Colbry is an Assistant Professor of Business Administration and Coordinator of the Master of Science in Leadership program at Cabrini College in Radnor, PA. Her experience spans across several change-based organizations. She has been recognized for working with organizations to help restructure their business processes. She has worked as an implementation consultant and trainer, assisting NGOs and nonprofit organizations. Stephanie's work includes a variety of consulting services such as organization structuring, strategic planning, change management, business process improvement, facilitation, financial management, and coaching. Her focus is on developing collaborative processes which foster transformation. Stephanie's current research emphasis is concerned with collaborative leadership and followership practices within change-based organizations, and also, sustainable leadership transformation in global conflict regions. She has presented at the International Leadership Association (ILA) conferences in Prague, Los Angeles, and Montreal. She has been a co-facilitator for the "Rising Leaders" program for the Greater Philadelphia Chamber of Commerce and has supported other leadership development projects in the Greater Philadelphia and Washington DC areas. Stephanie earned her Ph.D. in Organizational Leadership with a concentration in Nonprofit Management at Eastern University. She received her M.B.A. in Business Administration from Rider University, and B.S.B.A. in Marketing with a minor in Marine Science from Rider University.

Aram deKoven was born and raised in Westchester County, New York. Holding undergraduate degrees in Psychology and Music from the State University of

New York-Oswego, a Master's degree in Human Resources Management from Mercy College in Dobbs Ferry, NY, and a second Master's degree in Education and a doctorate in Curriculum and Instruction from Cornell University, Ithaca, NY. Dr. deKoven began teaching in after-school programs in Upstate New York working with at risk youth. Later he taught at the post-secondary level in Cornell University's teacher education program as a teaching assistant. From there he continued in teacher education at the State University of New York-Cortland as a visiting assistant professor of education. Following four years at Cortland, Dr. deKoven accepted a position at the University of Wisconsin-Eau Claire where he currently teaches educational technology, the history of American Education, and multicultural education to pre-service educators. All of Dr. deKoven's classes incorporate a highly critical lens that force his students to analyze the significant impact of race, class, affectional orientation, gender, and being an English language learner on educational opportunity and access in American schools. Dr. deKoven's research, publications, presentations, and intercultural immersion share this critical perceptive.

Stan M. Dura is an Assessment Program Manager for Western Governors University focusing on competency based assessment and has called the West Coast home for over 11 years. Before joining Western Governors University, Stan held various appointments in higher education, both within and outside the United States, at public and private institutions, teaching and developing curriculum for first year experience courses, academic advising, housing and residence life, and most recently, student affairs assessment and research. Stan is the Outgoing Chair of the Student Affairs Assessment Leaders (SAAL) and is also a member of the College Student Educators International (ACPA), Student Affairs Professional in Higher Education (NASPA), and the American Educational Research Association (AERA). He holds a M.A. in Student Development from Appalachian State University, B.A. in Psychology from Huntingdon College, and is nearing completion of his doctoral studies in Learning and Technology at the University of Nevada Las Vegas. Stan enjoys intellectual ideation, technology, and applying critical lenses and novel perspectives to student learning and organizational systems and process, and he has had the good fortune and honor of presenting at numerous conferences and consulting with various campuses and national organizations regarding student learning and innovations in residential and co-curricular programming and assessment practices.

Dawn M. Francis is an Assistant Professor of Communication at Cabrini College in Radnor, PA. She has over 20 years of experience in both academic and corporate settings. Her teaching and research are focused on communicating for social justice. Dawn currently teaches courses on narrative, nonfiction storytelling for the Common Good through digital technologies and social media. She also leads the College's faculty development committee, working with colleagues to design and deliver programming that helps faculty to integrate innovative pedagogies and social justice education into their curriculum. Dawn continually seeks ways to foster transformative learning experiences among her students and her peers in formal classroom settings and through compelling multimedia stories. In addition to her academic role, Dawn consults with organizations to architect solutions to achieve their business needs. For well over a decade, she has worked as a performance strategist, partnering with senior leaders in Fortune 500 companies to design, develop, and implement large-scale organizational change initiatives. Her clients span the pharmaceutical, telecommunications, IT, and payroll processing industries. Her areas of expertise include performance improvement, learning and development, and marketing communication. She has crafted solutions for domestic and global audiences. Dawn earned her Ed.D. in Higher Education — Academic Leadership from Widener University. She received her M.S. in Journalism from the E. W. Scripps School of Journalism at Ohio University, and a B.A. in English and Communication from Cabrini College.

Cath Fraser currently combines roles as a Research Leader, mentoring colleagues, and developing organizational projects, with independent research and writing contracts for other institutions across the higher education sector. Cath also facilitates academic writing retreats aimed at higher qualification completion or peer-reviewed publications. Current research interests include mentoring, staff development, and writing resources to support early-career teachers. In 2012, Cath was a Senior Visiting Fellow at the University of Windsor, Ontario.

Ryan Fuller (Ph.D., UC Santa Barbara; MBA San Francisco State University) is an Assistant Professor in the Speech Communication Department at the University of Arkansas at Little Rock, and an adjunct faculty at the University of Arkansas for Medical Sciences Fay Boozman College of Public Health. His research has been published in periodicals such as *Negotiation and Conflict Management Research*, *Journalism and Mass Communication Quarterly*, and the *Oxford Handbook of Internet Studies*. He is co-author of *Statistical Methods for Communication Researchers and Professionals* (Kendall Hunt). His research interests include conflict framing, crisis communication, mindfulness, organizational resiliency, and communication research methods. He lives in Little Rock, AR.

Arthur Gibb, CDR, served for 17 years as a naval aviator, including duty as Associate Chair in the Department of Political Science at the Naval Academy, and 15 months on the CNE-C6F staff in Naples, Italy, during which he served as one of the primary planning officers for the inaugural Africa Partnership Station (APS) mission. CDR Gibb completed his Ph.D. at the University of North Carolina — Chapel Hill, and holds a Masters in National Security Studies from Georgetown University. His dissertation focused on the use of the U.S. military and security assistance in post-Cold War foreign policy. CDR Gibb currently serves as the Chair of the Department of Leader Development and Research, actively leading efforts to integrate curricular concepts taught in the core courses with Midshipmen experience in leadership roles.

William F. Heinrich, Ph.D., is the Director of Assessment at the Michigan State University Hub for Innovation in Learning and Technology. He earned his doctorate in Higher, Adult, and Lifelong Education from MSU and works to enhance the value of co-curricular learning across the institution. His research has a dual focus on organizational assessment practice and policy along with undergraduate experiential learning in high-impact environments. Recent work focuses on using multiple perspectives to stretch normative practice in assessment, experiential learning, and critical thinking research.

Wesley S. Huey, CAPT, served for 20 years as a naval aviator, completing his operational career as commanding officer of an FA-18 squadron. He then earned his Ph.D. in Sociology, specializing in Social Psychology, from the University of Maryland College Park. His dissertation was titled *Innovation as Group Process: Hierarchy, Status, and the Dilemma of Participative Leadership*. Soon after reporting to the faculty at the U.S. Naval Academy, CAPT Huey established and became the first Chair of the Department of Leader Development and Research to integrate and expand curricular, cocurricular, and extracurricular leader development efforts for students, faculty, and staff. He was then selected to become Director of the Division of Leadership Education and Development, comprised of 43 military and civilian faculty teaching core and elective courses in military leadership and ethics, military law, sociology, psychology, and philosophy to 4500 Midshipmen.

Selena Kohel received her B.A. in Psychology and Piano Performance from the University of Wisconsin-Madison, her M.A. in Student Personnel Administration in Higher Education from New York University, and her Ph.D. in Interdisciplinary Studies, with concentrations in Counseling Psychology and Social Psychology, from the University of Wisconsin-Madison. She has worked in a variety of roles with an array of students at various institutions. Before falling in love with teaching, Dr. Kohel was employed as a student personnel administrator advising individual students on academic, career, and personal concerns; overseeing the development of student organizations, student leaders, and student staff; and facilitating diversity programming. During and since falling in love with teaching, Dr. Kohel has taught a variety of college-level courses at different institutions. Relevant courses taught at her current institution include: Personality Psychology; Social Psychology; Cross-Cultural Psychology; Race, Class, and Gender; and Counseling Psychology. Dr. Kohel is a strong believer in helping students develop their life skills, especially in regard to communicating, perspective-taking, critical-thinking, and acting in a responsible manner. Dr. Kohel's research interests include: teaching for cultural competence, teaching for participatory democracy, and exploring the role of social categorization in social inequality.

Janet L. Kottke, Ph.D., earned her M.S. and Ph.D. degrees in Industrial-Organizational Psychology from Iowa State University in Ames, Iowa. She is currently Professor of Psychology at California State University, San Bernardino, where she founded the Master's program in Industrial and Organizational Psychology. At various times during the program's evolution, she has served as director, recruitment coordinator, internship director, and outcome assessment coordinator. Dr. Kottke was honored with CSUSB's prestigious Outstanding Professor award in 2009, which recognized her achievements in teaching, scholarship, and service. Her primary scholarly works are in diversity, measurement, and pedagogy. She frequently presents at national conferences on pedagogical issues particularly relevant to practitioner-oriented curricula. She has published more than 45 referred journal articles and book chapters and has made nearly 200 presentations at local, regional, and national conferences. Currently, she is investigating the underlying constructs that define and predict employability. She has consulted with and for public and private organizations on organizational structure, human resource practices, and program evaluation.

Dandrielle Lewis is an Assistant Professor of Mathematics at University of Wisconsin-Eau Claire. She was born and raised in Elizabethtown, North Carolina. She received her Ph.D. in Mathematics from SUNY Binghamton University in 2011, her Master's degree in Mathematics from the University of Iowa, and her Bachelor of Science degree in Mathematics with a minor in Computer Science from Winston Salem State University. Her research lies in the area of Finite Group Theory, and she specializes in characterizations of subgroups of products of groups. She has taught Mathematics for the Educational Opportunity Program at Binghamton University and the Math and Science summer program at UWEC, these programs serving underrepresented groups from the inner cities of New York and Milwaukee, respectively. She is the Project Director for the Sonia Kovalevsky high school and middle school Math day for girls at UWEC, and she is a member of the UW Women and Science Advisory Board. Dr. Lewis is extremely passionate about doing research with undergraduates and creating opportunities for underrepresented groups and women in Science, Technology, Engineering, and Mathematics. She is a mentor for the Association for Women in Mathematics, the Wisconsin Alliance for Minority Participation research program, and many undergraduates across the country. One of her many passions includes grant writing to create and develop sustainable programs to impact academia, society, and communities at large.

Philippe Mairesse is an artist, a consultant and a researcher who works at the intersection between art and organizations. He earned a Ph.D. from the University for Humanistics in Utrecht (Netherlands) jointly with La Sorbonne University in Paris (France). His double thesis in humanization of organizations and in arts investigates the role of art for introducing more democracy into corporate meetings. Convinced that change towards a fairer world needs to make room for creation in everyday activity and work, he develops experimentations and theories on art-based methods for training and teaching managers and students. He is currently serving La Sorbonne University and co-chairs the National Research Project (ANR) 'Abrir: the arts to understand critical mutations in organizations'. He also leads an experimental and innovative art-based teaching project for the accounting Master in University Paris-Dauphine. He is a trainer for managers in the public sector and a consultant for creativity within work. His publications explore how and why art and aesthetics foster deeper reflexivity and sense-making within management practices and learning.

Kristen McIntyre (Ph.D., North Dakota State University) is an Associate Professor in the Department of Speech Communication at the University of Arkansas at Little Rock. She directs both the introductory communication course and the Communication Skill Center, a campus resource devoted to helping students, faculty, and staff develop and refine a variety of communication competencies. Her co-authored publications have appeared in *Communication Quarterly, Communication Teacher, Assessment & Evaluation in Higher Education*, and *Best Practices in Experiential and Service Learning in Communication*. Her research interests include communication education, communication training, service-learning, and communication curriculum assessment. She lives in Little Rock, AR.

Richard L. Miller received his Ph.D. in Social Psychology from Northwestern University in 1975. He has taught at Georgetown University, the University of Cologne, the University of Nebraska at Kearney, and is currently Chair of the Department of Psychology and Sociology at Texas A&M University – Kingsville. He worked for many years as the Director of applied behavioral science research projects for the Human Resources Research Organization (HumRRO) in Heidelberg, Germany, after which he set up a community college program for English speaking residents of Mallorca, Spain. Under his leadership, the UNK Department of Psychology was recognized as the 1999 Outstanding Teaching Department in the University of Nebraska system. At UNK, he served three terms as President of the UNK Chapter of Sigma Xi: The Scientific Research Society, three terms as President of the UNK Faculty Senate, and 15 years as Director of the Institutional Review Board. Rick is a past-President of the Rocky Mountain Psychological Association and serves as the Director of Departmental Consulting Services and e-book editor for the Society for the Teaching of Psychology. He is a Fellow of the American Psychological Association and the Association for Psychological Science. Rick has received several national teaching awards including the Robert Daniel Teaching Excellence Award from Division 2 of the American Psychological Association, and the US Professor of the Year award by CASE and the Carnegie Foundation for the Advancement of Teaching. In 2012, he received the Charles L. Brewer Distinguished Teaching of Psychology Award from the American Psychological Association.

Kevin Moore, Ed.D., is a nationally recognized entrepreneur and performance improvement/instructional design consultant. As an entrepreneur, Kevin has been a founder, owner, and/or executive of nine organizations and has over 30 years of experience designing and modifying instruction for learners. Kevin's experience includes needs assessments that address business needs and training requirements, physical and mental workload assessments, technology analysis, performance management systems design, technical and "soft" skills training design, and summative and formative evaluations of performance improvement programs. In addition, he has experience with the selection of appropriate training strategies and materials to address learner characteristics, course objectives, and sequencing of courses to fit curriculum needs and competency structures. Kevin's specialty is focusing on learner requirements for performance returns in any job-based situation. Recently, Kevin was given an opportunity to join the University of Tampa as the Director of Operations for the Innovation and Entrepreneurship Center. In this role, Kevin will bring his experience, technology, and educational background to help this outstanding team develop the most advanced empirical curriculum in entrepreneurship education.

Kevin M. Mullaney, CDR, served 15 years as a submarine officer before completing his doctorate in Industrial/Organizational Psychology at the University of Illinois Urbana-Champaign. He served for one year leading efforts to integrate and expand curricular, cocurricular, and extracurricular leader development opportunities as the head of the Leader Development and Research Department at the Naval Academy and is currently serving as the Director of Leadership Research, focused on consolidating assessment and research data collected as part of the curriculum and in conjunction with experiential leader development events to support an integrated, individualized leader development continuum for each student.

Andrea North-Samardzic is Lecturer in Organisational Behaviour at Deakin University where she teaches organizational behavior and leadership in postgraduate programs. She has previously occupied academic roles at Monash University, LUISS Guido Carli in Rome, and the University of New South Wales. Her research interests are in implicit theories of leadership, innovative teaching techniques in management and leadership, especially involving digital media, and equality and diversity within organizations.

Deborah A. Olson, Ph.D., earned her M.A. and Ph.D. degrees in Industrial/Organizational (I/O) Psychology from Wayne State University in Detroit, Michigan. She is currently an Associate Professor of Management and Leadership at the University of La Verne (ULV) in La Verne, California. Prior to joining ULV, she was a leadership development management consultant for over 25 years. As a consultant, she was the Vice President of Organizational Effectiveness and Management Development for Hay McBer and she also founded her own consultancy providing services to clients in the areas of executive development, human capital management, training and development processes, and team effectiveness. During her time as a consultant, she worked with over 350 organizations from both public and private sectors across North America. She has presented over 50 papers at regional, national, and international conferences, as well as numerous invited addresses. She has published more than 20 refereed journal articles and book chapters. Her current research focuses on the areas of career development, leadership and team effectiveness, human resource management practices, positive organizational behavior, and the use of talents to optimize the career success. She is also a coauthor of the recently published book *Mid and Later Career Issues: An Integrative Perspective* (2013).

David Owen, Ph.D., is a Senior Lecturer at the University of Bedfordshire Business School, UK, who has over 12 years of previous business experience in the electricity industry sector. He is currently the Course Leader for the MSc in Project Management course at the University of Bedfordshire and is the coordinator of the following postgraduate units: Project Management Tools and Techniques; Client Delivery Project; Project Management Dissertation; Oman M.B.A. Operations and

Project Management. He also is the coordinator of undergraduate units in Project Management and Operations Management, including versions of these units for the Department's Trans National Educational (TNE) partnerships in Hong Kong. David has pioneered the use of Virtual Learning Environment technology to enable group collaboration and assessment and has recently launched an online version of the M.Sc. in Project Management course. He is currently supervising four Ph.Ds. and his current research interests include Project Management: Complexity and Leadership; Effective E-Learning; and Sustainable Energy and Transport.

Elly Philpott is a Senior Research Fellow at the University of Bedfordshire Business School, UK, a Thesis Supervisor and Faculty Member for Laureate Online International, and a private business owner. She currently teaches Masters level students in the following subjects: Strategic Technology Management, Project Management Tools and Techniques, Contract and Procurement Management, the Dissertation; Business Research Methods; and a Client Delivery Project unit. She also teaches Decision Making with Risk and Uncertainty at D.B.A. level. She has supervised three Ph.Ds. to completion and is currently supervising two D.B.As. and seven Ph.Ds. She is a reviewer for a number of journals and has experience teaching and tutoring both European and international students, having held Visiting Lecturer posts in Poland and the Czech Republic. Her current research interests include Virtual Team Communities of Practice (VTCoPs), especially in projects and in online learning; innovation in SMEs; and university — business interaction.

Peter Richardson is Group Leader of the Business Management Team who deliver first and second year papers within the New Zealand Diploma in Business programme and facilitate third and fourth year business degree papers via an articulation agreement with the University of Waikato Management School. He also teaches economics and is a doctoral candidate with research interests in welfare economics and graduate employment outcomes. Peter has also worked in an international education environment in the Middle East and travelled extensively setting up recruitment and study pathways for international students.

Jennifer E. Rivera, Ph.D., is the Director of the Liberty Hyde Bailey Scholars Program, an interdisciplinary minor in Leadership in Integrated Learning. Her scholarship identifies teaching and learning components that impend or foster learning through experience. As a researcher and teacher, Dr. Rivera collaborates in the development, implementation, and evaluation of innovative educational programs that promote self-directed learning. Her publications and presentations highlight professional and personal reflections learned while working with communities to create, lead, and manage student and faculty growth within various educational settings.

Kenneth S. Shultz, Ph.D., earned his M.A. and Ph.D. degrees in Industrial-Organizational Psychology from Wayne State University in Detroit, Michigan. He also completed a National Institute on Aging funded post-doctoral fellowship in Social Gerontology at the Andrus Gerontology Center at the University of Southern California. Dr. Shultz is currently a professor in the Psychology

Department at California State University, San Bernardino (CSUSB), and serves as the Interim Director of their Center on Aging. Prior to joining CSUSB, he worked for four years for the City of Los Angeles as a personnel research analyst, where he conducted applied personnel psychology projects. Dr. Shultz also completed applied internships with United Airlines and UNISYS Corporation. He has presented papers and published articles on a wide variety of pedagogical issues, in addition to his substantive work in the areas of personnel selection, aging workforce issues, and retirement. Dr. Shultz has published four books (one edited) and nine book chapters, most recently coauthoring the book *Mid and Later Career Issues: An Integrative Perspective* (2013). He has also served as guest editor for a special issue of a journal on the Changing Nature of Retirement: An International Perspective for the *International Journal of Manpower* (http://tinyurl.com/6tvry2x).

Gemma Smyth is Associate Dean and Associate Professor at the University of Windsor Faculty of Law. She teaches Clinic Seminar, Dispute Resolution, and Access to Justice, and manages the academic components of the Clinic Law Program. Professor Smyth researches and writes in the areas of clinic law, dispute resolution and legal education. Most recently, she coauthored a book with Professors Sarah Buhler and Sarah Marsden on clinical legal education in Canada. Professor Smyth won teaching awards in 2005, 2009, and 2015. She is also active in the Windsor-Essex community, working with groups fighting for the elimination of poverty and for increased rights for older adults and women experiencing family violence. She is also active with the Association for Canadian Clinical Legal Education, and is Vice-President of the Canadian Association of Law Teachers. Prior to joining the Faculty of Law as a professor, Professor Smyth was Executive Director of University of Windsor Mediation Services and a mediator with an Ontario government ministry.

Emma Stenström, Associate Professor, Ph.D., is Director of the Research Center for Arts, Business & Culture and teaches leadership and organization at Stockholm School of Economics (SSE). Her research concerns mainly aesthetic, creative, contemplative, and innovative aspects of organizational practice and the humanistic side of management. Emma has published numerous scientific articles and book chapters, and her Ph.D. dissertation was even re-published in a popular version as a paperback. She is currently involved in a number of research projects including activity-based working, contemplative practices in leadership development, the cultural capital of airlines, and innovation in large systems. Several of her research projects are done in collaboration with other disciplines, in particular medicine, psychology, and fine arts. Apart from working at SSE, Emma has served as a guest professor at the University College of Arts, Crafts, and Design in Stockholm, and on the Board of Directors of several companies and organizations. With a background in emerging economies, she has also been teaching and conducting research in South Africa, India, Russia, and Serbia. Beside her academic career, Emma has made a career in media. Apart from hosting a TV show and running an award-winning blog, she is a columnist in the daily Swedish business paper *Dagens Industri* and has published more than 300 columns.

Joseph J. Thomas retired as a Lieutenant Colonel in the U.S. Marine Corps in 2004. He was the Director of the John A. Lejeune Leadership Institute at Marine Corps University. He currently serves as the Class of 1961 Chair and Distinguished Professor of Leadership Education (PLE) at the Naval Academy, taking a leading role in expanding leadership education programs, mentoring junior faculty, advising and assisting the Chair of the Leadership, Ethics and Law Department on leadership curriculum matters, teaching undergraduate core and elective courses, assisting with an innovative Master's degree program in leadership for military officers, and conducting research and scholarship in leadership development.

Charles Wankel, Professor of Management at St. John's University, New York, holds a doctorate from New York University. He has authored scores of books including best-selling textbooks, scholarly treatises, and edited volumes on sustainability, cutting-edge technologies and their use and implications for education and managing, poverty alleviation, and social entrepreneurship. His *Encyclopedia of Business in Today's World* received the American Library Association's Outstanding Business Reference Source Award. He has been a visiting professor in Lithuania at the Kaunas University of Technology (Fulbright Fellowship) and the University of Vilnius, (United Nations Development Program and Soros Open Society Foundation funding).

Laura A. Wankel, Ed.D., is the Senior Advisor for Strategic Initiatives at Northeastern University, a unique role designed to focus on student learning in an integrated way, not constrained by the traditional and artificial boundaries between the curriculum and co-curriculum. Previously, she served as the Vice President for Student Affairs at Northeastern University and Seton Hall University. Dr. Wankel has been actively involved in NASPA: Student Affairs Administrators in Higher Education, the premier professional association for the student affairs discipline, serving in numerous regional and national leadership roles including Chair of the Board of Directors. She holds an Ed.D. in higher education administration from Teachers College, Columbia University and has published several books on new technologies of higher education teaching and administration and has served on the editorial boards of the *NASPA Journal* and the *Journal of Student Affairs Research and Practice (JSARP)*. She has also served on the Board of Directors of the Association of Student Affairs at Catholic Colleges and Universities (ASACCU) and has presented on issues in higher education nationally as well as in Lithuania and Japan.

Rebecca J. White, Ph.D., is an entrepreneur and an educator and currently holds the Walter Chair of Entrepreneurship at the University of Tampa (UT). She received an M.B.A. and a Ph.D. from Virginia Tech University and a B.S. from Concord University. Her primary research and teaching interests are in opportunity recognition and entrepreneurship pedagogy. Dr. White has held a number of leadership roles in the United States Association for Small Business and Entrepreneurship (USASBE) serving as President in 2012. In 2015, Dr. White was selected to join the Justin G. Longnecker Fellows, a prestigious group of educators who have significantly impacted the entrepreneurship discipline. She has served as a member of the Executive Council of the Global Consortium of Entrepreneurship Centers for 8 years. Under her leadership, the entrepreneurship program at UT was named the 2014 Model Undergraduate Entrepreneurship program in the country. Dr. White was named the Tampa Bay Business Journal Business Woman of the Year 2010, was a 2006 Athena Award finalist, a 2005 recipient of the Freedoms Foundation Leavey Award for Excellence in Private Enterprise Education, and was an Ernst and Young Entrepreneur of the Year award winner in 2003. Prior to her work at UT, she built a nationally ranked entrepreneurship program at Northern Kentucky University. She was the founding director of the Women's Entrepreneurship Institute, an educational program for female entrepreneurs, offered jointly with the *New York Times*. She grew up in a family business and is the founder of several companies.

PART I
INTRODUCTION

Chapter 1

An Overview of Integrating Curricular and Co-Curricular Endeavors to Enhance Student Outcomes

Laura A. Wankel and Charles Wankel

> All genuine learning comes through experience
> John Dewey

Many of the skills sought by contemporary employers are ones that can be enhanced in students through their involvement in a diversity of activities and experiences. Through meaningful, active cognitive and emotional engagement, the application of knowledge and reflection, these skills can be developed and enriched. This can be a tonic ameliorating the problems emerging from the current situation. As the 21st century unfolds, the landscape of higher education is evolving rapidly and in significant ways. Forces for change are enveloping the postsecondary educational enterprise in unprecedented respects. Increasingly, those critical of the academy have become louder and more impatient, pressing for substantial changes to occur. Issues surrounding affordability, completion, flexibility, globalization, forecasts of a shortage of qualified individuals to meet employment needs, and a perceived skills gap of graduates continue to stimulate calls and responses for change. Additionally, technology and learning science research are creating new means and understanding of the process of learning itself.

The ways in which postsecondary education is delivered and consumed are increasingly more diverse. Some predict the unraveling, unbundling, or even demise of higher education as we know it. They cite the advent of MOOC's, various entrepreneurial initiatives departing from traditional structures and methods (some funded by leading foundations), and the movement to create more competency-based options for students (designed to reduce the amount of time it takes to earn a degree) as evidence of a major shift. Legislators too have been searching for ways to respond to the affordability issues and are seeking ways to develop educational options that will ensure that there are ample numbers of individuals who possess the skills necessary for the jobs of the future. Accrediting bodies and associations have been focusing more on outputs rather than inputs or credit hours and seat time to demonstrate learning (Craig, 2015; Selingo, 2013). Higher education is unquestionably an ecosystem under stress.

Employers in large numbers also are reporting that there is a skills gap between their needs and the competencies that college graduates possess (Manpower Group, 2013). In fact, many of the gaps identified focus on skills and attributes such as critical thinking, communication, problem solving, emotional intelligence, collaboration, creativity, intercultural competence, ethical decision-making and initiative (Hart Research Associates, 2015; Maguire Associates, 2012; Morrison, 2015; National Association of College and Employers, 2015; Savitz-Romer, Rowan-Kenyon, Zhang, & Fancsali, 2014).

As a side product of involvement in any of the wide diversity of activities, concomitant knowledge, and useful experiences, students often obtain the sorts of skills and know-how that contemporary employers are seeking. Such activities can actively engage learners cognitively and emotionally and, coupled with meaningful reflection, these skills can be further bolstered. In this context, it is more and more important for educators to identify approaches that can create and demonstrate meaningful student learning outcomes and to differentiate the value of their offerings in crowded, complex, and competitive environments.

Full consideration for creating deep and rich learning environments has long been a focal point for educators. Philosophers, psychologists, and educators alike have often addressed the need to integrate experience and "doing" into educational environments to increase relevance and produce more meaningful learning. One might argue that failing to do so could potentially lead to what Alfred North Whitehead referred to as "inert knowledge" in his 1929 essay "The Aims of Education." Indeed, experiential education and related active learning approaches have been used for decades with numerous findings of their benefit and impact on learning (Burch et al., 2014). Without doubt, the traditional notion that learning is confined to formal didactic instruction and solely to the acquisition of knowledge is inadequate to meet the needs of the contemporary environment.

New pedagogical paradigms emphasizing learner-centered approaches, along with technological advances enabling enhanced delivery and student engagement options, further catalyze the development of meaningful, active, and experiential learning (C. Wankel & P. Blessinger, 2012a, 2012b, 2012c, 2013; L. Wankel & P. Blessinger, 2012a, 2012b, 2012c). Additionally, we have long recognized that student learning, growth, and development are impacted by factors beyond formal instructional offerings (Astin, 1985, 1993; Kuh, Schuh, Whitt, and Associates, 1991; Pascarella & Terenzini, 1991; Tinto, 1987, 1993). In the current dynamic context, barriers that have typically separated the formal classroom environment from the co-curriculum have become blurred, enabling a focus on relevant learning outcomes designed to help students develop the requisite skills, competencies, attributes, and characteristics necessary to have a smooth transition from college to work and advanced study.

The term "co-curriculum," as we see it, is inclusive of learning that is directly related to a formal course of study or that might exist separate and apart from a formal course of study, as in cooperative education, internships, athletics, clubs, organizations, student employment and service, etc. While some may refer to these activities as extra-curricular, we see them all as part of the co-curriculum. All of these experiences hold the potential to contribute in meaningful and powerful ways to student learning. That is to say that learning happens everywhere and needs to be adequately identified, leveraged, and documented.

Documentation of learning that happens outside of formal instructional offerings is also a domain that is gaining traction. In the United Kingdom, the Higher Education Achievement Report (HEAR) is one such effort intended to capture the full array of students' achievements and learning (Higher Education Academy, 2015) and another initiative recently funded by the Lumina Foundation is focused on developing models of a comprehensive student record (Fain, 2015). These initiatives are all indicators of a rethink regarding the value and importance of co-curricular learning.

Efforts designed to increase the opportunities for students to apply knowledge into real-world settings and practice and navigate actual situations will facilitate integrative learning in powerful ways. Additionally, enabling students to develop proficiencies through experience and providing them with meaningful opportunities for reflection will enrich their learning and contribute significantly to developing their ability to articulate that learning. In this way, the value of the learning and related skills and competencies can be more clearly conveyed to others, whether that be potential or current employers, or in future educational settings. Consequently, this book will include examples of courses leveraging co-curricular opportunities as part of the program of study as well as co-curricular activities that exist as separate endeavors.

After this introductory chapter, Part II of this book, Approaches to Integrating the Curricular, Co-Curricular, and Extra Curricular, begins with Chapter 2, "Use of Practicum Classes to Solidify the Scientist-Practitioner Model in Master's Level Training," by Janet L. Kottke, Deborah A. Olson, and Kenneth S. Shultz. The authors of this chapter offer tangible examples of how to apply classroom concepts to organizational settings via a practicum course. Kottke, Olson, and Shultz take care to differentiate master's from doctoral program work and subsequently describe the curriculum of both an applied Master's in Industrial-Organizational Psychology and a Master's in Business Administration program. These practicum courses, the authors assert, serve as an exemplar of how to apply theory and research to organizational difficulties, providing students with needed experience gained through engagement in applied projects to positively impact both individual and organizational outcomes. The chapter authors moreover conclude that these approaches to designing and implementing practicum courses are applicable to a wide range of disciplines such as counseling psychology, education, and political science. Students representing varying levels of organizational experience, the authors conclude, can all benefit from these course-integrated projects.

In Chapter 3, "Integrating Curricular and Extracurricular programs to Enhance Leader Development at the U.S. Naval Academy," Wesley S. Huey,

Kevin M. Mullaney, Arthur Gibb, and Joseph J. Thomas discuss the United States Naval Academy's organizational and pedagogical endeavors to integrate curricular and extracurricular leader development programs. Recognizing the need to improve the integration process of these curricular and extracurricular programs, the authors also discuss the advantages a Web-based leader development portal poses through its evidence-based analysis, feedback, basic research, and program assessment elements. This chapter offers detailed descriptions of the Naval Academy's current methodology for leader development, expertly establishing the background and context.

Next, Chapter 4 by Philippe Mairesse, "Learning by Art-Making: The Inner-Outer Experience: An Experiment within a Master's Course in Audit, Control, and Accounting," touches on the some of the interesting roles and outcomes noticed when analyzing an experimental art-making workshop integrated into graduate accounting education at the University Paris Dauphine. Supported by an artist-coach and a researcher, students in this experimental workshop were required to produce artwork expressing their personal reflection on technical or theoretical issues they perceive as crucial in accounting. After reviewing the literature on art-based teaching and mapping outcome expectations, the author proposes to distinguish the four types of outcomes: instrumental, developmental, directed, and embedded. Processes mobilized in art-based teaching produce the first set of outcomes, while the second set are linked to the specific form of artwork engaged in by the teaching process. Observing that few theories explore the range of outcomes attributable to the form, the author draws on the experiment, as well as Winnicot's concepts of transition and intermediate objects to define the specific transformative quality of art forms. Simultaneously subjective and objective, internal and external productions, they enable the "inner-outer experience" through which knowing and self-development become possible. By investigating the special area where the delimitations between the self and the world are blurred and changing, the art-maker student adopts a posture of a natural researcher who creates knowledge at the moment he defines his self. The conditions for such an outcome are detailed by the author. This research opens the way for art-based methods focused on the deliverables required from the student, while recognizing that empowering the complexity of expression liberates access to knowing abilities and independent critical learning.

Following next in Chapter 5, "Application of Competency-Based Learning to Entrepreneurship Education: Integrating Curricular and Cocurricular Elements to Enhance Discipline Mastery," Rebecca J. White and Kevin Moore discuss the fast growing entrepreneurship discipline found in colleges and universities as well as the associated shortcomings of its development. In recognizing a widespread lack in integrating curricular and co-curricular elements in higher education entrepreneurship programs, White and Moore create a customized learning model using a five-phase competency development process. This model is designed to engage the learner, educator, and community volunteer in the learning and assessment process at both the individual and program levels.

In Chapter 6, "Bridging the Clinical-Doctrinal Divide: Clinician and Student Views of Teaching and Learning in Clinical Legal Programs," Gemma Smyth undertakes a detailed examination of the educational needs and perceptions of students and clinicians in Canadian legal clinics. In interviewing Ontario-based law students, clinicians, social workers, and community legal workers employed or studying at law school-affiliated legal clinics, Smyth solicited feedback on the diversity of learning experiences, hoping this could inform and shape future creations of clinical teaching and associated learning materials. Findings from these interviews reveal two critical observations: the existing literature and current teaching practices' underutilization of affective teaching, learning, and practice elements; and deep structural divides between doctrinal and clinical approaches to teaching and learning.

In Chapter 7, "Project Management: Practice-Based Learning in a UK University," by Elly Philpott and David Owens, discussions concerning practice-based teaching take center stage. Analyzing an MSc Project Management course unit that has international UK postgraduate students engaging with local communities, Philpott and Owens look at the value gained for participants as expressed in their individual reflective reports. The approximate 50 yearly students who participate in this unit are encouraged and supported in working for clients on three-month projects, such as preparing for local carnival events, with three objectives, and three deliverables (the "3-3-3" model of engagement). The authors describe the value created for external clients and for the university in terms of community feedback and sustainable engagement. By addressing unexpected outcomes, lessons learned, and the practicalities of reconciling practice-based teaching with a positive student experience, Philpott and Owns add to the literature.

The final chapter (Chapter 8) in Part II, "A Credit-Bearing Programmatic Approach to Community-Based Learning at a Metropolitan University: The UALR Speech Communication Department," by Kristen McIntyre and Ryan Fuller, puts our attention on the endeavors of the Department of Speech Communication at the University of Arkansas at Little Rock in fostering students' abilities to examine complex communication issues, problems, and dilemmas in order to make a difference. McIntyre and Fuller position problem-based learning, community-based learning, narrative ethnography, and research projects as an effective and meaningful way to achieve this aim. These activities are also positioned as helpful in assisting the department's ambition to encourage ethical, theory-informed recommendations to do no harm, affect positive change, and promote social justice in student's personal relationships, organizations, and communities. The authors moreover add to the literature by sharing the lessons learned through building a theoretical base for students to avail themselves with, integrating case approaches into the curriculum, and engaging resistance and failure.

In the first chapter (Chapter 9) of Part III, Integrating International Learning into Curricula, "The Somali Immersion Experience: An Intercultural Immersion," Dandrielle Lewis and Aram deKoven engage readers with a University of Wisconsin-Eau Claire (UWEC) program designed to enable their students to gain understanding and skills interacting with racial, ethnic, and cultural diversity; an experience sometimes not easily available in the predominantly white community in which the university is located. The Somali Immersion Experience (SIE) connects participants with Somali students in a collaborative nature, with both groups working together and jointly engaging in various endeavors to learn about Somali culture, traditions, and religion. The SEI spans 24 classroom hours and a week-long out-of-class immersion into the Somali community of Minneapolis/St. Paul, Minnesota. Through addressing, discussing, debating, and assessing sometimes sensitive topics and issues in a safe-space learning environment, participants are encouraged to reflect on their own lives and think outside the box. Recognizing the success and sustainability of the SEI program, the authors discuss the program's goals, practices, theories, strategies, assessment tools, and partnerships. Qualitative evidence in the form of the voices of students is included in this chapter in order to demonstrate some of the life-altering benefits of intercultural immersion programs.

Chapter 10, "Fostering Intercultural Competence through Short-Term Study Abroad," by Selena Kohel, investigates the intercultural learning acquired by Cottey College students enrolled in a brief 10-day study abroad journey to Thailand, a program conceived of by both the author and one of her colleagues. The program they created, Step into the World!: Thailand, focused on the regionally important issue of (un)sustainable tourism and incorporated Thai roles of culture and service. Students were required to complete a pre-course and a post-course survey, fill out an Intercultural Sensitivity Scale questionnaire, maintain a reflective journal, and write a personal impact statement, all of which provided the evidence the author uses to measure the course's impacts on their intercultural sensitivity, multicultural awareness, knowledge, and skills. These findings support the importance inside and outside classroom experiences have in enhancing student outcomes.

Part IV, Learning from Peers, opens with Chapter 11, "From Profit to Passion: What Business Students Learned from Circus Artists" by Emma Stenström, a chapter that explores the colorful context and rich learning that happens when Stockholm School of Economics business students and circus performers collaborate together in a mutual learning environment. The participating business students are all first-year Master's students in Management and the artists are all seasoned professionals, many of them running their own companies. Following the particular higher education course that brought these two communities together for five years running, Stenström utilizes interviews, observations, and reflections from roughly eighty business student participants to explore what they had learned through the collaborative endeavor and how this enabled many of the students to break the mold. Some of the areas of learning bolstered by the course include recognition of the importance of authenticity, presence, passion, and purpose.

Andrea North-Samardzic and Michael Cohen, in Chapter 12, "Peer Mentoring in Higher Education and the Development of Leadership Skills in Mentors," raise the question as to whether the development of leadership capabilities among mentors is attained through peer-mentoring programs in universities. In doing so, they add to the critical attention already expressed in reaction to proclamations from numerous mentoring programs that leadership skills are enhanced in mentors. Drawing on extensive scholarship on implicit leadership theories, North-Samardzic and Cohen argue two points: that mentors need to be leaders in the minds of their mentees to be considered leaders and that a greater focus on what leadership really is and how it can be manifested in the mentoring relationship needs to be in place. In carrying out a case study on a peer-mentoring program at Deakin University in Australia, the authors illustrate how properly developing leadership acumen in mentors can be accomplished.

Chapter 13, "Campus Community Integration on a Mission: Transformative Learning for Social Change," by Dawn M. Francis and Stephanie L. Colbry, explores how integrating students' curricular and cocurricular experiences can aid in Cabrini College's mission statement to provide every student with an "education of the heart." Analyzing the process used to unite a campus community around one shared vision of social change, they explore student's transformative learning experience as they endeavor to lead the change. Being case study driven, the chapter explains how a course instructor facilitated students' action in service of social transformation by using the Social Change Model of Leadership. Students' engagement in critically reflecting on their individual values, developing group values by negotiating differences among their classmates, and demonstrating leadership in alignment with community and societal values is facilitated through the instructor's application of an action research cycle. This process, Colbry and Francis assert, transforms students' understanding of social justice and motivates further actions in support of human rights issues located worldwide.

Chapter 14, "Student Team-Based Semester-Long Applied Research Projects in Local Businesses," by Anne Bradley, Peter Richardson, and Cath Fraser, concludes the penultimate unit by examining the "Applied Management" paper students pursuing a New Zealand Diploma in Business often complete. Over the course of an entire semester, Business and Management students undertaking this elective work collaboratively in groups to design and implement a research inquiry with a host organization. Bradley, Richardson, and Fraser expound upon how this alternative instructional model has been successful in assisting students making the transition to the workplace, touching upon many of the challenges and strategies encountered with such an endeavor. In recognizing how current literature endorses cocurricular learning, teamwork, and research activities, the authors ask why there appears to be very few higher education examples that combine all three pedagogies in an accredited study program.

The final unit, Leveraging Co-Curricular Endeavors, begins with Chapter 15, "Assessing Competencies: Extending the Traditional Co-Curricular Transcript to Include Measures of Students' Skills and Abilities," by Stan M. Dura. Acknowledging the issue of record low American public trust and confidence in higher education and the lack of direct evidence of student learning provided by higher education institutions, the chapter explores and responds to concerns raised by a diverse chorus of constituents and their calls for increased accountability and improved student learning. Dura, in rejecting previous trends of not questioning higher education's efficacy and value, addresses the dearth of current, direct evidence of student learning and discusses the limited value academic and cocurricular transcripts provide to students, educators, and employers. He instead suggests developing an outcomes-based cocurricular transcript as an extension to the traditional cocurricular transcript, the intention being to take advantage of the rich and numerous learning opportunities within the living laboratory of cocurricular experiences where students repeatedly demonstrate and hone their skills and competencies throughout their collegiate experience. In suggesting this change, the chapter takes care to explore some of the challenges associated with adopting an outcomes-based cocurricular transcript. Dura grounds his recommendation by discussing a number of examples and models of what such a program might look like and by providing insights and suggestions as to how it could be thoughtfully and effectively implemented.

Next, in Chapter 16, "Promoting Student Engagement in the Classroom and Beyond," Richard L. Miller deliberates ways in which instructors can promote course engagement through using four recently identified forms: skills engagement, participation engagement, emotional engagement, and performance engagement. Describing research that examined instructional practices and different high-impact, cocurricular activities (service learning, undergraduate research, learning communities, and internships/practica) with regard to how they affect the four forms of student engagement, the chapter positions such factors as classroom structure, individuation, and teacher support in being responsive to student questions, encouraging students to seek assistance, and assigning effective aids to learning as means to foster engagement. Key insights from this research, which indicate that undergraduate research and internships were generally more engaging than service learning or learning communities, are mulled over, with possible reasons for these findings addressed by Miller.

The final chapter of this book, Chapter 17, "Assessing Multiple Dimensions of Significant Learning," by Jennifer E. Rivera and William F. Heinrich, aims to match high-impact experiential learning with equally powerful assessment practices for gauging intended outcomes as well as embedded learning — those outcomes likely present but otherwise not generally assessed. The result gives learners and programmers direct access to a broad array of learning evidence. In observing three learning experiences analyzing individual student artifacts to identify multiple learning outcomes across domains, Rivera and Heinrich identify boundary-crossing skills and learning made visible through a multi-perspective assessment process as important outcomes. Data and feedback acquired through surfacing these embedded learning outcomes can be made available to the benefit of student, program, career, and institutional purposes.

We hope you will find this book to provide an overview of many approaches to bring cocurricular endeavors more deliberately and robustly into the higher educational enterprise. The stark separation of formal courses and the cocurriculum can be moved to education with boundaries that open to better support and leverage germane learning beyond courses. This undertaking will be guided by the purpose of better preparing learners for the real world opportunities they will be presented with after higher education.

References

Astin, A. W. (1985). Involvement: The cornerstone of excellence. *Change, 17*(4), 35–39.

Astin, A. W. (1993). *What matters in college? Four critical years revisited*. San Francisco, CA: Jossey-Bass.

Burch, G. F., Batchelor, J. H., Heller, N. A., Shaw, J., Kendall, J., & Turner, B. (2014). Experiential learning — What do we know? A meta-analysis of 40 years of research. *Developments in business simulation and experiential learning* (Vol. 41). *Orlando, FL: ABSEL Conference*.

Craig, R. (2015). *College disrupted: The great unbundling of higher education*. New York, NY: Palgrave Macmillan.

Fain, P. (2015, July 13). *Beyond the transcript*. Retrieved from https://www.insidehighered.com/news/2015/07/13/project-create-models-broader-form-student-transcript

Hart Research Associates. (2015). *Falling short? College learning and career success*. Washington, DC: Hart Research Associates. Retrieved from https://wwwaacu.org/leap/public-opinion-research/2015-survey-results

Higher Education Academy. (2015). *Higher education achievement report*. York, UK: Higher Education Academy. Retrieved from http://www.hear.ac.uk/about

Kuh, G. D., Schuh, J. H., Whitt, E. J., Andreas, R. E., Lyons, J. W., Strange, C. C., et al. (1991). *Involving colleges: Encouraging student learning and personal development through out-of-class experiences*. San Francisco, CA: Jossey-Bass.

Maguire Associates. (2012). *Survey of employers: The role of higher education in career development: employer perceptions*. Washington, DC: Chronicle of Higher Education. Retrieved from Chronicle.com/items/biz/pdf/Employers%20Survey.pdf

Manpower Group. (2013). *2013 talent shortage survey research results*. Milwaukee, WI: Manpower Group.

Morrison, N. (2015). Higher education is 'failing students and employers'. *Forbes Education*. Retrieved from http://www.forbes.com/sites/nickmorrison/2015/07/09/higher-education-is-failing-students-and-employers. Accessed on July 9.

National Association of College and Employers. (2015). *NACE job outlook 2015, Spring update report*. Bethlehem, PA: National Association of College Employers. Retrieved from http://www.naceweb.org/surveys/job-outlook.aspx

Pascarella, E. T., & Terenzini, P. T. (1991). *How college affects students: Findings and insights from twenty years of research*. San Francisco, CA: Jossey-Bass.

Savitz-Romer, M., Rowan-Kenyon, H., Zhang, X., & Fancsali, C. (2014). *Social-emotional and affective skills landscape analysis: An executive summary*. Columbia, MD: IMPAQ. Retrieved from http://www.impaqint.com/sites/default/files/files/ExecSummary_Noncognitive_Skills_Jan2015_0.pdf

Selingo, J. J. (2013). *College (un)bound: The future of higher education and what it means for students*. Boston, MA: New Harvest.

Tinto, V. (1987). *Leaving college: Rethinking the cause and cures of student attrition*. Chicago, IL: University of Chicago Press.

Tinto, V. (1993). *Leaving college: Rethinking the causes and cures of student attrition* (2nd ed.). Chicago, IL: University of Chicago Press.

Wankel, C., & Blessinger, P. (2012a). *Increasing student engagement and retention using online learning activities*. Bingley, UK: Emerald Group Publishing Limited.

Wankel, C., & Blessinger, P. (2012b). *Increasing student engagement and retention using immersive interfaces: Virtual worlds, gaming, and simulation.* Bingley, UK: Emerald Group Publishing Limited.

Wankel, C., & Blessinger, P. (2012c). *Increasing student engagement and retention using classroom technologies: Classroom response systems and mediated discourse technologies.* Bingley, UK: Emerald Group Publishing Limited.

Wankel, C., & Blessinger, P. (2013). *Increasing student engagement and retention in e-learning environments: Web 2.0 and blended learning technologies.* Bingley, UK: Emerald Group Publishing Limited.

Wankel, L., & Blessinger, P. (2012a). *Increasing student engagement and retention using social technologies.* Bingley, UK: Emerald Group Publishing Limited.

Wankel, L., & Blessinger, P. (2012b). *Increasing student engagement and retention using mobile applications: Smartphones, Skype and texting technologies.* Bingley, UK: Emerald Group Publishing Limited.

Wankel, L., & Blessinger, P. (2012c). *Increasing student engagement and retention using multi-media technologies: Video annotation, multimedia applications, videoconferencing and trans-media storytelling.* Bingley, UK: Emerald Group Publishing Limited.

PART II
APPROACHES TO INTEGRATING THE CURRICULAR, CO-CURRICULAR, AND EXTRA CURRICULAR

Chapter 2

Use of Practicum Classes to Solidify the Scientist-Practitioner Model in Master's Level Training

Janet L. Kottke, Deborah A. Olson and Kenneth S. Shultz

Abstract

Purpose — To demonstrate how applied projects integrated within master's level graduate programs in the organizational sciences provide students with experiences that facilitate the translation of classroom concepts into practices that positively impact individual, organizational, and societal level outcomes.

Methodology/approach — We discuss how the scientist-practitioner model guides our thinking regarding the development of cocurriculum options for master's level students. To give context, we provide thumbnail sketches of two applied programs — a master's of science degree program in industrial-organizational psychology and a master's of business administration (MBA) program — that serve as exemplars for linking practice with science.

Findings — We demonstrated, with specific examples, how practicum courses can bridge curricular and cocurricular offerings in stand-alone master's programs, thus offering a glimpse into the range of activities completed by master's students with little to over 20 years of work experience: job analysis, interview protocol development, program evaluation, talent acquisition, performance management, coaching, as well as training strategy ideation and delivery. We conclude the chapter with final reflections on the use of practicum classes in master's level training.

Originality/value — The practicum courses detailed serve as unique exemplars of how to apply theory and research to organizational problems, thus bridging science and practice in the organizational sciences.

Integrating Curricular and Co-Curricular Endeavors to Enhance Student Outcomes
Copyright © 2016 by Emerald Group Publishing Limited
All rights of reproduction in any form reserved
ISBN: 978-1-78635-064-0

Keywords: Graduate education; industrial-organizational (I-O) psychology; master's of business administration (MBA); practica; scientist-practitioner model

2.1.   Introduction

The ability to apply concepts from the classroom to organizational settings in which most students will eventually find themselves has been a perennial issue since the time of John Dewey (1938). The imperative of bringing theory to practice continues today with the reality of demographic changes in the workplace (Shultz & Olson, 2013), growing use of technology (Cascio, 2014), and the globalization of the workforce (Kraimer, Takeuchi, & Frese, 2014). In this chapter, we demonstrate how applied projects integrated within master's level graduate programs in the organizational sciences provide students with experiences that facilitate the translation of classroom concepts into practices that positively impact individual and organizational outcomes.

We use two specific exemplars to demonstrate the cocurricular design: (1) master's level students who are earning a degree in industrial-organizational (I-O) psychology and (2) students pursuing their master's of business administration (MBA). The master's in I-O psychology program is cohort-based and the majority of the students are early in their careers with relatively little full-time relevant work experience. The MBA students, conversely, are mid-career, with 5–20 years of full time, managerial experience and in a noncohort-based program. The two exemplars presented below show the importance of designing and implementing meaningful practicum courses to ensure that students of all levels of experience are able to meaningfully apply concepts through applied practicum experiences. However, as you will see, the approaches that we present are applicable to a wide variety of applied disciplines (e.g., education, political science, counseling psychology). Further, students who have varying levels of organizational experience — from entry level employees to managers — can benefit from the practical experiences we describe. And finally, thoughtful and purposeful design of practicum experiences can lead to important organizational outcomes.

We first briefly distinguish master's versus doctoral level training, emphasizing the more applied nature of most stand-alone master's programs compared to most doctoral training programs. Next, we outline how the scientist-practitioner (S-P) model structures and supports master's level training in applied areas. We then discuss traditional coursework and demonstrate how practicum courses bridge the gap between these two sets of curricular and cocurricular offerings in most stand-alone master's programs. Finally, we provide specific examples of applied experiences and projects completed by master's students who have a wide range of full time work experience (from little to over 20 years of work experience) and how practicum courses facilitate translation of theory to practice independent of the age or experience level of the students.

2.2. Master's versus Doctoral Level Training

The Society for Industrial and Organizational Psychology [SIOP] (1994) published the *Guidelines for Education and Training at the Master's Level in Industrial and Organizational Psychology* to guide graduate program development. In that document, it states that, "... master's level students will typically be consumers of I-O knowledge, rather than producers of new knowledge. As such, they are engaged in applying this knowledge to issues involving individuals and groups in organizational settings" (pp. 2−3). In addition, the document also notes that, "all master's level I-O practitioners should have knowledge of the various professional norms, standards, and guidelines relevant to the profession" (p. 14). While some of these issues are covered in formal content coursework, a practicum course is an ideal place to have the students' experience how these ideas apply within organizations. Further, master's level preparation in virtually all fields of knowledge focuses on deepening students' understanding of research outcomes within their discipline and the results that have been achieved when applied in organizational contexts. With this understanding, it is imperative that masters' level curricula take the next step to create opportunities for students to have meaningful experiences applying concepts learned in courses to see firsthand the impact they have, rather than simply reading about the summaries that others write about their experiences applying the concepts.

Furthermore, the *Guidelines* also discuss possible curriculum options for exposing future practitioners to the core competencies recommended in the *Guidelines*. These options include formal coursework, independent study, supervised experience (e.g., internships, practica), on-the-job training, and modeling or observation. This recommendation reinforces the significance of designing and facilitating practicum courses to prepare master's level practitioners for their eventual role in organizations.

Similarly, Bennis and O'Toole (2005), discussing the need for more applied experiences in MBA training, note that business programs were originally designed with the focus on the practice of management to expand the number of individuals who hold managerial roles and who could successfully apply key concepts to performance planning, training and motivating people, and nurturing a team and organizational culture that encourages employees to stay for the long term. To that end, professors who teach students in business schools have traditionally had extensive real-world experience in organizations, often as managers themselves before they became university professors. With the continued focus in the tenure review process on the importance of publishing in top tier management journals, Bennis and O'Toole note that it is often the case that tenured faculty have extensive publication records, but may never have worked outside of a university to deepen their understanding of organizational dynamics and the political processes that impact managerial problem solving and decision making with the press to achieve higher levels of performance in their work units. Thus, the focus on designing practicum for students and faculty to apply the concepts they are learning in the classroom to real-world problems is critical. Opportunities to observe the effect of the interventions developed during practicum experiences provide a rich learning opportunity for student development as well as for faculty to continue to bring value to the classroom cases, discussions, and the quality or substance of the assignments given in the courses offered in MBA programs (Bennis & O'Toole, 2005; Hughes, Bence, Grisoni, O'Regan, & Wornham, 2011). In addition, doing so will facilitate the outcome of focusing on the practice of management that is grounded in research and used to address problems and opportunities that managers face every day in their organizations (Bartunek & Rynes, 2014).

Therefore, we assert that practicum courses provide students with learning experiences that address many of the shortcomings noted by Bennis and O'Toole (2005) in some MBA programs. Ultimately, we are arguing that the S-P model be emphasized in applied master's level training, regardless of the discipline. In this chapter, however, we focus on I-O psychology and business masters' curricular and cocurricular program designs and provide specific examples that the authors have successfully implemented as part of their practicum courses.

2.3.   Scientist-Practitioner Model

The S-P model, as used in psychology, dates back to the 1949 Boulder Conference, which focused on clinical and counseling psychology (Zicker, 2012). Using the S-P model, master's level practitioners should be trained in both science and practice, where each perspective informs the other. Students learn about not only scientific methods but also practical applications of theories by translating them into processes and programs that address organizational issues and challenges. In addition, any graduate level program subscribing to the S-P model should provide opportunities not only to conduct research but also engage in applied practice (e.g., via internships, practica, and professor led consulting projects). While the S-P model of graduate level training has been espoused for more than a half century, the debate continues as to whether the S-P model truly exists in the specific courses and experiences given to master's level students as they complete their programs of study (cf. Aguinis & Cascio, 2008; Anderson, Herriot, & Hodgkinson, 2001; Cassidy, 2010; Cober, Silzer, & Erickson, 2009a, 2009b; Deadrick & Gibson, 2009; Hays-Thomas, 2006; Rupp & Beal, 2007). For example, Bennis and O'Toole (2005) argue that the pendulum has swung too far to the scientist side of the equation for MBA training. They note that in the early 20th century, master's level training in business was equated with vocational training, where most instructors were working managers. However, today almost the exact opposite is true; most business school professors are Ph.D. scientists with little or no business training or experience working in an organization outside of academia (Datar, Garvin, & Cullen, 2011). As illustrative of the issue, Bennis and O'Toole quip, "Today it is possible to find tenured professors of management who have never set foot inside a real business, except as customers" (p. 101). As practitioner-minded academics, we must provide students in applied master's programs with an opportunity to meld academic theories with practical application of the concepts to address organizational problems and opportunities (David, David, & David, 2011).

With the focus on ensuring that MBA programs link theory and practice, AACSB (2008) specifically states in its standards that teaching must engage students in the learning process through designing and implementing meaningful experiences as part of the curriculum. This acknowledges the essential nature of organizational challenges, problems, and processes, as multidimensional and complex, thereby needing to be understood through integrating theoretical frameworks with practical decision making (Bennis & O'Toole, 2005). The nature of learning about the complexities of organizational problems supports the importance of well-designed internship and practicum experiences that facilitate student application of concepts to address challenges faced by individuals, teams, and leaders as they seek to achieve specific results or outcomes within organizations. Relevance and application of course concepts are paramount in the learning process and assist our students not only to position themselves to actualize their own career aspirations but also to address important, complex, and difficult organizational problems. Thus, it is expected that the design of curricula will assist students in developing skills and applying concepts to address practical problems and challenges (AACSB, 2008).

As previously noted, we can appreciate the need for both science and practice. Further, we understand why some perceive that there is a divide between the academic and the practice in the organizational sciences. As Zicker (2012) noted, "The tension between the demands of the slow, cautious nature of science and the quick, results-oriented focus of the business community has been another tension that has been present from the start [of industrial psychology]" (p. 50). Thus, while scientifically oriented organizational researchers place emphasis on rigor and skepticism, practitioners typically place an emphasis on speed and conviction in decisions. To be clear, it is not that we would expect all master's level practitioners to be both scientists and practitioners, but rather to have a solid grounding in each area. In the next section of the chapter, we describe how we have bridged science and practice in the design of curricular and cocurricular experiences for our masters' students.

2.4. Traditional Coursework that Supports Applied Experiences

In this section, we provide an overview of the traditional coursework completed as part of a master's curriculum in industrial and organizational (I-O) psychology; we then share several applied projects to elucidate the applications of this coursework. The curriculum described contains the core components as prescribed by SIOP (1994) and is intended to provide students with the knowledge and skills needed to excel in applied settings (Weathington, Bergman, & Bergman, 2014; Zelin et al., 2015).

In the past, traditional coursework was conceptualized as face-to-face interaction in a physical classroom with the instructor lecturing and students taking notes. Now, the delivery of course content and interaction may be done via an online or video format in addition to face-to-face. Regardless of the method of delivery, many other aspects of traditional coursework have remained the same for a generation: a reliance on theory, research, and conceptualization of how theory and research are to be put into practice (Sitzmann, Kraiger, Stewart, & Wisher, 2006).

Even within a practitioner-oriented curriculum such as applied masters' programs, there is usually a heavy dose of theory and cases that demonstrate how those theories were applied, but little emphasis on designing experiences for the students to apply these learnings to address specific organizational problems and directly observe the results of their work.

As scientist-practitioners, we emphasize the science, with the belief that students need a firm foundation in science with the concomitant corollary that those students need as many opportunities as possible to apply the science in organizational settings. Although our master's curriculum is intended to help prepare students for their ultimate practice in organizations, the number of applied assignments will vary from course to course. To demonstrate how to integrate theory and practice, we begin by describing the master's in I-O psychology program as an exemplar of how to synthesize the S-P model. We begin by briefly describing the type of the courses offered and then share specific practicum assignments that demonstrate how students are trained as scientist-practitioners through our program. Our curriculum is consistent with, but tends to exceed, other master's curriculum offering a master's degree in I-O (cf. Tett, Walser, Brown, Simonet, & Tonidandel, 2011).

2.5.   Core Science: Research Methods and Statistics

The master's of science in I-O psychology program is a cohort-based program. As a result, students are required to take, in their first year, two advanced statistics courses and a research methods course. These courses constitute the core of the scientific method to which students are exposed. In the statistics courses, students learn descriptive, inferential, parametric statistics (e.g., ANOVA, regression), and nonparametric statistics (e.g., chi-square), as well as use computer programs (e.g., SPSS) to analyze data. In the research methods course, experimental design, as well as quasi-experimental and field research are discussed as approaches to collecting data to make decisions about hypotheses. These courses provide the basis for scientific action — conducting research, understanding the results, and being prepared to make critical judgments about the value of those findings for practice. Although research is often disparaged by practitioners (cf. Holton, 2004), the skill sets from these courses lay a foundation for effective decision making in applied settings. More specifically, we posit that effective thinking about how to approach a problem will be practical, regardless of the organizational context, whereas techniques learned to solve specific problems may no longer be useful as changes in technology and globalization continue to evolve (Neimeyer, Taylor, Rozensky, & Cox, 2014).

2.6.   Core I-O Content Courses

These courses constitute the traditional core of a program in I-O: job analysis, personnel selection, performance appraisal, organizational development, leadership, and motivation and reward systems. With reference to the "S" of the S-P model, these courses integrate theory and research. As an exemplar of this integration, personnel selection historically has relied on few theories, but has emphasized the vast amount of research that has been conducted over several decades to determine which techniques (e.g., cognitive testing) are most effective in selecting the employees most likely to succeed on the job (Schmitt, 2014). The job interview is among the most heavily researched among the selection techniques (Gatewood, Feild, & Barrick, 2010). As researchers continued to grapple with what features of the selection interview made it useful and valid (Posthuma, Morgeson, & Campion, 2002), it became apparent that the selection interview requires considerable cognitive processing on the part of the interviewer; ultimately this recognition led to revisions in how interview data were and are collected and processed (e.g., Dipboye, 1982; Macan & Dipboye, 1988). Thus, because of a renewed theoretical basis, the *structured* interview, with questions about past experiences in particular, has replaced the unstructured interview in the toolkit of the well-informed practitioner (Motowidlo et al., 1992). By comparison, work motivation, as an area of study within I-O psychology, contains multiple theories from which to draw conclusions about what initiates, directs, and sustains behavior in organizations over time (Latham & Pinder, 2005). The goal of the course is to help students understand the application of these ideas to people at work. Though the particular science-practice mix is likely to be different from course to course within the program, even from instructor to instructor, taken together, these courses are intended to reflect the core processes that are needed to manage human resources in organizations.

2.7. Additional Coursework Needed to Understand Human Resource Practice

In addition to the statistics, research methods, and core I-O courses already mentioned, the curriculum also includes courses in diversity, ethics, and legal issues relevant to master's level practitioners. These courses provide the needed understanding of complexity (i.e., diversity) and constraints (i.e., legal issues) on human resource processes and practices. As examples, within the legal course, students learn about the laws relevant to (mostly) personnel selection (e.g., Civil Rights Act of 1964 as amended in 1991). Though students are not expected to become proficient in the law *per se*, they are expected to comprehend how their practice may be impacted by legal requirements and constraints. Further, often the material in one course builds upon that in another course. For example, as noted earlier, the structured interview has more theoretical and research support than the unstructured interview (Wright, Lichtenfels, & Pursell, 1989); not coincidentally, the structured interview also has more support from case law in that an organization using the structured interview will likely find it more defensible if required to justify to a panel of judges (Gutman, Koppes, & Vodanovich, 2011; Williamson, Campion, Malos, Roehling, & Campion, 1997).

2.8. Examples of Applied Practicum Experiences: Master's in I-O Psychology Practicum: Overview

Though not the culminating experience for the MS I-O psychology program, the practicum course serves as an opportunity for students to integrate course content from the first year classes with the research methods and statistics courses. This course is situated within an intensive two-year master's of industrial and organizational psychology program. The program is cohort-based in which students, who enter in the fall of an academic year, typically progress through the coursework together. Prior to the practicum, students will have experienced several opportunities to apply and practice core concepts within courses. As one notable example, the personnel selection course requires students to undergo a mock structured selection interview for their final examination (Kottke, Valencia, & Shultz, 2013). In addition, as part of the performance assessment course, students will have conducted a performance appraisal coaching session as part of the final exam, as well as having conducted a job analysis as part of a group project. In addition, the students have, as part of their coursework, been required to develop or evaluate the templates for organizational programs (e.g., how to diagnose an organizational problem). In all cases, the background of theory is used to develop the assessments (cf. Linn, Baker, & Dunbar, 1991).

Another key element of the practicum course is the development, by each student, of a personal and professional mission statement (Morrisey, 1992). After the students have constructed their mission statements, they complete several surveys that help them understand their approaches to problems, networking, and teamwork. They will also receive considerable feedback from the instructor and peers about their oral presentation and team skills. As a critical, culminating assignment for the course, students create a developmental plan to help them bring additional focus to their second year in the program (Zimmerman, Bandura, & Martinez-Pons, 1992).

2.9. An Overview of the Approach Taken to Consulting Projects in the Practicum Class

Regardless of the focus of any given project, there are some commonalities in how the project progresses. First of all, the instructor identifies a project that is appropriate for the skill sets of the students (Troper & Lopez, 2009). The instructor communicates with the prospective client and once a clear project opportunity has been identified, the class is introduced to the client. With support and guidance from the instructor, the students form their own consulting organization. Typically, this organization consists of several teams with team leaders; frequently, the instructor serves as the overall project manager although, depending on the skill set of the students, an overall project manager may be selected from among the students. Once the structure is established, there is considerable interchange between the client and the students directly. At the conclusion of the project activities, a written report is presented to the client and usually a presentation. All work is supervised by the instructor of the practicum course.

2.10.   Master's in I-O Psychology Practicum: Specific Projects and their Learning Outcomes

2.10.1.   *A Classic I-O Project: Job Analyses and Interview Construction*

For this project, students conducted job analyses of a staff analyst position for a county government and created interview questions for that position and a statistical method analyst position. Students formed teams to conduct a series of interviews with the supervisor of the position and several job incumbents. Through these interviews, students clarified the accuracy of existing job descriptions, with regard to technical skills, and also identified additional soft skills that would enhance the effectiveness of staff analysts and statistical method analysts. The student teams then prepared interview questions that tapped into the identified interpersonal skills.

2.10.1.1.   How did students apply course concepts?

The most obvious course connection was the development of job descriptions through the use of job analysis, the foundation for nearly all personnel actions (Gael, 1984). Through conducting the interviews to collect job information from employees, students learned how to evaluate information and compare that information with existing job descriptions. By creating interview questions, students needed to think carefully about the features of the interview questions that would best capture the sought-for skills, thus applying the known research in the area (McDaniel, Whetzel, Schmidt, & Maurer, 1994). Students also identified what types of probes would represent the skills sought *and* be legally defensible (Williamson et al., 1997). Finally, students worked with each other and employees in a professional setting, which led to an acknowledgment about the need to be interpersonally appropriate across contexts. Students indicated great satisfaction with the experience, noting the project brought course content "to life" and, furthermore, required considerable effort to provide a quality product to a client.

2.10.2.   *Another Classic I-O Project: Organizational Diagnosis*

For this project, students worked to evaluate a client's request to determine if "boots on the ground" belief systems were consistent with the top management vision of organizational values. The specific company had begun as a family-run business in which everyone knew each other; the central values cherished by the founders were that employees felt cared for and that those employees subsequently performed well at their jobs. The client already had gathered data from a formal poll of employees conducted by an external agency but wanted to have a better understanding of a specific group of employees at one location with whom top management felt somewhat estranged geographically. Thus, teams of students developed interview protocols to gauge the extent to which the desired organizational culture was reflected at this remote site and then interviewed a dozen employees at the site. After the interviews, data were analyzed qualitatively, looking for alignment with the family values espoused by top management. The students compared the data from the quantitative poll of all employees working for the company that was broken out by geographical region, statements from top management, including those from company documents, and the data from the employee interviews. From these rich data sources, students determined that there was considerable evidence that employees, even at the remote location, did feel and exhibit the company spirit and appreciated the support that top management extended to them. Yet, there were opportunities for improvement, which led to recommendations developed by the student teams for top management to revisit their reward and promotion structures.

2.10.2.1. How did students apply course concepts?
The multiple facets of this project led not only to the application of the material from several courses but the integration of the material across those courses. Through the analysis of the quantitative and qualitative data, students applied critical and rational logic to evaluate different sources of information, which also made use of their statistical training and their developing research method skills. With their interviews of employees and managers, students identified issues related to training (Noe, Clarke, & Klein, 2014), leadership quality (DeRue, Nahrgang, Wellman, & Humphrey, 2011; Dulebohn, Bommer, Liden, Brouer, & Ferris, 2012), and reward structures (Lawler, 2000). Through their comparison of the relevant data from the different sources, students learned how organizational structure matched rewards, leadership, and limits on managerial action (cf. Coghlan & Shani, 2013). Students were enthusiastic about their experiences with the client: the work required application of a broad array of course material, giving the students an opportunity to assess and interpret the culture of an organization (Schein, 2010) and the effects of organizational practices on employee experience (Neuman, Edwards, & Raju, 1989).

2.10.3.   I-O Project with Societal Outcomes: Program Evaluation of a Health Education Initiative

For this final example, a client, representing a well-funded quasi-governmental agency charged with providing services to families and their children aged zero to five, wanted to know why the intervention offered by her agency did not seem to have the same impact as the education provided by an adjacent county's agency. Specifically, the key question centered on why, in one county, with a comparable target population, breastfeeding rates were considerably higher. Based on the information available to her, the type of education her agency was providing was identical to that provided by the other agency. The problem then for the students was to identify the source of the difference in breastfeeding rates. Students worked in teams viewing the issue from multiple angles. One team developed a survey targeting expectant mothers, asking about their awareness of breastfeeding and its benefits. Another team contacted hospitals in both regions to locate how well pediatricians and nurses were informing expectant mothers about breastfeeding. Yet another team contacted the educators in both regions to assess the true comparability of the education provided to mothers, both expectant and lactating. All teams used archival data extensively to supplement their own collected data. The project required a significant amount of coordination among the teams to share information as well as integration of the course material previously covered. Ultimately, the student consulting team determined that, though most materials provided to the target populations were nearly identical, the other county agency had a very effective advocate for breastfeeding who was making an outsized impact on the education of mothers. Based on this finding, students made several recommendations to the client, including the suggestion to develop a comparable champion for her agency.

2.10.3.1. How did students apply course concepts?

The nature of the project required the students to integrate concepts from organizational development (Coghlan & Shani, 2013), research methods, and training (Noe et al., 2014). Through the development of a meaningful and useful survey and how best to deliver the survey (e.g., online vs. paper copy), how to structure questions for busy professionals, and how to approach educators, students learned about the value of differential data collection methods (Creswell, 2013). Through the examination of the various data sources, student learned to evaluate, critically, the quality of data. By working with health educators, students assessed the type and quality of the programs provided to the target population. Through consistent interactions with the agency providing the service, students were able to evaluate the structure of the agency and its oversight of the service providers (Royse, Thyer, & Padgett, 2015). Working with the service providers as well as members of the target population, students learned how diversity might affect interpretations of data and subsequent recommendations (Cox, 1994). Thus, students developed cultural sensitivity as a result of the exposure to a broad range of people. With an integrative project, students reported both satisfaction and frustrations with the project. Frustrations derived from the difficulty in gathering data from such a broad spectrum of people (medical professionals, mothers from a myriad of backgrounds, and employees of governmental agencies). Despite the challenges of data collection and bringing together a disparate set of facts, students also expressed great satisfaction as they saw their recommendations being well received by the client as well as the members of the governing board of the agency.

2.10.4. *Summary of MS I-O Practicum*

As can be seen in the thumbnail descriptions of projects in Table 2.1, master's level I-O psychology graduate students gained valuable experiences that cemented course

Table 2.1: Practicum course projects listed with core curricula that form the basis for action in those projects.

Project title	Description of project activities and outcomes	Coursework applied
Development of Interview Questions for the Positions of Staff Analyst II (SA) and Statistical Methods Analyst (SMA)	*Context*: Large county government (employees — 18,000) in southern California, Department of Public Health *Activities*: Job analysis conducted for one position (Staff Analyst II) to update existing job description; students interviewed job incumbents and supervisors to assess the "soft" skills associated with SA and SMA positions *Outcomes*: Structured situational behavioral interview questions for each position and glossary of "soft" skills assessed	• Research methods • Personnel selection • Legal issues in organizations
Core Values, Sense of Family, and Built to Last	*Context*: Small (employees < 200) industrial service company based in Colorado with primary service, maintenance of petroleum pumping (i.e., derricks and associated hardware) *Activities*: Interviewed employees and middle managers, analyzed the resulting qualitative data for alignment with the company's core values, also analyzed survey data for corroboration with interview data *Outcomes*: Made recommendations to change human resource policies to address employee perceptions of inequities in compensation and promotion opportunities	• Research methods and statistics • Training • Leadership • Organizational development • Work motivation and reward systems • Legal issues in organizations
Baby Friendly County Comparisons	*Context*: County arm of state agency charged with providing services to children aged 0–5 and their parents or guardians *Activities*: Conducted analyses of the characteristics of two baby friendly hospitals, breastfeeding duration rates, and availability of supportive services to compare the target county outcomes with those of an adjacent county with putatively better outcomes; surveys, interviews, and archival data were primary data collection sources *Outcomes*: Recommendations for targeted education for service providers and mothers	• Research methods and statistics • Training • Leadership • Organizational development • Diversity

concepts and helped to solidify, adroitly, the connections to be found within the S-P model (cf. Zelin, Lider, Doverspike, Oliver, & Trusty, 2014; Zelin et al., 2015). In addition to the experiences on the practicum projects, students often were offered follow up internships by the sponsors of the projects, another testament to the ability of students to apply course concepts to organizational needs.

2.11.   Master's of Business Administration Practicum: Overview

By definition, MBA program curricula are designed to focus on the application of concepts and practices related to organizational outcomes that facilitate growth and financial success. The primary emphasis in most MBA programs is on strategy, finance, and marketing as the primary vehicles for creating organizational growth, both in terms of organizational size and financial success. Concentrations or elective classes are often offered in human resource management, leadership, and organizational behavior in most MBA programs, but these are not seen as important as strategy, finance, and marketing. More recently, the focus on the importance of people as *capital* in the organization whose impact can be measured has become an important factor for organizational leaders to integrate into their strategic decisions (Wright & McMahan, 2011) Measuring the impact of people on organizational outcomes and understanding how to design processes to optimize the selection, development, and performance of people have been researched for decades by I-O psychologists. It has only been more recently that AACSB (2008) has emphasized the importance of leadership and management in the MBA curriculum as issues related to organizational growth, diversity, globalization, network organizations, and the significance of the "war for talent" on the ability to execute the strategy of the organization.

2.11.1.   *Scientist-Practitioner Model: Integration of Coursework and Organizational Practices Focused on Human Capital Management*

The applied research of organizational psychologists who focus on using positive psychology principles to facilitate individual growth and supporting individuals in designing their jobs to optimize use of their talents to achieve important organizational outcomes has become a key process that managers can use to engage, motivate, and retain employees (Wrzesniewski, Berg, & Dutton, 2010). Similarly, research has been conducted for decades on the performance management process and the importance of giving and receiving feedback, both acknowledgment and suggestions for change, to facilitate the growth of individuals, as well as their ability to achieve organizational results (Stone & Heen, 2014). However, there are many challenges that managers face as they attempt to apply the principles of goal setting and feedback processes in productive ways to facilitate individual or team development and performance, rather than just filling out the form to satisfy "HR requirements" (Pulakos & O'Leary, 2011). Similarly, training and learning have been studied for decades, yet managers face the daily challenge of how to balance the time it takes to provide coaching and feedback to facilitate the development of their employees with the demands on their time to achieve organizational results — and avoid dealing with the defensiveness that often occurs when feedback is given (Argyris, 2004; Stone & Heen, 2014).

The MBA practicum that is described in this section was designed to facilitate the application of human capital management (HCM) theories, concepts, and research into the daily or weekly practices used by managers to achieve specific results of their organizations. The students in this MBA program are seasoned, full-time managers who are in a noncohort-based program. The focus for this practicum was on applying three key human capital concepts: (1) talent acquisition, (2) performance management, and (3) training, development, and learning. Before enrolling in the HCM practicum, MBA students took two courses in HCM to learn the theories and concepts, as well as complete case application assignments as are traditionally used in MBA coursework.

The case methodology is a long-standing approach used to bring theory to practice for MBA students, by providing them with an opportunity to learn from the challenges faced by organizations and their leaders, as well as the approaches used to address those challenges. A key element of the case based learning process is for students to develop recommendations about how to address the issues posed in the case through applying concepts and theories learned through the course readings and lectures. However, for some MBA students, the issues and challenges posed in the assigned cases are far removed from the experiences and challenges they face in their specific organizations and the type of work they are engaged in on a daily basis. As a result, this MBA practicum was designed to bridge that gap between theory and practice.

The MBA practicum unfolded over a 14-week period and was designed to bring the HCM concepts and theories into the daily tasks, meetings, and interactions of MBA students as they addressed their specific challenges and developed their own skills in HCM within the context of their current management position in their own organizational context. To apply these human capital concepts and translate them into specific behaviors, all MBA students hired an intern to work on a specific organizational project as part of the 14-week practicum. In the next section, we describe the specific concepts that the students learned as well as the activities and assignments that students were given to apply in their own organization to achieve specific results working with the interns whom they hired. Table 2.2 provides an overview of the practicum assignments and applications that the MBA students completed over the course of the 14 weeks.

2.11.2.   Talent Acquisition: Course Concepts and Practicum Applications

During the courses that MBA students completed as a prerequisite for the 14-week practicum, students learned about and completed cases focused on the key talent acquisition research and practical challenges that arise in the recruitment and selection processes. In this segment of the course, students focused on the importance of

Table 2.2: MBA practicum applications and assignments.

Processes in the practicum	Actions and student assignments (MBA student working with intern)	Linkage to course concepts and theories
Talent Acquisition	• Develop role description for intern (based on organizational tasks that need to be completed) • Create KSAOs and competencies that are linked to success in the intern role • Develop targeted interview questions and rating guide • Post role descriptions to develop candidate pool • Conduct interviews; rate candidates	• Role descriptions; KSAOs linked to performance outcomes • Attribution errors • Interviewing skills • Person-organization (P-O fit)
Performance Management: goals, feedback, linkage to talents	• Have intern complete talent assessment and craft assignments/tasks to be completed during the internship period to facilitate goal accomplishment • Establish goals and measures (for final intern project as well as weekly milestones) • Complete weekly reflections on tasks that are linked to talents and what needs to be changed for the next week. Tasks adjusted/changed (to the extent possible) each week to draw on intern's strengths and optimize performance • Provide informal feedback weekly; formal feedback at the mid-point of internship to update MBA students' HCM development plans	• Job crafting to link individual talents to job results (StrengthsFinder 2.0) • Goal setting and feedback processes • 2-way feedback between MBA student and intern; continuous communications • Recognition and acknowledgment (focus on strengths; weekly postings of actions taken to acknowledge others every week — minimum of 2)

Table 2.2: (*Continued*)

Processes in the practicum	Actions and student assignments (MBA student working with intern)	Linkage to course concepts and theories
Training, Development, and Learning Plans	• Create targeted training plans for intern linked to project tasks to be completed and building relationships with coworkers in the organization (focused on HCM concepts from coursework and how s/he would integrate behaviors and approaches with intern hired as well as current employees) • Intern works with MBA managers to create plan during the first week of the practicum with the focus on action learning, feedback • Development plans updated every 4 weeks during the practicum • Reflection at the end of the practicum "what did I learn, develop, what do I need to continue to focus on to expand my ability to apply HCM concepts to facilitate the engagement and development of people as we implement our strategy?"	• Linkage of training and development plans to the performance management plans (to impact results, these plans need to reinforce and support each other) • Action learning assignments; regular feedback on learning progress • Plans are written with specific actions embedded in the work that is to be completed during the practicum (some formal training courses may be offered, but the primary focus is on-the-job training with mentoring and coaching to support the learning of the interns)

human capital and how attracting and retaining people who possess the knowledge, skills, abilities, and other factors (KSAOs) that are directly related to the strategic outcomes of the organization will optimize individual performance, as well as organizational results (Wright & McMahan, 2011). Given that the practicum focused on completion of one specific project during the 14-week period, the MBA student (managing the intern) defined the project outcomes and worked with members of his or her team to identify the core KSAOs that would be linked to performance in the intern role to facilitate completion of the assigned project. This information was used to develop the position description that defined the KSAOs that were linked to the tasks and project to be completed during the practicum. In this process, MBA students also worked with their organization's human resources department to finalize the role description and ensure that it conformed with internal standards for the organization as well as legal requirements.

Once role descriptions were finalized and posted for applicants, MBA students studied the research and practices related to key selection processes and issues. Understanding the interviewing process and the impact of attribution errors and perceptual biases that impact candidates' ratings in selection interviews was the main focus. The reason for this is that leaders in organizations worldwide most frequently use employment interviews as a key element in the selection process (Wilk & Cappelli, 2003). Students learned about behavioral and situational interviewing approaches (Huffcutt, Conway, Roth, & Klehe, 2004) and how to use the KSAOs from the position descriptions they developed to create interview rating forms.

Targeted interview questions (behavioral and situational) were then developed that were linked to the KSAOs and follow up probing questions were drafted (Klehe & Latham, 2005). All interviews were conducted by a panel of MBA students taking this course. All MBA students reviewed the KSAOs and interview questions prior to interviewing candidates to ensure that everyone on the panel had the same understanding of the selection criteria and interview process. After the candidate completed the interview, the panel of MBA students met to discuss the data gathered during the interview and reach consensus on the final ratings for each candidate (Camp, Schulz, Vielhaber, & Wagner-Marsh, 2004). All members of the panel took notes to facilitate recall of specific behavioral examples and details that the candidates provided (Middendorf & Macan, 2002). Once the final candidate ratings were completed, the final decision that MBA students focused on was person-organization (P-O) fit. This was particularly salient given the short-term (14-week) internship period.

Using this process resulted in significant learning for the students who had a direct experience observing how their perceptual biases impacted their interpretation of the responses of the candidates. The research on interviewer biases and understanding how ratings of candidates can be inflated or deflated based on those biases was an essential learning outcome for the MBA students (Macan, 2009; Sacco, Scheu, Ryan, & Schmitt, 2003). The discussion of the data gathered from the interview among all MBA students on the panel reinforced the importance of having clear criteria established *before* the interviews are conducted so that the focus is on data related to those criteria rather than other factors which may or may not be related to performance (e.g., firmness of handshake, nonverbal mannerisms that appear to show confidence).

The importance of preparation for the selection process was a key learning outcome of this course. All of the MBA students who hired an intern as part of the practicum course reflected on the importance that the level of preparation for the selection of the interns, and noted that this does *not* consistently occur in their own organizations. Having had the experience of applying research on how to interview and select from a pool of candidates using more rigorous methods, allowed the MBA students to have a direct experience of how to apply the concepts related to research on selection interviewing and incorporate those into the practices that they used to select among a group of candidates.

The ratings from the interviews and the data from the final discussion among the panel were also used to create the training and development plans, as well as the performance management goals for the selected intern. Creating the performance goals and training plans for interns using the data from the selection process was an important element of understanding how HCM processes are interrelated and impact each other. The MBA students used the selection data to develop the onboarding process for the intern selected and to craft the job to optimize the use of the selected candidates KSAOs and talents to facilitate the interns' performance and early success in their role (Wrzesniewski et al., 2010).

2.11.3.   *Performance Management: Course Concepts and Practicum Applications*

Performance management practices have been studied for decades to identify the optimal design, yet the research has not had a consistent impact on the practices used by managers as they set goals and provide feedback (Pulakos & O'Leary, 2011). While there are many tactics that can improve the administration of performance management, the effectiveness of the process in terms of optimizing performance is directly impacted by the relationship and quality of communications between the manager and employee (Daniels, 2000; Granger & Hanover, 2012). Building on this organizational reality in the design of the performance management aspect of the practicum course, we specifically included activities that focused on developing the relationship between the MBA students and the interns each hired at the very beginning of the 14-week practicum. This began in the first meeting that occurred once the job offer was finalized by both parties.

To build the relationship, the initial focus was on understanding the talents of the MBA student and the intern. During the courses that each MBA student took prior to hiring their intern, each MBA student completed the StrengthsFinder Inventory (Rath, 2007) to identify his or her unique combination of talents. Based on the StrengthsFinder data, MBA students individually created a development plan focused on how to apply the human capital concepts using approaches that utilized their top five strengths. As part of the course, MBA students also focused on ways to recraft their current job (Wrzesniewski et al., 2010) so that they used their own talents more consistently as they completed projects and assignments in their organizations. Having completed this work already in support of their own performance management and learning, once the job offer was accepted, the MBA students asked their interns to complete the StrengthsFinder Inventory (Rath, 2007) prior to starting the internship. During the interview process, each intern had already received a detailed overview of the project to be completed by the end of the 14-week period. So to build the relationship and focus on optimizing performance though drawing on the talents of the MBA student and his or her intern, the first formal meeting focused on understanding each other's talents, how those talents impacted their approach to work and completing assignments and projects, and how each preferred to give and receive feedback.

The outcome of this first performance management meeting was that each understood the other's talents, how she or he preferred to give and receive feedback linked to their talents, as well as the MBA student's experience recrafting their own job assignments to optimize the use of strengths. MBA students also shared their development plans with their interns and asked for feedback and suggestions to adjust their own approach, particularly in areas where the MBA student and the intern had very different strengths; for example, an *Ideation* MBA student and an *Analytical* Intern would need to explore their preferred methods of thinking to ensure that they built trust into their relationship. Starting the performance management process by reinforcing the importance of openness and highlighting the fact that both the MBA student and the intern were learning about each other and how to best apply the human capital concepts to optimize performance and the results achieved by the end of the practicum was an important part of the relationship building between the MBA student (manager) and intern. Also, in this first meeting the MBA student and intern discussed how the project might be adjusted to ensure that interns used their strengths, using the StrengthsFinder data, throughout the practicum to achieve the highest level of results possible in the 14-week time frame.

The communications and meetings that occurred during the remainder of the first week focused on drafting lists of tasks that would be accomplished each week to measure progress toward completion of the project by the end of the 14-week practicum. The list of tasks were developed by the interns to ensure that they were linked to their strengths, from the StrengthsFinder data, and the MBA student (manager) reviewed them and offered additional ideas and suggestions. Another key element of the performance management process included having the MBA student (manager) make introductions between the interns and others in the department and organization who would work with and assist the interns in achieving the targeted results by the end of the practicum. Once this performance management groundwork was laid in the first week, formal meetings were then held at the beginning of each week to provide updates on task progress and establish a new, refined list of tasks that would be accomplished for the upcoming week. Informal meetings, communications, and e-mails were exchanged regularly so that there was regular feedback exchanged on progress each week during the practicum.

Because of the importance of giving recognition and acknowledgment on performance as well, both the MBA students and the interns had set the objective of providing a minimum of two formal acknowledgments to others each week to recognize and say "thank you" to those who helped them complete tasks or share information with them each week (Youssef-Morgan & Luthans, 2013). The assignment for all MBA students and interns was also to post summaries of the acknowledgments they gave each week on the shared, Web-based electronic Blackboard for the practicum course so that everyone who was in the practicum was able to read about the tactics that others used to recognize others and incorporate those ideas into their actions during the upcoming week. The process of setting goals on giving recognition and acknowledgment to those whom they were working with also made a strong impact on the culture of the teams that the interns were working within. Specifically, the frequency with which everyone on the team and in the departments were acknowledging others' performance and contributions increased through the actions that the MBA student (manager) and his or her intern were taking on a regular and consistent basis (positive emotional contagion). This acknowledgment was a side benefit of this process on the impact of the interactions among team members overall that was beyond the performance management actions that the interns and the MBA students were working on as part of the practicum.

During the 7th week of the practicum, each intern completed a formal, written feedback summary about his or her MBA student (manager). This summary described how well the manager (MBA student) was managing intern performance and crafting tasks in ways that allowed each to use his or her strengths on a weekly basis. This formal feedback also served as additional input to the MBA students about how effectively they were applying the HCM concepts in the work they were doing with their intern. The data from this formal written feedback was then used by the MBA students to update their performance plans for the practicum course. Once their plans were updated, MBA students shared their new plans with their interns and asked for the intern's feedback and suggestions to continue to apply the knowledge and skills from the concepts into their practices as managers. The actions taken by the MBA students (managers) and their interns through this practicum demonstrate the impact of the processes used when performance management occurs consistently and makes a positive impact on goal accomplishment, rather than becoming a form to be completed at the (arbitrary) end of a performance cycle (Pulakos & O'Leary, 2011).

2.11.4.   *Training, Development, and Learning: Course Concepts and Practicum Applications*

Training and development plans need to be linked directly to performance management goals to ensure that learning new knowledge and skills can be applied in a timely manner to achieve goals and results. If training is given and there is no opportunity to apply it immediately afterward, the information is soon forgotten and performance is not improved (Blume, Ford, Baldwin, & Huang, 2010). To ensure that the link between the performance management and the training plans were clear, during the first week of the practicum, MBA students identified specific training activities that would support the intern's learning. When developing the list of training activities, they identified two types: (1) development activities that would support the intern's ability to complete the tasks and (2) meetings and activities that would help the intern understand the organizational culture and "how we do things here" to ensure that the intern understood how to complete weekly tasks and their project using approaches that would work within the culture.

Receiving coaching about the cultural and political dynamics that exist within an organization and team is an essential part of assisting the interns in their success and helping them build relationships with others who need to be involved in the project (Olson & Jackson, 2009). At the end of the 14-week practicum, the interns consistently identified that understanding the culture and the politics was one of the most important parts of their training and development throughout the practicum. The interns reflected on how they had overestimated the importance of completing the project using their technical skills and analytical abilities and underestimated the importance of working with others to obtain their involvement and gather their ideas as a key part of the success of the project.

Action learning approaches were the primary process used for development throughout the practicum (Peters, 2013). As a process, action learning focuses on assigning a key project and providing feedback, coaching, development, and support to the individual(s) who are working on the project so that learning occurs within the context of completing the project and corresponding assigned tasks. The MBA students learned how to facilitate action learning outcomes through having regular interactions and feedback meetings with their interns. Specifically, learning how to ask questions of their interns and listening to the nature of the questions and requests from the interns helped the MBA students improve their coaching skills. The majority of the MBA students reported that their traditional coaching process was to tell the person who asked for help how to do the task and then have the person apply what they were told and report back on progress. For the MBA students, this coaching and training strategy often resulted in poor results and frustration in the relationship. Over time, lack of trust and avoidance were the result of this "coaching process." With their interns, the MBA students practiced asking questions about what was working and not working as they completed their weekly tasks. Asking questions often spurred the intern to think about new approaches and alternatives. This questioning strategy not only helped the intern identify more options, but it also allowed the MBA student to clearly see what training or development would be more helpful for the next week and then to provide that to the intern so that the information was available to the intern when she or he needed it to move forward on the project.

Far too often, the training process is designed to give people as much information as possible in a formal setting, then allow the person to access the information when it is needed. Unfortunately, people often forget what they learned during the formal training because at the time it was given to them, the information was not meaningful or they could not see how to apply it in their current work assignments. With action learning, information is given and exchanged in the context of the project, so the relevance and importance are clear and apparent. To facilitate the success of the learning process during the practicum, the developmental actions were written down and updated each week. The actions identified were linked to the tasks that needed to be accomplished as well as understanding the culture and the politics involved in completing the practicum project.

2.11.5.   *Summary of MBA Practicum*

At the end of the 14-week practicum, both the MBA students and interns reflected on what actions most contributed to their learning and development. They were also asked to link the actions they identified to their StrengthsFinder data so that they could identify how they had expanded their talents as a result of the practicum experience. Table 2.2 provides a visual summary of the actions that were taken to link theory to practice utilizing the S-P model.

2.12.   Final Reflections on the Use of Practicum Classes in Master's Level Training

In this chapter, we described how master's level education is different from the doctoral level, using master's in I-O psychology and business administration as exemplars. Understandably, the graduates of practitioner-oriented programs will be expected to develop competencies that can easily be applied to the workplace. As was recently noted by Zelin et al. (2015), "the benefit of graduate programs helping students to find practical experiences that they can utilize to start developing consulting skills that are not the traditional focus of graduate school training" (p. 128) is illustrated by the projects outlined in Tables 2.1 and 2.2. Thus, helping students to make the connection between the theories and concepts they are learning in core classes via the types of applied practicum projects described here is essential to the immediate and future success of graduates of these programs.

We also made a case for how traditional coursework lays the foundation for applied experiences. Providing meaningful experiences that facilitate student learning about how to translate theory to practice is vital for preparing master's level practitioners to be successful in their careers, once their degrees are conferred. Our primary goal in the chapter was to describe how practicum courses are especially useful in making the concepts from the traditional coursework meaningful for graduate students. Practica are particularly valued because the students function within an intact course while having professional, supervised guidance to apply course concepts to organizational problems. For programs in I-O psychology and for business administration, we provided many examples of how these important concepts could be practiced by both the novice practitioner (I-O) and the experienced professional (MBA), whether it was serving in a consulting role (I-O) or serving as a manager (MBA).

Throughout the chapter, we have linked theoretical concepts to action. For the MS I-O students, we described how in their practicum courses, they conducted job analyses, constructed interview protocols, assessed organizational culture, and evaluated a health education program. Through these projects, I-O students learned the importance of the foundational coursework of research methods, statistical analyses, personnel selection, organizational development, motivation, and leadership. MBA students, in their practicum, developed interview questions, which were used to select interns who were coached, trained, and evaluated by the MBA students throughout the remainder of the course term. MBA students learned how to link the concepts of talent acquisition, performance management, and training and development to the management of people in organizations. Although our examples are from applications of course material in MS I-O and MBA programs, we suggest the ideas we present can be useful for many professions. Again, we want to draw attention to the fact these practica included students from the beginning professional to the seasoned veteran — these learning opportunities are not unique to the student starting out but can and should be extended to those who are already working.

Finally, these practica provided valuable experiences not only for the individual students but also service for the organizations that were involved. In addition, faculty members who teach in these programs get the chance to develop and enhance their skills and abilities in applying ever evolving concepts and theories in the organizational sciences to real-world issues encountered in organizations, thus providing continuing education for faculty. In the end, our primary goal is to develop students — novice and seasoned — who will be able to make meaningful contributions to the organizations in which they work.

References

AACSB. (2008). *Final report of the AACSB international: Impact of research*. Tampa, FL: AACSB.

Aguinis, H., & Cascio, W. F. (2008). Narrowing the science-practice divide: A call to action. *The Industrial and Organizational Psychologist (TIP)*, *46*(2), 27–34.

Anderson, N., Herriot, P., & Hodgkinson, G. P. (2001). The practitioner-research divide in industrial, work, and organizational (IWO) psychology: Where are we now, and where do we go from here? *Journal of Occupational and Organizational Psychology*, *74*(4), 391–411. doi: 10.1348/096317901167451

Argyris, C. (2004). *Teaching smart people how to learn, Harvard business review on developing leaders*. Boston, MA: Harvard Business School Press.

Bartunek, J. M., & Rynes, S. L. (2014). Academics and practitioners are alike and unlike: The paradoxes of academic–practitioner relationships. *Journal of Management*, *40*(5), 1181–1201. doi: 10.1177/0149206314529160

Bennis, W. G., & O'Toole, J. (2005). How business schools lost their way. *Harvard Business Review*, *83*(5), 96–104.

Blume, B. D., Ford, J. K., Baldwin, T. T., & Huang, J. L. (2010). Transfer of training: A meta-analytic review. *Journal of Management*, *36*(4), 1065–1105. doi: 10.1177/0149206309352880

Camp, R., Schulz, E., Vielhaber, M., & Wagner-Marsh, F. (2004). Human resource professionals' perceptions of team interviews. *Journal of Managerial Psychology*, *19*(5), 490–505. doi: 10.1108/02683940410543588

Cascio, W. F. (2014). Looking back, looking forward: Technology in the workplace. In M. D. Coovert & L. F. Thompson (Eds.), *The psychology of workplace technology* (pp. 307–313). New York, NY: Routledge.

Cassidy, S. E. (2010). TIP-TOPICS for students: The value of applied experience: Bridging the scientist-practitioner gap in graduate school and beyond. *The Industrial and Organizational Psychologist (TIP)*, *48*(2), 120–130.

Cober, R., Silzer, R., & Erickson, A. (2009a). Science-practice gap in industrial-organizational psychology: Part I: Member data and perspective. *The Industrial and Organizational Psychologist (TIP)*, *47*(1), 97–105.

Cober, R., Silzer, R., & Erikson, A. (2009b). Science-practice gap in industrial-organizational psychology: Part II. *The Industrial and Organizational Psychologist (TIP)*, *47*(2), 103–110.

Coghlan, D., & Shani, A. B. (2013). Organizational-development research interventions. In H. S. Leonard, R. Lewis, A. M. Freedman, & J. Passmore (Eds.), *The Wiley-Blackwell handbook of the psychology of leadership, change, and organizational development* (pp. 443–460). Malden, MA: Wiley. doi: 10.1002/9781118326404.ch21

Cox, T. (1994). *Cultural diversity in organizations: Theory, research and practice*. San Francisco, CA: Berrett-Koehler Publishers.

Creswell, J. W. (2013). *Research design: Qualitative, quantitative, and mixed methods approaches*. Thousand Oaks, CA: Sage.

Daniels, A. C. (2000). *Bringing out the best in people: How to apply the astonishing power of positive reinforcement*. New York, NY: McGraw-Hill.

Datar, S. M., Garvin, D. A., & Cullen, P. G. (2011). Rethinking the MBA: Business education at a crossroads. *Journal of Management Development*, *30*(5), 451–462. doi: org/10.1108/02621711111132966

David, F. R., David, M. E., & David, F. R. (2011). What are business schools doing for business today? *Business Horizons*, *54*(1), 51–62. doi: 10.1016/j.bushor.2010.09.001

Deadrick, D. L., & Gibson, P. A. (2009). Revisiting the research-practice gap in HR: A longitudinal analysis. *Human Resource Management Review*, *19*(2), 144–153. doi: 10.1016/j.hrmr.2009.01.003

DeRue, D. S., Nahrgang, J. D., Wellman, N. E. D., & Humphrey, S. E. (2011). Trait and behavioral theories of leadership: An integration and meta-analytic test of their relative validity. *Personnel Psychology*, *64*(1), 7–52.

Dewey, J. (1938). *Education and experience*. New York, NY: Simon & Shuster.

Dipboye, R. L. (1982). Self-fulfilling prophecies in the selection-recruitment interview. *Academy of Management Review*, *7*(4), 579–586. doi: 10.5465/AMR.1982.4285247

Dulebohn, J. H., Bommer, W. H., Liden, R. C., Brouer, R. L., & Ferris, G. R. (2012). A meta-analysis of antecedents and consequences of leader-member exchange integrating the past with an eye toward the future. *Journal of Management*, *38*(6), 1715–1759.

Gael, S. (1984). *Job analysis: A guide to assessing work activities*. San Francisco, CA: Jossey-Bass.

Gatewood, R., Feild, H., & Barrick, M. (2010). *Human resource selection*. Independence, KY: Cengage Learning.

Granger, K., & Hanover, D. (2012). Transformational performance-based leadership: Addressing non-routine adaptive challenges. *Ivey Business Journal*, (January/February). Retrieved from http://iveybusinessjournal.com/publication/transformational-performance-based-leadership-addressing-non-routine-adaptive-challenges/

Gutman, A., Koppes, L. L., & Vodanovich, S. J. (2011). *EEO law and personnel practices* (3rd ed.). New York, NY: Routledge.

Hays-Thomas, R. (2006). Challenging the scientist-practitioner model: Questions about I-O education and training. *The Industrial and Organizational Psychologist (TIP)*, *44*(1), 47–53.

Holton, E. F. (2004). Implementing evidence-based practices: Time for a national movement? *Human Resource Development Review*, *3*(3), 187–188. doi: 10.1177/1534484304269055

Huffcutt, A. I., Conway, J. M., Roth, P. L., & Klehe, U. (2004). The impact of job complexity and study design on situational and behavioral description interview validity. *International Journal of Selection and Assessment*, *12*(3), 262–273. doi: 10.1111/j.0965-5X.2004.280_1.x

Hughes, T., Bence, D., Grisoni, L., O'Regan, N., & Wornham, D. (2011). Scholarship that matters: Academic–practitioner engagement in business and management. *Academy of Management Learning & Education*, *10*(1), 40–57.

Klehe, U., & Latham, G. (2005). The predictive and incremental validity of the situational and patterned behavior description interviews for team playing behavior. *International Journal of Selection and Assessment*, *13*(2), 108–115. doi: 10.1111/j.0965-5X.2005.00305.x

Kottke, J. L., Valencia, L. A., & Shultz, K. S. (2013). Using a simulated selection interview as a final examination in a graduate-level personnel selection class. *Psychology Learning and Teaching*, *12*(3), 290–296. doi: 10.2304/plat.2013.12.3.290

Kraimer, M. L., Takeuchi, R., & Frese, M. (2014). The global context and people at work: Special issue introduction. *Personnel Psychology*, *67*(1), 5–21. doi: 10.1111/peps.12067

Latham, G. P., & Pinder, C. C. (2005). Work motivation theory and research at the dawn of the twenty-first century. *Annual Review of Psychology*, *56*, 485–516. doi: 10.1146/annurev. psych.55.090902.142105

Lawler, E. E. (2000). *Rewarding excellence: Pay strategies for the new economy.* San Francisco, CA: Jossey-Bass.

Linn, R. L., Baker, E. L., & Dunbar, S. B. (1991). Complex, performance-based assessment: Expectations and validation criteria. *Educational Researcher*, *20*(8), 15–21.

Macan, T. H. (2009). The employment interview: A review of current studies and directions for future research. *Human Resource Management Review*, *19*(3), 203–218. doi: 10:1016/ j.hrmr.2009.03.006

Macan, T. H., & Dipboye, R. L. (1988). The effects of interviewers' initial impressions on information gathering. *Organizational Behavior and Human Decision Processes*, *42*(3), 364–387. doi: 10.1016/0749-5978(88)90006-4

McDaniel, M. A., Whetzel, D. L., Schmidt, F. L., & Maurer, S. D. (1994). The validity of employment interviews: A comprehensive review and meta-analysis. *Journal of Applied Psychology*, *79*(4), 599–616.

Middendorf, C. H., & Macan, T. H. (2002). Note-taking in the employment interview: Effects on recall and judgments. *Journal of Applied Psychology*, *87*(2), 293–303. doi: 10.1037/ 002-10.87.2.293

Morrisey, G. L. (1992). Your personal mission statement – A foundation for your future. *Training & Development*, *46*(11), 71–74.

Motowidlo, S. J., Carter, G. W., Dunnette, M. D., Tippins, N., Werner, S., Burnett, J. R., & Vaughan, M. J. (1992). Studies of the structured behavioral interview. *Journal of Applied Psychology*, *77*(5), 571. doi: 10.1037//0021-9010.77.5.571

Neimeyer, G. J., Taylor, J. M., Rozensky, R. H., & Cox, D. R. (2014). The diminishing durability of knowledge in professional psychology: A second look at specializations. *Professional Psychology: Research and Practice*, *45*(2), 92–98.

Neuman, G. A., Edwards, J. E., & Raju, N. S. (1989). Organizational development interventions: A meta-analysis of their effects on satisfaction and other attitudes. *Personnel Psychology*, *42*(3), 461–489.

Noe, R. A., Clarke, A. D., & Klein, H. J. (2014). Learning in the twenty-first-century workplace. *Annual Review of Organizational Psychology and Organizational Behavior*, *1*(1), 245–275.

Olson, D. A., & Jackson, D. (2009). Expanding leadership diversity through formal mentoring programs. *Journal of Leadership Studies*, *3*(1), 47–60. doi: 10.1002/jls.20095

Peters, M. (2013). Accomplish two for one with action learning. *Training and Development*, *67*(2), 52–57.

Posthuma, R. A., Morgeson, F. P., & Campion, M. A. (2002). Beyond employment interview validity: A comprehensive narrative review of recent research and trends over time. *Personnel Psychology*, *55*(1), 1–82.

Pulakos, E. D., & O'Leary, R. S. (2011). Why is performance management broken? *Industrial and Organizational Psychology*, *4*(2), 146–164. doi: 1754-9426/11

Rath, T. (2007). *StrengthsFinder 2.0*. New York, NY: Gallup Press.

Royse, D., Thyer, B., & Padgett, D. (2015). *Program evaluation: An introduction to an evidence-based approach*. Independence, KY: Cengage Learning.

Rupp, D. E., & Beal, D. (2007). Checking in the with scientist-practitioner model: How are we doing? *The Industrial and Organizational Psychologist (TIP)*, *45*(1), 35–40.

Sacco, J. M., Schau, C. R., Ryan, A. M., & Schmitt, M. (2003). An investigation of race and sex similarity effects in interviews: A multilevel approach to relational demography. *Journal of Applied Psychology*, *88*(5), 852–865. doi: 10.1037/0021-9010.88.5.852

Schein, E. H. (2010). *Organizational culture and leadership*. Hoboken, NJ: Wiley.

Schmitt, N. (2014). Personality and cognitive ability as predictors of effective performance at work. *Annual Review of Organizational Psychology and Organizational Behavior*, *1*(1), 45–65. doi: 10.1146/annurev-orgpsych-031413-091255

Shultz, K. S., & Olson, D. A. (2013). The changing nature of work and retirement. In M. Wang (Ed.), *The Oxford handbook of retirement* (pp. 543–558). New York, NY: Oxford University Press.

Sitzmann, T., Kraiger, K., Stewart, D., & Wisher, R. (2006). The comparative effectiveness of Web-based and classroom instruction: A meta-analysis. *Personnel Psychology*, *59*(3), 623–664. doi: 10.1111/j.1744-6570.2006.00049.x

Society for Industrial and Organizational Psychology, Inc. (1994). *Guidelines for education and training at the master's level in industrial/organizational psychology*. Arlington Heights, IL: Author. Retrieved from http://www.siop.org/guidelines.aspx

Stone, D., & Heen, S. (2014). *Thanks for the feedback: The science and art of receiving feedback well*. New York, NY: Penguin Books.

Tett, R. P., Walser, B., Brown, C., Simonet, D. V., & Tonidandel, S. (2011). SIOP graduate program benchmarking survey: Part 3: Curriculum and competencies. *The Industrial-Organizational Psychologist*, *50*(4), 69–90.

Troper, J., & Lopez, P. D. (2009). Empowering novice consultants: New ideas and structured approaches for consulting projects. *Consulting Psychology Journal: Practice and Research*, *61*(4), 335–352.

Weathington, B. L., Bergman, S. M., & Bergman, J. Z. (2014). Training science–practitioners: Broadening the training of industrial–organizational psychologists. *Industrial and Organizational Psychology*, *7*(1), 35–38.

Wilk, S. L., & Cappelli, P. (2003). Understanding the determinants of employer use of selection methods. *Personnel Psychology*, *56*, 103–124. doi: 10.1111/j.1744-6570.2003.tb00145.x

Williamson, L. G., Campion, J. E., Malos, S. B., Roehling, M. V., & Campion, M. A. (1997). Employment interview on trial: Linking interview structure with litigation outcomes. *Journal of Applied Psychology, 82*(6), 900. doi: 10.1037//0021-9010.82.6.900

Wright, P. M., Lichtenfels, P. A., & Pursell, E. D. (1989). The structured interview: Additional studies and a meta-analysis. *Journal of Occupational Psychology, 62*(3), 191–199. doi: 10.1111/j.2044-8325.1989.tb00491.x

Wright, P. M., & McMahan, G. C. (2011). Exploring human capital: Putting human back into strategic human resource management. *Human Resource Management Journal, 21*, 93–104. doi: 10:111/j.1748-8583.2010.00165.x

Wrzesniewski, A., Berg, J. M., & Dutton, J. E. (2010). Turn the job you have into the job you want. *Harvard Business Review, 88*(6), 114–117.

Youssef-Morgan, C. M., & Luthans, F. (2013). Positive leadership: Meaning and application across cultures. *Organizational Dynamics, 42*, 198–208. doi: 10.1016/j.orgdyn.2013.005

Zelin, A. I., Lider, M., Doverspike, D., Oliver, J., & Trusty, M. (2014). Competencies and experiences critical for entry-level success for industrial–organizational psychologists. *Industrial and Organizational Psychology, 7*(1), 65–71. doi: 10.1111/iops.12108

Zelin, A. I., Oliver, J., Chau, S., Bynum, B., Carter, G., Poteet, M. L., & Doverspike, D. (2015). Identifying the competencies, critical experiences, and career paths of I-O psychologists: Consulting. *The Industrial and Organizational Psychologist, 52*(4), 122–130.

Zicker, M. (2012). A brief history on the tension between the science and applied sides of I-O psychology. *The Industrial and Organizational Psychologist (TIP), 49*(3), 48–51.

Zimmerman, B. J., Bandura, A., & Martinez-Pons, M. (1992). Self-motivation for academic attainment: The role of self-efficacy beliefs and personal goal setting. *American Educational Research Journal, 29*(3), 663–676.

Chapter 3

Integrating Curricular and Extracurricular Programs to Enhance Leader Development at the U.S. Naval Academy

Wesley S. Huey, Kevin M. Mullaney, Arthur Gibb and Joseph J. Thomas

Abstract

Purpose — This chapter examines the integration of curricular and extracurricular approaches to learning.

Methodology/approach — The study is performed through a case study examination of leader development programs at the United States Naval Academy.

Findings — The Naval Academy's organizational and pedagogical approaches are grounded in the science of experiential learning and seek to integrate classroom instruction with the myriad leadership opportunities that are inherent in the design and function of the institution. Highlighting the example of the Class of 1977 Gettysburg Leadership Encounter, we show the impact on leadership development of explicitly linking curricular and extracurricular programs, and describe various tools that have proved effective reinforcing those linkages.

Originality/value — Students involved in this and other experiential programs and activities are better able to transfer the knowledge acquired in the classroom to the practical experience of leading their peers, and they lead with more confidence and better effectiveness. We conclude that this kind of integration has the potential not only to benefit the individuals involved but also to generate data on learning and development which could then be leveraged to enhance leader development through evidence-based analysis, feedback, and basic research.

Keywords: Experiential learning; leader development; leadership; curriculum development; experiential leadership development

Integrating Curricular and Co-Curricular Endeavors to Enhance Student Outcomes
Copyright © 2016 by Emerald Group Publishing Limited
All rights of reproduction in any form reserved
ISBN: 978-1-78635-064-0

3.1. Introduction

The U.S. Naval Academy provides opportunities for experiential leader development (ELD) as an element of student growth. Nearly 100% of Naval Academy graduates are commissioned as active-duty officers in one of the four military services. Central to the Naval Academy's mission is the preparation of graduates in mind and character to serve as ethical leaders over a career of service. The Naval Academy's curricular program in ethical leadership features a series of core academic courses grounded in social and behavioral science. Midshipmen take one leadership core course each of their four years at the Academy: NL 110 Preparing to Lead, NE 203 Ethics and Moral Reasoning for the Naval Leader, NL 310 Leadership Theory and Application, and NL 400 Law for the Junior Officer. These courses are taught by the Leadership Education and Development (LEAD) Division, one of five academic Divisions at the Naval Academy. Outside of class, students are assigned leadership positions within an overarching Brigade command structure and also occupy leadership roles in other extracurricular programs in which they apply leadership principles to learn how to lead effectively in diverse contexts. Three of these leader development experiences are described at length in an article by Huey, Smith, Thomas, and Carlson (2014).

Over the last several years, the Naval Academy has taken purposeful steps to integrate curricular and extracurricular programs to enhance the leader development experience for students, faculty, and staff. During this period, there has been a professionalization of the faculty who deliver the leadership curricular content. A leadership faculty that once consisted almost exclusively of rotational officer instructors on 2–3 year assignments has evolved into a more permanent faculty of Permanent Military Professors (senior Naval officers with relevant PhDs), Junior Permanent Military Professors (mid-grade Naval officers with relevant Master's degrees), and civilian tenure-track faculty in addition to a smaller group of rotational military instructors. LEAD Division leverages a unique collective skill-set that combines extensive military leadership experience with academic credentials to make more direct and purposeful connections between classroom content and leader experience outside the classroom. The leadership faculty engage midshipmen in seminars that prepare them for their extracurricular leadership experiences, facilitate mentor circles to assist students in making meaning of their unfolding experience, and assess relevant outcomes to further optimize the experience for future cohorts.

This chapter highlights the organizational and pedagogical approaches that have facilitated integration of curricular and extracurricular leader development programs at the Naval Academy. The chapter describes in general how this integration is accomplished by linking together Naval Academy curricular and extracurricular programs, and describes in detail an example of this integration — The Gettysburg Leadership Encounter. Finally, the chapter outlines a vision for how the process of integration can be improved through a Web-based data repository — the leader development portal — to enhance leader development by providing the structure and tools for evidence-based analysis, feedback, basic research, and program assessment.

3.2. Experiential Leader Development: Method and Outcome

A primary methodology for leader development at the U.S. Naval Academy is experiential leader development or ELD. Although it is not a new or novel concept, drawing on John Dewey's classic *Experience and Education* first published in the 1930s, ELD as a pedagogical approach within the larger field of leader development and education has been making great strides in the past decade. This general surge in the ELD approach mirrors the institutional experience of the Naval Academy. A more rigorous leader development program began there in the early 2000s with the formal assessment of existing leadership curricula. This assessment focused on the leadership classroom and employed traditional statistical assessment to evaluate curricular effectiveness. By 2008, Naval Academy leadership educators understood that classroom curricula and the traditional means to assess its effectiveness were insufficient to assess the full scope of student development as leaders, prompting leadership faculty to look beyond the classroom for complementary leader experi-ence, and the Naval Academy's foray into ELD began in earnest. For example, faculty in the LEAD Division pursued "skipper" qualification in the Naval Academy's summer sailing program for Midshipmen. Other LEAD faculty volun-teered to become hiking/backpacking instructors for the National Outdoor Leadership School (NOLS) in Lander, WY. Still other faculty volunteered to be more intimately involved with the development of student leadership positions or "stripers" who were tasked with the day-to-day administration of the student body otherwise known as the Brigade of Midshipmen. The common thread to all of these programs was that the learning environments provided immediate consequences to the students' plans, decisions, and actions.

LEAD faculty recognized the value of operationalizing the concepts they were teaching in the classroom and making reference to those concepts as key elements of the ELD experience. This insight spurred deliberate effort to integrate curricular and extracurricular programs, which will be discussed in the next section. In addi-tion, LEAD faculty began to incorporate other ELD activities into the academic year routine, such as Staff Rides, which entail walking tours of battlefields that place students in the footsteps of commanders whose plans, decisions, and actions could only be fully appreciated by seeing what was experienced. For instance, one Staff Ride involves a nearly 100 mile hike to gain an appreciation for the challenges of General Stonewall Jackson's "foot cavalry" during the 1862 Shenandoah Valley Campaign. These experiential opportunities were institutionalized so they persist as permanent features of the overall leader development program, for Midshipmen and faculty.

It can be said that the Naval Academy is merely parroting current trends and that there is little new in its attempt to broaden leader development. Other indivi-duals and institutions have staked their identities on this approach and are doing tremendous work to expand and validate the field (Sweeney, Kruger, Keith, & Judd, 2009). However, few have mastered both parts of this equation — well-developed leadership curricula (classroom) rooted in the social and behavioral sciences and a fully integrated experiential component to complement the classroom in very deliberate ways. Some have a classroom component *par excellence* while having only nominal experiential programs. Others have epic experiential programs unsupported by a rigorous classroom curriculum. The proper balance is difficult to achieve and varies according to institutional objectives. What, then, is the best balance of classroom instruction in leadership and reinforcing experiences? The Naval Academy has taken the following approach to this essential question.

3.3. Determining the Most Appropriate Leadership Curriculum

While there are countless undergraduate and graduate leadership courses and a growing number of major/minor/degree/specialization/certification offerings at both levels, the number of coherent, validated programs is relatively small. Kellerman (2012) claims that leader development is a "growth industry" in higher education, but like other industries in their infancy, lacks coherence. What passes for leadership curricula is often a conglomeration of management, behavioral science, and philosophy courses linked by loosely connected learning outcomes. Assessment of those outcomes is rarely attempted (Kellerman, 2012). Good programs should be able to map institutional learning outcomes to departmental or even course objectives. Instructors can then map those departmental or course objectives to assessment rubrics and even individual exam questions. Great programs should demonstrate the emphasis on specified elements of leader development (e.g., critical thinking, decision making, emotional intelligence, communication skills) across the curricula.

What are the components of a solid leadership curriculum? Based on development of the Naval Academy leadership curriculum over several years, the following basic elements emerge:

- Ethics, character, and moral responsibility.
- Decision theory.
- Effective communication.
- Leadership theory (e.g., trait, style, and situational approach, contingency, path-goal, and leader-member exchange theory and transformational, psychodynamic, and servant leadership approach).
- Fundamentals of applied behavioral and social science (e.g., social psychology, organizational psychology, culture and conflict theory, and cognitive science).
- Fundamentals of applied humanities (e.g., practical, context appropriate historical case studies, logic and applied philosophy).

3.4. Determining Complementary Experiential Programs

ELD is not for everyone. Universities and corporate training offices can offer a stimulating classroom environment to their students while at the same time providing excellent internships, study abroad opportunities, physically demanding practica, and other options that can be rightfully called ELD without explicitly tying the two learning environments together. Yet, by not tying the curriculum and ELD together with unifying language, complementary outcomes, and reinforcing assessment, the consequence can be a program that is sub-optimum. Linking the two elements of leader development is hard, time-consuming work. Above all, it demands close collaboration between faculty and staff across the enterprise.

The process begins with a simple identification of institutional outcomes and a translation of those outcomes into practical learning objectives. Once accomplished, these objectives can be the basis of curriculum development if none currently exists, or curriculum coordination where mature programs are in place. The Naval Academy has found that certain elements of the ELD experience are crucial; these include:

- Immediate feedback on decisions made in the form of consequences for the participant, especially when they come through dealing with adversity, is the most important element of ELD. Consequences can be physical in nature, involve professional reputation or pride, or involve monetary reward.
- "Epic" appeal. Participants should be convinced that the experience is worthwhile, exciting, rewarding, and nontrivial.
- Context-Relevant. The more the event appears to be tailor-made to the organization and individuals involved, the more participant enthusiasm is generated.
- Explicit commitment to the organization as well as personal gain. The experience should evince an organizational investment in the participant.

3.5. The States of Knowing and of Being

The U.S. Military Academy at West Point provides a brilliantly simple framework for conceptualizing leader development programs — Know/Do/Be (Sweeney et al., 2009). Simply put, there are things that must be learned (Know) through traditional classroom and practical applications. Skills and abilities must be exercised (Do) and the associated psychomotor applications assessed. Finally, embodiment of values (Be) and qualities that underpin the definition of leadership are required. It is this last point that is most difficult to define and assess. There are four states of being that characterize classical attributes of well-rounded leaders. Aspirants come into these states through careful and thorough preparation. They are:

- *Competence* can be defined in a number of ways. The prevailing competence model in the public sector defines competence as the set of knowledge, skills, abilities, and attitudes (KSAA) required to perform a given task. Of these four, measuring "knowledge" attainment is the most straight forward. Measuring skills and abilities can be more complex. Measuring attitude is difficult, particularly with self-reporting instruments. Specific assessment instruments and procedures used to measure elements of competence at the Naval Academy are discussed later in Section 3.9.

- *Ataraxia* (Ἀταραξία) is a Greek term typically associated with the Stoic philosophers and is generally interpreted as a state free of worry or preoccupation with that which is unimportant or beyond one's control. For contemporary leaders, achieving *Ataraxia* means being cool under pressure, focused on that which is truly important, and above petty or selfish squabbling. Assessing such an attribute is typically limited to guided observation from an experienced and vetted observer.
- *Virtus* is the Roman conception of character. Originally derived from the ideal "manly" virtues of valor, honor, and moral rectitude, today we interpret it as those qualities of character that determine one's fit for the public role of leadership — or placing the common interest and that of the organization one serves about one's own interest. When *virtus* approaches perfection, one achieves a state of *arete* (ἀρετή) or living up to one's full potential. There are many assessment tools that identify predispositions or qualities of character. Examples include Values in Action (VIA), elements of the Multi-Institutional Study of Leadership (MSL), or InfoMart's Character Assessment (Peterson & Seligman, 2004).
- *Intellectually curious* is the fourth and final state of being that will guarantee growth, adaptability, and continuous improvement. While considered by many to be innate, intellectual curiosity can be enhanced — it is the shared responsibility of the individual and the learning organization. Schools and training organizations can incentivize such curiosity by rewarding accomplishment of educational objectives. Selecting the appropriate incentive can be tricky work. Encouraging intrinsic motivation to learn is obviously the best method but that method is rarely obvious. Perhaps the best encouragement is the design and delivery of engaging material.

There are many other states of being generally considered essential to leadership. However these four collectively represent a quality, when found in an individual, that will transform organizations and individuals making up those organizations. Building programs to foster development in these domains demands resources and is also the product of focused and integrated curricula, complementary experiences, and sound assessment.

The very concept of Know/Do/Be as a developmental construct implies the integration of systems in two domains of learning — in the classroom and in the world of experience. The Naval Academy's approach to this integration is described in the next section.

3.6. Toward a Model of Applied Leadership Education — Driving the Transfer of Leadership Knowledge to Leadership Experience

You can't teach leadership.
Leadership is an art, not a science.
Leaders are born, not made.

Clichés abound in the leader development enterprise, even at national cathedrals of leadership development like the Naval Academy, where not very long ago leadership education as a process was almost entirely divorced from leadership development as an experience. In Annapolis, until the last decade, leadership educators were active-duty Navy and Marine Corps officers "on sabbatical" from operational service in fleet units, on two or three-year assignments to the Naval Academy's Department of Leadership, Ethics, and Law (LEL). These instructors were themselves often skeptical about whether leadership could be learned in a classroom. It is small wonder that their students, who have been called "Midshipmen" since the founding in 1845, aspiring to be operational officers like their leadership teachers, went through the motions of learning leadership in a classroom. They consumed the pseudo-science of leadership from industry press, immersed themselves in "scenario-based training" and case studies from across the "fields of leadership" — military, business, education, sports. Teachers and students alike implicitly accepted that leadership theory drilled and tested in the leadership and ethics classroom transferred wordlessly to the extracurricular leadership roles that are the hallmark of the service academy developmental experience. If leadership could not be learned in a classroom, at least it could be practiced outside the classroom — in the Brigade student hierarchy, on athletic fields, in extracurricular activities — under the watchful tutelage of leadership evaluators, themselves active service Navy and Marine Corps officers on two-year rotation from fleet units. While wearing the same uniform, leadership educators and leadership evaluators were in two separate and distinct orbits, as were the "education" and "development" domains they commanded.

This bifurcated mindset began to change in the mid-2000s, when the Naval Academy introduced professional academics and educators into its leadership faculty, replacing and complementing the professional officer faculty. Some of these educators were also active service or retired officers, having achieved terminal degrees in social or behavioral science disciplines at the end of operational careers. Armed with this dual pedigree as leadership scientists and practitioners, leadership educators understood that teaching and learning leadership and developing leadership must be integrated processes. In 2009, the Division of Leadership Education and Development or LEAD subsumed the Department of LEL, formally integrating the education and development domains in concept, name, and structure, if not yet in practice, and elevating the leadership education enterprise to the same organizational stratum as Engineering, Science, and Humanities.

Finally, in 2011, led by PhD naval officer faculty, the Naval Academy created the Department of Leader Development and Research or LDR, within the Division of Leadership Education and Development, whose explicit mission is to "integrate, expand, and assess the myriad ELD programs offered to Midshipmen across the four-year continuum." Under the auspices of LDR, the Naval Academy undertook to explicitly and purposefully connect its leadership and ethics education with its leader development experience. Leadership educators teamed with leadership evaluators to launch a series of jointly developed extracurricular projects designed explicitly to apply curricular objectives from core leadership and ethics courses to role-specific challenges in developmental experiences for Midshipmen leaders.

The first of these projects involved two of the quintessential summer leadership programs at Annapolis; the Plebe Summer detail, which is the cadre of upper-class midshipmen who train and educate incoming freshmen for six weeks as their "boot camp" crucible experience; and the Offshore Sail Training Program, in which Midshipmen crew 44-foot sailboats during three-week open-ocean voyages on the Eastern Seaboard. While these experiences have long been understood at Annapolis as formative leadership laboratories, only recently has that laboratory been informed by the scientific rigor and method that is the essence of laboratory settings in the physical sciences.

The integration of classroom instruction and experiential activities that enables ELD is rooted in Kolb's (1984) experiential learning cycle, wherein individuals make meaning of an experience through reflection and contextualization, and then experiment with new approaches or techniques to effect different outcomes in future experiences — see Figure 3.1.

Midshipmen encounter numerous experiential learning opportunities during their four years at the Naval Academy, ranging from their daily interaction with peers and officers in a structured, hierarchical environment, to their summer training and development experiences. The latter can include anything from serving with active-duty units in the Navy and Marine Corps to open-ocean sailing in a 44-foot sloop, from studying and traveling in foreign countries to trekking on Alaskan glaciers. Naval Academy leadership has for years touted the Academy as a "leadership laboratory," making the implicit assumption that a Midshipman's leadership is developed and improved through these many experiences. Unfortunately, the link between the classroom leadership curricula and these experiences has often been implicit, rather than explicit, and the belief that Midshipmen develop their leadership and character through these experiences is more of an assumption than

Experiential Learning Process

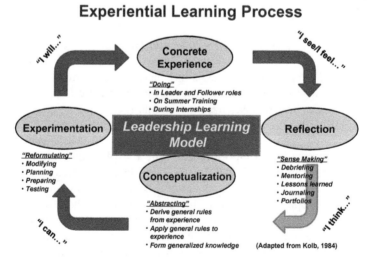

Figure 3.1: Experiential learning process. *Source*: Adapted from Kolb (1984).

a quantifiable outcome. Midshipmen themselves are generally quick to respond that they "learned a lot" from these experiences, but when pressed they often have difficulty identifying just what it was they learned, and, more importantly, how they will apply the leadership lessons from a given experience to their next leadership opportunity or experience.

Adapting Kolb's (1984) experiential learning model, the LDR department set out to design experiential learning environments in which Midshipmen more purposefully connect generalizable knowledge gained in leadership classrooms, with experience gained in leadership roles. These environments were conceived as developmental experiences for Midshipmen in which they could experiment with frameworks and concepts from core leadership classes to make meaning of the experience, that otherwise might escape notice as important for their development as leaders. For example, Transformational Leadership (Bass, 1998) is taught as a leadership style in the core course for third-year students, a style in which leaders seek to inspire and motivate followers by appealing to their emotions, their intellectual curiosity, and their shared values. In a seminar developed jointly by leadership educators and evaluators for the Plebe Detail, "detailers" learn that Transformational styles of leadership are particularly effective during Plebe Summer, when followers are developmentally primed and open to emotional appeals to meaning, purpose, and shared values. Without this deliberate prompting, detailers might likely miss the relevance of Transformational Leadership as a useful framework in the setting of Plebe Summer, or might apply the framework "accidentally" and thereby not fully grasp the lessons derived from the experience. With this prompting, detailers enter the experience of Plebe Summer prepared to experiment explicitly with Transformational styles of leadership, make sense of the response of their followers to their style as affirming or disaffirming of the style or of the way the style was deployed, and adjust in a way that is more fully informed by the theory. In other words, detailers become more theory-driven in their shaping of leadership experience, conceptualizing the experience with intention as Transformational Leadership in practice.

Pushing further to apply scientific method to Naval Academy leadership development programs, LDR launched a study in the summer 2012 of the Offshore Sail Training Program or OSTS, in which a PhD leadership educator and an experienced Naval Academy sail training instructor collaborated to divine through quantitative and qualitative methods — in-depth interviews and surveys of Naval Academy sailing program instructors — the elements of the sail training experience that were most relevant to leadership development. Findings indicated that elements of responsibility, risk and failure, and guided reflection were paramount to teaching leadership in the experience (Chabot, 2013). These elements were then reinforced in program courseware and in instructor training seminars, which themselves were conceived and delivered by leadership educators (LEAD faculty) to leadership evaluators (offshore sailing instructors). See Section 3.10 for more detail on this analysis.

LDR faculty also published a study (Huey et al., 2014) comparing the leader development outcomes achieved by three of the signature developmental programs at the Naval Academy — the two already mentioned, plus a wilderness leadership experience facilitated in the summer by the NOLS. These programs are products of synergy in which professional educators collaborate with practitioners to more deliberately drive the transfer of knowledge gained in the classroom to experience in leadership roles.

3.7. Influencing the Influencer — The Purposeful Development of Leadership Educators at USNA

> To put one's hand in a fire that consumes it is not necessarily to have an experience. The action and its consequence must be joined in perception. This relationship is what gives meaning; to grasp it is the objective of all intelligence. (John Dewey, Art as Experience, p. 44)

Dewey (1938) understood that education is most powerful when the experience of the learner is itself the teacher, rather than the person of the teacher. His de-centering of the teacher as the fount of learning in the educational setting was radical in his time and had enormous implications for the prevailing standard of teacher-centered classroom pedagogy. Yet Dewey emphasized that while the learner's experience in the educational setting was paramount, he was careful to note the importance of the teacher's role as mediator of that experience. The teacher's capacity to expertly shape (or fail to shape) the experience is the difference in the learner's experience being "educative" — invested with "continuity" and "interaction," elements he considered foundational to learning from experience — or *mis*-educative, that is, lacking one or both of these elements.

By "continuity," Dewey means that educative experience must import meaning from past experience, interleave with meaning in the present through perception and reasoning, and result in a transformed perspective for the future, including perhaps even the conditions under which future experiences occur. Taking the obvious example provided in Dewey's quote above, if one has no prior experience — through personal sensation or observation — of being burned by fire, and then fails to connect the burning sensation with the proximate cause in the experience of being burned, then the experience has no educative value. Dewey argues in fact the experience in this case is *mis*-educative, because the opportunity to learn and grow has been forgone despite the potential and many of the ingredients for growth, due to the failure of the learner to join cause with effect through perception and reasoning. The learner is doomed to burn herself again in the future and thus the experience lacks "continuity."

The second element of educative experience is interaction. Dewey's experiential model is inherently social, the product of disciplined exchange between teacher and learner. The value of the exchange is seen as a communal property emerging from shared interest in the intellectual growth and development of the group — through interaction with the course material, with the teacher and with each other, the group sets the conditions of educative experience as a social property of the learning environment. The teacher is but one element of the environment, though vitally important, for it is the teacher's command of the subject matter and skill in facilitating dialogue and interaction among students that sets the conditions for learning in the experience. So that experience in the classroom is educative rather than "mere" experience, the students must be stimulated into taking ownership of the experience — through purposeful and disciplined interaction with the teacher and other students — while yielding to the subject matter expertise and authority of the teacher.

The LDR department has applied Dewey's social principles of educative experience to the important task of developing Naval Academy faculty, staff, and coaches as "key influencers" of Midshipmen. In April 2015, for example, LDR faculty led a group of 45 Naval Academy staff officers and civilians, faculty members, and varsity athletic coaches on a visit to the Lincoln Memorial and Ford's Theater in Washington, DC, commemorating the 150th year since the assassination of President Lincoln. Drawing on ethical leadership principles embodied by Lincoln and enshrined in the leadership curriculum, such as a learning orientation, adaptability, and decisiveness, the experience centered on the interaction between the group and the facilitator, who guided reflection on Lincoln's leadership through historical narrative made more powerful by the rich symbolism of the Memorial and solemn dignity of the theater and boarding house across the street, where President Lincoln died. Lincoln's "adaptive leadership" was offered by the facilitator as the abstraction to be drawn from reflection on the month of April 1865, its relevance as a solution to modern military challenges emphasized to ensure the continuity of the experience for the group. From one History faculty participant, "I feel like this was a day I will not forget, and that I will become a better leader from this experience." A member of the athletic department staff commented "It's energized me to get back to non-fiction reading, particularly on the various aspects of Lincoln's legacy of leadership." At least part of the meaning of the experience for the group was the impact it would have on how they shape the development of Midshipmen as leaders. The fact that the group represented a diverse array of "influencers" from each of the Naval Academy "mission areas" — moral, mental, and physical — was an important element of the experience. Interaction among group members previously unacquainted brought a tapestry of perspective and point of view that enriched the experience for all. And not insignificant was the feeling of collegiality and unity of purpose that emerged from the experience. Other educative experiences for key influencers are now being planned to build on the success of the visit.

3.8. The Gettysburg Leadership Encounter

Perhaps the model of integration of curricular and extracurricular programs at the Naval Academy, this one aimed at Midshipmen development, is the Gettysburg Leadership Encounter. This weekend battlefield visit and seminar series held at Gettysburg College in Pennsylvania is designed to help rising seniors who have been selected for Brigade leadership positions prepare themselves to take on the challenges and responsibilities of command. Equally important is the emphasis on how the upcoming experience in a challenging leadership role will help them learn about the practice of leadership, strengthen their character, and facilitate their development as leaders ready to enter the Navy and Marine Corps.

While the Gettysburg Leadership Encounter itself qualifies as a Kolbian "concrete experience" (see Figure 3.1), it is more accurately a mechanism to facilitate the other phases of the Kolb cycle. Midshipmen are challenged to reflect on their experiences over the preceding three years in an effort to better understand their own emotional response to various leadership styles, ethical dilemmas, and tests of character. Seminars and small-group discussions allow them to both hear the perspectives of more experienced officers and to share their own ideas about what they have learned so far and how they want to apply these lessons to their coming leadership role. Guided tours of the battlefield allow for close examination of the leadership styles, characteristics, and decisions of Civil War leaders, with particular emphasis on how their actions reflected the themes of loyalty, standards, and action which are woven throughout the weekend experience.

The student participants in the Encounter are arguably the most accomplished leaders in the Brigade of Midshipmen. Roughly half are varsity team captains, almost all rising seniors, elected by their peers and approved by their coaches and the administration. The other half are rising seniors who have been selected by the Naval Academy officer leadership to be Company, Battalion, Regimental, and Brigade commanders in the coming fall. This group does not include the many Midshipmen who will hold supporting leadership positions — rather, these are Midshipmen who will wear the mantle of *command*. In addition to being among the most accomplished leaders in the Brigade, they are also in a unique position to learn even more about leadership from the experience of exercising their leadership in a command role. As with the seminars for Plebe Detailers discussed earlier, participants at Gettysburg focus on articulating their leadership vision and goals in a way that will be transformational for them, their teammates, and their company-mates. Collectively, they discuss the standards of behavior and performance each wants to model and instill and mechanisms for effectively holding others accountable to those standards in a challenging peer leadership environment. They leave the weekend with the building blocks necessary to articulate leadership development goals for themselves, performance goals for their respective teams or companies, and a vision statement which will provide the developmental and transformational context in which those goals are to be pursued.

Anecdotally, there are strong indications of the efficacy of the Gettysburg Encounter. Midshipman feedback on the weekend includes comments like "It provided me with a motivation for leading that I have never had before. It completely changed my perspective on what true leadership really means..." and "Gettysburg helped me understand that my standards and actions must align with the mission of the Naval Academy and the intent of the Commandant and Superintendent. The decisions I make will have a direct impact on how my unit carries out the mission." At a meeting with coaches from all varsity teams in the fall of 2014, several coaches with long Naval Academy tenure reported they had seen a noticeable difference in the leadership being demonstrated by their team captains, both on and off the field, since the inception of the Gettysburg Encounter. One example of this is a team captain who developed a leadership experience at a local war memorial for her team, linking lessons from the past to her team's individual and collective leadership development.

To close the Kolb cycle, these Midshipmen return to the Naval Academy in the fall and put their leadership vision into action, intentionally experimenting with the ideas and goals they began to develop at Gettysburg. Not surprisingly, this leads to both successes and failures, and hence another set of experiences which must be reflected upon and contextualized in order to make the most of them. LDR facilitates this meaning-making by holding a series of breakfast meetings throughout the year, bringing Gettysburg Midshipmen together in roundtables to discuss and share their experiences. Leadership educators facilitate the discussions, helping the Midshipmen reflect on the ongoing experience of leadership, in the process extracting lessons from their experience so far, reassessing their approaches, strategies, and tactics, and often setting new goals and designing new "experiments" to try to affect the results they want from their subordinates.

Some of the most powerful effects on leader development stimulated by this process do not emerge until participants have a chance to reflect on their successes and failures. At the end of each sports season and semester, the Midshipmen turning over command of their unit and the team captains finishing their season share their reflections on what they are glad they did, what they wish they had not done, and what they wish they had done. The staff is consistently impressed with the depth of these reflections. After a semester as a Company Commander, one young leader told his peers "I wish I had made more people mad," reflecting the difficulty of holding peers accountable to standards and expectations. One team captain shared his experiences of losing a close game to a rival. He was heart-broken and sat in the locker room with a towel over his head. When he got up to go to the bus, he realized for the first time that his whole team felt the same, but he had missed the opportunity to lead them. He had done nothing to help his team get through a difficult time. Another captain reflected that, because she had learned to take responsibility for her team, she was able to continue to be a leader after she was injured and could no longer compete and be the premiere on-field performer she once was. She found other ways to lead than "by example," because she understood her leadership was about more than just her performance on the field.

In addition to the continuous learning and development that happens as a result of the Gettysburg Encounter and the ensuing breakfast meetings, these leaders build a network of supportive peer leaders that emerges from the "Deweyan" interaction of the Encounter. The peer leadership dynamic at the Naval Academy makes holding others accountable to institutional standards difficult, even for the most confident and mature Midshipmen. Naval Academy leadership faculty know from classroom discussions and individual mentoring that almost all Midshipmen have a well-developed moral compass and generally want to do "the right thing," there is great pressure to conform to a social norm that stigmatizes peers for holding peers accountable to institutional standards, labeling them sell-outs. One result is that those chosen to fill positions of command often find themselves feeling alone in their efforts to drive transformational change. Gettysburg Encounter interaction develops personal ties across the Midshipman leader cohort that reinforces and strengthens the ability and resolve of these leaders to uphold standards and drive change. Company Commanders are now supported in their efforts by Team Captains in their companies, and Commanders within a Battalion can align standards and policies so that these are more likely to be seen and embraced as normative, rather than being dismissed as the illegitimate ideas of a single transitory leader. This has facilitated taking leadership risks, and, in addition to producing positive results with regard to company and team performance, has yielded valuable leadership lessons for the captains and commanders.

3.9.   Improving the Process of Integrating Curricular and Extracurricular Leader Development and Education: The Leader Development Portal

LEAD Division educators are now using scientific methodologies to improve the precision of ELD program development, to enhance midshipman leader development. In order to improve the *process* of, and fully capitalize on the *benefits* of, integrating curricular and extracurricular programs, LEAD Division is developing a mechanism to allow students, staff, and faculty from across the institution to tap into and have access to information that provides the grist for development and growth. This mechanism is envisioned to provide coherence and consistency for individual students across ELD experiences such that leader development experiences build upon one another.

The authors are calling it a web-based Leader Development Portal, the central organizing mechanism for the many curricular and extracurricular leader development efforts at the Naval Academy. The portal will support individualized profiles for each student in order to track their participation and store relevant artifacts from each of their leader development experiences. As an ancillary benefit, the portal will help facilitate basic research in leadership and provide the data required for program assessment.

3.9.1.   Curricular Integration: Leadership Wiki

The portal will also serve as an anchor for course material. With Naval Academy leadership curriculum standardized across four core courses, every student is exposed to the same leadership material. The portal will contain a leadership Wiki that provides details on the leadership concepts discussed in the core curriculum. In other words, the leadership Wiki would function much like Wikipedia as an online source for information on key leadership topics. One advantage of this approach is that students would be incentivized to engage with the portal as a resource for their classes. They would also have easy access to good summaries of key leadership concepts available to them if they wanted to revisit them at a later date. Web linkages built into the material pages would strengthen the conceptual linkages between key ideas that these courses seek to build. For instance, the curriculum includes discussions of leadership topics such as Transformational Leadership, sources of interpersonal power, tactics used in interpersonal influence, and intrinsic motivation theory. Links within the Wiki will strengthen the conceptual links between these concepts, showing how transformational leaders draw on specific sources of power (e.g., referent, expert, and legitimate power) and use specific influence tactics (rational persuasion, consultation, and inspirational appeals) to achieve intrinsic motivation in their followers. Additionally, faculty and staff from across the institution who lead ELD events but do not teach leadership classes (i.e., coaches, summer trainers, Language, Regional Expertise, and Culture (LREC) trip leaders) will have access to a resource that enables them to speak the same leadership language that their students are being taught in class. Program managers for large scale training events, such as Offshore Sail Training Squadron, could quickly put together a syllabus from a menu of Wiki topics as required reading for the staff who will be interacting with the students. Based on all of these potential uses, the leadership wiki will be a powerful tool to consolidate the curriculum and integrate it across extracurricular endeavors.

3.9.2. Curricular Artifacts: The Personal Leadership Portfolio

Every Midshipman takes a core leadership course each year. At several points during this curriculum, students complete assignments that reflect on their leadership experiences or ask them to define their aspirations and goals as leaders. Students are currently directed to store these reflective and aspirational documents in a Google share drive folder labeled as their Personal Leadership Portfolio (PLP). The PLP enables students to reach back and revisit their previous thoughts and track their growth to examine whether they have met their aspirational goals. The leader development portal will provide some additional formality and structure to the PLP. Inasmuch as the portal could be used to support extracurricular activities as is described in greater detail below, housing the PLP within the portal will enable students participating in extracurricular events to store goals and reflections generated during these events in a common location, thereby providing greater consolidation and continuity between curricular and extracurricular development (Figure 3.2).

3.9.3. Psychometric Feedback

Several of the topics in Naval Academy leadership courses investigate specific psychological constructs. In preparation for these discussions, students are often asked to complete measures of the psychological construct of interest, for example, a personality profile. Currently, students typically go to an external website that offers the measure of interest and brings their results into class. This approach is

Figure 3.2: Leader development portal screen shot: The personal leadership portfolio.

suboptimal for several reasons. First, although the measures are typically taken anonymously, the website has access to the student's IP address, so some level of attribution is possible. Second, unless the students choose to save their results, which seems unlikely, valuable and informative data is lost to further consideration. Instructors debriefing the results of these measures are typically doing so for an entire section in a one hour period. It may be difficult for students to get the feedback that is most relevant to them. Finally, core course instructors are not equally proficient in debriefing every construct discussed.

These personality measures could be taken on the portal with the results stored to the user's account. In addition to storing the results for future consideration, the portal could provide individualized feedback based on the results of the measure. For instance, students receiving a score above a threshold level on a measure of the personality trait "Conscientiousness" will receive a link to a page detailing the pros and cons of high Conscientiousness for leaders (see Figures 3.3 and 3.4). Once these results are added to the student's profile, they are available to the student from that time forward. Some psychological constructs are relatively constant and could be measured only once, thereby saving the student from taking the same measure again later for a different purpose. Other psychological constructs are more contextually dependent. These measures might be taken multiple times and the student could examine the differences. The student could also share their results upon request with faculty overseeing leader development events to allow for more focused leader development. For instance, the faculty representative overseeing a club could facilitate opportunities for an Introverted student leader to develop public speaking skills in a relatively nonthreatening environment.

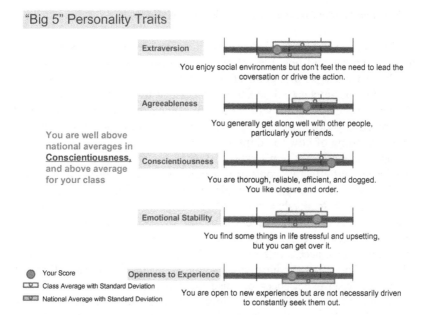

Figure 3.3: Leader development portal screen shot: Individualized feedback on personality traits.

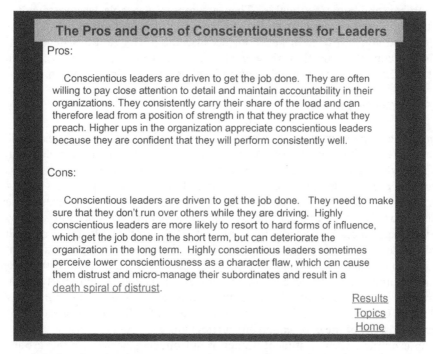

Figure 3.4: Leader development portal screen shot: Information tailored to the student to guide development.

3.9.4. Extracurricular Integration: Developmental Goals

Goal setting is essential for leader development because it requires leaders to envision possible futures and possible actions. With respect to the Kolb cycle of development, the process of setting goals effectively achieves the conceptualization stage, which provides the intellectual substance necessary to make sense of one's experience when given the opportunity to reflect. In other words, setting goals enables one to see more clearly how reality deviated from expectations, knowledge of which drives understanding of how to adapt and grow.

Based on Locke and Latham's extensive work on goal setting (Locke & Latham, 1990), we know that effective goals are specific, achievable, measurable, and actionable. The best way to form optimal goals for leader development is to draw on previous experiences in leadership roles. Effective goals should be part of the Kolb *cycle*, which implies that development is a recursive experience. In order for faculty guiding leader development to most effectively help students draw on past experiences, they must have access to some record of previous experiences. Too often this is not the case. Too often the hard work spent on feedback and reflection dissipates in the space between experiences because there is no synchronization between the faculty leading the events. The leader development portal provides an opportunity to close this loop by retaining feedback on a student's leadership strengths and weaknesses that can be used to create developmental goals. Inasmuch as these developmental goals address identified weaknesses, they should be more specific, more measurable, and more actionable. They are more actionable because faculty can craft the student's experiences by looking for specific opportunities to challenge the student and spur growth. In addition, because the portal captures developmental goals in a consistent location, these goals are more readily available to the participant after an experience is complete as an inspiration for reflection and growth.

3.9.5. Reflection Prompts

Many leadership experiences are naturally occurring in a student's life, especially as a student at a military institution. As Kolb's model of experiential learning portrays, and Dewey's concept of educative experience theorizes, simply having an experience is not sufficient for learning; learners must reflect on these experiences to update their schemas and formulate new theories of how the world works. The leader development portal can mechanize relevant leader development reflection for a wide array of experiences by providing a library of reflection prompts and a mechanism to record these reflections. For instance, if a faculty member is leading an overseas trip for which students are responsible for the planning and execution, that faculty member could create an "event" in the portal, invite the student participants to "join" the event, and assign the students to complete relevant reflections on their leadership experience by selecting from a library of reflection prompts that are direct extensions of the core leadership curriculum.

For example, when a student leader is introducing herself to the group she is leading on an overseas trip and establishing the structure to execute the mission,

Department of Leader Development and Research
Division of Leadership Education and Development
U.S. Naval Academy

USNA Leader Experiential Reflection Assignment

> For the Educator:
>
> This assignment is designed to assist USNA educators, leaders, coaches, and mentors who are helping midshipmen, as developing leaders, learn and grow from experience through reflection. It is offered as a starting point – adjustments are welcome. Please forward suggestions for improving the assignment to the Chair, Department of Leader Development and Research, USNA.

For the Midshipman:

This assignment is designed to benefit you in two ways: 1) help you make meaning of an experience you think is important for your growth as a leader; and 2) teach you a process you can use to make meaning of other experiences in the future. The process is drawn from Kolb's model of experiential learning.[1]

In three pages or less (double spaced), reflect in writing on a developmental experience from your leadership tenure as [insert USNA leader role here]. The paper should ultimately illustrate how you make meaning of the experience for the purpose of achieving greater insight in similarly patterned experiences in the future. Specifically:

1) Describe a 'concrete experience' from your tenure as a [USNA leader role]. "I saw/felt…"

Describe an experience as a [USNA leader role] characterized by situational factors that were novel, unexpected, ambiguous, unclear, and/or confusing. What did you see and hear? What did you feel during the experience?

2) Describe your 'Reflective Observation' of the experience. "I think…"

Why do you think it happened? Why was the experience important? What was the fundamental likeness of this experience to others in your past? How was it different from other similar experiences in your past – how was it novel, unexpected, ambiguous, unclear, and/or confusing? What concepts from your classroom experience apply here?

3) Describe your 'Abstract Conceptualization' of the experience. "I can…"

How might you think or behave differently next time to achieve different results? How can you use the insight you've gained from this reflection in the future?

4) Describe how you will 'Actively Experiment' with your insights gained in Step 3. "I will…"

Plan to actively apply the insights you've gained in Step 3 to relevant situations in the future. When you have actively experimented with your insights in new situations, take note of how others in the situation, the situation itself, and you, were changed by your experimentation. This is the 'concrete experience' that begins the cycle of experiential learning anew.

---

[1] Kolb, David A. 1984. *Experiential Learning: Experience as the Source of Learning and Development.*

Figure 3.5: U.S. Naval Academy experiential reflection prompt.

the faculty sponsor could assign a preparatory prompt before the meeting: "What structure/organization will your group need to succeed in its task? How will you introduce, develop and sustain this structure in your group?" and another for after the meeting: "Did your first meeting with your group meet your expectations? Why or why not?" These prompts will not only help the student leader be more effective in the moment but will also be available to her at the end of her experience as artifacts that she could use to make sense of her overall experience, guided perhaps by a final prompt: "Review the reflections that you have written during this leadership experience. Were the insights and judgments you made along the way accurate? How did they help or hinder you as a leader?" Imagine how especially valuable these artifacts will be for a student who did not succeed in her leadership.

While most leadership educators are interested in facilitating this type of leader development, few have the time, the expertise, or familiarity with the leadership curriculum to create and execute this reflection protocol. LEAD Division faculty have developed reflection prompts specifically for leadership courses, mentorship programs, summer leadership internships, and the Gettysburg Leadership Encounter, that focus on the specific developmental outcomes of those experiences. LDR also developed a more general reflection prompt based on Kolb's (1984) model of experiential learning that walks students through the cycle of learning from any specific experience, using evidence from Seibert and Daudelin (1999) that managers are particularly primed to learn from experiences that are novel, ambiguous, or unexpected — see Figure 3.5.

3.9.6. Feedback

Accurate feedback is one of the most essential elements for any type of development. Accurate external feedback enhances sense-making with respect to experiences and helps overcome the biases and perspectives that might be stunting growth. The leader development portal will serve as a clearinghouse to collect individualized feedback for students across a wide range of experiences. Two primary classes of feedback are envisioned: faculty and peer feedback. Beyond serving as a central hub to compile and retain feedback, the leader development portal provides a well suited platform for 360° peer feedback. High quality 360° feedback is very useful in diffusing common defense mechanisms in students that can derail development. Often it is easier to discredit the feedback one receives than to take responsibility for one's shortcomings. For instance, negative feedback from any given faculty member can be written off by deciding that it is the faculty member who is deficient. 360° from peers is much more difficult to disregard as it carries the weight of social consensus. Realistic feedback is often the wake-up call that young leaders need to instigate the desire for change and growth.

3.9.7. Contact Reports

Contact reports are a way to extend the focus on leader development across the curriculum and campus. Although the LEAD Division strives to interface with as many leader development events on campus as possible, it is inevitable that some events and experiences will not be accounted for. Contact reports enable faculty and staff to provide relatively free form leadership feedback to Midshipmen without formally creating an event on the portal. A faculty member could, for instance, enter a contact report highlighting a student's strengths and weaknesses in public speaking as observed in an English class. The feedback provided through the portal will go directly to the student's profile and instantly becomes a part of the story of leader development that each student is actively composing. This will enable the student to recall and focus on identified needs in future developmental events. Naval Academy leadership educators hypothesize that more faculty and staff will actively engage in leader development if they feel as though their efforts contribute to an integrated whole. Contact reports provide a relatively easy way for faculty and staff to provide this meaningful and actionable input.

3.10. Benefits of the Portal for Program Assessment: Programmatic Feedback/Assessment

The Naval Academy wants to be sure that leader development is effective in producing capable leaders for the fleet. The leader development portal will enable this by enhancing two forms of programmatic feedback. First, the portal will act as a clearinghouse for traditional feedback from ELD event participants. This feedback mechanism will be convenient to the students inasmuch as they are already regularly using the portal. The portal will facilitate assessment of leader development for programs and events for which leader development is an ancillary concern by delivering a ready-made product that requires minimal effort to execute. This will lead to more fine-grained assessment of leader development across the institution. In addition, a centralized data repository will stimulate a more consistent assessment to accommodate a wide array of leadership experiences across the curricular and extracurricular domain and, by providing consistency, enable a more valid comparison and assessment of the various programs.

Without the portal, the LEAD Division has been able to conduct in-depth assessment of experiential events on a small scale. For instance, an assessment was conducted to identify and enhance the leader development elements of the summer sailing program, the Offshore Sailing Training Squadron. The Sailing Center, which runs the program, is not equipped with the expertise or the time to assess the ELD occurring in their program. LEAD Division was able to design an assessment that specifically addressed the operant elements for successful ELD events: taking responsibility, experiencing risk of failure, and reflection on the experience (Chabot, 2013). Correlational analysis revealed a pattern of relationship suggesting that faculty feedback, guidance, and the provision of resources made Midshipmen experience greater sense of responsibility and opportunity to lead, which in turn led to more reflection on their experiences, more productive attitudes about stress, and greater confidence in their ability to lead (see Figure 3.6). Based on these results, instructor training for OSTS was changed to both highlight this pattern and give the instructors better tools to provide feedback and guidance.

The leader development portal promises much deeper and consistent assessment. Because the portal tracks each student as they develop, it enables a longitudinal assessment of development programs. Instead of simply getting instant programmatic feedback, researchers can start to assess each program in relation to more distal

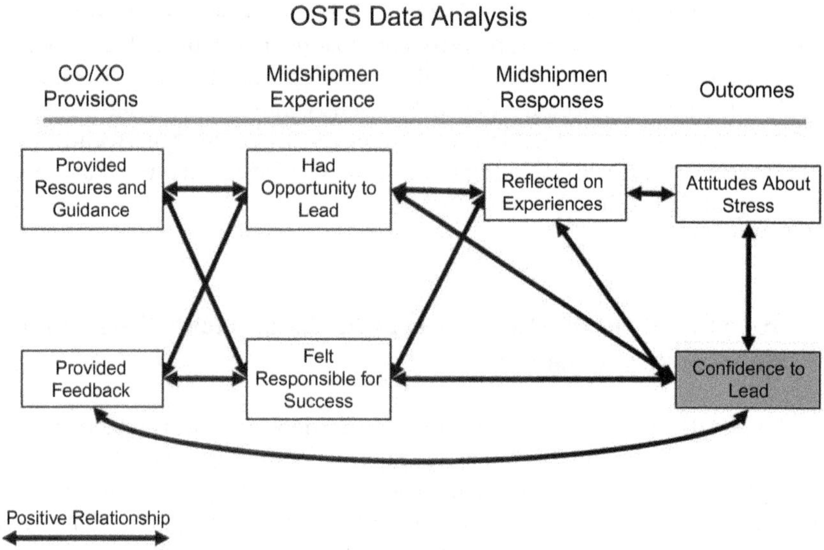

OSTS Data Analysis

Figure 3.6: OSTS data analysis.

outcomes. For instance, the Naval Academy is committed to developing seven gradu-ate attributes in its students, one of which is "Innovative," defined as "critical thin-kers and creative decision makers with a bias for action." Using the portal, assessments of innovation could be compared with the wide range of variables poten-tially resident in the portal to identify related traits and characteristics. Additional assessments of innovation could be completed in conjunction with relevant experien-tial events, such as capstone engineering project teams. Finally, moderating and med-iating experiences could be added into the analysis in an attempt to identify the key experiences associated with gains in innovation through the course of the undergrad-uate experience. This data could then inform institutional decisions on resource allo-cation to maximize return on investment.

3.11. Benefits of the Portal for Basic Leadership Research

Extracurricular events are often seen as a supplement to or extension of curricular activities. For educational domains that are largely experiential, such as leadership, these extracurricular events can be a fruitful site for basic research. In fact, with respect to leadership, harnessing extracurricular events for basic research using the leader development portal may be optimal.

Leadership as a construct is difficult to define and research. Leadership occurs in an array of varied contexts, and as a result generates outcomes that might be considered "good leadership" in one context, but not another. Because leadership entails interpersonal interactions, there are many levels of analysis that must be considered. Specifically, at the very least, research must account for the individual aspects of the leader and the follower, the relationship between the leader and the follower, and the dynamics and norms of the larger group or culture to which the leader and follower belong.

One of the ways leadership researchers deal with this complexity is through longitudinal research designs with a large array of variables. By studying leadership longitudinally, researchers are not forced to decide on a single measure of "good leadership"; rather, researchers can study multiple criteria of good leadership over time. Similarly, examining multiple leader development events longitudinally provides an array of leadership situations such that the context of leadership can be addressed as a predictive or moderating variable. Kenny and colleagues (2006) have developed a methodology, Social Relations Analysis, that accounts for the multiple levels of analysis occurring in leadership interactions through the analysis of networked groups. The data structure for this analysis is exactly the same as is used in 360°-degree feedback designs, a technique that integrates perspectives from the subject leader's supervisor, subordinates, and peers.

Thus, longitudinal analysis of a large array of variables addresses the most daunting challenges in leadership research. The leader development portal, in providing an infrastructure for developmental data, captures the data necessary to execute this optimal longitudinal design, with the large sample size required for statistical power. And by using this data for basic research, we can feed the knowledge gained in extracurricular development back into the curriculum.

3.12. Conclusion

With leader development at the very core of its charter, the Naval Academy is well served by being on the forefront of emerging trends in leadership education and leader development. One of these important trends is the purposeful linking together of leadership education and experience; the recursive interplay between the theory and practice of leadership. Building on Kolb's model of experiential learning, Naval Academy faculty are driving the transfer of knowledge from the classroom to the leadership experience to improve the educative value of the leadership laboratory at USNA. Naval Academy leadership educators make salient the relevant principles from leadership curricula "just in time" for the leadership experience, to prime Midshipmen for growth in those experiences. In addition, leadership educators guide reflection on these experiences as they unfold, to build Kolbian feedback loops that complete the cycle of experiential learning in present and future leadership experiences. Evidence from program assessments drives the design of ELD events to be most effective, where participants hold themselves accountable for achieving their given mission, experience the risk of failure if they do not act effectively, and reflect on their experiences to consolidate what they have learned and prepare them to try again. Naval Academy leadership educators welcome a future in which Web-based tools enhance experiential learning by making the curriculum, reflections tools, and assessment tools available to a wider swath of "influencers" on the faculty and staff, enabling educative experience for students on their developmental journey as leaders.

References

Bass, B. M. (1998). *Transformational leadership: Industrial, military, and educational impact.* Mahwah, NJ: Erlbaum.

Chabot, P. (2013). *Effectiveness of experiential leadership in offshore sail training squadron — Final report.* Unpublished manuscript.

Dewey, J. (1934). *Art as experience.* New York, NY: Penguin Group.

Dewey, J. (1938). *Logic: The theory of inquiry.* New York, NY: Holt, Rinehart, and Winston.

Huey, W. S., Smith, D. G., Thomas, J. J., & Carlson, C. R. (2014). The great outdoors: Comparing leader development programs at the U.S. Naval Academy. *The Journal of Experiential Education, 37*(4), 367–381.

Kellerman, B. (2012). *The end of leadership.* New York, NY: Harper Collins.

Kenny, D. A., Kashy, D. A., & Cook, W. L. (2006). *Dyadic data analysis.* New York, NY: Guilford Press.

Kolb, D. A. (1984). *Experiential learning.* Englewood Cliffs, NJ: Prentice Hall.

Locke, E. A., & Latham, G. P. (1990). *A theory of goal setting & task performance.* Englewood Cliffs, NJ: Prentice-Hall, Inc.

Peterson, C., & Seligman, M. E. P. (2004). *Character strengths and virtues: A handbook and classification.* Oxford: University Press.

Seibert, K. W., & Daudelin, M. W. (1999). *The role of reflection in managerial learning: Theory, research, and practice.* Westport, CN: Quorum Books.

Sweeney, P., Kruger, K., Keith, B., & Judd, T. (2009). *Building capacity to lead: The West Point system for leader development.* West Point, NY: United States Military Academy.

Chapter 4

Learning by Art-Making: The Inner-Outer Experience. An Experiment within a Master's Course in Audit, Control, and Accounting

Philippe Mairesse

Abstract

Purpose — This chapter analyzes art-based methods that focus on the deliverables required from the student in an academic exchange.

Methodology/approach — The study will focus on a group of second-year Master's students who, accompanied by an artist-coach and a researcher, were asked to produce an artwork reflecting their views on the technical or theoretical issues in accounting. These works were invented and realized in a four-day workshop and exhibition organized by the students.

Findings — Student submissions were found to fit into four types of outcomes: instrumental, developmental, directed, and embedded. The first two are produced by the processes mobilized in art-based teaching, while the second two are linked to the specific form of the artwork engaged in by the teaching process. Observing that few theories have explored the range of outcomes attributable to the form, the author draws on the experiment as well as Winnicot's concepts of transition and intermediate objects to define the specific transformative quality of art forms. By investigating the special area where the delimitations between the self and the world are blurred and changing, the art-maker student adopts a posture of a natural researcher who creates knowledge at the moment he defines his self — or to put it differently, through art-making, the student produces his/her self and his/her knowledge at the same time.

Originality/value — Recognizing that empowering the complexity of expression liberates access to knowing abilities and independent critical learning.

Integrating Curricular and Co-Curricular Endeavors to Enhance Student Outcomes
ISBN: 978-1-78635-064-0

Keywords: Research-oriented teaching; art-rooted knowledge; art-making; workshop; transitional objects; deep learning

The transition between the inside and the outside, concerning the independent and cocurricular resource of art when integrated into the classical institutional curricular, is the subject of this chapter. Dauphine University in Paris, a leading French institution in management and economics, belongs to the academic excellence cluster Paris Sciences and Humanities (PSL) that unites 21 institutions ranging from the hard sciences (physics, engineering, medical research) to social sciences and arts (fine and applied). Seeking the highest level in transdisciplinary research, the cluster fosters transversal innovative pedagogical projects aimed at defining new ways of teaching and learning. In this context, the directors of the Master's program in Control, Accounting, and Audit (CAA) decided to experiment with a one-week art-based workshop at the beginning of the second and final year. The course is compulsory and valuated with the normal number of ECTS credits. It draws on the 1998 European standard (LMD), asking institutions delivering a Master's degree to train students for research by helping them to acquire the desired skills: reflection, critical analysis, and integration. While the Master's first year program is mainly oriented toward acquiring techniques and skills for executing professional tasks based on reproducing what has been learned, the second year is directed toward acquiring a second level of competencies, where the young professional is capable of making critical observations and analysis, proposing solutions, and knowing how to communicate and manage ambitious projects. This level requires a high degree of involvement, independent thinking, and the ability to develop critical approaches and integrative processes. Because art-based teaching methods have been widely recognized as a good means to achieve such objectives (Cunliffe, Forray, & Knights, 2002; Dehler, Welsh, & Lewis, 2001; Eisner, 2002; Rooney, 2004; Schein, 2001; Wankel & Del Philippi, 2002; among others), an art-making workshop could help develop these skills. It could free the student's mind so that s/he becomes capable of creative thinking and can develop methods for acting efficiently in an uncertain and unknown context and respond to a high degree of quality requirements. In the field of accounting education, where art-based teaching experiments are scarce, our purpose was to open up the pathway by designing a first series of experiments. We had a second goal: by delineating the benefits and limitations of the method, we aimed at extending its validity to other fields. If art-making reveals potential benefits for accounting education where creative skills such as imagination, improvisation, or ease with uncertainty are not prioritized, we can legitimately suppose that the approach may be transferable to many other disciplines. Because such skills, together with critical thinking, are characterized (at least in France) as particularly necessary for the Master's and doctoral levels, we focused on Master's program students in their second year.

The first workshop, conceived and lead by the author and the Director of the Master's program, was based on our primary hypothesis that creation can foster better student involvement not only by creating strong team spirit but also by deepening the students' interest in the subjects studied. Based on this hypothesis, the students were asked to prepare an exhibition where their own works about crucial notions in accounting, audit, and control would be displayed. There were two objectives: first, by placing students in an unknown context, we would call for underused or underestimated skills such as imagination, critical analysis, adaptability, and personal thinking. The second idea was to immediately apply these skills by asking the students to produce works, which would express their own understating of key notions in accounting, audit, and control in a more complex and clear way. Similar to experiments in graduate or doctoral management education that use writing and poetry as an extension of the research process in which field notes are taken, not only purely verbally but through a mix of visual and verbal (Katz-Buonincontro, 2014), the idea was to push the students to produce complex and refined expressions of their knowledge of the core notions of accounting so that they could deepen their understating of these notions and their critical thinking.

The principle of the workshop was to enable the student's complex expression about scientific issues and knowledge by using various modes of representation: visual, discursive, embodied, and emotional. This was based on our secondary hypothesis, which was that complex expression through art gives access to complex ways of knowing and critical thinking; starting from the student's concern with accounting could result in higher involvement in learning and lead them to adopt a research posture.

To comply with the requirements of logical-rational argumentation, we adopted a classical research framing. The workshop was designed as an education research experiment: it was photographed, filmed, and recorded, with student acceptance, in order to collect material for study. Group interviews were conducted with the students every day of the workshop as well as six months later. The research objective was to explore if, and under which conditions, nonstandard art-making expressions on scientific themes foster a deepening of knowledge, instill a higher degree of reflection, and mobilize the student for research. The recordings, interviews, and observations conducted during and after the experiment by the leading team revealed a rich potential for investigating the role and outcomes of art-making in art-based teaching.

This chapter (1) reviews the main trends in theoretical approaches to art-based management education and suggests a new understanding of the role of art-making and artworks for teaching and learning, (2) recounts the experiment, (3) analyzes its outcomes, (4) indicates conditions for success and obstacles and limitations, and (5) suggests further investigations for research and teaching experiments.

4.1. Art-Based Approaches and the Issue with Their Implementation in Management Education

4.1.1. The Trend of Art-Based Approaches

Management education has long been following the model of the natural sciences over-valuing rationality and logic. The repeatability and predictability of quantitative approaches have long been reputed as the only legitimate basis for managerial action, together with rationalistic claims about manager objectivity (Beirne & Knight, 2007), within the general frame of a "technicized" cognitive culture and educational productivity (Eisner, 2004). However, real organizational life rather requires managers to act upon a basis of incomplete information and to solve problems they are part of instead of being detached from, which is not reflected in conventional management education that is primarily based on reason, rationality, and expertise (Ennals, 2014, p. 3). The critique is not new: almost half a century ago, March (1976) already commented on how "interesting" organizations supplement the "technology of reason" with a "technology of foolishness," based on the emergent and transitional nature of purpose, on inconsistency, and on the relaxation of functionally rational imperatives. Instead of opposing management as a science, to management as an art, Meisiek and Barry (2014) call for "the science of making management an art" where the manager has to play a variety of roles, among them the artist besides the manager-scientist (Hatch, Kostera, & Kozminski, 2007). They explain how art, with its attention to and expression of the human condition in a social context, is particularly adapted to educational purposes. Based on these premises, an art-based management education stream has developed within the frame of critical pedagogy, drawing on the conviction that rethinking the classical logical-rational frame calls for a renewed "aesthetic epistemology," which art-based learning could help to build (Nissley, 2002).

The art-based approach aims at incorporating the complexity of management and organizations and at making management education more transformational and emancipatory, overcoming the tendency to simplification of the organizational and environmental complexity (Dehler et al., 2001). It rejects the packaging mentality, rationalism, and the logic of passive learning, and operates a double move: first, it debunks rationalistic claims concerning the neutrality and objectivity of management thinking and practices, including ethical, social, and political issues. Second, it engages with the students rather than transmitting information and finds more open and mutually responsive ways of teaching through dialogue and debates (Beirne & Knight, 2007). By fostering dissensus rather than consensus, and appropriation rather than expertise, critical management education can be thought of as a vehicle for emancipation (Huault & Perret, 2011), aimed at better preparing the students to become independent learners capable of "complicated understanding." This means they become capable of combining scientific and symbolic ways of knowing and of incorporating multiple perspectives on interdisciplinary aspects of organizations and management (Dehler et al., 2001). This turn to more dynamic, subjective, and interactional approaches of management and education, grounded in art, should result in a better adapted two-eyed perspective (Irgens, 2014) for "seeing more and seeing differently" (Barry & Meisiek, 2010).

After a phase of experimental and marginal attempts, the art-based approach slowly became an official and supported trend in management education. The Carnegie report, "Rethinking Undergraduate Business Education: Liberal Learning for the Profession" (2011), states that the core components of liberal arts education (analytical thinking, multiple framing, the reflective exploration of meaning, and practical reasoning) can and should be integrated into the undergraduate business curriculum by putting emphasis on the reflective exploration of meaning (Spee & Fraiberg, 2015). It concerns, in particular, the meaning of action for the self or the meaning of learning for the students. The culture of rationality and efficiency is aimed at specifying, with absolute certainty, expectations and procedures related to students, which is suitable for training them to achieve tasks they are asked to do. The arts, on the contrary, foster another kind of motivation for tasks they themselves choose to do. This is why arts could serve as a model for redesigning better educational systems (Eisner, 2002).

4.2.   The Issue with Art-Based Teaching Methods

Despite such a long-lasting trend of practices and theories concerning the renewal of management education through the arts, along with its emerging recognition, many difficulties remain in applying art-based methods to classical management education. Statler and Guillet de Monthoux (2015), among others, point out opposing viewpoints concerning how and why arts and humanities should be applied to management education.

The practical implementation of such approaches in management education meets a first major issue, namely, that it can generate anxiety and resistance among students used to traditional rationalistic methods. Another problem can emerge from the faculty itself and its propensity to stick to conventional distance, superiority, and expertise, which thus jeopardizes both the dialogical and critical stances of the critical approach (Beirne & Knight, 2007), especially when encountering students' resistance. A third issue is the risk of seeing the arts used for subtly reinforcing established management practices or conceptions rather than stimulating independent thinking, a risk which the call to radical art traditions like community or forum theater (Boal, 1979) tries to avoid (Beirne & Knight, 2007). The hope is to directly engage with people and build trust in order to question what is normal and routine, and thereby interrogate the role of authority and hierarchy. Countering the dominance of the expert and his/her authority by enabling co-construction and dialogue is not easy. This is what Mack (2013) calls the "aesthetic risk" in management education.

The major issue, however, is to evaluate the effects of such a pedagogy on the skills and competencies (Barry & Meisiek, 2014; Berthoin Antal, 2009). Though Rooney (2004) listed the types of effects to consider — improvement of learning abilities, relational and self-organizational skills, and cognitive abilities (comprehension of symbols, interpretation, and problem-solving), among others — it remains difficult to assert precisely how to attain these effects, which art-based features to use, as well as how to implement them within the scope of classical institutions.

Behind this lies the issue of understanding how students would acquire competence through art-making or -perceiving. Sutherland (2013) states we lack an empirically grounded work focusing on the underlying experiential learning processes of participants in such art-based education methods in management and leadership. The present study seeks to be such a work.

4.3.   Understanding Why and How Art-Based Teaching Methods Work

4.3.1.   The Focus on Experience

Rationally theorizing or analyzing our sometimes chaotic social environment is not separated from intuitively experiencing it: we feel, think, and act simultaneously. Critical management and pedagogy aims at reintroducing the importance and value of experience, with its opacity, complexity, and illuminating, multilayered nature. The intention is to enhance a more qualitative experience of the organizational world, recentering organizing and organizations around the lived experience, feelings, motivations, beliefs, and interactions of members.

Taylor and Hansen (2005) suggest that art practices in organizational life enable capturing lived experiences and the tacit knowledge of day-to-day organizational reality. It resonates with the notion of aesthetic experience according to Dewey (1934/2005). Very distinct from the aesthetic of beauty, aesthetic experience is focused on expression as a creative act. It is triggered by the impetus to address the situation, the world, and others, and it is aimed at reaching unity in what otherwise remains inchoate. In aesthetic experience, structure is felt and immediately recognized. "When unity is of the sort already described, the experience has esthetic character even though it is not, dominantly, an esthetic experience" (Dewey, 1934/2005, p. 44). It is aimed at the construction of a meaningful unity through qualities and qualitative relations as well as through analytic-rational reasoning. Such an experience is grounded in the inextricable entanglement between the practical domain of action and feeling, and the abstract domain of thought and concepts.

The ability to reach for unity and coherence in a disparate flux of events and information is identified as a growing organizational competence. Teaching this skill can be achieved by introducing the experience of art-making or art-perceiving in management education, in order to experience a different relation to organizing, organizations, and their flows of uncertain and contradictory information.

4.3.2.   The Expected Effects of Art-Based Teaching Methods

In this section, I will use the term "art forms" to speak of art products, art objects, or artworks: painting, objects, images, performances, photographs, drawings, sculptures, and the same. "Form" is a multi-meaning term, which I will here consider in its limited sense of material realization.

The review of the existing literature on management education reveals that two kinds of premises concerning art and its effects are mobilized in order to explain how art-based methods may help in acquiring a greater capacity to manage the experiential, social, human, and complex dimension of organizations, in addition to its productive and profitable aspects. The presumed outcomes of art-experience are attributed by the literature:

- to the specific processes mobilized by art, or
- to the qualitative relation to art products (or forms).

Both have transformative effects on experience and knowledge if introduced in well-designed curricula.

4.3.3. The Instrumental Expected Effects of Art Processes

On the one hand, the process of creation has an instrumental value. By breaking with preestablished plans, it is supposedly suitable for preparing future managers to act in disturbed and changing environments. Art-based methods foster the ability to face uncertainty, ambiguity, ill-defined issues, and the complexity of contemporary organizations by developing nonlogical and nonrational capabilities for perceiving, describing, and relating differently to this complexity (Adler, 2006; Barry & Meisiek, 2010; Cunliffe et al., 2002; Darso, 2004; Eisner, 2002; Hatch, 1997; Le Theule & Fronda, 2002; Springborg, 2012; Sutherland, 2013; Taylor & Ladkin, 2009). The processes of creation are characterized by extreme adaptability, improvisation, *ad hoc* procedures, variability, and implicitness, among others. The appeal to such ways of doing counters the hegemony of functionalist and controllable processes in traditional management education and practice and makes more room for experience in management learning and doing. Several of these processes correspond to a mode of action close to the actual activity of managers. Teaching students to critically build their own knowledge by assembling ideas resembles the manager making *ad hoc* decisions or the artist making a collage; reflecting on art-making or art-perceiving induces students to reflect on their own experience and think of different possible professional or educational practices and skills (Madden & Smith, 2013), such as the capacity to face ambiguity and complexity, nonlogical and nonrational capabilities, flexible purposing, and *ad hoc* bricolage.

4.3.4. The Developmental Expected Effects of Art Processes

On the other hand, art-based methods and processes of creation mobilize an intuitive, sensible, emotional, and embodied experience. Instead of being oriented toward instrumental goals, their transformative action leads to the development of distinctive thinking skills aimed at communicating a kind of meaning that language is not able to transmit, qualified as "ineffable" (Biggs, 2004; Eisner, 2002). Art makes abstract notions tangible (Barry & Meisiek, 2014) and represents ideas that are otherwise not easy to process (Eisner, 2002), thus nurturing reflexivity, sensitive engagement, and critical thinking (Beirne & Knight, 2007; Hill & Lloyd, 2015; Statler, 2014; Sutherland, 2013).

Critical thinking is empowered by the fact that art does not come with prefabricated and fixed interpretations (Barry & Meisiek, 2014), and develops the capacity to tolerate contradictions and paradoxes (Parush & Koivunen, 2014). They cause us to see and experience the changing world before appropriate concepts and words can describe it (Statler & Guillet de Monthoux, 2015). By producing ideas and re-configuring knowledge, art enables a re-formation of intelligence and gives access to a specific form of knowledge (Mack, 2013; Strati, 2007). This emerges partly from a phenomenological conception of the experience of art-making or art-perceiving, pertaining to notions such as practice-as-theory, practice-as-learning, participative inquiry, reflective practice, practice-as-research (Bennett, Wright & Blom, 2013), embodied ethics, and an avenue to consciousness (Eisner, 2002).

Viewing art and creative processes as a kind of knowledge provides a core for a developmental pedagogy, which promotes "growth of mind" and enables "the most complex forms of thinking," namely "artistically rooted forms of thinking" (Eisner, 2002) where cognition and perception fuse together. The specific knowledge acquired through art pertains to presentational knowing. Among the four types of knowing identified by Heron and Reason (1997) — experiential, propositional, presentational, and practical — presentational knowing is an implicit embodied knowing requiring aesthetic-artistic forms of representation and serves to build a bridge between experiential and propositional knowing. The major role given to imaging (be it visual, musical, poetic, or literary) in art processes can help provide the student with presentational modes of inquiry: metaphors and analogies are core ways of thinking beyond scientific rationality and accessing a different level of meaning. In summary, the focus on processes is expected to produce developmental outcomes: acquiring presentational knowing, the ability to deal with contradictions and paradoxes, access to embodied implicit knowledge, consciousness, and growth of mind.

The role and outcomes of processes of creation have been quite widely investigated for practical objectives, for example, developing general skills such as attention to detail and to what is overlooked, caring for the counter-intuitive, the ability to diagnose changing environments, the awareness of the different ways that oneself, as well as others, understand issues, and so on. Improvisational or forum theater, poetry, or storytelling, among others, bring in a radically critical and playful exploration of the social and ethical aspects of organizations (Katz-Buonincontro, 2014). Processes of creation are also mobilized widely for developmental and knowledge purposes, for example, through the art of performance and happening, where the meaning or content of the work is intrinsically linked with the process of performing.

However, the role and outcomes of art forms has been studied less, though Taylor and Ladkin (2009) identified "process and result" as two key dimensions when they mapped the types of art-based methods used for the development of managers and leaders. Barry and Meisiek (2010), investigating the role of art products, argue that the cultivation of collective mindfulness involves "analogous artifacts," particularly artistic ones, which provide analogical suggestive representations of the organizational situation. Related to notions like "boundary objects"

(Carlile, 2002) or "evocative objects" (Turkle, 2007), analogous artifacts open up a range of potential meanings in an unplanned and autonomous way. Here the art product is considered relative to its meaning, and more specifically to the "work that art does," which the authors express by the term "workart." Though the notion of the "analogous artifact" is powerful and can provide a good idea of what is an artwork, it is not considered in its physical and aesthetic properties but again relative to a process (a "work") aimed at producing results occurring after the perception of the "workart." The role and effects of the art form remain to be studied at depth.

First, in order to better understand the role of art-making and the specific quality of art products in management and accounting education, I will draw on Eisner's "artistically rooted forms of thinking," which he defines by six components:

- experiencing qualitative relationships and making judgments,
- flexible purposing,
- the inextricability of form and content,
- the nonuniversality of propositional form,
- the importance of the medium, and
- the aesthetic satisfaction the action itself makes possible.

Crossing Eisner's typology of art-rooted thinking with a four-entries table (experience/knowledge — process/form), we can map out the expected art-based outcomes for management education. Among the six above listed components, one fits into the "effects of process" category: flexible purposing is part of the creation process and its improvisation dimension. The five others cannot be attributed to processes but rather to forms. They contribute to defining two other kinds of possible effects of introducing art into education.

4.3.5. The Embedded Expected Effects of Art Forms

A first category of effects resulting from the confrontation with art forms concerns knowledge and can be characterized as the embedding of knowledge in materiality. The inextricability of form and content relates to the specific "art-rooted" form of knowledge, where materiality and intellectuality, cognition and perception, are merged into one. Making judgments is an expression of this specific kind of knowledge based on intimate feelings and convictions that can nevertheless be stated as generalities.

4.3.6. The Directed Expected Effects of Art Forms

A second category of effects resides in the direct experience of art forms. The first thing we can say is that experience is immediately affected by the medium. Unlike texts, which we perceive almost identically regardless of the way they were written, printed, enlarged or spoken, paintings and sculptures are perceived as totally distinct experiences. The first effect of the confrontation with art forms is to trigger our attention to the medium and its materiality. A second effect is that experiencing the art forms mobilizes us through the pleasure and aesthetic satisfaction it makes possible, such as the experience of art-making. According to Dewey, this aesthetic satisfaction occurs based on the specific attention given to relationships and disparateness, heterogeneity, and unity. Whether in perceiving or making art, aesthetic experience is a question of attention to the relationships between the different elements of the artwork. It "selects what is congruous and dyes what is selected with its color, thereby giving qualitative unity to material externally disparate and dissimilar" and providing "unity in and through the varied parts of an experience" (Dewey, 1934/2005, p. 44). Confronting art forms develops the ability to pay attention to the qualitative relationship between disparate elements in order to improve their relationships toward a greater unity. Because they call for attention, focus, and mobilize intentionality, this last category of effects can be called "directed."

Table 4.1 provides a summary of the different expected effects of the confrontation with art in education, according to the literature. The issue is that only half of the table is investigated, mainly through the attention to processes and their transformative effects on experience and knowledge. The attention to form, and the transformative effects of form-making, is more embryonic and difficult to bring out due to the overestimated role of symbolic thinking linked to the domination of logic-rationale.

Here, there is a research and experimental challenge in investigating and theorizing the effects of nonsymbolic approaches to art forms in management education through the direct experience of art-making. I will first explore one possible

Table 4.1: Art-based expected outcomes in management education.

Art-based outcomes	Processes	Forms
Experience	*Instrumental:* – Face ambiguity and complexity – Nonlogical, nonrational capabilities – Flexible purposing – *Ad hoc* bricolage	*Directed:* – Making – Aesthetic experience – Importance of the medium – Aesthetic satisfaction of action – Qualitative relationships
Knowledge	*Developmental:* – Access to embodied implicit knowledge – Meaningful contradictions and paradoxes – Consciousness, growth of mind	*Embedded:* – Inextricability of form and content – Cognition mixed with perception – Judgments – Presentational knowing

theoretical interpretation of the function of art forms, before broaching the empirical part of the chapter.

4.4. A Transitional Interpretation of Art Forms and Their Function

Researchers and scholars have theorized their own use and production of art forms to communicate, illustrate, or make their intellectual argument (Moriceau, 2012; Nissley, Taylor, & Houden, 2004; Steyaert & Hjorth, 2002; Szendy, 2012; Taylor, 2000; among others). Such forms present the intellectual meaning and knowledge of the researcher to their audience. The latter experience and co-construct a different kind of knowledge by interacting with the researcher through the art form. Dramaturgy, for example, externalizes and emphasizes various inner experiences, then confronts them on stage, and at last enables the "spect-actors" to re-internalize and appropriate the experience. As Woodward and Ellison (2010) indicate concerning the performing arts, viewers take an aesthetic object into themselves and in turn project themselves into the aesthetic object. We could say that the outer world invades the inner self and vice versa in a typical move, which I suggest is not only proper to dramaturgy but to art-making in general. Shaping (one's interior) life by creating (external) material forms is the specific quality of "making" art — or of aesthetics as a philosophy of life.

Not far from what Barry and Meisiek (2010) indicate about the "analogous artifacts," the projection of the inner to the outside and vice versa relates to what Winnicot describes as the constitutive paradox of the infant's development. The mother and child together create the illusion of a "created reality" through what Winnicot calls "transitional objects." For the safe development of the self, the realm of illusion and its transitional objects has to be an accepted paradox, an "intermediate area of experience, unchallenged in respect of its belonging to inner or external (shared) reality." Winnicot adds that this area "throughout life is retained in the intense experiencing that belongs to the arts and to religion and to imaginative living, and to creative scientific work" (Winnicot, 1971, p. 14). "Transitional" refers to the transition the infant passes through, from being merged with the mother to being separated, by crossing an intermediary zone where reality and creation are blurred. Called a zone for play, or third space, or transitional space, it can be understood as the space where the limits between me and not-me are being created and experimented, a space materialized through entities both merged and separated, as parts of the inner and the outer worlds simultaneously. Our relation to transitional objects is specific: we have to create them, destroy them, possess then lose them, before and in order to be able to *use* them. This constitutes the process of becoming an individual subject distinct from one's objects, by separating oneself from the objects with which we were first confused.

If the intermediary zone is a necessary condition for the child's development, adults also need a personal intermediate area, filled with "not-me objects" through which they construct their own illusion of an objective-subjective reality. Relating inner and outer reality needs the safe intermediate area where the objective or subjective quality of reality is not challenged. Religion, art, culture, and science represent these safe areas (Winnicot, 1971, pp. 18–19). The "not-me" or transitional objects in these overlapping zones of adult realities are un-invested versions of the seminal infant's transitional object such as artworks, theories, and beliefs incorporating more and more common cultural interests. Understanding artworks as this kind of object helps to understand their role in the development of the grown-up, in the same way the transitional object serves in the infant's development.

In Winnicot's view, the development process passes through the paradox of accepting the lack of distinction between objectivity and subjectivity, or between inner and outer experience, in order to separate the self from the environment. We could call it the basic process of learning: if a self can be said to have its own inner reality, distinct from the outer real world, it is because s/he is continuously testing the objectivity-subjectivity distinction in intermediate areas where s/he can experience "inner-outer" things, events, and beings (Winnicot, 1971, p. 11). Consequently, the limits of a self could be called "inside peripheries" (or the self can be said to be externally centered). The paradox also links individuals to others and the collective since the illusion-disillusion process is initially performed by mother and child inseparably. Sharing illusions about objective and subjective realities is both an inner experience and a collective one. When several members enjoy their own personal intermediate zones without trying to impose their illusion on others (what the students did in the experiment), they may be pleased to find a certain degree of overlap. This is where a common experience is created, linking the members of a group (Winnicot, 1971, p. 14) within the space "where the necessary madness of childhood can be revisited and where cultural experience and creativity can occur" (Woodward & Ellison, 2010).

Knowledge, understood as the construction of a database concerning the outer world, is highly dependent on the experience of inner versus outer reality, which according to Winnicot and object-relation theory has to be experienced through "me-not-me" objects for adults: objects that take the inner experience as an external environment and the reverse. "Aesthetic experience" could identify the collective and individual experience of a transitional state between inside and outside, objective and subjective, merging and distinction, which needs intermediate "objects," whose status is uncertain and shifting. We can now understand the insistence on uncertainty, ambiguity, and ill-defined issues when it comes to the interest of art for teaching and learning. More than learning to manage uncertainty, the question is how to experience the double certainty of inner and outer objects in order for the student to sharpen his/her own delimitations and the acuteness of his/her "knowledge," understood as: *what can be said about the outside from the inside.*

The experimental workshop we designed was aimed precisely at exploring if, and under which conditions, nonstandard art-based expressions of scientific themes, considered as intermediate objects, foster a deepening of knowledge, instill a higher degree of reflection, and mobilize the student to conduct research. The example analyzed in this chapter aims at demonstrating the potential of such artworks-based approaches, even in the context of the strong rationalist-scientific thinking dominant among accountancy students.

4.5.   The Art-Making Workshop Experiment

4.5.1.   Methodology

The assignment was to create artworks and organize an art exhibition within four days. The experiment was built on two convictions. First, the students were motivated to study accountancy, audit, and control; almost half of them were planning to do research, and the second half were following professional apprenticeship training in conjunction with their university courses. We had to start from their own involvement and concerns about their graduate studies. Then, there was an obvious gap between the requirement of organizing an art exhibition of high quality and the lack of any artistic skill or knowledge among the students. It would have been impossible and counter-productive in the allotted time to try to teach them art history, art-making, or art theory as a preliminary for the workshop. The initial idea was to inject some adapted artistic information and examples according to the progress of the work. But I quickly felt this would have been a disincentive and a return to the traditional position of expert and authority, threatening the dialogical and open way of teaching we wanted to establish. Consequently, absolutely no artistic reference was given throughout the workshop. The only "artistic" requirement was to express convincingly one's ideas about central notions in accounting, audit, or control. The starting phase consisted of a two-hour round table discussion where each student revealed his or her motivations and interests in studying in the Master's program. Then groups were formed according to similarities in interests and worked in the afternoon at deepening their reflection. The five themes chosen by the five groups were: the International Financial Report Standards (IFRS), fraud in accountancy, social responsibility, the domination of figures, and change in complex environments. The assignment was to produce a short speech at the end of the day to be given to the whole class, expressing the convictions and issues the group worked out. They were also asked to make the speech as responsive and moving as possible in order to communicate the meaning they wanted to convey more extensively. The second phase was to write down the text and shape it into a manifesto, tract, poster, note, slogan, or other textual format. Then each group was asked to translate their text into a nonverbal form, be it a performance, image, object, drawing, or something else. No indication about the form was given. This phase started with the group brainstorming and producing ideas, schemas, and commented drawings in notebooks. The selected idea to be realized was then translated into a time, money, and resources organization schedule and the remaining day and a half was devoted to producing the artwork with their limited available skills and techniques. Some advice was given to the groups, who all completed their artwork (installation or assemblage), which they displayed in the exhibition space, choosing carefully the place for the art and text they had shaped. These included a poster (IFRS), a tract (social responsibility), a framed short notice (fraud), wild writing on cardboard (change), and a performance (the domination of figures). The opening party was a success.

Practically, the workshop was conducted by an artist-researcher (the author), whose role was to design the setting, support the students, keep track of time with regular checkpoints, organize the progression toward the final deliverable, and collect data (record and observe). A young researcher helped as an assistant. The instructions were as follows:

- Artworks must express the students' understanding of central notions concerning audit, control, or accounting.
- Phase One: Start from the student's concerns about accounting, audit, and control. Ask them to express those concerns collectively by verbal and nonverbal means and to make a first statement about the issue(s) that concern them.
- Phase Two: Form groups with similar concerns and work together to produce a "manifesto": a completed form of writing (poster, slogan, tracts …). A short public presentation (performing the statement) to the whole class by each group concludes day one.
- Phase Three: Translate the manifesto visually. Any form is possible. No art education, information, or examples were delivered to the students.
- Each group of five to six students was given a budget they could use freely for buying material or services outside.
- The exhibition displaying the writings and the artworks was organized in the main reception room in the university and open for one night only. The visitors were the other students and faculty, the dean, exterior researchers and teachers, artists, and critics. It received unanimous acclaim.

4.5.1.1. An excerpt of the activity of one of the five groups

— I'm not satisfied with this, something is wrong, don't you think?
— I agree, I don't know what's wrong or what to change … Try to keep close to your feeling and imagine what a better work would look like.

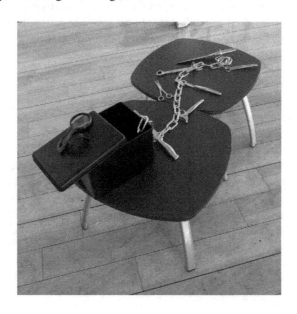

Three hours before the opening, the students in the small group of five have lost the enthusiasm they had yesterday evening. I too feel annoyed and see no solution to their problem. The strange object they have created looks weird, heavy, and improper when yesterday we all thought it was acute, subtle, and beautifully threatening, like the international accounting norms the students have chosen to comment. The assemblage of sharpened knives, scissors, cutters, and other razor-edged instruments, all made of stainless steel attached to a steel chain lingering on the table, is supposed to describe the double-edged power of IFRS, the International Financial Reporting Standard, which the students see as dangerous and counter-productive if used by nonexperts. They have worked on the theme for three days, wondering whether research in accounting should aim at looking for the best methods for applying the IFRS or at criticizing norms and suggesting other ways of regulation. Doing research as normalizing or de-normalizing the standards was the issue around which the group gathered at the beginning of the workshop. The curious sculpture they created lies on the wide table, slightly threatening, inert, waiting for more — like the students waiting for inspiration, one after another approaching the object and trying a different arrangement, another configuration, vainly. I withdraw from the group and leave them alone with the issue.

Two hours later they fuss in all directions in the exhibition room, looking for the best place to install the rectified artwork. They do not like the spot they had first chosen and try different solutions, moving around two small black coffee tables they found. Finally we agree on a space near the entrance, close to the window where they post a large typographic statement concerning IFRS norms. The sculpture-assemblage is now finalized: the snaky chain of blunt instruments emerges out of a black metallic box with an open lid and the ensemble is displayed on the two black coffee tables stuck together. The box comes from a previous idea they had about a pile of boxes symbolizing successive levels of norms behind norms, similarly to Russian nesting dolls, corresponding to different levels of administration from local to international. The idea was given up for the blunt assemblage, but now the black box takes on its full double meaning by hiding and displaying, controlling and releasing the dangerous instrument. When entering the space, visitors keep out of reach, cautiously considering the object from a certain distance as if it could jump at them. Their work and the whole show are a success; the other artworks displayed by the five groups of students are very different one from another, but they all demonstrate a complex degree of visual, verbal, and spatial expression serving a critical reflection. During the opening night, the students stand beside their work and proudly comment on them for the visitors — other students, professors, the university dean, researchers, invited artists and critiques, and family. Four hours later, the show is over, we pack up and distribute the artworks in several offices and storage rooms.

4.6. Discussion

The research objective was to explore if, and under which conditions, nonstandard art-making expressions about scientific themes foster a deepening of knowledge, instill a higher degree of reflection, and mobilize the student for research. The teaching objectives were the learning of desired management skills, namely:

- being capable of critical observation and analysis,
- the ability to propose solutions,

- knowing how to communicate and manage ambitious projects,
- proving a high degree of involvement,
- independent thinking, and
- the ability to develop integrative processes.

We can first notice that the workshop complies with the previously listed objectives of critical management education. The core components of liberal arts education identified by the Carnegie Report are present in the experiment: "analytical thinking" is active during the reflection on one's motivations and concerns about accounting issues; a successive and "multiple framing" of the themes results from their successive translations from oral expression to written text to visual expression to exhibiting to commenting; a "reflective exploration of meaning" is not only achieved but constitutes the basis of the work; finally, "practical reasoning" is dominantly used in the realization phase.

The workshop resulted in mobilizing hidden competencies. It enacted a situation similar to challenging professional situations: the students were immersed in a field in which they had almost no information or skills, and they became capable of mobilizing unexpected competencies ("We drew on competencies we didn't know we had," one student said). They were dealing with problems they were part of, in the most personal sense. Some students questioned their own value ("Facing a critique I'd say: yes, but I am not good at this, I know it's not my ability"), while others discovered the excitement of being concerned with success or failure, and being responsible for something larger than themselves ("We want to make it, for me it would be a failure if we can't"; "What will we show on Friday? Maybe we won't have anything to show, it will be embarrassing, for the Master's [program], the university; we're under a lot of pressure"). Their decisions were directly part of the production, more like interventions than detached abstract decisions. Finally, they played a variety of roles, including accountancy student, team manager, budget controller, artist, critic, and audience.

The competencies they mobilized were of the kind we were looking for. Their productions showed a high degree of critical thinking: each small group developed their ideas by critically investigating the core accounting and strategy notions they had chosen to deal with (fraud, the domination of numbers, change in a complex environment, social responsibility, and international accounting norms). They all investigated the ambiguity and paradoxes of these notions (the inevitability of fraud, the ambivalence of norms, and so on). Confronted with unexpected situations and practical problems when realizing their "form," they all proved to have a good capacity for proposing solutions and adapting to the unexpected, which the on-time opening and success of the exhibition demonstrated.

They all managed their project (time, budget, roles, quality control, etc.) with a high degree of involvement and performance (deadlines, completeness, coherence between concepts and realizations, etc.). Their independent thinking is clear through the unconventional works they produced: none of the works is a copy or an imitation of a current visual production available on the Internet or other media. Finally, all groups went through integrative processes taking into account the different personalities, competencies, and relations to time in order to reach a cohesive collective oriented toward a common goal that they all reached.

In summary, the workshop apparently resulted in the expected outcomes in terms of critical thinking, management skills, and adaptation to unexpected situations and problems. In order to further explore these outcomes in detail, I will focus on the interviews conducted during and after the workshop. These interviews allow for a more precise understanding of the different kinds of effects produced by the workshop on students' learning, according to the classification of Table 4.1.

4.6.1. *Instrumental Outcomes*

Interviews reveal almost no concerns from the students regarding the instrumental outcomes listed in the process/experience category: facing ambiguity, ill-defined problems, the appeal to nonlogical capabilities, and flexible purposing. Very few students expressed a concern about the absence of logic ("We are not here for that, we're not expected to produce such things") or flexible purposing ("We had ideas but we had to change," "We did not understand why we couldn't put all our ideas in one"). Only one instrumental effect was widely active: *ad hoc* actions and bricolage were spontaneously adopted. It is clearly visible in the artworks themselves and the process of their fabrication. Without any specific instructions or requirements, all the groups built *ad hoc* assemblages of disparate materials — cardboard, wood, tape, toys, balloons, paper puppets, cutlery, and so on. What can stand as evidence of the obviousness of such actions in such contexts does not appear in the interviews. *Ad hoc* actions, unexpected associations, and bricolage were not considered as a problem or a second best choice by the students, but were deliberately chosen as the best way to answer the challenge (e.g.,, installing bicycle wheels on top of cardboard boxes in order to comment on change, or filling a tennis net with balance sheets, for criticizing fraud).

4.6.2. *Developmental Outcomes*

Consciousness and growth of mind remain until now a hypothesis. Neither the students' comments nor the actions during the workshop showed any concern with contradictions and paradoxes, except for the quite usual comments on the opposition between art, understood as freedom, and the requirement to respect the schedules, experienced as a constraint. The "access to embodied implicit knowledge" remains to be explored as we did not assess the students' knowledge improvements.

Finally, developmental outcomes — and instrumental ones to a minor extent — appear to be purely theoretical: no evidence of such outcomes can be firmly stated from the experiment. Most of the expressed and observed outcomes correspond to the "embedded" and "directed" categories.

4.6.3.   Directed Outcomes

"Directed outcomes" refer to the transformative effects of form and making on experience. They consist mainly in (Table 4.1) aesthetic experience, awareness of the importance of the medium, encountering the aesthetic satisfaction of action, and development of qualitative relationships. The development of qualitative relationships was first attested by the "team-building effect": a strong linking was created within the group by the workshop, qualified six months later as one of its undisputable results by the students. Experiencing the quality of relationships was also effective concerning the perception, improvement, and aesthetic of the created artworks. The students played easily with various materials, gluing, assembling, juxtaposing elements in order to attain a coherent united whole (Dewey, 1934/2005), what some of them described with vague words such as "it works" or "it doesn't work."

The importance of the medium was obvious to almost all students who carefully chose how to materialize their ideas, through which shapes, objects, colors, and size. They expressed in their comments how important action was for reaching the kind of satisfaction they were looking for:

> We really want to realize it, it would be a failure if we cannot make it.
> We did something really interesting, we really are into the making. The first thing I want to do is to rush into it and see if it works.
> We will make something, we'd never thought we were capable of that.
> We'll be proud of what we've made.

The satisfaction they express can be said to be of the aesthetic kind in Foucault's sense of the aesthetic of the self (Foucault, 2001): a doing which enables the self to reach its own truth and value.

4.6.4.   Embedded Outcomes

"Embedded outcomes" consist in awareness of the embedding of knowledge into materiality (see Table 4.1): becoming conscious of the inextricability of form and content, the fact that cognition is mixed with perception, concerns about judgements and the dominance of presentational knowing.

Firstly, the main and almost unanimous observation by the students after the workshop is that it fostered a high and unusual level of reflection that they associated with the act of making:

> It pushed our thinking to the limit;
> It has been a long time since I have thought that much;
> A very positive side is that we thought a lot.

When asked why it is so unusual to think deeply in a second-year Master's program, the answer is enlightening: "We thought about it and we transformed that thinking into an artwork."

> What is unusual is to think about what counts for us, our values, and think of it in physical forms.
> You never ask yourself what is important for me in accounting that I want to turn into an artwork.
> It is not like solving an equation; we were trying to look for something. We had no idea where we wanted to go, what we had to do, and we had to think anyway.
> "It's like in research." "Research is when you try to invent something which doesn't exist, in the Master's [program] we don't really work on that, but in the workshop we did."

These words constitute quite good attempts at defining presentational knowing as a characteristic of the workshop. All students were at ease with turning their thinking into nonverbal forms, demonstrating an unusual ability to connect knowledge with presentational forms of expression and worked at ease with the inextricability of form and content.

Second, the students also characterize the relation between creation and analytical thinking. Instead of an opposition, they identify a continuum from language to nonverbal thinking, the continuity being named analysis ("We went beyond our usual values; continuing with analysis beyond writing and speaking, this is creation"). This is an unexpected result: contrary to scholarly interpretations, students, even when confronted with art-making from a radically rationalist domain, do not oppose art analytically. It opens up a promising path for further research: if the opposition between analytical rational processes and artistic or aesthetic approaches is not experienced by the participants as an opposition but as a continuum, it requires a different use of art-based methods, less oppositional and more integrated into analytical curricula, for which our experiment could serve as a model.

One student expressed clearly what all were showing by their attitude during the opening:

> It is amazing how we can stand and look at our work and discover what we've meant.

Doing so, he was connecting cognition with perception in such a simple way that it almost seemed naïve. Less naïve were the students' ways of creating meaning by working out physical shapes: here again they attain cognition through making and perception of their own making.

Lastly, many students' comments concern judgments and the expert position. Here again, the scholarly interpretation of an opposition between the authoritarian expert posture and participative dialogical methods is not corroborated. Unanimous students' critique retrieved from the interviews focuses instead on the evaluation process, arguing that the notation procedure (attribution of credits) can lead to destroying trust and fostering strategic behaviors, masking the involvement in creation under adaptive responses to hypothesized requirements. Judgement itself is not problematic if it concerns the qualitative appreciation of the aesthetic result (form); in case of disagreement, the student must be allowed to decide what to do ("It's our opinion that counts; you come and help us but in the end it's our idea, our opinion"). Expert judgment, if it helps to achieve a high quality result, is recognized by all students as a positive element for producing a successful exhibition ("It helps us to excel; in the end we'll be proud of ourselves"; "We often reach the right result with him, even if it goes through ... difficult paths, like you have to go back to the beginning and start again, but in the end we succeed, that's what counts").

4.7.   A Preliminary Conclusion

"A preliminary conclusion" is that the noticeable outcomes pertain mainly to the "directed" (experiencing the art form) and "embedded" (embedding of knowledge in materiality) categories (Table 4.1). Making the artwork, orienting reflection toward the type of thinking research requires the importance of the material for formulating their purpose, and the aesthetic satisfaction in the end (directed outcomes) are quoted by all students as key elements in the success of the experiment. "Embedded" outcomes (inextricability of form and content, cognition mixed with perception, "art-rooted" thinking) appear in their intellectual and visual productions: when, for example, they welcome visitors to the show, they stand by their artwork and explain their ideas about norms, fraud, or social responsibility by indicating, describing, and referring to their artwork.

The fact that mainly directed and embedded outcomes were gathered, with almost none that were instrumental or developmental, clearly positions the experiment in the "form" column of the table more than the "process" one. The effects of the workshop did not result from the processes that creation triggered (except for *ad hoc* actions and bricolage). They mainly resulted from art-making and the confrontation with the realized objects.

Table 4.2 displays the observed effects for each of the five groups, according to the interviews analysis.

4.8.   Conclusion

My research questions were: (1) Does complex expression through art give access to complex knowledge and critical thinking? (2) Do students' engagement with what they consider to be crucial result in higher indirect learning? (3) Do students' concerns with their subject and higher involvement lead them to a research attitude? (4) Does the experiment help understand the role of art forms in such learnings?

Table 4.2: Student interviews analysis, sorted by expected outcomes categories.

Expected outcomes		Gr 1 change	Gr 2 fraud	Gr 3 SR	Gr 4 num.	Gr 5 norms
Instrumental	Facing ambiguity and complexity			✓		
	Nonlogical, nonrational capabilities			✓		
	Flexible purposing			✓	✓	
	Ad hoc bricolage					
Developmental	Access to embodied implicit knowledge				✓	
	Meaningful contradiction and paradoxes					
	Presentational knowing			✓		
	Consciousness, growth of mind	✓		✓		
Directed	Making	✓✓	✓✓	✓✓	✓✓	✓✓
	Aesthetic experience	✓✓	✓✓	✓✓	✓✓	✓✓
	Importance of the medium	✓✓	✓✓	✓✓	✓✓	✓✓
	Aesthetic satisfaction of action	✓	✓✓	✓	✓✓	✓✓
	Qualitative relationships	✓	✓✓	✓✓		✓✓
Embedded	Inextricability of form and content	✓✓	✓	✓✓	✓✓	✓✓
	Cognition mixed with perception					✓✓
	Judgments			✓✓		✓✓
	Art-rooted thinking	✓✓			✓✓	✓✓
	Access to embodied implicit knowledge	✓	✓			✓

A first conclusion answering questions 1–3 is that the desired deepening of knowledge was acquired by all students, accompanied by a high degree of reflection and critical thinking, visible in the production itself: all works were critical concerning the explored issues in accounting and control. The degree of reflection instilled by the workshop was qualified by the students as similar to the kind of reflection necessary for research and was closely linked to the production of art forms expressing ideas concerning the technical issues of accounting and control. They expressed how translating their thinking into visual and nonverbal forms was crucial in the process of deepening their involvement and their research attitude. The observation of the students' behaviors during the workshop, as well as their comments, also demonstrated they were appealing to and developing high-level competencies, such as the capacity to propose solutions, independent thinking, reflexivity on one's knowledge, and the ability to manage challenging projects.

Though research-oriented ways of thinking were explicitly told by the students to have been a particularly important outcome of the workshop, whether they turned more toward research or developed a research attitude after and in relation with the workshop was not examined for this session. Nevertheless, enough clues convinced us to repeat the experiment next year at the doctoral level in order to demonstrate the potential of the approach to develop a research attitude.

A second conclusion answering my fourth research question is that the "result," the artwork, the artifact becomes the focal point around which "deep learning" (Watagodakumbura, 2013) takes place. What the students expressed is that form and art-making functioned as *a (different) formulation of the thought*. This can be explained as a formulation, which goes *further than verbal formulation* but which is *still qualified as analysis*. Furthermore, the reflection that led to the form, or that was expressed by it, is defined by the students as being deeper than usual, having the quality specific to research. In summary, the art form they produced was for them an analytical nonsymbolic formulation of thought, elevating learning to research.

> I'd never thought, first, that we were capable of doing this, second, that our idea could be visualized like this and that we could do it in one day;
> The first thing I want to do is to embark on the realization;
> Now that we have this idea of suspending the net from the ceiling, I realize it will have a much stronger impact.

Beyond symbols or metaphors, the created assemblages *are* in a way the idea: the net *does* contain balance sheets, the Earth *is* dominated by a number, the blunt scissors and knives *do* form a double-edged dangerous instrument. They are the idea in the sense that they formulate it "beyond speech and writing" as the students indicate. The long-lasting effect on the students (the final interviews conducted six months later provided more outcomes than the first ones carried out during the workshop) and their positive appreciation are linked to the success of the show and the numerous positive comments they received on opening night. They succeeded in an achievement, which gave the experience its completeness and meaning: "We have an experience when the material experienced runs its course to fulfillment (...). A piece of work is finished in a way that is satisfactory; a problem receives its solution; a game is played through; a situation is so rounded out that its close is a consummation and not a cessation" (Dewey, 1934/2005, p. 205). The students did not separate knowledge from the physical form of their creation, and when they expressed that "we had to think and transform our thinking into a physical shape," they linked their inside (knowledge) with the outside (shaping of objects) without clear delimitations. They did not turn into artists at the end of the workshop. On the contrary, it seems that producing art forms has only an interest for them if it expresses better than words their thinking about the gist of their discipline.

My main conclusion is the transitional hypothesis: following the outcomes of the experiment, which seemed to confirm the transitional interpretation of the role of art forms, I suggest (to be confirmed by further research) that artworks, more than being instrumental or developmental artifacts implied in self-transformation processes, serve as intermediate objects that allow for the development of learning as research, and that improving knowledge needs the support of "aesthetic" forms — aesthetic meaning the property of an intermediate object to be both inside and outside, created and given, subjective and objective — such as artworks. Experiencing these properties of intermediate objects is more a state than a process: it is the state of being here and there, looking at the object and creating it, being looked at by the object which does not exist, being the other in oneself, and so on. The specific state one attains by experiencing creation is called catharsis by Vygotsky (1925/1971), illumination by the poet, and contemplation by the philosopher. I would like to call it *learning*. A production of "knowledge" always is a creation of the world (Hermann-Pillath, 1993), which makes it at the same time an illusion. Learning, understood as knowledge creation, is thus related to experiencing the state of transition where we do not know if the world is given or if we create it, if we are distinct from our objects or fused with them.

Applying these ideas to teaching-learning collectives could foster a different way of conceiving education and promote the use of art-based methods in an integrated way. Students are supposed to "complicate their own understanding" and form knowledge of a different kind. This is an impossible task unless they find the support of specific objects with which they can experience the intermediate state between inside and outside, inner and outer worlds, subjectivity and objectivity, and so on. Only by meeting such transitional objects, and/or by creating them, can they manage their own inner delimitations and form themselves by making art forms, after which they can make statements concerning the outer world: this is knowing and learning by investigating the transitional area where the inner and outer experiences are one. A possible way of proposing transitional learning objects is to suggest that they produce artworks, precisely because creating a thing happens in the intermediate area where me and not-me, inner and outer, ideas and things, reflection and action merge together before they split apart and give birth to a researcher and his research, a manager and her decisions, or a student and her learning development. The production of such forms, progressively labeled "artworks," which are used to evaluate the student, does not come about miraculously, but is the result of, and expresses, a continuous effort mutually achieved by teachers and students — the same effort we provided during the workshop, that is, the students, myself, and the teaching team. The effort not only consists in mastering practicalities and production skills but implicitly involves reflecting on the relation between the externalized production of shapes and the internal construction of the self (sometimes explicitly; e.g., one student questioned her ability to bring a contribution to the group, when in fact she was doing brilliantly). The students were evaluated not only on proving theoretical or factual knowledge but also (and centrally) on demonstrating their ability to produce and reflect on their own knowledge about production — which amounts to knowledge-in-practice. More than learning from the teacher, they had to "form" themselves, which happens through organizing the production of aesthetic "forms": forms whose exteriority and interiority are exchangeable. One group of students, for example, organized themselves as a production line, selecting the better "workers" and "managing" their production in order to create hundreds of small paper paste characters — as a critical expression of social responsibility practices.

"Learning" then means developing a particular state of mind considering exteriorities as interiorities, centered on peripheral perceptions, events, or facts *as if they were interiorities*. Such a state of mind allows for intensifying the self in spite of and through its dispersion, crossing inner borders in order to develop a hold on the outside, shaping the in-between. The art-maker student adopts a posture of a natural researcher who creates knowing at the moment he defines his self — or, to put it differently, by art-making the student produces his self and his knowledge at the same time. Artworks happen along the way, like cornerstones, landmarks, or memories of future travels yet to come. To read the students' productions as traces of a future being, to guess next turns and speculate on alternatives is the guidance teachers should provide. Such results, based on empowering the complexity of expression, open the way for art-making based methods focusing more on the (aesthetic) form of the deliverables required from the student than on the process of learning and recognize that empowering the complexity of expression liberates access to sophisticated knowing abilities and independent critical learning.

4.9. Limitations, Conditions, and Further Research

4.9.1. Credibility of Analysis

Though evidence of interesting outcomes arise from the production of the workshop and/or student comments, we did not assess the students afterward. Assessments concerning the mobilized knowledge and the change in the consciousness of the students' knowledge should have been done before and after the experiment. As it is, there is sufficient evidence of a good probability that the appeal to art-making results in the expected learning as to promote further experiments and research.

4.9.2. Dependability

One important factor that was not tackled in our experiment is the personality of the artist-coach leading the workshop. Though it is possible to detail the criteria for a successful experiment and find other good facilitators, it remains difficult to analyze how much of the success (or limitations) of the experiment can be attributed to the personality of the author. Different coaches would organize the workshop differently. What should be preserved is the focus on the production of "art" not as art but as the expression of the student's knowledge.

4.9.3. Confirmability

The experiment needs to be repeated at the same and different levels (Masters and Doctorate) in different fields. Further results will confirm or inform this first study. We invite researchers to develop their own experiments in the direction of art-making within classical curricula in order to enhance, promote, and broaden the scope and legitimacy of this approach. Some limitations would especially have to be explored in a deeper way. As indicated earlier, the introduction of art-making into classical education systems risks encountering anxiety and resistance; the faculty has a propensity to stick to their role as experts and to reinforce the dichotomy between knowledge and ignorance. We met these risks and they must not be underestimated, especially when we know that art-based methods instill a zone of indeterminacy between the inside and the outside, which is difficult to accept. Some points have to be investigated further.

- The mediating role of the internal faculty was not sufficiently explored. Their role is probably crucial in many ways: not only do they guarantee the security and institutional recognition of the process and legitimate the external resources but they also install the "intermediate area" where the subjective-objective distinction concerning knowledge in the field is questioned. This requires closely assisting the students in deepening their own reflexive exploration of the knowledge they already have and pushing the boundaries.

- The guidance by an external coach whose legitimacy is based on recognized expertise: it is a crucial point that needs to be explored deeper. In particular, how would the personalities of the different coaches impact the validity of the workshop? His/her expertise would be to assist the students when they encounter roadblocks in ideation for their artifacts. A secondary issue is the degree to which the coaching has to focus on the result, not the process or the method.

- *The grading issue*: should there be no grade, credits, or notation to jeopardize the process as students state? While I overcame the compulsory evaluation in our case by giving each the student the maximum grade, this is not a satisfactory solution. Why not grade students on their reflection papers about the experience (a critical component of experiential learning with which we did not experiment)?

- Pacing and timing are crucial. A tight schedule with many checkpoints and individual-collective intermediary presentations helps. The intensity of the experience is linked to its shortness. But how short can it be? And how long are the students required to be present? This was one of the main questions the students and the faculty had after our experiment. The issue is not easy to solve, as the pace of creation can be particularly slow and fast at the same time, requiring persistent and intense involvement, but it also passes through "blank page" periods where nothing happens.

- The necessity of aesthetic judgment: it must be assumed but it brings in inevitable tensions attached to it. In order to minimize the difficulties in receiving qualitative judgments, they should be uttered quickly, softly, and firmly but always with the possibility that they can be refused.

4.9.4.   *Transferability*

By integrating an art-making workshop into an accounting program, we intended to put ourselves in the most difficult context, due to the high degree of logical-rational paradigm in that field. The good result we encountered causes us to expect a good probability of success in transferring the experiment to other fields. The condition is to start from the students' involvement in their own disciplines and ask them to work on notions with which they are concerned and familiar. However, we did meet a limitation linked to the last component listed in the Carnegie Report: practical reasoning. In our experiment of art-based teaching, practical reasoning applies to art-making and not to accounting or other professional techniques. It remains to be investigated whether art-making can also foster practical reasoning concerning professional issues. Our next study and experiment will investigate and try to solve the issue, by making more room for elaborating on student concerns in their field. It may be necessary to appeal to supplementary faculty resources, and it will be time consuming, but there may be a way to transfer competencies immediately from art-making to accounting on a research level, providing we manage to keep all the experiences in the intermediate zone. I would hypothesize that the key point, in order to prevent a logical-rational stance from taking over, is to use professional reasoning as artifacts, in the same way we use materials: as intermediate objects with no clear delimitation, transitional in the sense that, at the exact moment they are created out of nothing, they exist as if they had existed for a long time, and vice versa. This is how artworks "work," and pedagogy through art-making generate critical teaching and learning.

4.9.5. Professionalism

A last point in the form of a hypothesis concerns the professionalism of learning. Responses to assignments for management students are supposed to train them to later manage and produce results for a firm. Producing forms that shape the self at the same time that they respond to an imposed constraint could train students to understand how to manage people's work in a way that makes sense. I conclude by proposing the idea that, if working life is supposed to become more meaningful and management is supposed to develop a more humanistic and sustainable dimension, then art-making could be one way to introduce critical reflexivity and a global aesthetic-analytical approach in business studies or management practices. It would enhance and "teach" the "aesthetic dimension" of organizational life and production, understood as the capacity for valuing the mutual construction of selves and collectives *by* circulating the results of productive activity towards the outside — which most firms often do not develop or do so only at a minimum.

References

Adler, N. (2006). The arts and leadership: Now that we can do anything, what will we do? *Academy of Management Learning & Education, 5*(4), 486—499.

Barry, D., & Meisiek, S. (2010). Seeing more and seeing differently: Sensemaking, mindfulness, and the workarts. *Organization Studies, 31*(11), 1505—1530.

Barry, D., & Meisiek, S. (2014). Discovering the business studio. *Journal of Management Education, 39*(1), 153—175.

Beirne, M., & Knight, S. (2007). From community theatre to critical management studies: A dramatic contribution to reflective learning? *Management Learning, 38*(5), 591—611.

Bennett, D., Wright, D., & Blom, D. (2013). The artistic practice-research-teaching (ART) nexus: Translating the information flow. *Journal of University Teaching and Learning Practice, 7*(2), 1—21.

Berthoin Antal, A. (2009). *Transforming organisations with the arts. Research framework for evaluating the effects of artistic interventions in organizations.* Research report. Gothenburg: TILLT Europe.

Biggs, M. (2004). Learning from experience: Approaches to the experiential component of practice-based research. Paper presented at the Forsknung, Reflektion, Utveckling conference, Sigtuna, Sweden.

Boal, A. (1979). *Theatre of the oppressed.* London: Pluto Press.

Carlile, P. (2002). A pragmatic view of knowledge and boundaries: Boundary objects in new product development. *Organization Science, 13*(4), 442–455.

Cunliffe, A., Forray, J., & Knights, D. (2002). Considering management education: Insights from critical management studies. *Journal of Management Education, 26*(5), 489–495.

Darso, L. (2004). *Artful creation: Learning-tales of arts-in-business.* Copenhagen: Samfundslitteratur.

Dehler, G., Welsh, M., & Lewis, M. (2001). Critical pedagogy in the "new paradigm". *Management Learning, 32*(4), 493–511.

Dewey, J. (1934/2005). *Art as experience.* New York, NY: Penguin Group.

Eisner, E. (2002). *The arts and the creation of mind.* New Haven, CT: Yale University Press.

Eisner, E. (2004). What can education learn from the arts about the practice of education? *International Journal of Education and the Arts, 5*(4), 1–13.

Ennals, R. (Ed.). (2014). *Responsible management: Corporate responsibility and working life.* Heidelberg: Springer.

Foucault, M. (2001). *Fearless speech.* Los Angeles, CA: Semiotext(e).

Hatch, M. J. (1997). *Organization theory, modern, symbolic and postmodern perspectives.* Oxford, UK: Oxford University Press.

Hatch, M. J., Kostera, M., & Kozminski, A. (2007). *The three faces of leadership: Manager, artist, priest.* Hoboken, NJ: Wiley-Blackwell.

Hermann-Pillath, C. (1993). New knowledge as creation: Notes when reading Nietzsche on evolution, power and knowledge. *Journal of Social and Evolutionary Systems, 16*(1), 25–44.

Heron, J., & Reason, P. (1997). A participatory inquiry paradigm. *Qualitative Inquiry, 3*(3), 274–294.

Hill, G., & Lloyd, K. (2015). A practice-led inquiry into the use of still images as a tool for reflective practice and organisational inquiry. *International Journal of Professional Management, 10*(2).

Huault, I., & Perret, V. (2011). Critical management education as vehicle for emancipation: Exploring the philosophy of Jacques Ranciere. *M@n@gement, 14*(5), 281–309.

Irgens, E. (2014). Art, science and the challenge of management education. *Scandinavian Journal of Management, 30*(1), 86–94.

Katz-Buonincontro, J. (2014). Decorative integration or relevant learning? A literature review of studio arts-based management education with recommendations for reaching and research. *Journal of Management Education, 39*(1), 81–115.

Le Theule, M. A., & Fronda, Y. (2002). L'organisation en tension entre routine et création: un autre regard sur l'instrumentation. In *Technologie et management de l'information, enjeux et impact dans la comptabilité, le contrôle et l'audit* (CD ROM). France.

Mack, K. (2013). Taking an aesthetic risk in management education: Reflections on an artistic-aesthetic approach. *Management Learning, 44*(3), 286–304.

Madden, L. T., & Smith, A. D. (2013). Using photographs to integrate liberal arts learning in business education. *Journal of Management Education, 39*(1), 116–140.

March, J. (1976). The technology of foolishness. In J. March & J. Olsen (Eds.), *Ambiguity and choice in organizations* (pp. 69–81). Oslo: Universitetsförlaget.

Meisiek, S., & Barry, D. (2014). The science of making management an art. *Scandinavian Journal of Management, 30*(1), 134–141.

Moriceau, J. L. (2012). I thought I only had to have an idea, and to write it clearly. Paper presented at the 6th Art of Management and Organizations conference. York, UK.

Nissley, N. (2002). Art-based learning in management education. In C. Wankel & B. Del Philippi (Eds.), *Rethinking management education for the 21st century* (pp. 27–61). Charlotte, NC: Information Age Publishing.

Nissley, N., Taylor, S., & Houden, L. (2004). The politics of performance in organizational theatre-based training and interventions. *Organization Studies, 25*(5), 817–839.

Parush, T., & Koivunen, N. (2014). Paradoxes, double binds, and the construction of "creative" managerial selves in art-based leadership development. *Scandinavian Journal of Management, 30*(1), 104–113.

Rooney, R. (2004). *Arts-based teaching and learning: Review of the literature.* Washington, DC: VSA Arts.

Schein, E. (2001). The role of art and the artist. *Organizational Aesthetics, 2*(1), 1–4.

Spee, J., & Fraiberg, A. (2015). Topics, texts, and critical approaches: Integrating dimensions of liberal learning in an undergraduate management course. *Journal of Management Education, 39*(1), 56–80.

Springborg, K. (2012). Art-based methods in management education from the symbolic, connectionist, and embodied perspective. Paper presented at the 6th Art of Management and Organization conference, York, UK.

Statler, M. (2014). Developing wisdom in a business school? Critical reflections on pedagogical practice. *Management Learning, 45*(4), 397–417.

Statler, M., & Guillet de Monthoux, P. (2015). Humanities and arts in management education: The emerging Carnegie paradigm. *Journal of Management Education, 39*(1), 3–15.

Steyaert, C., & Hjorth, D. (2002). Thou are a scholar, speak to it … on spaces of speech: A script. *Human Relations, 55*(7), 767–797.

Strati, A. (2007). Sensible knowledge and practice-based learning. *Management Learning, 38*(1), 61–77.

Sutherland, I. (2013). Arts-based methods in leadership development: Affording aesthetic workspaces, reflexivity and memories with momentum. *Management Learning, 44*(1), 25–43.

Szendy, E. (2012). Du changement au mouvement: Application de la méthodologie du Traceur au cas de la transformation du Musée National des Arts et Traditions Populaires en un musée des civilisations de l'Europe et de la Méditerranée. Doctoral dissertation. CNAM: Paris.

Taylor, S. S. (2000). Aesthetic knowledge in academia: Capitalist pigs at the Academy of Management. *Journal of Management Inquiry, 9*(3), 304–328.

Taylor, S., & Hansen, H. (2005). Finding form: Looking at the field of organizational aesthetics. *Journal of Management Studies, 42*(6), 1211–1231.

Taylor, S., & Ladkin, D. (2009). Understanding arts-based methods in managerial development. *Academy of Management Learning and Education, 8*(1), 55–69.

Turkle, S. (2007). *Evocative objects: Things we think with.* Cambridge, MA: MIT Press.

Vygotsky, L. (1925/1971). *The psychology of art.* Cambridge, MA: MIT Press.

Wankel, C., & Del Philippi, B. (Eds.). (2002). *Rethinking management education for the 21st century.* Charlotte, NC: Information Age Publishing.

Watagodakumbura, C. (2013). Authentic learning experience: Subtle but useful ways to provide it in practice. *Contemporary Issues in Education Research, 6*(3), 299–304.

Winnicot, D. W. (1971). *Playing and reality*. Chatham, UK: Routledge.

Woodward, I., & Ellison, D. (2010). Aesthetic experience, transitional objects and the third
space: The fusion of audience and aesthetic objects in the performing arts. *Thesis Eleven,
103*(1), 45–53.

Chapter 5

Application of Competency-Based Learning to Entrepreneurship Education: Integrating Curricular and Cocurricular Elements to Enhance Discipline Mastery

Rebecca J. White and Kevin Moore

Abstract

Purpose — Entrepreneurship is one of the fastest growing disciplines at colleges and universities today. Programs span campuses offering traditional coursework and a variety of experiential learning options for students from all majors. While most agree that as much learning, if not more, occurs outside of the classroom, there has not been a model for integrating curricular and cocurricular components in entrepreneurship programs. Moreover, there has not been clear agreement on how to assess value from these programs.

Methodology/approach — To resolve this, we used a five-phase competency development process to create a customized learning model that engages the learner, the educator, and the community volunteer in the learning and assessment process at both the individual and program levels. This chapter presents a case study in a private, metropolitan university of 8200 students. The case study presents the problem and rationale, a history and overview of the application of competency-based education, and a five-stage process used to develop the model and apply the model to achieve a customized learning path for students in entrepreneurship.

Findings — The five-stage model of competency-based education can be applied to develop a customized learning approach and assessment path for students who study entrepreneurship. The use of a technology support platform can extend and simplify the use of this model and allow for the integration of curricular and cocurricular components of an experiential education.

Integrating Curricular and Co-Curricular Endeavors to Enhance Student Outcomes
Copyright © 2016 by Emerald Group Publishing Limited
All rights of reproduction in any form reserved
ISBN: 978-1-78635-064-0

Originality/value – This is a unique approach to integrating curricular and cocurricular education to provide a holistic experiential education for learners. The value of this program extends to faculty who assess learning and volunteers who participate in the learning experience. Specific attention is given to the challenges and process for curriculum mapping and the use of this model for assessment.

Keywords: Competency-based learning; assessment of learning; experiential education; curriculum mapping; cocurricular program assessment; entrepreneurship education

5.1. Introduction

Competency-based learning models have been used for the past 40 years to enhance human performance in the workplace (Ennis, 2008). Introduced by McClelland in the early 1970s, competencies were recognized as significant predictors of employee performance and success (McClelland, 1973). Often more associated with training than education, these models have also been widely adopted in the development of curricula for vocational and technical education.

However, more recently the health disciplines and other advanced education systems have used competency-based learning to develop and assess mastery of knowledge and skills.

The concept and practice of using competencies to define and measure performance has been widely researched and defined. For our purposes, we define a competency as the capability of applying or using knowledge, skills, abilities, behaviors, and personal characteristics to successfully perform in a given domain. Personal characteristics include mental/intellectual/cognitive, social/emotional/attitudinal, and physical/psychomotor attributes necessary for success (Dubois, 1993; Lucia & Lepsinger, 1999; Boyatzis, 1982; Fogg, 1999) as well as internal and external constraints, environments, and relationships related to performance. Motivations and perceptions of the activity and one's self or talent are also viewed as influential in competently and successfully performing in a given role (Boyatzis, 1982; Fulmer & Conger, 2004; Gangani, McLean, & Braden, 2006; Sandberg, 2000). It should be noted that this definition of competency is more inclusive than "knowledge and skill" and focuses on the application of knowledge, skill, attitude, and the ability to meet complex demands by drawing on many psychosocial resources (Gordon et al., 2009; Schratz et al., 2013).

Competency-based education (CBE) is a framework for designing and implementing education that focuses on the desired performance capabilities of the learner within this broad definitional context. While attaining a level of "competence" has long been the goal of traditional educational systems. These traditional models of curriculum design have largely been based on the delineation of intended learning objectives of instruction. Courses and curricula are then created based on these learning objectives that focus on identifying and measuring what a learner should know. By contrast, CBE makes the acquisition of selected competencies explicit by establishing observable and measurable performance metrics that learners must *demonstrate* to be deemed "competent." Whereas traditional education tends to focus on what and how learners are taught, CBE is focused on whether or not learners can demonstrate application of learning to solve problems, communicate effectively, perform procedures, and make appropriate decisions within a given context.

Working with a structured and validated competency model provides the designer of education programs with powerful capabilities. Among those are the ability to map competency, abilities, and behaviors to curricular and cocurricular learning events. Using the competency model also allows us to sharpen our capability to create assessment programs and adapt the program based on knowledge and tasks at the individual level. A competency definition is used to create the learning path and a competency set can be used to adapt the path as long as it is valid and relevant to the entrepreneurial experience. This creates a system of learning that is centered on the individual learner and leverages the competency structure to adapt curricular and cocurricular activities.

In recent years, educators in the field of entrepreneurship have been seeking a model to define key learning outcomes for entrepreneurship education and a way to integrate curricular and cocurricular programs. CBE models provide a meaningful solution to these challenges.

In this chapter, we describe the application of CBE to the discipline of entrepreneurship. Campion et al. (2011) identify four key strengths of CBE that uniquely align with the current needs in entrepreneurship education. First, CBE is based on competency sets of knowledge, skills, abilities, and other characteristics (KSAOs) of high performance in a domain. These include behaviors demonstrating abilities that then can be used to assess degree to competency. This design allows for clear assessment of learning in any educational program that is experiential by design. Second, CBE allows for distinguishing between top performers and average performers thus there is a fit with the traditional grading models. Third, CBE allows for change over time in competencies, offering an opportunity to evaluate individual growth in competencies. Finally, the use of CBE models to design an educational program provides an opportunity to tie models of learning directly to best practice in the field.

Over the past 20 years, entrepreneurship as a field of research and study has grown in interest to both scholars and practitioners. For several decades, research was primarily focused on the activity undertaken by entrepreneurs in the launching of a new business organization (the process of entrepreneurship) rather than on the entrepreneurs' personal characteristics or traits (Gartner, 1985; Low & MacMillan, 1988; McGrath & MacMillan, 2000). Similarly, entrepreneurship pedagogy focused primarily on implementation of a business concept for many years. For example, nearly 20 years ago, Kourilsky characterized entrepreneurship education in the following manner.

> Current entrepreneurship education tends to migrate towards its natural focus of "least resistance" – the traditional business management process areas ... (1995, p. 14)

Once not even considered a discipline in many business schools, entrepreneurship education has blossomed into one of the fastest growing fields of study in the world. And, as educational institutions have rushed to get on the "entrepreneurship education growth wave," they have cobbled together programs that range from degree programs in business and other colleges (most often engineering or the arts) to those that are exclusively experience and activities-based programs (no course offerings) to those that have a combination of both curricular and cocurricular elements. The result has been a proliferation of programs and experiences designed to "educate" students on the application of an entrepreneurial mindset often built without clear methods of assessment of learning.

Today leaders in the discipline are advocating that entrepreneurship education is an instrument of empowerment for individuals and a tool for transforming markets, businesses, industries, economies, and communities (Morris, 2013). However, educators in the field have acknowledged that traditional pedagogy is not sufficient and that teaching entrepreneurship may be considered more like the study of other "crafts" such as medicine and architecture (White, Hertz, & D'Souza, 2011). The result has been a new interest in CBE as a foundation for curriculum design and learning assessment.

A few scholars have attempted to explore competencies as a way to understand entrepreneurial behavior. For example, Wing Yan Man (2006) empirically explored entrepreneurial behaviors through a competency framework and identified six behavioral patterns in the entrepreneurial learning construct. More recently, Morris, Webb, Fu, and Singhal (2013) identified 13 competencies demonstrated by successful entrepreneurs. However, these early attempts have not been based on models of competency modeling or best practices in CBE and have not integrated the cocurricular elements of study.

In this chapter, we will provide a case for the application of CBE to entrepreneurship education. We begin with an overview of CBE best practices and illustrate how the competency model development process can be leveraged to identify the KSAOs exhibited by master entrepreneurs. We also examine how application of CBE can provide a direct pathway to more thorough and meaningful entrepreneurship education assessment. Our intent in this chapter is to illustrate the process we used to leverage best practices, tools, and technology in competency modeling to align our curricular and cocurricular learning programs.

5.2. Competency-Based Learning Models

Historically competency-based learning models were designed for individuals in organizations and were based on specific work functions within a structured role. The implementation and focus on "competency modeling has been an important innovation in that it is a way to get organizations to pay attention to job-related information and employee skills in the management of employees" (Campion et al., 2011, p. 1). Like many disciplines, competency modeling has gone through some significant growing pains through the years. Literature in competency modeling wrestled with two underlying questions: First, the need for further definition around what a competency is and what it is not and secondly, a clearer understanding of the conditions in which to apply the competency model.

The definition of "competency" dominated the early competency literature. As late as 1997, The Society of Industrial and Organizational Psychology (SIOP) established a task force consisting of leading researchers and practitioners to focus on the following five questions:

1. What is a competency?
2. What is the difference between competency modeling and job analysis?
3. Why are competencies so appealing in the most comprehensive literature review on competency modeling?
4. Should competency models be validated?
5. What is the future of competency modeling?

For two years, the task force investigated these questions and, based upon a comprehensive literature review, concluded that even with the most knowledgeable competency modeler or researcher that there was no single agreed upon definition of competency. They did agree upon a number of principles, however. Those included that a job analysis is much more "work focused" while competency modeling is "individual" focused and neither is a singular approach to describing the working environment. Competency models should be validated using a process and involving those who do the work. Finally, while there exists a significant need for further research along specific areas there is great hope for the discipline of competency modeling (Shippmann et al., 2000).

Indeed the discipline of competency modeling, while struggling with some direction, was clearly making headway. Recently, the overall push to understand competency modeling and apply these concepts to education through competency-based education (CBE) has been gaining significant backing. While CBE has played a role in traditional education venues for decades, application at the college/university level has used a different model (Shapiro, 2014). However, this is changing in large part to a political push to design and deliver affordable degree programs. Despite concerns among professors, there are increasing numbers of universities moving in the direction of competency-based programs (Ordonez, 2014).

More recently, the field of medical education has taken CBE to new levels by applying competency models within their curriculum with a large commitment from their community. competency-based medical education (CBME) is a hot topic with researchers seeking more powerful definitions, a framework for applying competency modeling and the dissemination into supporting fields such as public health and social work education (Ervin, Carter, & Robinson, 2013; Frank et al., 2013; Newell & Nelson-Gardell, 2014). The advances in CBME have given educators and curriculum/instructional designers validated tools to apply in the development of their own competency models. Through the application of CBE methods to other areas such as engineering education and tourism management, a theoretical toolset has been developed. These tools include definition acceptance, competency frame-work design, benchmarking methodologies, assessment methodologies, and validation methodologies (Cecil & Krohn, 2012; Ervin et al., 2013; Frank et al., 2013; Kasser, Hitchins, Frank, & Zhao, 2013; Mirzazadeh et al., 2013; Newell, 2013).

5.3.   Entrepreneurship Education

In this chapter, we discuss the application of CBE to entrepreneurship education. The practice of buying and selling goods and services and starting new ventures has been a vital part of the business economy for centuries. Based on Schumpeter's (1934) process of creative destruction, business scholars from economics and marketing provided support for the value of innovation for economic growth. Yet, for decades, business colleges only weakly acknowledged the importance of the founder and the early stages of business development. There were a few academic pioneers such as Penrose (1955) who focused research on the role of the entrepreneur and Stinchcombe (1965) who directed the attention of organizational theorists to the risk associated with young firms, a concept he referred to as a "liability of newness." However, until the 1970s, the startup and early stages of a business were taken as forgone conclusions and the important and interesting research questions were primarily focused on how to manage the enterprise that had grown beyond the earliest stages of development.

The roots of the study of entrepreneurship as a distinct discipline and as we know it today began to emerge in business schools in the early 1970s. However, research questions focused on small firms were primarily examining the similarities and differences between small and large firms and/or the traits of successful entrepreneurs (Hornaday & Bunker, 1970; Mancuso, 1974). Large firms were considered by the top academics as the important and interesting players in the marketplace. However, in response to market demand, new programs provided by the Small Business Administration (SBA) began to grow and Small Business Development Centers (SBDCs) exploded in number. In the academic world, scholars began to examine traits of successful business owners, best practices among small firms and the impact of this significant group on the economy. The results were dramatic and the field continued to expand in the 1980s. By the mid-1980s, small business had been clearly differentiated from entrepreneurship (Carland, Hoy, Boulton, & Carland, 1984) and scholarly exploration of the process and skills necessary to start and fund wealth-creating firms took root. Simultaneously, there was an explosion of degrees and programs in business colleges focusing on the study of new venture creation of high growth firms. The number of schools teaching a new venture or similar course grew from a few dozen in the early 1980s to more than 1600 20 years later (Katz, 2004; Kuratko, 2004; Solomon, Duffy, & Tarabishy, 2002).

In 2000, the notion of an entrepreneurial mindset was formulated (McGrath & MacMillan, 2000) and the next decade was marked by a movement to expand entrepreneurship education beyond the business college and even the academic community and into the world of practice. Accelerators and educational programs for entrepreneurs have exploded both on university campuses and in communities across the United States and worldwide. And, at the same time, entrepreneurship programs in other disciplines such as engineering and the arts (Streeter & Jacquette, 2004) have grown.

The result is that the discipline has been striving for academic legitimacy (Brazeal & Herbert, 1999; Kuratko, 2004, 2005; Neck & Greene, 2011; Solomon et al., 2002). Questions regarding how entrepreneurship is taught and who is best positioned to teach have not been fully addressed. According to Neck and Greene (2011), the "academic field and the practical field of entrepreneurship have consistently been at odds." Often their differences are around such questions as whether entrepreneurs are born or made, whether the discipline can be taught, and whether there are universal principles of entrepreneurship (Caird, 1992; Henry, Hill, & Leitch, 2005a, 2005b; Kirby, 2004). This lack of agreement on both content and pedagogy in entrepreneurship education has led to a lack of consistency among courses and curricula. For example, in a review of entrepreneurship course syllabi, Fiet (2001) found that entrepreneurship courses encompassed 116 topics but overlapped only on one-third. Henry et al. (2005a) summarized this state by suggesting that the content developed by scholars differed "to such an extent that it is difficult to determine if they even have a common purpose" (p. 103).

In spite of this, entrepreneurship has become one of the most popular areas of study on many campuses with students from all disciplines interested in business startup. For example, a recent gallop poll suggested that 8 out of 10 high school students want to be entrepreneurs (Calderon, 2011). Entrepreneurship programs are experiential in nature and therefore can be quite costly. The outcome is that billions of dollars are spent on the discipline as schools add programs, centers, new space for creative endeavors, and new people to provide learning opportunities. In addition, groups such as Start up Weekend make claims about their ability to serve as the best educational program available for nascent entrepreneurs. As a result, the pressure is increasing for entrepreneurship educators to create value for their stakeholders and demonstrate impact. Yet it remains unclear how we define an educated and prepared graduate of entrepreneurship education.

Gaining clarity around impact is complicated by the experiential nature of the programs. In fact, it can be argued that the majority of learning takes place outside of the classroom. Programs such as boot camps, competitions, and networking events provide the opportunity for students to learn basic skills required for success in new venture creation. However, measuring learning in these environments has been mostly anecdotal to date and has not provided an avenue for longitudinal program assessment nor the opportunity for continuous improvement based upon multiple evaluations.

In recent years, academic groups such as the United States Association for Small Business and Entrepreneurship (USASBE) and the Global Consortium of Entrepreneurship (GCEC) have provided opportunity for dialogue about the direction of the discipline. In these forums, it has become apparent that educators are seeking a model for defining key learning outcomes for entrepreneurship education and for integration of curricular and cocurricular programs. CBE models provide a meaningful solution to these challenges.

5.4.   Entrepreneurship Education and Assessment

Few studies have examined the short-term or long-term effects of entrepreneurship education on student attitudes, behaviors, and professional competencies (Duval-Couetil, 2013; Pittaway, Hannon, Gibb, & Thompson, 2009). To date, the literature has focused on the development of programs with an assumption that by offering well-designed courses and curricula, students will increase their knowledge and skills and that this will lead to an increased likelihood of success in the workplace and as founders of new ventures. However, few studies have tested this assumption (Dickson, Solomon, & Weaver, 2008; Gorman, Hanlon, & King, 1997).

There are two primary forms of assessment that have begun to take root in business education. The use of the first, which is a form of *summative evaluation*, involves measuring what students do and do not know at a specific point in time. This trend has been driven by AACSB's accreditation and "Assurance of Learning" program. In this method of measurement, each degree program develops a list of learning objectives and identifies measures for each that are reviewed periodically for a sample of students. More recently, there has been a movement toward a second form of assessment as a learning tool. These efforts have been focused on *formative assessment* (Moskal, Ellis, & Keon, 2008; Pringle & Michel, 2007), a form of evaluation that provides continuous feedback to students that can be used to accelerate and improve learning.

According to Duval-Couetil (2013) assessment of entrepreneurship, education programs have several unique challenges. These include (1) it is a young and ill-defined discipline; (2) there is significant diversity among programs; (3) it emphasizes practice and instructors include both academic educators and practitioners; and (4) it is assumed that both venture creation and economic development are the primary outcomes. In order to address these unique challenges, we turned to competency-based learning models. These validated models offer the opportunity to clearly address the first three as well as an avenue to expand the field beyond the narrow perspective of outcomes limited to venture creation and economic development. Thus, by applying CBE to entrepreneurship education, we believe the current challenges of assessment can be addressed.

5.5.   Integrating Curricular and Cocurricular Programs through a Competency Learning Model

Over the years, entrepreneurship programs on most campuses have taken one of a few paths. Often these programs begin with an inspired faculty champion. However, sometimes the impetus for an entrepreneurship program begins with an administrator who is eager to offer this popular major on campus. A third pathway is often a successful entrepreneur donor who has reached financial success and wants to give back to his or her academic institution by endowing an entrepreneurship program. Either way, programs may begin as a course or two in the management department or less frequently, the marketing department, and then grow into minors and often majors in entrepreneurship. Alternatively, some programs will begin with a full major and an endowed Center.

Academic content developed through entrepreneurship scholarship grew in parallel to these programs. More and more young faculty were drawn to the field and increasing numbers of seasoned faculty began to add to our understanding of entrepreneurship as opportunities increased. In a study funded by the Kauffman Foundation, Katz (2004) found that the number of chairs and professorships in entrepreneurship and related fields in the United States grew 71 percent, from 237 in 1999 to 406 in 2003. Globally, he identified 563 endowed positions around the world, up from 271 in 1999. These translated into a quarter of a billion dollars being spent on newly endowed positions from 2000 to 2004.

Historically, centers of entrepreneurship were developed to either support the academic program by providing opportunities for experiential learning and/or scholarship or as standalone programs, often funded by a successful donor, to provide continuing educational programs for the community. Centers most frequently were either focused on teaching, scholarship, service to the community or some combination of the three. For those center and programs focused on experiential learning, centers became the main avenue to connect students to the business community through speaker programs, boot camps, competitions, accelerators, and other opportunities to network and build entrepreneurial skills while in college.

Parents, employers, and educators have long realized the pedagogical value in these programs as they have watched the development of nascent entrepreneurs over their academic careers; however, they have not had clear measures of learning associated with these programs. In order to resolve this, we used a five-phase competency program development process (Figure 5.1). The process begins with a competency identification and validation process followed by curriculum mapping, a customization

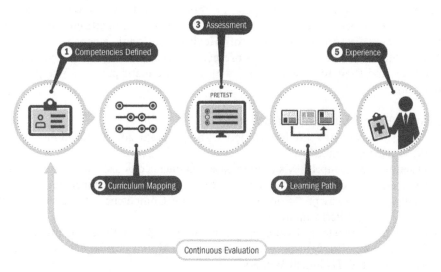

Figure 5.1: Five Phase Competency Program Development Model.

process and learning path and assessment of performance. This process gives us a competency structure or a complete competency model. The competency structure will allow for mapping curricular and cocurricular activities to the competency model. Creating a competency definition or even a competency definition and a set of associated behaviors is inadequate for assessment or the mapping to learning objectives.

5.6.   Five-Phase Competency Program Development Process

5.6.1.   *Competency Model and Validation Process*

While there is a significant push to apply competency models within higher education, it is important to note that our goal in establishing the competency model was not necessarily to allow credit to be given for past experiences and accelerate the student through the program. While recognizing and building on those life experiences within the structure, our goal was entirely on the instructional design and the ability to personalize the curricular and cocurricular activities to provide a rich learning experience. Overtly, we did have a goal to add legitimate learning principles by applying the competency structure to our cocurricular activities. In this way, it would be possible to give a certificate or even badges (success-based criteria) based on the interaction of the students with the cocurricular activities alone.

While developing a competency model for entrepreneurs is a daunting task, using expertise in that field was afforded to our development process. As noted in the biographies, one of the primary authors for this chapter is one of the founders of TiER1 Performance Solutions. TiER1 specializes in human performance with past experiences working in competency modeling with the United States Air Force Human Performance Wing, large commercial organizations, and government agencies (National Institute of Health, National Science Foundation, NASA) which was essential. For our project, we leveraged TiER1's expertise, past experience, and their four-phase competency development process. The process is listed below:

- Phase 1: Establish the competency structure
  - Work with key stakeholders to define the program goals and intended use of the competency model.
  - Determine the competency structure based on intended goals: Two-Level Structure: Competency and Necessary Ability, Three-Level Structure: Competency, Necessary Ability, and Behaviors: Four-Level Structure: Competency, Necessary Ability, Behaviors, and Performance Criteria.
  - Create the Competency Evaluation Team: Subject Matter Experts (Entrepreneurs), Entrepreneur Educators, Curriculum/Instructional Designers, Competency Modelers, and Technical Writers.
- Phase 2: Develop Competency and Ability Statements

- Conduct a Literature Review of Competency Statements within the subject area and associated subject areas.
- Develop a high level draft of Competency and Necessary Ability statements.
- Conduct a Comparative analysis with other competency frameworks from associated domains (e.g., Management and Leadership).
- Review with the Competency Evaluation Team.
- Conduct interviews using focus groups, nominal group process, and individual interviewing.
- Synthesize and consolidate.
- Validate and rank competencies with the Competency Evaluation Team.
- Conduct a larger scale field test of the Competency and Necessary Ability structure and gather data.
- Phase 3: Develop the Competency Matrix
  - Develop the entire Competency Matrix (Two-Level, Three-Level, or Four-Level).
    - Level 1 is the Competency with an overall definition. Typically there are between 7 and 16 competencies defined within a domain.
    - Level 2 is the Necessary Ability with definitions. Typically there are between 5 and 7 necessary abilities for every competency.
    - Level 3 is the Effective Behavior with definitions. This is a level of granularity where the individual understands at the task level what is required. There are between 4 and 8 effective behaviors for each of the necessary abilities identified.
    - Level 4 is the Performance Requirement. This begins to form the basis for assessment and level of mastery of the competency. Awareness of the behavior, application of the behavior or a higher order thinking to lead the behavior.
  - Develop the Associated Performance Statements to each behavior.

    In this model, each competency forms a "Competency Set" within the structure. For example, *Management* is the *Competency* and includes Planning, Standardization, Controlling, and Delegation as *Necessary Abilities*. The effective *Behaviors* for the Planning Necessary Ability are Able to sequence actions, Able to confirm practicality of plans, Able to identify variables in the plan, and the Ability to break down a goal. For this Competency set, each level is critical to understand for the individual to perform and attain mastery.
- Phase 4: Validate the Competency Model
  - Implement large scale validation process

For validation, we used a web competency validation tool from TiER1 (see screen shot below) that allowed for the collection and alignment of demographic data to the entrepreneurs selection of Competency and Necessary Ability in a priority sort activity. Subjects were invited to participate in the validation model via this platform. This allowed us to validate the competency model on both priority of Competency and Necessary Ability relative to the entrepreneurs experience level as well as a variety of business and entrepreneur level demographic variables.

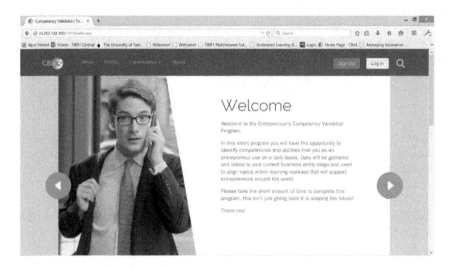

5.6.2. Curriculum Mapping

The process of mapping existing curriculum is not a trivial matter as it takes time, must be thorough, and a process must be established to make it continuous. Research on mapping curriculum to competency models is sparse at best and most assume it is straightforward process. This area of research is a rich opportunity and the importance of the mapping process for Personal Learning Pathways is critical. See Figure 5.2 for a process overview of the mapping process. However, as Ervin et al. (2013) discovered the mapping process has several notable problems: Interpretation of skill/competency, philosophical interpretation; difficulty determining the proficiency level; background of rater (faculty); and the relationship between each competency. In addition, the process requires a team approach and must involve all those who teach within the program. Involving the entire faculty in teams helps avoid problems later with other issues such as scheduling for faculty on off teaching days or on sabbatical, time required to map to the competency, and interpretation and structure of each learning objective by instructors at the course level.

In order to integrate our curriculum with the cocurricular programs, we first reviewed all of our courses to ensure the curriculum is aligned with the competency model. Overall the mapping process resulted in an evaluation of 24 curricular hours of entrepreneurship coursework for an undergraduate major. The programs reviewed included three speaker series programs, a multilevel competition and bootcamp program, a student run and student attended conference, pitch competitions, business plan competitions, an accelerator, an internship program, and a mentoring and shadowing program. We also provided students with an option to request a review of programs not offered through the university center (similar to the process of reviewing transfer courses).

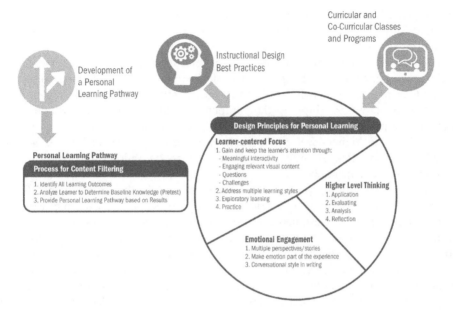

Figure 5.2: Competency Mapping Process.

The mapping process, while tedious, can be a highly creative exercise and produce an overall evaluation of the curriculum that is highly valuable. As an AACSB accredited college of business, we used their Assurance of Learning model as a first step. We then leveraged a Web-based curriculum mapping tool that allowed us to visually see the overall curriculum and cocurriculum relative to the competency model down to the behaviors/learning objectives. The result of this process was the *Spartan Entrepreneur Curriculum Map* and the associated competencies from the visual mapping tool. The curriculum mapping process has four levels:

1. Mapping the curriculum to the competency model.
2. Mapping each individual course to the Necessary Abilities and Behaviors within competency model.
3. Developing learning objectives for each cocurricular activity within the program and mapping Competency − Ability − Behavior within the competency model.
4. Assigning and mapping the performance requirement (if required) to the assessment within the courses and across the curriculum.

Curriculum design is different from course level design and this is accounted for in the structure of the competency model. Using the syllabi and the instructional faculty, we examined the curriculum relative to the competency and abilities in the model. Global discussion questions included examining assumptions and opinions about how to define a competent entrepreneur and identifying the abilities graduates of the program should possess. More specific to the program, discussions examined program and curriculum gaps and redundancies and how to improve at the program (curriculum) level. In addition, discussions on the performance level required for each course and the type of assessment used within the learning environment were essential to truly assess those behaviors. We created a high-level process "thought" document that we used to determine the level of course, lesson, topic and aligned to the language within the competency structure. This also allowed us to create learning objectives and begin the process of aligning our cocurricular activities. Mapping the competency model to each individual course was then supported within the structure of the competency model as seen in Figure 5.2. The higher-level curriculum mapping courses typically will be associated with competencies and within those courses the abilities and behaviors will be addressed appropriately.

Through the mapping process, we identified gaps in the program that we did not account for in the regular curriculum design process. For example, we found that students enter as freshmen and do not have an opportunity to take courses until they are accepted in the business college as juniors. In order to provide an opportunity for students to engage sooner, we added a freshman course for students interested in entrepreneurship. Through our discussions, we also found that students often have limited opportunities to engage in programming in late evening hours and on the weekends. To remedy this, we were able to add a live and learn component by specifying a dorm for students declaring an interest or major in entrepreneurship and adding supportive programming for this group. In addition, we increased the hours of access to the entrepreneurship center by adding new space that is staffed later hours. Thus, the process of mapping the curriculum to the competency model had many unintended but very positive outcomes.

5.6.3. *Personalization and Assessment*

The *Spartan Entrepreneur Curriculum Map* platform provided us with a way to determine a base level of entrepreneurial competency for each student entering the system. In addition to completing this assessment, each participating student completes two validated behavioral and personality assessments. Combined with the competency assessment, these two allowed us to create a baseline for each entering student. The first of these is the DISCflex® built on a behavior assessment tool based on the *DISC* theory of psychologist William Moulton Marston, which centers on four different behavioral traits: dominance, inducement, submission, and compliance. The second is the EMP (Entrepreneurial Mindset Profile). Developed by the Leadership Development Institute at Eckerd College (a Network Associate of the Center for Creative Leadership), the EMP is an assessment tool based on extensive research into the traits, motivations, and skills of entrepreneurs. The EMP assesses the "entrepreneurial mindset" and how it affects growth, innovation, and an entrepreneur's overall success.

Students can take the three assessments at any point in their academic career; however, we seek to make students aware of the opportunity and encourage them to enter the process as soon as they identify an interest in entrepreneurship. Since students from any major can participate in the cocurricular programs, the assessments are not limited to entrepreneurship majors.

5.6.4. Customized and Adaptive Learning Path

Once a student's advisor receives the results of the two assessments, the student meets with a center advisor to map out his or her learning path. In order to create an adaptive model that students and faculty could use to manage and assess individual learning, we developed an electronic platform, *The Entrepreneurship Collective (TEC)* to aid in the tracking process. As with most entrepreneurship programs, we faced the challenge of how to build and maintain an engaged learning community that included students, faculty, and volunteers. For example, most programs have entrepreneurs in residence, entrepreneurs and other business leaders from the community who judge and mentor and provide internships and speakers from the community and other academic institutions. Furthermore, most center leaders are then faced with building a method for engaging these individuals and scheduling programming. The creation of an electronic process for this activity is particularly valuable because it allows a pathway to seamlessly engage all key stakeholders in the learning process. In addition, it allows for selective information sharing so that student information can be kept confidential. Finally, the model allows a platform for graduates to stay involved in the program and thus enhance the opportunity to gather longitudinal data on alumni (to learn more about the electronic model please contact the authors).

5.6.5. Assessment

The entire model was created to provide an opportunity to better assess learning in entrepreneurship and to provide a learning model that would overcome the challenges outlined earlier in this chapter. By integrating the curriculum with cocurricular student offerings via a scientific process and utilizing technology to collect data and review progress, faculty and administrators have a way to track and assess learning. The key benefit then becomes a way to help students customize learning and for programs to assess not only individual learning but to also provide collective data on students at any point in time, in any course or program or to track the progress of the program and its students and graduates over time. Ultimately job performance and impact of new companies built can be assessed and can become a valuable aid to continuous improvement of academic programs in entrepreneurship.

To assess the model, we intend to develop a governance plan for each of the programs in the cocurricular program. Governance and maintenance plans must consist of continuous evaluation at all levels of the alignment process (please refer to Figure 5.3).

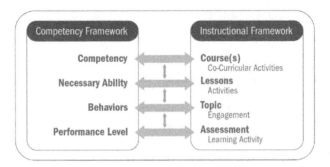

Figure 5.3: Program Structure and Assessment.

5.7. Conclusion

Our overarching goal was to use competency modeling for the purpose of creating a more powerful learning environment. We created a comprehensive model and validated that model not just on competency, ability, and behavior but linked the priority of those elements based on stage of the business, education level, and experience level of the entrepreneur. The model is self-evolving and thus becomes more valuable and precise as we continue to collect significant amounts of data across multiple demographics as well as multiple host institutions. As other faculties and institutions leverage the model, we can begin to collectively add legitimacy to many of the amazing things programs and people are doing to advance entrepreneurship using a singular scale. The four-level structure of the model (*Competency − Necessary Ability − Behavior − Performance Level*) adds significant power to the utility in curriculum design and evaluation.

Assessment of learning with a competency model allows us to not only measure the overall program but also the learner and learning activity. Using written tests, experiential activities, project work, and so on, provided the designer of the content some guidance on the level of mastery for each behavior or ability. The mapping of the curricular and cocurricular activities was our intended goal but in reality we were able to design more powerful and engaged learning programs for our students. Through this process, we were able to add legitimacy to each learning objectives that was written and placed in our syllabi. This is true for both the Terminal Learning Objectives and the Enabling Learning Objectives for the classes and the cocurricular activities.

While this process is extremely valuable in allowing us to create more aligned and powerful learning programs there were both intended and hidden elements that we discovered to be helpful. The process:

- Allowed us to evaluate our curriculum in a purposeful manner and align this to entrepreneurs.
- Allowed us to evaluate courses, lessons, topics, and methods of assessment in meaningful ways.
- Allowed us to evaluate and align our cocurricular activities to competency and ability statements providing legitimate linkages and assurance of learning to these activities.

- Provided useful data on the entrepreneurial ecosystem and how our curriculum/cocurricular activities align.
- Provided opportunity for us to modify our elements within programs (Incubator Application and selection process, Speaker selection and learning objectives process for these events, and others).
- Provided opportunities for us to think about our advising capability for our majors and minors in a meaningful way.
- Allowed us to personalize a path for individual students who come to our program with different levels of experience such as nascent entrepreneurs and students, military veterans, business owners, and service providers.

Finally, it goes without saying that the team we assembled to do this project is critical. The opportunity to leverage TiER1 Performance Solutions and their technology and tools for process and experience gave us an advantage. The tools themselves allowed us to reach out to many entrepreneurs around the world, in many sized businesses, at every stage, at every level, to validate the model and add both quantitative and qualitative data to the process and outreach to the entrepreneurial community for validation. Having individuals who can go deep in theory and practice of entrepreneurship education, formally trained in theories of learning and teaching instructional designers, competency modeling professionals with significant experience in both theory and practice, and supportive faculty who understand and want to drive toward these far reaching goals is clearly an advantage when undertaking a project of this magnitude.

While we learned a tremendous amount and created a system of learning that uses the flow of data to encompass what entrepreneurs are actually doing, develop a more precise theory and practice of teaching and learning in entrepreneurship education, and identify a path for continuous assessment and evaluation, there is a note of caution. The model is foundational as a reference point but years and years of teaching and learning experience should not be discounted. Entrepreneurship is a complex and dynamic theater in which to play. While this is one potentially valuable tool, other models and methods should not be discounted. In the end, the model merely *guides* design — it should not *drive* design.

Applying this model was especially valuable to the field of entrepreneurship education, however, it can also be used in any discipline that employs experiential learning and/or engages the student learner with the practitioner via cocurricular activities. We believe the principles of developing and accessing learning via CBE models and customized learning paths has universal application.

References

Boyatzis, R. E. (1982). *The competent manager: A model for effective performance.* New York, NY: Wiley.

Brazeal, D. V., & Herbert, T. T. (1999). The genesis of entrepreneurship. *Entrepreneurship Theory and Practice, 23*(3), 29–45.

Caird, S. (1992). Problems with the identification of enterprise competencies. *Management Education and Development, 23*(1), 9.

Calderon, V. (2011). *U.S. students' entrepreneurial energy waiting to be tapped.* Gallup. Retrieved from http://www.gallup.com/poll/150077/students-entrepreneurial-energy-waiting-tapped.aspx

Campion, M. A., Fink, A. A., Ruggeberg, B. J., Carr, L., Phillips, G. M., & Odman, R. B. (2011). Doing competencies well: Best practices in competency modeling. *Personnel Psychology, 64*(1), 225−262.

Carland, J. W., Hoy, F., Boulton, W. R., & Carland, J. A. C. (1984). Differentiating entrepreneurs from small business owners: A conceptualization. *Academy of Management Review, 9*(2), 354−359.

Cecil, A., & Krohn, B. (2012). The process of developing a competency-based academic curriculum in tourism management. *Journal of Teaching in Travel & Tourism, 12*(2), 129−145.

Dickson, P. H., Solomon, G. T., & Weaver, K. M. (2008). Entrepreneurial selection and success: Does education matter? *Journal of Small Business and Enterprise Development, 15*(2), 239−258.

Dubois, D. D. (1993). *Competency-based performance improvement: A strategy for organizational change.* Amherst, MA: HRD Press, Inc.

Duval-Couetil, N. (2013). Assessing the impact of entrepreneurship education programs: Challenges and approaches. *Journal of Small Business Management, 51*(3), 394−409.

Ennis, M. R. (2008). *Competency models: A review of the literature and the role of the employment and training administration (ETA).* Office of Policy Development and Research, Employment and Training Administration, US Department of Labor.

Ervin, L., Carter, B., & Robinson, P. (2013). Curriculum mapping: Not as straightforward as it sounds. *Journal of Vocational Education and Training, 65*(3), 309−318.

Fiet, J. O. (2001). The theoretical side of teaching entrepreneurship. *Journal of Business Venturing, 16*(1), 1−24.

Fogg, C. D. (1999). *Implementing your strategic plan: How to turn "intent" into effective action for sustainable change.* New York, NY: American Management Association.

Frank, J. R., Mungrod, R., Ahmed, Y., Wang, M., De Rossi, S., & Horsley, T. (2013). Toward a definition of competency-based education in medicine: A systematic review of published definitions. *Medical Teacher, 32*(8), 631−637.

Fulmer, R. M., & Conger, J. A. (2004). Identifying talent. *Executive Excellence, 21*(4), 11.

Gangani, N., McLean, G. N., & Braden, R. A. (2006). A competency-based human resources development strategy. *Performance Improvement Quarterly, 19*(1), 127−139.

Gartner, W. B. (1985). A conceptual framework for describing the phenomenon of new venture creation. *Academy of Management Review, 10*(4), 696−706.

Gordon, J., Halász, G., Krawczyk, M., Leney, T., Michel, A., Pepper, D., ... Wiśniewski, J. (2009). *Key competences in Europe: Opening doors for lifelong learners Warsaw.* CASE Centre for Social and Economic Research, on behalf of CASE Network.

Gorman, G., Hanlon, D., & King, W. (1997). Some research perspectives on entrepreneurial education, enterprise education and education for small business management: A ten year review. *International Small Business Journal, 15*(3), 56−77.

Henry, C., Hill, F., & Leitch, C. (2005a). Entrepreneurship education and training: Can entrepreneurship be taught? Part I. *Education and Training, 47*(2), 98−111.

Henry, C., Hill, F., & Leitch, C. (2005b). Entrepreneurship education and training: Can entrepreneurship be taught? Part II. *Education and Training, 47*(2−3), 158−169.

Hornaday, J. A., & Bunker, C. S. (1970). The nature of the entrepreneur. *Personnel Psychology, 23*(1), 47−54.

Kasser, J., Hitchins, D., Frank, M., & Zhao, Y. Y. (2013). A framework for benchmarking competency assessment models. *Systems Engineering, 16*(1), 29–44.

Katz, J. A. (2004). The chronology and intellectual trajectory of American entrepreneurship education. *Journal of Business Venturing, 18*(2), 283–300.

Kirby, D. A. (2004). Entrepreneurship education: Can business schools meet the challenge? *Education and Training, 46*(8–9), 510–519.

Kourilsky, M. L. (1995). Entrepreneurship education: Opportunity in search of a curriculum. *Business Education Forum, 50*(1), 11–15.

Kuratko, D. (2004, January). Entrepreneurship education in the 21st century: From legitimization to leadership. Paper presented at the United States Association for Small Business and Entrepreneurship (USASBE) National conference, Dallas, TX.

Kuratko, D. (2005). The emergence of entrepreneurship education: Development, trends, and challenges. *Entrepreneurship Theory and Practice, 29*(5), 20.

Low, M. B., & MacMillan, I. C. (1988). Entrepreneurship: Past research and future challenges. *Journal of management, 14*(2), 139–161.

Lucia, A. D., & Lepsinger, R. (1999). *Art & science of competency models*. San Francisco, CA: Jossey-Bass.

Mancuso, J. R. (1974). What it takes to be an entrepreneur: A questionnaire approach. *Journal of Small Business Management, 12*(4), 16–22.

McClelland, D. C. (1973). Testing for competence rather than for "intelligence". *American Psychologist, 28*(1), 1–14.

McGrath, R. G., & MacMillan, I. C. (2000). *The entrepreneurial mindset: Strategies for continuously creating opportunity in an age of uncertainty* (Vol. 284). Boston, MA: Harvard Business Press.

Mirzazadeh, A., Hejri, S. M., Jalili, M., Asghari, F., Labaf, A., Siyahkal, M. S., & Saleh, N. (2013). Defining a competency framework: The first step toward competency based medical education. *Acta Medica Iranica, 52*(9), 710–716.

Morris, M. H. (2013). Entrepreneurship as empowerment and transformation. Paper presented at the Global Consortium of Entrepreneurship Centers, Kansas City, MO.

Morris, M. H., Webb, J., Fu, J., & Singhal, S. (2013). A competency-based perspective on entrepreneurship education: Conceptual and empirical insights. *Journal of Small Business Management, 51*(3), 352–369.

Moskal, P., Ellis, T., & Keon, T. (2008). Summary of assessment in higher education and the management of student-learning data. *Academy of Management Learning and Education, 7*(2), 269–278.

Neck, H., & Greene, P. (2011). Entrepreneurship education: Known worlds and new frontiers. *Journal of Small Business Management, 49*(1), 55–70.

Newell, M. E. (2013). Patients of the future: A survey of school nurse competencies with implications for nurse executives in the acute care settings. *Nursing Administration Quarterly, 37*(3), 254–265.

Newell, J. M., & Nelson-Gardell, D. (2014). A competency-based approach to teaching professionals self-care: An ethical consideration for social work educators. *Journal of Social Work Education, 50*(3), 427–439.

Ordonez, B. (2014). Competency-based education: Changing the traditional college degree power, policy, and practice. *New Horizons in Adult Education and Human Resource Development, 26*(4), 47–53.

Penrose, E. (1955). Limits to the growth and size of firms. *The American Economic Review, 45*(2), 531–543.

Pittaway, L., Hannon, P., Gibb, A., & Thompson, J. (2009). Assessment practice in enterprise education. *International Journal of Entrepreneurial Behaviour Research*, *15*(1), 71–93.

Pringle, C., & Michel, M. (2007). Assessment practices in AACSB-accredited business schools. *Journal of Education for Business*, *82*(4), 202–211.

Sandberg, J. (2000). Understanding human competence at work: An interpretative approach. *The Academy of Management Journal*, *43*(1), 9–25.

Schratz, M., Laiminger, A., MacKay, F. K. P., Křížková, E., Kirkham, G. A., Baráth, T., & Söderberg, T. (2013). *The art and science of leading a school: Central5: A Central European view on competencies for school leaders: Final report of the project: International co-operation for school leadership involving Austria, the Czech Republic, Hungary, Slovakia, Slovenia, Sweden 2013*. Budapest, Hungary: Tempus Public Foundation.

Schumpeter, J. A. (1934). *The theory of economic development: An inquiry into profits, capital, credit, interest, and the business cycle*. New York, NY: Oxford University Press.

Shapiro, J. (2014). Competency-based degrees: Coming soon to a campus near you. *Chronicle of Higher Education*, February 17. Retrieved from http://chronicle.com/article/Competency-Based-Degree-/144769

Shippmann, J. S., Ash, R. A., Batjtsta, M., Carr, L., Eyde, L. D., Hesketh, B., … Sanchez, J. I. (2000). The practice of competency modeling. *Personnel Psychology*, *53*(3), 703–707.

Solomon, G. T., Duffy, S., & Tarabishy, A. (2002). The state of entrepreneurship education in the United States: A nationwide survey and analysis. *International Journal of Entrepreneurship Education*, *1*(1), 21.

Stinchcombe, A. L. (1965). Social structure and organizations. In J. March (Ed.), *Handbook of organizations* (pp. 142–193). Chicago, IL: Rand McNally.

Streeter, D., & Jacquette, J. (2004). University-wide entrepreneurship education: Alternative models and current trends. *Southern Rural Sociology*, *20*(2), 27.

White, R. J., Hertz, G. T., & D'Souza, R. D. (2011). Teaching a craft – Enhancing entrepreneurship education. *Small Business Institute Journal*, *7*(2), 1–14.

Wing Yan Man, T. (2006). Exploring the behavioural patterns of entrepreneurial learning: A competency approach. *Education + Training*, *48*(5), 309–321.

Chapter 6

Bridging the Clinical-Doctrinal Divide: Clinician and Student Views of Teaching and Learning in Clinical Legal Programs

Gemma Smyth

Abstract

Purpose — The initial purpose of this study was to examine the educational needs and perceptions of students and clinicians in Canadian legal clinics.

Methodology/approach — The author conducted a literature review of leading educational materials in Canada and the United States focusing on required or preferred competencies for law students. The author then interviewed law students, clinicians, social workers, and community legal workers from across Ontario, Canada, all of whom were working or studying at law school-affiliated legal clinics. Interview subjects were asked a series of questions about their learning experiences in hopes of informing the creation of clinical teaching and learning materials.

Findings — The data revealed an under-reliance of the affective elements of teaching, learning, and practice in both existing literature and current teaching practices. The data also revealed deep structural divides between doctrinal and clinical teaching and learning approaches.

Originality/value — Without further integration between these two approaches, students and, ultimately, communities and clients will not reap the benefits possible from an integrated curriculum.

Keywords: Clinical legal education; clinical/doctrinal divide; law school curricula; affective learning in law; supervision in the clinical setting; curriculum integration

Integrating Curricular and Co-Curricular Endeavors to Enhance Student Outcomes
Copyright © 2016 by Emerald Group Publishing Limited
All rights of reproduction in any form reserved
ISBN: 978-1-78635-064-0

6.1. Introduction

How can clinical and doctrinal legal education work more effectively together? How can the doctrinal curriculum support the clinical curriculum? What methods and modes of education are most appropriate to prepare students for the skills, attitudes, and knowledge required in a clinical setting? These questions are central to the work of educating law students, both in order to support deeper student learning and to better integrate a fully realized theory-practice curricula in the modern law school. The clinical/doctrinal divide (perceived or otherwise) has, for the author, functioned as a barrier to integrating competent, sophisticated, critical, and activist approaches to clinical legal education. For clarity, "doctrinal" refers to the standard law school curriculum, which, despite significant recent changes, remains dominated by larger classes with primarily lecture-style content delivery. "Clinical" refers to an experiential education program in which law students work under supervision on cases with real-life implications. The study described in this chapter investigates the clinical/doctrinal through the eyes of clinicians and clinical students. While the initial aim of the study was to inform the creation of educational materials, the data gathered showed quite clearly the significant structural barriers to integrating clinical and doctrinal legal education. Part 1 of this chapter outlines the context in which the study took place, as well as some history of clinical and doctrinal approaches to legal education in North America. Part 2 describes the methodology, literature review, and instrument design of this research study of clinicians and students across Ontario, Canada. Part 3 analyses the study data in light of other comparable studies across Canada and the United States, and examines how this study might influence law schools aiming to integrate clinics in their curricula. Ultimately, this chapter concludes that the clinic/doctrine divide, however much a product of perception or reality — is dangerous and unproductive for students and for the overall mission of legal education. This divide leads to silos, mutual disrespect, and — unchecked — to power-based relationships between clinics and law schools that undermine students' and clients' experiences. Above all, this chapter is a call for deep dialogue between clinics and law schools that goes beyond the skills/doctrine debate to a shared student, community, and client-focused mission.

6.2. Part 1: Context

This study took place in Ontario, Canada, a jurisdiction with the greatest number of legal clinics per capita in Canada, mostly due to higher rates of government funding. The clinics at each Ontario law school that take on the greatest number of clients are called "Student Legal Aid Service Society" (SLASS) clinics, designated as such under the Legal Aid Services Act, S.O. 1998, c. 26. There are also clinics called "community legal clinics" affiliated with law schools: specifically, Legal Assistance of Windsor (LAW, affiliated with the Faculty of Law, University of Windsor), and Parkdale Community Legal Services (affiliated with Osgoode Hall Law School, Toronto). Each law school hosts a number of other clinics; for the purpose of this study, the author focused on SLASS and community legal clinics because of their longer history with student placements and the greater total number of students placed there. As well, these clinics have the fewest differences in case load, areas of law, and population served that made comparison between clinics easier.

Each clinic hosts a number of students including volunteers, paid summer students, and for-credit placements. Each has a training or education program affiliated with the clinic, although they vary in intensity and scope. Some clinics have mandatory courses affiliated with them, some offer intensives, and others offer a course of study throughout the academic year. Each clinic hosts law students who are currently enrolled in an affiliated law school. Although some students are in their first year, most are in their second or third and final year of law school. The majority of clinic employees are lawyers, but community legal workers and social workers are also employed by clinics.

All clinics in this study work almost exclusively with poverty law matters. "Poverty law" is a defined area of practice that involves housing law, social benefits (disability entitlements, welfare, and so on), immigration and refugee, summary criminal offenses (offenses without the chance of imprisonment), and other legal areas that disproportionately affect people living in poverty. Some clinics also take on student clients in their areas of practice. Some clinics also provide social work services, and others engage in community development, law reform, and other systemic work. Primary student tasks include interviewing and counseling clients, appearing in front of administrative tribunals and courts, negotiating with the opposing party, maintaining files, writing letters and submissions, working ethically and professionally in their designated role, and a wide variety of other tasks. Many clinics also require students to conduct public legal education sessions and to support community groups using traditional and nontraditional advocacy.

Two additional items are worth noting here. First, the legal clinics here have a mix of governance models. Some are controlled by the Deans of law schools. Others have advisory boards, while others have community governance boards. All receive most of their funding from an arms-length government funder. None function primarily through a law school or social work course, but most have courses affiliated with them. Almost all clinic employees in Canada are not hired as professors or full-time instructors.

Clinics function relatively apart from the larger and rather specific teaching and learning environment in law schools. Students do not take the majority of their courses using a clinical model, and no law school in Canada has yet mandated a clinical placement. Thus, the majority of a law student's education is delivered through doctrinal courses. Like American law schools, Canadian law schools are heavily influenced by the casebook model of legal education, developed by Christopher Langdell (Goebel, 1995; Kimball, 2009; Moline, 2004). Although we now take university-based law schools for granted, lawyers were previously educated primarily through an apprentice-style system in which novices worked under experienced lawyers. Seeking to move legal education into universities, Langdell argued that "Law, considered as a science, consists of certain principles or doctrines … [t]he shortest and best, if not the only way of mastering the doctrine effectually is by studying the cases in which it is embodied" (Langdell, 1871, p. vi). Langdell developed the casebook method of teaching and learning in which cases written by judges were dissected to establish their purpose, effects, rationale, reasoning, and logic. This methodology paved the way for the three-year, university-based legal education, which now dominates the training of lawyers across North America and in many other jurisdictions around the world.

While the Langdellian method most certainly has benefits, it also relegates most forms of active learning outside the Socratic to the sidelines. Thus, many students graduate from law school with significant knowledge of doctrine, but very little understanding of practice and, consequently, little understanding of how the two interact. Although outside the purview of this study, Canadian provinces and territories still require students to article, which is, essentially, the requirement that graduated law students complete bar examinations and a period of apprentice-style work under a licensed lawyer. This is not required in the majority of American states. It is also important to note that clinics have existed alongside — and sometimes in spite of — the dominant casebook method of teaching and learning (Martin Barry, Dubin, & Joy, 2000). In both Canada and the United States, clinics grew out of social movement activism in the civil rights era (Abel, 1993; Lowry, 1972; Zemans, 1997). Impetus for law school-based clinics came from a variety of sources but was most championed by law students and legal academics. The degree of curricular integration and acceptance by the rest of legal academics and law schools has been very mixed. Survey respondents discuss this particular point at some length later in this chapter.

Critics of the current Langdell-inspired model of legal education were once relatively marginal; however, dissenting voices have grown steadily louder over the past decades with reports such as Carnegie (Sullivan, Colby, Wegner, Bond, & Shulman, 2007); MacCrate (American Bar Association, 1992); Stuckey (2007); and, in Canada, the *Futures Report* (Canadian Bar Association, 2014) calling for significant reform to legal education. No report has recommended the elimination of law school as we know it; rather, all reports have recommended, among other things, increased attention to experiential and clinical legal education. To some extent, law schools have listened. Many have expanded existing clinical programs, externships, and other place-based learning. Law schools have also increased experiential learning content. However, from the perspective of the clinicians interviewed for this project, significant questions remain about exactly how and what law students learn in the classroom and how it overlaps (or departs) from clinical expectations. While there are various explanations for these departures, the data gathered in this study raises questions about how live-client clinics and doctrinal teaching and learning can be meaningfully integrated for optimum student learning.

6.3.   Part 2: The Project

6.3.1.   *Project Background*

In 2013, the University of Windsor funded a two-year project to develop online, open source educational materials for students working in two University-affiliated legal clinics, Legal Assistance of Windsor (LAW) and Community Legal Aid (CLA). This project was inspired by practical need above all else. Due to various challenges with curriculum and resources (including time), Windsor's clinical teaching staff had difficulty incorporating adequate learning for clinical law students entering their first clinical placement — a concern that was echoed by the clinicians interviewed for this project. Because the materials were intended to be open source, the author embarked on a study aimed at understanding what clinicians and law students needed in terms of educational materials. As occurs in many studies, what actually arose from the data gave insights beyond the initial purpose. Clinicians and students were not entirely clear about what materials would be useful to them, but gave fascinating insights into the operation of doctrinal and clinical legal education showing that structural reform is required to achieve true integration.

6.3.2. The Study — Description

The primary aim of the research study was to understand what clinicians want students to know at various points in their clinical placements, as well as how clinicians educate their students, the role of the law school in clinical legal education, and what materials they might like to use in their own clinics. The study also aimed to understand how students perceived the education they received before, during and after their clinical placements, and what materials might have supported their learning. Because of ethical and privacy constraints in obtaining student contact information from other institutions, students interviewed for this study were limited to University of Windsor clinic students working during the period during which the study took place. Funding was also limited to a certain number of interview hours and funding was available for a limited period of time. Due to potential conflicts of interest with the PI, who has professional relationships with many of the research subjects, an independent researcher contacted clinicians (including social workers, lawyers, and community legal workers) working at community legal clinics. The only criteria for eligibility was that the clinician be employed at a legal clinic and supervise students as part of their role. The possible number of respondents at the time (the total number of employees who supervised clinics at law school-affiliated legal clinics) for the study was 44, with responses from 11; hence, the clinician response rate was 25%. Research ethics constraints also limited access to students at other institutions; hence, the researcher chose a sample of beginner, intermediate, and advanced clinical students from CLA and LAW. The total sample size was intended to be 12 students (four from each "level" of clinic experience), and the total number of students interviewed was 11 during the time frame allotted through research ethics. The sample size was relatively small, but considering the total number of clinicians in Ontario at the time was also small, a 25% response rate can be considered significant enough to draw preliminary conclusions. In the future, a pan-Canadian study would provide greater depth of information.

6.3.3. Methodology, Instrument Design, and Literature Review

The survey instrument included both quantitative and qualitative design aspects, with semi-structured, voluntary in-person and telephone interviews. In-person interviews were chosen because the interviewer sought depth of perspective and wanted freedom for the interviewer to probe further as necessary. As well, the researcher hoped in-person interviews would garner a greater response rate. The survey included forced choice and open questions. The forced choice questions asked the respondent to comment on a Likert scale the relevance of a particular set of competencies, with the opportunity to add their own competencies. The study relied on a theoretical thematic analysis as outlined by Braun and Clarke (2006), as questions were drawn from a rich array of competencies already described in the legal education literature. However, the study also tried to allow for an inductive approach insofar as participants were encouraged to express opinions outside the prescribed competencies (Braun & Clarke, 2006).

The competencies themselves were drawn from a literature review of the foundational published pieces setting out preferred competencies in law students and lawyers. A list of forced choice competencies is contained in the appendix. The literature review included the most commonly cited books, articles, and reports on lawyering competencies including Shultz and Zedeck's 26 lawyering effectiveness factors (Shultz & Zedeck, 2009), competencies identified in the Carnegie Report (Sullivan et al., 2007), and the MacCrate Report (American Bar Association Section of Legal Education & Admissions to the Bar, 1992). Because these competencies were mostly situated in the wider law school (although some reports included experiential and clinical learning components), the literature review also drew on clinic-specific articles, books, and reports that identified particular clinical competencies including work by Imai (2002), Sameer Ashar (2008), and Roy Stuckey and co-authors (Stuckey 2007). This generated a list of over 150 competencies, which were then narrowed by eliminating those that overlapped and grouping similar competences together. The survey also included a series of open-ended questions that allowed participants to further explore the themes by expanding in ways that might not have been adequately covered in the initial questions.

Data collection took place over three months. Interviews with participants in locations outside of Windsor took place via telephone or webcam while interviews with participants within the city of Windsor were conducted in person. In person, interviews took place in a private office setting. To avoid a potential conflict of interest resulting from the author's professional connection to potential participants, an independent researcher was hired to conduct interviews. The independent researcher was a doctorate-level social work student at the University of Windsor. Two other student researchers were hired to transcribe interviews and support data analysis. Both were third year law students who were not currently placed at either clinic. Neither had access to identifying information from the interview subjects.

6.3.4. Sample/Participants

Student participants from the two Windsor clinics (LAW and CLA) were invited to participate. Samples of six students from each clinic (beginner experience;

intermediate experience; advanced experience) were randomly selected for participation. Securing participation from students with varying levels of experience served to ensure a balance between homogeneity and heterogeneity within the small sample. To select the sample, the primary investigator developed a list of students who had volunteered, taken credit, and/or been employed at each of the two clinics within the past two years. Each student was then categorized by level of experience within the clinic. The primary investigator (PI) used simple random sampling to invite two students from each category to participate. Each student was allowed 48 hours to respond to the invitation before another student from the same category would be invited to participate. This process was repeated until the PI came as close as possible to the target sample of 12 students.

Professionals involved in the supervision of students from six Student Legal Aid Services Society (SLASS) clinics and two community legal clinics (Legal Assistance of Windsor and Parkdale Community Legal Services) were invited to participate as part of the clinician sample group.

6.3.5. Data Collection and Ethical Considerations

This research project obtained Research Ethics Board approval from the University of Windsor on June 17, 2013. From the commencement of the data collection to completion, the researchers made two requests to the Board for minor revisions regarding classification of participants. All revisions were approved before being implemented. Email addresses for all clinician participants were obtained from an online listserv and provided to the independent researcher for the sole purpose of inviting participation in the study. Email addresses for all student participants were accessed from the clinic administration and provided to the independent researcher with the sole purpose of inviting participation in the study. To ensure anonymity of participants to the principal investigator, the independent researcher coded the raw data before it was delivered for analysis. The code indicated a letter value for each individual clinic and a number value to indicate the profession/level of experience of the participant. After the data were analyzed, the code was released. All information collected was kept in locked cabinets or under the supervision of an approved researcher at all times. All researchers underwent TCPS2 training (Government of Canada, 2014) prior to beginning the study.

Data analysis began with the transcription of audio data. The transcriber was involved in neither the interviewing of the participants nor final data analysis so as to maintain the anonymity of the research subjects. The raw text data were delivered to the principle investigator and research assistant for coding to identify and label themes. The researchers undertook a thematic analysis to identify patterns and themes within the data collected. The researchers relied on a contextual method of interpretation, partway between essentialist and constructivist approaches. As Braun and Clarke wrote, the researchers attempted to "acknowledge the ways individuals make meaning of their experience, and, in turn, the ways the broader social context impinges on those meanings, while retaining focus on the material and other limits of 'reality'" (Braun & Clarke, 2006, p. 81). Thus, the researchers attempted to understand and reflect what interview subjects explicitly stated, as well as well as unpack possible contextual assumptions and effects that impacted these realities.

For each theme, the researchers developed a title and definition for the theme and identified any exclusions to the category. The variance in themes among and between various subsamples was considered for analysis. Code titles were developed based on the literature review described above. Variance in these themes was collected separately and, where appropriate, given a separate title. The researchers engaged in a double-coding process to increase the validity of the coding results. To ensure validity of information gathered from the samples, a subsample of each group was first coded, and then coding was compared for applicability to the remainder of the sample. Themes were counted for prevalence, but the researchers also noted "outlier" data or unusual statements that might provide a particularly insightful note for the purpose of the study or that stood out as an explanation or point that the researchers had not previously accounted for. While some of the findings reported in this chapter are descriptive, the PI has also attempted to decipher and interpret underlying assumptions and ideas that come alive in the data.

6.3.6. *Limitations*

There are several limitations to this study. First, the study only includes data from Ontario clinics. Because these clinics are government-funded rather than university funded or run through a law school course, the nature of the institutional culture was more limited than it is in reality. However, the type of clinic examined in this study remains the most prevalent type in Canadian clinical legal education. Further, the students surveyed were only from Windsor. While the law school experience is not significantly different from school to school in Ontario (except, perhaps for a new law school at Lakehead University), certainly a greater diversity of students would have given greater depth to the student responses. The PI also has limited understanding of why certain clinicians did not participate and what they might have added to the study. What are the differences between the clinicians who did not participate and those who did? Undoubtedly, clinicians are busy, but it is also possible that those who were more interested in the subject of this study responded. There were also limitations due to the PI being unable to listen directly to the recordings. This was necessary for anonymity and confidentiality, but also meant that the PI relied on the written word, rather than the more nuanced voice recordings.

6.4.   Part 3: Findings

Although a number of themes emerged from this research, for the purposes of this chapter, two shed particular light on the development of work-integrated learning in law schools. First, the clinicians and students surveyed demonstrated significant gaps in what they considered important competencies along the learning journey from novice to advanced learner. Both clinicians and students — although more notably clinicians — also discussed a number of affective elements in the clinical teaching and learning experience that did not appear to align neatly with the competencies used for this study. Concerns about the emotionally challenging nature of clinical work were also echoed throughout the study, perhaps speaking to the need to pay closer attention to the integration of affective learning in both doctrinal and clinical teaching. Second, in the eyes of clinicians and students, the doctrinal and clinical curricula do not seem to be meaningfully integrated. As discussed further below, some of these findings confirm outcomes from other studies in Canada and North America, although with some variation. The final section of this chapter will address potential curricular changes that might ease the wide gap between clinical and doctrinal learning to support improved student experience and mastery-level competency development.

6.5. Theme 1: Defining Competence

6.5.1. *Novice Students*

As described earlier, clinicians and students were first asked to identify the most important skills student should possess before they enter their clinic placement. Both respondent groups were asked to choose from a forced choice set of options and then asked to expand on others not already captured. Students without prior clinical experience were grouped as "novices."

For novice students in the forced choice section (see Table 6.1), clinicians identified "ability to demonstrate respect for and alliance with clients" as the most important competency for novice students (50%), followed by knowledge of the law and procedures at the clinic (33%). Organization, understanding one's own limits, ability to identify learning gaps and needs and the ability to learn from supervision

Table 6.1: Most important skills for students before they enter a clinical placement (clinicians vs. students).

Clinicians	Students
(1) Ability to demonstrate respect for/ alliance with client (50%)	(1) Client interviewing (33%)
(2) Knowledge of law and procedures at clinic (33%)	(2) Knowledge of law and procedures practiced at the clinic; research (18%)
(3) Organization; Understanding one's own limits; ability to identify learning gaps and needs; ability to learn from supervision (all 25%)	(3) Organization; oral advocacy skills; professional letter writing; ability to draw out information; how client experience impacts case (all 9%)

were identified as equally important by 25% of respondents. Of note, competencies such as decision-making, leadership, oral advocacy, policy analysis, understanding other community resources, and conflict resolution were not listed as the most important skills before entering the clinic.

Clinicians also identified a significant number of competencies outside those offered as possible options. These included: "open-minded," "fearlessness," "ability to empathize, compassion, an understanding of social structures and power structures," "interested in a social justice setting," "understanding and empathy," "maturity and responsibility to deal with really sensitive issues," and willingness to engage. As one respondent stated, "I guess [my answer] would be open-minded because it's a pretty steep learning curve and a lot of times, students are not the same after a clinical placement in terms of learning about the law, about the community and about themselves." Another clinician said, "I think the most important is ... an ability to work without grudge on work that may seem meaningless."

In stark contrast, novice clinic students identified tangible skills they considered important before entering a clinical placement (see Table 6.1). For about one third of students, client interviewing was identified as the most important skill to know before entering a clinical placement. As the reader might intuit, client interviewing is the first task most students complete when they meet with a client. Eighteen percent of students also identified knowledge of the law and procedures at the clinic and research. Again, these are practical skills required at the next stage of clinical work. A variety of competencies were identified in the third most commonly cited category at 9%, including organization, oral advocacy, and letter writing.

6.5.2.   Theme 1: Analysis

Clearly, what students and clinicians view as core competencies for a novice student bear little resemblance to one another, save for the shared "knowledge of the law and procedures at the clinic" and organization (slight overlap). For students, the concept of interviewing a client for the first time was the most immediate and pressing concern, as most of them had never met a client in a professional role before. Students were simply seeking information about what they needed to do most immediately. Another possible interpretation is that novice students view their roles in rather technocratic ways. They have never seen the full scope of a case from first interview, through the sometimes very long arch through negotiation, perhaps mediation, submission writing, and perhaps hearing. Ability to delve into the *quality* of a client relationship, rather than seeing the case as a set of technocratic steps, might be difficult for a novice. A clinician's view may be that "ability to demonstrate respect for and alliance with clients" is an important skill during the client interview, but that it also permeates every interaction a student has with a client. For a student focused on (and perhaps fearful of) each individual task, and with limited knowledge of the overall arch of clients' disputes, "being able" to interview a client, perhaps without regard to the quality of the relationship, would naturally be identified as a dominant skill.

There are several possible explanations for other pieces of this data. First, as later data will confirm, clinicians tended to demonstrate a "kitchen sink" approach to teaching and learning for students, in which nearly all competencies were considered of almost equal importance. Their expectations did not differentiate dramatically for novice versus experienced students. One explanation for this might be that clinicians have been in the field so long that they have lost perspective on what students know upon beginning a placement. Another is the culture of law, which has a well-documented history of high expectations of its employees with relatively little personal (particularly emotional) support (Pierce, 1995; Saab Fortney, 2000). This is not to say that there is poor treatment of students at clinics, but that the general culture of law is not necessarily attentive to personal wellbeing. Yet another, simpler, explanation, is that clinical training programs — despite differentiating themselves from law schools — have not developed adequate education programs for students that identify and scaffold learning outcomes, identify threshold learning concepts and bottlenecks, and so on. This specific question was not asked of participants and is therefore speculative, but may provide some rationale for these findings.

Another possible theory is that clinicians view certain traits as teachable and therefore unimportant, whereas competencies are part of a student's ethical or personal make-up — and perhaps unteachable. For example, for the clinician who considered ability to work hard without begrudging the effort, a student who has a strong work ethic is preferable to a student who does not demonstrate this aptitude — whether or not this is something specifically noted in clinical training. Perhaps, then, the question here is more about whether certain competencies can be learned, and which cannot. Several clinicians alluded to this in their interviews. One stated, "if you're ... being judgmental and you don't believe in your client and you don't have any ethical values or considerations, I'm not going to be able to do much with you and actually you're not going to be much good to anybody." Here, this attitudinal approach to clients (demonstrating fundamental respect for clients) and having no ethical — or, here, perhaps *moral* values — was considered unteachable. Another clinician quite clearly differentiated between what was considered teachable and what was not:

> [a]bility to work with others, ability to take instruction ... when they make a mistake and come forward ... ability to take criticism. I think they're important before they come to us ... You know, we hire students usually after first year, so their skills as lawyers is going to be very little .... Other skills ... can be taught, but not these four ...

It was beyond the scope of this study to review the competencies taught by every law school in this study; however, it would not be unreasonable to state that these skills are likely not addressed in the law school curriculum. They are certainly outside the competencies mandated by the Federation of Canadian Law Societies (2009).

Also noteworthy is the nature of the competencies identified by clinicians as both the most important in the forced-choice section ("ability to demonstrate respect for and alliance with clients") and the open section of the survey, the majority of which are affective in nature. It is helpful here to consider the concept of emotional intelligence ("EQ"), a concept coined by Salovey and Mayer (1990) and popularized by Daniel Goleman (2006). Goleman identified five areas of EQ competence: intrapersonal, interpersonal, adaptability, stress management, and general mood. The competencies mentioned by the clinicians fall squarely within these categories. Consider Table 6.2, outlining Goleman's five categories and various clinician responses.

EQ is a desirable trait in many contexts, including in law. Goleman's book itself identifies myriad ways EQ is helpful in the workplace, particularly for leaders (Goleman, 2006; Goleman, Boyatzis, & McKee, 2013). Marjorie Silver, a leading legal academic in alternative approaches to legal practice and education, wrote about the idea in 1999. Legal academics and others have linked emotional intelligence to increased professionalism (Montgomery, 2007–2008) and improved leadership ability (Palmer, Walls, Burgess, & Stough, 2001). In her work analyzing interview data from practicing lawyers, Irene Taylor found that corporate lawyers demonstrated higher than average levels of some EQ competencies such as independence and optimism (Taylor, 2002a, 2002b, 2003, 2004). Some of the traits identified in Goleman's studies are also found in the studies from which the forced choice competences in this study

Table 6.2: Daniel Goleman's EQ and clinicians' responses.

Goleman's EQ category	Clinicians' responses
Intrapersonal	"fearless" "interested in people" "interested in a social justice setting" "Certainly they have a heightened sense of their own self-importance that will ruin the work they do at the clinic" (importance of humility) "maturity" "[students must be] honest about their own limitations and their own internal complex"
Interpersonal	"ability to demonstrate respect for and alliance with clients" "[a]bility to work with others, ability to take instruction ..."
Adaptability	"when they make a mistake and come forward ... ability to take criticism." "willingness to engage" "ability to work without grudge on work that may seem ... meaningless"
Stress management	"ability to deal with really sensitive issues"
General mood	"open-minded" "empathy" "compassion"

were drawn. For example, the "character" competencies from Shultz and Zedeck (2009) (passion and engagement, diligence, integrity/honesty, stress management, among others) were echoed in the additional competencies identified by clinicians.

However, unique to this data is the clinicians' emphasis on commitment to social justice principles. Shultz and Zedeck, for example, identified "community involvement and service" as one of the 26 competencies; in the clinic setting, however, this charity-model approach was not considered desirable. As noted earlier, clinicians appeared to prefer community-based approaches to working with clients ("... an understanding of social structures and power structures," "interested in a social justice setting"). The concept of the lawyer as ally dominated the responses, much more so than a benevolent service model. These competences were more likely to be echoed in the clinical legal education literature (Ashar, 2008; Imai, 2002). The implications of this will be discussed later in this chapter.

6.5.3. *Defining Competence: Intermediate and Advanced Students*

The next part of the study explored how students and clinicians thought teaching and learning competencies should change over time, as students gained greater experience working at the clinic (see Table 6.3). This section shared significant thematic similarity with the novice students. Clinicians expected students to be better at time management (42% of respondents) and better organized (27%). Students identified improvement in organization (36%) and time management (27%); however, the similarities end there. Clinicians expected improvements in the affective domain again, expecting improvements in confidence as well as deepened understanding of a wide range of social justice-related competences such as "insight into poverty law issues."

Students — speaking from their own experiences — reported improvements in ethics and knowledge of law and procedure. For example, one student noted, "I learned how to work with co-workers, group leaders, and review counsel" (interesting to note based on an earlier comment that working with peers is an

Table 6.3: Most important competences for intermediate and advanced students — clinicians and student responses.

Clinicians	Students
Better at time management; more confident (42%)	Organization ("I found my own system") (36%)
"Deeper and more mature understanding of how the law interacts with clients"; "Deeper insight into poverty law issues"; "Deeper understanding of the meaning of justice" (33%)	Time management (including efficiency); ethics, including privilege, confidentiality (27%)
Better organized (27%)	Knowledge of law and procedures (18%)

unteachable skill). Of note are other students who described a tangible difference in professional identity: "[m]y work became more fluid, less bound by these strict guidelines." Few students mentioned social justice work specifically, but when it was mentioned it was in less-than-optimistic terms. As one student said, "[y]ou can either get more interested in social justice, or maybe disillusioned and burned out." This concept of burn out and disillusionment came up again in the following section of the survey.

6.5.4.   *Threshold Concepts and Roadblocks*

Respondents were also asked to identify areas in which students often struggle, in hopes of identifying concepts and materials that could support students through these more challenging areas (Table 6.4). For clinicians, the most common response (58%) was time management, followed by organization (50%), both of which capture a similar skill set. Combined, a mix of these two skills was important for every clinician interviewed. It is notable that in the forced choice portion of the survey, the areas most identified as problematic for students (time management and organization) were only briefly mentioned by students (organization was mentioned by 9% of students and time management not at all).

Beyond this commonly held view for clinicians, the areas in which students struggled were wide-ranging. In this section, clinicians tended to identify a diverse range of areas in which students struggle, resulting in a data set that included

Table 6.4: Areas in which students often struggle — views from clinicians and students.

Clinicians' views	Students' views
(1) Time management (58%)	(1) Memo submission drafting; ability to learn from supervision (27%)
(2) Organization (50%)	(2) Conflict resolution; understanding one's own limits; active listening (18%)
(3) Professional letter writing; understanding how client experience impacts case (33%)	(3) Organization; decision-making; supervision; self-care; oral advocacy skills; identifying policy issues; confidentiality and privilege; understanding one's own limits; ability to draw out information (9%)
(4) Self-care; good judgment; identify facts and legal issues; research; understanding one's own limits; ability to draw out information; plain language communication (25%)	

everything from professional letter writing, understanding how the client's experience impacts the case, self-care, good judgment, research, and plain language communication. Students continued to identify more basic legal and professional skills as areas of struggle (memo submissions, conflict resolution).

However, one area in particular stands out: approaches to supervising students. A major way students learn in a clinic is through supervision; sometimes one-on-one in discussion of particular cases and strategies, and sometimes in case rounds and small group supervision. For students, a significant number identified "the ability to learn from supervision" as a struggle. In a clinic, supervision occurs in a small group or one-on-one setting with supervisors and peers. Because of the nature of this question and the ensuing comments, it appears students struggled with supervision from the supervising professionals at the clinics, mostly lawyers. As one student succinctly stated, "[c]ompetencies are irrelevant if we don't have good supervision." Although clinicians seemed to favor competencies that were client- and social justice focused, and although they had high expectations from the outset of students' placements, most discussion of supervision focused primarily on following instructions and being independent. One clinician noted, "[i]f they come [to the clinic], assuming they know what they're doing ... they're going to waste their time ... Follow instructions!" Another clinician stated, "I expect the students to come more confident in dealing with clients and resolving issues and less, I don't want to say needy but that's kind of what I mean." In contrast, when asked what good supervision looked like, one student said, "[s]upervisors should lead by example." Another clinician was more nuanced, expressing concern about giving students too much information at once, and overwhelming them. This clinician stated: "[y]ou know, they have some initial security as their role as a lawyer, then I can expand that. But, if I'm asking them to do everything and look at everything, they don't feel they have any competency anywhere, then that's just scary." Clearly, students value good supervision; however, clinicians expressed a range of approaches to supervision, some of which would be effective for certain types of students, but not others. It is also unclear from the data whether students simply did not have the skill to facilitate good supervision; for example, ability to receive feedback is an important skill to facilitate good supervisory relationships. Students did not rank this skill highly.

When asked to expand on other challenges in their clinical experiences, students identified a wide variety of problems. One student echoed what the clinicians saw as problematic (time management and organization), but for a different reason. As she said, "I had really no idea how to keep track of all my cases ... Initially, it was like drinking from a fire hose because there's so much information coming at you." So, for the student the problem was more about the sheer volume of material and information, along with having a heavy caseload with no clear organizational system.

As discussed above, students also discussed the challenges working in a social justice clinic setting with few resources: "I think we often also just find that we don't have the resources to fight certain fights." This combination of being completely overloaded with practical information, along with the sinking reality of working within a system that actively keeps people poor was reflected in the survey data; however, students did not seem to have the language or worldview held by clinicians that allowed them to get through the day-to-day challenges of this environment. One clinician expressed this problem as follows:

> It's hard ... I feel sorry for students when they first see how poorly their clients are treated by the law. They know that life is unfair and unfair things happen, but when they witness it, when they see it, when they don't have a remedy, it becomes very difficult for them.

This is a well-documented difficulty for law students, particularly those working in a legal clinic environment (Buhler, 2013; Gavigan, 1999). This emotional reality reveals the disconnect between "law on the books" and law as it operates in people's lives. The casebook method does not require students to engage with actual people whose lives change from day-to-day, who might not be able to afford a bus pass, never mind a lawyer, or who — even when they win a case — might not be able to enforce the decision. This can come as a shock to some students on a quite basic level. As one clinician reported, "One of the students said, 'My clients are so difficult. I just wish, I like the law piece, I just don't like my clients.'"

Clinicians cared deeply not only about how students' realizations about the nature of the law would impact their wellbeing but also about the institutional structures that exacerbated their struggles. One clinician stated,

> [l]aw is set up in such a way that it's pretty horrible, right, even without doing the clinical experience. It's a stressful experience ... I think they're almost up to $18,000 for tuition, they're all stressed out about trying to get a job and OCI's ["on campus interviews"] and it ... doesn't matter what I do when I tell them prepare as much as you can ... it's always a nightmare with time management ....

It was this statement more than any other that revealed the price that is paid by students by having a curriculum that is not aligned, in an environment that places so much emphasis on getting a job.

Few students or clinicians spoke about the importance of self-reflection in a direct way. In expanding on views regarding self-reflection and work management, one clinician stated, "I can see very clearly whether [the student] is having difficulty dealing with the client ... It reflects in their work and then the client suffers ... I need [students] to be honest about their limitations and their own internal complex." Although the students certainly demonstrated commitment and interest in the clinic, this type of self-reflection did not appear in the survey data. It is perhaps this self-reflection that could improve students' performance and well-being. This will be expanded upon later in the chapter.

6.5.5. *Transferable Competencies*

In the next section of the survey, students and clinicians were both asked which competencies introduced or reinforced in law school were transferable to clinic practice. Overwhelmingly, the answer from both students and clinicians was nothing, or very little. One student responded, "[v]ery little. I think law school does a good job of teaching you how to think like a lawyer and to structure your arguments in a 'lawyerly' way ... But it doesn't really do much to teach you how to do the day-to-day." When asked to identify transferable skills, a full 81% of students' answers were some variation of "[n]ot really" or "[n]one at all, I'd say." The interviewer was instructed to probe students on specific courses that were most relevant. Students mentioned Legal Writing, Criminal, Civil Procedure, Evidence and Access to Justice (this is a course unique to Windsor Law. It is a mandatory first year course focusing on social justice approaches to law and legal systems.). Some students identified these skills and a seminar course that sometimes accompanies the clinical placement. However, when asked to identify what skills they learned, students had great difficulty identifying specifics.

Clinicians also held this "two worlds apart" view. In fact, clinicians were palpably cynical about what is being taught in law schools. One clinician was clearly confused by the question: "I'm not sure they're going to learn [clinical work] in other academic courses." Another said, "I think our clinic course and the clinic, they're going to learn a lot of the skills ... I'm not sure they're going to learn it through other academic courses." When asked whether students would learn particular competencies, such as cultural competency, one clinician said, "[c]ultural competence would not be discussed at all in law school."

During the course of this study, the student group interviewed underwent curricular changes that made a legal ethics course mandatory. One clinician commented that even when students were made to take this course, they continued to make serious ethical errors in the clinic. This clinician said, "There's such a difference between talking about ethical situations and everyone saying, 'I'll be ethical! I'll be ethical!' and then when they're faced with it do you recognize this is an ethical issue?... When you're sitting in a classroom, it's different because there isn't somebody who's going to feel the immediate impact of this work, so [clinics] make it much more real." When asked if, perhaps, students were not as competent in certain areas as the clinicians might have expected, one clinician stated, "it doesn't matter what year they're in. I always treat them as if they know nothing."

Clinicians and students were asked where they thought certain competencies should be taught: classroom, clinic, a combination or both, and/or elsewhere. Two main operating theories dominated these responses. First, some respondents thought that law school doctrinal classes should introduce the competencies surveyed in this study, and that the clinic should reinforce them in an integrated curriculum model. One clinician argued that, "[i]f some of these skills were taught in the classroom, whether it's in law school or through the clinic course and then they're reinforced during their time in the clinic, I think they're going to be in a better position." Another clinician responded, that "these competencies should be taught everywhere." The second operating theory posited that: "law school can't teach anything as well as the clinics" (clinician).

Students were unanimous in their view that client interviewing (including active listening and ability to draw out information) was best learned in a clinic. About a third of students also noted that legal writing (including professional letter writing, memo, or submission drafting) was also best learned with clinic, along with ethics and a number of other competencies.

6.5.6. *Implications*

What can we learn about teaching and learning in law school from this study? The easiest answer is to fall into the centuries-old debate between law as intellectual inquiry and law as a practice (described above). Indeed, there are many in the legal academics who would not consider preparation for a clinical placement or any work-integrated learning as appropriate content for law school. However, based on this and other data, as well as external pressures described above — and most importantly for students — debate must become more nuanced. In this study, it was clear that both students and clinicians were cynical about the utility of law school vis-à-vis clinical legal education. Again, there are several explanations for these views, many of which are common challenges across professional disciplines while others are unique to law school. First, it is not uncommon for professionals in the field to consider new apprentices as the proverbial "empty vessel." To be fair to law schools, many reports have confirmed the ability of law schools to introduce students to basic concepts, high-level legal reasoning, forms of government and legislation, and a wide range of other foundational and intellectually-rigorous concepts (Sullivan et al., 2007; Canadian Bar Association, 2014). However, a few assessment-related challenges make *transferability* of this knowledge problematic. Testing in law school remains largely summative rather than formative (with some notable exceptions such as Legal Research and Writing). There is very little pressure to really understand much until the final exam, which is traditionally worth 100% of a student's grade. Even when essays are assigned, they again are usually submitted at the end of the term and deal with a narrow area of law. Hence, so long as law schools rely on these forms of assessment, there is little incentive for students to learn the material early or to be able to retain it so they can use it in a clinical setting. Second, the casebook method is not conducive to application in real-life scenarios. Of particular note here is that the substantive content of casebooks provides no insight into how a lawyer might actually engage with a client in interviewing, counseling, negotiation, working with opposing parties, strategizing, and so on. Thus, we have a problem of both form and substance.

While legal education has significant deficiencies, based on this study, it is clear that clinics can also do more to support student learning. Some of these reforms can occur internally, with basic scaffolding of concepts into introductory, intermediate, and mastery-level learning outcomes. The "firehose" approach referenced earlier by one student simply is not conducive to learning, particularly if students must apply concepts with real clients almost immediately. It would also be useful for clinics to sort out which competencies they consider innate and unteachable, and which others could be taught. If certain competencies are considered mandatory for clinic work and are not taught, perhaps students should be screened beforehand to ensure they possess these qualities. Otherwise, a clinical placement has the potential to be frustrating for both student and clinician. Is the clinic the ideal place to identify potential ethical and practice barriers and to work with students at that point, with an aim to improve or at least diminish their negative impact? These data also raise questions about the viability of mandatory clinical placements. This is not a current policy at any Canadian law school but has been the subject of discussion in other jurisdictions (Tokarz, Lopez, Maisel, & Seibel, 2013).

For clinic pedagogy, this study revealed the very wide range of what is considered effective teaching and learning practice. The clinicians interviewed varied widely in their expectations of students, how they should be taught and supervised, and what students should know upon entering a program. Despite the clinic being a learning environment, there was notably little discussion of reflective practice or other teaching and learning pedagogies supportive of self-directed and lifelong learning. Being able to follow instructions is indeed a competency, but the expectations expressed by clinicians require students to use judgment, ethical and moral reasoning, critical thinking, and other high-level skills beyond following instructions. Indeed, this is what being a lawyer is all about.

This study also revealed some gaps in the literature on competencies. While many of the studies more than adequately captured the major concerns of clinicians, the affective pieces, described above, were mostly missing. This includes competences to support students in dealing with the emotionally difficult nature of clinic work. There were also gaps in the realities of resourcing cases. Students did struggle with the reality of making decisions about clients' lives within the limits of available resources. This would not only be a useful tool for the immediate clinical experience, it would be a lifelong competency regardless of the area of practice. There were also some gaps in the studies used for the literature review, but referenced in studies subsequently used for analysis. These mostly fell within the area of emotional intelligence including students' confidence, enthusiasm, positivity, maturity, ability to empathize, and so on. One clinician perhaps reflected why clinicians de-emphasized the importance of learning the law and ranked attitudinal competencies more highly: "I think you can learn the law very quickly ... but coming in open to this learning and to this experience is very important."

Although the original aim of this study was to inform creation of teaching and learning materials, the data gathered clearly showed that there are far deeper structural barriers at play in law schools. There are also long-standing prejudices and institutional barriers that can stand in the way of truly integrated, student-centered curricula. Whether perceived or real, the academic/practice divide can resemble a caste-like system in which academics receive better treatment (pay and benefits, hours, workload, more flexibility) than clinicians and other "non-academic" staff (Kennedy, 2004). This is, of course, not universally true, but does play out in many clinics. Clinics are often also physically siloed from law schools. While being close to the communities served by clinics is important, the physical separation can sometimes be perceived as an intellectual divide as well. The data were also somewhat depressing considering that clinics have existed in Ontario law schools and elsewhere across North America for more than 40 years. That law schools and clinics have not been able to find a path toward a more integrated curriculum that provides a meaningful pathway to learning for law students is, simply, no longer acceptable. This study charts a preliminary path to work-integrated learning by identifying student competencies for both clinics and law schools. These competencies, and others identified by respondents, go far beyond "practice readiness," although a degree of this is indeed important. The goal here is to graduate students who have mastered skills and attitudes to allow them to think and practice critically and ethically on behalf of clients, communities, and groups who are in desperate need of their work.

Acknowledgments

The author gratefully acknowledges the University of Windsor and the Law Foundation of Ontario for funding this and related work. Research assistance was expertly provided by Ms. Shawna Labadie, Ms. Rosie Malik, and Ms. Christa Yu. For challenging conversations about the clinical-doctrinal divide in law that improved this work, thank you to Dr. Chantal Morton, Dr. Annie Rochette, and Marion Overholt. Particular thanks to the staff of the Centre for Teaching and Learning at the University of Windsor including Dr. Alan Wright and Professor Nick Baker. Thanks, also, to the research subjects — students, lawyers, social workers, and community legal workers — whose thoughtful responses shaped my understanding of legal education.

References

Abel, J. (1993). Ideology and the emergence of legal aid in Saskatchewan. *Dalhousie Law Journal, 16*, 125–168.

American Bar Association Section of Legal Education and Admissions to the Bar. (1992). *Legal education and professional development — An educational continuum.* Report on the task force on law schools and the profession: Narrowing the gap. Chicago, IL: American Bar Association.

Ashar, S. (2008). Law clinics and collective mobilization. *Clinical Law Review, 14*, 355–414.

Braun, V., & Clarke, V. (2006). Using thematic analysis in psychology. *Qualitative Research in Psychology, 3*(2), 77–101.

Buhler, S. (2013). Painful injustices: Encountering social suffering in clinical legal education. *Clinical Law Review, 19*, 405–428.

Canadian Bar Association. (2014). *Futures: Transforming the delivery of legal services in Canada.* Ottawa, CA: Canadian Bar Association.

Federation of Canadian Law Societies. (2009, October). *Task force on the Canadian common law degree: Final report.* Retrieved from http://flsc.ca/wp-content/uploads/2014/10/admission8.pdf

Gavigan, S. (1999). Poverty law, theory, and practice: The place of class and gender in access to justice. In E. Comack (Ed.), *Locating law: Race/class/gender connections* (pp. 208–230). Halifax, CA: Fernwood.

Goebel, J. (1995). *A history of the school of law.* New York, NY: New York University Press.

Goleman, D. (2006). *Emotional intelligence: 10th anniversary edition.* New York, NY: Bantam.

Goleman, D., Boyatzis, R., & McKee, A. (2013). *Primal leadership: Unleashing the power of emotional intelligence.* Cambridge, MA: Harvard Business Review Press.

Government of Canada. (2014). *Tri-council policy statement 2.* Retrieved from http://www. pre.ethics.gc.ca/eng/policy-politique/initiatives/tcps2-eptc2/Default/

Imai, S. (2002). Counter-pedagogy for social justice: Core skills for community lawyering. *Clinical Law Review, 9,* 195–216.

Kennedy, D. (2004). *Legal education and the reproduction of hierarchy: A polemic against the system: A critical edition.* New York, NY: NYU Press.

Kimball, B. (2009). *The inception of modern professional education: C. C. Langdell, 1826–1906.* Raleigh, NC: University of North Carolina Press.

Langdell, C. C. (1871). *A selection of cases on the law of contracts.* Boston, MA: Little, Brown & Co.

Legal Aid Services Act, S.O. 1998. c. 26.

Lowry, D. R. (1972). A plea for clinical law. *Canadian Bar Review, 50,* 183.

Martin Barry, M., Dubin, J. C., & Joy, P. (2000). Clinical education for this millennium: The third wave. *Clinical Law Review, 7*(1), 1.

Moline, B. J. (2004). Early American legal education. *Washburn Law Journal, 42,* 775–802.

Montgomery, J. E. (2007–2008). Incorporating emotional intelligence concepts to legal education: Strengthening the professionalism of law students. *University of Toledo Law Review, 39,* 323–352.

Palmer, B., Walls, M., Burgess, Z., & Stough, C. (2001). Emotional intelligence and effective leadership. *Leadership and Organizational Development Journal, 22*(1), 5–10.

Pierce, J. L. (1995). *Gender trials.* Berkeley, CA: University of California Press.

Saab Fortney, S. (2000). Soul for sale: An empirical study of associate satisfaction, law firm culture, and the effects of the billable hour requirements. *University of Missouri-Kansas City Law Review, 69*(2), 239–309.

Salovey, P., & Mayer, J. D. (1990). Emotional intelligence, imagination, cognition and personality. *Imagination, Cognition and Personality, 9*(3), 185–211.

Shultz, M. M., & Zedeck, S. (2009). *Final research report: Identification, development and validation of predictors for successful lawyering.* Social Science Research Network. Retrieved from http://works.bepress.com/marjorie_shultz/14

Silver, M. A. (1999). Emotional intelligence and legal education. *Psychology, Public Policy and Law, 5*(4), 1173–1200.

Stuckey, R. (2007). Best practices for legal education: A vision and a road map. Clinical Legal Education Association, Pennsylvania.

Sullivan, W. M., Colby, A., Wegner, J. W., Bond, L., & Shulman, L. S. (2007). *Educating lawyers: Preparation for the profession of law.* San Francisco, CA: Jossey-Bass.

Taylor, I. (2002a). Canada's top 25 corporate litigators. *Lexpert Magazine,* July.

Taylor, I. (2002b). Canada's top 30 corporate dealmakers. *Lexpert Magazine,* November.

Taylor, I. (2003). Carpe diem! Canada's top 25 women lawyers. *Lexpert Magazine,* September.

Taylor, I. (2004). Top 40: 40 and under 40. *Lexpert Magazine,* November.

Tokarz, K., Lopez, A. S., Maisel, P., & Seibel, R. F. (2013). Legal education at a crossroads: Innovation, integration, and pluralism required! *Washington University Journal of Law and Policy, 43*(Summer), 11.

Zemans, F. (1997). The dream is still alive: Twenty-five years of Parkdale community legal services and the Osgoode hall law school intensive program in poverty law. *Osgoode Hall Law Journal, 35*(3–4), 499–534.

APPENDIX

Competencies

(1) How important are the following **general management skills** for entry level and intermediate students?
   (a) Organization
   (b) Time management
   (c) Decision-making
   (d) Leadership
   (e) Collaboration with peers, supervisors, other professions, etc.
   (f) Conflict resolution skills, including negotiation and representation at mediation
   (g) Supervision (ability to supervise others)
   (h) Self-care, "work-life balance," coping with stress, emotional wellness
   (i) Good judgment in uncertain situations
(2) How important are the following **legal knowledge, skills, values and ethics** for entry level and intermediate students?
   (a) Knowledge of the substantive law and procedures practiced at your clinic (i.e., OW, ODSP, Criminal)
   (b) Ability to develop accurate, well-reasoned legal argument
   (c) Oral advocacy skills
   (d) Identifying facts and legal issues
   (e) Identifying policy issues
   (f) Selecting and applying relevant research sources, including legislation and case law
   (g) Understanding of confidentiality and privilege
   (h) Cultural competence
   (i) Ability to identify ethical dilemmas
   (j) Understanding of the limits of the student's own abilities — when to seek out supervisor
(3) How important are the following **communication skills** for entry level and intermediate students?
   (a) Professional letter writing
   (b) Memo/submission drafting
   (c) Grammar and spelling (written)
   (d) Active listening skills
   (e) Ability to draw out information
   (f) Plain language communication suitable to the purpose and audience (written and oral)
(4) How important are the following **community lawyering skills** for entry level and intermediate students?
   (a) Awareness of how systems impact clients' lived experiences and understanding of how the law and legal practices act to marginalize clients

(b) Knowledge of how clients lived experiences may impact their legal case (i.e., disabilities, poverty, domestic violence)

(c) Knowledge of community resources and supports suitable for a wide range of clients

(d) Knowledge of other professionals' roles/comfort in accessing

(e) Ability to analyze and implement preventative conflict resolution techniques/ interventions

(f) Ability to demonstrate respect for the client and act as an ally

(5) How important are the following **learning/ongoing development Skills** for entry level and intermediate students?

(a) Ability to reflect on and learn from experience

(b) Ability to identify learning gaps/needs

(c) Ability to recognize learning style

(d) Ability to access needed learning materials

(e) Ability to integrate new knowledge into ongoing practice

(f) Continuous goal setting and development

Chapter 7

Project Management: Practice-Based Learning in a UK University

Elly Philpott and David Owen

Abstract

Purpose — The chapter evaluates the value of practice-based teaching and learning on a UK postgraduate unit and describes the development of conceptual models for the student practice-based experience.

Methodology/approach — Student experience is explored through the use of an in-depth case study. Student understanding is explored through an exit survey of students.

Findings — Student experience of the unit was positive and negative. Positive experiences stem from good client communications, a motivated student team, and the buzz of a real project. Positive experiences appear to lead to a perception of pride in outcomes and personal transferrable skills. Negative experiences stem from the lack of life experience, language difficulties, client unavailability, lack of subject knowledge, and literature gaps which left students feeling ill-equipped to deal with the international group context. Negative experiences lead to stress and poor group development.

Research limitations — The study is based on a single simple case. The methodology has sought to reduce problems with internal validity and bias. The data collection and analysis methods are repeatable and we encourage other academics to test our conceptual models and conclusions.

Originality/value — Conceptual models for positive and negative experience are proposed.

The study suggests there is a balance to be sought between providing a positive student experience and practical learning. Practice-based learning

Integrating Curricular and Co-Curricular Endeavors to Enhance Student Outcomes
Copyright © 2016 by Emerald Group Publishing Limited
All rights of reproduction in any form reserved
ISBN: 978-1-78635-064-0

adds significant value to the student in terms of improved understanding of hard and soft tools, but may need to be based upon positive and negative experience.

Keywords: Practice; learning; postgraduate; project; experiential; value

7.1. Introduction

Simon (1967) espoused that the mission of a business school was to provide students with a science based education that they could readily apply. He further described how traditional barriers between business and business schools would need to be lowered. He foresaw that this would need to be done in three ways. (1) Have a business school that understands the problems that managers face and incorporate problem solving into educational experiences; (2) conduct research that generates scientific knowledge to improve the world and guide managerial problem solving; (3) create actionable knowledge acquired through science and the business context (Rousseau, 2012; Simon, 1967).

Lucas and Milford (2009) state that a study "for business" recognizes that there is a vocational element to education and students should be adequately prepared for employment. They discuss how in recent years employability has become a central issue within higher education. Interestingly, the authors go on to state that a study "about business" should recognize that education can fulfill a wider role, that of allowing students to study the role of business in society, incorporating sociological, legal, economic, or ethical aspects. They further proffer that, business curricula must therefore take account of the diversity and dynamism of subject knowledge; approaches that emphasize technique over context will develop only partial knowledge and understanding while recognizing that business educators are also under pressure to include "useful" knowledge within the curriculum.

At the University of Bedfordshire Business School in the United Kingdom, a practice-based ethos has been embraced. Practice-based teaching draws heavily upon the concepts of experiential learning, learning by doing, and action learning. As a business school, we ensure that students learn by doing and the "doing" part involves solving problems for local businesses.

Understanding the problems that business people face is done through regular events and contact points, boundary-spanning personnel uniquely responsible for business development with external businesses, regular university-business activities, the incorporation of external panels of business practitioners who are involved in course design and assessment, and finally the employment of Professors of Practice whose role is to support a practice-based ethos by facilitating sustainable contact with local businesses. We conduct positivistic and phenomenological research that extends the extant literature and provides practical recommendations for businesses.

In addition, we conduct market research to inform the design and delivery of our courses. We call this Research Informed Curriculum Design (RICD) (Bentley et al., 2013). Most importantly from a student learning perspective, we facilitate students acquiring actionable knowledge through the implementation of a practice-based teaching and learning experience. In doing so, we address "learning about businesses" and "learning for business." Business courses at the University of Bedfordshire are designed with this tenet at their core and all learning outcomes from the course level to the unit level have learning outcomes structured along the lines of "skills" and "knowledge." In doing all these things we have truly embraced Simon's (1967) and Lucas and Milford's (2009) visions.

In the Business School, we run a number of executive and specialist courses at the postgraduate level. While the literature in this area predominantly deals with practice-based teaching and learning in MBAs, health, and the delivery of STEM subjects, the unit of analysis in this chapter is a professionally accredited Masters in Science in Project Management (MSc PM). Berggren and Söderlund (2008) argue that given the increasing and important role of projects in society and the fact that projects should be schools for leaders, project managers must not be content with only following the discussions of management education — they should be taking the lead in the development. Winter, Smith, Morris, and Cicmil (2006) discussed the need for new research in relation to the developing practice to extend the field beyond its current intellectual foundations and to connect it more closely to the challenges of contemporary project management practice.

Postgraduate Project Management courses require an eclectic mix of theory from other disciplines. For example, our course utilizes hard decision tools from decision sciences and operations and soft tools from human resource management and cultural studies. Larson and Drexler (2010) emphasize that project management is a sociotechnical discipline that combines sophisticated quantitative tools with quintessential people skills. The MSc in Project Management at the University of Bedfordshire was designed to provide knowledge and skills in all these areas while providing opportunity to apply tools and knowledge practically. The practical elements of the course are evidenced specifically in a unit called the "Client Delivery Project." The unit is based on our bespoke "3-3-3 model" of working with external clients. The 3-3-3 acronym describes the fact that the students work with client briefs that have 3 objectives, 3 deliverables, and have to be delivered in three months. This is an internal model that we have developed over the last five years.

Unlike the extant literature on learning pedagogies and project management, here we address this approach to learning through the lens of the student. Our approach is empirical and deliberately student-centric. This chapter addresses the issue of whether students perceive practice-based learning to improve their understanding of hard and soft project management tools. It also seeks to address whether practice-based learning improves a student's university experience. In this chapter, we first embed the idea of practice-based teaching in the extant literature. We then introduce a case study of practice-based teaching which is built around international postgraduate students on the MSc in Project Management. The research questions addressed are the following:

(1) What is the improvement in the understanding of hard and soft project management tools through having completed a practice-based unit?
(2) How does a practice-based unit affect the student experience?

Unit impact data is gathered from the quantitative analysis of a small exit survey and anecdotal evidence. Student experience data are gathered from the qualitative analysis of students' reflective reports. A number of measures for student experience for practice-based projects are subsequently proposed and wider outcomes for the university, teaching staff, the students, and the community are discussed. Finally limitations of the study are discussed, and opportunities for further research are tabled.

7.2. Literature

In order to position the concept of practice-based teaching and learning in the wider literature, we will discuss the historical impetus for the pedagogical approach and then the three underlying theories that underlie the practice-based teaching and learning at the University of Bedfordshire.

Interest in practice-based teaching and learning in business schools has been around intermittently since Simon's (1967) work however interest has ebbed and flowed throughout that period. In the United Kingdom where the majority of universities are still public institutions, there has been resurgence in practice-based teaching and learning between 2005 and 2010 largely seeded by available government funding. Lead by the UK's Open University, a number of interested universities, Business Schools amongst them, came together to pool good practice. The Open University's Centre for Excellence in Teaching and Learning (CETL) was funded by the Higher Education Funding Council for a period of five years between 2005 and 2010 (Open University, 2015). A number of initiatives were seeded and good practice shared. Our university was involved in this initiative and a practice-based ethos was quickly developed in the Business School subsequent to the CETL activity.

Practice-based teaching and learning in a postgraduate business course refers to a combination of approaches. It in effect marries the work of Dewey, Kolb, Berggren, and Söderlund (experiential learning) with that of Revans (action learning) and his followers with theory from Argyris (learning through doing) and Gibbs (the importance of critical reflection for learning).

Experiential learning originally stems from the early works of Dewey and other notable scholars of human learning and development: Kurt Lewin, Jean Piaget, William James, Carl Jung, Paulo Freire, Carl Rogers, and others — who put experience in the center of their theories (Kolb & Fry, 1975; Kolb & Kolb, 2005). Kolb (1984, 2015) later developed a model of experiential learning based on six propositions: (1) Learning is best conceived as a process, not in terms of outcomes; (2) All learning is relearning; (3) Learning requires the resolution of conflicts between dialectically opposed modes of adaption to the world; (4) Learning is a holistic process of adaption to the world; (5) Learning results from synergetic transactions between the person and the environment; (6) Learning is the process of creating knowledge (Kolb & Kolb, 2005). Experiential learning takes place when it is as evident that there is a cycle of concrete experience, observation and reflection on that experience, formation of abstract concepts based upon the reflection and finally some kind of testing of those new concepts. In defining experiential learning in this way, he highlighted the importance of reflection which was picked up and elaborated upon by Gibbs (1988) who provided a framework for reflection which is often used as a reflection template for students. Practice-based teaching in our context embraces the Kolb cycle and Gibbs framework. Students are required to reflect upon their experiences of action learning. The Gibbs framework includes the following activities: description of the activity, feelings about the activity, evaluation of the activity, conclusions and finally actions going forward. Action learning is an approach to individual and organizational development and is widely used in a variety of public, private, and third sector organizations (Brook & Milner, 2014; Brook, Pedler, & Burgoyne, 2012) based on the work of Revans (1998) in the 1960s action learning revolves around the solving of a problem usually by a group. Sometimes referred to as Problem-Based Learning (PBL), this form of learning now has a number of different flavors within UK Higher Education which include the following: self-managed action learning (Bourner, 2011) and critical action learning (Lawless, 2008; Rigg & Trehan, 2004; Vince, 2008). The differences between the two approaches are largely down to the degree of facilitation involved on the part of the tutor and have evolved from a pragmatic need to deal with ever-increasing class sizes. In our context, "the problem" is the client's problem which has to be derived and validated with the client, after which it has to be solved by agreeing clearly defined objectives and deliverables, and then implementing and controlling a project to produce the agreed deliverables.

Later authors such as Berggren and Söderlund (2008) have explored experiential learning under a project management lens and have proffered the idea of a "social twist" to experiential learning in order to respond to the challenges of a Mode 2 society (socially distributed, application-oriented, transdisciplinary and subject to multiple accountabilities (Gibbons, Limoges, Nowotny, Schwartzman, & Trow, 1994)) and to explore how knowledge coproduction can be brought into project management training. In response to criticisms of Kolb in the area of failures to reconcile personal and social learning, Berggren and Söderlund proffer an expanded learning cycle. The expanded cycle emphasizes the additional need to integrate processes of articulation and reflection to allow for the abstraction of knowledge by the individual. In our context, articulation is achieved through the requirement for group and individual presentation at intermittent stages throughout the Client Delivery unit and reflection is achieved by the students having to produce a reflective report on their individual learning and future personal development plans.

Argyris (1993) in his seminal book on organizational inquiry purported that learning occurred when one detects and corrects error and that error is any mismatch between what we intend an action to produce and what actually happens when we implement that action. It is a mismatch between intentions and results.

He also said that learning also occurs when we produce a match between intentions and results for the first time. Practice-based teaching in our context allows errors and matches to be experienced and therefore learning to occur. The mismatch between theory and practice is lived in the context of the uses and limitations of project management tools that they have been taught. We do not consider this approach to be Community-Based Learning or service learning because the aim is not social good but to solve a specific problem for a business or social enterprise. Moreover, in out unit the student activity falls outside of Mooney and Edwards' (2001) Hierarchy of Community Based Learning. Student activity here is an out of class within the local business community but it has no determinate social action (unless the business is a social enterprise). It does however entail structured reflection, acquiring skills, it doesn't by itself qualify for curriculum credit, but it does render a service. It may however have social benefits for international students as it exposes them to a local business community and for local businesses that experience international input to their businesses.

In summary, our concept of practice-based teaching and learning draws heavily upon the experiential learning, action learning, and learning by doing.

7.3. Methodology

7.3.1. *The Case Study*

The Client Delivery Project unit which is the source of our data aims to enable students to develop and enhance a broad spectrum of project management skills; provide them with an understanding of the dilemmas and issues inherent in project management; and provide the opportunity to analyze and evaluate a range of tools and techniques used in project management, alongside performance, change and commitment issues. This means that students get to use and evaluate hard and soft tools of project management. The unit enables students to learn from their experience of managing a real project by critically assessing a range of project management models and tools, choosing from them in a flexible way to fit organizational demands in a given practical situation. Project management involves a deliberate and reflective assumption of role, and students are encouraged to reflect on their performance as project manager or as team member. Students draw heavily on content from other units to make sense of their assigned projects and implement practical solutions for a real client. Principle units drawn on are Project Management Tools and Techniques (hard tools) and the Human Side of Management (soft tools).

Students attending the course come from many undergraduate disciplines and have undertaken undergraduate degrees around the world. Some have professional experience. All students are considering a career as professional project managers. Alumni have moved into project management roles in construction, events, IT, health, and education.

Table 7.1: Showing the numbers enrolled and pass rates for the MSc in project management 2012–2014.

Year	Number enrolled	Number passed	Number failed	Average grade[a]	Pass rate (%)	Fail rate (%)	AB+ rate (%)	Non submission rate (%)
2011–2012	22	22	0	10.4	100	0	45	0
2012–2013	58	55	3	10.1	95	5	41	3
2013–2014	37	36	1	11.0	97	3[b]	51	3

[a]The university uses a 16 point scale for grading. 10 is a C+. 11 is a B−.
[b]Failing students have the opportunity to retake the unit with the next cohort.

The 2013–2014 cohort represented what Yin (2014) would call a common case; a single case which represented an opportunity to understand social processes related to some theoretical interest. The theoretical interest is the relationship between practice and perceived understanding of hard and soft project management tools, and the relationship between practice and student experience.

7.3.2. The Case Context

The MSc PM course admits three cohorts a year, October, February, and March with part time and distance learning variants. The 2013–2014 cohort contained students from more than 10 countries. All teaching and communication in class was in English. Table 7.1 provides a picture of the course in terms of typical numbers enrolled, pass rates, and average grades.

7.3.3. The 3-3-3 Practice-Based Model

Project management is essentially a practical discipline. Whilst the subject incorporates an eclectic mix of theoretical concepts and models from other disciplines, its fundamental nature is one of using theory, models, and techniques to achieve concrete outcomes. As such, practice is an essential part of acquiring the skills of project management. Layered upon this is the idea of tools being hard and soft. Hard tools are those typically used within project initiation documents for example, business case, objectives, deliverables, a plan, a critical path, WBS, org structure, stakeholder and communications plan, risk and quality assessment. Soft tools are those associated with theories of human interaction; effective team working, leadership, motivation, effective communication, negotiation, and conflict resolution. Students are exposed to hard and soft tools in previous units and are assessed on their separate unit knowledge with some limited theoretical and practical application. The Client Delivery unit however brings together this skill and knowledge and forces students to apply and evaluate hard and soft tools simultaneously.

To heighten the experience and make it more real for students, we simulate real projects by working with real clients to solve real business problems. This forms part of our Business School ethos. This 3-3-3 model applied within the Client Delivery unit of the course enables practice-based teaching and learning with the involvement of external clients. The students learn by doing; are involved in action learning, and undertake experiential learning through their own reflection. They are given a project brief and are involved in their assigned groups in formulating three objectives with three related deliverables that have to be delivered within three months from March to May each year. They are then assessed on their project approach and the success of their deliverables, then on their personal reflection.

7.3.4.   The Client Delivery Unit Assessments

The unit has two assessments. The first has two parts. Part 1 is a group interim report — in practice this is a project initiation document of 1500 words — outlining how each student group intends to address the project brief. Individual viva voce are conducted to obtain an individual mark for this activity. A viva voce is an oral examination of work done. Assignment 1 part 2 is a final group report following completion of the project reflecting on the outcomes and tools evaluated and used. Assignment 2 is an individual report reflecting on the impact of human factors on the project and identifying personal learning throughout the project and future personal learning objectives. To facilitate this, students are encouraged to keep a personal log of their thoughts and experiences throughout the project and provided with the Gibbs framework to guide their personal analysis. Formative feedback on ongoing issues and assessments is given throughout the 12 week period of the project.

7.3.5.   Typical 3-3-3 Student Briefs for 2013–2014

The 2013–2014 students (our cohort) worked on client projects between March and May that year. The cohort, one of three that year, was split into groups using a combination of techniques which were informed by Belbin tests, previous group experience, the requirement to ensure mixed cultural groups and internal guidelines which include no lone females. Where possible we tried to ensure that one of the students was also a Projects In Complex Environments (PRINCE2®) practitioner. PRINCE2® is a methodology developed by the Office of Government Commerce in the United Kingdom (UK Government, 2015). Project managers undertake formal assessment to become foundation or practitioner qualified. Table 7.2 shows the clients, client problems, and project objectives for each student group.

In order to answer the question, what is the improvement in understanding of hard and soft project management tools through having completed a practice-based unit? In this instance, the unit of analysis is a student cohort that completed the Client Delivery unit between 2013 and 2014. The Client Delivery unit is the last unit in the course and directly precedes the dissertation. All learning outcomes for previous units had been specifically designed to reflect students' knowledge of and skills

Table 7.2: Showing the client, the client problems, and the related project objectives.

Title of project	Client	Client problem	Objectives
Cultifest	UKCCA	Funds needed	Hold an event Raise funds Produce a sustainability plan
VIP tent	UKCCA	Service level required was unknown by the client	Research best practice Benchmark existing client offering Make recommendations
Course feasibility	UKCCA	Training needs unknown	Conduct market analysis Conduct competitor analysis Produce feasibility report
Friends Scheme	Festive Road	Social media marketing gap	Research best practice Benchmark Existing client offering Make recommendations
Creative spaces	Festive Road	New premises needed urgently	Research facilities available Analyze and map client requirements Make recommendations
Give back	Supermarket	Impending legislation on food waste — options needed to reduce food to land fill	Research legislation on perishable foods Research uses of perishable foods in a specific location Make recommendations on the uses of and logistics issues for sustainable reuse

in using hard and soft project management tools. Students are required to have achieved an adequate level of understanding and skills in previous units before starting the Client Delivery unit. Any perception of improvement after completing the Client Delivery unit would show value added by the practice-based teaching and learning approach in the unit. On Completion of the Client Delivery Project unit, the student should be able to do the following:

- Demonstrate a depth of knowledge of appropriate hard and soft project management tools and relevant theory and critically evaluate when to apply them during a project life cycle.
- Demonstrate the application of your project management knowledge and understanding to work in a team to plan, communicate, implement, control, evaluate, and feedback lessons learnt, as well as manage stakeholders and benchmark and critically evaluate performance.

7.3.6. Research Design

Prior to all data collection and analysis, ethics approval was sought and granted at a faculty level commensurate with university policy. An appropriate research design was considered in order to answer the question, *"What is the improvement in the understanding of hard and soft project management tools through having completed a practice-based unit?"* The research question clearly involved an independent variable (learning in the unit) and a dependent variable (improvement in skills and knowledge in hard and soft project management tools). A quantitative method is therefore suitable for this type of data collection. This is an exploratory study so wider validity testing is not an aim. As such, we are exploring a relationship and not testing hypotheses. The author was in a privileged position as the tutor for the unit with access to the required data. This data was collected from a simple exit survey for students using SurveyMonkey software which explored students' perceived level of skill and knowledge before and after the unit in the area of hard and soft project management tools. Four simple questions were developed and the survey was introduced and contextualized. Students were invited to complete the survey after completing the unit after all assessment marks had been returned in order to reduce any halo effect. A seven point Likert scale was used for the survey. To avoid compromise of the scale due to social desirability (students wishing to look good to their tutor), all responses were anonymous. Students were informed that by completing the survey, they would be providing informed consent for their data to be used anonymously.

In order to answer the question, *how does a practice-based unit affect the student experience?* The approach took a little more thought. The research design was more difficult to define because there are no existing measures for university experience as it related to practice-based teaching and learning. For this reason, a dependent−independent relationship was harder to define. As an exploratory study, and with access to rich qualitative data where students had assessed their own learning in individual reflective studies, it was possible to develop attributes of what constituted a good and bad experience. Students were familiar with the process of writing reflective reports using a Gibbs framework having completed three earlier reports during the course. A qualitative approach was therefore taken for this part of the research and the Gibbs framework provided the framework by which data was collected. Thirty-two reflective scripts were available for analysis from the 2013 to 2014 cohort.

A reflective report, in methodological terms, is both a document and a physical artefact. Yin (2014, p. 106) describes the strengths of using these types of data source as they can be used to provide insight into cultural features and technical operations; they are stable, unobtrusive, specific, and broad. In terms of weaknesses selectivity and availability may be a problem. In this instance, bias selectivity was overcome by using reflective scripts from all students in the cohort. Reporting bias was overcome by searching for both positive and negative experiences within each script. This was subsequently validated by an academic with no interest in the outcome of the research to eliminate any reporting bias, capture any emissions, or question any possible misinterpretation. Availability was not an issue because the author had full access to all scripts. Scripts were completely anonymized and combined into one document and no personal data was used in the reporting of the combined results.

A total of 59 thousand words were analyzed using NVIVO software to elucidate positive and negative experiences described by students. Example quotes illustrating positive and negative experiences are listed here.

> Positive example — "I have learnt how to motivate people, maintain time, co-ordination within group, combined efforts, team spirit, communication, respect to other opinions, etc. These were my great personal achievements from this project."
>
> Negative example — "In our project we faced some problems, mainly communication."

All of the negative and then positive experiences were coded into positive and negative nodes representing emergent themes and then sorted into trees to aid conceptual clarity, prompt to code richly, and identify patterns (Bazeley, 2007, p. 103). This process was done a number of times. This produced conceptual models for positive and negative experiences.

The findings, discussion, and analysis are presented in later sections.

7.4.   Findings

7.4.1.   *Outcomes in Terms of Perceived Understanding*

The Client Delivery Project unit takes place before the final dissertation at a time when students have finished all other units on the course. At that point, students are expected to have a good knowledge of project management and they should have an adequate theoretical understanding and skill with hard and soft tools of project management. In 2013–2014, after completion of the Client Delivery unit, we asked the students about their level of understanding of hard and soft tools of project management tools. We used a Likert scale of 1–7, where 1 was "very poor" and 7 "excellent," to capture levels of agreement with the following questions:

- What was your level of understanding of project management hard tools prior to the project unit?
- What was your level of understanding of project management hard tools after the project unit?
- What was your level of understanding of project management soft tools prior to the project unit?
- What was your level of understanding of project management soft tools after the project unit?

Hard tools were defined as the traditional tools associated with the four phases of project management; those that might be found specifically in any project initiation document, for example, work break down structure, organizational structure plans, Gantt charts, and risk and quality assessment. Soft tools are those associated with managing people, for example, leadership, team management, motivation, negotiation, and conflict resolution.

Thirty two of thirty six answered the question on soft tools. Thirty one of thirty six answered the question on hard tools. Tables 7.3 and 7.4 show the students' perception of their understanding of hard and soft tools before and after the unit. The results show a significant positive shift in understanding for both hard and soft tools as a result of the Client Delivery Project unit. After completion, for hard tools, the percentage of students that considered their understanding to be "good" and above went from 29% to 100%. For soft tools, this figure went from 45% to 100%.

7.4.2.   Outcomes in Terms of Reflective Reports

A reflective report is an individual document produced by students after the main client project is completed. It gives a student an opportunity to reflect on his or her own personal learning and allows the student to plan any further learning required. A qualitative analysis of the primary reflective language used by the students using NVIVO software produced the following conceptual frameworks for positive and negative experiences.

Positive experiences appear interrelated. However notable in the conceptual model for the students' positive experience are the start and end nodes. Positive experiences seem to stem from good client communications, team motivation, and the buzz of being involved in a real project. Positive experiences seem to lead to pride in outcomes and professional transferable skills.

Negative experiences also appear to be interrelated. Notable in the conceptual model for the students' negative experiences are the start and end points. Negative experiences stem from lack of life experience, language difficulties, client unavailability,

Table 7.3: Showing student understanding of soft project management tools before and after the unit.

Understanding of project management soft tools	Very poor	Poor	Inadequate	Adequate	Good	Very good	Excellent	Responses	Weighted average
% Before the unit	6.25	9.38	40.63	15.63	18.75	9.38	0.00	32	3.59
% After the unit	0.00	0.00	0.00	0.00	9.38	68.75	21.88	32	6.13

Table 7.4: Showing student understanding of hard project management tools before and after the unit.

Understanding of project management hard tools	Very poor	Poor	Inadequate	Adequate	Good	Very good	Excellent	Responses	Weighted average
% Before the unit	3.23	6.45	25.81	19.35	32.26	12.90	0.00	31	4.10
% After the unit	0.00	0.00	0.00	0.00	12.90	54.84	32.26	31	6.19

lack of project management knowledge, and finally the fact that project management theory from the literature appears insufficient to address the international project group context. This leads to stress and poor group development.

7.5.   Discussion

What is the improvement in understanding of hard and soft project management tools through having completed a practice-based unit? — in other words, what is the value added to the student through having completed a practice-based unit following the completion of conventional units designed to embed hard and soft project management tools?

If we consider this unit a proxy for practice-based learning, then the outcomes illustrate that students clearly believe the practice-based unit improves their knowledge of hard and soft tools. For soft tools, only 29% of students in the 2013−2014 cohort considered their knowledge and skills to be adequate to excellent before the unit despite the majority having been assessed as having adequate skills and knowledge by previous assessment. After the unit, this rose to 100%.

For hard tools, only 45% considered their knowledge and skills to be adequate to excellent before the unit. After the unit, this rose to 100%. In addition to this, they clearly consider improvement in their skills and knowledge as a positive experience. Figure 7.1 also demonstrates that in addition to improvements in skills and knowledge other outcomes such as improved communication skills and increased confidence were also cited.

Does practice-based teaching affect a student's university experience? Our conceptual models (Figures 7.1 and 7.2) clearly show positive and negative experiences and how data nodes within each are interrelated. One approach to analyze these models is to consider nodes that appear to be starting points and end points because from a practitioner perspective, these are areas that can be influenced to through instructional design to improve a student experience.

It is clear that positive experiences appear to stem from good client communications, good client engagement, team motivation, and the buzz of a real project. Students perceive these to lead to pride in the group's outcomes and professional transferrable skills as evidenced by statements like the following:

> I was able to use other soft skills such as negotiation, presentation, analytical and organizational skills while carrying out the project. These skills are transferrable and could be used in future projects.
> … and the transferable skills-conducting survey, research will help me to reuse in any other activity like this either in a project or everyday life. During the PGD/MSC course we got a good theoretical knowledge of project management. Afterwards, an opportunity to apply the theoretical knowledge in the real life {the Client delivery unit} was, I believe, not only complementary to our theoretical knowledge but also very important for professional life.

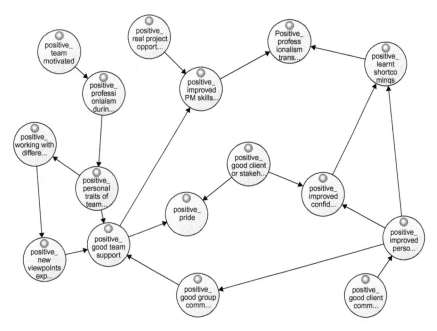

Figure 7.1: Conceptual Framework for Positive Student Experience.

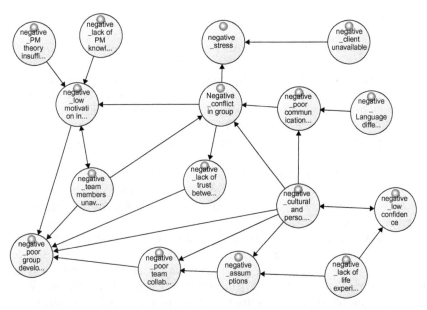

Figure 7.2: Conceptual Framework for Negative Student Experience.

Intermediate data nodes suggest that positive client/stakeholder feedback, the inter-personal relationships within the group, and the realization of individual short comings in terms of skills and knowledge influence the outcomes. Negative experiences stem from lack of life experience, language difficulties, clients being unavailable, the group leader's lack of project management knowledge and the fact that despite having studied the literature in terms of the human side of management, the students felt that the theory was inadequate in describing or helping them to cope with their immediate experiences. Students perceived this to eventually lead to stress and poor group development. This is evidenced in the following statements:

> ... I had also to face some difficulties regarding formation of group.
> ... we were taken out of our comfort zone and put with unfamiliar faces and people. Before we became a group the six members we did not really have any relationship among ourselves.
> The pressure of having various tasks to do I sometimes found stressful but I can see how this situation has better prepared me for the future.
> Arranging the time and date of group meetings was a little bit problematic as group members came from different places and they had jobs in different dates and times.
> In the begin was the project was outside my comfort zone as I am used to IT based project but this didn't stop me giving everything to make sure the project was completed successfully.
> ... we faced difficulties while allocating tasks to every individual because of the very human nature that everybody was feeling his/her part is more complicated.
> Having a different "view of the world" does lead to conflict within the group.
> Communication skills sometimes created some problems, as different member of the group has got different English accent.
> Some motivation theories didn't help the project in fact I found them much of a hindrance as they can't be applied to everybody. In fact people from the eastern hemisphere are motivated by different things from the western hemisphere of the world.
> ... Project suffers some mismanagement and coordination gap.

The Client Delivery Project is the last unit before the dissertation. Given the experiences described and the unit's proximity to the end of the course, we can safely infer that the practice-based teaching unit affects the overall students experience in positive and negative ways.

We could act to improve the student experience by acting to secure a positive experience and reduce the negative experiences. We could improve the positive experiences by further facilitating good client communications and client engagement or removing the real client altogether by simulation perhaps. We could improve team motivation by reverting to previously dropped assessment methods like peer review or by further incentivizing performance. The down side of doing this is that we risk introducing unknown negative experiences or worst still reducing the value to the student of learning to deal with conflict or building confidence through being forced to deal with a real client.

We could act to reduce negative experiences by restricting course applicants to those with work experience, tightening our English language requirements, and replacing a real client with a simulated client. We could further select group leaders for PM competence. Finally, we could support primary research in the area of motivating international project teams, using the results to inform our own teaching and thereby fill perceived gaps in the literature. While the practicalities of these activities can be debated this author feels that in doing so we may be at risk of "throwing the baby away with the bath water."

7.6. Teaching Outcomes — Should We Actively Improve the Student Experience in Practice-Based Units?

In the current Higher Education Institution (HEI) environment, there is a lot of effort being made to improve the student experience. Practice-based teaching and learning and exposure of international students to local environments can be fraught with danger for both the university and for the student. Without proper planning, the international student and home student experience can be sullied if students are exposed to scenarios where their personal or group experience is poor. There is institutional pressure to improve the student experience and practice-based units are no exception to this rule. The problem with practice-based units is they are largely out of the control of teaching staff. This represents both a risk and an opportunity for rich learning.

In terms of improving the unit experience and therefore the university experience, our results would suggest that the design and review of the course could address a number of areas. However, in seeking to artificially create positive experiences and weigh a negative student experience with the demands of real business, we are creating a more artificial environment for students. Real-world projects are messy and difficult with clients that are independent and often difficult to communicate with. International project teams have multicultural teams with varying levels of English language skill. Perhaps a more fitting approach would be to accept the negative experience of practice-based learning as a "real-world plus" and take a hit on overall student experience. As a scholar–practitioner, this is my personal preference; however in a HEI world where student experience is fast becoming a differentiator between institutions offering similar courses, this may be a harder approach to defend with HEI executives.

Our research suggests that appropriate "experience measures" for international and home students on practice-based learning courses might include the following areas.

- Pride in group/project outcomes
- Transferrable skills and knowledge for professional life (e.g., theory, hard, and soft)

- Other transferrable skills (e.g., confidence, communication, language, life experience, presentations)
- Transferrable knowledge from the group interaction (e.g., new personal contacts, time management, conflict resolution, negotiation)
- Transferrable knowledge from the client interaction
- Ability to cope with project stress
- Ability to work in a group or lead a group
- Ability to work in an international student team

Apart from the potential development of "experience measures" for practice-based teaching, the Client Delivery Project unit has also provided us with rich teaching experience and the opportunity to produce teaching cases based around the real project experiences.

7.6.1. *Value Added for the Community*

The benefits to the local community have become evident for this type of practice-based teaching and learning. Not only have businesses benefited from the project deliverables gratis but networking has increased outside the university and students have maintained relationships with their clients after graduating. For example, 10 students from the cohort in the case study continued a relationship with the local Carnival having worked for the UK Centre for Carnival Arts. Association with the university going forward offers many organizations a degree of credibility that was missing before. For example, staff have been invited to join company boards as nonexecutive offices, another organization felt that the association with the university increased its chances of successfully applying for government funding.

7.6.2. *Value Added for the University*

The Client Delivery Project has exposed the capabilities of our students to local organizations. This has largely been positive. As momentum builds up and more projects are completed, we are able to show a portfolio of projects to prospective clients. This helps business development in the future.

7.6.3. *Value Added for the Students*

Anecdotal evidence shows us that our students having completed a project with real clients is a differentiator for them in the market place. One student recalled how an interview was progressing slowly until she mentioned having worked on a project with a real client. At which point the interviewer became animated and the student was offered the job. Others have used their experience from the Client Delivery unit to decide on a career path in a specific area of project management, while others have used it to decide specific areas to avoid. Others have concluded that project management is not for them while others have adapted so poorly to group work that they have decided to go it alone, starting their own businesses.

7.6.4. *Unexpected Outcomes*

One unexpected outcome for the unit was related to a negative experience on the part of one of the students. A parent complained independently to the department that his adult child had been put under unacceptable stress during the Client Delivery Project unit. This was taken seriously and additional support measures were made manifest within the unit materials for future students to consider.

This was unexpected and a shock to staff. In the United Kingdom, there is a phenomenon called "helicopter parenting" and this may well have been an example of this phenomena. But if we are to attempt to simulate real work environments for our students, we also need to expect the real-world stresses that come with this approach. Institutions need to ensure that student support and pastoral care are fit for purpose. However, again, as a scholar−practitioner, I am mindful not to throw the baby away with the bathwater by doing this. Students need to develop resilience and a university environment is a safe place in which to do this unlike in the real world.

7.7. Limitations

An exit survey was used to gauge students' understanding of hard tools and soft tools prior to undertaking the unit. Students were therefore asked to undertake a retrospective assessment of their prior knowledge. This may present a degree of methodological concern. However, students started the unit having already been assessed on their understanding and skills in prior units. Students were aware of prior unit marks at this point and therefore had an awareness of their own abilities. One could argue that undertaking the unit could have influenced their view of their own starting point and this combined with a human compulsion to appear to do well may have led students to state their understanding at the start of the unit to be adequate. Despite students having been assessed as reaching an adequate level of understanding and skills through previous assessment, some students actually perceived their starting point to be less than adequate (see Tables 7.3 and 7.4). This may also be interpreted as students' bias to over-emphasize achievement in the unit or a discrepancy between academic threshold criteria and a student's confidence level in their abilities. This area requires further study.

A second point of concern that was also considered was the generalization of hard and soft tools, making it difficult for someone with a strong background in some soft/hard tools but weaknesses in others to answer the question precisely. However a composite measure was deemed sufficient for this study because the learning outcomes for the unit use threshold criteria that are themselves composite. This aspect of the study will however be given further thought for ongoing research.

7.8. Conclusion

Practice-based learning appears to add value to conventional delivery in specialized postgraduate courses in terms of students improved understanding of hard and soft tools and value to staff and the local business community. Engaging with the local community provides value for all involved however downsides may include the fact that negative experience gained by virtue of the "real" experience may affect the student's university experience *per se*. However, those tasked with implementing this pedagogy should weigh the long-term advantages of a real-world experience against short-term institutional measures of student experience.

Practice-based learning exposes students to real-world pressures and associated stress. Institutions therefore need to ensure that the requisite student support and pastoral care are available to counteract these risks.

In terms of an unexpected theoretical contribution we became aware that although the guiding theories of experiential learning, action learning and learning through doing stand, there appears to be little research contextualize these theories in terms of university-business community activities. "Community learning" and "service learning" contextualize the experiential learning approach and manifest an overall societal aim — the public good. There appears no equivalent for private good. The term "open learning" is used widely to describe free access to materials and resources for the purpose of learning. In this context perhaps what we have is Practice-Based Learning in an "Open Business Learning" context. Here the resources are the students and the beneficiaries are all the stakeholders involved.

We plan to assimilate the learning into subsequent course revisions and incorporate our findings into revised course content and course delivery. We are currently evaluating the results of a second (2014−2015) cohort which will represent a longitudinal case. A second study will also formally look to explore the relationship between experiences reported in reflective reports with the university's unit exit survey in terms of communication and confidence. We will also consider the limitations of this study and explore a possible discontinuity between prior assignment threshold levels and student confidence going into the Client Delivery Project unit.

The research approach adopted here is considered to be broadly repeatable due to the data collection methods used. We invite other academics who teach project management in a practice-based way to repeat our approach, test our experiential measures, and compare notes on our findings.

References

Argyris, C. (1993). *Knowledge for action: A guide to overcoming barriers to organizational change*. San Francisco, CA: Jossey-Bass.

Bazeley, P. (2007). *Qualitative data analysis with NVIVO*. Los Angeles, CA: Sage.

Bentley, Y., Duan, Y., Richardson, D., Philpott, E., Ong, V., & Owen, V. (2013). Research-informed curriculum design for a master's-level program in project management. *Journal of Management Education, 37*(5), 651−682.

Berggren, C., & Söderlund, J. (2008). Rethinking project management education: Social twists and knowledge co-production. *International Journal of Project Management, 26*(3), 286−296.

Bourner, T. (2011). Developing self-managed action learning (SMAL). *Action Learning: Research and Practice, 8*(2), 117−127.

Brook, C., & Milner, C. (2014). Reflections on 'creative' action learning in business education: Some issues in its theory and practice. *Teaching in Higher Education, 19*(2), 126−137.

Brook, C., Pedler, M., & Burgoyne, J. (2012). Some debates and challenges in the literature on action learning: The state of the art since Revans. *Human Resource Development International, 15*(3), 269−282.

Gibbons, M., Limoges, C., Nowotny, H., Schwartzman, S., & Trow, M. (1994). *The new production of knowledge: The dynamics of science and research in contemporary societies.* London: Sage.

Gibbs, G. (1988). *Learning by doing: A guide to teaching and learning methods.* London: Further Education Unit.

Kolb, A. Y., & Kolb, D. A. (2005). Learning styles and learning spaces: Enhancing experiential learning in higher education. *Academy of Management Learning & Education, 4*(2), 193−212.

Kolb, D. A. (1984). *Experiential learning: Experience as the source of learning and development.* Englewood Cliffs, NJ: Prentice-Hall.

Kolb, D. A. (2015). *Experiential learning: Experience as the source of learning and development* (2nd ed.). Upper Saddle River, NJ: Pearson Education Inc.

Kolb, D. A., & Fry, R. E. (1975). Towards an applied theory of experiential learning. In C. L. Cooper (Ed.), *Theories of group processes: Wiley series on individuals, groups, and organizations* (pp. 33−58). London: Wiley.

Larson, E., & Drexler, J. A. (2010). Project management in real time: A service-learning project. *Journal of Management Education, 34*(4), 551−573.

Lawless, A. (2008). Action learning as legitimate peripheral participation. *Action Learning: Research and Practice, 5*(2), 117−129.

Lucas, U., & Milford, P. (2009). Key aspects of teaching and learning in accounting, business and management. In H. Fry, S. Ketteridge, & S. Marshall (Eds.), *A handbook for teaching and learning in higher education: Enhancing academic practice* (3rd ed., pp. 382−404). New York, NY: Routledge.

Mooney, A., & Edwards, B. (2001). Experiential learning in sociology: Service learning and other community-based learning initiatives. *Teaching Sociology, 29*(2), 181−194.

Open University. (2015). *Centre for excellence in teaching and learning.* Retrieved from http://www.open.ac.uk/opencetl/practice-based-professional-learning

Revans, R. W. (1998). *ABC of action learning.* London: Lemos and Crane.

Rigg, C., & Trehan, K. (2004). Reflections on working with critical action learning. *Action Learning: Research & Practice, 1*(2), 149−165.

Rousseau, D. M. (2012). Designing a better business school: Channelling Herbert Simon, addressing the critics, and developing actionable knowledge for professionalizing managers. *Journal of Management Studies, 49*(3), 600−618.

Simon, H. A. (1967). The business school: A problem in organizational design. *Journal of Management Studies, 4*(1), 1−16.

UK Government. (2015). *Best management practice portfolio*. Retrieved from https://www.gov.uk/government/publications/best-management-practice-portfolio/about-the-office-of-government-commerce

Vince, R. (2008). Learning-in-action and learning inaction: Advancing the theory and practice of critical action learning. *Action Learning: Research and Practice, 5*(2), 93–104.

Winter, M., Smith, C., Morris, P., & Cicmil, S. (2006). Directions for future research in project management: The main findings of a UK government-funded research network. *International Journal of Project Management, 24*(8), 638–649.

Yin, K. (2014). *Case study research: Design and methods*. Los Angeles, CA: Sage.

Chapter 8

A Credit-Bearing Programmatic Approach to Community-Based Learning at a Metropolitan University: The UALR Speech Communication Department

Kristen McIntyre and Ryan Fuller

Abstract

Purpose — The chapter focuses on how engaging undergraduate and graduate students at a metropolitan university through community-based experiential learning can help them make a difference in their personal relationships, in their workplaces and in their communities.

Methodology/approach — The chapter explores the University of Arkansas at Little Rock Department of Speech Communication's integrated approach to undergraduate and graduate curriculum that focuses on four types of casing complex problems and making positive, ethical recommendations to make a difference. Specifically, the chapter explores how problem-based learning; service-learning; narrative ethnography; and research projects can be used as meaningful ways to case complex communication issues and to make ethical, theory-informed recommendations to not only do no harm but also affect positive change and promote social justice in students' personal relationships, organizations, and communities.

Practical implications — Lessons learned from the programmatic approach are shared that include building a theoretical base for students to draw from, integrating case approaches into the curriculum, and engaging resistance and failure. Chapter recommendations promote using theory as a lever for learning, building meaningful relationships with stakeholders, and adopting a process orientation that embraces failure.

Integrating Curricular and Co-Curricular Endeavors to Enhance Student Outcomes
Copyright © 2016 by Emerald Group Publishing Limited
All rights of reproduction in any form reserved
ISBN: 978-1-78635-064-0

Originality/value – The chapter offers a review of four undergraduate courses and four graduate courses, with explicit applications of the four case approaches. Additionally, learning objectives, major assignment descriptions, and assessment approaches are detailed for each course.

Keywords: Experiential learning; case method; communication; applied communication; ethics; programmatic curriculum

8.1. A Programmatic Approach to Community-Based Learning at a Metropolitan University

The purpose of this chapter is to investigate how the Department of Speech Communication at the University of Arkansas, Little Rock, has successfully integrated meaningful experiences that expand beyond the walls of classroom learning into both the undergraduate and graduate programs. The chapter overviews curricular commonalities spanning the undergraduate and graduate levels, shares lessons learned, and makes recommendations for other departments that are interested in a similar approach. For the purposes of this chapter, we focus on our unique approach to case study instruction that underscores a meaningful reflection on the ethical implications of our communication practices.

The department orients both undergraduate and graduate programs to emphasize the application of theory to real-world issues and problems (Frey & Cissna, 2009) and foregrounds experience as a foundation of student learning (Kolb, 1984; Kolb & Kolb, 2005). In line with this approach, the department has integrated case-based learning throughout its BA in Speech Communication and MA in Applied Communication Studies programs. Starting with the first one semester undergraduate course, SPCH 1300 (the introductory speech communication course in the department, serving as the prerequisite for all upper-level courses) students engage in case studies based on their past and current lived experience as well as participate in service-learning. Throughout the department's curriculum, undergraduate courses draw on personal and service experiences to analyze conflict management, work with difference, diffuse innovations, craft persuasive speeches, and improve personal relationships, to name a few. At the graduate level, students' final projects address real-world issues in the greater Little Rock, AR, area. Students collect and analyze data, and complete a paper and presentation with analysis and recommendations informed by theory. Example projects include anti-bullying communication initiatives at elementary and middle schools, social media use during a flu epidemic, message effectiveness in the Mayflower, AR ExxonMobil oil spill, and parent-teacher communication. After graduating, many of our students attain positions as communication specialists/directors, managers, nonprofit volunteer coordinators, as well as professional development consultants for local organizations.

Guided by the notion of *good people, speaking well* (cf. Quintilian), the department has adopted an ethical stance. Within our case-based curricular approach is a department-wide emphasis on ethical communication practices. Starting with the basic communication course (SPCH 1300), students are introduced to ethical dilemmas of communication (e.g., responsibility, integrity, fairness, truthfulness/honesty, respect, grace), which they apply to a conflict in their own lives and reflect on why it produces a dilemma. In other courses as well, students draw on experience to tease out ethical communication implications from their cases. In graduate level courses, students reflect on experiences in the field, considering research ethics as they conduct their own projects and making ethical recommendations to construct better social worlds. In summary, the department works to provide students with meaningful learning via purposeful lived experience and service-based case studies as well as an emphasis on wrestling with ethical communication practices within each case situation.

8.2. About UALR and the Speech Communication Department

In the following section, we introduce the context in which the department is situated. The University of Arkansas at Little Rock (UALR) is a metropolitan university with approximately 12,000 students (undergraduate and graduate). It is one of the two universities in Arkansas that are classified by the Carnegie Foundation for the Advancement of Teaching as a community-engaged institution (New England Resource Center for Higher Education, 2015). The mission of the University of Arkansas at Little Rock is to:

> develop the intellect of students; to discover and disseminate knowledge; to serve and strengthen society by enhancing awareness in scientific, technical, and cultural arenas; and to promote humane sensitivities and understanding of interdependence. Within this broad mission are the responsibilities to use quality instruction to instill in students a lifelong desire to learn; to use knowledge in ways that will contribute to society; and to apply the resources and research skills of the University community to the service of the city, the state, the nation, and the world in ways that will benefit humanity. (University of Arkansas at Little Rock, 1988, para. 6)

In line with this community-engaged mission, the Department of Speech Communication emphasizes an ethical, applied approach to the study of communication. Specifically, the department's mission to *foster the co-creation of better social worlds* is a commitment to ethical goals in communication processes and practices. Faculty applied scholarship attends to these ethical issues as does instruction by focusing on contemporary social issues and seeking to advance the understanding of communication in practical settings (*Journal of Applied Communication Research*, n.d.). For example, faculty research has examined: (a) how people make positive life changes in response to cancer diagnoses, (b) how leaders can create opportunities after a crisis, (c) how dialogue can be fostered across faith traditions, or (d) how positive organizational cultures can be created and sustained. The faculty's research seeks to *make a difference* in how communication is practiced in personal and professional environments.

Because an applied communication focus permeates instruction, faculty align learning experiences and assessment across our undergraduate and graduate degree programs. Across our programs, our graduates should be able to (1) formulate an argument/thesis; (2) make analytical claims using communication theory; and (3) offer ethically responsible, theory-informed recommendations to improve communication practices. To achieve these ends, department faculty adopt *case method* with an emphasis on *communication ethics* across the curriculum.

8.3. Casing: A Framework for Real-World Communication Issues

In the following section, we introduce the case method as an approach to instruction and specify the unique way that it is used throughout the department. In effect, we argue for the value of case instruction, but contrast traditional case learning with *enactments* that privilege a focus on student lived experience. *Enactment* is a deliberate word choice for the department. An *enactment* situates reality as a social construction (Berger & Luckmann, 1991); that is, the environment is neither objective nor a biased perception, but rather something that we actively create and which then influences us.

In the traditional sense, *case instruction* refers to the use of short- to medium-length, preformulated narrative dilemmas that are authentic and relevant to the course material, and which put students into decision-making roles (Garvin, 2003). Cases address complex phenomena with uncertain or ambiguous outcomes, provide a basis for reflection and classroom discussion, and stimulate critical thinking (Graham & Cline, 1980; McManus, 1986). However, traditional cases can often be far removed from students' lived experiences.

Substantial attention has been given to *case-based instruction*, emphasizing both the advantages and disadvantages for student learning (Mostert, 2007). Some of the student-centered advantages of traditional case method pedagogy include emphasizing context-dependent, practical problem-solving; providing opportunities for vicarious learning; analyzing problematic situations from multiple perspectives; developing analytical and problem-solving skills; and involving learners in their own learning. Some challenges of case-based instruction include familiarizing students with case teaching, relating cases to a theoretical base, and dealing with case complexity in class discussions and written analyses (Mostert, 2007). Other critiques of the traditional case method include a focus on the exceptional (i.e., organizational crisis) rather than some of the more commonplace aspects of interpersonal, group, organizational, or community contexts (Dorn, 1999). In essence, the more traditional use of case method, while undoubtedly valuable in many respects, focuses on a preformulated write up that may fail to connect with students' experiences.

In an effort to address some of these critiques, throughout our undergraduate and graduate programs, we carefully draw upon or construct specific student lived experiences for examining real communication issues that affect interpersonal relationships, groups, organizations, and communities. Our focus turns attention to actively *casing* (note the gerund; e.g., Charmaz & Bryant, 2011) communication practices that are part of students' experiences as a participant or observer. Consequently, *casing* privileges experiential learning (Kolb, 1984; Kolb & Kolb, 2005), a pedagogical approach that promotes the integration of four adaptive learning modes to engage all learners and to achieve the intended learning goal(s): concrete experience, reflective observation, abstract conceptualization, and active experimentation. Concrete experience invites learners to fully involve themselves in new experiences (Kolb, 1984). Reflective observation creates an opportunity for learners to "observe their experiences from many perspectives" (Kolb, 1984, p. 30). In the abstract conceptualization mode, learners "must be able to create concepts that integrate their observations into logically sound theories" (Kolb, 1984, p. 30). Finally, the active experimentation mode asks learners "to use these theories to make decisions and solve problems" (Kolb, 1984, p. 30). When all four modes are included in a structured learning experience, learners are much more likely to internalize the new knowledge and/or skill, increasing comprehension, retention, and application of the learned material.

When *casing*, students offer rich and thick descriptions of experienced contexts (Geertz, 1973) inclusive of the meaning construction process that occurs by the participants in these contexts, analyze them by connecting data to theory, and make recommendations that are grounded in ethics. This approach reveals important shifts in how they conceptualize communication and ultimately helps them to recognize and implement communication practices to affect changes in their professional and personal relationships. Specifically, *casing* is enacted in our undergraduate and graduate courses through (1) problem-based learning, (2) service-learning, (3) narrative ethnography/self-reflection, and (4) real research projects in undergraduate and graduate programs.

8.3.1. Problem-Based Learning

One enactment of *casing* communication issues is problem-based learning (PBL). In PBL, instructors introduce nuanced and open-ended problems, leading to an investigation from which subject matter content and instruction emerge (Edens, 2000). With this approach, students own and actively try to solve the problem. The instructor facilitates the process by monitoring, asking questions, and coaching. PBL originated in medicine as an alternative to traditional medical education and has diffused into health, legal, education, and social science fields, including communication (Ahlfeldt & Overland, 2002). In communication, teacher-scholars have implemented PBL in courses such as business and professional communication (Allen & Rooney, 1998; Brzovic & Matz, 2009; Pennell & Miles, 2009), intercultural communication (Saatci, 2008), public relations (Attansey, Okigbo, & Schmidt, 2007), public speaking (Sellnow & Ahlfeldt, 2005), and research methods (Roberts, 2001). PBL is different from the traditional case narrative where students read and debate what could or be done; rather, they shape the context and reflect on their communication practices. Students who participate in PBL activities demonstrate critical thinking and teamwork skills (Attansey et al., 2007; Pennell & Miles, 2009; Sellnow & Ahlfeldt, 2005) and effective (i.e., persuasive) rhetoric (Smart, Hicks, & Melton, 2013).

8.3.2. Service-Learning

Another enactment of *casing* complex issues is service-learning or learning through organized and meaningful community service activities (Britt, 2012; McIntyre & Sellnow, 2014). Specifically, service-learning is "a teaching and learning strategy that integrates meaningful community service with instruction and reflection to enrich the learning experience, teach civic responsibility, and strengthen communities" (Seifer & Connors, 2007, p. 4). Extending beyond volunteerism, service-learning is an "educational experience in which students participate in an organized service activity that meets community needs" and consequently "gain further understanding of course content, a broader appreciation of the discipline, and an enhanced sense of civic responsibility" (Bringle & Hatcher, 1995, p. 112). Benefits of service-learning include concretizing abstract theories and encouraging critical thinking about the subject matter; raising awareness of and critical thinking about social issues and students' values and choices as societal members; and, addressing human needs related to social inequality (Britt, 2012). Challenges of service-learning include institutional commitment, alliance with community agencies, student inducements, and integration into the curriculum (Gujarathi & McQuade, 2002).

Service-learning activities have been integrated into academic curricula and student organizations across colleges and universities (American Association of State Colleges and Universities, 2013). Because the communication discipline is concerned with the quality of communication theory and how it informs practice, teacher-scholars have embraced service-learning as a way for students to reflect on the dialectic of communication theory and communication practice (Applegate & Morreale, 1999). For example, recent communication education scholarship critically assesses service-learning in the basic communication course (often a general education requirement in college curriculum) (McIntyre, Douglas, Holley, & Sandor, 2009; McIntyre & Sellnow, 2014), business and professional communication (Littlefield, 2006), crisis communication (Maresh-Fuehrer, 2015), group communication (Mize Smith, 2014), health communication (Bute & Kopchick, 2009), intercultural communication (Littlefield, Freed, & Rick, 2012), interpersonal/family communication (Vaughn, 2009), public speaking (Martinez, 2004), and research methods (Liu, 2011).

8.3.3. Narrative Ethnography/Self-Reflection

Another enactment that *cases* communication practices is narrative ethnography, which attempts to establish "the centrality of personal experience and identity in the social construction of knowledge" (Goodall, 2004, p. 187). As scholars, ethno-graphers attempt to reveal the complexity of communication (Goodall, 2004). In scholarship of teaching literature, researchers have focused on ways for students to learn by reflecting on meaningful personal experience and connecting it to course content (Hubbs & Brand, 2005). That is, teacher-scholars put students in the role of researcher, investigating and legitimizing their own experiences as worthy of reflection. Reflection takes "the unprocessed, raw material of experience and engaging with it as a way to make sense of what has occurred. It involves exploring often messy and confused events and focusing on the thoughts and emo-tions that accompany them" (Boud, 2001, p. 10). By reflecting on personal experi-ence, students become aware of their communication practices and how they learn (Voss, 1988), and are able to assimilate and apply concepts to current or future events (Connor-Greene, 2000; Croxton & Berger, 2001). Moreover, ongoing reflec-tion prompts students to make connections between their experiences and their coursework, and provides a collection of stories from which to derive analytical claims about effective or ineffective communication practices. Challenges to reflec-tion include time and work required, different perceptions about assignments, inhibition of free expression, and uncertainty about what critical reflection is (Chabon & Lee-Wilkerson, 2006).

8.3.4. Research Projects

A final enactment that *cases* authentic communication issues is the research project. Research projects provide an active outlet for applying theoretical concepts to real-life problems, and a few studies have discussed how to engage students in authentic research projects (Bergstrom & Bullis, 1999; Liu, 2011). However, scholars have cri-tiqued the dominant mode of translation of communication research (and teaching of it) to undergraduate and graduate students (Kahl, 2010b); that is, without direct application, students may struggle to use the knowledge to *make a difference*. Apparent from reviews of empirical methods instruction is that such training is often not taught in a way for them to see how they can use their research methods knowledge to address a problem or a need in the community (Liu, 2011). Challenges of such projects include students' feelings of uncertainty and perceptions about the amount of work (Liu, 2011). Benefits to students include improving their confidence in using research to address *real-world* problems and their awareness of community needs and research resources available to address them.

This section detailed four enactments used to *case* real-life problems: PBL, service-learning, narrative ethnography, and research projects. These approaches to learning all focus on learning by doing and reflecting (Kolb, 1984), a process that makes learners active in their own learning, fosters greater self-awareness, and gen-erates greater sensitivity to social issues and the role of communication. In the fol-lowing, we address communication ethics as a distinct *casing* theme across the undergraduate and graduate curricula.

8.4. Communication Ethics

This section defines *ethics* and *applied ethics*, relates them to the communication discipline, and addresses generally how they align with the Speech Communication Department's mission. *Ethics* is concerned with standards of conduct typically based upon normative systems, philosophical schools, and/or religious traditions that guide judgments about right/wrong and good/bad (Seeger, Sellnow, Ulmer, & Novak, 2009). *Applied ethics* "addresses the day-to-day problems of good human conduct" (Seeger et al., 2009, p. 281). An applied orientation toward communication ethics attends to issues in real-life communication choices and how they relate to values, standards, and norms.

Communication scholars recognize the significance of addressing ethics in both theory and practice (Andersen, 2000; Arnett, 1986; Arnett, Arneson, & Bell, 2006; Johannesen, 2001; Seeger et al., 2009). Because "questions of right and wrong arise whenever people communicate," communication scholars and educators adopted a "Credo for Ethical Communication" (National Communication Association, 1999, para. 1). The preamble of the Credo states: "Ethical communication is fundamental to responsible thinking, decision-making, and the development of relationships and communities within and across contexts, cultures, channels, and media" (National Communication Association, 1999, para. 1).

Given concerns about failure to address ethical dimensions of communication in the classroom (McCaleb & Dean, 1987), communication departments have integrated ethics into curricula (Christians & Lambeth, 1996). In a survey of department heads, 81% of programs offered modules dedicated to ethics and 39% had standalone ethics courses (Christians & Lambeth, 1996). The authors of that study, however, concluded that the "jury is still out on whether ethics will become a central area of communication studies" (p. 236). Challenges in teaching ethics included difficulties in evaluating students' exams and written work because they concluded "ethics was a matter of opinion," or that the course received mixed reviews because it did not "resolve enough issues or give them help" (p. 241).

Seeger et al. (2009, p. 280) acknowledge that examining real-world communication ethics is difficult "because of the complexity of moral questions, lack of clarity regarding ethical standards, and traditional emphasis on 'amoral' approaches in many applied communication contexts." These same authors address how in order to be relevant to daily ethical choices that people face, the standards must focus on the local context "where narrower parameters can be drawn and agreed on value traditions identified" (p. 282). This pragmatic view contrasts with universal ethics, which searches for generalizations. Where there are competing value positions, Seeger et al. (2009) recommend being aware of the ethical implications of communication choices and sorting through conflicting value positions by prioritizing them for a particular setting.

Seeger et al. (2009) provide a useful frame to integrate ethics into the curriculum by addressing goals. They introduce: *do no harm*, *affect positive outcomes*, and *promote social justice* goals of applied communication work. These goals enable us to discuss ethics and fit with our program and mission. We define these and provide examples of research that illustrates these goals. *Do no harm* assesses outcomes or consequences and balances potential risks with benefits. Do no harm is one of the main concerns of most Internal Review Boards: the risks presented to participants is minimal. *Affect positive outcomes* not only avoids harm but also seeks to create benefits. An example is a study designed to give back to the research site, such as conducting a needs assessment and developing and executing a training plan for organizational members. *Promote social justice* moves beyond understanding a topic and seeks to transform society by addressing pressing social inequities (Hartnett, 2010). An example is a study looking at information provision to marginalized stakeholder groups during crises, with the goal to incorporate such groups into crisis planning and response in a much more effective way.

In effect, *casing* provides students with a way to reflect on dilemmas in everyday communication choices, and help them understand how they can make a difference in their own lives and in their communities.

8.5. Case Method, Communication Ethics, and UALR Speech Communication Department

Case method and ethics are appropriate and compatible approaches to the study of communication issues in undergraduate and graduate programs. Ethical issues are complex, and case method is ideally suited as a holistic approach to complex problems. Research by Canary (2007) demonstrated that case method was an effective format for ethics instruction. What follows is a series of exemplars, four from the undergraduate program,

- *SPCH 1300: Speech Communication Fundamentals*
- *SPCH 3320: Advanced Public Speaking*
- *SPCH 3323: Conflict Management*
- *SPCH 4300/4301: Senior Capstone*

and four from the graduate program,

- *SPCH 7321: Organizational Communication Theory*
- *SPCH 7350: Crisis Communication*
- *SPCH 7352: Organizational Communication Training*
- *SPCH 8301: Master's Research Project*

that illustrate how we help students *case* complex issues, take a position on communication issues, and make ethically informed, positive communication recommendations.

8.5.1. Undergraduate Courses

8.5.1.1. SPCH 1300: Speech communication fundamentals
SPCH 1300 is the introductory speech communication course in the department, serving as the prerequisite for all upper-level courses and is an approved course for

the university general education core. Uniquely grounded in the theme of civility, the course introduces students to foundational communication principles governing our interactions with others, structural components of public speaking, and conflict management strategies in interpersonal communication contexts. Civility is defined as the "choice we make to consider others' thoughts and feelings in our communication and general behavior" (Lane, Abigail, & Gooch, 2014, p. 336). Consequently, the curriculum uses both *narrative ethnography/reflection* and *service-learning* approaches for the following learning objectives:

- Apply foundational communication principles to a variety of contexts.
- Present speeches in an organized manner.
- Use technology to draft components of a presentation.
- Locate, evaluate, and integrate online research into a presentation.
- Recognize, name, and analyze effective and ineffective/unethical communication behaviors.
- Generate communication-based solutions to problematic/unethical communication behavior.
- Articulate the relationship between communication and positive community change.

Within the two case modes, ethics is woven into the fabric of the SPCH 1300 curriculum, specifically with an emphasis on *do no harm* and *affect positive outcomes*. The course introduces the tenet *promote social justice* (Seeger et al., 2009). Ethical implications of communication are operationalized in the following way for students:

Trustworthiness: the degree to which the accuracy of our ideas and shared information can be used by others to make decisions, maintaining the trust needed for a healthy community.

Integrity: modeling our values for others by holding ourselves accountable to the same standards that we hold others to and keeping promises that we make to others (even when no one is "watching").

Concern for Community: committing to the practice of daily actions, interactions, and performances of engaged citizens that promote a cocreated community experience.

Fairness: considering all sides of the conflict without showing favor to our own interests.

Respect: actively listening to and showing regard for the ideas of others before evaluating and responding to their messages.

Responsibility: holding ourselves accountable for our choices, actions, and communication with others.

Restraint: refraining from insulting others or participating in negative communication (even when others are participating in negative communication with us).

Caring with Grace: understanding and meeting the needs of the people we interact with. Specifically, approaching all that we do with a positive attitude (even if the situation may not necessarily warrant one), showing forgiveness through our communication to those who may not necessarily deserve it (also known as turning the other cheek or treating others the way we'd like to be treated), and interpreting others' communicative intentions compassionately and positively (so, rather than immediately assuming the worst from someone, give them the benefit of the doubt — it's quite possible that this person has absolutely no idea that his/her message hurt/upset/angered us) (Department of Speech Communication, 2014, p. 5).

Students are tasked with identifying and analyzing ethical implications of poor/unethical/ineffective communication across a variety of communication contexts as they move through the course.

Two major assignments are grounded in case *narrative ethnography/reflection* and the ethical goals of *do no harm* and *affect positive outcomes*. The first assignment is the Positive Communication Video. In the video, students identify a person in their lives whom they consider to be an effective, positive communicator, analyze the communication behaviors of their chosen individual, and identify and explain two ethical implications of communication modeled by their identified exemplar. The second assignment is the Interpersonal Communication Paper. In the paper, students identify a personal relationship, past or present, that experienced or is experiencing tension. Students select and define relevant communication concepts and ethical implications of communication related to the case. Those same concepts and ethical implications are then used to analyze the role of communication in creating tension. Finally, students make communication-based recommendations for themselves and their respective partners for ethically navigating the tension.

Introducing the ethical communication goal of *promote social justice*, the use of a *service-learning* framework is found in the third major assignment, the Informative Service Speech. Students first complete a preservice reflection worksheet where they are asked to describe what they feel their responsibility to the world is as well as their immediate community. They are also asked if they have volunteered before, what they think their service experience for the course will be like, and whether or not they think their four hours of service will make a difference. After students serve for a minimum of four hours at an instructor-approved, nonprofit organization, they complete a postservice worksheet that helps them process their service experience in preparation for the speech. Students brainstorm relevant stories from their experience, identify and define applicable communication concepts and foundational communication principles for understanding and analyzing the communicative interactions during their service hours, and reflect on how ethical implications of communication help promote positive community change.

While four hours may seem inconsequential, the amount of service does not necessarily correlate with the quality of learning (McIntyre & Sellnow, 2014). Rather, the quality of the reflective process surrounding the service experience is key to facilitating student connection making. Consequently, structured SPCH 1300 reflective components integral to the *narrative ethnography* and *service-learning* case approaches help to transform a seemingly short student lived experience into a meaningful, high impact learning opportunity (Brogan, Gilles, & Woodard, 2014; Kahl, 2010a). Formal, internal assessment of the SPCH 1300 program supports extant findings that these particular case pedagogies work well to facilitate student achievement of SPCH 1300 course learning outcomes (Novak, Markey, & Allen, 2007). Specifically, foundational communication principle pre- and post-tests indicate that students better understand the inherent complexity of communication. Additionally, students' use of presentational structure in a public speech improves significantly from the introductory speech to the informative speech. Finally, by the end of the semester, the majority of students noticeably improve their ability to identify, define, and apply foundational communication principles, concepts, and ethical implications in a variety of communication contexts.

What is perhaps the most compelling indication of pedagogical success are the responses documented in course evaluations. Many of our SPCH 1300 students complete their service-learning with organizations that work with underserved populations, including inner-city youth, homeless, and women's shelters, for example. In course evaluations, we have received several qualitative comments specifically from minority students who have taken the course, who have affirmed its positive impact in dealing with issues that first-generation college students experience such as "cultural suicide" as well as the "imposter syndrome" (Brookfield, 2006). For example, our students repeatedly comment that their service models the importance of college and good citizenship behaviors to youth in their communities. In support of these comments, 95% of SPCH 1300 students indicated in the course post-survey that they will continue being involved in their communities. One student specifically commented, "I am always involded [sic] in my community and I think it is a wonderful thing to do and I appreciate that UALR Speech Department makes it part of the program."

8.5.1.2. SPCH 3320: Advanced public speaking

Building on the introductory public speaking material and the *service-learning* framework in SPCH 1300, this course promotes public speaking as a civic responsibility and focuses on understanding the ethics of speaking, in the expectation that students will "develop what the ancient rhetoricians called civic virtue" (Hogan, Hayes Andrews, Andrews, & Williams, 2014, p. 8). Working within Motley's (1997) communication orientation to public speaking that emphasizes connection instead of perfection, students develop rhetorical knowledge and skills to be engaged citizen-critics. The SPCH 3320 curriculum is heavily cased in *PBL* and *service-learning pedagogy*, and consequently promotes the development of ethical communication commitments to *affect positive outcomes* and to *promote social justice* in the following objectives:

- Answer the Course Big Questions: What makes a persuasive speech effective? What are the ethical implications of the speeches we make? What role does public speaking play in creating better social worlds?
- Deliver public presentations that are organized using macrostructure.
- Deliver public presentations that assert claims supported by credible evidence.
- Use appropriate self-disclosure, stories, examples, and translation of statistics to engage an audience throughout a public presentation.
- Evaluate through a written formal self-assessment their ability to meet course and unit learning outcomes.

Using the *PBL* approach, students first identify a social issue of personal importance, which serves as the problem they work to understand and address all semester (Edens, 2000). Once students commit to a social issue, they then identify a local nonprofit organization that aligns with their chosen issue, layering the *PBL* with *service-learning* pedagogy. Many students choose to continue serving with the service site from their SPCH 1300 course experience. Similar to SPCH 1300, students complete a preservice reflection assignment. After receiving instructor approval, students complete a service agreement form with the nonprofit organization site supervisor. Students then, over the course of the semester, complete a minimum of eight hours of service separated into four unique site visits of at least two hours each. The required service hours provide students with valuable lived experiences that function in three specific ways: (1) to provide students with an opportunity to develop a deeper understanding of the complexity of their social issue, (2) to help students build their personal credibility and confidence during their speeches, and (3) provide students with an opportunity to experience how public speaking can positively impact our community in meaningful ways. A service verification form and an accompanying structured journal reflection are submitted for each service visit.

As students research their respective social issues and complete their service hours, they build and present small presentations in preparation for the Persuasive Speech of Policy, a major deliverable for the course. As advocated by problem-based and service-learning literature, the policy speech functions as the public dissemination of students' experiences (Heffernan & Cone, 2001) and shifts their speaking into the realm of advocacy. Structured using Motivated Sequence (Hogan et al., 2014) to emphasize the ethical goal of *promoting social justice*, the policy speech establishes a narrowed problem related to the student's social issue, introduces a plan that is designed to address the problem by including an audience-centered call to action, and outlines the support for the plan as well as the costs and benefits of implementing the plan. The entire UALR campus is invited to attend the presentations via the university listserv (1000 + faculty and staff) and social media outlets. Speakers also formally invite family, friends, and nonprofit site supervisors and colleagues to attend.

The primary form of assessment in the course is unique in that a competency-based education (CBE) framework is used. In CBE, the curriculum is driven by learning objectives aligned with the development and mastery of practical, societal needs (Grant, 1979). As students develop their public speaking skills and civic virtue, they are provided written and oral feedback (but no grades), engage in reflexive self-assessment, and revise written and oral work until competency is met. Students create a formal portfolio argument for their midterm and final grades based on provided criteria. The portfolio consists of a comprehensive reflective self-assessment paper included in a three-ring binder with supporting evidence (class notes, reading notes, drafts of work, final versions of work, etc.).

In the act of self-assessing, students must explicitly discuss how they have met each learning objective, as evidenced by their supporting work and explanations, as well as explain the value of meeting the objective as it relates to effective public speaking. Students regularly reflect on their dramatic shifts from a performance orientation to communication orientation, acknowledging the service requirement as the impetus for helping them to embrace their civic responsibility as public speaking advocates for community change. A secondary form of assessment is gauging student understanding of foundational communication principles via the pre- and post-tests used in SPCH 1300.

8.5.1.3. SPCH 3323: Conflict management

Conflict is defined as "the interaction of interdependent people who perceive incompatibility and possible interference as a result of incompatibility" (Folger, Poole, & Stutman, 2013, p. 4). Conflict management then centers on how we interact with our relational partners to shift our interdependence and/or alter our perceptions of incompatibility and interference. In effect, issues related to values, norms, and standards permeate conflict; some conflicts are moral conflicts (Pearce & Littlejohn, 1997), and students learn throughout the class that how they label or name conflict issues is value-laden and implicates parties as responsible (Putnam, 2010). The focus draws on *narrative ethnography, PBL,* and *a research project* to accomplish the following learning objectives:

- Define various elements of conflict and understand the potential for altering them;
- Understand and apply psychological and communication theories to explain how and why conflict occurs;
- Know how conflict occurs in different relationships and contexts;
- Manage disputes more effectively;
- Make positive, ethical, and theory-informed recommendations for improving conflict management.

The first method of casing complex communication problems and issues is by *narrative ethnography*. This occurs in stages, through two assignments. The first assignment asks students to identify a meaningful conflict in their lives where they know a considerable amount about how the conflict unfolded. They then analyze the dispute according to how it shapes and is shaped by the relationship and how communication patterns contribute to escalation or de-escalation in a self-perpetuating manner. To build on their skills and improve their own relationships, students are then asked to write about and actively try to manage a meaningful conflict in their lives. Specifically, they develop an argument around how the theory explains the conflict and the effectiveness of the theory or its implications in managing the conflict. In essence, they are directly attempting to *affect positive change* in their own lives and the lives of others.

As their culminating experience in the course, students engage in both *PBL* and a *research project* to case communication issues. They participate in a simulated labor-management negotiation, which is a discipline hearing for an employee who violated ethical standards of the company by allegedly stealing, but who is otherwise regarded as a person of good character (Geist, 1984). Each team creates a strategy for negotiating with the other side, develops arguments for their positions, and assesses each side's leverage in bargaining. Also, before the negotiation, they meet with each other to establish ground rules for bargaining such as turn-taking. During the negotiation, teams offer proposals and counterproposals and take breaks to caucus and discuss further strategy. The negotiation is filmed; the video and strategy materials and agreements are shared with both teams to analyze. Following the negotiation, students take on the role of researcher by writing a research paper based on the exercise they took part in. Specifically, they take a stand on communication issues and argue how and why the negotiation reached a particular outcome. Moreover, they also craft ethically informed communication recommendations to either *do no harm* or *affect positive change* in the negotiation and in labor-management negotiations in general.

Student learning is assessed in several ways in this course. First, writing assignments — including narrative ethnography and research projects — are evaluated based on how well students connect data with theory and how realistic their recommendations are. Second, overall student learning is assessed based on pre- and post-tests that address some common misconceptions about conflict communication.

8.5.1.4. SPCH 4300/4110: Senior capstone

For over 20 years, the departmental capstone course sequence has served as the culminating deep learning experience for our majors (and for our department). In this course, we assess our students' ability to meet our overall program learning outcomes:

- Demonstrate an accurate understanding of assigned theories in the discipline;
- Demonstrate effective oral communication skills in the public speaking context;
- Apply one communication theory to a real-world situation in a final capstone paper and presentation.

Cased heavily in *narrative ethnography/reflection* and focused on the ethic of *affect positive outcomes*, students first write a formal case study paper. To provide the context for analysis, students are tasked with recording conversations they engage in over the course of 10 days. Based on the documented conversations, students then identify a meaningful interpersonal relationship represented in the conversations. Following this, students identify a meaningful and relevant communication theory to use for analysis of the dialogue. Students continue to capture conversation moments and use the recorded discourse as data, which is then analyzed through the chosen theoretic lens. After analysis is complete and students identify claims grounded in their chosen theory, they make ethical recommendations for positive communication moves in the relationship. Theoretically grounded communication recommendations are provided for what the student can enact his/herself, then shift to suggestions for the partner featured in the relationship, and finally move outward to the general other. Second, once the case study paper is complete, students transition the paper to a 20–25 minute public presentation. Students are then paired with a faculty mentor from the department who coaches them in preparation for the formal presentation day.

Assessment of the capstone sequence takes place in two steps. First, the faculty member teaching capstone engages students in a revision process throughout the semester until the case study paper meets competency. Second, external stakeholders, including alumni of our program, prominent community members, and upper campus administrators, are invited to assess the capstone presentations. Assessment data collected from participating faculty and external stakeholders consistently indicates that our capstone students model effective presentational structure, knowledgeably explain complex communication theories in relevant and accessible ways, use theory to make unique claims supported by savvy discourse analysis, and provide clear and practical theory-based recommendations for positively navigating interpersonal communication contexts.

8.5.2. Graduate Courses

8.5.2.1. SPCH 7321: Organizational communication theory

This course defines organizational communication as the cocreation of relational symbolic actions that create and constrain ethical and effective processes and goals. This focuses on *organizing* rather than *organization* (Weick, 1995). Given the definition of organizational communication, the course is framed with a focus on mindfulness. Mindfulness is "the process of drawing novel distinctions" (Langer & Moldoveanu, 2000, pp. 1), while mindlessness relies on rules and routines developed from the past, regardless of present state of affairs. Making novel distinctions has benefits, such as an increased awareness of one's surroundings, openness to new information, generation of different categories, and recognition of multiple viewpoints (Langer, 1989). According to Langer (1989, p. 11), "The creation of new categories … is a mindful activity. Mindlessness sets in when we rely too rigidly on categories and distinctions created in the past (masculine/feminine, old/young, success/failure). Once distinctions are created, they take on a life of their own" (1989, p. 11). This course is designed to help graduate students improve their leadership and organizational communication skills, and enacts *narrative ethnography* and *PBL* for the following learning objectives:

- Recognize mindful and mindless communication practices and their role in organizing;
- Apply communication theories to complex, communication issues in organizing;
- Make ethically and theoretically informed recommendations to improve organizing.

Two assignments ask students to focus on "critical incidents," a form of *narrative ethnography* that connects course concepts to personal experience. Critical incidents are defined as events that were "unexpected" or "surprising" in nature (Oliver & Roos, 2003), and in turn memorable for a lesson learned. The criticality of an incident is determined by the justification, significance, and meaning that individuals attach to them. In both assignments, students write a short personal case study in which they take a stand on how their communication was effective or ineffective as a leader, describe the case, make analytical claims using communication theory, and then make ethically informed, positive recommendations for themselves and others implicated in the case.

Another assignment is an interactive *PBL* assignment, which presents students with a genuine and complex problem facing all types of organizations: data breach (Veltsos, 2012). Data breaches undermine the legitimacy of the organization as a steward of customers' personally identifying information (PII) because these data can be sold by criminals. Students are placed in one of four teams: a company, a security vendor, journalists, and police. Team assignment is based on students' employment, volunteer activities, and coursework. This case begins with an unconfirmed breach. Law officers and journalists receive leaked correspondence. A rapid succession of information ensues and creates considerable uncertainty. The case concludes with the discovery of a confirmed breach precipitated by an infected e-mail account that allowed hackers to copy one million customers' PII. Following the exercise, students discuss it and then write a research paper.

In all written assignments, students apply concepts of mindfulness and mindlessness and make recommendations. Assessing mindfulness involves looking for students' applications of the terms that define it — new categories; different routines; and multiple perspectives — to evidence from the case. Where they critique themselves or others for mindlessness (applying old categories, over reliance on routines, and working from a single perspective), ethical recommendations to address these concerns are expected.

8.5.2.2. SPCH 7350: Effective crisis communication

This course defines a crisis as "… a specific, *unexpected*, and *non-routine* event or series of events that create high levels of *uncertainty* and simultaneously present an organization with both *opportunities* for and *threats* to its *high-priority goals*" (Ulmer, Sellnow, & Seeger, 2014, p. 8). Thus, crisis communication problematizes "the messages and meaning construction processes in all forms of human interaction and coordination that surround these threatening and high uncertainty events" (Sellnow & Seeger, 2013, p. 2). The course is framed by the Discourse of Renewal (Ulmer et al., 2014), an alternative approach to crisis communication that examines how leaders identify opportunities arising out of the crisis and respond naturally to express concern for all stakeholders rather than shielding the company from blame. Moreover, the theory foregrounds ethical communication because it promotes crises as revealing rather than building character. Hence, it reinforces the notion that leaders should know and communicate their values, for these provide clarity in confusing times such as crises. The ultimate goal in this class is to help students to better conceptually understand crises in order to produce effective crisis communication. With this in mind, the course uses *PBL, narrative ethnography*, and *research projects* to achieve the following course objectives:

- Define crisis in a meaningful, mindful, and productive manner;
- Explain in depth the Discourse of Renewal approach to managing crises;

- Analyze the effectiveness or ineffectiveness of crisis communication using the Discourse of Renewal approach;
- Construct a communication-based solution to a crisis based upon the Discourse of Renewal.

This course adopts two approaches to *PBL* that case complex issues related to crisis communication. This includes site visits (i.e., field trips) as a class to learn about such topics as crisis planning and crisis response. For example, the class tours a restaurant on a busy intersection in Little Rock, AR, and hears from the owner-operator. Students learn about crisis planning from a restaurateur who has dealt with crime issues, food-safety concerns, and public protest because corporate headquarters became involved in social issues. The class also visits the statewide Emergency Operations Center located in Little Rock to learn about preparing for emergencies and responding to public stakeholders, including news media. After hearing about guidelines for engaging news media, students are placed into teams representing different stakeholders (local hospital, emergency response, and department of health) to formulate a response to a public health crisis. They then participate in a mock press conference that includes potential ethical dilemmas arising from competing values (e.g., public access to information vs. protecting privacy codified by law). Following the press conference, students receive real-time feedback from communication personnel in the department of health and from each other.

A second instance of *PBL* presents students with a "ripped from the headlines" news story, asks them to critique the effectiveness of crisis communication, and make ethical recommendations informed by Discourse of Renewal. Stories are topical, and students first work individually to determine how a case fits the definition of a crisis, critique the responses, and make communication recommendations to move beyond the crisis. They then return to the class to cull the best ideas to create a crisis response plan.

Because Discourse of Renewal centers on values and how crisis reveals rather than builds character, this course uses an exercise related to *narrative ethnography/personal reflection*. Values are tied to ethics inasmuch as they are what we consider we ought to do, and what we consider right or wrong and good or bad. Moreover, values are what we turn to in times of crisis to provide clarity on how to respond. Specifically, students brainstorm as many personal values as they have. Examples include ethical principles mentioned earlier, such as responsibility, integrity, fairness, restraint, concern for community, etc. In another round, students identify their three core values. In a final round, they create a personal philosophy of leadership based on core values and aligned with goals. To enhance their public commitment to their values, they read their philosophy in front of their classmates.

A final approach uses the *research project*, and asks students to identify a topical crisis or potential crisis of their choice, and to put themselves in the role of consultant to analyze crisis response according to Discourse of Renewal, and to make ethically based, positive recommendations both for the organization in question and also for other similar organizations.

This course employs multiple modes of assessment to address student learning. Writing assignments — PBL and research — are evaluated on whether students successfully apply concepts from Discourse of Renewal, and whether the recommendations could reasonably *affect positive outcomes* by improving effective crisis communication. Other forms of assessment include students' perceptions of skill development and changes in attitudes/beliefs regarding crisis communication. For example, following their visit to the department of health, students are surveyed on their perceptions of crisis communication skills, including improvements on working as a team, remaining calm in the face of negative comments, and putting themselves in others' shoes, for example (Anderson, Swenson, & Kinsella, 2014). Regarding attitude changes, students are assessed on misconceptions about crisis communication, including a common misconception about crises building character (Ulmer et al., 2014). Following repetition from different methods of casing communication issues, particularly the core values exercise, students shift from believing that crises build character to crises reveal character.

8.5.2.3. SPCH 7352: Organizational communication training

The pedagogy of this course is closely linked with the SPCH 3320 in its emphasis of skills goals and engaged citizenry via *service-learning*. Specifically, the course has partnered for the past five years with a handful of community partners including Our House, a local shelter for the working homeless, AmeriCorps via our UALR Children International organization, and currently partners with Immerse Arkansas (IA), a nonprofit organization that works with youth who have aged out of the foster care system.

Kolb's (1984) Cycle of Experiential Learning serves as the primary theoretical framework of the course's promoted training approach. Using *service-learning, narrative ethnography/reflection* and *research project* as well as a focus on the ethics of *affect positive outcomes* and *promote social justice*, graduate students, in partnership with IA, work toward the following learning objectives:

- Answer the course Big Questions: What are the key principles grounding the design and facilitation of communication trainings? What ethical implications should communication trainers consider? How can communication trainings co-construct better social worlds?
- Ground specific, observable, measurable, and attainable intended learning outcomes in needs assessment results.
- Facilitate an experiential learning communication training plan that incorporates Kolb's (1984) Cycle of Experiential Learning.
- Assess the success of an experiential learning communication training to meet intended learning outcomes.
- Articulate the relationship between communication expertise and civic responsibility.

First, student work is cased through a general framework of *service-learning* and *research project*. Graduate students are informed the first day that the class is linked with a community client (Immerse Arkansas) and the course will be used to develop, facilitate, and assess professional communication trainings for the IA youth. As students learn about the process of developing a training, they are also engaging *in* the process with the community client. The class is given quantitative and qualitative needs assessment data collected prior to the beginning of class. Collectively, students analyze the data, identifying key areas for communication training interventions. The class then creates two or three training packages grounded in the needs assessment analysis for the client to choose from. Past training packages have included workshops on ethical communication, building and maintaining relationships in the workplace, conflict management, and active listening.

Once the client selects a training package, the class separates into teams to tackle specific communication skills-training contained in the package. Teams then develop focus group questions and meet with the IA youth to gather additional data to help inform their training choices. After students draft their respective training plans, they meet with the youth again, this time during IA's once-a-week community dinners. Teams then have an opportunity to add finishing touches to the training and training materials and to develop a training post-assessment before the IA youth come to campus to participate in the trainings. The *research project* framework becomes more prominent as teams create an executive summary comparing the needs assessment and post-assessment data to determine if the training fostered the anticipated learning outcomes.

Multiple forms of assessment exist in the course. First, the community client provides feedback throughout the training development process and representative IA staff attend and assess the trainings providing valuable stakeholder data to both the graduate students and the instructor. Second, training participants (IA youth) assess the overall effectiveness of the training via the post-assessment. Additionally, peers in the course are required to attend and assess the trainings using the same rubric as the instructor. Third, trainers assess themselves through structured video reflection assignments associated with a 5-minute research report talk, a 15-minute team discussion activity, and the 60-minute training. Finally, this course, like SPCH 3320, uses CBE as the holistic assessment approach of the course learning objectives. What differs in the CBE approach for this course is the cocreation of final letter grade criteria. Working together, the graduate students and instructor create the criteria to operationalize the course learning objectives. Students then use the cocreated criteria to structure their reflective self-assessment portfolios.

8.5.2.4. SPCH 8301: Master's research project

The research project represents the culminating *casing* experience for our graduate students in that we situate them as communication consultants. Students are tasked with enacting the department's mission to cocreate positive applied communication scholarship through the investigation and problem-solving of real-life communication problems at the community level. Often students analyze local and/or national organizations and contexts to better understand how communication is creating and promoting productive and/or harmful organizational culture (see Appendix). Other students develop, facilitate, and/or assess communication trainings. Yet other students work with organizations to assess responses to past crises or crisis response preparedness.

Assessment of the master's research project is twofold. First, students must defend their final paper in a traditional committee defense. Second, students must present the findings of their final research project to an external audience. Presentations must focus on the application of relevant communication theory to improve communication within the designated context. Consequently, students often present their findings directly to the case organization. Students may also present at local, regional, and/or national conferences or in appropriate campus and community venues.

These exemplar courses reveal casing of complex communication issues from interpersonal relationships to pressing social issues. In each example, we reviewed how students case communication problems, how these connect to ethical principles or dilemmas, and how we assess student learning. In the following section, we address lessons learned and recommendations for other departments considering similar curricular implementations.

8.6.   Lessons Learned/Recommendations

Up to this point, we introduced four enactments of *casing* (PBL, service-learning, narrative ethnography, and research projects) that take an ethical focus on communication and addressed how these are integrated in our undergraduate and graduate programs in communication. Reflection on these enactments revealed three lessons learned and three recommendations for cross-disciplinary teacher-scholars who wish to introduce these approaches in their programs. A first lesson learned relates to establishing a theoretical basis from which students operate. A second lesson learned addresses the difficulties in integrating these approaches into the curriculum. A third lesson learned focuses on students' resistance and concerns about failure. With each of these lessons learned, we provide recommendations for implementing a similar programmatic approach.

8.6.1.   *Theoretical Foundation*

The successful application of theory is a learned skill and one with which our students initially struggle. Undergraduate and graduate students alike often question the relevance or usefulness of theory and are often intimidated by academic scholarship, finding the research difficult to understand and the theories too complex. In order to better prepare our students for their engagements with a variety of communication theories in our program, the SPCH 1300 curriculum was designed specifically to prepare students for theory-based case reflections in the major. Specifically, curricular scaffolding is used to provide multiple opportunities of repetitive skill building related to the identification and application of communication concepts and ethical implications of communication across major assignments in a variety of contexts. Rather than focus on the specific concepts, SPCH 1300 students practice the skill of positive application of communication knowledge. As new majors in our program, students transition this introductory skill set to more sophisticated positive application and promotion of specific communication theories in courses such as SPCH 3320: Advanced Public Speaking and SPCH 3323: Conflict Management. Repetition further refines their theoretic skill set and students' communication knowledge deepens as they identify, understand, and apply relevant theories across the variety of nuanced case issues in the curriculum.

8.6.1.1. Recommendation: Use theory as the lever for learning

The key to meaningful experiential learning in the classroom is structured reflection. To that end, we recommend an explicit integration of structured reflection that promotes theory as the primary lens for sense making and organization of the experience. Without this specific guidance, it is likely that students will make improper connections, or no connections at all, on their own and learning will fall short. Specifically, without a concrete theoretical grounding, students' haphazard reflections may reinforce reasoning fallacies and perpetuate communication misconceptions. Preparing students for this type of scholarly reflection requires a thorough overview of the theory, practice applying the theory prior to the experiential component(s) of the course, and a careful debrief discussion with moments of affirmation and correction to help students further navigate the complexities inherent in using communication theory to better understand and assess a lived experience. As students move through the layered experiences and accompanying skill building in our program, they begin to reframe communication theories as important, useful tools for understanding and cocreating better social worlds.

8.6.2. *Integration Challenges*

While our curriculum approaches clearly foster engagement and student learning, building consensus across multiple stakeholder groups is challenging. Many faculty struggle to balance academic freedom with the kind of standardization a programmatic approach such as ours requires. The consistency in learning experiences across courses involves buy-in from the entire faculty. In the set-up of service-learning, faculty can also feel overwhelmed by the significant investment of time and energy upfront that is often necessary to ensure the course experiences are structured to facilitate and meet learning objectives. Finding community partners that are both a good match for the desired learning experiences and a good match in terms of co-educators can often be a trial-and-error process until a strong partnership is established. Finally, given that students already find themselves over-extended, juggling school with families and jobs, the uncertainty and complexity of the *casing* approach can be somewhat overwhelming for students. Understandably, both undergraduate and graduate students initially resist the messiness of learning through cases and wrestle with ownership of their learning when the answer is not black and white or provided in a multiple-choice option.

8.6.2.1. Recommendation: Engage in meaningful conversations with stakeholders

First and foremost, ongoing faculty conversations and commitment are imperative to a comprehensive curricular approach. Our programmatic buy-in did not happen overnight. The *casing* approach in our curriculum has evolved over the past 20 years. However, the commitment to *casing* has been an explicit, transparent component of program curriculum discussed openly and passionately during the faculty interview process. As potential colleagues consider departmental fit, we are upfront about the importance of department-wide buy-in for this unique learning approach. Additionally, framing the departmental ethical stance required several formal and informal discussions as we investigated ways we could consistently and transparently operationalize ethics for students across our respective courses. We started by discussing what the *big questions* (Bain, 2004) were for our courses, finding ways we could infuse an emphasis on communication ethics for each course. Once big questions were established, curriculum adjustments accordingly followed.

Specifically, we recommend exchanging syllabi to better understand the opportunities each course offers for intersections with the *casing* approaches. Continuing conversations can strengthen faculty's ability to help students transfer learning from his/her course to other courses in the program by making specific references to past or future learning moments in other courses. Second, in the integration of service-learning approaches, we recommend starting with a few hours of well-designed service and reflection. Faculty already have plenty to manage; however, including a service experience into a course does not necessarily need to be burdensome. In fact, a few carefully structured service hours and reflection can be extremely efficient in meeting service-learning outcomes in meaningful and memorable ways without overwhelming faculty (McIntyre & Sellnow, 2014). Additionally, we encourage the use of a Memorandum of Understanding (MoU) for community partnerships that span the length of a course (or longer). The MoU should provide a concrete description of the nature of the partnership. It is important to include language in the MoU that highlights the partnership as a co-created learning experience and delineates the role and agreed upon responsibilities of the community partner as co-educator. Additionally, it may be prudent to include language that acknowledges that student-created deliverables are products of the learning process and may not necessarily be viable for client use. At the end of the course, a debriefing session is essential to review the reciprocity of the partnership in terms of value-added experiences for both the learning in the course and deliverables for the organization. The next lesson learned explicitly addresses recommendations for navigating student buy-in.

8.6.3. Student Resistance and Failure

In the U.S. educational system, the focus on grades can sometimes generate resistance and suspicion among students toward trying new things. Focusing on grades can also get in the way of students seeing themselves as active in their own learning. This rings true with our experience with different enactments of casing communication issues. For example, we sometimes wrangle with our students over the particular modality of *casing* communication, such as service-learning, PBL, or narrative ethnography. In some cases, this is because they are uncertain about how they are going to be evaluated, and this typically comes from an orientation of doing it right and being evaluated as a success or failure. At the same time, students may resist an ethical focus because that opens a potential host of issues, again because there are ways of viewing this as *right* or "correct." Sometimes students resist an ethics focus because they view these issues as matters of opinion or to issues better left to priests and philosophers. They do not feel in a position to render ethical judgments.

8.6.3.1. Recommendation: Adopt a process orientation and embrace failure
In order to create an invitational learning environment for our students, we have framed case learning and ethics with a process orientation that embraces failure (Sitkin, 1996). Consequently, we recommend that others who seek to integrate these case enactments or ethics focus on a process orientation. We frame failure as an opportunity for students to learn and develop. This approach recognizes that we are not always the best at what we do when we do it the first time, and this provides us with an opportunity for personal growth. The process orientation also shifts away from a focus on individual character traits (success/failure, ethical/unethical) and instead frames these as behaviors we can change. Sometimes failure is due to superficial connection of course concepts to a case. Other times it is a failure to recognize the ethical implications of our own communication choices. To bolster students' engagement in this reflective process, we embrace rewriting and revision. This helps students to develop deeper connections between communication issues and theory, between theory and positive, ethical communication recommendations and between reflexivity and positive, personal growth.

8.7.   Conclusion

We began with the notion that there is a world outside of the walls of the classroom, and that faculty are charged with helping students to *make a difference* by providing opportunities to engage in and reflect upon meaningful experiences. To that end, we introduced the UALR Speech Communication Department, situated in a community-engaged university setting, and introduced an integrated approach to undergraduate and graduate curriculum that focuses on four types of *casing* complex problems and proposing positive, ethical recommendations to make a difference. We introduced PBL; service-learning; narrative ethnography; and research projects. Each of these was positioned as a way to examine complex communication issues and to make ethical, theory-informed recommendations to not only *do no harm* but also *affect positive change* in students' personal relationships, organizations, communities, and beyond.

Reflecting on the place of lived experience-based learning in our courses, we derived lessons learned and recommendations. Our lessons included building a theoretical base for students to draw from, integrating case approaches into the curriculum, and engaging resistance and failure. Our recommendations centered on using theory as a lever for learning, building meaningful relationships with stakeholders, and adopting a process orientation that embraces failure. Although these are not a panacea to all of the challenges of integrating meaningful cocurricular experiences into classroom learning, they go a long way to engage students, faculty, alumni, and the larger community in the work that we do.

References

Ahlfeldt, S., & Overland, K. (2002, September). Service and problem based learning: Challenges for the engaged communication scholar. *North Dakota Journal of Speech & Theatre, 15*, 73–78. Retrieved from http://0-web.a.ebscohost.com.iii-server.ualr.edu/ehost/pdfviewer/pdfviewer?sid=83be199a-65dd-41c2-9109-30cc6404f1be%40sessionmgr4002&vid=9&hid=4104

Allen, R., & Rooney, P. (1998). Designing a problem-based learning environment for ESL students in business communication. *Business Communication Weekly, 61*(2), 48–56.

American Association of State Colleges and Universities. (2013). *About ADP*. Retrieved from http://www.aascu.org/programs/ADP/

Andersen, K. E. (2000). Developments in communication ethics: The ethics commission, code of professional responsibilities, Credo for ethical communication. *JACA: Journal of the Association for Communication Administration, 29*(1), 131–144. Retrieved from http://0-web.a.ebscohost.com.iii-server.ualr.edu/ehost/pdfviewer/pdfviewer?sid=83be199a-65dd

Anderson, B., Swenson, R., & Kinsella, J. (2014). Responding in real-time: Creating a social media crisis simulator for the classroom. *Communication Teacher, 28*(2), 85–95. doi: 10.1080/17404622.2013.865766

Applegate, J. L., & Morreale, S. P. (1999). Service-learning in communication: A natural partnership. In E. Droge & B. Ortega Murphy (Eds.), *Voices of strong democracy: Concepts and models for service-learning in communication studies* (pp. ix–xiv). Washington, DC: American Association for Higher Education.

Arnett, R. C. (1986). *Communication and community: Implications of Martin Buber's dialogue.* Carbondale, IL: Southern Illinois UP.

Arnett, R. C., Arneson, P., & Bell, L. M. (2006). Communication ethics: The dialogic turn. *The Review of Communication, 6*(1–2), 62–92. doi: 10.1080/15358590600763334

Attansey, M., Okigbo, C., & Schmidt, M. (2007). Preparing PR students for the brave new world: Students' perceptions of problem-based learning. *Public Relations Quarterly, 52*(2), 29. Retrieved from http://0-search.ebscohost.com.iii-server.ualr.edu/login.aspx?direct=true&db=ufh&AN=31809493&site=ehost-live&scope=site

Bain, K. (2004). *What the best college teachers do.* Cambridge, MA: Harvard University Press.

Berger, P. L., & Luckmann, T. (1991). *The social construction of reality: A treatise in the sociology of knowledge.* Harmondsworth, UK: Penguin.

Bergstrom, M. J., & Bullis, C. (1999). Integrating service-learning into the communication curriculum at a research university: From institutionalization to assessment of effectiveness. In E. Droge & B. Ortega Murphy (Eds.), *Voices of strong democracy: Concepts and models for service-learning in communication studies* (pp. 25–33). Washington, DC: American Association for Higher Education.

Boud, D. (2001). Using journal writing to enhance reflective practice. *New Directions for Adult and Continuing Education, 2001*(90), 9–18. doi: 10.1002/ace.16

Bringle, R. G., & Hatcher, J. A. (1995). A service-learning curriculum for faculty. *Michigan Journal of Community Service-learning, 2*(1), 112–122. Retrieved from http://hdl.handle.net/1805/4591

Britt, L. L. (2012). Why we use service-learning: A report outlining a typology of three approaches to this form of communication pedagogy. *Communication Education, 61*(1), 80–88. doi: 10.1080/03634523.2011.632017

Brogan, S. M., Gilles, E. E., & Woodard, T. J. (2014). Corresponding with the past, writing the future: A community-based service learning project. *Kentucky Journal of Communication, 33*(1), 12–25. Retrieved from http://0-web.a.ebscohost.com.iii-server.ualr.edu/ehost/pdfviewer/pdfviewer?sid=262f3c23-19df-46f4-8f4f-f22b67cc7aea%40sessionmgr4003&vid=6&hid=4104

Brookfield, S. (2006). *The skillful teacher: On technique, trust, and responsiveness in the classroom* (2nd ed.). San Francisco, CA: Jossey-Bass.

Brzovic, K., & Matz, S. I. (2009). Students advise Fortune 500 company: Designing a problem-based learning community. *Business Communication Quarterly, 72*(1), 21–34. doi: 10.1177/1080569908321439

Bute, J. J., & Kopchick, C. L. (2009). Health communication and health education: Empowering students to educate their communities. *Communication Teacher, 23*(2), 71–76. doi: 10.1080/17404620902780221

Canary, H. E. (2007). Teaching ethics in communication courses: An investigation of instructional methods, course foci, and student outcomes. *Communication Education, 56*(2), 193–208. doi: 10.1080/03634520601113660

Chabon, S. S., & Lee-Wilkerson, D. (2006). Use of journal writing in the assessment of CSD students' learning about Diversity: A method worthy of reflection. *Communication Disorders Quarterly, 27*(3), 146–158. doi: 10.1177/15257401060270030301

Charmaz, K., & Bryant, A. (2011). Grounded theory and credibility. In D. Silverman (Ed.), *Qualitative research* (3rd ed., pp. 291–309). Thousand Oaks, CA: Sage.

Christians, C. G., & Lambeth, E. B. (1996). The status of ethics instruction in communication departments. *Communication Education, 45*(3), 236–243. doi: 10.1080/03634529609379052

Connor-Greene, P. A. (2000). Making connections: Evaluating the effectiveness of journal writing in enhancing student learning. *Teaching of Psychology, 27*(1), 44–46. doi: 10.1207/S15328023TOP2701_10

Croxton, C. A., & Berger, R. C. (2001). *Journal writing: Does it promote long term retention of course concepts?* National Teaching and Online Forum. Retrieved from http://www.ntfl.com/html/sf/jounral/htm

Department of Speech Communication. (2014). SPCH 1300 course manual. In S. D. Lane, R. A. Abigail, & J. C. Gooch (Eds.), *Communication in a civil society* (2nd custom ed.). Boston, MA: Pearson Education.

Dorn, E. M. (1999). Case method instruction in the business writing classroom. *Business Communication Quarterly, 62*(1), 41–60. doi: 10.1177/108056999906200104

Edens, K. M. (2000). Preparing problem solvers for the 21st century through problem-based learning. *College Teaching, 48*(2), 55–60. doi: 10.1080/87567550009595813

Frey, L. R., & Cissna, K. N. (Eds.). (2009). *Routledge handbook of applied communication research*. New York, NY: Routledge.

Garvin, D. A. (2003). Making the case: Professional education for the world of practice. *Harvard Magazine.* Retrieved from http://harvardmagazine.com/2003/09/making-the-case-html

Geertz, C. (1973). *The interpretation of cultures: Selected essays* (Vol. 5019*)*. New York, NY: Basic books.

Geist, P. (1984, May). Bargaining simulation unit: An instructional tool for the organization communication course. Paper presented at the International Communication Association Annual Meeting, San Francisco, CA.

Goodall, H. L. Jr. (2004). Commentary: Narrative ethnography as applied communication research. *Journal of Applied Communication Research, 32*(3), 185–194. doi: 10.1080/0090988042000240130

Graham, P. T., & Cline, P. C. (1980). The case method: A basic teaching approach. *Theory into practice, 19*(2), 112–116. doi: 10.1080/00405848009542883

Grant, G. (1979). *On competence: A critical analysis of competence-based reforms in higher education*. San Francisco, CA: Jossey-Bass.

Gujarathi, M. R., & McQuade, R. J. (2002). Service-learning in business schools: A case study in an intermediate accounting course. *Journal of Education for Business, 77*(3), 144–150. doi: 10.1080/08832320209599063

Hartnett, S. J. (2010). Communication, social justice, and joyful commitment. *Western Journal of Communication, 74*(1), 68–93. doi: 10.1080/10570310903463778

Heffernan, K., & Cone, R. (2001). *"Course organization." Fundamentals of service-learning course construction*. Providence, RI: Campus Compact.

Hogan, J. M., Hayes Andrews, P., Andrews, J. R., & Williams, G. (2014). *Public speaking and civic engagement* (3rd ed.). Boston, MA: Pearson Education.

Hubbs, D. L., & Brand, C. F. (2005). The paper mirror: Understanding reflective journaling. *Journal of Experiential Education, 28*(1), 60–71. doi: 10.1177/105382590502800107

Johannesen, R. L. (2001). *Ethics in human communication* (5th ed.). Prospect Heights, IL: Waveland.

Kahl, D. H. (2010a). Connecting autoethnography with service learning: A critical communication pedagogical approach. *Communication Teacher, 24*(4), 221–228. doi: 10.1080/17404622.2010.513036

Kahl, D. H. Jr. (2010b). Making a difference: (Re)connecting communication scholarship with pedagogy. *Journal of Applied Communication Research, 38*(3), 298–302. doi: 10.1080/00909882.2010.490845

Kolb, A. Y., & Kolb, D. A. (2005). Learning styles and learning spaces: Enhancing experiential learning in higher education. *Academy of Management Learning & Education, 4*(2), 193–212. doi: 10.5465/AMLE.2005.17268566

Kolb, D. A. (1984). *Experiential learning: Experience as the source of learning and development*. Englewood Cliffs, NJ: Prentice Hall.

Lane, S. D., Abigail, R. A., & Gooch, J. C. (2014). *Communication in a civil society*. Boston, MA: Pearson.

Langer, E. J. (1989). *Mindfulness*. Philadelphia, PA: De Capo Press.

Langer, E. J., & Moldoveanu, M. (2000). The construct of mindfulness. *Journal of Social Issues, 56*(1), 1–9. doi: 10.1111/0022-4537.00148

Littlefield, H. (2006). Service learning in business communication: Real-world challenges develop real-world skills. *Business Communication Quarterly, 69*(3), 319–322. doi: 10.1177/1080569906069003 11

Littlefield, R. S., Freed, T. B., & Rick, J. M. (2012). "Getting out of your bubble": Incorporating service learning in the intercultural communication course. *Journal of the Communication, Speech & Theatre Association of North Dakota, 52*, 2553–2558. Retrieved from http://0-web.a.ebscohost.com.iii-server.ualr.edu/ehost/pdfviewer/pdfviewer?sid=262f3c23-19df-46f4-8f4f-f22b67cc7aea%40sessionmgr4003&vid=9&hid=4104

Liu, M. (2011). Fostering civic engagement in the communication research methods course. *Communication Teacher, 25*(3), 166–174. doi: 10.1080/17404622.2011.579908

Maresh-Fuehrer, M. M. (2015). Service-learning in crisis communication education: Revisiting Coombs' objectives for the crisis communication course. *Communication Teacher, 29*(3), 173–190. doi: 10.1080/17404622.2015.1028554

Martinez, S. P. (2004). Informative connections: Enhancing public speaking assignments with service learning. *Communication Teacher, 18*(1), 23–25. doi: 10.1080/1740462032000142158

McCaleb, J. L., & Dean, K. W. (1987). Ethics and communication education: Empowering teachers. *Communication Education, 36*(4), 410–416. doi: 10.1080/03634528709378696

McIntyre, K. A., Douglas, M. T., Holley, N., & Sandor, S. L. (2009). Service-learning in the basic communication course. In D. W. Worley (Ed.), *Best practices in experiential and service learning in communication*. Dubuque, IA: Kendall/Hunt Publishing Company.

McIntyre, K. A., & Sellnow, D. D. (2014). A little bit can go a long way: An examination of required service in the basic communication course. *Communication Teacher, 28*(1), 57–73. doi: 10.1080/17404622.2013.843012

McManus, J. L. (1986). "Live" case study/journal record in adolescent psychology. *Teaching of Psychology, 13*(2), 70–74. doi: 10.1207/s15328023top1302_5

Mize Smith, J. (2014). Making change out of change: Integrating service-learning into small group communication. *Kentucky Journal of Communication, 33*(2), 66–78. Retrieved from http://0-web.a.ebscohost.com.iii-server.ualr.edu/ehost/pdfviewer/pdfviewer?sid=262f3c23-19df-46f4-8f4f-f22b67cc7aea%40sessionmgr4003&vid=12&hid=4104

Mostert, M. P. (2007). Challenges of case-based teaching. *The Behavior Analyst Today, 8*(4), 434. doi: 10.1037/h0100632

Motley, M. T. (1997). *Overcoming your fear of public speaking: A proven method*. Boston, MA: Houghton Mifflin.

National Communication Association. (1999). *Credo for ethical communication*. Retrieved from http://www.natcom.org/policies/External/EthicalComm.htm

New England Resource Center for Higher Education. (2015). *Carnegie community engagement classification*. Retrieved from http://nerche.org/index.php?option=com_content&view=article&id=341&Itemid=92

Novak, J. M., Markey, V., & Allen, M. (2007). Evaluating cognitive outcomes of service learning in higher education: A meta-analysis. *Communication Research Reports, 24*(2), 149–157. doi: 10.1080/08824090701304881

Oliver, D., & Roos, J. (2003). Dealing with the unexpected: Critical incidents in the LEGO Mindstorms team. *Human Relations, 56*(9), 1055–1080. doi: 10.1177/0018726703569002

Pearce, W. B., & Littlejohn, S. W. (1997). *Moral conflict: When social worlds collide*. Thousand Oaks, CA: Sage.

Pennell, M., & Miles, L. (2009). "It actually made me think": Problem-based learning in the business communications classroom. *Business Communication Quarterly, 72*(4), 377–394. doi: 10.1177/1080569909349482

Putnam, L. L. (2010). Communication as changing the negotiation game. *Journal of Applied Communication Research, 38*(4), 325–335. doi: 10.1080/00909882.2010.513999

Roberts, F. (2001). Teaching research methods using a problem-based learning approach. *Communication Teacher, 16*(1), 6–8. Retrieved from http://0-web.a.ebscohost.com.iii-server.ualr.edu/ehost/pdfviewer/pdfviewer?sid=262f3c23-19df-46f4-8f4f-f22b67cc7aea%40sessionmgr4003&vid=15&hid=4104

Saatci, E. (2008). Problem-based learning in an intercultural business communication course: Communication challenges in intercultural relationships in internationalizing small-or medium-sized enterprises. *Journal of Business and Technical Communication, 22*(2), 237–260. doi: 10.1177/1050651907311931

Seeger, M. W., Sellnow, T. L., Ulmer, R. R., & Novak, J. (2009). Applied communication ethics: A summary and critique of the research literature. In L. R. Frey & K. N. Cissna (Eds.), *Routledge handbook of applied communication research* (pp. 280–306). New York, NY: Routledge.

Seifer, S. D., & Connors, K. (Eds.). (2007). *Community campus partnerships for health: Faculty toolkit for service-learning in higher education.* Scotts Valley, CA: National Service-Learning Clearinghouse. Retrieved from https://ccph.memberclicks.net/assets/Documents/FocusAreas/he_toolkit.pdf

Sellnow, D. D., & Ahlfeldt, S. L. (2005). Fostering critical thinking and teamwork skills via a problem-based learning (PBL) approach to public speaking fundamentals. *Communication Teacher, 19*(1), 33–38. doi: 10.1080/1740462042000339258

Sellnow, T. L., & Seeger, M. W. (2013). *Theorizing crisis communication.* Malden, MA: Wiley.

Sitkin, S. (1996). Learning through failure: The strategy of small losses. In M. D. Cohen & L. S. Sproull (Eds.), *Organizational learning* (pp. 541–578). Thousand Oaks, CA: Sage.

Ulmer, R. R., Sellnow, T. L., & Seeger, M. W. (2014). *Effective crisis communication.* Thousand Oaks, CA: Sage.

University of Arkansas at Little Rock. (1988). *Mission.* Retrieved from http://ualr.edu/about/mission/

Vaughn, M. (2009). Video family memoirs: Service-learning in a family communication course. *Communication Teacher, 23*(4), 153–157. doi: 10.1080/17404620903218791

Veltsos, J. R. (2012). An analysis of data breach notifications as negative news. *Business and Professional Communication Quarterly, 75*(2), 192–207. doi: 10.1177/1080569912443081

Voss, M. M. (1988). The light at the end of the journal: A teacher learns about learning. *Language Arts, 65*(7), 669–674. Retrieved from http://www.jstor.org/stable/41411441

Weick, K. E. (1995). *Sensemaking in organizations.* Thousand Oaks, CA: Sage.

APPENDIX

Example Master's Research Projects

Focus: Organizational culture

- *A New Revolution of Communication and Leadership: A Cultural Analysis of a Hospital Administrative Department*
- *Communication Excellence Theory: Stories of Communication Excellence between Physicians and Patients at Arkansas Children's Hospital*
- *A Cultural Analysis of a Youth Development Center: Creating Tomorrow's Leaders*
- *Bridging the Divide: Recruitment Offices' Perceptions of their Communicative Relationships with their Campuses*
- *Bridging the Gap: Improving Parent-Teacher Communication*
- *Positive Communication in Debate: How Debaters Think About and Practice Communication.*

Focus: Communication trainings

- *"We Are More Similar than Different": An Assessment of the Impact of Communication Training on Pakistani Students' Cultural Mindsets*
- *Listen Up: Listening Training for Student Organizations*
- *Assessing Communication Excellence in an Elementary School Anti-bullying Program*
- *Best Practices in Communication Center Training and Training Assessment.*

Focus: Crises or crisis response preparedness

- *The Red River Floodway Expansion Project: Best Practices in Risk Communication Modeled by the Manitoba Floodway Authority*
- *Arkansas' Response to Hurricane Katrina: Effective Crisis Communication in Public Health*
- *A Little Birdie Told Me: H1N1 Information and Misinformation Exchange on Twitter*
- *The Discourse of Renewal and the Obesity Crisis in the Arkansas Delta*
- *Effective Crisis Communication: Lessons Learned from the Deepwater Horizon Oil Spill.*

PART III
INTEGRATING INTERNATIONAL LEARNING INTO CURRICULA

Chapter 9

The Somali Immersion Experience: An Intercultural Immersion

Dandrielle Lewis and Aram deKoven

Abstract

Purpose — This chapter provides the structure of an engaging intercultural, out of class, integrative curricular Somali Immersion Experience (SIE) offered to University of Wisconsin-Eau Claire Education Studies majors and nonmajors who are not exposed to many different races, ethnicities, and people from different cultures because of the demographics of Eau Claire.

Methodology/approach — SIE participants complete 24 classroom hours and a weeklong immersion into the Somali Community of Minneapolis/St. Paul, Minnesota. Critical Race Theory provides the framework for the coursework. Quantitative data is collected via pre- and post-SIE online surveys and classroom assignments. Qualitative data is collected via summative papers and reflective sessions.

Findings — The results indicate that participants develop understanding and knowledge of Somali culture, religious practices, life styles and school lives, as well as their performance in teaching, reading, mathematics, and social studies to nonnative speakers of English. The participants' preconceived notions about Somalians, Muslims, and Islam were based on what they saw portrayed in the media. After the SIE, participants expressed how much knowledge they gained about best practices in English as a Second Language instruction, communicating: "Somalians and Muslims are a peaceful people." One participant exclaimed "I have learned more in a week than I have learned during my field teaching experience and more than I have learned by taking a semester long class."

Originality/value — This chapter offers help to individuals and institutions wanting to improve students' exposure to diversity through domestic immersions.

Integrating Curricular and Co-Curricular Endeavors to Enhance Student Outcomes
Copyright © 2016 by Emerald Group Publishing Limited
All rights of reproduction in any form reserved
ISBN: 978-1-78635-064-0

Keywords: Intercultural immersions; English as a Second Language learners

Education Studies (ES) majors at University of Wisconsin-Eau Claire (UWEC) are taught about teaching to diverse groups. After completing the ES program, students are prepared for teaching in a classroom. However, because of the demographics in the Eau Claire Area School District (ECASD), where most students complete their field experience and student teaching, ES majors are not exposed to many different races, ethnicities, and people from different cultures. The students' lack of exposure is what makes their Somali Immersion Experience (SIE) fascinating and both personally and professionally rewarding because it provides an educational intersection where preservice educators can develop and grow their cultural competencies. The SIE merges ES, Sociology, Geography, and Political Science in a hands-on and engaging experience, an experience that would be the dream of any educator. This chapter reports on the SIE and how the curriculum and practices of the SIE provide an out of class cocurricular opportunity for UWEC ES majors and nonmajors to gain experience working with diverse groups, particularly Somalis.

9.1. Background and Goals of the Somali Immersion Program

The SIE was conceived by UWEC professor Dr. Kate Reynolds in the 2009–2010 academic year with the help of Dr. Aram deKoven, and currently, Drs. Dandrielle Lewis and Aram deKoven, professors at UWEC, are facilitators of the Somali Immersion program. The SIE program has been offered for five years, and is offered once a year during the winter academic session. The SIE includes 24 classroom hours and a weeklong immersion into the Somali community of Minneapolis/ St. Paul (MSP). The Somali community is known as "Little Mogadishu" because it is the center of the largest concentration of Somalis in this nation and one of the largest populations of Somalis outside of Somalia.

UWEC is a predominately White institution. However, the demographics are changing. For example, in fall 2014, UWEC admitted its largest diverse incoming freshman cohort. At UWEC, there are few diversity courses offered. For example, Dr. Aram deKoven teaches *Race, Class, and Gender Studies*. Other courses offered are: *Language in Culture and Society*, *African American History*, and *African American Civil Rights Movement*. For ES majors who want to teach in diverse schools and desire more experience with students of color, the SIE gives them that opportunity. The Somali community was chosen for several reasons: (1) English is a common second language for many Somalis, (2) They are the largest underrepresented group in the MSP area, (3) To build a partnership between the Somali community, which lacks external educational opportunities, and UWEC, which lacks in diversity, to develop a bridge to strengthen those areas of weaknesses, and (4) The research interests of Dr. deKoven include the impact of race, class, gender, and affectional orientation on educational access and success. The goals of the SIE align with the mission and values of the National Education Association (NEA).

The mission of the NEA is "to advocate for education professionals and to unite our members and the nation to fulfill the promise of public education to prepare every student to succeed in a diverse and interdependent world." The core values that guide their work are: "equal opportunity, a just society, democracy, professionalism, partnership, and collective action" (NEA Handbook, 2015, p. 7). Our goals include:

1. Gathering information about Somali culture, traditions, and religion from scholarly presentations, readings, and observation.
2. Being able to express a deep awareness of how learners' race, background knowledge and experiences, culture, religion, and gender impact school environments.
3. Being able to articulate the complexities of urban immigrants' lives and large populations of one culture in one school (specifically, high incidence populations of nonnative speakers).
4. Identifying examples of experiences of first-generation immigrants to the United States and connecting them to their own ancestral stories.
5. Demonstrating strategies for building equity into public education for nonnative English speakers and an ability to advocate on behalf of nonnative English speakers and their needs.
6. Being able to express an understanding of the privileges of the White, middle-class Americans, who are not immigrants.

The Somali Immersion curriculum and related activities are developed and designed for the UWEC participants to learn about the history and culture of the Somali people, the struggles and joys of being an immigrant, and the difficulties of being a second language learner. Subsequently, this increased awareness aids the participants, many of whom are now graduates of UWEC, to be guided by well-rounded information, rooted in a sense of social justice, and in the ultimate knowledge of human equality.

The SIE is significant and relevant to current teacher and higher education needs because classrooms are becoming more diverse, and educators must be able to teach effectively and communicate with students from different backgrounds. Teaching a diverse classroom effectively includes having an awareness of diverse student needs, understanding where the students come from and who they are, communicating with English as a Second Language (ESL) students, and designing problems and activities to engage all students. The more experience the educators have, the better they are able to reach and connect with all students in the classroom, and the SIE provides such experience.

9.2.   Theoretical Framework

The SIE challenges participants to reflect on their own lives and think using new ideas instead of traditional and expected ideas by addressing, discussing, debating, and assessing sensitive topics and issues in a safe learning environment where they are challenged but not judged. The SIE is framed by service and Critical Race Theory (CRT) provides the conceptual framework for SIE coursework.

9.3. Critical Race Theory

To prepare SIE participants for asset-based service-learning work, explained in greater detail in the next section, we turn to CRT to guide the immersion practicum and pre-program coursework. In addition to a basic understanding of CRT, SIE participants must have an understanding of implicit, or subconscious bias. Together these two concepts prepare students for critical introspection and culturally competent asset-based fieldwork.

CRT is attributed to the work of the pioneering legal scholar Bell (1992). CRT is a framework for understanding and making sense of social phenomenon. CRT holds, among other tenets, that race and racism are central and permanent concepts in society, which are essential to be considered when analyzing and interpreting the world in which we live. Also, CRT maintains that "race" as a system for human classification, has no biological or scientific grounds, but rather, race is a construct conceived by humans to institutionalize power and privilege along color lines (Bell, 1992). Furthermore, CRT argues that race-based discrimination is a normal part of everyday life in the United States, not an aberration (Ladson-Billings, 2015). CRT is guided by, and accepts what are known as counter narratives for attempting to understand how racism operates and what it looks like in the United States today. Rather than listening only to the voices of power, the media, wealthy citizens, and those with elevated degrees, through counter narratives we hear the perspectives of those often silenced, and we gain a clearer picture of how race-based social phenomenon emerge today. Two of the classroom lectures of the SIE are counter narratives.

The SIE uses CRT to unmask racist policies, practices, and ideologies. In current times these are more often hidden, rather than visible in overt expressions of racial hatred. These policies and practices are cloaked in the "business as usual" mentality of the day-to-day operations of society (Gillborn, 2008; Matsuda, Lawrnece, Delgado, & Crenshaw, 1993; Yosso, Smith, Ceja, & Solorzano, 2009). Participants in the SIE are interested in creating social justice by narrowing racial divides. As such, they are taught to focus their mental attention on solving race-based inequalities by analyzing the operations of bureaucratic systems, such as school districts, rather than suggesting ways that persons of color can adapt or modify their lives to better meet the needs and requirements of society as a whole (Banks, 2001; Gay & Kirkland, 2003; Singleton & Linton, 2006; Yosso, 2005).

The SIE seeks to prepare participants to carry out equitable program participation that does not discriminate or favor based on race, class, gender, affectional orientation, or English language skill. The SIE also seeks to go further by having participants begin to develop the tools for deeply analyzing their own relationship to power and privilege. To accomplish this, the SIE also turns to research on implicit bias.

We understand that it is not simply enough for one to say, "I am not racist." It is more truthful and impactful to acknowledge that everyone harbors bias and prejudice to one degree or another (Banaji & Greenwald, 2013; Dasgupta, McGhee, & Greenwald, 2000; Vedantam, 2010). To see difference is in fact a human trait, and this is not cause for concern. However, when we attribute value or worth to the differences we see, then race-based discrimination emerges (Dasgupta et al., 2000). Research on implicit bias is clear, as humans have bias and are susceptible to acting out on these biases (Bargh & Morsella, 2008; Eagleman, 2011; Steele, 1997; Steele & Aronson, 1995). The SIE informs participants about the power of subconsciously held bias, not only in shaping word views but also in possibly altering outcomes for those people who they come in contact with. The first essential step is to take an open and honest inventory of our own biases, name them, and then seek to prevent them from governing our thoughts and actions. This process is hard and needs to be on going.

The SIE requires that participants be willing to uncover and analyze their implicit or subconscious biases. This is absolutely essential for equitable and inclusive program participation. SIE faculty and staff cannot have meaningful and honest conversations about discrimination and inequality without first acknowledging and identifying each of our own roles and culpabilities living and participating in a society that favors some groups at the expense of others. To deny this reality would eliminate the possibility of an asset-based working relationship between the SIE of UWEC and the Somali community.

9.4. Service: An Asset-Based Mindset

The SIE uses an asset-based approach, which acknowledges that a great deal of our bias and prejudice are deeply rooted in core beliefs, values, and understandings. Many of these deeply held ideas impact the way we think and feel about others, and these values can in turn affect the way we treat and interact with those around us. An asset-based approach forces participants to identify, analyze, and possibly modify core beliefs, attitudes, and values. The use of an asset-based approach makes that which is often unconscious, conscious so that we can actively address and seek to control the effects of growing up in a society that consistently sends messages about what or who is "inferior" or "superior." Simply put, an asset-based mindset ensures that SIE participants enter their immersion experience not thinking that their way of knowing, thinking, and communicating is any better or worse than the people with whom they will work.

We are acutely aware of the transformational power that intercultural immersions can have on student and faculty learning. Intercultural immersions, when properly facilitated, can broaden perspectives, widen and diversify social networks, and create pathways for critically reflective introspection. For many, intercultural immersions completely alter, for the better, the way a participant sees the world in which they live, nothing short of a complete paradigm shift. We revel in the possibility that participants could experience such a powerful learning opportunity. However, this learning must not come at the expense or detriment of the SIE partners. Intercultural immersions can, and should be done well, with respect, shared admiration, and collaboration.

> Reciprocity is the key to community service learning; this is what differentiates it from philanthropy and charity. The reciprocity involved (with service learning) is, however, asymmetrical. (Camacho, 2004, p. 31)

We acknowledge that this is a service-learning opportunity for primarily White, middle class, English speaking college students. The Somalis, for the SIE, are often from economically stressed homes and are frequently English learners. Our UWEC students have privilege and power relative to our Somali partners, a reality we do not wish to exacerbate. To this end, the facilitators of the SIE aim to employ the following three core principles:

1. Giving in the spirit of service,
2. Serving with reciprocity, and
3. Working in collaboration.

The giving of time and energy to serve a worthy cause is an essential part of the college experience. The SIE is conducted in the "spirit of service." Participants are reminded that one of the goals of the SIE is to provide valuable, asset-based service of the highest quality, reliability, and caring support.[1] While many service-learning opportunities are linked to course grades, student club points, and graduation requirements, the SIE is not. However, we would ultimately like to have the SIE count toward service-learning "credit" in the future because many participants and colleagues have expressed the value in this program and believe the SIE satisfies the criteria for service-learning opportunities. Over the years, we have tried offering the SIE for credit and noncredit. Currently, the SIE is offered for nongraduation credit. The reasoning is as follows:

1. By not offering the SIE for credit, we attract a wider range of student participants, not from one major or discipline only.
2. We draw participants who are intrinsically motivated to participate for no other reason than interest in the subject matter. This produces a higher level of engagement and involvement of the participants.
3. By not offering the SIE as a class, we can require fewer writing assignments and reading exercises and focus more on discussions, lecture, and collaboration.
4. The program costs are significantly lower for participants, and
5. We do not conflict with one of our underlying principles, which is to not create a situation where programmatic requirements might trump offering genuine service and support.

---

1. For this reason, the SIE eliminated the course credit option.

The SIE should meet the needs of both the people we are working with and the needs of the SIE, the participants, and UWEC. We have done our best to listen to the wishes of our collaborators and ambassadors to learn how best to serve them. For example, we may have participants who wish to focus on teaching Math concepts, but our Somali partners would rather our students teach technical language skills. In this scenario, the SIE participants, however skilled in Math Education, would teach and seek help teaching technical English skills if needed. Another example is the time the actual SIE is offered. For UWEC students and faculty, the spring and summer sessions are better for running the SIE. However, we have learned that the schools we work with prefer the winter session because we can provide maximum support for their teachers at a time that does not conflict with testing days or Muslim holidays. A culturally sensitive service relationship should be balanced, where both parties are benefiting.

Finally, we believe that service is something that is done with people, not to them or for them. Selected participants of the SIE are challenged to answer the following three questions:

1. Do you feel that part of your service is to help the people you are working with become more like you, or think more like you?
2. Do you feel "sorry" for the people you are working with?
3. Do you feel that nothing you learn from your service relationships will inspire positive changes in your attitudes, values, and/or actions?

If a SIE participant answers "yes" to any of these questions, then we must work with the participant to address any conceptual misunderstanding. It is important to the existing relationship with our Somali partners and to the integrity of the program that all participants be comfortable answering "no" to the above questions. All students in the SIE must be willing and able to work in Somali neighborhoods and schools with an asset-based mindset. We mention this because selecting participants who want a genuine service-learning opportunity is crucial to a successful SIE.

The SIE requires that all participants agree to not use their involvement in the program as an opportunity to proselytize because that would deeply offend the Somalis. We wish to never lose sight that we want to provide a valuable asset-based service. Participants are encouraged to be open minded and to grow while serving the Somali community.

9.5.   Cultural Ambassadors

Guided by an understanding of CRT and implicit bias training, we sought to build meaningful working and friendly relationships with Somali community partners and stake holders. One central element to the success of the SIE has been our relationships with key players in the Somali community. Before the SIE began, we met with a wide range of people to talk about the program and its goals. We intentionally brought unfinished ideas to the table discussions to seek input from our Somali colleagues and to employ those ideas. After several meetings in MSP, we met an individual who was very interested in partnering with us. Abdirizak Bihi, known to all as "Bihi" met with us many times over lunch, coffee, and dinner. We worked to build the relationship with Bihi and the Somali community just as much as we worked to design an intercultural immersion for UWEC students. The tenor of our relationship was key as we would be asking for a large commitment of each of our partners in the future, especially Bihi.

Bihi turned out to be a famous individual in the Somali community, in MSP, and around the world. He is widely known as a highly trusted person, and he is respected by the residents of "Little Mogadishu," Somali schools, teachers, politicians, and by the community Elders. Bihi has great favor in Little Mogadishu, and as a result the good will and trust, was to some extent, passed along to the SIE by our Somali partners. This is an important element for the SIE because the Somali community has long been subjected to harsh and often unjust treatment and scrutiny by outsiders. Through a combination of racism, language discrimination, religious misunderstandings, socioeconomic woes, and a barrage of United States law enforcement officers seeking to apprehend individuals accused of supporting Al-Shabbat and other identified terrorist organizations, a good deal of skepticism and mistrust has developed between some Somalis and some White non-Somalis.[2]

Bihi was instrumental in implementing the initial ideas, plans, and goals of the SIE in the Somali community. For example, he would speak Somali to community members and leaders and say "These guys are OK. They are teachers, and they are here to help with good hearts and minds." With the endorsement of Bihi, nearly everything we asked for was granted. Bihi introduced us and participants to teachers in Somali schools, school officials, residents, business owners, and Somali Elders. Without his efforts, our work would have been much more difficult and perhaps impossible.

Another central partnership was our relationship with the two predominately Somali schools, which we will call School A and School B. We sought schools that served primarily Somali youth, and initially we sent out approximately 10 letters seeking partnerships with MSP-area schools in Minnesota and schools in Wisconsin. In some cases, we were granted phone meetings with school officials, but it was not until we mentioned the name Bihi that we heard our first "yes."[3]

The SIE is entering its sixth year and is a sustainable program. We have developed strong relationships with School A, a public middle school, and School B, a public charter school. Guided by critical practices and understandings and equitable and racially conscious leadership, these schools have a cohort of culturally competent educators, and they appreciate having UWEC participants teach and

---

2. For this reason, our choice to rent two large black Suburbans may have been a poor choice for shuttling our participants through the neighborhood.

3. It helped that the SIE was rooted in a Teacher Education program. Later we learned that for many Somalis being a teacher is a profession worthy of great respect and admiration.

collaborate with their teachers. For these reasons, our relationships have been strong and enduring. The SIE maintains these bonds with partners by keeping regular contact throughout the school year, constantly seeking and getting teacher and staff feedback about our participants, ensuring that we are meeting administrators and teacher needs and expectations, and building into our grants some money to help the Somali schools purchase needed books and equipment.

Even though there was no general formula or equation for building firm partnering and working relationships, CRT and implicit bias training were important first steps for SIE facilitators to have positive working relationships with the Somali community and schools that serve students of color. Establishing a productive working relationship with SIE participants, Somali partners and partnering schools are essential to having a successful SIE.

In addition to helping us gain access to schools, Bihi established connections with the local Mosque, Imams, Somali Museum and Cultural Center, Brian Coyle Center, and the Somali Elders. These connections were made a great deal easier by asking Bihi to initiate the collaboration.

9.6. Classroom Practice and Coursework

Prior to being placed in one of the two partnering Somali schools in MSP, participants are required to take and complete 20 hours of classroom-based instruction. The 20 hours consists of five classes, four hours each, and these classes provide the groundwork for working effectively and equitably with Somali youth and ESL students. The coursework is selected to provide maximum context and depth for understanding the unique situation that is faced by many Somalis in MSP. An outline of the five pre-immersion classes, including lectures, topics, and other activities is given in Table 9.1.

Table 9.1: Classroom meeting schedule.

Class (timeframe)	Topic(s)
Class 1 (5:30–9:30 p.m.)	• Introductions and norming the group • Overview of SIE goals, expectations, reading assignments, assessments, journals, final summative paper • Complete pre-SIE online survey • Watch Somali culture documentary • Discuss history and impetus for immigration "Your Guide to Somali Culture" and "The Letter: An American town and the 'Somali Invasion'." This includes a debriefing discussion • Dr. Aram deKoven lecture: Introduction to CRT and implicit race-based bias • Homework/reading assigned

Table 9.1: (*Continued*)

Class (timeframe)	Topic(s)
Class 2 (5:30–9:30 p.m.)	• Know-Want to know-Learn (KWL) exercise • Discussion of participants' ancestors' immigrant stories, oral tales, and myths • Abdirizak Bihi lecture: Patterns of Somali culture, daily lives in Somalia compared to MSP, the Somali diaspora, immigration, and the Somali-American experience
Class 3 (5:30–9:30 p.m.)	• Dr. Dandrielle Lewis lecture: Race, Gender, Math: my journey and experiences that Math led to me • Dr. Stephen Hill lecture: The Politics of Somali, Eastern Africa, and World Relations of Somalia • Dr. Stephen Hill leads discussion of White privilege and the ramifications within our public schools • Homework/reading assigned
Class 4 (5:30–9:30 p.m.)	• Geography professor or Historian lecture: The History of Africa focusing on Eastern Africa and History from Ancient Times to Present of Somalia • The geography professor or Historian also leads discussion on Somali immigration to Barron, Wisconsin • Homework/reading assigned
Class 5 (5:30–9:30 p.m.)	• TESOL person or Foreign Language professor lecture/ workshop: Effective Instructional techniques for Teaching Literacy Acquisition and Critical Reading Skills to Diverse Learners and ESL students • Participants work through activities and handouts that teach them how to work effectively with ESL students • Dr. deKoven discusses the tenets and beliefs of working productively and maintaining positive interactions in religious discussions • Discuss and prepare for SIE in MSP departure • Homework/reading assigned
Class 6 (5:30–9:30 p.m.)	• Program follow up and debrief • Complete KWL exercise and post-SIE online surveys • Focus groups and turn in summative papers

9.7.   The Weeklong Somali Immersion Experience in MSP

The SIE was not only educational. It was awe-inspiring. The SIE was a six-day immersion into the MSP Somali community, "Little Mogadishu." On the first day, participants arrived in MSP were given the opportunity to settle in the hotel, and got the opportunity to meet a female Somali film director, Fathia Absie. In an intimate and informal setting, she discussed her phenomenal journey to America from Somalia, the life lessons she learned along her journey, and the way her experiences impacted her life, beliefs, and views of America. The participants asked her questions during the discussion, and this interaction marked the beginning of an introspective journey of the participants from UWEC by making them reevaluate their own lives, privileges, and opportunities. Participants walked away from the discussion saying: "She is awesome"; "I do not know if I could have come to America at that same age and survived"; "She is an amazing leader"; "She is beautiful"; "She is intelligent, very smart, and she inspired me." Some participants cried because they were moved and overwhelmed with the similarities between the family values of the Somali people and the White and Hmong cultures. The participants realized that in many ways the Somali people were not very different from themselves. After this discussion, the participants dined at an Indian restaurant with their cohort, the facilitators of the SIE, professors, and Bihi.

On days 2–6, the classroom immersion at two predominately Somali schools, "School A" and "School B" occurred. Participants were placed into classrooms according to their majors and were matched, as close as possible, to work with teachers in their fields of expertise. Cooperating teachers were encouraged to use our participants in any way that they deemed useful. However, the SIE facilitators preferred that cooperating teachers engage our participants in their classrooms with high-impact practices such as designing and teaching lessons, small group instruction, and/or providing one-on-one student support. Additionally, all of our cooperating teachers modeled culturally relevant teaching practices in their classrooms.

School days started at 7 a.m. and ended at 3 p.m. After school, we embarked on various adventures/expeditions in MSP to expose the participants and further immerse them into the Somali community. The expeditions included visiting: the Somali Museum, the Mosque in the Somali community, and the Somali Mall. The three listed venues were chosen because the experiences involved learning about Somali culture and Islam, and giving the participants the opportunity to get Henna tattoos at the Somali Mall.

The founder, owner, and curator, of the Somali Museum, and his daughter guided us through the Museum. This was significant because the daughter is a college student at Metropolitan State University in MSP majoring in Urban Education. A professor of Urban Education at Metropolitan State joined us during our museum visit, and brought three of her Somali students with her. Touring the museum consisted of taking a journey and learning how Somalians preserved their milk and meat in Somalia, viewing traditional clothing and wedding attire, historical pieces, places, and statues in Somalia, pictures of political presidents, traveling guides, and standing inside a decorated hut from a Somalian village.

After the museum tour, the college students from Metropolitan State and UWEC discussed their majors, the classroom settings and what they learned during their field experiences, teaching stories, their career goals, and the grade levels and subjects they wanted to teach. They also discussed diversity classes being offered at their respective institutions. UWEC students exclaimed "I wish we had Urban Education as an option to major in at our school," and "I have learned more in a week than I've learned during my field teaching experience and more than I've learned by taking a semester long class." Metropolitan State students exclaimed "After doing field experience in MSP schools, I know teaching and giving back to my community is what I want to do in life." Although similarities existed among their students, UWEC participants expressed a desire to teach more diverse students.

Visiting the Mosque in the Somali community with Bihi was a life changing experience. The Imams, who are the preachers of the Mosque, invited us to observe their evening prayer. It is important to note that we did not ask to observe a prayer service, but rather we were invited to join. This gesture was significant because evening prayer is a very private time for the Somalis, and the men and women pray in separate rooms. However, they made an exception for us, a group which consisted of mostly women, and they allowed us to be in the same room as the men. Bihi explained and translated the prayers. The Somalis welcomed us into their lives and personal time as if we were family, and they did not make us feel unwelcome or awkward. After the prayer time, the Imams and a few of the Elders sat with us and answered questions that the participants had, which ranged from discussing the similarities and differences between Islam and Christianity, prayer in schools, politics, and Somali values. The participants were shocked and amazed at how similar their religious beliefs were with Islam, and they admired and respected how they were welcomed by the Somali community into this private setting. They also admired the high value that Somalis have for education, professors, and teachers. There was a mutual respect and admiration for each other, their respective cultures, and where they came from.

During another evening, participants had the opportunity to learn more about the Islamic culture by engaging in conversations with the Elders of the Somali community. The Somali Elders are the *de facto* governing body of Little Mogadishu. With the help of Bihi, as our translator, we exchanged stories. For example, at the time of this discussion, there was a bombing in Paris that involved Islamic extremists. The participants and the Elders discussed politics, and the Elders made it very clear that they did not support any wrongdoing that occurred. Other topics of discussion included the hierarchy of who handled crimes, community issues, and family problems. It turned out that even though formal authorities, like the police, may be contacted for crimes, issues, and concerns, the Somali community has another system similar to court. The court consists of the Elders and the parties involved in the crime or problem. Female participants were given the opportunity to have the women Elders make their scarves into hijabs, this opportunity crossing cultural barriers. In exchange for this meeting with the Elders, we offered cooked camel meat as a gift, the latter being warmly received. After offering the gift of food, we ate some of it with them because Somalis believe "it is better to eat some of it with your guests rather than leaving it for them to eat."

Participants also volunteered at the Brian Coyle Center, where Somali students go after school for tutoring and fun activities. The participants tutored and helped students with their homework, read books to specific age groups, organized book donations, and showed Somali students educational activities on the computer. They also played basketball, tossed the football around, played games, and hula hooped. Engaging in physical education with the students, outside of a classroom setting, was fun and exciting for the participants. In fact, they did not want to leave.

Other experiences included assessing their immersion classroom experiences, as a group, during a reflection session at the hotel. We asked the participants guided questions. For example, one question was, what are you learning about ESL students from a teacher perspective? One of the responses was "As teachers we need to plan lessons that engage students at every learning level, and this includes covering the same material but having exercises/activities that provide a range of difficulty levels." Participants also wanted to engage students more by doing more group work activities. This was insightful because the participants began to think about the environment and space they want to create in their own classrooms when they start their teaching careers. Specifically, they reflected on their ECASD field experiences and compared that experience to the SIE. Further, they discussed and assessed very sensitive topics about race and privilege in schools and in the Eau Claire community versus the Somali community and the impacts that the privileges had on the students, their values, their beliefs, and their ability to succeed or be held back educationally. The SIE provided a safe learning environment where they could discuss these topics openly and freely.

Other experiences included international dining meal options. Some of the evening meals were mandatory, and others were not. Restaurants and foods that many of our students had never visited or been exposed to were options. For example, a few choices were Somalian, Ethiopian, Eritrean, Indian, and Japanese restaurants. SIE meal time was used to further explore cultural traditions and to strengthen bonds between participants and facilitators. We often invited guests and collaborators to join us for dinner.

9.8.   Guided Reflection and Assessment

Guided reflection and assessment throughout the SIE is formative and critical for both the participants and the facilitators. We use this to improve their learning, address areas where they need work, and help us realize where the participants are struggling and provide immediate feedback. Research in teacher education supports and encourages guided reflection and assessment. For example, Stiggins (2002) suggested an effective way to provide these experiences is through modeling assessment strategies in teacher education classes. In a study on backward assessment and guided reflection, Song (2008, p. 1) stated "The results showed significant improvement in participants' teaching and their students' learning after they adopted 'backward' assessment and guided reflective practice."

The SIE has an annual assessment plan built into the program. We use the data collected from participants, partnering schools, community partners, and program leaders to ensure that the goals and objectives of the program are being met. We meet before, during, and after the SIE to ensure that operations and activities move forward as planned. Data from Somali community partners is gathered informally at the end of the weeklong immersion into Little Mogadishu. Information is collected via face-to-face meetings, e-mail correspondences, and phone conversations. For the partnering schools, gathering information includes face-to-face meetings with school officials and teachers and phone interviews. This information is reviewed and is used to make improvements to the program in subsequent years. The SIE has Institutional Review Board approval for conducting research with human subjects. Data gathered about the impact of the program on participants is formalized. We incorporate three forms of analysis: two are quantitative and one is qualitative.

The quantitative information for the SIE was collected using two survey instruments. Both surveys are administered pre- and post-SIE. One of the two instruments has been research-validated, the Multicultural Awareness Knowledge Skills Survey—Teacher Version (MAKSS-T) (D'Andrea, Daniels, & Heck, 1991; D'Andrea, Daniels, & Noonan, 2003). This survey was originally designed to gauge teachers' knowledge, awareness, and abilities to interact productively in intercultural environments, the goals of which perfectly align with the goals of the SIE. The second survey instrument was adapted from the MAKSS-T for use with questions that directly pertained to working within the SIE.

For example, we ask questions relating to Somali customs, language, traditions, and religious beliefs. We asked the following questions on both the pre- and post-SIE surveys. The information presented in Figures 9.1–9.3 represents individual pre- and post-program responses on a scale from "no familiarity" to "thorough."

In addition to questions asked specifically about the Somalis, more generalizable questions were asked about participants' abilities to prepare and carry out culturally relevant instructions.

Pre- and post-surveys, completed by the participants, are used as collected data to help secure funding for the program. When asked "what did you learn about teaching reading/literacy to non-native English speakers?" one participant's response was "I learned that it is important to use symbols and pictures when

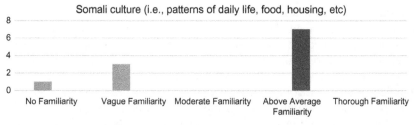

Figure 9.1: How FAMILIAR are you with Somali Culture (patterns of daily life, food, and/or housing)?

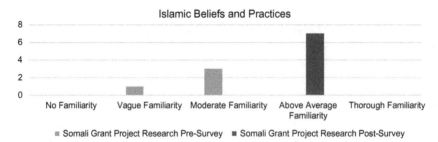

Figure 9.2: How FAMILIAR are you with the following topics: Islamic beliefs and practices?

Figure 9.3: After participating in this Somali Intercultural Immersion Experience, how would you rate your understanding of the impact of the way you think and act when interacting with persons of different cultural backgrounds?

working with English Language Learners (ELL) students. Pictures are universal and can help students understand what is going on. It is also important when teaching reading to ELL students that they are frequently asked comprehension questions. It is easier for them to read English words but very difficult for them to apply what they have read." UWEC Domestic Intercultural Immersions program provides grant funding to help sustain the SIE, and data exhibiting participant growth strengthens our grant proposals.

Quantitative data provides the immersion planners with a useful snapshot of the impact of the program on participants. Increases in knowledge and competencies between the start and conclusion of the program are viewed as evidence of the overall effectiveness of the program. Furthermore, the size and range of the positive change can be analyzed. If some of the focus areas are realizing only slight increases in measured understanding and competencies then modifications can and have been made.

In addition, the quantitative data has been very useful in analyzing the effectiveness of the SIE. Since the quantitative measurement devices have remained the same, we can easily compare and contrast any of the immersions five years of operation. For the most part we have found that consistently over the years, the SIE has helped participants make large gains in understanding and competencies with regard to working in culturally diverse settings. However, there have been a few things that have changed as a result of the data that we have collected. For example, we found that many participants were left with lingering questions regarding Islam and its core tenets. As a result of this discovery, we added more course content, guest speakers, and group discussions around Muslims and Islam. Another example of how the program has been shaped by the data we collect is the fact that we increased the amount of information that participants acquire regarding effective classroom strategies for working with English learners. The feedback we received indicated clearly that this was an area of concern for both teacher education and nonteacher education participants.

Finally, the qualitative data has provided us with a good system for documenting our successes to our funders, the media, and as a tool for program promotion. While we, the program planners, find mixed method analyses to be most effective, many prefer to see only numeric presentations of the effectiveness of the program. In addition to providing information for making corrections and adjustments to make the program more impactful for students, the qualitative data has enabled us to effectively and concisely present the effectiveness of the program.

Qualitative data was collected and analyzed using constant comparative method in order to develop a Grounded Theory (Glaser & Strauss, 1967). During the final on campus meeting after the weeklong immersion has been completed, participants are convened and broken up into two focus groups. Each group is asked the same set of post-SIE questions. These questions are drawn directly from the MAKSS-T. In the focus groups, participants provide long-form responses to the questions. A system of selective coding was incorporated to analyze the qualitative data whereby we were looking for data to emerge in categories revolving around similar patterns, groupings, and/or themes. Exemplars of these themes are presented below.

Together, both the quantitative and qualitative data provide a detailed picture of the ability of the SIE to deepen, alter, and improve participant knowledge and skills revolving around (a) their ability to work equitably and effectively with Somalis and (b) regarding their ability to understand and process higher level understandings about race and racism in the United States today. This detailed feedback for the SIE has enabled its organizers to bolster certain components, add new ones, and eliminate others. This data provides an essential component that has enabled the SIE facilitators to provide the best possible program for participants and for our Somali collaborators.

9.9. Summative Papers and Results

Two to three weeks after the SIE, UWEC participants meet with us for one last time to complete the "L" part of the KWL exercise, complete post surveys, reflect on their experiences, and turn in their summative papers. According to Chappius and Chappius (2007, para. 7), summative assessments "are used to make some sort of judgment, such as to determine what grade a student will receive on a classroom assignment, measure program effectiveness, or determine whether a school has made adequate yearly progress." They also state that summative assessment "typically documents how much learning has occurred at a point in time; its purpose is to measure the level of student, school, or program success." For the SIE, summative papers were used to help measure the effectiveness of our program.

Harlen and Crick (2002, p. 1) identified and synthesized "research evidence about the impact of summative assessment and tests on students' motivation for learning." Their review "identified more positive messages that identify action that can be taken to ensure that the benefits of summative assessment" (Harlen & Crick, 2002, p. 75) and many of their suggested practices are implemented in the goals of the SIE. "Implementing strategies for encouraging self-regulation in learning and positive interpersonal relationships" (Harlen & Crick, 2002, p. 76) is one specific practice attributing success to the SIE. According to McCombs (2003, pp. 16–18), the strategies include:

- Fostering caring personal relationships among students and between students and teacher,
- Helping students to challenge themselves and think for themselves while learning,
- Helping students to take some responsibility for learning to learn,
- Supporting students in directing their own learning,
- Providing students with some choice and control over their learning process, and
- Encouraging collaboration and the use of other students as resources for learning.

For their summative papers, participants were asked to "Write an essay/summative paper to critically reflect on and evaluate your SIE and its contribution to your cognitive and personal growth." The feedback was profound and significant, and their responses included what they learned about Somalia, politics, religion, biases (including their own), teacher and multicultural education, the impact of the SIE on their own lives, and their support and recommendation of the Somali Immersion program. Because a major portion of the success and sustainability of the SIE is based on the voices and experiences of the participants, samples of the feedback, arranged by similarity of topic, follow.

Before the Somali Immersion program, many participants did not know about Somali culture, Islam, and where Somalia was located on a map. Many students also admitted that their only exposure to diversity in a classroom came from a UWEC course on *Race Studies*. According to Student C:

> Because I am an ES major, I am required to take *Race Studies*, which is a cultural diversity class, and I absolutely loved it and learned a tremendous amount. But, this Immersion blew that class out of the water.

Throughout the SIE, participants asked many questions about Islam because they thought it was a radical religion based on what they saw on television, and they identified the major differences between Islam and Christianity. When the participants had the opportunity to speak with the religious leaders and Elders of Little

Mogadishu, they began to fully understand the similarities as opposed to the differences. Student D said:

> The media portrays Islam as a violent and terrorist-driven religion, when really Muslims are extremely peaceful and passionate people. I found it amazing that they are devoted to praying five times a day. I was surprised on how much Islam, Christianity, and Judaism, are similar.

Many participants had no experience working in a diverse community and school population because of the demographics of Eau Claire. As future educators, the participants expressed their gratitude for gaining this experience during the SIE. Student A wrote:

> Observing and working with amazing teachers at School A (one of the predominately Somali schools) was an experience that I will never forget. I had the opportunity for the first time in my life to work with English Language Learners. I was able to learn about the methods that my teacher used to help the new-to-country students learn English in the most efficient ways possible. My classroom was extremely diverse and the majority of my classroom was made up of students who recently came to the United States from Somali. I was very sad when I finished my last day working with them.

Although the participants did not collaborate on their papers, similar ideas emerged when they wrote about the open discussion they had with undergraduate Somali students majoring in Urban Education at Metropolitan State University. Student A voiced:

> I was able to even meet friends that were my own age! We had the opportunity to discuss important issues such as race, current education problems, and shared our dreams. Members from my Somali Immersion trip and I bonded with the fellow future teachers from Metropolitan State. I learned so much just from having life conversations with them and will enjoy remaining in contact with them all.

Each student mentioned discussions with the Elders of the Somali community, but only one student included details. Student E said:

> The one thing I will never forget is how much the Elders respected teachers (not very many people do anymore). They said, "Somali children has three parents: (1) their biological parents, (2) other Somali parents, and (3) their teacher." This was remarkable to know how much the Somali community trust and believe that teachers will do their best for their child's education. I was deeply honored by that.

We expected the SIE to positively impact the participants as individuals pursuing careers in education by allowing them to make connections with a new culture. The feedback exceeded our expectations because we also received feedback addressing the impact of the SIE and its benefits for Eau Claire. Student B asserted:

> This experience not only benefited myself, but the city of Eau Claire as well. Why? Because when we came back we told our stories, which will hopefully show people that becoming more acceptable of diversity is a win for everyone. I completely recommend this program for educators or anyone for that matter.

Student C communicated:

> The Somali Immersion was the best experience I have had in four years at UWEC. It pushed me to broaden my views, destroy stereotypes, and open my heart to a whole community. We experienced life, real life diversity, and were welcomed with open arms. This is something Eau Claire doesn't have much of. How many diversity classes do we have at UWEC that challenge students both religiously, culturally, and require them to reflect on their own lives? This is exactly what the Immersion did. I learned that the Somali people are a severely misunderstood people, and as educated Americans we can do something to help these people and help ourselves understand their culture. The amount of content I learned in one week would take two semesters at UWEC. This is what makes this program irreplaceable, and I support this program 100%. I would recommend this Immersion to any field of study, education majors or not. Having a different perspective and understanding another people can be nothing but beneficial. Any stereotype that I had going into this trip was shattered.

As a Black Mathematics professor and facilitator of the SIE at UWEC, I realize that sustaining the Somali Immersion program is not only feasible, but it is needed. Participants acquire desired knowledge of diverse groups and cultures, and implement acquired knowledge and experiences into their lives, undergraduate majors, and careers as future educators. The following comments from Student C sum up why this program must continue to grow and make progress.

> Imagine if Political Science majors, Science, Public Relations, Agricultural, or even Actuarial Science majors all stepped out of their comfort zone and experienced this culture and their stereotypes were also shattered. How much would this change the university, media, and even politics? Eau Claire claims diversity and we claim the power of [and]. What if we were both welcoming [and] understanding of other cultures or we expand horizons [and] discover cultures, other

than our own. Imagine how the environment would change for the better. This is something that I would love to see implemented into this already amazing school.

The feedback from the participants shows that the goals of the Somali Immersion program are being met and surpassed through the SIE. Participants are provided a platform where they can be exposed to and immersed in a different culture, discuss sensitive topics without being judged, and ask questions to members of the Somali community. Through discussions, reflection sessions, writing, and self-introspection, participants become the truest expression of themselves.

9.10. Outcomes

The SIE does more than expose the UWEC participants to Somali students, their cultures, and their communities. The interaction between the UWEC participants, the Somali students, and the Somali community enables the UWEC participants to realize that more similarities exist between them than their preconceived notions. In addition, when differences do surface, these differences are embraced and cherished, as they make up the richness that binds this complex tapestry that is the United States. Because of the existing similarities, the participants of the SIE can enter classrooms after their graduation as educators who know and understand that although diverse students may look different than who they are used to seeing, they have similar values and life expectations and can connect with them as individuals, the latter enabling them to engage diverse students successfully.

This program advances not only the student participants and the Somali community but also their departments, campus, and communities at large where they will teach and apply what they have learned. For example, Dr. Lewis is the project director for an annual Sonia Kovalevsky (SK) high school and middle school mathematics day at UWEC. While co-facilitating the SIE, she met teachers at one of the predominately Somali schools in MSP. After returning to UWEC from the SIE, she decided to extend recruiting efforts for the SK day and invited these teachers to bring a bus of students to the event. The teachers brought 20 young Somali and Hispanic girls to participate. Funding for their travel was secured from the Dean of the College of Arts and Sciences and STEM admissions. These efforts were significant because for many of the girls who attended from MSP, it was their first trip to a UW school and Eau Claire, Wisconsin. This was also the first time UWEC had a group of Somali students visit our campus. At SK day 2014, we had no African-American/Black ethnicity participation, but in 2015, we had 20% African-American/Black participation. More data and information about the Somali students involvement at this event is provided in Lewis (2015, para. 11). Another example is one of the student participants gave a presentation on the transformative experience of the Somali Immersion program during the Faculty Led Immersion Week at UWEC. Presenting at this venue allowed the SIE to be publicized to the entire UWEC community.

9.11.   Conclusion

The collaboration between the Somali Immersion program and the Somali community in MSP is beneficial for both the UWEC and the Somali communities. The key principles and components of the SIE that would be applicable to similar programs are: expose undergraduates and students to diverse cultures, challenge them to become more aware of diverse students' needs, equip them with skills that will make them better and more effective teachers, provide them with teaching experience working with nonnative English speakers, encourage them to become advocates of diverse students by showing them what is needed within the diverse communities, increase diversity and recruiting efforts to be more inclusive, and learn that we are not very different than the diverse communities we work with. We are changing biases and the environments and cultures at UWEC and within the Somali community. Great communication with partners involved in the immersion experience and the key principles and components attributed to our success.

SIE participants develop understanding and knowledge of Somali culture, religious practices, life styles and school lives, as well as their performance in teaching, reading, mathematics, and social studies to nonnative speakers of English. Thus, through an integrative curricular SIE participants are enhanced intellectually and interculturally, the experience promoting excellence and diversity in a globally competitive workforce. The Somali Intercultural Immersion has been, and is, a successful program because it is truly a collaborative effort. The program revolves around creating and sustaining positive relationships. These relationships are framed by a deeply critical understanding of self, in conjunction with a fearless desire to speak about the impact of race, class, and cultural power structures on everyday people and their lives. The SIE owes its success to a greater extent to the Somali partners who have invested their time, energy, and intellect into making this program work for Somali students, Somali families, teachers, and UWEC students. Some elements of the program are malleable. For example, the staff may change and the courses may deviate. For the SIE and programs similar to ours to be successful, it is our belief that the core assumptions and intellectual underpinnings described in this chapter must remain constant.

References

Banaji, M. R., & Greenwald, A. G. (2013). *Blindspot: Hidden biases of good people*. New York, NY: Delacorte Press.

Banks, J. A. (2001). Multicultural education: Historical development, dimension, and practice. In J. Strouse (Ed.), *Exploring socio-cultural themes in education*. Upper Saddle River, NJ: Merrill Press.

Bargh, J., & Morsella, E. (2008). The unconscious mind. *Perspectives on Psychological Science, 3*(1), 73–79.

Bell, D. (1992). *Faces at the bottom of the well: The permanence of racism*. New York, NY: Basic Books.

Camacho, M. M. (2004). Power and privilege: Community service learning in Tijuana. *Michigan Journal of Community Service Learning, 10*(3), 31.

Chappius, S., & Chappius, J. (2007). The best value in formative assessment. *Educational Leadership Magazine: Informative Assessment, 4*(65), 14–19.

D'Andrea, M., Daniels, J., & Heck, R. (1991). Evaluating the impact of multicultural counseling training. *Journal of Counseling and Development, 70*(1), 143–150.

D'Andrea, M., Daniels, J., & Noonan, M. J. (2003). New developments in the assessment of multicultural competence: The multicultural awareness, knowledge, and skills survey for teachers. In D. Pope-Davis, H. Coleman, W. Liu, & R. L. Tororek (Eds.), *The handbook of multicultural competencies in counseling and psychology* (pp. 154–168). Thousand Oaks, CA: Sage.

Dasgupta, N., McGhee, D. E., & Greenwald, A. G. (2000). Automatic preferences for white Americans: Eliminating the family explanation. *Journal of Experimental Psychology, 36*, 316–328.

Eagleman, D. (2011). *Incognito: The secret lives of the brain.* New York, NY: Pantheon Books.

Gay, G., & Kirkland, K. (2003). Developing cultural critical consciousness and self-reflection in preservice teacher education. *Theory into Practice, 42*(3), 181–187.

Gillborn, D. (2008). *Racism and education: Coincidence or conspiracy?* New York, NY: Routledge.

Glaser, B., & Strauss, A. (1967). *The discovery of grounded theory.* Chicago, IL: Aldine.

Harlen, W., & Crick, R. D. (2002). A systematic review of the impact of summative assessment and tests on students' motivation for learning (EPPI-Centre Review, version 1.1). In *Research evidence in education library* (Issue 1, pp. 1–77). London: EPPI-Centre, Social Science Unit, Institute of Education.

Ladson-Billings, G. (2015, April 8). *Critical race theory in education.* University of North Carolina Ashville [video file]. Retrieved from https://www.youtube.com/watch?v= katwPTn-nhE

Lewis, D. (2015, September). Increasing diversity and inclusion for women in STEM. *Notices of the American Mathematical Society, 62*(8), 920–922.

Matsuda, M. J., Lawrnece, C. R., Delgado, R., & Crenshaw, K. W. (1993). *Words that wound: Critical race theory, assaultive speech, and the first amendment.* Boulder, CO: Westview Press.

McCombs, B. L. (2003, April). Defining tools for teacher reflection: The Assessment of Learner-Centered Practices (ALCP). Paper presented at the 84th Annual Meeting of the American Educational Research Association, Chicago, IL.

NEA Handbook. (2015). NEA Handbook (p. 7). National Education Association of the United States. Retrieved from www.nea.org/home/19322.htm

Singleton, G. E., & Linton, C. (2006). *Courageous conversations about race.* Thousand Oaks, CA: Corwin Press.

Song, K. (2008). Impact of backward assessment and guided reflection on social studies education: A four-step teaching cycle. *International Journal of Social Education, 23*(1), 118–138.

Steele, C. M. (1997). A threat in the air: How stereotypes shape intellectual identity and performance. *American Psychologist, 52*(6), 613–629.

Steele, C. M., & Aronson, J. (1995). Stereotype threat and the intellectual test performance of African Americans. *Journal of Personality and Social Psychology, 69*(5), 797–811.

Stiggins, R. J. (2002). Assessment crisis: The absence of assessment for learning. *Phi Delta Kappan, 83*(10), 758–765.

Vedantam, S. (2010). *The hidden brain: How our unconscious minds elect presidents, control markets, wage wars, and save our lives.* New York, NY: Random House.

Yosso, T. J. (2005). Whose culture has capital? A critical race theory discussion of community cultural wealth. *Race Ethnicity and Education, 8*(1), 69–91.

Yosso, T. J., Smith, W. A., Ceja, M., & Solorzano, D. G. (2009). Critical race theory, racial microaggressions, and campus racial climate for Latino/a undergraduates. *Harvard Educational Review, 79*(4), 659–690.

Chapter 10

Fostering Intercultural Competence through Short-Term Study Abroad

Selena Kohel

Abstract

Purpose − This chapter analyzes the impact of intercultural academic experiences on students in the areas of intercultural sensitivity and multicultural awareness, knowledge, and skills.

Methodology/approach − Cottey College's mission statement includes a clause about educating students to be useful members of a global society (*Mission*, n.d., para. 1). Toward achieving the mission, each of Cottey College's second year students is offered an international experience over spring break that is largely paid for by endowed funds. For spring break 2015, the author of this chapter and a colleague offered a trip to Thailand. To participate, students were required to take part in a Step into the World!: Thailand course that was intended to prepare them to successfully navigate, and later reflect upon, their experience abroad. The trip portion of the course spanned 10 days. To measure what impacts the course may have had, students were asked to complete a pre-course and post-course survey, the Intercultural Sensitivity Scale (Fritz, Möllenberg, & Chen, 2002), and to complete journal entries and a personal impact statement by which their multicultural awareness, knowledge, and skills were assessed.

Findings − Analysis of the results suggests the Step into the World!: Thailand course had a positive impact on the majority of students' intercultural sensitivity and multicultural awareness, knowledge, and skills.

Originality/value − The findings support the importance of intentionally combining inside and outside of the classroom experiences to enhance student outcomes.

Integrating Curricular and Co-Curricular Endeavors to Enhance Student Outcomes
Copyright © 2016 by Emerald Group Publishing Limited
All rights of reproduction in any form reserved
ISBN: 978-1-78635-064-0

Keywords: Intercultural sensitivity; multicultural awareness, knowledge and skills; global citizenship; short-term study abroad

Toward achieving the mission of fostering students' value as members of a global society, each of Cottey College's second year students, who is in good standing, is offered an international experience over spring break that involves a trip to a European location. Locations have included Paris, Florence and Rome, London, Madrid, and Barcelona. While on the trip, students are required to take part in a bus tour and a walking tour, two educational modules, and a farewell dinner. On some trips, they also have been required to attend a performance. The rest of the time is theirs to use as they deem fit. To participate, students are required to partake in a Step into the World! class that is intended to prepare them to successfully navigate, and later reflect upon, their travels abroad. The class is graded pass/fail.

For spring break 2015, a colleague and I offered an "alternative trip" to Thailand. We wanted to offer students an opportunity to experience that which is further away from that to which they may be accustomed. Also, we wanted to offer students an opportunity to connect more broadly and deeply with the people, culture, and/or country to which they would be traveling, taking time constraints into account. To accomplish our aims, we developed a program that focused on sustainable/unsustainable tourism, incorporating the roles of culture and service in regard to Thailand. Like with the European trips, students were required to participate in a Step into the World! class before and after traveling to Thailand. The class was graded with letter grades.

10.1.   Step into the World!: Thailand: Framework

Although the focus of the Step into the World! course my colleague and I co-coordinated was on Thailand, the course was not about Thailand *per se*, and although the focus of the Step into the World!: Thailand course was on sustainable/unsustainable tourism, incorporating the roles of culture and service, we did not intend for the course to be discipline-based. We structured the course to provide a framework that students could use in the future, abroad as well as within the United States, as all interactions have the potential to be cross-cultural (Arredondo et al., 1996; Fouad & Brown, 2000; Pedersen, 2000; Sue, Arredondo, & McDavis, 1992). The framework was based on the American Psychological Association's [APA's] (2002) *Guidelines on Multicultural Education, Training, Research, Practice, and Organizational Change for Psychologists*.

The authors of the APA's (2002) *Guidelines on Multicultural Education, Training, Research, Practice, and Organizational Change for Psychologists* highlighted the importance of recognizing culture. The guidelines follow. Although the guidelines were written for psychologists to work more effectively cross-culturally, for the Step into the World!: Thailand course, the guidelines were applied to both the instructors and students to interact more effectively cross-culturally — with those they would meet on the trip portion of the course and with one another.

- "Guideline #1: Psychologists are encouraged to recognize that, as cultural beings, they may hold attitudes and beliefs that can detrimentally influence their perceptions of and interactions with individuals who are ethnically and racially different from themselves." (p. 17)

- "Guideline #2: Psychologists are encouraged to recognize the importance of multicultural sensitivity/responsiveness, knowledge, and understanding about ethnically and racially different individuals." (p. 25)

- "Guideline #3: As educators, psychologists are encouraged to employ the constructs of multiculturalism and diversity in psychological education." (p. 30)

- "Guideline #4: Culturally sensitive psychological researchers are encouraged to recognize the importance of conducting culture-centered and ethical psychological research among persons from ethnic, linguistic, and racial minority backgrounds." (p. 36)

- "Guideline #5: Psychologists strive to apply culturally-appropriate skills in clinical and other applied psychological practices." (p. 43)

- "Guideline #6: Psychologists are encouraged to use organizational change processes to support culturally informed organizational (policy) development and practices." (p. 50)

In Guideline #1, the authors of APA's (2002) *Guidelines on Multicultural Education, Training, Research, Practice, and Organizational Change for Psychologists* addressed the importance of developing self-awareness, in particular of being aware of how our beliefs, feelings, and values have been shaped by our personal, social, and cultural identities and ways in which our assumptions of what is right, wrong, good, and bad may impact those with whom we find ourselves to be similar or different. When holding greater power, those who hold negative attitudes toward those with whom they find themselves to be different, in the form of prejudice which is based on inaccurate or incomplete information, may engage in discriminatory behaviors. In being aware of our worldviews and ways in which they may impact our thoughts and actions toward others, we may be better able to come to understand others — as separate from ourselves (Ibrahim, 1999) and to have more effective interactions.

In Guideline #2, the authors of APA's (2002) *Guidelines on Multicultural Education, Training, Research, Practice, and Organizational Change for Psychologists* addressed the importance of developing a broad knowledge base and below surface level understanding of others, including the content, valence, and salience of their personal, social, and cultural identities (Root, 1999; Sellers, Smith, Shelton, Rowley, & Chavous, 1998). A broad knowledge base of others includes their socio-political histories and current day realities and ways in which groups with which they identify may have been or are marginalized or oppressed (Crocker, Major, & Steele, 1998; Santiago-Rivera, Arredondo, & Gallardo-Cooper, 2002).

In Guidelines #3–#6, the authors of APA's (2002) *Guidelines on Multicultural Education, Training, Research, Practice, and Organizational Change for Psychologists* addressed the importance of developing skills by applying our awareness and knowledge described in Guidelines #1 and #2 in practical settings using culturally relevant practices (Pope-Davis & Coleman, 1997; Sue, 1997). For example, as the demographics in the United States continue to shift, existing therapeutic practices that largely focus on a subset of the population, White and middle class, may be seen as less and less sufficient to treat growing subsets of the population. To more effectively treat the latter, the authors cited the importance of exploring differences as well as similarities, using assessment tools that are culturally suitable, taking into account culture in case conceptualizations, and being able to use a wide array of interventions (Dana, 1998; Ivey & Ivey, 1999; Parham, White, & Ajamu, 1999; Prieto, McNeill, Walls, & Gomez, 2001).

The authors of the APA's (2002) *Guidelines on Multicultural Education, Training, Research, Practice, and Organizational Change for Psychologists* noted both theory and research to assist us in developing our multicultural awareness, knowledge, and skills as described in Guidelines #1–#6. The first step is akin to Guideline #1 — to be aware of our beliefs, feelings, and values and in what ways they are related to our in-groups and out-groups (Devine, Plant, & Buswell, 2000; Gaertner & Dovidio, 2000). The next step is to continually try to disassociate automatic positive feelings toward our in-groups and automatic negative feelings toward our out-groups. Relevant and accurate information about our out-groups — akin to Guideline #2, appropriate mood, and motivation may aid in this (Fiske, 1998). Increased contact with out-groups may help in this (Pettigrew, 1998), especially if the contact involves equal status and perspective-taking (Finlay & Stephan, 2000; Galinsky & Moskowitz, 2000).

10.2.   Step into the World!: Thailand: The Class

My colleague and I structured the Step into the World!: Thailand class to support students' development of multicultural awareness, knowledge, and skills. To introduce the students to the course framework, we asked them to read Bennett's (1979) "Overcoming the Golden Rule: Sympathy and Empathy." We did not ask them to read the APA's (2002) *Guidelines on Multicultural Education, Training, Research, Practice, and Organizational Change for Psychologists* as collectively the students in the course intended to pursue a variety of majors and Bennett's article may be applied within different disciplines yet closely aligns with APA's *Guidelines*. In his article, Bennett relates sympathy to the Golden Rule, by which people assume similarity and may or may not address or respond to others in ways that are beneficial to them. Bennett relates empathy to the Platinum Rule, by which people assess similarities and differences so that they may address or respond to others in ways that are beneficial to them (Bennett, 1979). Aligned with APA's Guidelines #1 and #2, my colleague and I encouraged students to ascribe to empathy or the Platinum Rule for the purposes of the course and to try to understand before to judge. Bennett (1979) provided six steps by which one may develop empathy: "assuming difference," "knowing self" (p. 209), "suspending self" (p. 210), "allowing guided imagination," "allowing empathic experience" (p. 211), and "reestablishing self" (p. 212). Students identified in which stage they believed they were. The majority of the students identified themselves to be in "allowing empathic experience." Students also shared scenarios they envisioned occurring on the trip for which they believed practicing empathy would be appropriate and possible.

To further introduce the students to the course framework, the first day of class, we asked the students to select subtopics upon which they would focus, in small groups, throughout the course to generate a class video on intercultural experiences. The subtopics follow.

- Why is it important to have intercultural experiences?
- Why is it important to know your own culture(s) to have successful intercultural experiences?
- What habits of mind and behavior facilitate successful intercultural experiences?
- What knowledge facilitates successful intercultural experiences?
- What skills facilitate successful intercultural experiences?

The second subtopic aligns with APA's Guideline #1, the fourth subtopic aligns with APA's Guideline #2, and the fifth subtopic aligns with APA's Guidelines #3–#6. We asked students to garner content for their subtopics from course happenings, outside of class research, and self-reflection.

Although we considered the answers to all of the above questions in the portion of the Step into the World!: Thailand course that took place in the United States, we focused on the last three questions in particular. My colleague and I anticipated that the students would be able to find or discover appropriate answers to the first two questions more readily on their own than the last three questions. In addition, for the second question, we asked students to repeatedly reflect on their culture, Thai culture, and the role of culture in their and others' lives across written journal entries and a personal impact statement.

With a focus on the last three questions in particular, Step into the World!: Thailand course content and pedagogy followed the APA's *Guidelines*. In alignment with APA's Guideline #1, we regularly asked students to try to withhold or address any automatic negative judgments. In alignment with APA's Guideline #2, we frequently encouraged students to seek further information and to strive to understand others' perspectives from others' perspectives. In alignment with APA's Guidelines #2–#6, we structured each class to provide students with relevant and accurate information and hands-on experience regarding Thai language and culture. Each class contained additional content, as well, to meet the overall learning objectives of the course.

10.3.   Weekly Lessons: Focus on Language

10.3.1.   Information and Practice

The first class, we asked students to select Thai nicknames to be used throughout the classes and trip. The use of informal names that in some way describe those who hold them is very widespread in Thailand. My colleague and I wanted to encourage students to internalize this cultural information, as well as to learn and practice some basic Thai words I thought they would encounter while in Thailand. We asked students to select nicknames that characterized them in some way from the words associated with the different letters and sounds in the Thai alphabet. In following classes, class began with a name game to provide students practice in saying and remembering one another's names, and thus 24 basic Thai words.

The following classes, I taught students phrases for a variety of occasions. I also taught them what polite particles to use and when. (Polite particles are used widely by Thais to show respect to the listener.) For students who wanted to learn more of the language, I provided access to a Thai language book/cd for tourists and a Thai language book/cd for beginners.

I taught students basic phrases to which I expected they would be exposed or might find use for regularly, the knowledge and skill of which would facilitate inter-actions while in Thailand. Phrases included those that might be heard when meeting someone for the first time, committing a cultural faux pas, reassuring someone (or being reassured), receiving a kind gesture, and trying to communicate.

To develop their language skills, after new phrases were taught, my colleague and I asked the students to form into small, set practice groups. In each group was someone I had identified as most able to approximate the Thai language to that point, to serve as a role model, and to provide feedback. We then asked students to incorporate the new phrases they had learned into a skit(s) or a real life activity(ies) that was intended to resemble what they may encounter in Thailand. In one skit, group members took turns greeting others in their group by stating, asking, or answering, "Hello," "My name is," "What is your name?," "It is nice to meet you," "How are you?," and "Good-bye." Those, while not speaking, observed. In another skit, each group member took a turn committing a cultural faux pas against another group member. The former would then say, "Excuse me," and the latter would respond with, "It is okay." Again, those, while not speaking, observed.

Sometimes, as stated earlier, we asked students to practice their language as a whole class. In one class, my colleague and I gave students the opportunity to try a variety of snacks they would find in Thailand, for example, shredded dry pork, pork rinds, shrimp chips, pickled mango with chili, tamarind candy, Pocky sticks, grass jelly, Thai tea, and yogurt drinks. Students chose whether or not they wanted to be a possessor of a snack. The students without snacks were responsible for ask-ing those with snacks, "May I have the snack please?" The latter were to oblige, according to the Thai principle of kreng jai, which is to put others' wants and needs before your own, and to respond, "Yes," while handing over portions of or their entire snacks. The receivers were to say, "Thank you," and the givers were to say, "You are welcome."

Students then exchanged roles. Those with snacks became those without snacks and vice versa. The proprietors of the snacks were responsible for asking those without snacks to, "Try it," in other words, to try their specific snacks whether they wanted to do so or not. The latter were to accept, according to the Thai principle of kreng jai, and to respond with, "Thank you." This was followed by the initiator saying, "You are welcome."

In addition to providing an opportunity for students to develop their language skills, in alignment with APA's Guideline #1, we intended the two previous skits to give students opportunities to navigate aspects of Thai culture with which they may have some difficulty, based on a trip that took place in 2013 and based on current participants' answers to the question of which aspect of Thai culture did they believe they might have the most difficulty adjusting. Participants on a trip that took place in 2013 seemed to have difficulty with the Thai food they encountered in Thailand, leaving much Thai food untouched at breakfasts and lunches and choosing foods more familiar to them for dinners and snacks. The majority of the current participants answered that they believed they might have the most difficulty adjusting to sharing with others. Thus, we intended the two previous skits to give students opportunities to become familiar with what I believed they were likely to encounter in Thailand and to manage their emotions, as well.

In another class, as two first year students — a student from Thailand and a student from the United States who had participated in a high school exchange program in Thailand, presented, I interspersed comments to the class in Thai. I had taught the students some of the words. I had not taught them all of the words. I encouraged the students to use the phrases they had studied to help decipher what I was saying, for example, "Could you please speak slower?," and "I only speak a little Thai. Do you speak English?"

I also taught the students phrases I thought would prove useful during specific events on our itinerary, such as our cultural exchange with students at Ratchapat Thonburi University and our homestay at Baan Mae Kam Pong. For our cultural exchange with students at Ratchapat Thonburi University, our students would be teaching the Thai students how to make dreamcatchers and the Thai students would be teaching our students how to make krathongs (i.e., banana leaf floats) and to carve decorative watermelons. To prepare, I taught the students variations of the phrase, "Am I doing this right?" To develop their language skills, when the students were learning how to make dreamcatchers in the United States to be able to teach the Thai students in Thailand, I asked them to, in Thai, ask for and give one another appropriate feedback on their dreamcatchers. I also taught the students a question I thought they may encounter, and the appropriate answer to the question, as they dined on home-cooked meals in villagers' homes in Baan Mae Kam Pong: "Does it taste good?" and "It tastes good."

10.4.   Weekly Lessons: Focus on Culture

10.4.1.   *Information and Practice*

Across multiple classes, we taught the students traditional Thai cultural norms that are still widely held and asked them to enact them during class both in the United States and in Thailand. We told them that they would see Thai people who did not exercise these norms but that it was important that they do, unless a norm violated one of their ethical or moral principles. When we asked the students why we were asking them to act in ways that not all Thais would act, one student responded that as outsiders it was important for us to show that we know the norms, whereas Thais are assumed to know the norms and to choose whether or not to follow them. I followed with, based on my experiences in Thailand, some Thais may have negative preconceptions of us, coming from the United States, based on media portrayals they've seen, and I emphasized the importance of making positive impressions so that we may gain greater access and insight regarding Thai people, Thai culture, and Thailand. Several times throughout the course, I also emphasized the importance of showing respect in Thailand, as a cultural norm and a means of sustainable tourism. Also, in "being Thai," the students may come to better understand the people, culture, and country of Thailand.

We taught the students that Thailand figuratively translates to the "land of smiles," which is exemplified by sunook (i.e., fun), jai yen (i.e., a cool heart), and mai bpen rai (i.e., it is okay). The "smiles" in "land of smiles" refers not only to feelings of happiness but to a form of expression that is intended to facilitate smooth interpersonal interactions. We also taught the students concrete ways in which they may embody sunook, jai yen, and mai bpen rai both in the classroom and abroad.

We taught the students that on a continuum from individualistic to collectivistic that Thais have been found to be more collectivistic (Hofstede Centre, n.d., para. 5). We taught them that emanating from this, Thais believe in raksah naa (i.e., saving face) and kreng jai (i.e., considering others before oneself). We also taught them concrete ways in which they may demonstrate raksah naa and kreng jai both in the classroom and abroad.

Additionally, we taught the students that on a continuum from low power distance to high power distance that Thais have been found to have higher power distance (Hofstede Centre, n.d., para. 3), which may be shown through the reverence paid to the royal family, monks and Buddha images and the differential treatment of those of higher socio-economic status and/or age. We taught the students concrete ways in which they may be expected to act according to their station as it would be in Thailand (and if they were Thai). We also taught the students about the status of different groups in Thai society. Groups included girls and women, people who are perceived as gender non-conforming, people who identify as lesbian or gay, and people with darker skin. In one class, students were shown a succession of pictures of people who would have varying status in Thailand. For each picture, students were asked to exhibit the proper level at which to hold their heads and at which to hold their hands for the Thai greeting and were asked to express the proper polite particle.

Many Thai cultural norms arise from Buddhism, which is the predominant religion in Thailand. We taught the students concrete ways in which they may exhibit these Thai cultural norms both in the classroom and abroad. For example, my colleague and I asked our students to step over the classroom threshold when entering and leaving and asked our students to take off their shoes at the classroom door. We also taught them Thai cultural norms specific to behavior regarding monks, temples, Buddha images, and spirit houses.

10.5. Weekly Lessons: Focus on Additional Areas

To further meet the overall learning objectives of the course, my colleague and I supplemented the lessons on Thai language and culture. Additional content included information on logistics of the class and trip, sustainable/unsustainable tourism, and service. To reinforce the overall learning objectives, we reserved one class period for review activities intended to be fun.

In regard to sustainable/unsustainable tourism, we asked students to watch the movie *The Last Elephants in Thailand* (Dherscher's Channel, 2012) ahead of class. The movie documents cruelty elephants in Thailand may experience, including to prepare them to entertain, for example, by painting pictures, or otherwise serve, for example, by providing rides to tourists. The movie contains examples of repercussions of unsustainable tourism. During class, my colleague presented information on sustainable/unsustainable tourism. Following this, students engaged in a discussion as to how they participate in sustainable/unsustainable practices in the United States and what our group's sustainable/unsustainable practices may look like in Thailand.

In regard to service, we asked students to engage in a discussion on the definition of service. I then presented information on servant leadership and the four service projects in Thailand in which we would be participating that were based on servant leadership. Servant leadership is working with others to accomplish their aims. As such, servant leadership is in alignment with APA's Guideline #2, empathy and the Platinum Rule. The four service projects included planting wild orchids in the forest with members of Maejo University and the surrounding community; teaching English, weaving baskets and putting together tea pillows with villagers in Baan Mae Kam Pong; feeding and bathing rescued elephants at the Elephant Nature Park; and planting corals in the Gulf of Thailand.

In regard to review activities, we gave students the opportunity to demonstrate what they had learned from the classes before within the context of a meal and a game. My colleague and I brought to class different dishes the students may find in Thailand, that is, salabao, green chicken curry, red squash curry, jasmine rice, and Thai custard. In small groups, they approached the serving table. One person from each group was asked to demonstrate the appropriate way to use utensils in Thai culture for the group to be able to eat. I'm happy to report no one was left hungry. Also in small groups, students participated in a jeopardy-like game in which they selected a category, that is, logistics, language, culture, sustainable/unsustainable tourism, or service, were asked a question pertaining to the category, and received

100 points for each correct answer. The members of the winning team won their choice of prizes, for example, Thai ice coffee, Thai tea, yogurt drinks, Mama instant noodles, or Lobo seasoning mixes.

10.6.   Step into the World!: Thailand: The Trip

We required the students to partake in all activities while on the trip. We asked them to emulate Thai culture, practice sustainable tourism, and engage in service as much as possible. Activities were scheduled almost every day from early morning till early evening (Table 10.1).

Table 10.1: Step into the World!: Thailand: The Trip.

Date and Time	Activity
Monday, March 9	
PM	• Arrived at Suvarnabhumi Airport
Tuesday, March 10	
AM	• Explored old Bangkok (i.e., stopped at Pak Klong Talad, the biggest fresh flowers market in Bangkok; took a long-tail boat ride along the Chao Praya River; stopped at Wat Arun, Temple of the Dawn; continued along the Thonburi canals)
PM	• Participated in a cultural exchange (i.e., created joint paintings, dreamcatchers, krathongs, and/or decorative watermelons) with students at Ratchapat Thonburi University
Wednesday, March 11	
AM	• Spoke with the Director of the Thai Ecotourism and Adventure Travel Association
	• Visited Wat Pho, the Temple of the Reclining Buddha
PM	• Visited the Grand Palace and Wat Phra Keow, the Temple of the Emerald Buddha
	• Explored marketplaces on Thanon Khaosan and in Chinatown
Thursday, March 12	
AM and PM	• Visited Ayutthaya (biked around the ruins of the old capital)
	• Took an overnight train to Chiang Mai
Friday, March 13	
AM	• Explored Chiang Mai (i.e., visited Baan Doi Pui, a Hmong Hilltribe Village; visited Wat Phra That Doi Suthep)
PM	• Volunteered with Mae Jo University returning wild orchids to the forest
	• Observed/shopped for local arts and crafts at the Chiang Mai Night Bazaar

Table 10.1: (*Continued*)

Date and Time	Activity
Saturday, March 14	
AM	• At a food market, explored ingredients we would use to cook; shopped
	• Took a Thai cooking class
PM	• At Wat Sri Supan, the Silver Temple, chatted with a monk on Buddhism and meditation; practiced sitting and walking meditation
	• Explored the making of Thai arts in the Wua Lai community, a community in which only a few households continue to produce silver wares at home
	• Observed/shopped for local arts and crafts at the Wua Lai Walking Street
Sunday, March 15	
AM	• Explored Baan Mae Kam Pong, a Community Based Tourism village
PM	• Ate home-cooked meals at villagers' homes
	• Observed/shopped for local arts and crafts at the Thapae Walking Street
Monday, March 16	
AM and PM	• Explored and volunteered at the Elephant Nature Center (i.e., fed and bathed rescued elephants)
	• Continued to explore and volunteer at the Elephant Nature Center
	• Took an overnight bus to Hua Hin
Tuesday, March 17	
AM	• Continued via vans and speedboat to Koh Talu (i.e., Talu Island)
PM	• Trekked to the scenic view point
	• Went squid fishing
Wednesday, March 18	
AM	• Explored and volunteered at a turtle nursery (i.e., fed the turtles, implanted transmitters, released turtles, and picked up garbage along the shore)
PM	• Took part in coral planting instructed by an expert in marine life and coral reefs
	• Went snorkeling to see the corals we had planted, and beyond
	• Went on a night trek to find hermit crabs and chicken crabs
Thursday, March 19	
AM	• Had a leisurely morning
PM	• Returned via speedboat and bus to Bangkok
Friday, March 20	
AM	• Departed Suvarnabhumi Airport

10.7.   Assessment

10.7.1.   *Learning Objectives*

Upon completion of the Step into the World!: Thailand class and trip, we hoped that the students would be able to demonstrate the following Cottey College learning objectives:

- respects diversity,
- thinks critically, and
- acts responsibly.

Also upon completion of the course, we hoped the students would be able to demonstrate the following course learning objectives:

- describe the Platinum Rule,
- describe key components of Thai culture,
- differentiate between sustainable and unsustainable tourism practices,
- describe different types of service,
- embody and facilitate others' intercultural competence, and
- articulate the impact made on them and by them regarding culture, tourism, and service.

To assess gains from the Step into the World! course, my colleague and I put into place several measures. Measures included a survey on intercultural sensitivity, journals, personal impact statements, and a class video. I detail the findings from the survey, journals, and personal impact statements below.

10.8.   Intercultural Sensitivity Scale

10.8.1.   *Design and Procedure*

We used on-line surveys to collect data. One week before the start of class, my colleague and I asked each student to complete a standardized measure that assesses intercultural sensitivity. One week after the end of class (which occurred two weeks after the trip), we asked each student to complete the standardized measure again. We made the surveys available on SurveyMonkey. We sent direct e-mails to students from Survey Monkey asking them to participate. In addition, we posted messages on the Cottey College message board asking students to check their e-mail and to participate in the study. We gave students approximately one week to complete each survey. We secured Institutional Review Board approval prior to recruitment for the pre-survey.

10.8.2. Participants

Nineteen of the twenty-four students who participated in the course completed both the pre-survey and post-survey. All participants were traditionally aged college students between the ages of 19 and 24, $M = 19.84$. All participants were White women and United States citizens.

10.8.3. Instrumentation

We comprised the overall online survey of a consent form, quantitative survey (i.e., one standardized measure and a demographic questionnaire), and thank you. The standardized measure, the Intercultural Sensitivity Scale (Fritz, Möllenberg, & Chen, 2002) was made up of 24-items and five factors: "interaction confidence" (p. 168), "interaction engagement" (p. 167), "interaction attentiveness" (p. 168), "respect for cultural differences" (p. 167), and "interaction enjoyment" (p. 168). Sample questions for interaction confidence included: "I find it very hard to talk in front of people from different cultures" and "I always know what to say when interacting with people from different cultures" (p. 171). Sample questions for interaction engagement included: "I am open-minded to people from different cultures" and "I avoid those situations where I will have to deal with culturally-distinct persons" (p. 170). Sample questions for interaction attentiveness included: "I am sensitive to my culturally-distinct counterpart's subtle meanings during our interaction" and "I am very observant when interacting with people from different cultures" (p. 171). Sample questions for respect for cultural differences included: "I think my culture is better than other cultures" and "I respect the values of people from different cultures" (p. 170). Sample questions for interaction enjoyment included: "I get upset easily when interacting with people from different cultures" and "I often get discouraged when I am with people from different cultures" (p. 171). Students responded to each item on a Likert-type scale of 1 (*strongly disagree*) to 5 (*strongly agree*).

10.8.4. Statistical Analysis

Prior to the analysis, we removed the data from the respondents who did not complete both the pre-survey and post-survey. We reverse-scored the responses, as appropriate, so that higher means reflect more intercultural sensitivity. We assessed internal consistency coefficients to ensure adequate reliability (i.e., .70 and above). We gleaned demographic information and scale descriptives. We conducted a Paired-Sample Wilcoxon Signed Rank Test to assess whether or not the Step into the World!: Thailand course may have had an impact on intercultural sensitivity.

We assessed intercultural sensitivity using the 24-item Intercultural Sensitivity Scale (Fritz et al., 2002). Participants indicated the degree to which they felt "interaction confidence" (p. 168), "interaction engagement" (p. 167), "interaction attentiveness" (p. 168), "respect for cultural differences" (p. 167), and "interaction

Table 10.2: Descriptive Statistics.

	Sample sizes	Cronbach's alphas	Ranges	Means	Standard deviations
Pre-survey	19	.88	3.50–4.58	3.95	.36
Post-survey	19	.86	3.71–5.00	4.25	.33

enjoyment" (p. 168) on a scale of 1 (*strongly disagree*) to 5 (*strongly agree*). Scale descriptives include number of respondents, internal consistency coefficients, ranges, means, and standard deviations. The number of respondents who completed both the pre-survey and post-survey equaled 19. The reliability coefficients for the pre-survey and post-survey were .88 and .86, respectively. The range for the pre-survey was 3.50–4.58 and for the post survey was 3.71–5.00. The mean for the pre-survey was 3.95 ($SD = .36$) and for the post-survey was 4.25 ($SD = .33$) (Table 10.2). A Paired-Sample Wilcoxon Signed Rank Test was conducted to determine if the Step into the World!: Thailand course had an impact on intercultural sensitivity. Post-survey scores were higher than pre-survey scores at a statistically significant level, $Z = -3.10$, $p = .002$. The result suggests the Step into the World!: Thailand course had a positive impact on intercultural sensitivity, barring outside factors that may have influenced students' intercultural sensitivity.

10.8.5. Journals and Personal Impact Statements

My colleague and I asked each student to submit three journal entries — one shortly before the start of the trip, one during the trip, and one shortly after the trip. The journal entries were to form the basis for personal impact statements. The questions for the three journal entries were approximately the same. We asked the students to incorporate their experiences in Thailand into their responses for their second and third journals. The questions attended to personal goals for the trip (i.e., "describe two things you'd like to realistically achieve by the end of the Thailand trip; provide a minimum of one way for each of how you will assess whether or not you've reached your goals"). They also focused on how each student described her culture and Thai culture (i.e., "describe your culture; provide a minimum of two major concepts with a minimum of one piece of concrete evidence for each") and (i.e., "describe Thai culture; provide a minimum of two major concepts with a minimum of one piece of concrete evidence for each"). The questions addressed how each student defined and enacted sustainable/unsustainable tourism (i.e., "describe unsustainable tourism; provide a minimum of two major concepts with a minimum of one piece of concrete evidence for each of how you and/or others have engaged in unsustainable tourism") and (i.e., "describe sustainable tourism; provide a minimum of two major concepts with a minimum of one piece of concrete evidence for each of how you and/or others have engaged in sustainable tourism"). They referred to how each student defined and enacted service (i.e., "describe service; provide a minimum of two major concepts with a minimum of one piece of concrete evidence for each of how you and/or others have engaged in service").

My colleague and I asked each student to submit a personal impact statement one week after the trip. We asked each student to review her journal entries and to reflect upon her progress on her goals for the trip (i.e., "describe a minimum of two things you achieved by the end of the Thailand trip; provide a minimum of one way for each of how you know you reached your goals"). We also asked each student to reflect upon the role of culture (i.e., "describe your culture and describe Thai culture; reflect on the role of culture in your and others' lives"), sustainable/unsustainable tourism (i.e., "describe unsustainable tourism and describe sustainable tourism; reflect on the role of unsustainable and sustainable tourism in your and others' lives"), and service in her and others' lives (i.e., "describe service; reflect on the role of service in your and others' lives"). We also asked each student to reflect upon what she will take forward from the trip portion of Step into the World!: Thailand (i.e., "describe a minimum of two things you will apply in the future from the Thailand trip; provide a minimum of one way for each of how you envision applying your experience").

10.8.6. Analysis

We conducted an examination of students' journals and personal impact statements to determine if the course's learning objectives had been met. Each of the learning objectives seems to have been met to some degree. As students began the course in different places in regard to their interests, knowledge, and skills, and thus may have engaged in Step into the World!: Thailand in different ways, a uniformity of responses was not expected nor wanted. Of the 24 students who participated, 21 students seemed to make progress regarding the majority of the learning objectives. Three students did not. For their personal impact statements, two students wrote considerably of experiences not related to the course. They gave specific, concrete examples of how they had engaged in sustainability and service before the course but did not reflect on how their experiences in Thailand added to those. Another student wrote that she plans to focus on how people are similar in her future travels as she believes differences are minor compared to similarities and to focus on differences is "futile."

A restatement of the learning objectives for the course follows with quotes from students' journals and personal impact statements to demonstrate the growth that took place. The quotes themselves exemplify students' performance regarding the learning objective of being able to articulate the impact made on them and by them regarding culture, tourism, and service. As inferred above, the quotes may not be representative of all the students who participated in the course. However, they lend support for similar experiences to take place.

When taken together, the quotes highlight the importance of having a firm knowledge and skill base that may further be operationalized, reinforced, clarified, and expanded upon. For Step into the World!: Thailand, the development of that knowledge and skill base took place in the classroom. The rest took place outside.

The classroom portion of Step into the World!: Thailand helped in students' learning in that their anxiety dissipated as they developed a basis of information, knowledge, and skills to use and upon which to build. The following students' quotes lend support for this supposition:

> "I have to admit that I was terrified of the idea of going to Thailand because I didn't know their culture and I didn't want to offend any-one within their own country. My feelings of anxiety of course were subsided as I gained more knowledge about Thai language, customs, hierarchy, and mannerisms through class and my actual experience in Thailand."
>
> "A proficient knowledge of Thai culture played a key role in having a successful trip over in Thailand. I remember catching myself once when I dropped a 50 baht bill; I was tempted to step on it so it would not blow away, but I refrained, knowing that was disrespectful to Thais!"
>
> "The Step into the World! class we took was very helpful, and it gave me a stronger foundation to accomplish my personal goals I set beforehand. The ability to adapt to foreign surroundings easier and to generate a better understanding of Thai culture are the goals I made shortly before our travels began."

Some or all of the information, knowledge, and skills taught in the classroom may have been readily forgotten once students left the classroom. However, once in Thailand, students were placed in many situations that called for what they had been taught, which facilitated greater risk-taking to use the information, knowledge, and skills. The following student's quote lends support for this supposition:

> I have always had a difficult time learning languages, but being immersed in Thailand around people who only spoke Thai gave me the opportunity to truly make progress in this. When there is no other choice but to make as much effort as is possible, that's what you do. One week into the trip, we spent an afternoon in Mae Kam Pong Village in the mountains of Chiang Mai. We split into four different groups, and had a homemade lunch in a local's home. There was a minor mistake when my group ended up without one of our profes-sors or tour guides to accompany us and translate. Our host didn't speak English, and throughout the seven of us, we had a memo pad and a laminated card with around twenty Thai terms that we had learned in class. It was challenging, but I left feeling positive about the experience.

Students in that group later told us they had introduced themselves to their host, asked for their host's name, and taken the dishes from their meal to the kitchen to be of help.

10.8.7. *Respects Diversity*

The trip portion also helped in students' learning in that they were placed in situations that facilitated broader thinking and experiences. For example, in regard to the learning outcome of respects diversity, one student wrote:

> The first goal I set was to allow myself to broaden my horizons through an open-minded approach to new ideas. One experience that specifically challenged me while I was in Thailand was squid fishing. I am generally a very animal friendly person and the thought of fishing has always disturbed me. Even as a child I refused to eat the fish I had accidentally caught. This being said, I made the decision to branch out and at least observe this unique activity. By the end of the boating trip I had caught a squid and made a connection with the local fishermen which has been a large part of my interpersonal understanding of the Thai way. I overcame my fear of taking an animal's life and broadened my understanding of Thai people through being open-minded to this new experience.

10.8.8. *Thinks Critically*

Similar to respects diversity but in regard to the learning objective of thinks critically, one student wrote:

> Initially, my two personal goals for this trip were to better understand spirit houses and to better understand the principles behind Buddhist monks and their lifestyles. I definitely achieved those goals. For example, I have seen so many spirit houses at hotels, markets, homes and temples. I saw them in upscale areas and developing areas. At first, I did not understand why less wealthy families would spend their funds on food that ants would eat, but I know now that it is an important part of their culture. Though I will not be putting a spirit house in my yard, I really respect its beauty and message for Thai people: it is an offering of food and drink to spirits on the ground that was broken by the family. For the second goal, visiting many temples and actually meeting with a monk strongly influenced my outcome. Though I am Christian, and not Buddhist, myself, I was able to appreciate the various beliefs of their teachings. The main concern I had with Buddhism and the monks was that women cannot be officially ordained in Thailand, and that they cannot touch monks because it would make the monks "impure." Before visiting Thailand, I also felt offended that women could not enter many ordination halls and certain grounds on temples. While in the end, I still do not agree with the "same, but different" (per the monk we met) concepts for

male and female Buddhists, I have reached a level of comprehension and respect. Our tour guide, Phii Toy, explained that Buddhist women want to get good karma, and comply by the rules, like not being allowed in ordination halls. I understand her stance and respect it. However, I was pleased to learn that Sri Lanka and a temple in West Thailand ordain women as Buddhist monks!

The student was able to think critically and to perspective-take as to the usefulness of spirit houses and separation of women and men in Buddhism.

10.8.9. *Acts Responsibly*

In regard to the learning objective of acts responsibly, my colleague and I wanted the students to understand the meaning of and to take part in servant leadership. Thus, we arranged the four service-learning projects noted earlier for our time in Thailand. We also wanted students to view service broadly and to take it upon themselves to engage in varying kinds of service. The following quotes reveal this took place. One student wrote:

We had discussed in my small group about how service takes on many forms. It can be the service projects that we were involved in. It could be picking up trash along a hike and camping it back with you to throw away, or it can even be as simple as smiling at someone or listening to their story or their cause.

Feeding turtles in a turtle nursery and releasing them into the sea were not service-learning opportunities we had anticipated but ones that were well-received. One student wrote:

I know I truly put others before myself, both the turtles and my peers, in this project. I am vegetarian and very against touching dead animals intended for consumption. Even in my jobs as a nanny and as a baby-sitter, I would avoid it at all costs, or wear gloves if the children really wanted me to make them hotdogs or steak instead of pizza. Thus, it was a big deal for me to reach my hand into the bucket of dead fish to feed the hungry turtles. While I washed my hands thoroughly afterwards, I was not bothered as much as I thought I would be. It felt good to put the turtles' needs before my personal qualms and beliefs.

We were given the opportunity to release three turtles that were ready to be on their own. Only three students were needed to handle the turtles. I asked all the students who really wanted to be one of those who released a turtle to speak to the group so three could be chosen. In her third journal, the student above wrote:

Being from [a beach community], I have grown up learning about sea turtles at the local [marine center]. I've also grown up seeing sites marked off on the beach with pegs and neon tape, delineating the areas mother sea turtles had laid their eggs. Thus, it would have been a dream to actually be able to hold a sea turtle and help it begin a new chapter of its life! However, when I saw how emotional [another student] was, and how eager the other five were, I knew it would be morally right to let them actually release the turtles.

10.8.10. Describes the Platinum Rule

The trip portion of Step into the World!: Thailand aided students' learning in that students were further able to operationalize, to reinforce, or to clarify concepts we had covered in the classroom. In regard to the learning objective of being able to describe the Platinum Rule, students' quotes included:

> "The Platinum Rule differs from the Golden Rule, and they can be applied in different situations in order to reach the best outcome. The Platinum Rule states that others should be treated the way they wish to be, as opposed to how you want to be treated. It is important to know which is the most relevant while being a tourist, and to keep both in mind in different situations. Monks, for example, are not supposed to come into physical contact with females. We had the opportunity to chat with a monk, and learn meditation with him. Everybody had a great time learning from him, and seemed to appreciate him as a person and the fact that he took the time out of his day to do this for us, but when we left, we did not shake his hand. We crouched down and walked away, which is how he wanted to be treated. If we applied the Golden Rule to this situation, it would have been extremely disrespectful."
>
> "We were expected to adopt the Platinum Rule, which means treating people the way that they want to be treated, which I made my main goal. I felt like I accomplished my goal by trying to speak Thai, eating in the Thai way, greeting others in Thai, and practicing Thai mannerisms."

The students were able to identify specific, concrete examples of and to enact the Platinum Rule.

10.8.11. Describes Key Components of Thai Culture

In regard to the learning objective of being able to describe key components of Thai culture, multiple students mentioned collectivism, power distance, and Buddhism in their personal impact statements. Regarding collectivism, students noted party size and interdependence. Students' quotes included:

> "I anticipated Thai culture would be collectivistic. I would not be living with Thai families, so I thought it might be hard to witness this.

However, it was manifested in other ways. I rarely saw just one person in a car or sitting alone at a table in a restaurant. I would often see two or even three Thai people on a scooter riding along the road, and it seemed like most people dined out with their family, friends or companions. Even in ads, like for a local gym in Thailand, I saw groups of friends pictured more often than just one person."

"In Thai culture, the collectivism is much more apparent. When shopping in many of the markets that we visited, it was interesting to see the competing vendors helping each other out, between finding change or suggesting something to buy."

These students were able to view and identify real life examples of collectivism.

Regarding power distance, multiple students wrote of their revelation of the extent to which the Thai royal family is revered. One student wrote, "Though I learned about the monarchy and the importance of the king in Thai people's lives, I did not anticipate his image and the queen's to be everywhere, on our tour bus, on street signs, in Koh Talu's office." Another student wrote, "It was really incredible to me seeing how much the Thai people respect their Royal Family, and how publically they respect the King. Seeing all the shrines dedicated to the King was really amazing and moving to me." The students were able to reinforce the information they had learned regarding power distance in Thailand.

Regarding Buddhism, students wrote of gaining a better understanding of Buddhism and Buddhism's influence on Thai culture. Students' quotes included:

"Buddhism wasn't as complex as I thought it was going to be, but without the monk sharing the meaning of Buddhism, I wouldn't have understood as clearly. I was able to have a primary source in finding out information of their faith."

"I learned that it is not exactly a religion, but a way of life, because they do not worship a higher being (though they follow the lessons of the Buddha and respect his image). I was very interested in the concept of karma and doing good deeds to achieve nirvana."

"At the beginning of the trip I thought that the Thai culture was long-term oriented and the American culture was short-term oriented. After meeting with the monk in the temple, I realized that both cultures are short-term orientated, meaning that they focus on the here and now. The difference is that the American culture focuses on the here and now for selfish reasons, mainly instant gratification, whereas the Thai culture focuses on living in the here and now to help them reach enlightenment through Buddhism."

The students were able to clarify what they had understood about Buddhism.

10.8.12. *Differentiates between Sustainable and Unsustainable Tourism Practices*

In regard to the learning objective of being able to differentiate between sustainable and unsustainable tourism, students commented on social, cultural, environmental, and economic forms of sustainable and unsustainable tourism. Students' quotes included:

> "Unsustainable tourism involves actions that destroy cultures, social structures, or the environment either knowingly or unknowingly. For example mocking Buddhist statues, taking a picture of certain Buddhist images, a woman touching a monk, or consuming more than necessary, especially since Thai's don't recycle plastic and they drink a lot of filtered water out of water bottles, are ways of being an unsustainable tourist. However, sustainable tourism involves doing research before going to another country and while you're there applying that knowledge. While in Thailand we spoke the language, practiced certain mannerisms like stepping over the threshold, doing the appropriate wai to someone, listening to new information at the elephant rescue center and during the orchid planting, or picking up trash on the beach at Koh Talu are ways of being a sustainable tourist because we were a part of the culture as it was, we weren't trying to change it, and we also were trying to leave the places that we had visited in better conditions than when we had come upon them."

> "An emphasis in our Step into the World!: Thailand class was acting as a sustainable tourist instead of an unsustainable tourist. I had never been able to put a word on this concept before. Sustainable tourists make an effort to only leave a positive impact on the place they are visiting. A sustainable tourist may make the conscious decision to eat in a local restaurant as opposed to a McDonald's, take a bike to get around instead of a taxi, or even to turn off the lights and air conditioning in their hotel before leaving for the day to preserve energy resources."

> "This meant that we stayed in places that had ecofriendly practices in place, such as turning off electricity twice a day, to visiting and supporting a village that allowed tourists to experience authentic Thai culture while not changing for the attraction and attention. By participating in these practices I have gained a better understanding of what being a sustainable tourist means and how I can go about traveling and distinguishing between good and bad actions."

10.8.13. *Describes Different Types of Service*

In regard to the learning objective of being able to describe service, students described a variety of service, with a focus on servant leadership, and noted the importance of service overall. Of note, although servant leadership is based on someone else's goals, students were able to see how both others and they benefitted. Students' quotes included:

> "Serving in a different country is a little different because it requires learning a new culture, but what is interesting is that by learning their culture we were already doing service, listening to the reasons behind their projects, spreading that knowledge and performing our service projects were all forms of service. Service comes in all forms and sizes, the small acts of service mattered just as much as the big acts of service."
>
> "Taking part in the service projects helped me understand everything that Thailand is doing to help their society and culture as well as showing us what we can do to support them without intruding and pushing our ideas of what we thought they needed."
>
> "In Thailand, we participated in a lot of service projects like feeding and caring for elephants, planting orchids, releasing turtles and picking up trash on the beach. These activities benefited us because we got the opportunity to help others. However, the Thai people benefited more because they had tourists that tried to impact their environment in a positive manner. They made us conscious of our actions and how to engage in projects that benefited the country. Service is not easy because you have to learn a substantial amount before you can try to do something beneficial for someone else. I have volunteered before, but the service we did in Thailand opened my eyes to just how much more I can contribute to others, especially to my own people. You do not always have to give money."
>
> "The service projects we participated in definitely helped both the environment and people we visited as well as ourselves. By releasing sea turtles, we helped the animals and the conservatory, because we spread its message through our pictures and speech to friends and family. We also benefitted, learning more about the species and what we can do to help them worldwide."

10.8.14. *Embodies and Facilitates Others' Intercultural Competence*

In regard to the learning objective of embodying and facilitating others' intercultural competence, many students wrote of employing Thai cultural norms and the relationship between their "being Thai," sustainable tourism, and service. In addition, one student wrote:

> Over the course of this trip, I feel like I've been able to gain a much greater understanding of how to interact with another culture. Learning how to act when traveling and visiting within Thailand by

partaking in their customs and mannerisms has allowed me to not only become a better traveler but also learn about another culture. This trip helped me become a better traveler by teaching me that when you travel, learning about what that culture expects and how to interact in the most polite ways is one of the greatest ways to have a good experience when visiting another place. By knowing that most Thai's don't raise their voices and do smile allowed for better interaction with local business. I feel I had a better experience overall by acknowledging their mannerisms and being polite by their cultural standards.

The student articulated awareness, knowledge, and skills that are essential components of intercultural competence. Another student wrote:

My first goal was to step out of my box, especially when it came to speaking the language more. I actually accomplished my goal when we went to Chiang Mai and we had lunch in the villagers' homes. With the small amount of words and phrases that I did know in Thai, I asked our hostess what her name was and how she was doing and the group that I was with had responded with our names and we repeatedly told her that the food was delicious.

The student provided a positive model for other students to follow.

10.8.15. *Articulates the Impact Made on Them and by Them Regarding Culture, Tourism, and Service*

To add to what has been stated above, themes that seemed to predominate as to how students would use their Step into the World!: Thailand experience in the future include incorporating aspects of Thai culture into their lives, continuing their intercultural learning, and engaging in more sustainable practices and a wider variety of service. Given Cottey College's mission of educating students to be useful members of a global society (Cottey College, n.d., para. 1), below, I focus on students' quotes regarding continuing their intercultural learning. Some students wrote of attitudes with which they would approach further intercultural learning. Students' quotes included:

"My next goal is to try my best to view everything from other cultures non-ethnocentrically. We have been discussing ethnocentrism a lot in my Language & Culture class too, but actually experiencing very foreign cultures has led me to appreciate what I have actually been learning."
"After coming back from Thailand, I realized that there is more that I want to do. I want to travel more and learn more about other

cultures. I want to immerse myself in other cultures just like I did with the Thailand trip. I want to go back-packing through other countries and spend time with locals like homestay so I can gain more cultural experiences."

Other students wrote of actions they would take differently for future travels. Students' quotes included:

"While I learned many things about Thai culture before I went, I should have made more time to practice the language. Compared with some of my experiences visiting France (where I could converse in the language), I would have learned more and felt more comfortable interacting with Thai people if I could speak more Thai." "My second goal would be to prepare myself more by doing more research and practicing the mannerisms and language more because knowing these things and doing them makes a difference. By being Thai or at least trying made a huge difference, the Thai people were more willing to help us, some of them were shocked, but it also put a smile on their faces because I think it showed them that we cared enough to try."

Taken together, the quotes encompass multicultural awareness, knowledge, and skills needed for intercultural competence.

10.8.16.   *Class Video*

Lastly, students completed a video that expressed the importance of having intercultural experiences and how to prepare to have successful intercultural experiences. The video was based on information covered in class in the United States, experiences on the trip in Thailand, outside research, and self-reflection.

10.9.   Conclusion

Similar to many other institutions of higher learning, Cottey College's mission statement includes a clause about educating students to be useful members of a global society (Cottey College, n.d., para. 1). My colleague and I had the great fortune to be able to try to reach this goal, and various objectives, through both inside and outside of the classroom learning. Multiple quotes from students' journals and personal impact statements provide support for the importance of combining inside and outside of the classroom learning, especially in regard to trying to develop multicultural awareness, knowledge, and skills. The positive and statistically significant difference in the pre-survey and post-survey scores on the Intercultural Sensitivity Scale suggests the same.

I also learned, and believe became and can continue to become a better educator, through combining inside and outside of the classroom learning. As someone who teaches Cross-Cultural Psychology and as someone who is an advocate for social justice, I was able to see, specifically and concretely, in what ways my teaching is meeting, and not meeting, my institution's and my own professional and personal goals and to alter course, accordingly. Taken together, the students who participated in the course, my colleague, and myself may be more useful members of a global society for having had the opportunity to connect our experiences in and out of the classroom.

References

American Psychological Association. (2002). Guidelines on multicultural education, training, research, practice, and organizational change for psychologists. *American Psychologist, 58*(5), 377–402.

Arredondo, P., Toporek, R., Brown, S. P., Jones, J., Locke, D. C., Sanchez, J., & Stadler, H. (1996). Operationalization of the multicultural counseling competencies. *Journal of Multicultural Counseling and Development, 24*(1), 42–78.

Bennett, M. J. (1979). Overcoming the golden rule: Sympathy and empathy. In D. Nimmo (Ed.), *Communication yearbook 3* (pp. 191–214). Washington, DC: International Communication Association.

Cottey College. (n.d.). *Mission, vision, learning outcomes, and values.* Retrieved from http://www.cottey.edu/future-students/the-cottey-advantage/mission/

Crocker, J., Major, B., & Steele, C. (1998). Social stigma. In D. T. Gilbert & S. T. Fiske (Eds.), *The handbook of social psychology* (pp. 504–553). New York, NY: McGraw-Hill.

Dana, R. H. (1998). *Understanding cultural identity in intervention and assessment.* Thousand Oaks, CA: Sage.

Devine, P. G., Plant, E. A., & Buswell, B. N. (2000). Breaking the prejudice habit: Progress and obstacles. In S. Oskamp (Ed.), *Reducing prejudice and discrimination* (pp. 185–208). Mahwah, NJ: Erlbaum.

Dherscher's Channel. (2012, January 4). *The last elephants in Thailand* [Video file]. Retrieved from https://www.youtube.com/watch?v=vy0H37xD3E8

Finlay, K. A., & Stephan, W. G. (2000). Improving intergroup relations: The effects of empathy on racial attitudes. *Journal of Applied Social Psychology, 30*(8), 1720–1737.

Fiske, S. T. (1998). Stereotyping, prejudice, and discrimination. In D. T. Gilbert & S. T. Fiske (Eds.), *The handbook of social psychology* (pp. 357–411). New York, NY: McGraw-Hill.

Fouad, N. A., & Brown, M. (2000). Race, ethnicity, culture, class and human development. In S. D. Brown & R. W. Lent (Eds.), *Handbook of counseling psychology* (pp. 379–410). New York, NY: Wiley.

Fritz, W., Möllenberg, A., & Chen, G.-M. (2002). Measuring intercultural sensitivity in different cultural contexts. *Intercultural Communication Studies, 11*(2), 165–176.

Gaertner, S. L., & Dovidio, J. F. (2000). *Reducing intergroup bias: The common ingroup identity model.* Philadelphia, PA: Brunner/Mazel.

Galinsky, A. D., & Moskowitz, G. B. (2000). Perspective-taking: Decreasing stereotype expression, stereotype accessibility, and in-group favoritism. *Journal of Personality & Social Psychology, 78*(4), 708–724.

Hofstede Centre. (n.d.). *Strategy, culture, change.* Retrieved from http://geert-hofstede.com/thailand.html

Ibrahim, F. A. (1999). Transcultural counseling: Existential worldview theory and cultural identity. In J. McFadden (Ed.), *Transcultural counseling* (pp. 23–58). Alexandria, VA: American Counseling Association.

Ivey, A., & Ivey, M. (1999). *Intentional interviewing and counseling: Facilitating multicultural development.* Pacific Grove, CA: Brooks/Cole.

Parham, T. A., White, J. L., & Ajamu, A. (1999). *The psychology of blacks: An African centered perspective.* Upper Saddle River, NJ: Prentice Hall.

Pedersen, P. (2000). *Hidden messages in culture-centered counseling: A triad training model.* Thousand Oaks, CA: Sage.

Pettigrew, T. F. (1998). Applying social psychology to international social issues. *Journal of Social Issues, 54*(4), 663–675.

Pope-Davis, D. B., & Coleman, H. L. K. (1997). *Multicultural counseling competencies: Assessment, education and training, and supervision.* Thousand Oaks, CA: Sage.

Prieto, L. R., McNeill, B. W., Walls, R. G., & Gomez, S. P. (2001). Chicanas/os and mental health services: An overview of utilization, counselor preference and assessment issues. *The Counseling Psychologist, 29*(1), 18–54.

Root, M. P. P. (1999). The biracial baby boom: Understanding ecological constructions of racial identity in the 21st century. In R. H. Sheets & E. R. Hollins (Eds.), *Racial and ethnic identity in school practices: Aspects of human development* (pp. 67–89). Mahwah, NJ: Erlbaum.

Santiago-Rivera, A., Arredondo, P., & Gallardo-Cooper, M. (2002). *Counseling latinos and la familia: A practitioner's guide.* Thousand Oaks, CA: Sage.

Sellers, R. M., Smith, M. A., Shelton, J. N., Rowley, S. A., & Chavous, T. M. (1998). Multidimensional model of racial identity: A reconceptualization of African American racial identity. *Personality & Social Psychology Review, 2*(1), 18–39.

Sue, D. (1997). Multicultural training. *International Journal of Intercultural Relations, 21*(2), 175–193.

Sue, D. W., Arredondo, P., & McDavis, R. J. (1992). Multicultural counseling competencies and standards: A call to the profession. *Journal of Counseling and Development, 70*(4), 477–483.

PART IV
LEARNING FROM PEERS

Chapter 11

From Profit to Passion: What Business Students Learned from Circus Artists

Emma Stenström

Abstract

Purpose — This chapter examines the infusion of liberal arts studies into traditional business education.

Methodology/approach — The object of study will be the collaboration between representatives of the University of Dance and Circus and the Master-level students of the Stockholm School of Economics. Evidence of the effect of this collaboration will be drawn from interviews, observations, and reflections gathered from the business students.

Findings — This study and its related counterparts show that liberal arts studies incorporated into business programs enhance creativity, professional judgment, social contribution, and personal fulfillment in students. The addition of multiple framing was found to be particularly healthy to the students' educational development.

Originality/value — The involvement of creative processes in business education leads to a more fulfilling and beneficial program for students.

Keywords: Circus management; creative entrepreneurship; interdisciplinary collaboration; contemplative action; embodied learning; art-based business education

11.1. Introduction

What happens when you put business students and circus artists together in a common course? Why would you do it, and what will they learn?

When we created such a course, we thought that it would be good for both groups to broaden their perspectives. The circus artists, who were mostly

Integrating Curricular and Co-Curricular Endeavors to Enhance Student Outcomes
Copyright © 2016 by Emerald Group Publishing Limited
All rights of reproduction in any form reserved
ISBN: 978-1-78635-064-0

self-employed, could learn about entrepreneurship from the business students, and the business students could learn communication skills from the circus artists. However, it turned out that what they learned went much deeper than that — and took some surprising turns.

In this chapter, we will focus on some of the lessons the business students pointed out as being the most important. Some of them were expected, others not, but all of them also taught us what might be missing in traditional business education.

It might not be circus per se that is missing in the business school, but rather the broadening of horizons, and, most important, the addressing of some very basic human questions — at least if one is to believe what these students discovered through the course.

11.2.   The Set-up

The course was a joint initiative of the Stockholm School of Economics, hereafter called the business school, the University College of Dance and Circus, hereafter called the circus school, and Sweden's most well-known contemporary circus, Cirkus Cirkör. It started as part of an interdisciplinary research project about the role of contemporary circus in society, but when the course turned out to be popular and appreciated by the students, it was repeated over five years. While it gave credits, it was seen more as a cocurricular activity, since it was not part of the traditional curricula of neither the business nor the circus school.

The circus artists were all professional artists. Most of them were running companies, and some were very successful artists, with an international reputation. The business students were all first-year master students in management, all of them with a bachelor in business administration from different schools. Most of them had previous work experience and about half of them were international students, mainly from Europe.

Both groups received credits for the course and the business students were also graded. Faculty came from both the business and the circus world and there were always two course directors, one from the business school and one from the circus school. Equality and mutuality were two important principles governing the course.

However, in this chapter, the focus will be on the business students and what they learned from the course and the collaboration with circus artists. The material used is interviews with and observations of approximately 80 business students during three years of the course and hundreds of pages of written material in the form of the students' reflections after the course. All quotations not marked otherwise are picked from the students' written reflections.

11.3.   Educational Philosophy

There were several reasons for why we at the business school chose to work with a circus, the main one being that we already ran a research project on contemporary circuses, and this course started as part of that research project. We wanted to see what would come out of such collaboration, and in particular what the business students could learn from circus artists. We therefore kept, on purpose, the course design as open and explorative as possible.

The course was built on an academic foundation, mainly from the field of cultural and creative industries and cultural economics (Caves, 2000; Hartley, 2005; Hesmondhalgh, 2002; Howkins, 2001; Throsby, 2010). We were curious to see what bringing in contemporary circuses in business education could teach us about the exchange between arts and business, both what art and artists can bring to business life (Adler, 2006, 2011; Austin & Devin, 2003; Darsoe, 2004; Mayeur, 2006; Mugnier, 2006) and the many benefits of arts-based education (Nissley, 2010; Scharmer & Kaufer, 2010; Taylor & Ladkin, 2009). Since we started the course in 2009, there have been other business schools that followed. Recently, EDHEC in France announced, for example, its collaboration with Cirque du Soleil with the purpose to train their business students in creative business (Bradshaw, 2015).

Learning about creative companies is necessary for any business today. Experiences are gaining in importance over goods and services, esthetics is getting more attention, and creativity is becoming a primary asset (Boltanski & Chiapello, 2005; Guillet de Monthoux, 2004; Reckwitz, 2012). Therefore, we realized that it was important for our business students, no matter where they were heading, to learn more about esthetics, experiences, and creativity.

Within the circus industry there are different types of organizations. Apart from traditional circuses, traveling around, and street performers, there are large companies like the Canadian contemporary circus Cirque du Soleil. Cirque du Soleil has thousands of people employed and generates close to a billion dollars in revenues. They have become role models for other businesses with their "blue ocean strategy" (Kim & Mauborgne, 2005) but are sometimes criticized within the circus community for being "too commercial," as the artists pointed out in the course. However, there are also small, artistic circus companies across the globe, struggling with balancing the cultural and commercial, as all artistic enterprises (Bourdieu, 1986).

What we did not expect, but what became the main outcome, was that the students also discovered a lot about issues that are common in contemporary leader and entrepreneurship research (Beer, Eisenstat, Foote, Fredberg, & Norrgren, 2011; Gelles, 2015; George, 2003; Sarasvathy, 2008; Scharmer & Kaufer, 2013; Sinclair, 2007) such as the importance of authenticity, presence, passion, and purpose. This raised questions about what we teach in business education in general, which is a discussion that has received a lot of attention in recent years (Colby, Ehrlich, Sullivan, Dolle, & Shulman, 2011; Datar, David, & Cullen, 2010; Khurana, 2010; Moldoveanu & Martin, 2008; Nussbaum, 2010).

Over the years the course developed but the general principles remained the same. We ran the course collaboratively. For example, if the topic were sales there would be someone from the business school lecturing about sales from an academic perspective, someone from the circus talking about how a circus sells its performances, and finally a street performer, sharing the secrets of selling on the street. This multiple framing of issues was an important principle in the course.

In general, we provided lectures and seminars about topics such as cultural and creative industries, the experience economy, negotiation and sales, the use of arts and design in business, and creative leadership, among others, and then we let the two groups of students design one workshop each. Both groups were given the same task: provide the other group with valuable knowledge from your own field of expertize. Since we were curious about the outcomes, we gave them as much freedom as possible.

The first workshop was set up by the circus artists in the suburbs of Stockholm and contained physical exercises, using the different circus disciplines. The second workshop was set up by the business students and changed over time. During the first year it was more about general topics, such as leadership and innovation, and later became more of a consulting workshop on how to develop each circus artist's enterprise. The idea behind the workshops was that the two groups should not only learn from each other but they should also discover what they could provide to the other. In other words, the workshops had the intention to create mutual benefits for both groups.

A common experience for both groups were that they put words on their tacit knowledge and that they saw, in the encounter with the others, the value of their skills and knowledge. As one business student described afterward:

> To some extent we did not know what sort of knowledge we could pass to the circus students. As management students, we spend so much time with each other, that the knowledge we obtain over the years becomes perceived as common knowledge, even though it is actually gained through hard work and years of education. When we actually apply the tools we learn, they sound rather unimpressive … However, when presented to people who have not seen these tools before, they actually have a strong impact, which is something that I learned through working with the circus artists.

Nevertheless, more important was that the students and artists saw many similarities between management and circuses. As one business student put it, "There are quite evident comparisons such as the juggler who has many balls in the air and multi-tasking skills of successful managers. Many of the words such as 'control', 'balance', and 'focus' are keywords for circus artists as well as for managers." Exploring these similarities, but also different ways of approaching them, became critical issues in the course.

11.4. The Art of Balance

One of the more obvious qualities of both management and circuses is balance, as the students and artists soon discovered. At the business school, balance is a returning theme, from the balance sheets in accounting to the market equilibrium in economics. Still, few students had reflected on what balance means.

Is it a space in-between, or a combination of opposites? A place where forces meet, where there is an equal amount of demand and supply, assets and liabilities, effort and ease, strength and flexibility, masculinity and femininity, energy and gravity, work and rest, what?

Balance can be seen both as positive, such as in life-work balance, and negative in the sense "boring." "Walking the tightrope," one of those circus concepts that are used metaphorically, tends, for instance, to mean that one has to balance between two opposing views with little room for compromise.

In the workshops, the business students were invited to try balancing on a tight-rope and then reflect on the experience. Balance became an embodied experience, which brought new insights. As one of the students put it, "Balance is movement and can never be captured."

Just saying or hearing it is one thing, but it is different when you experience it with your whole body and then discuss it with people who have spent years practicing balance. The insight becomes deeper, more embodied, than in an accounting class.

Consider, for example, how a tightrope walker describes balance in a book about circus:

> Balance is a constant movement in and out of equilibrium. An eternal quest for the perfect poise. No matter how much you aspire to succeed, you only move swiftly in, and then out. As soon as you've attained balance you lose it. If you try to hold on to it, you will fall. (Björfors & Balkfors Lind, 2009, p. 61)

These kinds of statements evoked discussion. What would that mean in management? That you constantly have to move, develop, and change if you want to attain balance?

As soon as you've achieved *balance you lose it. If you try to hold on to it, you will fall.* Are many companies accused of gaining and losing balance? Instead of continuing to develop and innovate, they tried to grab onto that balance they had achieved, and then they fell. Just in the same way as we often do in life. When everything feels perfect, we try to hold onto that feeling, and then we fall.

In management this can take the form of being afraid to lose a position, status, brand, or money, and grabbing onto it desperately instead of developing. One might then lose it all. These were the kinds of reflections the business students made after having experienced and discussed balance with the circus artists. That balance as movement became the main insight for many of the students who translated it into a need for developing for management.

Apart from reflections on what a concept such as balance might mean in practice, another insight from the workshops became how important it is to learn how to recover from a fall and attain balance again. "Problems will arise, but as the acrobats emphasized, it is more important that you be confident that you can solve them because going out of balance will happen and it is important to know that one can get back into balance." Knowing how to fall is an important skill that is lacking in management, according to several of the students. Also, since falling is rarely practiced, it becomes difficult to trust that you can get back into balance.

11.5. Trust is in the Air

Trust has become one of those familiar themes in the business school. Trust is necessary in society, in organizations, in customer relations. As with so many of these concepts, the meaning for the individual student is rarely explored. What does it mean to trust? How does it feel?

Of particular importance in the course was to discover how hard the acrobats worked with trust and how it was not something that came naturally but rather was an acquired quality:

> Once I've let go of my trapeze and I'm in the air, I'm past the point of no return ... All I can do then is to fly and to have trust ... I have to believe that all the hours of training and preparation are engraved in me ... If I see that my aim is off, my whole consciousness tells me to make a correction. But that is just what I should refrain from doing! The catcher corrects, I have to let go and do everything to prevent myself from doing anything at all. I surrender myself and trust ....
> (Björfors & Balkfors Lind, 2009, p. 95)

This description seems to have created some of the significant insights for the business students. What if trust is not something you can take for granted? If it is hard work? Alternatively, as one of the business students described it after the course, "Trust is a big task, an everyday work. You build it up slowly, incrementally."

As with balance, trust is regarded as something temporary. "To have trust is not something you learn once and for all. Having trust is something that needs to be conquered again and again and again" (Björfors & Balkfors Lind, 2009, p. 95).

When the artists described how they worked daily with developing trust it also became clear how trust and emotional issues were related and how important it was to think of it as a relationship. A business student reflected upon it:

> Seeing the interaction between the acrobats showed that in order for them to be successful they have to completely [immerse] themselves into the situation and trust the other person completely. To me what was most interesting was the fact that both the artists commented on the fact that they could feel instantly if there was tension between them and that it hindered the trust. Therefore, they had to deal with all the uncomfortable situations up front in order to strengthen the relationship and be able to work together.

It is easy to imagine how this would have implications for management. Trust is not something you acquire once and forever; trust is created in a relationship and constantly needs to be recreated. Trust is, in other words, a temporary and relational quality, which might even go against our natural instincts.

Two of the artists, Louise von Euler Bjurholm and Henrik Agger, who took one of the first versions of the course, later engaged themselves in a research project about their discipline, pair acrobatics. For one year, they both answered four questions everyday about their physical and mental states and their experience of the contact between them. They also used many recordings as well as diaries. These reflections led to a Master's project entitled "Extreme Symbiosis."

According to them, trust and cooperation are not the same things, although they are interdependent. Cooperation is the tool to create trust, and since trust continuously goes up and down, cooperation can be forced to build up trust when trust is low. In that sense, trust is forced (von Euler Bjurholm, 2013).

Some of the business students doubted that they would ever come across these kinds of trustful relationships in business life:

> The ability to completely let go of a situation and let trust guide your actions and communication is a value that I can only dream of in business relationships. Due to several reasons, I don't believe that any such relationship I will ever have, will reach the same level of trust as the acrobats'. However, to strive for this state of trust is truly desirable, as it constitutes a genuine, mutually beneficial, and authentic relationship where all parties communicate at the same level.

Others were skeptical of the role of trust in business life and business school:

> A few years in business school (among aspiring young professionals) have taught me one valuable lesson — never trust anybody. The "up-or-out"-culture is based on individual performance, and the motivation to work as teams is extremely small.

This is, of course, remarkable and requires attention. Do we not encourage our students to trust each other; do we not encourage trust? The amount of value placed on trust is one of the major areas of concern for those worrying about the future of business education (Colby et al., 2011).

One of the business students also made the link between trust, diversity, and inclusion and believed business can learn from the circus:

> In the circus world, people with completely different skills and sometimes visions have learned to cooperate and to trust each other. They have learned to overcome their differences and to take a collective responsibility, yet still valuing everyone's uniqueness. I believe that this ability to combine diversity and inclusion is a key success factor when it comes to creating good teams and the circus world appears to have come a lot further than the business sector within this area.

11.6. Precious Presence

Circuses as a contemplative space might not be the first association that comes to your mind but there are contemplative elements within the practice. One of the more obvious points is the need for being present, which is also something that is attracting much attention in the business community.

In recent years it has, for instance, become familiar to offer mindfulness training in corporations, especially in Silicon Valley. Mindfulness is originally a Buddhist concept but it has successfully been translated, and ripped of its religious meaning, to Western society with the help of scientific proofs of its many benefits (Gelles, 2015).

One of the main forces behind the mindfulness movement is Jon Kabat-Zinn, Professor of Medicine and founder of Mindfulness-Based Stress Reduction (MBSR), an eight-week long training in mindfulness. He defines mindfulness as "paying attention in a particular way, on purpose, in the present moment, and non-judgmentally" (Kabat-Zinn, 1994).

Without ever mentioning the word "mindfulness" it was present in the learning that took place during the course, especially the juggling part where a juggler sounds very similar to Jon Kabat-Zinn:

> When I juggle, it is as if I leave all that has been and all that will be and I walk into the room of now. The strange thing is that after a while in the now-room, I feel like I'm in all times at once ... In the present, time grows. (Björfors & Balkfors Lind, 2009, p. 89)

The room of now, leaving what has been (the past) and what will be (the future) behind, is the expansion of the present moment. These words could be taken straight out of a book on mindfulness. However, instead of sitting quietly in meditation the students experienced mindfulness through juggling.

Circus is a lot about presence. Apart from the need for the artists to be present, in the deepest sense, to perform the acts, the acts themselves either use or create presence. Think of the magician, for example, whose tricks rely on his or her ability to direct the audience's focus elsewhere, or the acrobat who creates maximum presence within the audience. In traditional Swedish circuses, the audience is, for instance, asked to show "largest possible silence" before an acrobatic act.

Within the course, the learning took place both in the direct embodied experience and in the discussions afterward between artists and business students. Two of the students reflected on the importance of being present to be creative:

> Now I know that if I need to find new ideas, one of the ways I can do it is to forget about the deadlines, stop thinking about the final result I want to get, about the word "must," and just relax and switch my attention to anything that is around me. As one of the artists told me, "You do not know in advance what ideas will come of your current situation, so just pay attention and try to catch it when a new idea is shown to you."

Being in the present moment is also believed to be one of the precious qualities in leadership. We become more compassionate and open in interactions, and we might see others less as the means to achieve an end. Further, the practice of being present is said to decrease levels of stress, increase creativity, improve listening skills, help managers make more ethical decisions, negotiate better, and become more effective

(Gelles, 2015; Sinclair, 2007; Tan, 2012). Therefore learning how to be present, through meditation or juggling, might help in management:

> What also struck a cord in the course was that juggling is described not as an art of catching but rather as an art of throwing. "Catching is not primary, throwing is …." (Björfors & Balkfors Lind, 2009, p. 89)

This made sense among the business students who started to reflect on how they began many projects without really paying attention to how they would be able to catch them. The juggling experience made some of them consider a change of focus toward paying more attention to how different projects are set up instead of just trying like crazy to catch them. This can also be interpreted as a step toward a more mindful approach to management learned through juggling.

11.7. The Central Element of Embodiment

Perhaps the most important element of the course, seen from the business students' perspective, was that it included explicitly embodied experiences. Without having tried to juggle, walk on tightropes, perform acrobatics feats, direct a performance, or perform a clown act, the business students would never have learned as much. It was first and foremost the embodied experience that made them deeply reflect on the meaning of topics such as balance, trust, and presence.

In the circus, the connection between body and mind comes naturally. The body might even be superior to the mind. Louise, one of the acrobat pair we have already met, reflects upon her and her partner Henrik's practice:

> In many of our exercises I cannot decide by my intellect to do this or that, rather it is a series of tiny little steps, which build up trust and memory in the body that makes it able to perform. Of course, this takes place in interaction with the intellect. But I think for me it is the physical sensation that can convince the intellect to do something and not vice versa. It is in the body I feel I have the control or not. (von Euler Bjurholm, 2013, n. p.)

Perhaps it is the same in management, although we rarely address it, thus forgetting that management is also an embodied practice (Ladkin, 2008; Sinclair, 2007). Bringing the body to class was also one of the most valuable lessons for the business students. As one student expressed it, "The most important area of transferable knowledge for business people can be identified as bodily knowledge — the physical experience of self-confidence, trust, and openness."

Another student related the body to trust and to another kind of knowledge that is seldom addressed in business education and noted that he also started to trust his fellow students more after the physical exercises:

> Business students were forced to use primarily their bodies, not their minds, in different tasks ... The difficulties and effort required were felt through the body, creating a kind of knowledge based on experience in a bodily form. Returning to school the next day I strongly felt that I trusted and could cooperate better with those in my workshop group.

We already know that there is a strong connection between the body and mind, but still we teach as if our students were only minds. Louise describes, for example, her and Henrik's learning in the following terms:

> In the beginning it was mostly about what our teacher told us to do, listening to his instructions (theory) and trying to transform it into the body (practice). But the instructions became increasingly embodied; when it had become our bodies' language we were able to use theory by ourselves. (von Euler Bjurholm, 2013)

Does this apply for management as well? As a professor, I have many times observed how important movement is in the classroom. It is through the body the teaching takes place. If I move toward a student, if I lean over, it encourages the student to talk, I illustrate different concepts with my body, I use my voice to emphasize certain points. I change the pace through standing up versus sitting down, I move around the classroom to make sure that every student is involved. Teaching is for sure an embodied practice, yet very little of it was covered during pedagogical training. I am forever grateful to my theater training and my yoga practice because that is where I learned how to teach.

For the circus artists, physical intelligence is key and they also know the importance of taking care of the body. Food, sleep, practice, emotions, everything affects our bodies and therefore the work. From Louise's diary:

> We had forgotten the sandwiches we normally eat before the show, this was not good for the mood or the nerves ... in the number we got nervous and stressed. Technically it went ok, but we did not have a feeling or a sense of each other. The technique became dominant and the character work between us secondary. (von Euler Bjurholm, 2013, n. p.)

The lack of food, or energy, created a distance in the relationship and an emphasis on technique instead of character, which is just one of many things we can relate to whether we are acrobats, professors, or managers. Much of management is practiced as if we did not have any bodies. We stay up late, we sit still, we do not get enough sleep, and we eat badly. Perhaps that also creates distance and an overemphasis on technique. Several students noted that there are things to be learned from circus artists like Louise, "The body and mind work in close cooperation, where a tired body affects the mind as much as a tired mind affects the body, and similarly with a vigorous state."

11.8. Turning Failure into Success

The attitude toward failure was another topic that gained much attention since there were major differences between the business students and the circus artists. "While the artists accepted failure as an outcome that could become reality, business students saw it as something unimaginable."

In another student's eyes, the same goes on in business:

> In business, failure is not accepted and highly career-critical. Therefore, it is avoided at any cost. Even if a failure occurs, people have little experience in how to handle this situation. In many settings, even talking about failures is frowned upon so that even peers are prevented to learn from each other's mistakes. Leaders or managers rarely admit if they are wrong and thus do not set good examples. The personal risk of failing is very high.

What seems to be the case here is fear; fear of failure. Another business student expressed it: "In the business world, failing is intolerable. Investors, managers, and recruiters demand your CV to be filled with successes stories only. Once you have a major failure while occupying an important position, your further career is highly questionable."

The artists viewed fear of failure differently. One artist expressed it this way: "I have taught myself not to be afraid of being afraid. When I'm about to do something difficult, I usually visualize taking my fear by the hand, and then jump in" (Björfors & Balkfors Lind, 2009, p. 69). They also talked about failing as part of the process, "A fall, a failure, a crash: this is a theme very present in the field of circus .... It is one of the most valuable elements of practical knowledge we have as circus artists. We need to go through it to attain control" (von Euler Bjurholm, 2013, n. p.).

This created a lot of sometimes heated discussions in the classroom. At one point a business student said that it was more dangerous to fail in the business world since one could lose one's job. At the circus, there were no jobs to be lost, only temporary contracts. This made some of the circus artists very upset, and they pointed out that failing in acrobatics might mean that you lose not your job or your contract, but your life. Therefore, it is not because of less risk that artists accept failures; failing is rather an inevitable part of the creative process.

Failure was also associated to risk, and once again there are perceived differences between business students and circus artists:

> While artists have learned to use risk, we seem to have learned to avoid risk at all times.
> In business, risk is most often seen as something negative and a feature to avoid to a high extent, most of the artists explained that risk is an essential part of their everyday work and they welcomed risk.

The different views on risk came as a surprise to everybody, including faculty. The artists pushed for the importance of taking risks and accepting failures to learn and develop and the business students learned, "Therefore, inspired by artists, the business can start changing the solely negative connotations associated with failure and see it as the essential element in the learning process. Without trying to do more and in a new way, our society is doomed for stagnation."

In general, the students saw a connection between acceptance of failures and development, which, they also translated into management implications. "In order to really improve the business world's risk averse mentality, I think that we need to focus more on the opportunities that each situation offers and really understand the strong link between failures and development."

The circus discipline that most clearly builds on failure is of course the clown, and it is perhaps a reason for why so many people are afraid of clowns (coulrophobia). It might be related to fear of failure.

In traditional circuses, the clown has an important role, providing a temporary relief between the death-defying acts of acrobatics. The audience can rest a bit and relieve tension through laughter. In a contemporary circus, the clown usually works with social criticism through showing social vulnerabilities and doing things against the norm.

However, the clown can also teach us how to turn failures into success, as one of the business students discovered, "Using a failure as an opportunity also means that you cannot analyze all the risk and possible downfalls because according to the clown you only have about one second to react upon the moment. If you wait too long the opportunity is gone."

11.9. Creative Courage

Creativity is one of those perhaps evident areas where business students and circus artists can exchange ideas. For most of them, the major point of learning was how rewarding it felt to meet people from a completely different area, and many wrote about the benefit of having discovered that. "My most important learning outcome: Be more open to new ways and approaches."

The collaboration in itself also showed the value of working with people with different mindsets. "… Understanding different ways of thinking, interacting with people with diverse mindsets that were yet unfamiliar to me broadened my horizon. The workshop broke down prejudices and stereotypical assumptions on both sides and encouraged outside-the-box-thinking." The understanding and broadening of mindsets might be one of the important, but sometimes forgotten, aspects of business education (Colby et al., 2011; Martin, 2009; Moldoveanu & Martin, 2008).

One way to accomplish it is to broaden the education through collaborations like this one. Perhaps it is especially important if the culture values conformity, which is usually the case with business schools, at least according to the students who participated in the course. One student recalled a conversation he had with one of the circus artists, "I remember one artist asking me after passing by a group of students in the corridor: — Why does everybody look the same here? — Does everybody think in the same way as well? — Oh yes, was my answer. — That's strange, he said."

Many seem to agree that the business world values conformity while the circus world values diversity. Conformity rarely enhances creativity, which might also impede entrepreneurial thinking. One student wrote after the course:

> To me it seems that lots of artists have the courage to break with societal norms. Business students on the other hand lack that bravery and therefore stick to the beaten track. This is a reason why most of us chose a corporate career rather than becoming successful entrepreneurs. In this sense I believe that business students are much more risk averse than circus people, but that through interaction with the artists these aversions might be reduced. Therefore, I believe that the workshop accomplished something that is usually very difficult for business schools to achieve: It enhanced entrepreneurial thinking.

"It enhanced entrepreneurial thinking" was both an unexpected and a positive comment about the course. While we had originally thought the circus artists would learn about entrepreneurship from the business students, the learning went the other way as well. The business students learned entrepreneurial thinking from the circus artists.

Many of the management students were also eager to learn about different methods of creativity from the circus artists, and some were impressed, "The circus-way-of-doing-things: listen-observing-while-doing and plan for spontaneity will gain foothold in the business world since innovation and creativeness are becoming more important."

Others observed that there were not only one kind of creative method but a number of different methods. "It was really interesting to see how the different artists use different methods in order to be creative."

Today everyone is expected to be creative. The German sociologist Andreas Reckwitz, among others, describes how creativity used to be something that was primarily associated with the arts but now has expanded to all areas. Creativity has changed from being something extraordinary to being something normal and normative. Non-creativity is close to pathology and nobody wants to be considered non-creative (Reckwitz, 2012).

One big benefit of the course was that some of the business students also saw and acknowledged their creativity:

> I noticed that I, and probably many other business students, am much more creative than what I thought. During our discussions, I was able to come up with pretty creative solutions and that was nice. It gave me a little bit of a morale boost, which I think is rather important. It is important because in order to dare to be creative, one must feel that one has something interesting to offer. And many business students probably do not think of themselves as creative. So, to understand that one actually is creative is important because it works like a self-fulfilling prophecy.

This student raised an important question for those of us who work in management education: do we make our students believe they are creative? Do we encourage an identity of being creative? If one is to believe this group of students, who come from many different business schools, the answer is no, we do not. So this might be a problem since having a creative self-identity is one of the qualities to look for in a creative individual (Amabile, 1997).

Several of the business students rejected the notion that the circus is more creative than business life. One even suggested that creativity within the arts has to fit into that art genre while in business you can do anything. Business, therefore, leaves room for more creativity than the arts. Others were more skeptical. They believed creativity is important in business, but that it was not always encouraged in all companies, or in business education, mainly because, as we have already seen, failures are not. "You are never encouraged to improvise, to apply a trial and error approach, and mistakes are not appreciated. But maybe mistakes are the essence of the creative process." Or, in another student's words, "Circus is about imagination, fantasy, dreams, entertainment — the impossible. The business world is based on the opposite basic principles; structure, reality, plans, control — the possible."

These quotations illustrate the difference between an entrepreneurial mindset, where imagination and fantasy of course are important, and a managerial mindset, where the outcomes are already defined (Sarasvathy, 2008). But it also tells the story about the view of business as something that does not include imagination, dreams, and entertainment; as something that is realistic, serious, and perhaps even boring. Business, in these students' eyes, seems to be a place without magic.

As one of the business students noticed, there were also differences in the ambitions between the business school and the circus school. While the business school, according to this student, declared on its website that 94% of graduates have jobs within three months of graduation, the circus school presented themselves in the following words, "We do not train people for today's demands; we aim at that which will come. Our students and their visions will challenge the present and change the world!"

Perhaps business education has something to learn from arts education. Those who have criticized business education in recent years notice the lack of an entrepreneurial mindset among business students. Colby et al. (2011) believes, for example, that entrepreneurship and innovation are areas where there is a largely unrealized potential for integrating arts in the business curricula since it helps students develop an ability to frame problems in multiple ways, to deal with complexity and uncertainty, to think creatively, and, perhaps most important of all, "to search for and find passion" (p. 158).

11.10.   Inside-out or Outside-in?

The major and unexpected outcome of the course was that it started much existential questioning. What am I here for? What should I do with my life?

These kinds of questions could, of course, be discussed in a traditional class, but the advantage of putting two widely different groups (business students and circus artists) together is that they saw alternative paths more clearly. One business student described his interpretation like this:

> I observed that both groups use oppositional strategies when it comes to career planning. The business students use pretty much an outside-in strategy creation technique: They look at the job market and identify jobs or industries that are most attractive to them for reasons like high salaries, demanding tasks, challenging activities and good development opportunities. These are often industries like management consulting and investment banking. Then they look for the job requirements in those fields. Based on this analysis they develop a strategy that enables them to fulfill these requirements. It includes choosing a good university, studying a lot, going on exchange, learning new languages, engagements in lots of extra-curricular activities, internships, etc. In other words: They become what the high-potential job market wants them to be. The artists on the other hand follow an inside-out strategy development procedure. They look at their skills, talents and passions — at what they are good at and what they like doing. Then they start developing those skills and start working on different performances. In the end they hope that somebody likes what they do and that they will be able to earn money with their art. In other words: They become what they want to be and hope that the market likes it.

The different paths were interpreted as different kinds of motivation. While the circus artists were thought to be intrinsically motivated, the business students were driven by external measures of success or were extrinsically motivated.

Many students seemed to see a link between passion and motivation. Finding and following their passions became an important goal for many of them after having met with the circus artists. One student explained how she saw the difference between the two groups:

> One topic that I thought a lot about during and after the workshop is career choice and life planning. I noticed a big difference between the business students and the artists. Most of the business students have a very rational approach: after college they decide to go to business school and pursue an education that will later enable them to find a job that secures their future. Many of the students do not really know what they want to do in life but by choosing this path the probability of being financially successful in the future is pretty high. It is a path that is very common and broadly accepted in society. Most of the artists, on the other hand, started to do something they liked, although they never knew if they would ever be able to earn any

> money from it. They started with their passion and tried to develop it,
> to be able to make a living from it some day.

This might of course not be true, but the interesting thing is the interpretation. The passion of the circus artists, and the lack of passion among business students, was a theme that came back many times. For some students it became a reminder that they needed to find that passion they had before starting business school, a passion they rarely met in business school. One wrote, "I got to revisit a lot of the things that I left behind a very long time ago," and another one reflected in more general terms:

> Some people live their life by devoting it to their passion. You live to
> work and work consists of the things you enjoy the most. You do not
> expect to earn money, to make life easy or to live it as "ordinary" peo-
> ple. You have a gift or a passion, and you devote all your time to this
> activity. As a business student you rarely meet people like this,
> because we work to live. Work is necessary in order to survive; work
> is what gives you the money which you later can spend on vacation, a
> big house, luxury products and services that facilitate your everyday
> life.

A reason for why business students are more extrinsically motivated and artists more intrinsically motivated could be their different education. Arts education is much more focused on the individual student, classes are smaller, students receive individual feedback, and they work closely with their professors, while business education is much more mass-produced, which creates less room for individuals to develop their passion and puts more focus on external measures such as grades or, later, salaries. We might, therefore, have designed business education to create individuals who are more extrinsically motivated, and it might also affect their learning. "Many business students are very focused on receiving good grades, rather than learning something and developing themselves."

The business students also feel a strong pressure to perform according to somebody else's standard. One business student analyzed these different forms of motivation and their effect on others:

> When business students and circus artists come together, it is a meet-
> ing between two very different worlds. Each world has prejudices
> about the other. The circus artists think the business students are cold
> and unfriendly while the business students think that the circus artists
> are a bit crazy and weird. I can understand the prejudices that the two
> worlds of business and circus have of the other. Of course business
> students can seem unfriendly, but maybe they have to be to endure in
> their world of feeling the constant external pressure to perform. I can
> also understand why circus artists can seem a bit crazy, they do not
> act according to the expected norms of behavior.

Beside this "constant pressure to perform," some business students also seem to be uncertain about their choices and afraid of not having made the right choice themselves. As one business student expressed it, "It's threatening to meet people that have made completely different choices from us. What about if they are right?"

Who decides what is a good choice? Is it you, or is it someone outside, who gives you status? What is more important in the long run? These are the kind of questions that were discussed a lot during the workshops.

For many business students, this became the key take-away from the course, which tells us a lot about business education in general — and what is lacking in it:

> The workshop has reminded me to turn that coin around from time to time and to look at both sides! As most people in business schools, I often pay too much attention to what other people like professors, recruiters or the job market want me to be. I should rather pay more attention to my skills, talents, expectations and passions, and do what I want to do, to become who I want to be. The workshop has helped me to keep in mind that my personal development should be based on both the inside and the outside view of myself.

Addressing these kinds of existential questions, the source of all creation, might be the biggest contribution arts can bring to business. While we have tended to focus either on the products or expressions of artistic work or the processes, perhaps now is the time to concentrate on the source behind all creation (Scharmer & Kaufer, 2010, 2013). This becomes particularly important when creating something new in entrepreneurship and innovation, for example (Scharmer, 2009), which is also what one of the business students observed:

> In the innovation workshop organized by us, we tried to explain how we look at innovation. We showed some diagrams and charts, which the artists had some difficulties understanding. After all how can one boil down this complex process to a graphic on the board? Also, moreover how can you innovate full heartedly if you are not really sincere in what you are doing?

As the students themselves noted, finding one's own passion and drive might be more important than ever, and the arts might even serve as a role model in a society where people want to work creatively and follow their passion. The discussion therefore had management implications:

> The main conclusion is then, that managing the talents of my generation possibly will be like managing artists — at least, because intrinsic motivators will be shared. This serves as a strong indicator that creative leadership has a clear role in future management and that management as a discipline will have to seek new inspirations.

However, most important of all, meeting with the circus artists and discussing each other's dreams had implications for individual students, such as this one:

> To hope and have the imagination to do that what we truly wish for and follow our dreams, can only be described as — a life worth living for. Dreams are the reason for our being, to pursue them is exactly why we are here, to be happy. Finding one's dream and then simply go for it, is a lesson one can definitely learn from the circus. However, the biggest risk of all must be to be stuck in a life with no joy.

11.11.   Leading with Authenticity

It is not all about finding and fulfilling your own passion; it is also about helping others to do it. This perspective was partly lacking in the course. The discussions often stopped at what the artists and students wanted, not what they could do for others, although we know that serving others and fulfilling a higher purpose is the basis for leadership (Beer et al., 2011).

Some business students even seemed surprised to find traces of that kind of thinking among the circus artists, as if it was something they had never come across in business school. One student noted, slightly surprised, "The circus artists looked upon good leaders as selfless people: they give to others without knowing if they will receive something in return. Their primary wish is to do something good, rather than to be perceived as significant persons by others."

Would it be different in business? Why? In leadership theory, we talk a lot about the importance of having a higher purpose, of leading with authenticity, but also of leading with less ego (Scharmer & Kaufer, 2013; Sinclair, 2007).

While the higher purpose was not always evident, some of the other teachings in contemporary leadership theory seemed to happen in this course. For instance, authenticity became a topic and several of the students wrote that they believed the artists would make good, authentic leaders since they were so true to themselves. "I think that I met a couple of authentic leaders. They exhibited genuine passion, had a strong conviction, were originals not copies, and they based their actions on their values. I think that artists can be great leaders."

Authentic leadership is suggested to emerge from self-awareness. To be authentic you must know your true self (beliefs, preferences, values, strengths, and weaknesses) and act in accord with that true self. However, it is not the whole story. Authentic leaders must also understand what drives them and balance their intrinsic and extrinsic motivations. In other words, they are driven both by inner values, such as personal growth and helping people to develop, and external validation, like financial rewards and recognition.

Since leaders cannot succeed on their own, authentic leaders build support teams that can advise them in times of difficulty and celebrate with them in moments of success. And, perhaps most important of all, authentic leaders lead with a higher purpose, not just fulfilling their own goals but actually serving others and wanting to make a difference in the world. In short, authentic leaders show a passion for their purpose, practice their values and principles, and lead with both their hearts and their heads (George, 2003).

For some of the business students, the course even created a change in the direction their lives took. Some started their companies. Others remembered that they had an artistic background themselves, "I am now willing to find a way of combining my business & economics education with my artistic knowledge in order to do something that would make a difference, something that I would really enjoy doing instead of only enjoying the benefits it brings."

Once again, we come back to the existential questions of following your own passion, and not only performing according to someone else's standard of doing things that make a difference, but exploring what you are meant to do and your dreams. Perhaps that should be the goal of any education, whether it is in business or the arts. And perhaps that is what mostly has gone missing in our professional educations (Deresiewicz, 2014). Or as one business student expressed it in her reflection after the course:

> A young woman, with a particular belief in the economy of hearts, is riding her bike home.... She thinks back one year, to the time before she started the master program in management. She was uncertain of her capabilities, she was afraid that her dreams were naïve. This time, she is riding her bike with confidence, thinking of the adventures ahead of her. Thinking that those days in Alby enhanced what had started to grow. Those circus artists gave of their passion and devotion, they were not afraid of failure since failure is part of the game. Instead, they trusted themselves and by doing so they transformed the trust in others. The feeling that manifested itself in the girl ... many years ago is back. Everything is possible again and it is allowed, and even encouraged, to dream those big dreams.

11.12.   Conclusions

Regarding the implications for business education, the course showed that what can be accomplished is in line with what others have suggested. The study from Carnegie Foundation Studies in Higher Education suggests, for example, the integration of liberal arts in business education in order to enhance creativity, professional judgment, social contribution, and personal fulfillment. In particular there is, according to the Carnegie Report, a need to add *multiple framing*, involving the questioning of assumptions and dealing with ambiguity, and *the reflective exploration of meaning*, which raises "questions such as what difference does a particular understanding or approach to things make to who I am, how I engage the world, and what it is reasonable for me to imagine and hope" (Colby et al., 2011, p. 60). We believe that this course stimulated both.

Multiple framing became an obvious theme throughout the course since the business students and the circus artists came from such different backgrounds and since we deliberately worked with presenting perspectives from both the business and the circus world.

Reflective exploration of meaning became the main outcome, as has been shown above, since there were so many questions about passion and drive: what you want to do in your life, which path you choose and why, and what you can contribute with.

There are also other authors who have emphasized the need to introduce a more multidisciplinary way of thinking in order to break from the ordinary numbers-only, ethically blind view of the world which business education has developed into (Agier & March, 2011). Understanding that there are different ways of thinking and encouraging the use of different models is another important task for business education (Moldoveanu & Martin, 2008). This seems to have been, at least partially, accomplished through the course.

While it is not always addressed explicitly by those criticizing business education (Colby et al., 2011; Datar et al., 2010; Khurana, 2010; Moldoveanu & Martin, 2008), the lack of a discussion about these kinds of existential questions seems to be one of the serious problems. If the students do not know or trust their passion, they will continue to look outside for rewards, which might create a lot of the problems we have in society today. Further, as a society, we might miss many entrepreneurs and innovators.

This chapter has only covered a small portion of all the benefits that came out of the course and collaboration between business students and circus artists. There are, of course, many more. Still, it shows how traditional business education might be lacking certain qualities that might be even more important in the future, such as the ability to find one's own passion and drive from within, to find meaning, to learn how to improvise and handle failures, to see things from multiple perspectives, to believe in one's own abilities, including being creative, to embrace diversity, to dream and see opportunities, to integrate the body and the mind, and to contribute to society, among other things.

Summing up, in more detail, the course shed light on:

- The benefits of bringing different disciplines together since it gives the students an opportunity not only to learn about others but also to see and value their knowledge and skills and to put words on their tacit knowledge. In the case of the business students, they learned that they were also creative although it had not been encouraged in their business education.
- How one can learn from having multiple perspectives on a certain topic, for example "sales," which were looked at from both a business and artistic point of view, an academic and practical view, and from an informal and formal point of view by bringing in academics and practitioners from business, circuses, and street performers. What seems important is to treat the different perspectives equally, make sure they are always included at all different levels, from faculty to actual projects, and to make sure the course and collaboration are mutually beneficial.
- That there is a lot to learn about management from specific disciplines within the circus, for example how "balance," which is something both the manager and the tightrope dancer strive for, is never permanent.

- How useful it can be to look at leadership from another perspective and how this came to include aspects such as values, communication, trust, diversity, inclusion, improvisation, and, not the least but often forgotten in business education, the body.
- How creativity is not always encouraged at the business school and how it involves being open to diversity, uncertainty, and failures; how it takes time and always involves risks; how one can learn from those criticizing, and from failing.
- How business education might stimulate more of a managerial rather than an entrepreneurial mindset, and that there is a lot to learn about entrepreneurship from artists, especially when it comes to seeing opportunities, to find and build on one's own passion, to have and follow dreams, and to create what is usually not considered serious but rather frivolous among academic scholars in business: magic.
- The importance of reflecting upon the meaning of work and from where motivation comes, from the inside or from the outside.
- The need to raise and discuss existential questions in order to get to the source behind all creation, whether of a business or a performance.

References

Adler, N. (2006). The arts and leadership: Now that we can do anything, what will we do? *Academy of Management Learning and Education*, 5(4), 466–499.

Adler, N. (2011). Leading beautifully: The creative economy and beyond. *Journal of Management Inquiry*, 20(3), 208–221.

Agier, M., & March, J. (2011). *The roots, rituals, and rhetorics of change: North American business schools after the second world war*. Palo Alto, CA: Stanford Business Press.

Amabile, T. (1997). Motivating creativity in organizations: On doing what you love and loving what you do. *California Management Review*, 40(1), 39–58.

Austin, R., & Devin, L. (2003). *Artful making: What managers need to know about how artists work*. Upper Saddle River, NJ: FT Prentice Hall.

Beer, M., Eisenstat, R., Foote, N., Fredberg, T., & Norrgren, F. (2011). *Higher ambition: How great leaders create economic and social value*. Cambridge, MA: Harvard Business Review Press.

Björfors, T., & Balkfors Lind, K. (2009). *Inside a circus heart*. Stockholm: Cirkus Cirkör.

Boltanski, L., & Chiapello, E. (2005). *The new spirit of capitalism*. London: Verso.

Bourdieu, P. (1986). *Distinction: A social critique of the judgement of taste*. London: Routledge.

Bradshaw, D. (2015). Edhec business students join the circus. *Financial Times*, February 19.

Caves, R. (2000). *Creative industries*. Cambridge, MA: Harvard University Press.

Colby, A., Ehrlich, T., Sullivan, W., Dolle, J., & Shulman, L. (2011). *Rethinking undergraduate business education: Liberal learning for the profession*. San Francisco, CA: Jossey-Bass.

Darsoe, L. (2004). *Artful creation: Learning-tales of arts-in-business*. Copenhagen: Samfundslitteratur.

Datar, S., David, G., & Cullen, P. (2010). *Rethinking the MBA: Business education at a crossroads*. Cambridge, MA: Harvard Business Review Press.

Deresiewicz, W. (2014). *Excellent sheep: The miseducation of the American elite and the way to a meaningful life*. New York, NY: Free Press.

Gelles, D. (2015). *Mindful work: How meditation is changing business from the inside out.* London: Profile Books.

George, B. (2003). *Authentic leadership: Rediscovering the secrets to creating lasting value.* San Francisco, CA: Jossey-Bass.

Guillet de Monthoux, P. (2004). *The art firm: Aesthetics management and metaphysical marketing, from Wagner to Wilson.* Palo Alto, CA: Stanford University Press.

Hartley, J. (Ed.). (2005). *Creative industries.* Oxford: Blackwell.

Hesmondhalgh, D. (2002). *The cultural industries.* London: Sage.

Howkins, J. (2001). *The creative economy: How people make money from ideas.* London: Allen Lane, The Penguin Press.

Kabat-Zinn, J. (1994). *Wherever you go, there you are: Mindfulness meditation in everyday life.* New York, NY: Hyperion Books.

Khurana, R. (2010). *From higher aims to hired hands: The social transformation of American business schools and the unfulfilled promise of management as a profession.* Princeton, NJ: Princeton University Press.

Kim, C., & Mauborgne, R. (2005). *Blue ocean strategy. How to create uncontested market space and make competition irrelevant.* Cambridge MA: Harvard Business Review Press.

Ladkin, D. (2008). Leading beautifully: How mastery, congruence, and purpose create an aesthetic of embodied leadership practice. *Leadership Quarterly, 19*(1), 31–41.

Martin, R. (2009). *The design of business: Why design thinking is the next competitive advantage.* Cambridge, MA: Harvard Business Press.

Mayeur, C. (2006). *Le manager à l'ècoute de l'artiste.* Paris: Éditions d'organisation.

Moldoveanu, M., & Martin, R. (2008). *The future of the MBA: Designing the thinker of the future.* Oxford: Oxford University Press.

Mugnier, H. (2006). *Art et management. Du fantasme à la réalité.* Paris: Les éditions demos.

Nissley, N. (2010). Arts-based learning at work: Economic downturns, innovation upturns, and the eminent practicality of arts in business. *Journal of Business Strategy, 31*(4), 8–20.

Nussbaum, M. (2010). *Not for profit: Why democracy needs the humanities.* Princeton, NJ: Princeton University Press.

Reckwitz, A. (2012). *Die Erfindung der Kreativität — Zum Prozess gesellschaftlicher Ästhetisierung [The invention of creativity — On the aestheticisation of society].* Berlin: Suhrkamp.

Sarasvathy, S. (2008). *Effectuation.* Cheltenham: Edward Elgar Publishing.

Scharmer, O. (2009). *Theory U: Leading from the future as it emerges: The social technology of presencing.* San Francisco, CA: Berrett-Koehler Publishers.

Scharmer, O., & Kaufer, K. (2010). In front of the blank canvas: Sensing emerging futures. *Journal of Business Strategy, 31*(4), 21–29.

Scharmer, O., & Kaufer, K. (2013). *Leading from the emerging future: From ego-system to eco-system economies.* San Francisco, CA: Berrett-Koehler Publishers.

Sinclair, A. (2007). *Leadership for the disillusioned: Moving beyond myths and heroes to leading that liberates.* Crows Nest: Allen & Unwin.

Tan, C.-M. (2012). *Search inside yourself: The unexpected path to achieving success, happiness (and world peace).* San Francisco, CA: Harper One, Harper Collins Publishing.

Taylor, S., & Ladkin, D. (2009). Understanding arts-based methods in managerial development. *Academy of Management Learning & Education, 8*(1), 55–69.

Throsby, D. (2010). *The economics of cultural policy.* New York, NY: Cambridge University Press.

von Euler Bjurholm, L. (2013). Extreme symbiosis. Master's thesis, University College of Dance and Circus in Stockholm, Sweden.

Chapter 12

Peer Mentoring in Higher Education and the Development of Leadership Skills in Mentors

Andrea North-Samardzic and Michael Cohen

Abstract

Purpose — We examine the question of whether peer-mentoring programs in higher education develop leadership skills in student mentors.

Methodology/approach — The various forms of peer mentoring are discussed, as well as the benefits that these programs can bestow on mentors. We then turn to a discussion of the relationship between peer mentoring and leadership, and place particular emphasis on implicit leadership theories and the research in this area. A case study of a large peer-mentoring program at an Australian university is undertaken and the various aspects of implicit leadership theory are examined in the light of comments collected from both mentees and mentors.

Findings — Evidence of implicit leadership skills of mentors was seen in the responses of mentees. However, the explicit treatment of leadership skills in the peer-mentoring program needs to be approached in a more deliberate manner if students are to benefit fully from the experience of mentoring.

Originality/value — While the results of this study were inconclusive, it does provide a basis for further inspection of leadership development within peer-mentoring communities.

Keywords: Implicit leadership theory; mentoring programs; higher education; peer mentoring

Integrating Curricular and Co-Curricular Endeavors to Enhance Student Outcomes
Copyright © 2016 by Emerald Group Publishing Limited
All rights of reproduction in any form reserved
ISBN: 978-1-78635-064-0

12.1.   Introduction

Mentoring in higher education institutions can make a significant impact on student outcomes. There are a variety of mentoring programs that provide benefits for both mentors and mentees (Christie, 2014), such as formal programs with peer mentors, as well as informal mentoring relationships with members of faculty and student advisors (Driscoll, Parkes, Tilley-Lubbs, Brill, & Pitts Bannister, 2009). Given the time and funding dedicated to formal peer-mentoring programs at colleges and universities around the world, in this chapter we focus our attention specifically on such programs.

Jacobi's (1991) extensive review reinforced that view that mentoring is critical for the student experience, with subsequent research extolling the benefits of mentoring programs. However, Crisp and Cruz (2009) caution that measuring the exact nature of student outcomes is challenging, particularly attributing improved outcomes specifically to mentoring programs. We take heed of such caution and in this chapter examine one oft-cited outcome of peer-mentoring programs: leadership.

While it is frequently stated that peer mentoring develops the leadership capabilities of mentors, we take a critical look at this assumption and ask, "do peer-mentoring programs actually develop mentors to be leaders?" This is an important question to ask given that the leadership development aspect of peer-mentoring programs is so attractive that one of the recommendations from an influential US-wide study on developing leadership capacity in students in general is that they have mentoring relationships (Dugan & Komives, 2007).

The chapter proceeds as follows. First, the general aspects of a peer-mentoring program are described. We then examine implicit leadership theory (ILT) and its usefulness for understanding leadership in the context of peer mentoring. This is followed by a discussion of the leadership aspects of such a program before applying ILT to analyze a peer-mentoring program in an Australian university. Finally, we draw some conclusions that point to the need for further research if leadership is to be an important factor in the design of such programs.

12.2.   Peer Mentoring

Peer-mentoring schemes differ greatly across institutions, and it is challenging to have a "universal definition" that encompasses such diversity (Collings, Swanson, & Watkins, 2015). However, there are common elements that traverse institutional contexts. In most instances, incoming first-year students are matched with a more senior student as an advisor to assist in their transition into higher education or advanced degrees, with mentors often having more than one mentee in order to form a group (Heirdsfield, Walker, Walsh, & Wilss, 2008; Terrion & Leonard, 2007). Unlike a peer tutor, who usually provides academic guidance on specific subjects and assignments, peer mentors advise mentees on the *hidden curriculum*, the skills and competencies required to meet the objectives of the official curricula

(Collings, et al., 2015). Importantly, human development and the improvement of student outcomes is the essential premise of mentoring schemes (Allen & Eby, 2011).

Jacobi's (1991) conceptualization of mentoring relationships continues to be used by researchers as analytical categories: emotional and psychological support, assistance with career and professional development, and role-modeling. This was later extended by Crisp (2009), and Nora and Crisp (2007) to include academic subject knowledge support and was further refined by Colvin and Ashman (2010) to identify the roles that mentors play and not just the functions of mentoring relationships.

Colvin and Ashman's (2010) findings pointed to five roles of peer mentors. The most dominant was "learning coach," accounting for nearly half of all responses. Here, students facilitate their mentees develop academic skills and strategies for their study programs. The next most common roles were "student advocate" (mentors act as a liaison between mentees and faculty) and "connecting link" (introducing students to campus resources). The least common roles were "peer leader" via role-modeling and "trusted friend." A more recent study on these roles by Holt and Lopez (2014) prioritized them as "learning coach," "trusted friend," "connecting link," "peer leader," then "student advocate." Even though the roles were prioritized differently, they illustrate that unlike other mentor relationships, peer mentors serve more psychosocial functions than career-related functions and provide increased social support (Ensher, Thomas, & Murphy, 2001).

According to Terrion and Leonard's (2007) peer mentors must have certain attributes to fulfill these roles. These include the ability and willingness to commit time, matching of gender and race (though whether gender and race matching leads to improved outcomes has mixed findings), more university experience than mentees, and academic achievement; prior mentoring experience was not considered to be necessary. To fulfill the career-related function of the mentoring relationship, prerequisites include having a similar program of study and motivation for self-enhancement. To fulfill the psychosocial function, peer mentors must have suitable communication skills, supportiveness, trustworthiness, empathy, a personality match to their mentee, enthusiasm, and flexibility (both in terms of scheduling meetings as well as in dealing with the variety of topics that might be raised unexpectedly).

While activities can be as varied as off-campus visits to professionals in their future fields or volunteer work, the most common activity tends to be weekly or fortnightly meetings to discuss academic matters such as study tips, advice on interacting with professors in class, or how to manage course loads (Rodger & Tremblay, 2003). This usually occurs through mentors offering support, advising on campus resources, and sharing past experiences (Fox & Stevenson, 2006). It is worth noting that such meetings and interactions are becoming increasingly electronic with students using digital platforms and technologies such as learning management systems (Shrestha, May, Edirisingha, Burke, & Linsey, 2009) and other forms of computer-mediated communication (Ensher, Heun, & Blanchard, 2003; Leidenfrost, Strassnig, Schabmann, Spiel, & Carbon, 2011).

As peer-mentoring schemes are designed to assist students, whether they achieve the intended outcomes has been the object of significant attention. Findings are mixed which is often attributed to the variation in programs across institutions (Crisp & Cruz, 2009). An additional issue is the difficulty of abstracting the individual mentor from the mentoring program insofar as that when looking to examine the outcomes of mentoring programs such as satisfaction, it is challenging to determine whether the outcomes were the result of the individual mentor or program factors (Collings et al., 2015). However, several scholars (as cited in the following paragraph) agree that mentoring has significant benefits for both mentees and mentors.

As a result of mentoring programs, mentees are argued to experience increased student satisfaction (Allen, Russell, & Maetzke, 1997; Collings et al., 2015) and can also significantly improve their grades (Leidenfrost et al., 2011; Rodger & Tremblay, 2003). In turn, mentors develop improved interpersonal and communication skills and enhanced social networks (Good, Halpin, & Halpin, 2000; Hall & Jaugietis, 2011; Harmon, 2006; Heirdsfield et al., 2008; Kiyama & Luca, 2013; Reyes, 2011), better time management and organizational skills (Hall & Jaugietis, 2011), as well as enhanced self-awareness (Harmon, 2006). There are also challenges for mentors, the most significant being mentee engagement, as well as experiencing difficulties sustaining communications and having mentees ask for assistance (Colvin & Ashman, 2010; Heirdsfield et al., 2008; Holt & Berwise, 2012). However, the outcomes we are most concerned with here are leadership skills and/or capabilities. To inform our discussion of peer mentoring and leadership, first we must consider the literature on leadership theory, specifically implicit leadership theory (ILT). In the following section, we discuss the notion of implicit leadership theories (ILTs) and how understanding what the follower thinks of the leader, what the mentee thinks of the mentor, is paramount for developing student mentors' leadership capabilities.

12.3.   Implicit Leadership Theories

Research on implicit leadership theories is longstanding, first receiving attention in the 1970s (Eden & Leviathan, 1975; Lord, Binning, Rush, & Thomas, 1978; Rush, Thomas, & Lord, 1977). Arising from the area of social cognition, and in particular Rosch's (1999) work on the structure of natural categories, the concept of a leader prototype or implicit leadership theory emerged to recognize that individual followers possess different mental constructs of what constitutes "a leader." In turn, these implicit leadership theories influence followers' expectations of, and reactions to, others. That is, whether someone is perceived to be a leader and also an effective leader at that depends on the nature and content of the follower's implicit theory of leadership. In the context of a mentor/mentee relationship, ILT states that mentors are only leaders if their mentees consider them as such. The more closely leaders are perceived to possess characteristics that match the followers' prototype of a leader, the more likely it is that they will allow the leaders to exert leadership influence on them, and the more the leaders will be perceived as effective by the followers.

The development of an implicit leadership theory by followers is a relatively slow process that results from extensive experience within a specific context (Sherman, 1996). Although prototypes are conceived of as existing at the individual level, their nature can be influenced by factors that operate at the more macro level, such as the larger systems of meaning that are present within a society or even a particular organization (Weick, 1995). More recently it has been recognized that not only are implicit leadership theories developed through external stimuli (Shondrick & Lord, 2010) they are also influenced by changing understandings of our own sense of self (Shondrick, Dinh, & Lord, 2010).

The traditional approach to eliciting implicit theories asks people to generate lists of characteristics in response to a single cue (e.g., "manager"). One weakness of this approach is that if a characteristic is not mentioned — this is, it is non-generated by the respondent — then it is assumed it is not part of the respondent's implicit theory of leadership. Yet, if asked about a non-generated characteristic being prototypical, respondents can easily identify whether or not the characteristic fits their implicit theory; thus some researchers adopted a two-stage approach. Researchers began with individual item generation, but then combined the listed characteristics of numerous individuals to produce an inclusive, collective list (Offermann, Kennedy, & Wirtz, 1994). This list of attributes is then given to other respondents who are asked to indicate the extent to which these attributes are typical of a leader in order to produce prototypicality ratings. This technique of presenting items to respondents to rate was found to be more effective and convenient for measuring prototypes.

Research on implicit leadership theories has become very popular with a recent review of trends in leadership publications ranking it the 12th most researched topic in leadership research between 2000 and 2012 (Dinh et al., 2014). As pointed out by Schyns and Schilling (2011), the majority of empirical research has focused on attributes of effective leadership that commonly comprise peoples' implicit leadership theories. However, not everyone's implicit theory of leadership is about effective leadership. Indeed, Foti, Bray, Thompson, and Allgood (2012) as well as Schyns and Schilling (2011) illustrated that while positive attributes dominate such lay theories, they contain both effective and ineffective leadership characteristics. This has changed over time with earlier research (see e.g., Offermann et al., 1994) showing more positive content of implicit leadership theories.

The changing nature of implicit leadership theories is an advantage not given other leadership theories. Theorizing on the nature of prototypes using connectionist-based framework has emphasized their dynamic nature (Hanges, Lord, & Dickson, 2000; Lord, Brown, Harvey, & Hall, 2001). Within the connectionist model, it is argued each time leadership prototypes are used they are recreated rather than stored and retrieved from long-term memory. As such, implicit leadership theories are not static or inflexible.

An appreciation of followers is another hallmark that sets apart research on implicit leadership theories from other bodies of scholarship. Indeed, this is another advantage of taking the implicit leadership theory perspective for leadership research: it is inherently follower centric. For example Hoyt, Burnette, and Innella's (2012) study showed that individuals are more likely to be influenced by leadership role models if they held the belief that leaders were made, not born. Those who believed leaders were born and not made when presented with role models reported less confidence in their leadership abilities and also performed more poorly on the associated task. Similarly, it has also been shown that if a person's self-perception matches their implicit leadership theory, they are more likely to take on a leadership identity (DeRue & Ashford, 2010). Here we can see that research on implicit leadership theories encompasses a broader view of leadership, looking not just at the leader but also the process of influence. This points to the vast complexities governing implicit leadership theories, making it a challenging topic to pursue. Indeed, there are few instruments that seek to uncover the stated preferences for leadership and unpack the hidden beliefs that influence leadership perceptions (Schyns, Felfe, & Blank, 2007). This is crucial as the notion of "implicit" means that people are largely unaware that these prototypes and schemas are influencing their perceptions (Epitropaki, Sy, Martin, Tram-Quon, & Topakas, 2013). How this impacts of peer mentors as leaders is thus our central concern.

12.4.   Peer Mentoring and Leadership

A number of scholars have argued that mentors improve in leadership as a result of acting as a mentor. In Townsend, Delves, Kidd, and Figg's (2011) study, mentors commented on their fellow mentors behaving as leaders. Similarly, Taylor et al. (2013, p. 101) conclusion on the outcomes of a peer-mentoring program in a medical school was, "we also feel more confident that the pervasive 'hidden curriculum' of medical school is safely fostered under the *leadership* (emphasis added) of our best students who are themselves provided with a constructive opportunity to role model the positive aspects of professionalism for their peers." Other scholars put forward similar assertions about mentors being better equipped for leadership as a result of their participation in peer-mentoring schemes (see e.g., Colvin & Ashman, 2010; Good et al., 2000; Hall & Jaugietis, 2011).

Endemic to peer-mentoring schemes is "peer leadership" which includes the "basic principles of peer education, leadership, and mentoring" (Esplin, Seabold, & Pinnegar, 2012, p. 86). The literature on this is much broader as a peer leader "provides leadership in (a) variety of contexts and can range from being an individual mentor, a group leader, head of an organization, or community leader" (Cuseo, 2010, p. 4). As identified by Ender and Kay (2001), peer leaders are involved in residential life and orientation programs, as well as roles such as student ambassadors, alumni mentors, academic tutors, or orientation ambassadors (Cuseo, 2010). Peer leaders can be mentors but this is not always the case.

There is some conceptual confusion in the literature, which is not surprising given there are overlaps between mentoring and leadership (Ragins & Kram, 2007). For example Esplin et al. (2012) use the Purdue Promise program as an illustration of peer leadership but then refer to the participants as mentors, not leaders. Esplin et al. (2012) use the terms interchangeably where as other scholars point to leadership as a role or a function within the mentoring relationship (see e.g., Colvin & Ashman, 2010; Holt & Lopez, 2014). Others use mentoring and leadership in tandem without distinction (see also Shook & Keup, 2012) something that is common in the aforementioned peer leadership literature.

Our issue is that it appears leadership is included in the peer-mentoring agenda often without a proper analysis or indeed even acknowledgment of what leadership really is. Mentors are cast in the role as "peer leader" and develop "leadership skills" but scholarship is decidedly lacking on what leadership actually is or what are considered to be leadership skills. The only explanation appears to be that a "peer leader" is a role model who sets an example (Colvin & Ashman, 2010), mere lip service to a significant body of scholarship. This is where there is a problem in research on peer mentoring and leadership: there is a lack of theoretical understanding of leadership. Without this understanding, how can we convincingly say that mentors are leaders or develop leadership skills?

There are some notable exceptions. Barnes (2014) used the Social Change Model of Leadership Development to examine whether participation as peer mentors enabled students to develop their socially responsible leadership capacity. However, the program under study had mentees who were not in higher education but were students in grades 1–12 and thus is not directly related to our target population in higher education. Additionally, the study did not examine whether acting as a mentor enhanced leadership capacity but whether the mentors who chose to participate in the program exhibited more socially responsible leadership. Campbell, Smith, Dugan, and Komives (2012) also used the Social Change Model of Leadership Development to examine the impact mentoring relationship has on leadership capabilities but only looked at mentees, not mentors. The Social Change Model of Leadership Development is particularly appealing as it was developed by leadership scholars specifically to apply to students in higher education institutions and emphasizes socially responsible action (Komives & Wagner, 2012). Where the Model falls short is in the analysis of the relationship between leader and follower. If mentors are leaders, are their mentees their followers? This seems likely. As such, how mentors and mentees interact as leaders and followers needs further attention.

12.5.   A Case Study in Detecting Leadership within a Peer-Mentoring Program

How can an understanding of implicit leadership theories offer a more compelling perspective for the development of leadership capabilities of student peer mentors? As we argued previously, implicit leadership theory implies that mentors are only leaders if their mentees consider them as such. Having students rate themselves on whether they have developed leadership skills does not properly assess whether they are actually leaders or developing their leadership abilities in the context of the mentor-mentee relationship.

We now consider if we can find evidence of student leadership in the historical records of a large and popular peer-mentoring program in higher education. Deakin University has three campuses in and around the city of Melbourne in Australia. The university is currently ranked 45th in the Times Higher Education (THE) list of the world's top 100 universities under 50 years old. Deakin has over 50,000 students, with a third choosing to study wholly in the cloud (i.e., online). The Faculty of Business and Law is one of the four faculties at Deakin, and it offers popular student-mentoring programs for both undergraduate and postgraduate students.

12.5.1.   *Description of the Program at Deakin*

The Faculty website describes the program in the following terms: "Mentors are current Business and Law students who are able to provide first-hand experience, advice and suggestions to make your time more enjoyable and easy." The aim of the program is to assist the transition of new students into university life. There are two major facets to this aim: first, to assist students to deal with the somewhat complex and novel institutional aspects of university life (e.g., clarification of academic expectations, referral to relevant support services in both the faculty and university, advice about coursework tasks, examination preparation, etc.); second, to facilitate the social integration of the mentee into a new environment. This second aspect is of particular importance at Deakin given the large number of students who have recently arrived in Australia to begin their tertiary education.

The programs run for six weeks at the start of the trimester and consist of weekly meetings of mentors and mentees. The content of each meeting is semi-structured so that all information needed by new students can be imparted, and the opportunity to discuss issues that are of concern to mentees is available at each meeting. The program also conducts a series of social events so that new students have an opportunity to build social networks.

At the end of the six-week program, mentors complete an evaluation of their experience as mentors. Additionally, they are required to submit weekly online journals detailing the following:

- How many times they meet with mentees
- Day of meeting/s
- Mode of communication, for example, face-to-face, e-mail
- The main issues addressed
- Positive aspects of the meeting
- The most challenging aspects
- Level of mentee engagement
- Whether they used the meeting agenda or not
- A brief summary of additional issues.

Where possible students are allocated to mentors studying the same or similar course or discipline; most groups consist of between two and four students.

Table 12.1: Enrollment of mentors and mentees 2013–2015.

Enrollment for trimester 1	Undergraduate program		Postgraduate program	
	Number of mentors	**Number of mentees**	**Number of mentors**	**Number of mentees**
2013	70	236	36	151
2014	67	347	38	185
2015	87	400	44	237

Mentors are explicitly excluded from acting as tutors; for example mentors may not directly answer assessment questions, or provide a copy of their own course notes or assignment, or assist in writing an assignment.

Table 12.1 contains the enrollment statistics for these mentoring programs. The Faculty operates on a trimester calendar, where the 3rd trimester is roughly equivalent to the Summer term. The popularity of the program is evident from the growth in the number of enrollments and the fact that the program is entirely voluntary indicates that students derive value from participation in the program.

12.5.2.   Developing Leadership in Mentors

The success of this program depends upon the availability of suitable mentors. Thus a major aspect of the program is the recruitment and training of students to act as mentors — which is where the connection between mentoring and leadership arises. The question that we wish to answer is whether peer-mentoring programs succeed in providing evidence of the development of leadership skills, and so it is to the cohort of mentors that we look for answers.

To be clear, along with many other such programs, the peer-mentoring program at Deakin does aspire to imparting leadership skills to its mentors. The recruitment of mentors specifically mentioned the following benefits from participation in the program:

- Development of skills in communication, organization, and leadership
- Acquisition of experiences which add value to the student's CV
- Networking opportunities with other mentors and mentees
- A sense of achievement of helping others by sharing experiences.

Aspiring mentors are given the following information, to assist them in understanding the selection criteria.

Volunteer mentors are chosen for their:

- ability to assist and support new students in their transition to University
- commitment to helping others and supporting their University community

- enthusiastic, approachable, motivated and reliable nature
- have an interest in furthering your leadership, communication, organization and time management skills
- knowledge of University and Faculty support services
- good, consistent academic results with a WAM (weighted average academic results) greater than 60%. (*Source*: http://www.deakin.edu.au/business/students/mentor-program/be-mentor)

Volunteers are interviewed, and if successful are given a one-day training course. They are also offered opportunities to socialize with other mentors. Many of the volunteers formally participated in the program as mentee, and they often state one of the reasons for wishing to become a mentor is some form of "giving back" to the program.

At the conclusion of each six-week program mentors are afforded the opportunity to evaluate the program. The evaluation process is similar to that for the mentees, and besides technical issues concerning the program there are open-ended question such as the following: "Please reflect on your experience of being in the mentor program and write down your thoughts."

An analysis of 118 responses by mentors to this and similar open-ended questions found that only 11 mentors (9.3% of respondents) mentioned leadership. The program was strongly endorsed when leadership was mentioned, as the following quotes illustrate:

> Mentor 1:
>
> Being a mentor is a great enjoyment. The program functions as a platform where you can display your abilities in communication, leadership and spirit of teamwork. Share with your mentees your experience at Deakin and it will be a fruitful journey.
>
> Mentor 2:
>
> [The] mentor program gives me good experiences. I have opportunity to meet people from different cultural backgrounds. I can improve my leadership skills and help other students to be successful in their study at Deakin. Before I joined mentor program, I didn't realize that I can help other students to adjust in Deakin university environment. I am more confident to voice my opinion and get involved in group discussion. This program helped me to expand my network, which is very important to support my career in the future.

There are at least two alternative explanations for the low frequency with which leadership is discussed. It is possible that the mentor did not in fact develop or use leadership skills in the program. Alternatively, it is possible that leadership skills are so implicit in the process of mentoring that the mentors were unaware that they were in fact developing and using these skills.

Students who wished to become mentors were required to apply through a competitive process. An examination of the answers to the questions on the application form to be appointed as a mentor allows a better understanding of how leadership is viewed by this cohort of mentors. Applicants are required to answer the following questions on the application form:

- Why do you want to become a student mentor?
- What skills and qualities could you bring to your role as a student mentor?
- What other relevant work, volunteer, or other experience do you have to prepare you for this role?

An analysis of the responses of 106 applications reveal that 65 applicants (61%) mention *leader* or *leadership* at least once in their answer to these questions. Many of the responses indicate that the applicants view leadership as a vital part of the process of mentoring and teamwork, as evidenced by the following examples:

> Applicant 1:
>
> I highly value communication, listening and speaking with people, to understand, share and learn, and my skills reflect this. I have been a leader for many years in various endeavors both at university and high school before that. I have trained as a Public Speaker and Debater. I strongly support giving everyone the opportunity to speak and be heard. Moreover, I am diligent and dedicated and will help my Mentees find the support they need as new university students. I am also organized and prompt, I follow instructions and am capable of working in a team, one-on-one and independently.
>
> Applicant 2:
>
> I believe this role would enhance my interaction and leadership skills so as to provide myself with experience I can use in the work-force. Additionally, I remembered when I first started university in a new environment with people I did not know and that a friendly face is all I needed to fit in. I want to be that that person whom my mentees can come up to and know that I will to the best of my ability provide advice or be there to listen to any problems they may be having.
>
> Applicant 3:
>
> When I first started university, I was very much looking forward to this new academic journey however I did experience a sense of loneliness as I didn't know anyone. I know what these new students would be feeling and I am hoping to provide them with a friendly face and someone they can talk to whether it be about their new surroundings or if they need some advice about their studies. I would also like to expand my leadership and management skills. It will be a challenge to balance schooling, work and mentoring but I believe this experience would be very beneficial to my life in the workforce.

12.5.3.   *How Do Mentees Regard the Leadership Skills of Their Mentors?*

We stated earlier that having students rate themselves on whether they have developed leadership skills does not properly assess whether they are actually leaders or developing their leadership abilities in the context of the mentor-mentee relationship. Indeed, mentors may think they are "doing leadership" because it is mentioned in the recruitment and selection material. This seems a likely conclusion as when leadership is referred to in their feedback, it is mentioned alongside the other "skills" in the recruitment and selection material. Do mentors think they are "doing leadership" because we have told them they will be developing these skills? In order to answer this question we examine how the mentees view their mentors. Providing support, guidance, advice, and social networks may be part of the mentee's ideas of what being a leader is, the implicit leadership theories of the mentees.

At the end of each program students are invited to evaluate the program via an online survey. A total of 368 responses have been received by mentees over this two-year period. In addition to specific issues that the directors of the mentoring program would like to evaluate, there are open-ended questions such as "The most rewarding aspect about being mentored was ...." An analysis of the responses to this particular question shows that both major aims of the program are well covered. By far, the most common response was that their mentor provided guidance and support on how to navigate their higher education experience followed by opportunities for friendship and social connections. The following two comments (which are fairly representative) are provided to illustrate this:

Student 1:

Getting tips and information about anything and everything related to studying in Deakin and staying in Melbourne. If I had not joined the program, I would find myself wandering around campus and wasting time trying to figure out on my own how things run around Deakin. Being mentored has helped me settle down in Deakin quickly and I can concentrate on studying without having to worry about certain things. And besides, I made a new friend who I can relate to very well.

Student 2:

Meeting different people from different backgrounds. To benefit from the experiences of another international student. Not so much lonely face to face communication. I met new people from diverse cultural backgrounds. This really helped in my learning process about my new life in Australia! All and above, I knew someone i.e. my mentor who will help me out if I ever faced with any difficulty in the university. Always had someone to contact with regard to academics. She can help me to understand master study life and solve many problems. Initial guidance to adopt the new environment.

Not once in the 368 evaluations that were examined did the word "leader," "leadership," or even "role-model" appear — yet almost all comments related positively to the assistance that mentors, who were initially strangers, provided to mentees. This is a surprising result. We argued above that based on implicit leadership theory research, mentors are only leaders if their mentees consider them as such. We now have to consider the possibility that although the mentors believe that they had developed leadership skills, the mentees did not see them from this perspective. According to implicit leadership theory, they did not achieve leadership capabilities. This begs the question as to whether leadership is a significant factor in the mentoring relationship.

12.6. Conclusion

We have argued that asking students directly what, if anything, they have learnt about leadership in any situation will produce unreliable responses. To test if a particular peer-mentoring program has in fact enhanced leadership skills requires a more indirect approach. Ideally, those being mentored would be a less biased source of information, but in the case study that we examined there was no direct comment about leadership from mentees. Furthermore, mentors are likely parroting back the information provided in recruitment and selection material. This does not mean that leadership was not in effect but rather that for peer-mentoring programs to properly address student leadership capabilities, the concept of leadership must be approached in a more deliberate and meaningful way.

For this to occur we believe peer-mentoring programs, both in design and development must ask several questions:

- How do we define leadership?
- What are leadership skills?
- Can they be developed in the context of a peer-mentoring program, through training and/or the process of peer mentoring?
- How can the mentors be seen as leaders in the eyes of the mentees?

Given that everyone has different conceptualizations of a leader, and various different implicit theories of leadership, student mentors must be aware that to be a leader in the context of their mentoring relationship depends on whether their mentees see them as a leader.

We regard our findings as inconclusive. Nevertheless, we do believe that they raise the question as to whether acting as a peer mentor really does develop leadership capabilities for students in higher education. This is not to say that peer-mentoring programs are not beneficial. Indeed, they are shown to have extremely beneficial outcomes for mentors and mentees alike. Whether leadership is one of those outcomes requires much needed further research. We argue that attention to implicit leadership theories, particularly those of mentees, is a fruitful avenue for future scholarship.

References

Allen, T. D., & Eby, L. T. (2011). *The Blackwell handbook of mentoring: A multiple perspectives approach*. Malden, MA: Wiley.

Allen, T. D., Russell, J. E., & Maetzke, S. B. (1997). Formal peer mentoring factors related to proteges' satisfaction and willingness to mentor others. *Group & Organization Management, 22*(4), 488–507.

Barnes, S. R. (2014). *Exploring the socially responsible leadership capacity of college student leaders who mentor*. Master's thesis, University of Nebraska-Lincoln, Lincoln, NE.

Campbell, C. M., Smith, M., Dugan, J. P., & Komives, S. R. (2012). Mentors and college student leadership outcomes: The importance of position and process. *The Review of Higher Education, 35*(4), 595–625.

Christie, H. (2014). Peer mentoring in higher education: Issues of power and control. *Teaching in Higher Education, 19*(8), 955–965.

Collings, R., Swanson, V., & Watkins, R. (2015). Peer mentoring during the transition to university: Assessing the usage of a formal scheme within the UK. *Studies in Higher Education* (forthcoming). doi:10.1080/03075079.2015.1007939

Colvin, J. W., & Ashman, M. (2010). Roles, risks, and benefits of peer mentoring relationships in higher education. *Mentoring & Tutoring: Partnership in Learning, 18*(2), 121–134.

Crisp, G. (2009). Conceptualization and initial validation of the College Student Mentoring Scale (CSMS). *Journal of College Student Development, 50*(2), 177–194.

Crisp, G., & Cruz, I. (2009). Mentoring college students: A critical review of the literature between 1990 and 2007. *Research in Higher Education, 50*(6), 525–545.

Cuseo, J. (2010). Peer leadership: Definition, description, and classification. *E-Source for College Transitions, 7*(5), 3–5.

DeRue, D. S., & Ashford, S. J. (2010). Who will lead and who will follow? A social process of leadership identity construction in organizations. *Academy of Management Review, 35*(4), 627–647.

Dinh, J. E., Lord, R. G., Gardner, W. L., Meuser, J. D., Liden, R. C., & Hu, J. (2014). Leadership theory and research in the new millennium: Current theoretical trends and changing perspectives. *The Leadership Quarterly, 25*(1), 36–62.

Driscoll, L. G., Parkes, K. A., Tilley-Lubbs, G. A., Brill, J. M., & Pitts Bannister, V. R. (2009). Navigating the lonely sea: Peer mentoring and collaboration among aspiring women scholars. *Mentoring & Tutoring: Partnership in Learning, 17*(1), 5–21.

Dugan, J. P., & Komives, S. R. (2007). *Developing leadership capacity in college students*. College Park, MD: National Clearinghouse for Leadership Programs.

Eden, D., & Leviathan, U. (1975). Implicit leadership theory as a determinant of the factor structure underlying supervisory behavior. *Journal of Applied Psychology, 60*(6), 736–741.

Ender, S. C., & Kay, K. (2001). Peer leadership programs: A rationale and review of the literature [Monograph]. In S. L. Hamid (Ed.), *Peer leadership: A primer on program essentials: The first-year experience monograph series no. 32* (pp. 1–11). Columbia, SC: National Resource Center for the First-Year Experience and Students in Transition, University of South Carolina.

Ensher, E. A., Heun, C., & Blanchard, A. (2003). Online mentoring and computer-mediated communication: New directions in research. *Journal of Vocational Behavior, 63*(2), 264–288.

Ensher, E. A., Thomas, C., & Murphy, S. E. (2001). Comparison of traditional, step-ahead, and peer mentoring on protégés' support, satisfaction, and perceptions of career success: A social exchange perspective. *Journal of Business and Psychology, 15*(3), 419–438.

Epitropaki, O., Sy, T., Martin, R., Tram-Quon, S., & Topakas, A. (2013). Implicit leadership and followership theories "in the wild": Taking stock of information-processing approaches to leadership and followership in organizational settings. *The Leadership Quarterly*, *24*(6), 858–881.

Esplin, P., Seabold, J., & Pinnegar, F. (2012). The architecture of a high-impact and sustainable peer leader program: A blueprint for success. *New Directions for Higher Education*, *2012*(157), 85–100.

Foti, R. J., Bray, B. C., Thompson, N. J., & Allgood, S. F. (2012). Know thy self, know thy leader: Contributions of a pattern-oriented approach to examining leader perceptions. *The Leadership Quarterly*, *23*(4), 702–717.

Fox, A., & Stevenson, L. (2006). Exploring the effectiveness of peer mentoring of accounting and finance students in higher education. *Accounting Education: An International Journal*, *15*(2), 189–202.

Good, J. M., Halpin, G., & Halpin, G. (2000). A promising prospect for minority retention: Students becoming peer mentors. *Journal of Negro Education*, *69*(4), 375–383.

Hall, R., & Jaugietis, Z. (2011). Developing peer mentoring through evaluation. *Innovative Higher Education*, *36*(1), 41–52.

Hanges, P., Lord, R., & Dickson, M. (2000). An information-processing perspective on leadership and culture: A case for connectionist architecture. *Applied Psychology*, *49*(1), 133–161.

Harmon, B. (2006). A qualitative study of the learning processes and outcomes associated with students who serve as peer mentors. *Journal of the First-Year Experience & Students in Transition*, *18*(2), 53–82.

Heirdsfield, A. M., Walker, S., Walsh, K., & Wilss, L. (2008). Peer mentoring for first-year teacher education students: The mentors' experience. *Mentoring & Tutoring: Partnership in Learning*, *16*(2), 109–124.

Holt, L., & Berwise, C. (2012). Illuminating the process of peer mentoring: An examination and comparison of peer mentors' and first-year students' experiences. *Journal of the First-Year Experience & Students in Transition*, *24*(1), 19–43.

Holt, L. J., & Lopez, M. J. (2014). Characteristics and correlates of supportive peer mentoring: A mixed methods study. *Mentoring & Tutoring: Partnership in Learning*, *22*(5), 1–18.

Hoyt, C. L., Burnette, J. L., & Innella, A. N. (2012). I can do that the impact of implicit theories on leadership role model effectiveness. *Personality and Social Psychology Bulletin*, *38*(2), 257–268.

Jacobi, M. (1991). Mentoring and undergraduate academic success: A literature review. *Review of Educational Research*, *61*(4), 505–532.

Kiyama, J. M., & Luca, S. G. (2013). Structured opportunities: Exploring the social and academic benefits for peer mentors in retention programs. *Journal of College Student Retention: Research, Theory and Practice*, *15*(4), 489–514.

Komives, S. R., & Wagner, W. (2012). *Leadership for a better world: Understanding the social change model of leadership development.* San Francisco, CA: Wiley.

Leidenfrost, B., Strassnig, B., Schabmann, A., Spiel, C., & Carbon, C. C. (2011). Peer mentoring styles and their contribution to academic success among mentees: A person-oriented study in higher education. *Mentoring & Tutoring: Partnership in Learning*, *19*(3), 347–364.

Lord, R. G., Binning, J. F., Rush, M. C., & Thomas, J. C. (1978). The effect of performance cues and leader behavior on questionnaire ratings of leadership behavior. *Organizational Behavior and Human Performance*, *21*(1), 27–39.

Lord, R. G., Brown, D. J., Harvey, J. L., & Hall, R. J. (2001). Contextual constraints on prototype generation and their multilevel consequences for leadership perceptions. *The Leadership Quarterly*, *12*(3), 311–338.

Nora, A., & Crisp, G. (2007). Mentoring students: Conceptualizing and validating the multi-dimensions of a support system. *Journal of College Student Retention: Research, Theory and Practice, 9*(3), 337–356.

Offermann, L. R., Kennedy, J. K., & Wirtz, P. W. (1994). Implicit leadership theories: Content, structure, and generalizability. *The Leadership Quarterly, 5*(1), 43–58.

Ragins, B. R., & Kram, K. E. (2007). *The handbook of mentoring at work: Theory, research, and practice.* Thousand Oaks, CA: Sage.

Reyes, M. E. (2011). A sophomore-to-junior mentoring program that works: The SAM program at the university of Texas Pan American. *Journal of College Student Retention: Research, Theory and Practice, 13*(3), 373–382.

Rodger, S., & Tremblay, P. F. (2003). The effects of a peer mentoring program on academic success among first year university students. *Canadian Journal of Higher Education, 33*(3), 1–17.

Rosch, E. (1999). Principles of categorization. In E. Margolis & S. Laurence (Eds.), *Concepts: Core readings* (pp. 189–206). Cambridge, MA: Massachusetts Institute of Technology.

Rush, M. C., Thomas, J. C., & Lord, R. G. (1977). Implicit leadership theory: A potential threat to the internal validity of leader behavior questionnaires. *Organizational Behavior and Human Performance, 20*(1), 93–110.

Schyns, B., Felfe, J., & Blank, H. (2007). Is charisma hyper-romanticism? Empirical evidence from new data and a meta-analysis. *Applied Psychology, 56*(4), 505–527.

Schyns, B., & Schilling, J. (2011). Implicit leadership theories: Think leader, think effective? *Journal of Management Inquiry, 20*(2), 141–150.

Sherman, J. W. (1996). Development and mental representation of stereotypes. *Journal of Personality and Social Psychology, 70*(6), 1126.

Shondrick, S. J., Dinh, J. E., & Lord, R. G. (2010). Developments in implicit leadership theory and cognitive science: Applications to improving measurement and understanding alternatives to hierarchical leadership. *The Leadership Quarterly, 21*(6), 959–978.

Shondrick, S. J., & Lord, R. G. (2010). Implicit leadership and followership theories: Dynamic structures for leadership perceptions, memory, and leader-follower processes. *International Review of Industrial and Organizational Psychology, 25*, 1–30.

Shook, J. L., & Keup, J. R. (2012). The benefits of peer leader programs: An overview from the literature. *New Directions for Higher Education, 2012*(157), 5–16.

Shrestha, C. H., May, S., Edirisingha, P., Burke, L., & Linsey, T. (2009). From face-to-face to e-mentoring: Does the "e" add any value for mentors? *International Journal of Teaching and Learning in Higher Education, 20*(2), 116–124.

Taylor, J. S., Faghri, S., Aggarwal, N., Zeller, K., Dollase, R., & Reis, S. P. (2013). Developing a peer-mentor program for medical students. *Teaching and Learning in Medicine, 25*(1), 97–102.

Terrion, J. L., & Leonard, D. (2007). A taxonomy of the characteristics of student peer mentors in higher education: Findings from a literature review. *Mentoring & Tutoring, 15*(2), 149–164.

Townsend, R. A., Delves, M., Kidd, T., & Figg, B. (2011). Undergraduate student peer mentoring in a multi-faculty, multi-campus university context. *Journal of Peer Learning, 4*(1), 37–49.

Weick, K. E. (1995). *Sensemaking in organizations* (Vol. 3). *Thousand Oaks, CA: Sage.*

Chapter 13

Campus Community Integration on a Mission: Transformative Learning for Social Change

Dawn M. Francis and Stephanie L. Colbry

Abstract

Purpose — This chapter explains how the Social Change Model of Leadership served as the process for uniting the campus on Cabrini Day around one shared vision of Leadership for Social Change. It also uses Mezirow's theory of transformative learning to examine the resulting transformation that occurred among students engaged in this process.

Methodology/approach — In an effort to showcase students' transformation into leaders for social change, the chapter focuses expressly on students enrolled in one particular course. These students worked together to develop a live simulation for Cabrini Day that brought campus community members through the real-world experiences of unaccompanied immigrant minors fleeing to the United States to escape violence in their home countries. The chapter employs an action research methodology to describe how, when, and why these students became transformed. Students' planning steps, actions within the live simulation event, and reflections on their actions were analyzed using the individual, group, and community values of the Social Change Model, as well as the tenets of transformative learning theory.

Findings — Findings reveal that the Social Change Model is a viable process for integrating curricular and cocurricular endeavors on campus. Findings also show that this process can lead to transformative student learning outcomes.

Originality/value — Integrating curricular and cocurricular experiences on college campuses can lead to significant student learning outcomes and experiences.

Keywords: Leadership; social change; transformative learning; integration; curricular; cocurricular

Integrating Curricular and Co-Curricular Endeavors to Enhance Student Outcomes
Copyright © 2016 by Emerald Group Publishing Limited
All rights of reproduction in any form reserved
ISBN: 978-1-78635-064-0

13.1.   Introduction

Every year, on the second Tuesday of November, members of the Cabrini College community come together to celebrate Cabrini Day. Cabrini Day is a campus-wide day of educational programming focused on the mission of the institution. The mission is to provide each student with an "Education of the Heart." These words, once spoken by the College's namesake Saint Frances Xavier Cabrini, urge learners of all faiths to use their education to bring about positive social change.

Initial and on-going mission-focused education is provided to everyone on campus — namely, the students, faculty, staff, administration, and Board of Trustees. Undergraduate students, in particular, are introduced to the mission through the College's Justice Matters core curriculum. Here, within a progression of courses labeled Engagements with the Common Good (ECG), students become aware of their shared humanity and responsibility to work in service of others. As the College's 2014–2015 Undergraduate Catalog (2014) states:

> The outcome of Engagements with the Common Good is that students will be civically engaged: working for peace and justice and against poverty and oppression and increasingly growing in their compassionate concern and ability to advocate for all human beings. More specifically, this core and common curriculum focuses on achieving the student learning outcome of Responsibility for Social Justice. (p. 87)

ECG courses range in focus and span a 100, 200, and 300 level, culminating in a major-specific capstone experience in students' senior year. ECG topics include: dating and domestic violence; hunger and homelessness; global poverty; foster care; immigration law; race and gender equality; and more. Common across all ECG courses is the objective to build students' knowledge, skills, values, and habits to benefit the Common Good.

Annually, the faculty who teach ECG courses are especially encouraged to have their students actively participate in Cabrini Day as a cocurricular experience. The objective is to have these students educate others in the campus community about their ECG-focused topic of injustice. In doing so, students are showcasing their academic excellence, leadership development, and commitment to social justice.

13.2.   Cabrini Day 2014: Lead for Change

As co-chairs of Cabrini Day 2014, we as co-authors of this chapter led the initiative to integrate the curricular experiences of the ECG courses with the cocurricular experience of Cabrini Day. We worked across faculty in all academic disciplines who teach ECG courses to unite the campus community around one shared vision of "Leadership for Social Change," our theme for the day.

Among the many events that took place on Cabrini Day 2014, one in particular encouraged students to work with their ECG faculty member to take a leadership role in advocating for social justice. This event was termed Lead for Change. For this event, students worked with their professors to produce mission-focused presentations, live simulations, round-table discussions, multimedia stories, and the like. Students were required as part of these presentations to educate audiences on the root causes of their injustice, as well as to inform them of how to take action to bring about important social change.

The Lead for Change event was competitive, too. Audience members who came to the event were given a ballot to vote for the top three presentations that moved them the most to take action. The first-place winner received a $100 check from the College made out to the charity most closely aligned with their social justice topic. The second and third place winners received $75 and $50 checks, respectively, for their charities. Over 80 presenters participated in the Lead for Change event.

The real reward, however, was witnessing students' transformation through this curricular and cocurricular integration. Students appeared to deeply understand the meaning of social justice, in addition to their responsibility for the inherent dignity of all human persons around the globe.

Thus, in this chapter, the information presented addresses the following research questions: (1) What *process* was implemented to effectively unite the campus around one shared vision of Leadership for Social Change? (2) How did this process *impact* student learning — and organizational learning — outcomes? This chapter will answer these questions by introducing the process model for leading change on Cabrini Day, as well as explaining how this model allowed for transformative learning to occur. The process will be illustrated through a descriptive case example of a particular ECG course where students engaged with the model and took action in service of meaningful social change. The resulting impact of their social action will be shared.

13.3. Overview: The Social Change Model of Leadership Development

The Social Change Model has its foundation in relational dynamics with a strong focus on creating change for the improvement of one's community (Figure 13.1). The Higher Education Research Institute of UCLA developed the Social Change Model to address larger local and global social issues, focusing on empowering college students to be the future generation to embrace and advocate for change (Astin & Astin, 1996; Wagner, Ostick, & Komives, 2006). Central to the model's design is the need for these students to understand themselves, to appreciate others, and to work as a group to bring about sustainable change in social issues (Wagner et al., 2006).

Within higher education, the Social Change Model has been utilized by curricular and cocurricular leaders alike as an effective framework for engaging students to grow in their understanding of themselves, as well as to energize them to work in service of social change. According to Jacoby (1996), the Social Change Model allows for experiential learning, whereby students participate in activities that address the needs of the community, structured intentionally to promote leadership development and transformation.

A key component of this model is its movement away from a leader-centric approach toward a community-based, collaborative approach. The model is intended to be inclusive with a goal of developing leadership qualities for all involved (Wagner et al., 2006). In this model, leadership is viewed as a process and the values of equity, social justice, self-knowledge, personal empowerment, colla-boration, citizenship, and service are explicitly promoted (Wagner et al., 2006). Astin and Astin (2000) and Wagner et al. (2006) would support the argument that leadership is a process, not a role. They posit the process allows for change to be fostered through the transformation of oneself, facilitating collaboration at a group level and then throughout the community.

The model (Figure 13.1) depicts leadership development and transformation occurring within three distinct stages, which consists of seven specific values (Wagner et al., 2006):

- Stage One: This stage has an *individual* focus, which is comprised of consciousness of self, congruence, and commitment.
- Stage Two: This stage has a *group* focus, which is comprised of common purpose, collaboration, and controversy with civility.
- Stage Three: This stage has a *community* focus, which is comprised of citizenship resulting in societal change.

Seven values — termed the Seven C's — are fostered among students in each stage of the Social Change Model. The summaries of these values that appear in Table 13.1 pull from a synthesis of research on the model (Astin & Astin, 1996, 2000; Komives, Lucas, & McMahon, 1998; Wagner et al., 2006).

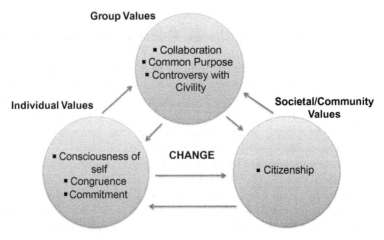

Figure 13.1: Social Change Model.

Table 13.1: The Seven C's of the Social Change Model.

Individual	
Consciousness of self	Being aware of one's beliefs, values, attitudes, and emotions that motivate one to take action.
Congruence	Thinking, feeling, and acting in ways that are authentic, consistent, genuine, and honest.
Commitment	Motivating oneself with an energy that drives collective action, which is built on passion, intensity, and discipline.
Group	
Collaboration	Working together to serve common goals holding; holding one another mutually accountable and responsible; empowering one's self and others through trust building.
Common purpose	Possessing common goals and shared values.
Controversy with civility	Recognizing different viewpoints that are made transparent and allowing for open discussion with civility.
Community	
Citizenship	Acknowledging shared human dignity; having individual and group take responsibility to improve the community; harnessing leadership development that results in positive social change.

13.4.   Application of the Social Change Model to Cabrini College's ECGS

Students enrolled in Cabrini College's Justice Matters core curriculum courses, Engagements with the Common Good (ECG), learn how to advocate for social justice. ECG faculty facilitate students' leadership development by moving them through the three stages of the Social Change Model and cultivating their formation of the seven values. As part of this process, faculty stress the importance of personal empowerment and group collaboration in order to evoke socially just, community-based change.

In truth, ECG courses can create significant dissonance for students who enter with certain worldviews and are forced to examine them for their validity. Here, students are being challenged to question their existing values and beliefs about certain populations and their right to live in dignity. As the students come to understand the root causes of injustice that affect these populations, they often become more open to different viewpoints. In the classroom setting, students negotiate their differences in viewpoints with one another, and many come to a new, shared understanding of injustice from which to take action and advocate for change.

Without these important moments of self-awareness and personal controversy that occur in Stage One of the Social Change Model, students would lack the impetus to come together in Stage Two and work collaboratively to achieve a common purpose. Fueled by these shifts in their mindset, students become energized and enlivened to engage with the community in Stage Three to actively advocate for social change.

13.5.   Transformative Learning Theory

As stated earlier, the goal of Cabrini Day is to transform students' understanding of social justice and have them demonstrate publicly their support for the Common Good. Students' transformation begins in their ECG courses where they explore notions of justice and human rights in ways that challenge their existing perceptions of the world. This type of learning that challenges one's worldview and results in personal perspective transformation bears the traits of Mezirow's (1991) transformation theory of adult learning.

Transformative learning theory emerged from Mezirow's research in the late 1970s that studied women's return to college through reentry programs at two-year institutions (as cited in Baumgartner, 2012). These programs provided a pathway for women to further their education or ready themselves for the workforce after an extended period of time. Through survey research and interviews with these program participants, Mezirow found that their experiences precipitated a shift in their meaning perspectives. Meaning perspectives are comprised of meaning schemes — also referred to as habits of mind — that govern how individuals interpret their experiences. They represent a person's implicit beliefs, values, attitudes, and assumptions (Cranton, 2008; Mezirow, 1990b, 2000; Taylor, 2007). Meaning perspectives are transformed when individuals revise their beliefs, values, attitudes, and assumptions based upon their new worldview.

Mezirow (2000) conceived of this shift in meaning perspectives as occurring through a multi-phase process that begins with a disorienting dilemma and concludes with a decision to take action based on this transformed perspective. In many ways, the leadership development process that occurs within the Social Change Model bears congruence with the transformative learning process. The 10 phases in this process include:

> (1) Experiencing a disorienting dilemma; (2) Undergoing self-examination with feelings of fear, anger, guilt, or shame; (3) Conducting a critical assessment of internalized assumptions and feeling a sense of alienation from traditional social expectations; (4) Relating discontent to the similar experiences of others; recognizing the problem and process of transformation are shared; (5) Exploring options for new roles, relationships, and ways of acting; (6) Planning a course of action; (7) Acquiring the knowledge and skills for implementing a new course of action; (8) Trying out new roles and assessing them; (9) Building competence and self-confidence in new roles; (10) Reintegrating into one's life with the new perspective. (Cranton, 2006, p. 20; Mezirow, 2000, p. 22)

The process of transformative learning is constructivist and relational in nature (Cranton, 2000; Kasl & Elias, 2000; Kegan, 2000). Within a constructivist frame, the theory posits that we interpret new experiences as a result of our past experiences. As stated by Cranton and Taylor (2012), "We uncritically assimilate perspectives from our social world, community, and culture. Those perspectives include distortions, stereotypes, and prejudices" (p. 6). They influence the decisions we make and the actions we take. Then, one day, when we are presented with a new experience that challenges our existing expectations, "we may reject the discrepant perspective or enter into a process that could lead to a transformed perspective" (p. 6).

Baumgartner (2012) revealed that Mezirow's theory of transformative learning was criticized in the late 1980s by two researchers who found the theory to be too focused on the individual and not centered enough on social change. She reported, "Mezirow ... countered that social action was only one goal of education. He argued that individual transformation could lead to social action" (p. 104). Later, in 2006, "Mezirow responded that transformative learning theory is a foundation for learning how to take social action" (Baumgartner, 2012, p. 110). This quote, of course, brings us back to the Social Change Model where we observe individual transformation being linked to community-based social action, perhaps — if Mezirow is right — as a result of transformative learning.

The following section will describe how transformative learning has the potential to occur through the stages in the Social Change Model.

13.6.   Transformative Learning through the Social Change Model

13.6.1.   *Stage One: Consciousness of Self; Congruence; Commitment*

Recall that Stage One is focused on the individual and individual values. The model, when applied to a university setting, regards college students as individuals who are "able to effect positive change for the betterment of others, the community, and society" (Astin & Astin, 1996, p. 16). All students, therefore, have the capacity to be leaders. The process of leadership is realized not only through the actions of individuals, but through the actions of a group working from a core set of shared values to drive change. Those contributors who worked to formulate the Social Change Model "suggest that a conscious focus on **values** should be at the core of any leadership development effort" (Astin & Astin, 1996, p. 16). Thus, they maintain, this leadership development process should prompt student leaders to examine their own personal values.

Students' examination of their personal values begins in Stage One with a consciousness of self — meaning, to be self-aware. According to the originators of the Social Change Model, social change begins with self-awareness. "Enhanced self-awareness facilitates the group process, not only because it leads to a better understanding of others, but also because it aids in the development of trust, an essential ingredient in effective collaboration" (Astin & Astin, 1996, pp. 31–32). Each student leader must, therefore, pose the following reflective questions to themselves:

> What are my values? What kinds of social changes do I really care about? What are my skills, strengths, and talents? How can I best contribute to the group's common purpose, to the leadership process, to social change? (p. 32)

While the questions may appear straight forward, the critical self-reflection they provoke can be deeply upsetting when students are asked to question their own tacit values and the values of others around them who may ascribe to a dominant ideology. Take, for example, a social issue like immigration reform that evokes deep political and cultural divides. Some students will hold steadfast to the notion that all immigrants who enter into the country illegally are doing so to steal jobs from Americans. They assimilated these "values, beliefs, and assumptions from [their] family, community, and culture" (Cranton & Taylor, 2012, p. 7). When exposed to alternate realities, such as the stories of some immigrants — many of them children — coming to the United States to escape violence in their home countries, students are faced with a choice. Do they revise their tacit values, beliefs, and assumptions believing they are now too oppressive, or do they remain wedded to society's dominant perspectives? The root of social change lies in their response. If they choose to revise their values, not only are they taking the first step to social action; they are also taking the first step in the transformative learning process.

Once students begin to revise their taken-for-granted values, beliefs, and assumptions, they now have the opportunity to behave in a manner that is consistent with these revised notions. In doing so, they are acting with congruence. When students in their role as leaders come together around a common concern their "collective congruence can begin a movement for social change" (Astin & Astin, 1996, p. 37).

Of course, this movement for change requires commitment on the part of students. Commitment requires energy, effort, and passion. It has both rational and affective dimensions. For example, some students may become involved in an effort out of a sense of obligation to the group, while others possess a true passion for the cause. Regardless of the motivation, the originators of the Social Change Model contend, a person's heart must drive their actions. They state:

> The connection to your heart and to your values comes in part from **Consciousness of Self** and in part from **Congruence**. Unless a fit can be found between who you are and what you do in the group leadership activity, you will find yourself doing the minimum, making a lackluster, half-hearted attempt, and relying mostly on others instead of actively engaging yourself. (Astin & Astin, 1996, p. 40)

The model's value of commitment, in that it engages both the mind and the heart, has the potential to produce transformative learning. Tisdell (2012) writes about various types of transformational learning experiences. She describes one that takes place when individuals join together to effect social change in the community. In this context, she states, "People meet; their eyes and hearts and minds engage. They work together to make their communities better as they challenge systems of privilege and oppression, in what is often referred to as *emancipatory learning* (emphasis in original) efforts" (p. 22). According to Mezirow (1990a), "Acting upon these emancipatory insights, a praxis, is also necessary. The learner must have the will to act upon his or her new convictions" (pp. 354–355). He continues, "Praxis is a requisite condition of transformative learning" (p. 356). Note, also, that scholars of transformative learning theory describe this praxis as on-going — "a continuing process of action, critical reflection, and dialogue" (Shapiro, Wasserman, & Gallegos, 2012, p. 366).

With a greater consciousness of self and a commitment to acting upon one's critically examined beliefs, students enter into Stage Two of the Social Change Model where they plan for this praxis.

13.6.2.   Stage Two: Collaboration; Common Purpose; Controversy with Civility

Stage Two of the Social Change Model is focused on group values and group process. Once individuals commit themselves to action, as in the previous stage, they come together here in ways that deepen their trust of one another and empower them to take action. Stage Two is relational. Thus, from a leadership development perspective, students are negotiating ways of working with each other to achieve a common goal, exploring differences and capitalizing on the strengths of each other.

In Stage Two, the group values of collaboration and common purpose are closely linked. "Collaboration mobilizes and enhances the power of the group through the members' commitment to the common purpose" (Astin & Astin, 1996, p. 48). Effective collaboration is borne out of shared responsibility and accountability for the group's mutual goal. The trust-filled relationship upon which collaboration rests can spur members to eschew their individual aims and embrace the group's common purpose. With collaboration, members pull from among their collective talents to generate a shared vision for change.

Within the Social Change Model, collaboration is regarded as "being most centrally about how people value and relate to each other across differences in values, ideas, affiliations, visions, and identities (e.g., race, gender, culture, religion, sexual orientation, class, etc.)" (Astin & Astin, 1996, p. 49). Collaboration is not merely task-focused. "It is also a powerful way to learn about ourselves and others in the process" (p. 49).

As stated earlier, transformative learning theory is also relational in nature. Group work and dialogue serve as the "contexts and means for personal and social transformation" (Shapiro et al., 2012, p. 355). The process of dialoguing with others, whereby diverse viewpoints are shared and examined in an open and trusting exchange, is referred to as discourse in the transformative learning literature.

Mezirow originally termed this application of dialogue "rational discourse" (Mezirow, 1991); however, he later changed it to "reflective discourse," Baumgartner (2012) explains, "perhaps ... to portray more accurately the role of reflection and to distance himself from the critiques of transformative learning being too cognitive and rational" (p. 109). As the theory evolved, it began to integrate more emotional, spiritual, and extrarational dimensions (Dirkx, 2001). Transformative learning, Mezirow came to state, can occur as people shift their existing "points of view by 'trying on another's point of view'" (Baumgartner, 2012, p. 109).

Trying on other points of view occurs as "learners share their experiences and resources with each other to create new knowledge" (Cranton, 2006, p. 5). Creating new knowledge through these interpersonal interactions has both rational and affective dimensions; meaning, these trusting relationships allow for the safe exploration of feelings and validation of one's emotions (Taylor, 2000). Often, as a result of assessing one's uncritically assimilated assumptions in this manner, a plan for action is formulated and ultimately executed. Those who come together as a group to take action begin to redefine themselves and construct new meaning about the world around them.

In the Social Change Model, the value of common purpose links all three value sets — individual, group, and community (Astin & Astin, 1996, p. 56). The group value of common purpose relies on group members being self-aware and committed to change. Moreover, it sustains the group when tensions result during the implementation of the plan for change. Additionally, it propels the group to work in service of the Common Good with the goal of realizing the desired change.

Common purpose unites a group and allows for "transformative dialogic moments" (Shapiro et al., 2012, p. 357). These moments are often generated by dissonance within the group. Dissonance comes from "recognizing two fundamental realities of any creative effort: (1) that differences in viewpoint are inevitable, and (2) that such differences must be aired openly but with civility" (Wagner, 2006, p. 9). This concept is revealed in the third group value — controversy with civility.

Shapiro et al. (2012) put forth, "We must constantly challenge ourselves not to assume that our fellow human beings inhabit the same reality that we do" (p. 357). While this is true, they cite the group as playing a vital role in allowing for the exploration of both difference and oneness. "The group provides the container or holding environment to hold the complexity of seemingly incompatible personal narratives or ideas" (p. 357). They go on to characterize certain groups as transformative. Those, they say, that are focused on a critical analysis of systemic challenges "seek social emancipation and social change for social justice" (p. 360). They seek this as a result of personal self-awareness and the recognition of their collective role in supporting systemic change.

Returning to the earlier reference to immigration reform in Stage One of the Social Change Model, students who enter into Stage Two come having critically reflected on their values, beliefs, and assumptions of undocumented immigrants. As such, their previously unexamined habits of mind — *and* habits of heart — are now more open to change. Change can occur through dialogue with group members, albeit this discourse can evoke controversy and feelings of ill will. However, if students remain focused on the common purpose of addressing the systemic causes of injustice, they are more likely to find a way to write a new narrative — one of compatibility and collaboration — in service of the Common Good.

As the group works together to achieve systemic change, they often become more passionately connected to the community and society they are seeking to serve. This step in the leadership development process brings us to the final value set in the Social Change Model — community/societal values.

13.6.3. Stage Three: Citizenship; Change

Stage Three of the Social Change Model moves the leadership group toward its shared purpose of creating meaningful change for social groups that are marginalized or experiencing injustice. As the model itself was formulated for leaders in a higher education setting, it is reasonable to consider the model's goal of educating and developing leaders "to make a better world and a better society for self and others" (Astin & Astin, 1996, p. 21).

Student leaders demonstrate their community/societal values through a leadership development activity. One such activity might include educating community members on the root causes of undocumented minors coming to the United States, and then organizing a bus trip to lobby elected officials on their behalf. The reason for the demonstration being, as the originators of the model envisioned it, citizenship is not merely being a member of a leadership group. "Rather, it implies

active engagement of the individual (and the leadership group) in an effort to serve that community, as well as a 'citizen's mind' — a set of values and beliefs that connect an individual in a responsible manner to others" (Astin & Astin, 1996, p. 65). It also involves, they state, having sincere compassion for others. Student leaders, in this sense, engage with their caring hearts to become active citizens of the world and live the philosophy of service beyond one's self.

As with the community/societal value of citizenship, transformative learning also requires action from a transformed state of being. "Transformative learning is ... about change and empowerment" (Merriam & Kim, 2012, p. 68). While the theory most certainly highlights individual change and empowerment, the outcome of such can be group empowerment that drives social change. In this regard, the transformative learning process bears a distinct likeness to the Social Change Model. Meaning, they both share the fundamental assumption of *change* — change among individuals born out of self-analysis, change facilitated by trusting relationships within a group, and change that prompts social action from a newly constructed worldview.

13.7.   Fostering Transformative Learning

Within a higher education setting, leadership development is often facilitated among students by faculty as curricular leaders and by staff members as cocurricular leaders. These individuals provide a supportive environment for learning and change to occur. While much has been written in this literature review about the student as a learner in the transformative learning process, it is also imperative to acknowledge the significant role curricular and cocurricular leaders play in facilitating transformative learning and social change.

According to Ettling (2012), "The TL practitioner is increasingly identified as a promoter of a more just world order and as a facilitator of new levels of awareness of our cosmic interdependence" (p. 540). These practitioners, she maintains, "have a predisposition to educate for change" (p. 536). Educating for change in higher education requires the practitioner to foster trust among students, to model respect for differences, to self-disclose, often through story, and to be transparent with one's intentions (Ettling, 2012).

While TL practitioners lay the foundation for collaboration among members of the learning group, they must also seek to make learners uncomfortable by asking them challenging questions that get them to question what they believe, the origins of their beliefs, and why they hold fast to these beliefs. In other words, they need to engage learners in critical self-reflection — often by sharing viewpoints incongruent with students' own — in order to provoke them to "validate [their] beliefs through the experiences of others who share universal values" (Mezirow, 1997, p. 9). This, then, provides students with the option to revise their previously unexamined assumptions.

Once students revise their assumptions, the TL practitioner can then move them to action in support of their new understanding. Action may include involving students in the design and execution of a research project, which is termed participatory action research. Action research is one methodology Merriam and Kim (2012) suggest for studying transformative learning. The following section of this chapter describes the action research methodology and applies it to a particular case — namely, students engaged in a research project to bring about social change.

13.8. Action Research Method

The action research process is a natural part of teaching. Within their classroom, teachers are continuously observing, collecting data, and changing classroom practices to improve student learning. In this way, action research can be utilized as an effective tool to aid educators to improve practices in their classrooms through intentional reflection and observation (Calhoun, 1994). Reason and Bradbury (as cited in Popplewell & Hayman, 2012) define action research in this way:

> A participatory, democratic process concerned with developing practical knowing in pursuit of worthwhile human purposes ... It seeks to bring together action and reflection, theory and practice, in participation with others, in the pursuit of practical solutions to issues of pressing concern to people and more generally the flourishing of individual persons and their communities. (p. 2)

According to Dick (2006) action research is different than other types of research based on its process of systematic reflection. This systemic reflection can effectively bring about positive change in both students and communities. Lewin, who is considered by some to be the founder of action research (Popplewell & Hayman, 2012), stated that it is "the powerful notion that human systems could only be understood and changed" if all members within the community are involved in the inquiry process itself (as cited in Brydon-Miller, Greenwood, & Maguire, 2003, p. 12).

13.8.1. What Action Researchers Believe

Action research is best utilized in environments that are conducive for teaching and learning (Ozanne & Saatcioglu, 2008). According to Puckett, Harkavy, and Romer (2000) action research is an effective research methodology for helping academic researchers and practitioners collaborate effectively to identify and analyze opportunities and problems, as well as to find solutions or present new models that can be tested within the larger learning community.

> Action researchers believe that knowledge is socially constructed and plural. They highlight the importance of reflexivity in the production of knowledge; good action researchers should continually question what they think they know, their approach, the choices they make

during the research process and what they do with their findings. (Popplewell & Hayman, 2012, p. 3)

Action research encourages researchers to participate with the community, not as observers, but as active members (Nyden, Figert, Shibley, & Burrows, 1997). Strand, Marullo, Cutforth, Stoecker, and Donohue (2003) argues that action research must be collaborative in nature where the community need or goal and pedagogical content coexist. The ultimate goal of action research is social change and social action, which promotes social justice (Strand et al., 2003).

13.8.2. Why Choose Action Research?

In the context of this study, action research was chosen as an appropriate framework to discuss why, when, and how students involved in the Cabrini Day Lead for Change activity became transformed. Coghlan and Brannick's (2001) Action Research Cycle (Figure 13.2) was specifically chosen from among other action research processes based upon its focus on providing context and purpose for social action, as well as its initial step of constructing new understanding about the social issue that laid the groundwork for transformation.

In action research, the community is involved with the entire learning cycle. In fact, effective integration and buy-in of the community ensures the results of the study are relevant and beneficial to the community (Wagner et al., 2006). Broadly speaking, researchers and the community must enjoy a strong relationship with one another in order to effectively establish an action research project. This type of relationship allows for understanding and navigating community needs, agendas, and constraints. Students who have direct personal contact with members of the community are able to utilize the knowledge and experience of all community members. They learn through first-hand experience.

Students in this study had direct personal contact with members of the larger Cabrini College community throughout their action research process. They worked together to identify the needs of the community through a shared goal, creating social change to address social problems.

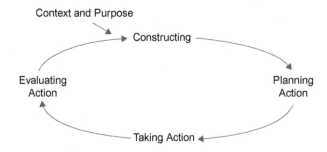

Figure 13.2: Coghlan and Brannick's action research cycle.

13.9. Data Collection and Analysis

The essential criterion in studies that rely on reflection and observation is appropriately selecting participants based on shared experience (Creswell, 2007; Moustakas, 1994). Van Kaam (1959, 1966) suggested that participants be selected so as to have a great variety of situations in which transformation has been experienced … distinguishing that which is constant from that which varies dependent upon different situations (Van Kaam, 1959, p. 67). Participants need to have an interest in understanding the nature and meaning of their experiences, be willing to participate in interviews and focus groups, and allow permission to have their artifacts utilized for future community development (Moustakas, 1994).

The researchers in this study used criterion sampling to select an active case study with willing participants from the community under study. The researchers, through criterion sampling, were able to identify those participants who actively participated in an ECG Learning Community at Cabrini College, whereby they explored through reflection and action how to become engaged leaders of social justice.

In this study, the appropriateness of the sample that met the proposed criteria was more important than quantity or randomness. According to Morse (1991) this means finding "good" informants who are willing and able to reflect and share with the researcher. "An appropriate sample is guided by informant characteristics and by the type of information needed by the researcher" (Morse, 1991, p. 135).

To best display students' transformation, a case study utilizing Coghlan and Brannick's (2001) Action Research Cycle was selected. Planning documentation, simulation artifacts, excerpts from students' written, audio, and video-based reflections, students' evaluation of their actions, and reflections from the professor will be shared. The process of data collection and analysis within action research (Stringer, 2014) includes the following:

- Selecting an area or focus through the effective identification of a community opportunity or problem where action is needed. Questions asked during this process are: What significant things happened? Describe the events. Who was involved, what did they do? What picture emerges? How did I/the group feel?
- Data collection involves collecting existing data from multiple data sources (identified above) that provides a foundation for the case under investigation. Questions asked during this process are: Why did this happen? What caused it? What helped, what hindered? What was expected? What assumptions were made? What really struck the group? What other experience or thinking highlighted the experience differently, if any?
- Organizing data through the appropriate collection of events and artifacts is crucial. Questions asked during this process are: So what does this mean for practice? What is needed? How? What can be done differently? What steps will need to be built to put these new insights into practice?
- Analyzing and interpreting data requires a collaborative process where artifacts, interviews, and reflection journals are synthesized into specific themes resulting in

a community model. Questions asked during this process are: What could have been done differently? What was learned, what new insights were gained? What was confirmed? What is needed for future development?

13.10.   Application of the Action Research Cycle

Coghlan and Brannick's (2001) Action Research Cycle leads researchers to effective action and evaluation of a given opportunity or problem. Contained within this section is an explanation of how the action researchers in Cabrini College's fall 2014 ECG 100 LC course went through the following steps in Coghlan and Brannick's (2001) model: Context and Purpose; Constructing, Planning Action, Taking Action, Evaluating Action. In accordance with action research methodology (Stringer, 2014), data collection in this study identified key themes and assumptions that highlight the experiences of students transformed within the case.

13.11.   Case Participants

Mezirow (1990a) was referring to adult educators when he said, "We do all have a professional obligation to become skilled in the strategies and tactics of social action education and to share this expertise where we can with those with whom we have a sense of solidarity" (p. 358). In writing about emancipatory education and transformative learning Mezirow stresses that "every adult educator has a responsibility for fostering critical self-reflection and helping learners plan to take action" (p. 357).

Dr. Jerry Zurek, professor and chair of the Communication Department at Cabrini College, has been an emancipatory adult educator for more than 40 years. Each semester in his ECG 100 course titled "Our Interdependent World," Zurek seeks to build students' knowledge, habits, values, and skills to benefit the Common Good. He actively employs an Action Research approach, working alongside his first-year students to identify global human rights violations, challenging students' sociocultural prejudices during the research process, partnering with them to action plan, and supporting them as they take action to address injustice.

In the fall of 2014, Zurek's ECG 100 learning community (LC) students examined the lives of young adults both in the United States and around the world. Special attention was given to young adults struggling to live while facing extreme hardship. The ultimate goal of the course was to educate students to become "engaged citizens of the world," a key tenet of the College's mission. Zurek sought to meet this goal by fostering a global understanding among students for integral human development and the role of the United States in other nations. He also sought to develop students' analytical skills by asking them to "examine the root causes of major international economic and social issues and their relationship" to students' lives (Zurek, 2014, para. 4). Zurek sought to shape students' moral and ethical lenses, as well as their problem solving and team building skills. Ultimately, he focused on preparing students to lead positive change based on their growing social justice mindset.

The venue for students' action in service of social change was the Lead for Change event on Cabrini Day 2014.

13.12. Description of the Sample

Zurek's ECG 100 LC course in fall 2014 consisted of 17 students, all first-semester, first-year Communication majors. These students signed up to participate in the Communication LC in order to form friendships within this cohort group in their major. Students in the COM LC take three courses together in their first semester at Cabrini College. These courses include an introductory course in the COM major, the ECG 100 LC course, and a College Success course. Students also participate in enrichment activities together, such as taking field trips to COM-related venues like the Newseum in Washington, DC, and attending speaker events on campus. In the COM LC, students establish a close bond with one another, as well as a familiar, collaborative relationship with their professors in these courses.

A classroom coach in the ECG 100 LC course also offered students guidance and support, both inside and outside the class. This coach was an undergraduate COM student and student leader in the COM Department who participated in the course previously, and who was invited to serve in this role by Zurek. Besides learning from the coach, the students also learned from three Cabrini Missioners who attended and actively contributed their insights to the class. These missioners work in Cabrini missions and schools across the world, supporting and advancing the work of the Missionary Sisters of the Sacred Heart whose founder, St. Frances Xavier Cabrini, is the patron saint of immigrants.

13.13. Case Study: Our Interdependent World

13.13.1. Background

On Cabrini Day 2014, all 17 of Zurek's ECG 100 LC students, as well as the classroom coach and Cabrini Missioners, executed a public educational experience for the College community. Their experience focused on the plight of unaccompanied minors fleeing Central America due to violence and poverty. They called this live simulation event #RefugeesSeekingSafety. Students' leadership for social action in this simulation occurred through a semester-long action learning process. The process follows Coghlan and Brannick's (2001) action research cycle as articulated by Popplewell and Hayman (2012). In this cycle:

> Action Researchers first establish the context and purpose of the research and form collaborative working relationships. Once this is

done, researchers and participants jointly construct the issues, plan action, take action and then evaluate this action — a cycle that is repeated throughout the research process. (p. 4)

13.13.2.   *Context and Purpose*

The context for the research experience was set from the very beginning of the fall 2014 semester as Zurek introduced students to his ECG 100 LC course and shared its theme, "A Global Family Portrait of Young Adults." Through this introduction Zurek began to help these first-year Communication students understand their global interdependence. As students read stories of young adults facing severe hardship, they were challenged to examine their own beliefs and explore their connectedness to social groups that had once seemed so foreign.

Zurek also awakened students to the realization that they could take immediate and important action for the poorest and most vulnerable young adults in the United States and around the world. He enabled students to understand that the purpose of the course was to grow their social consciousness and get them to act in a leadership capacity to support systemic change. Here, he explained that students would be able to share their knowledge and lead for change on Cabrini Day 2014.

13.13.3.   *Constructing*

In the early part of the semester, students studied the condition of teens and young adults in dire situations worldwide. Special focus was given to homeless youth in the United States, refugees in Syria displaced by the country's civil war, and unaccompanied minors who are refugees seeking safety from violence in countries like Guatemala, Honduras, and El Salvador. As Zurek partnered with students to help them unpack the root causes of the injustices among these populations, he also worked with them to construct a civic literacy frame that was action-oriented in its approach, compelling them to see the necessity of working for the dignity of all human beings.

Once students came to this shared understanding and became aware of their capacity to effect change, Zurek worked to foster among them the seven critical values of leadership (Astin & Astin, 1996) — the Seven C's. He assigned course readings, reflection assignments, and class discussions designed to help students gain a greater *consciousness of self*. One such assignment required students to write a reflection titled "Syria through the eyes of an 18-year-old." Zurek asked students to write their 300- to 500-word reflection as though they were an 18-year-old Syrian living in the midst of war. Students were asked to share what they would be thinking in the current state, as well as their thoughts about the future, if this were their reality.

Assignments such as this one were developed to prompt students to adopt another perspective and construct a new reality. They were also designed to have students examine their values and assumptions and consider ways in which their own actions were in *congruence* with their beliefs. Critically reflective assignments such as this one were intended to build students' *commitment* to action and social change on behalf of those persons suffering human rights atrocities.

13.13.4.   Planning Action

Planning for Cabrini Day 2014 began in earnest in October 2014. Zurek first asked students to read the bestselling text *Enrique's Journey* that tells the story of a Honduran boy who risks tremendous peril to travel to the United States in search of his mother. He then sought to foster critical reflection by having students imagine this journey as though they were taking it alongside of Enrique. How would you feel? he asked his students. They needed to write a reflection paper titled "If I were with Enrique."

With this contextual understanding of the immigration reform debate, students were allotted five class periods and told they needed to work together to prepare their Cabrini Day 2014 presentation on Central American teens fleeing their home countries. Zurek structured each of the five classes to focus on these topics, respectively: Why do they leave? What happens to them when they get to the United States? What can we do to help? How will we present this information on Cabrini Day? Rehearsal, what worked and what did not?

In preparation for each class period, Zurek assigned students several news articles for homework, as well as a short reflection on these articles. In class, students worked as a team with Zurek, the classroom coach, and the Cabrini Missioners to strategize and design an experience that would be immersive and provocative to audiences. In his role as professor, Zurek was careful to guide the planning process while allowing the students to lead and work collaboratively toward their goal. Zurek's classroom coach was integral to students' leadership development as well. She assisted them with organizing outside of class, reminded them of deadlines, and helped them stay on track.

In this way, Zurek and his classroom coach sought to facilitate the Group Values of the Seven C's. They fostered an environment of *collaboration* during the planning process. They brought students together around the *common purpose* of developing a meaningful Cabrini Day 2014 experience, helping students understand their shared responsibility and authority (Wagner, 2006), as well as their accountability to one another. They also guided students to design an experience that was informed by their newly examined and shifting individual values pertaining to the immigration debate. Both insisted upon *controversy with civility*, recognizing that diverse viewpoints can create tensions but always bringing students back to the shared goal of leading change for the Common Good.

13.13.5.   Taking Action

On the day of the event, it was time for these students to share their individual and group values with the campus community, thereby exhibiting a Seven C of *citizenship*. Students' developed a live simulation for the Cabrini Day 2014 Lead for Change event that put participants into the shoes of an unaccompanied minor fleeing a Central American country and facing extreme peril. Participants included fellow undergraduate students in all College majors, full-time and part-time faculty, and members of the administration. The experience consisted of the following steps.

13.13.5.1. Introduction and Notice of Identity

Participants encountered a table at the entrance to the live simulation where one of the ECG 100 LC students introduced the experience. The student said:

> What you're about to experience is something adults, teens, and young children in Central America experience everyday. They are starting in their home country and fleeing to the United States to escape gang violence and achieve a safer, better quality of life. Here is a card with an identity of a young person who actually made this journey. In this simulation, *you* will take this person's journey. See if you make it to the United States.

Participants received imitation money and one of six identities, which consisted of a boy or girl from Honduras, Guatemala, or El Salvador. The identities from Guatemala were on yellow index cards, Honduras on orange index cards, and El Salvador on green index cards. Each card gave a summary of a different young person and his or her journey. For example, one card said:

> Cecilia Reyes, age 16. This is her fifth time trying to leave Honduras. She hired a smuggler to get out of the country to go to the United States for freedom. She traveled alone for a month's time. She was beaten and robbed. She arrived in Texas at a gas station where armed smugglers demanded their $1,000 pay.

With their identity card and money in hand, participants walked to the appropriate color-coded index card on the floor to begin their simulated journey to the United States as an unaccompanied minor.

13.13.5.2. Encountering Danger

As participants started their journey in Honduras, Guatemala, or El Salvador, they encountered more ECG 100 LC students and Cabrini Missioners playing the role of gang members who were there to threaten, rob, or thwart participants' journey in whatever way possible. Based upon each participant's identity, the corresponding gang member would have a script. For example, Cecilia's identity prompted the gang member to say, "How many times is this for you? Keep trying; you're not going to make it." The gang members used intimidation tactics and took participants' money. The gang members would then step out of role to educate participants on an aspect of the struggle to get to the United States. Cecilia's gang member said, "These gangs threaten people until they get what they want. If you don't give them what they want, they will kill you. They don't have a problem killing people of any age."

Once participants moved beyond the gang member intimidation portion of the simulation, they encountered two more ECG 100 LC students who explained that more than 55,000 young children experience what they just experienced on a daily basis. These students went on to say that these children leave their homes and those they know and love as refugees, not immigrants. The students then led participants to the simulated United States border so they could find out the result of their journey.

13.13.5.3. At the Border

At the border, participants met additional ECG 100 LC students who explained the fate of unaccompanied minors who reach the border. They described how these young migrants would often turn themselves in to border patrol agents, only to be placed in overcrowded detention centers that provide shelter but little else like a shower, a blanket, or a warm meal. At times, students shared, the Department of Homeland Security would move these minors from shelters to group homes as they worked to locate their family, or until other care options became available.

13.13.5.4. Advocacy

After participants learned about the border experience, they encountered six ECG 100 LC students who comprised an Advocacy Team. Two of these six people debriefed the experience for participants. They said:

> Even though what you just went through was a simulation, what you witnessed is actually happening in society today. Young children in Central American countries are making this perilous journey to the United States for safety and to escape dangers back home. How can we help these young people when they arrive at our country?

These students also told participants about three key actions they can take to help unaccompanied minors. These actions included: supporting organizations creating jobs in refugees' home countries, working to fix the immigration court system, and lastly, seeing these young children as refugees in need of shelter and safety. Students very explicitly stated, "These are refugees seeking asylum, not immigrants trying to steal our jobs. They aren't coming here because they want to, but because they have to."

Participants were then led to a table with two computers where they could click to "like" the students' Facebook page for Refugees Seeking Safety or the Catholic Relief Services' (CRS) website where they could find more information on this topic. Lastly, the ECG 100 LC students directed participants to a table to sign a poster that said, "I Understand What It Means to be an Unaccompanied Minor." On this table, participants could also write down suggestions to help these unaccompanied minors, and upperclassmen would then take them to their United States Congress person when they went to lobby later in the semester. As participants exited the live simulation, they were given a paper with all the ways to continue to interact with this issue and take action by following #RefugeesSeekingSafety on social media.

13.13.5.5. Evaluating Action

Later that afternoon on Cabrini Day, these ECG 100 LC students were awarded first place for their presentation at the Lead for Change event. They received a $100 check from the College made out to CRS for their work with youth in Central America. Given the outstanding number of votes they received from participants who experienced the live simulation at the event, these ECG 100 LC students appeared to *change* participants' perspective on the immigration debate. They worked together to develop as leaders and achieve what Wagner (2006) says is "the ultimate goal of leadership development ... positive social change" (p. 9).

Following this Cabrini Day experience, Zurek assigned students the task of creating a #RefugeesSeekingSafety website. He explained his intention was to share it with CRS so that the experience could be replicated at all CRS-partner institutions, which include Cabrini College and other colleges across the United States.

Zurek also asked students to reflect upon what they learned as a result of leading the live simulation. He asked them to share these thoughts through the lenses of human rights and Catholic Social Teaching. Students shared their insights with one another in the classroom, as well as on their individual blogs and in their final papers.

Section 13.20 will present these reflections. It will link students' process to the Social Change Model, and the impact of the process to transformative learning theory.

13.14. Analysis and Interpretation

As explained through the #RefugeesSeekingSafety case study example, the Social Change Model served as the process for effectively uniting the campus around one shared vision of Leadership for Social Change. Here, the impact of that process on student learning — and organizational learning — outcomes are considered. The impact will be analyzed through the reflections of six specific students who were members of Zurek's ECG 100 LC in Fall 2014. These six students were the most reflective, the most forthcoming with their reflections, the most engaged with the action research project for Cabrini Day, and the most active in continuing to advocate for social justice.

Below is an analysis and interpretation of the experiences of these students in the ECG 100 LC, as well as the experiences of the professor. Pseudonyms are used in place of students' real names. Information is presented according to the Individual, Group, and Community Values of the Social Change Model. It is critiqued for its transformative learning impact.

13.14.1. Individual Values

In this step of the Social Change Model, the following five key themes emerged: (1) students' personalization of human rights issues affected them emotionally and opened them up to change; (2) students' mindsets formed through dominant ideologies were challenged and subsequently shifted; (3) students began to feel a sense of personal responsibility for global justice; (4) students recognized their interdependence with their global human family; and (5) students felt empowered and motivated to unite with others for social change.

13.14.1.1. Personalization and its Emotional Impact

This ECG 100 LC course focused on teens and young adults who are living in difficult and volatile conditions around the globe. Being young as well meant that the ECG 100 LC students were able to imagine their life in the shoes of these youth experiencing injustice. As Kara said:

> I feel a connection to the unaccompanied minors crossing the border because we are so close in age. It really puts things into perspective, if things had worked out just a little bit differently I could have been the one fleeing violence, illegally crossing the border, risking everything for just a chance at a better life. That is what makes me want to help, the fact that I understand what it's like to be sixteen, seventeen and eighteen years old, and I know that children that age should not be forced to do what these children are doing.

Amy reflected on the unaccompanied minors' journey from Central America to the United States and said, "In order to stop the cycle of missed birthdays and milestones of life … I would also risk everything to be with my family again if we were ever separated." Erica, on the other hand, stated emphatically that she would never be able to make the journey north, and she was also certain her younger sister could not as well. Personalization opened these students up emotionally to the realities of the young immigrants' struggles.

13.14.1.2. Mindsets Challenged and Shifted

A number of students reflected on their ignorance of global justice issues before joining the class. They acknowledged a disinterest in international affairs, stating that they didn't recognize its relevance to their lives. As Amanda stated, "I had little to no knowledge on what really goes on in the world. I also did not care about what happened outside my little circle of news."

Kara shared a similar view. She said, "For me, when I first started learning about it, I was of the mindset that this is something really awful that's happening, but it's happening in another country." As the class continued, Amanda and Kara began to see the interconnections between their lives and the lives of others who bear persecution across the globe. "It … made me realize that this is real life," Amanda said. "Just because it is not happening to me personally does not mean that it does not exist."

Maura cited her family's influence in shaping her mindset about global issues. She stated:

> Before we started talking about unaccompanied minors, I thought …
> they were coming in and taking our jobs. That was my mindset

because that's what the adults in my life always thought. So, I thought I had to think that way. But then learning and reading *Enrique's Journey*, reading the articles and all the stories that [Dr. Zurek] posted online for us to read, it really opened my mind and broke my heart.

Just like Maura, other students referenced their heart being broken by their learning experience as well. Mia revealed, "It broke my heart to read these stories about the young adults going through problems that they should not have to go through. My desire to help people in need gets stronger as the year goes on." This desire manifested for students as a feeling of personal responsibility.

13.14.1.3. Personal Responsibility for Global Justice
Once students felt personally connected to the issues of injustice and began to shift their mindsets, many felt a deep sense of personal responsibility to lead the change they would like to see. Kara said:

> When I learned about how involved we in the United States actual are in the problems that are going on there, and I learned how involved we are in the drug trade, I felt like we had ... I had this obligation to then go in and help ... because we are part of the problem.

Mia concurred with this feeling of obligation saying, "I feel like if I do not give back to those who need it that I will seem ungrateful for all that I have." Fellow students like Amanda also felt this call to act. She stated, "Whenever I see or hear about a struggle in the world, near or far from me, I always want to jump right up and help. This [course] has turned me into a completely different person but I am glad it happened."

13.14.1.4. Recognition of Interdependence
Students came to recognize their interdependence with people around the world as they studied the root causes of injustices like poverty, homelessness, drug violence, and war. Studying root causes appeared to shatter their presuppositions. Kara explained:

> Many people think that the problem of immigration starts and ends at the U.S./Mexico border but it starts long before that, in the Latin American countries they are coming from. If the situation was better in their home countries, if gangs were not such a big problem, then they would not need to come here. The drug trade is feeding the problem as well because the gangs are heavily involved in the drug trade. The bigger problem is we are feeding the demand for the drug; we in the U.S. are only adding to the major problem of the drug trade and in turn we are feeding the gangs and the violence in these countries.

Kara went on to say, "I feel like because of this class I see the world as a more global and interconnected world. That has allowed me to envision these people as my neighbors and their problems as not just theirs but as my own as well." Amy agreed saying that learning about those affected by the root causes of injustice awakened her to new realizations. "I also never thought learning about them would have such a big impact on the way I see the world and how we are all connected," she said. "No matter where you live or how you live, everyone is connected through their desires, hopes and dreams."

13.14.1.5. Empowered and Motivated to Act
According to Zurek, "As [students] learned about the suffering of their fellow humans, they sought out more information, and were moved to educate others and finally to advocate for systemic change." As Erica said, "If more people are educated then we can begin to take action."

Rather than feeling daunted by the suffering of others, many students felt energized. Instead of feeling insignificant, they felt empowered. Mia said, "Even though we were few in number, we eventually could make a difference. This was the beginning of my leadership development, which is one element of Cabrini's mission."

Students attributed their leadership development and commitment to change to their passion for justice. For example, Kara said, "I feel like with all of the passion we have for these kids we could make a big difference and make a real change." Mia wrote about this passion fueling advocacy. "Without advocacy, there would be little positive change," she said.

What is important, Kara said, is to not simply learn about these issues of systemic social injustice and stop there. She stated:

> Most importantly [this course] taught me that I can do something to help them and not only help them with the current problem they have but help them to improve their lives overall. We cannot just learn about these situations, feel bad for them and just move on. We also cannot just say something must be done, we have to go out and do it.

13.14.1.6. Transformation through Individual Values
As these reflections indicate, the students in this class examined their own personal values — tacit or expressed — and became more self-aware. By questioning their beliefs and assumptions, they began to revise them to become more congruent with their own developing worldview, not simply accepting the values of family, friends, and the status quo. For these students, their learning was both rational and emotional. Many times, they spoke about their hearts being broken, especially as they personalized the injustice and put themselves into the shoes of others.

It would appear that students' broken hearts are driving their desire to take action. At the end of this stage, students of like mindsets are coming together as a group around a common concern — namely, the plight of unaccompanied minors risking the dangerous journey to the United States. There is evidence of students' leadership and commitment, and it is built on their passion, intensity, and sense of responsibility for global justice.

13.14.2.   *Group Values*

In this step of the Social Change Model, the following three key themes emerged: (1) students negotiated their differences in viewpoints in a civil manner to form a supportive group; (2) students found immeasurable value in the guidance of their classroom coach who facilitated their collaboration by modeling leadership and passion for social justice; and (3) the public nature of students' live simulation brought them together to achieve a common purpose while still allowing them to take a personal stand on what they were learning about immigration. These themes came forth through observation of the students taking action as a group on Cabrini Day, as well as an analysis of their documented group reflections, and reflections by Zurek, the course instructor.

13.14.2.1.   Students Negotiated Differences

Students stressed the uncomfortable nature of sharing their different beliefs, values, and viewpoints with the group. Kara acknowledged:

> I had to sit back and reflect on my own personal actions to bring my
> best qualities to the table ... while recognizing that bringing the group
> together could become hostile if my attitude were to become negative.

Despite this dissonance, students came to understand that they could develop a comfort level with one another. Exercising controversy with civility, students worked to make sure everyone's voice was heard in a respectful way. This built trust and allowed members to remain comfortable in their differences while also building a harmonious relationship.

According to Zurek, students' focus on a common goal enabled them to pull together. Erica demonstrated this focus when she said:

> With very different beliefs, ideas, and viewpoints, it can easily become
> a very stressful situation to work together as a group. I found myself
> having to be comforted by the larger group to set aside my own perso-
> nal emotions to meet group goals.

As a group, students developed the ability to bring out the strengths in one another. Consequently, they became more committed to the common goal and more motivated and passionate to lead for change.

13.14.2.2.   Classroom Coach Facilitated Collaboration

Students reported the classroom coach played a significant part in their group process, as well as their leadership development. Zurek felt the same way. He said,

"The classroom coach was a key to success. A natural leader herself, the coach ... possesses intrinsic motivation to work for social justice. She is enthusiastic and passionate, with a desire to inspire these students."

Inspire, she did. Students reported that the coach's passion for the subject matter fueled their own passion. It also encouraged them to develop a deeper understanding of social justice and work in service of the Common Good. As Erica said:

> I can say ... she honestly pushed me personally to get involved with this simulation because in high school I never was involved in social justice. I never was passionate about it ... and just to ... hear what she had to say, she's honestly a big reason why ... I was involved in the simulation ... and honestly got me more into social justice than I realized.

Amy agreed saying, "She was so passionate about social justice issues. It lit a fire in me because she lit up the room when she spoke about these issues." In addition to inspiring students, the coach also served to organize students outside of class. She answered questions, gave suggestions, and contributed to the group's cohesion. Moreover, students reported that she helped them develop as leaders.

13.14.2.3. Public Platform Gave Common Purpose

"Cabrini Day brought the students together and concentrated their energy," Zurek said. Indeed, this cocurricular event provided the public platform for students to showcase their common purpose. Kara articulated this purpose when she said:

> Ensuring that everyone is treated like a human being, and everybody has the same rights, and everybody has the same basic necessities is essential for us to fight together for.

Fighting together for change meant students needed to become educated on human rights. They needed a trust-filled environment to engage in heated conversation and critical reflection. They also needed to recognize their own responsibility in bringing about systemic change. Zurek felt they did so in the course. He said, "Students deepened their insight and commitment as they internalized the conclusions they had come to about human rights themes." The clearer the themes became to students, the stronger the group's cohesion became to their common purpose.

13.14.2.4. Transformation through Group Values

As these comments from the students and the course instructor indicate, students negotiated ways of working with one another in order to achieve their common purpose. This process was wrought with friction as students navigated their discomfort of sharing viewpoints that were not supported by all. In the end, however, students realized their collective goal was bigger and more important than their individual viewpoints. They were propelled to raise awareness of the human rights issues surrounding the treatment of unaccompanied minors from Central America. With

Cabrini Day as their platform for being heard, students set aside individual differences to deliver a shared vision for change.

13.14.3. Community Values

In this step of the Social Change Model, the following significant theme emerged: (1) students lived the mission of the College on Cabrini Day and personally came to understand what it means to "Do Something Extraordinary" — the College's tagline.

13.14.3.1. Students Lived the Mission
In fact, students used these words themselves, saying the meaning of them suddenly became clear through their live simulation event. Erica said:

> Everyone that walked through the simulation was ... involved with Cabrini somehow; whether they were a student, a teacher, or a worker. They were all proud to know that students from Cabrini created this, let alone freshmen. I overheard one or two people talking about how well this goes along with the mission of the college. I was shocked to hear that. Taking a step back and actually seeing and hearing the feedback, I can see how those people said that now. Cabrini College's mission is to Do Something Extraordinary. We did exactly just that.

Others agreed saying they were really proud of shifting participants' mindsets about immigration through their simulation. They felt they met their goal of raising awareness "about the dangers and risks these refugees take in order to create better lives for themselves and their families," as Amy said. To this end, Zurek reflected, the goal of the course was not simply to transfer knowledge, but to formulate students' moral character. He stated that this outcome was achieved as a result of "a combination of factors [that] came together in a moment of grace."

13.14.3.2. Transformation through Community Values
As these reflections convey, students joined together as a leadership group to spark a public dialogue about immigration reform and social justice. Their simulation actively engaged members of the community in a conversation about a highly politicized issue with seemingly no solution. The students challenged this assumption. They challenged audiences — just as they had challenged themselves — to open their minds and their hearts to a more intimate reality of the plight of immigrant minors. As such, they exhibited citizenship through their service to the Common Good and helped others feel empowered and inspired to join them in leading change.

In the end, they came to see the truth in Wagner's (2006) writing about the Social Change Model. As she states, "All students can do leadership. Leadership development is not reserved for students holding leadership positions, but is for any student wanting to engage with others to create change" (p. 8).

13.15.   Conclusion

How is it possible to "Educate a Heart"? This is, after all, the mission of Cabrini College. As described in this chapter, the answer lies in the integration of students' curricular and cocurricular experiences. It begins first in the classroom. Here, as part of an action research cycle, faculty introduce students to poignant stories of hardship and injustice. They ask students to relate these stories to their own lives; to personalize the injustice; and to examine their values, beliefs, and assumptions.

Once students' hearts are broken through these compelling stories, faculty give context to students and discuss why these injustices are taking place. In other words, they unpack the root causes. Through this examination students become motivated to address these causes, to come together around a common purpose, and to lay aside individual differences in service of the Common Good. With this shared vision and plan for change in place, faculty provide students with the forum to take action. Students, recognizing their responsibility as engaged citizens of the world, educate others on the injustice. They lead positive change with — and for — the community.

Students, like the ones in Zurek's ECG 100 LC course, educated hearts on Cabrini Day. They did so in conjunction with their faculty members who used the Social Change Model in their courses to express leadership as a process. As part of this process, faculty promoted the values of equity, social justice, collaboration, citizenship, and service to foster transformative learning and group empowerment. The result is that students came to see their shared humanity and responsibility to work together in service of others.

In short, educating hearts can be achieved through the thoughtful implementation of the Social Change Model. Here at Cabrini College, the model effectively linked curricular and cocurricular experiences on Cabrini Day and united the campus around one shared vision of Leadership for Social Change. It also transformed students' worldviews and encouraged them to continue to apply their academic excellence and commitment to social justice to lead for positive social change.

References

Astin, A. W., & Astin, H. S. (1996). *Guidebook for a social change model of leadership development*. Los Angeles, CA: Higher Education Research Institute.

Astin, A. W., & Astin, H. S. (Eds.). (2000). *Leadership reconsidered: Engaging higher education in social change*. Battle Creek, MI: W. K. Kellogg Foundation.

Baumgartner, L. (2012). Mezirow's theory of transformative learning from 1975 to present. In E. W. Taylor & P. Cranton (Eds.), *The handbook of transformative learning: Theory, research, and practice* (pp. 99–115). San Francisco, CA: Wiley.

Brydon-Miller, M., Greenwood, D., & Maguire, P. (2003). Why action research? In A. Campbell (Ed.), *Action research in education* (pp. 9–27). Thousand Oaks, CA: Sage.

Cabrini College. (2014). *Undergraduate catalog 2014–15*. Retrieved from http://www.cabrini.edu/Academics/Resources-and-Support/Undergraduate-Catalog/

Calhoun, E. F. (1994). *How to use action research in the self-renewing school.* Alexandria, VA: ASCD.

Coghlan, D., & Brannick, T. (2001). *Doing action research in your own organization.* London: Sage.

Cranton, P. (2000). Individual differences and transformative learning. In J. Mezirow (Ed.), *Learning as transformation: Critical perspectives on a theory in progress.* San Francisco, CA: Jossey-Bass.

Cranton, P. (2006). *Understanding and promoting transformative learning: A guide for educators of adults* (2nd ed.). San Francisco, CA: Jossey-Bass.

Cranton, P. (2008). *Basic theoretical terms and concepts: Overview.* Unpublished manuscript. Retrieved from http://transformativelearningbermuda.com/uploads/Basic_Theoretical_Terms_and_Concepts_of_TL.doc

Cranton, P., & Taylor, E. W. (2012). Transformative learning theory: Seeking a more unified theory. In E. W. Taylor & P. Cranton (Eds.), *The handbook of transformative learning: Theory, research, and practice* (pp. 3–20). San Francisco, CA: Wiley.

Creswell, J. W. (2007). *Qualitative inquiry & research design.* Thousand Oaks, CA: Sage.

Dick, B. (2006). Action research literature. *Action Research, 4*(4), 439–458.

Dirkx, J. (2001). Images, transformative learning, and the work of soul. *Adult Learning, 12*(3), 15–16.

Ettling, D. (2012). Educator as change agent: Ethics of transformative learning. In E. W. Taylor & P. Cranton (Eds.), *The handbook of transformative learning: Theory, research, and practice* (pp. 536–551). San Francisco, CA: Wiley.

Jacoby, K. (1996). Service-learning in today's higher education. In K. Jacoby (Ed.), *Service-learning in higher education* (pp. 3–25). San Francisco, CA: Jossey-Bass.

Kasl, E., & Elias, D. (2000). Creating new habits of mind in small groups. In J. Mezirow (Ed.), *Learning as transformation: Critical perspectives on a theory in progress.* San Francisco, CA: Jossey-Bass.

Kegan, R. (2000). What "form" transforms? A constructivist-developmental approach to transformative learning. In J. Mezirow (Ed.), *Learning as transformation: Critical perspectives on a theory in progress* (pp. 35–69). San Francisco, CA: Jossey-Bass.

Komives, S. R., Lucas, N., & McMahon, T. R. (1998). *Exploring leadership: For college students who want to make a difference.* San Francisco, CA: Jossey-Bass Publishers.

Merriam, S. B., & Kim, S. (2012). Studying transformative learning: What methodology? In E. W. Taylor & P. Cranton (Eds.), *The handbook of transformative learning: Theory, research, and practice* (pp. 355–372). San Francisco, CA: Wiley.

Mezirow, J. (1990a). Conclusion: Toward transformative learning and emancipatory education. In J. Mezirow (Ed.), *Fostering critical reflection in adulthood: A guide to transformative and emancipatory learning* (pp. 354–376). San Francisco, CA: Jossey-Bass.

Mezirow, J. (1990b). How critical reflection triggers transformative learning. In J. Mezirow (Ed.), *Fostering critical reflection in adulthood: A guide to transformative and emancipatory learning* (pp. 1–20). San Francisco, CA: Jossey-Bass.

Mezirow, J. (1991). *Transformative dimensions of adult learning.* San Francisco, CA: Jossey-Bass.

Mezirow, J. (1997). Transformative learning: Theory to practice. In S. Imel, J. M. Ross-Gordon, & J. E. Coryell (Eds.), *New directions for adult and continuing education* (Vol. 74, pp. 5–12). San Francisco, CA: Jossey-Bass.

Mezirow, J. (2000). Learning to think like an adult: Core concepts of transformation theory. In J. Mezirow (Ed.), *Learning as transformation: Critical perspectives on a theory in progress* (pp. 3–33). San Francisco, CA: Jossey-Bass.

Morse, J. (1991). On the evaluation of qualitative proposals. *Qualitative Health Research, 1*(2), 147–151.

Moustakas, C. (1994). *Phenomenological research methods*. Thousand Oaks, CA: Sage.

Nyden, P. W., Figert, A. E., Shibley, M., & Burrows, D. (1997). *Building community: Social science in action*. Thousand Oaks, CA: Pine Forge Press.

Ozanne, J. L., & Saatcioglu, B. (2008). Participatory action research. *Journal of Consumer Research, 35*(3), 423–439.

Popplewell, R., & Hayman, R. (2012). *Where, how, and why action research approaches used by international development non-governmental organisations?* International NGO Training and Research Centre, Briefing Paper 32, pp. 1–16.

Puckett, J. L., Harkavy, I., & Romer, D. (2000, Fall). Action research as an approach for improving service, teaching and research. (Special issue). *Michigan Journal of Community Service Learning*, 113–118.

Reason, P., & Bradbury, H. (2001). Inquiry and participation in search of a world worthy of human aspiration. In P. Reason & H. Bradbury (Eds.), *Handbook of action research: Participative inquiry and practice* (pp. 1–14). London: Sage.

Shapiro, S. A., Wasserman, I. L., & Gallegos, P. V. (2012). Group work and dialogue: Spaces and processes for transformative learning in relationships. In E. W. Taylor & P. Cranton (Eds.), *The handbook of transformative learning: Theory, research, and practice* (pp. 355–372). San Francisco, CA: Wiley.

Strand, K., Marullo, S., Cutforth, N., Stoecker, R., & Donohue, P. (2003). *Origins and principles of community-based research*. San Francisco, CA: Jossey-Bass.

Stringer, E. (2014). *Action research* (4th ed.). Thousand Oaks, CA: Sage.

Taylor, E. W. (2000). Analyzing research on transformative learning theory. In J. Mezirow (Eds.), *Learning as transformation: Critical perspectives on a theory in progress* (pp. 285–328). San Francisco, CA: Jossey-Bass.

Taylor, E. W. (2007). An update of transformative learning theory: A critical review of the empirical research (1999–2005). *International Journal of Lifelong Education, 26*(2), 173–191.

Tisdell, E. J. (2012). Themes and variations of transformational learning: Interdisciplinary perspectives on forms that transform. In E. W. Taylor & P. Cranton (Eds.), *The handbook of transformative learning: Theory, research, and practice* (pp. 21–36). San Francisco, CA: Wiley.

Van Kaam, A. (1959). Phenomenological analysis: Exemplified by a study of experiences of really feeling understood. *Journal of Individual Psychology, 15*(1), 66–72.

Van Kaam, A. (1966). *Existential foundations of psychology*. Pittsburgh, PA: Duquesne University Press.

Wagner, W. (2006). The social change model of leadership: A brief overview. *Concepts & Connections: A Publication for Leadership Educators, 15*(1), 8–10.

Wagner, W., Ostick, D. T., & Komives, S. R. (2006). *Leadership for a better world: Understanding the social change model of leadership development*. San Francisco, CA: Jossey-Bass.

Zurek, J. (2014). *Syllabus for ECG 100 our interdependent world*. Retrieved from https://ecg100.wordpress.com/syllabus/

Chapter 14

Student Team-Based Semester-Long Applied Research Projects in Local Businesses

Anne Bradley, Peter Richardson and Cath Fraser

Abstract

Purpose — This chapter describes an alternative model to out-of-the-classroom learning which has been highly successful in assisting students in New Zealand to make the transition to either the workplace, or to higher qualifications.

Methodology/approach — The final paper within the New Zealand Diploma in Business is 'Applied Management' in which students work in groups to design and implement a semester-long research inquiry with a host organisation. The authors discuss the challenges and strategies associated with delivering this paper and reference three current studies which relate to this student cohort: the first about students' perceptions of cooperative learning in groups, and the alternate selection and assessment techniques the university has been trialling; the second about a Maori mentoring pilot pairing students with mentors in the workplace; and third, examining students' experiences and expectations of the Diploma as a pathway into degree study.

Findings — Our story offers an example of how a focus on quality and accountability to local business stakeholders has created a successful co-curricular learning environment, and suggests the value of combining the three strands of research, teamwork and co-curricular projects.

Originality/value — While the context is of a small, regional institute, many of the elements of good practice will be transferable to other higher education providers.

Keywords: Student research; group projects; business immersion; work placements

Integrating Curricular and Co-Curricular Endeavors to Enhance Student Outcomes
ISBN: 978-1-78635-064-0

14.1.   Introduction

14.1.1.   The New Zealand Higher Education Sector and the Employability Imperative

The higher education sector in New Zealand traverses quite an array of provision and provider models. Our eight universities, the youngest of which was established as recently as 2000, account for 33% of our post-secondary students. The remaining two thirds are dispersed between 18 Institutes of Technology and Polytechnics (ITPs), two colleges of education, three wananga (a publicly owned tertiary institution that provides education in a Maori cultural context) and an ever-changing array of private training establishments (PTEs), with 604 registered at the time of writing. In consequence, there is a correspondingly wide range of subject, level and quality within the courses on offer. There are also multiple provider agreements where introductory courses and entry level qualifications from one institute receive credits in recognition of prior learning, and ensure enrolment, or contribute to higher level qualifications awarded by another. The government's *Tertiary Education Strategy 2014–2019* (Ministry of Education [MOE], 2014) specifically calls for a more 'outward facing' and 'high-performing' (p. 2) tertiary education system, with strong links to industry and the global economy. The economic outcomes sought include employment, relevant skills and knowledge for labour productivity, and better access to skilled employees for business. The same document notes that 'In any given year in New Zealand, about 250,000 new jobs are created, and a similar number cease' (p. 9) but that while this is a relative constant, the combined after-effects of the recent global financial crisis, with national challenges such as the large rebuild needed after a significant earthquake in the South Island's largest city of Christchurch, mean that there is currently a considerable mismatch between the job market and the available labour pool. Employers are once again starting to find it difficult to attract people with an appropriate range of both specific and transferable skills, and narrowing this gap has become the number one priority for higher education organisations in our country, as well as further afield. There is therefore an emphatic and overt focus on employability as a graduate outcome, nationally and individually for each institute. There is a strong element of 'social exchange' (Haar & Brougham, 2012) or shared interest here: students need robust career options and well-paid professional roles, and human resources are widely recognised as the most valuable asset in organisations (Lee & Bruvold, 2010; Schaufeli, Bakker, & Salanova, 2006; Yamamoto, 2013). Good connections between industry and providers are seen as the key to meeting the needs of both parties (MOE, 2014). This is an imperative with which all higher education providers are familiar, and is certainly a key driver in our own institution's qualification development and delivery.

14.1.2.   BoPP and the Applied Management Course

The Bay of Plenty Polytechnic (BoPP) is a small/medium-sized regional organisation in New Zealand's ITP network, delivering certificate, diploma and undergraduate degree programmes with strong pathways established for our students to feed into partner universities for post-graduate study. A core aspect of our business is vocational and professional training; in today's competitive market, we have to be highly responsive to the changing needs of the workplace, and maintain a very close scrutiny over the quality of what we offer and the value ascribed to our qualifications. We are always mindful of the imperatives established by the government's strategic plans as outlined above and these are incorporated in our own vision statement of 'Eke Panuku — Reaching our potential together' and the aim of 'Contributing to the realisation of the national tertiary education strategy' (https://www.boppoly.ac.nz/). BoPP offers programmes which are designed to enable students to progress towards, and ultimately achieve an employment-enabling qualification which has strong local support from the business world, and external quality approval ensuring credit recognition by other providers. The 'School of Business' faculty is focussed on providing education courses for the local, national, and the international market, and one of our flagship programmes is the New Zealand Diploma in Business, a 'nationally recognised qualification' (New Zealand Qualifications Authority [NZQA], n.d.) that allows learners to gain a broad range of general business skills and knowledge, followed by an opportunity to focus on career related options such as accountancy, banking, finance, management, marketing and tourism. Students must complete 12 level 5 and 6 papers (100 and 200 undergraduate level) including a number of compulsory and optional requirements determined by NZQA. The Applied Management paper we offer is one of these, and is deliberately pitched as a transitional paper, to assist students to move from their diploma-level study, to either employment, or onto further undergraduate study with a partner university, to complete a four year Bachelor of Management Studies, or a three year Bachelor of Business Analysis or Bachelor of Tourism qualification. Research skills and co-curricular workplace learning are the paper's central foci, and students are encouraged to wait until their final semester before tackling this paper, as it draws extensively on cumulative prior learning. Earlier papers have required students to complete smaller tasks involving host organisations, and the concept is that these will have served as a training platform for a semester-long, self-directed group project within a local business. The official descriptor states: 'Students will identify a managerial problem, and research and apply management concepts and tools to find and recommend possible solutions to the problem' (NZQA, 2011). By seeking to move students from a theory and concept-based learning environment, to a practical and applied setting, the Applied Management paper is following a well-established and growing trend for offering co-curricular learning opportunities — a trend now well traversed in the literature.

14.2. Literature Review

14.2.1. *Co-curricular Learning — Benefits and Challenges*

'Time and time again' says Andrews (2013), 'employers tell us that a degree alone is not indicative of a well-rounded graduate' (p. 1). Higher education providers need to reassess their role: it is no longer enough just to provide the opportunities for students to achieve good academic results, rather we now need a wider curriculum to develop the range of skills and attributes students will need to succeed in the many and varied roles they will encounter in future life. Part of this objective can be achieved by offering flexible qualifications which allow students to build an academic record by selecting papers which match their interests and aspirations — as is the case with the large number of papers students can select from in the Diploma in Business. However, the other part of the equation is the 'co-curriculum': the activities beyond the classroom that are instigated and facilitated by effective learning programmes, but that are nonetheless closely related to classroom learning and coursework (Andrews, 2013; Storey, 2010). Supervised co-curricular activities include variations like work/field placements, internships, business mentors, role shadowing, work/study assignments and co-constructed research projects (Storey, 2010). The common intention is to provide the opportunity to integrate skills acquired through study with actual applied experience (Leung, Ng, & Chan, 2011). The literature notes three categories of benefits which arise from participation in such endeavours: benefits to the organisation, to the employer, and to the learners. Organisations benefit, says Gutowski (2006), through industry recognition and marketing as a place where students receive a holistic education, and as a provider of quality graduates. Advantages to employers include the introduction to some prospective job-seekers as well as gaining evidence or answers to a business issue which has been formally investigated under tutor supervision (Cicekli, 2013). But the main recipients of gains from co-curricular activities are the learners, for whom involvement can be a transformative experience, strengthening their engagement and commitment to their study pathway, and confidence in their career decisions. Hamrick, Evans, and Schuh (2002) provide a useful framework of five categories of outcomes that can be expected from the co-curricular experience: educated persons; skilled workers; democratic citizens; self-aware and interpersonally sensitive individuals; and life skills managers. Other lists outline the learning outcomes which accrue, for example the following from Penn State University (2006): knowledge acquisition/application; cognitive competency, life skills and self-knowledge, personal integrity and values, intercultural development, and leadership and active citizenship. Arguably, all these outcomes are essential to assist the graduate not just in their first destination after graduating, but further forward, and throughout their life journey. Already discussed in the introduction to this chapter, is the way in which employability has emerged at the forefront of much of our higher education work. Employability is almost always the prime reason students give for enroling in a qualification (Leung et al., 2011; Storey, 2010) and one of the Key Reporting Indicators required by government agencies (MOE, 2014). There is an extensive literature around the qualities organisations need and seek from newly recruited graduates, but a useful synthesis is provided by the meta-analysis undertaken by Cicekli (2013) which looked at 28 international studies, with sample sizes varying from 12 to 872 employers. Cicekli concluded that 'although some employers seek education-specific or industry/job-specific qualities, most qualities sought are generic qualities' (p. 53). These generic skills/competencies required by organisations in the 21st century were: communication, interpersonal, and teamwork skills; Cognitive skills; motivation, willingness and enthusiasm; data/information- and technology-related skills; time management and ability to work under pressure; being ethical; leadership skills; personality/character (including honesty, self-confidence and conscientiousness); and previous work/internship experience. How are employers identifying these attributes? Through the reputation of the credentialing organisation, through grades, and — equally importantly — through evidence of accomplishments and experience in co-curricular activities (Cicekli, 2013). The benefits of co-curricular work and learning are therefore well established, and one might expect to see this element more widely embedded across multiple disciplines in higher education — yet the reality is often that such initiatives are voluntary additions which students can opt in and out of, or, where they are part of required course work, are still relatively ad hoc and can vary from year to year, reliant on the course convenor's own contacts and networks. The Advisory Board Company (2011) cites a study conducted by the Student Affairs Leadership Council drawn from more than 30 universities in the United States and Canada, advocating for an urgent address of the status of co-curricular activities in a climate of fiscal pressure and funding cuts. The challenges, they say, are threefold: 'accreditation, budget constraints, and the need to demonstrate impact' (p. 2). The Council's research addressed the issue of accreditation of programmes by governing bodies (in New Zealand's case this is the four yearly Self-Assessment External Evaluation and Review process, supported by internal Annual Programme Evaluation Review processes), saying that co-curricular learning outcomes are increasingly playing a bigger role in accreditation, where education providers have defined learning outcomes for these activities, and well-developed plans to assess them. The onus, therefore, is on the institution to ensure that the co-curricular portion of a qualification is an integrated and essential element, supported by all the criteria which surround in-class, taught units of learning. Similarly, confronting ongoing budgetary constraints means that divisions are under 'greater pressure than ever' to demonstrate that they are investing funds in programmes 'that effectively support student learning and development' (The Advisory Board Company, 2011, p. 5). Clearly those who provide and value co-curricular learning experiences need to find ways to collect data and systematically document learning outside the classroom. With co-curricular learning widely extolled for the opportunities it offers in intellectual, social, moral and emotional development (e.g. Hamrick et al., 2002), a key issue, long recognised, is that there has never been an efficient way to document shifts in capability (Gutowski, 2006). This is a dilemma for courses such as our credit-bearing Applied Management paper, and to some extent has driven much of our decision-making around the course's shape and scope. Biggs (2003) outlines the importance of assessment as a primary driver of student learning — what is measured is what matters to students, and the amount of choice the prescription allows in terms of content (the Applied Management prescription is included as the appendix as an example of one in which there is considerable leeway for contextualisation), provides the catalyst for self-directed and problem-based approaches to teaching and learning that have enormous potential value for learners, once the considerable challenges in planning and facilitation have been met. The flex available within a course of co-curricular learning cuts to the heart of educational philosophy as Biggs sees it: are students here to pass a course, and gain a qualification, or are they here to develop a professional life? If this were not argument enough, there is also a well-established drive to chronicle the development of graduate attributes beyond content knowledge as a strategic focus in tertiary education (Barrie, 2004; Cicekli, 2013). Once again employability is at the forefront, with these attributes' primary purpose to place students in a far better position for their future careers (Storey, 2010). Gutowski (2006) suggests that alongside academic transcripts which serve to demonstrate the outcome 'educated persons', perhaps the co-curricular transcript, by capturing students' education outside the classroom, can demonstrate the rest of these soft skills/generic learning outcomes. Together, academic and co-curricular transcripts would communicate the entire scope of students' education — their experiences and the knowledge, skills, and abilities acquired through the entirety of their higher education career. Another example of a solution to credentialing external learning is the 'place-based framework' referred to by Spalding, Williams, and Wise (2014) for designing and assessing learning outcomes. This cyclical, six-step model attempts to combine 'direct measures of student learning where they demonstrate what they know and can do, with indirect assessment where students report perceived changes in attitudes and knowledge and skills' (para. 28). Methods include surveys, journaling, mid-term reflections, legacy projects and transition binders, photos, reflection, and case study results and findings. No examples of research-reports-reflections assessments, such as the approach taken by the Applied Management course discussed in this chapter, were found.

14.2.2.   Groups and Teamwork

The other field of literature with which our version of an extended work-based co-curricular immersion closely resonates is that of group work, prominent in both higher education and organisational workplaces. There is a vast body of research in both education and management disciplines on the benefits of 'teamwork' in achieving desired outcomes, and teams have become a key approach to structuring both work and learning over the past two decades (Appleblaum & Blatt, 1994; Bosworth & Hamilton, 1994; Hernandez, 2002; Jackson, 1995; Tarricone & Luca, 2002; Zakarian & Kusian, 1999), however, research also suggests that the potential value of team work is frequently not realised (Rotfield, 1998; Van der Vegt & Bunderson, 2005; Verderber & Serey, 1996). Hernandez (2002) states 'employers … need employees who know how to work effectively with others. Self-managed teams are performing increased amounts of work in many organisations today' (p. 74) and he also acknowledges that team learning can promote students' engagement and thinking skills. Baker and Clark (2011) cite evidence that students who learn in groups develop increased intercultural understanding and tolerance, improved interpersonal skills, higher level thinking skills and that they are better prepared for the modern participative workplace. Priority One of New Zealand's Tertiary Education Strategy states 'The priority is to ensure that the skills people develop in tertiary education are well matched to labour market needs' (MOE, 2014, para. 5), so that group and team work is clearly a valuable course component. However, in the workplace and in the classroom, simply putting people in groups does not create effective teams, with typical issues including 'unclear goals, mis-management, conflict and unequal participation' (Hansen, 2006, p. 12). This is further exacerbated when students are completing an assessed task situated outside the classroom, involving a complex range of project and relationship management skills. The requirement to assess individual achievement within such assessments, usually via some sort of peer evaluation (Gutowski, 2006) often results in a self-destructive spiral of conflict and self-justification. Thus, spending time on group formation and development (Tuckman, 1965) is a key to successful completion of the assignment tasks, and team facilitation and support is an important element of the teacher's role. Bosworth and Hamilton (1994) highlight the importance of a supportive environment which provides 'scaffolding' until individuals and teams develop the skills and understanding that enable them to function independently. Importantly, group learning differs from engaging in group conversations. Group learning, also known as cooperative learning, suggests the use of reflection or sharing past experiences to explain current understanding. These reflections and experiences are individualised and strengthened in multiple settings, within and outside the classroom, developing a well-rounded learner. Self-awareness is obviously important, and one of the essential pre-conditions of successful collaborative learning is individual accountability but in practice, 'social loafing' and inequitable participation are constant threats to the process, with an especially high level of student reporting, say Baker and Clark (2011), in culturally diverse groups. These authors advocate specific training for teachers in higher education institutes around group formation, group operation, and group and individual assessment considerations, to ensure that the group learning process is a rewarding experience for all participants. Further, education practitioners in New Zealand tertiary institutions, where the student body consists of a diverse mixture of domestic and international students from a range of educational, cultural and societal backgrounds, require solutions developed *in situ* to encourage pedagogically sound and culturally accommodating group management frameworks that fit our distinct national profile. The particular response developed by the Applied Management paper to harness and integrate the benefits of both co-curricular experiences and group learning, is a good example of an attempt to provide just such a solution.

14.3.   A Practical Implementation: About the Applied Management Paper

The New Zealand Qualifications Authority (NZQA) course prescription for Applied Management (see the appendix), a 20 credit, level 6 paper, is unusual in that it does not specify content, but rather outlines three assessment tasks that students must complete. Students (working in teams of up to six) select a management topic or issue and develop a research proposal, using a local organisation as a case study, and carry out primary and secondary research to diagnose and analyse the issue and develop practical recommendations which they present orally and in a report. These tasks represent 75% of the overall mark for the paper, and address Learning Outcomes 1 and 2: identifying a problem and writing a proposal, and then reporting on the findings from their research. They also individually evaluate the project in a separate assignment worth 25% of their total mark, which completes Learning Outcome 3: critically reviewing the process (New Zealand Qualifications Authority, 2011). The course prescription for Applied Management is included at the end of this chapter (see the appendix). In order to achieve this, students must negotiate access to a local organisation, which will provide the 'case' for the project, and must lead an on-going process of data collection and discussion with organisational members, and satisfy organisational managers that ethical and professional standards are being upheld. Class time at the start of the paper is focussed on developing a research proposal to meet the sponsor's business needs, understanding the role of a literature review, creating primary data collection instruments and writing supporting documentation. Once the proposal is approved the students manage the research, analysis and reporting processes as an independent learning project supported by the course lecturers — or tutors, as we call our academic teaching staff. Outputs are submitted for final assessment, but also presented to the business management. Students must also complete a comprehensive individual evaluation of the quality of the project, the effectiveness of the team and their own contribution, which introduces an element of reflection vital to the experiential learning process (Baker & Clark, 2011; Kolb, 2014). Thus, students can gain a number of benefits from this course: transferable employment skills such as collaboration, project management, problem solving, communication and conflict resolution, together with the development of a relationship with the organisation involved, research skills and increased knowledge and understanding of a particular management topic, as depicted in Figure 14.1.

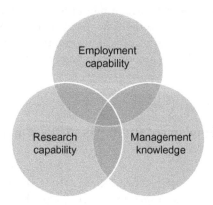

Figure 14.1: The three outcome competencies for applied management graduates.

Students often comment that they enjoy this paper, because it is 'real'. This example of integrated curricular and co-curricular learning has multiple benefits for learners; however, successful completion of the course requires the application of a complex range of knowledge and skills and places a major emphasis on students as independent, self-motivated learners. Most participants have no prior research experience, very little experience working in or managing teams, no project management experience and few of the independent learning skills assumed by this approach. In addition to this, Information Technology students have the option to complete the paper as part of the Diploma in Applied Computing Level 6, and come to the process with little or no knowledge of the management theory and practice which the Diploma in business students have been studying for the past two years. Over recent iterations of delivery, workshops and mini-lectures have been developed to cover key management topics, team dynamics, research methods and academic writing skills, and provide an increasing level of support, structure and guidance for teams via small group tutorials, which has resulted in excellent course completion rates. However, the effect of this was that delivery had become progressively more traditional and 'teacher-focussed' over the past few years, which has not facilitated the skill development needed for learners to carry out their research projects and manage their teams effectively and independently. We are trying to rectify this slip, and shift our practice back to better reflect adult learning theory which advocates student-centeredness (e.g. Biggs, 2003), as well as align with our organisation's vision of 'Students — first, last and always!' It has therefore been vital to develop a clear strategy for the preparation and facilitation of student teams in order that the potential value of their off-campus semester's work can be gained, and this is the topic of a current action research project involving a professional inquiry into the delivery of the course. This new approach will include visits from a number of senior managers from successful local businesses to discuss current local business issues, and the implementation and evaluation of enquiry learning approaches involving specific team-based, cooperative learning strategies to try and improve the preparation of groups of learners and equip them to work in teams, carry out and write up their research and gain the benefit of the new knowledge and experience they need in their future careers (Bosworth & Hamilton, 1994; Gibbs, Rust, Jenkins, & Jaques, 1994; Hansen, 2006; Michaelsen, Bauman-Knight, & Fink, 2002).

14.4.   An Evolving Delivery: Preparing the Students

14.4.1.   *An Emphasis on Group Work*

Students presenting for their first Applied Management class will probably be expecting the typical learning environment: seats set up in rows facing the whiteboard and data-show screen, where they can place themselves according to their need for anonymity or engagement. In short, they anticipate a fairly traditional educational experience focussed on teacher-led discussion, most likely involving a number of power-point slides and video clips. They are often surprised to learn that in this paper, unlike all the others, they are in charge: it is the students who select the topic, identify the subject of their project and decide what, when and how they will carry it out, within defined parameters. These students are in their second or third year of study, and usually include a range of ages; the majority straight from secondary school but a sprinkling of mature learners too, with a mix of gender and culture and a small percentage of international students. Yet despite the diversity on offer, most appear to have experienced minimal interaction with their peers, and their learning experiences to date are often not especially memorable. Indeed, if you ask them what they have learned from their studies so far, the answer is most often rather shockingly sketchy, and may only slightly increase with further prompting and questioning.

The existing knowledge students generally bring to this paper is therefore minimal, and in order to address this, a series of workshops were developed to refresh students' understanding of the core management principles they are required to apply in their projects. However, as mentioned above, over time the effect of this was that the paper became increasingly delivered as a 'taught' paper, with teacher-led classes absorbing much of the classroom time at the cost of developing effective research and team work skills, and getting students underway with their co-curricular placements as expeditiously as possible. It has become an on-going challenge to achieve congruence between a desire to impart the necessary knowledge and the understanding that traditional teaching methods are the least effective means of achieving this (Bosworth & Hamilton, 1994; Knight & Wood, 2005; Kolb, 2014), and that effective teaching and learning involves a partnership between a community of learners engaged in 'as real as possible' activities that simultaneously build knowledge and skills, facilitated by a structure, environment and people that support them. Most of these students have past experience completing group assignments with varied results, and there is evidence of a dramatic increase in group work amongst business faculty across the Western world (Hansen, 2006; Hernandez, 2002). However, studies show that many students are simply put into groups with little or no preparation, and minimal support or structure to enable them to work effectively as a team, manage a project and deal with conflict (Ettington & Camp, 2002; Hansen, 2006), and so the idea of a semester-long group assignment which forms 75% of the summative assessment for the paper fills many of them with apprehension and unease. Early findings from our current study on student perspectives of collaborative assessment indicate that, although students acknowledge the potential benefits of completing assignments in groups, they have clear concerns about equitable contribution and evaluation. Structured team formation, monitoring and evaluation activities are important strategies for managing such issues (Bosworth & Hamilton, 1994; Gibbs et al., 1994; Hansen, 2006). Hansen (2006) notes recent graduate comments about teamwork such as 'Teamwork skills are a must at my job. The many group projects really gave me a taste for how to deal with group dynamics' (p. 17).

14.4.2. Team Formation

Since almost all the semester will be spent conducting their group research into some aspect of an external organisation's business, we make sure the first sessions of the course prepare the students to establish strong working relationships and good decision-making about group development. Teams are not formed until week 3 of the course, and a number of activities are completed during these first weeks that enable the formation of 'strategic teams' — that is, diverse teams with a range of existing knowledge, skills and attitudes. Such activities include Belbin's 'Teams Roles Analysis' (Belbin, 2010) which is available on-line from www.Belbin.com, and a checklist of skills and personality traits that enables students to individually self-evaluate their own strengths and what they can contribute to a team. We also cover an introduction to interpretivist and positivist research perspectives which allows students to locate themselves on a continuum between the two approaches, with a view to working with a team from a similar research perspective. The team formation process involves sharing a summary of individual team behaviours, skills, traits and perspectives and working together to join students in balanced teams. Small class numbers enable this to be done in a supportive and open manner, facilitating a balance between student preferences, such as 'I want to work with my friends', and the need to ensure equitable, well balanced teams. Student teams are then required to produce a Team Charter, including their goals, expectations, roles and responsibilities for each team member and a timeline for project completion.

14.4.3. Progress Monitoring

Until recently, monitoring of team progress was carried out via informal discussions during team tutorials with the teacher, with the result that often conflict and other problems were not addressed in a structured way, or not identified at all due to the reluctance of team members to criticise each other, until the final evaluation at the end of the project, when it was too late to act. A new initiative has been introduced which provides a structured approach to formative feedback and monitoring of team performance part-way through the semester, in the form of a mid-semester review (Figure 14.2), which is completed first in 'cross over groups' each containing a member from each of the research teams, and individual mid-semester evaluations completed by each team member about each individual on their team (Figure 14.3). The individual evaluations are collated by the teacher and a summary of the overall evaluation is given to each team member, to encourage honesty via anonymity.

The purpose of this process is to encourage students to share issues and ideas with each other across different teams, identify any issues and provide the opportunity for resolution or improvement prior to project completion. These mid-way evaluations are also useful as a source of data — not just about student achievement and learning, but also about perceptions of value, and skills development. Students also learn about giving and receiving feedback, and reflect on this in their journals — which also constitute another source of data.

MID SEMESTER REVIEW

    1. Complete individually
    2. Discuss in your cross-over group
    3. Share ideas with your project team and identify key action points.

The most enjoyable thing for me in the paper so far this semester has been:

The most challenging thing for me in this paper so far this semester has been:

The most interesting or useful thing for me in this paper so far this semester has been:

One thing we have done as a team which has helped us to work effectively and learn is:

One thing which goes wrong or we have had trouble with in our team is:

One thing we need from the tutor is:

Figure 14.2: Mid-semester review. *Source*: Adapted from Gibbs et al. (1994).

14.4.4. *Evaluating Individual Contribution and Team Performance*

The final piece of assessment for this paper is an individual evaluation of the project, including the effectiveness of the team, the quality of the research process and outcomes, and key learning about the research topic, which carries a considerable weighting of 25% of the overall grade for the paper. Previously, this had been completed either as a 'journal' during the course or as a reflective essay, and these were submitted at the end of the semester — with mixed results. Many students evidently did not understand how to reflect on their experiences of co-curricular learning outside the normal academic setting, and failed to evaluate critical elements in sufficient depth during the semester, and so gained minimal benefit from the process. The teaching team has now introduced a weekly on-line journal with open questions focussed on independent tasks and classroom activities that week, intended to engage students in a continuous process of reflection and action, and guide them in the development of reflective thinking skills. The journal is completed and marked each week, and this provides an effective mechanism for structured formative feedback throughout the course. The group research report, including an oral presentation of the project, forms the major piece of summative assessment for this course, carrying a weighting of 60% of a student's final grade. Measurement of individual contribution to such substantial group projects is fraught with potential for conflict, and a number of strategies have been developed to manage this dynamic and create equitable outcomes for each participant; however collaborative learning experts all agree that there is no magic formula and some conflict is inevitable in the unpredictable world of teamwork (Bosworth & Hamilton, 1994; Gibbs et al., 1994; Hansen, 2006). The first touchpoint in this process is the mid-semester review and feedback process, which facilitates early detection and resolution of problems. In addition, students are now each required to submit a short, individual literature review from which the secondary research section of the research report is

GROUP MEMBER EVALUATION FORM					
Team Member _____					
Professionalism			Rating Scale: 1 (low) to 5 (high)		
Expectation:	1	2	3	4	5
Prompt attendance at team meetings					
Meets deadlines					
Contributes fair share of workload					
Teamwork					
Develops/discusses ideas & makes constructive suggestions					
Listens and incorporates team feedback in own work task					
Is a good listener and encourages others to contribute					
Academic Standards					
Written work delivered as agreed, (quality & quantity)					
Demonstrates a grasp of theory and links to project (referenced correctly)					
Demonstrates critical thinking/evaluation skills					
Overall comments					
What specific suggestion would you make to this person for work on future projects?					
What was this person's most valuable contribution to the group?					

Figure 14.3: Individual evaluation. *Source*: Adapted from Bosworth and Hamilton (1994).

developed. This is marked separately and added to the group report mark to provide individual differentiation, and to ensure that every team member has completed wider reading and can contribute to the development of recommendations at the end of the project. Students are required to complete a final individual evaluation of each team member (Figure 14.3) at the end of the course, and this feeds into the allocation of final individual marks for the report. This approach to evaluation has received an extremely positive response from the governing agency, NZQA, with the Applied Management marking rubric and assessment instructions published as an exemplar in 2012. The action research we are currently undertaking will help us determine the continued efficacy of these assessment methods, as well as trialling a range of cooperative learning tools and techniques in the quest to better prepare students for their co-curricular engagement.

14.4.5.   The Research Requirement

Once students have formed their groups we embark on the central focus of the paper: that students conduct meaningful, relevant research in a local organisation. This requires them to understand and apply research skills including the development of a research proposal, creating appropriate research instruments, collecting and analysing primary data, undertaking a literature review and synthesising their findings to develop a set of practical recommendations for the organisation. This is the first time these students have undertaken a formal business research project. There is therefore a need for students to acquire an understanding of relevant research methods, the research process, research ethics and indeed the language of research. They also need to factor in their responsibilities to their external, workplace sponsors, as well as satisfying tutors' expectations. These elements, alongside team formation, are also covered in the early weeks of the course. Research skills development is facilitated through the gamut of typical teaching resources: readings, exemplars, class discussions, group analysis of successful and less useful accounts of research into similar topics, panels of invited researchers from outside the programme, video clips and so on. It is the need to interweave the diverse demands this paper presents that has led to the re-development of the delivery of this course. The co-curricular, outside the classroom learning seeks to engage these students in meaningful learning that enhances not only their knowledge of the subject, but also provides them with opportunities to develop skills and attitudes that will be useful and relevant to them in their future professional lives. Our research to date suggests that team-based enquiry learning and problem-based learning strategies promise to simultaneously expose students to the necessary knowledge and skills in team work, research skills and understanding of the topic (Barrett & Moore, 2011). Feedback from past students confirms that the skills and research experience they gain in this paper specifically help them as they progress to higher level study and employment.

14.4.6.   Making the Connection with Business Sponsors

Implicit within this process is the development of a working relationship with key members of a real business (or not-for-profit organisation) which will become the case study for the student teams' research, and this is an important axis of real connection between the institution and its external stakeholders. Working with a real business is fundamental to completion of the paper, provides students with a sense of relevance and meaning to their study, and creates an applied understanding of their research topic (Hansen, 2006). The process begins with student teams brainstorming possible businesses or industries which interest them. In practice, many projects develop from students' own contacts and networks in the community, including friends and relations, and past and current employers. Where students are unable to generate their own leads, the tutor may offer suggestions — particularly likely where students come from outside the region, or country. Students are responsible for making initial contact with the organisation, gaining access and agreement of parameters and ethical considerations, and on-going communication during the project. This is overseen by the tutor, who provides a formal letter of introduction explaining the course requirements and contact details for feedback or queries. A confidentiality agreement template is available which can be signed by the students and the organisation representative who is approving the project, and many organisations request anonymity in the written research report to protect themselves from the potential for commercially sensitive information to become public. Once students have connected with an organisation which is keen to sponsor a research project, it is up to the students to develop a proposal which outlines the research topic, scope, method(s), ethics, analysis and reporting. Data collection cannot begin until the proposal document has been approved by the tutor, and a record of the student teams, project topics and sponsoring organisations has been submitted to our institute's Research Committee, although actual approval is granted by the class tutor and School of Business' Research Leader. The following are examples of research inquiries completed by student teams in previous years:

- How can (a local surf and skate retailer) effectively integrate and engage seasonal staff to maximise productivity during the summer season?
- How effective was the change management strategy during the recent re-structure of (a local kiwifruit packhouse), and what recommendations can be made to increase the effectiveness of these changes?
- How does the organisational culture at (a local telecommunications business) affect team performance, and what changes can be made to create a more productive culture?
- How well does the current structure at (the local regional council) meet the needs of the organisation and its stakeholders, and what improvements could be made to the current structure to facilitate the achievement of organisational aims?
- What motivation strategies are in place at (a local supermarket), how effective are they and what recommendations can be made to increase staff satisfaction and motivation?
- What is the level of staff engagement at (a local pre-school), and what strategies can be implemented to increase engagement?
- How are systems and procedures (at a local aged care provider) impacting performance, and what recommendations can be made to improve the workflow?
- What is the current level of motivation and satisfaction amongst volunteers at (a local charity), and what strategies can be recommended to engage voluntary workers?

Once the proposal has been accepted, the student teams manage their own projects — utilising the introductory material covered in early classes about group management, communication, monitoring, recording and so on. Research teams meet with the tutor on a weekly basis, and there are often instances of friction and debate, but the general principle is to assist the student teams to find their own solutions, wherever possible. At the agreed deadline, groups are required to submit a full report of the research, including their conclusions and any recommendations for the business sponsor, and present their findings to the class. A copy of the report is also made available to the business sponsor. Local businesses vary in their attitude towards these projects. Most often projects are treated purely as academic in purpose and although mangers may read the report, the result is limited in terms of action or implementation. In terms of the credentialing requirements, an organisation's only responsibility is to 'host' the student group. However, we are slowly building a track record of occasions when projects are initiated by a business which has identified specific issues for research and is prepared to implement practical recommendations resulting from the project, which of course is immensely satisfying for the student team and course tutors.

14.5.   How Do We Know it Works?

Satisfied customers — both students and the business partners who host them — are of course important, but such anecdotal and informal feedback needs to be supported with more rigorous evidence, especially when a paper occupies a fairly pivotal position within a larger qualification. As described above, the New Zealand Diploma in Business level 6 is a 240 credit qualification made up of a selection of twelve 20 credit courses or papers that can be completed part or full-time, and are offered by a number of NZQA accredited ITPs and PTEs. Our organisation, BoPP, offers the Diploma as a face-to-face lecture/tutorial delivery or as an online blended model. One of the major benefits and points of difference for the BOPP Diploma students is that they receive a guaranteed full credit of their diploma courses into the University of Waikato's (UOW) business degrees Bachelor of Management Studies (BMS), Bachelor of Business Analysis (Financial) (BBA(Fin)) and Bachelor of Tourism (B Tour). The guaranteed credit is conditional upon a student receiving a B grade average over all papers. The 636 Applied Management paper is one that can be chosen as an elective in the Diploma in Business qualification and for the Diploma in Applied Computing level 6 but is also a compulsory course for students who wish to graduate with a New Zealand Institute of Management level 5 Diploma in Management. Since the Applied Management paper traverses a number of qualifications, and may be a key experience in preparing our students for a successful transition to degree study with our university partner UOW, it is vital that we understand the student experience and expectations of their co-curricular learning experience, and the Diploma as a whole.

14.5.1.   Collecting Evidence

In addition to responsibility to our academic partners, and our students, part of our organisation's strategic goals for the next five years is to grow a pervasive research culture, and recent or current research inquiries related to the New Zealand Diploma in Business sit within this vision. Mention has already been made of the action research underway on student perspectives of group work and collaborative assessment within the Applied Management paper. Since this study will rely largely on students self-reporting, ongoing attempts to cross-reference results with other forms of data will include use of achievement grades compared with previous cohorts and other Diploma papers, as well as integrating findings from complementary studies. A second related research project is a recent exercise of pairing Maori Diploma students as mentees with a Maori mentor currently working in a business workplace related to the student's career aspirations; another opportunity for co-curricular learning opportunities, but which in this case, is outside the actual programme of study. This is discussed in more detail below. The largest study taking place at time of writing is a research project which has been examining our students' first destination intentions, and questioning how successful this programme is as a pathway in preparing graduates for higher qualifications and employability in their field. While this survey includes all the Diploma graduates, and not just those who undertook the Applied Management paper, it does provide useful insights regarding students' immediate employability goals and destinations, and emphasises the close relationship between education providers and business/industry. The online survey of Diploma graduates from 2009 to 2014 included a series of questions identifying demographic characteristics, followed by a number of closed and open questions that were dependent on whether the respondent continued on to enrol with the UOW and complete a business degree or alternatively finished studies after the Diploma. Students were also asked a series of rating questions in terms of their Diploma and degree experiences and were able to expand on those ratings with key reasons, including a comparison of their initial expectations and graduate outcomes. In contrast to the other two studies which drew on techniques of coding and theming in keeping with qualitative research conventions, data analysis for the survey results was statistical, and the following account summarises the most significant correlations and frequencies of responses. Seventy per cent of valid responses (71) were female which is consistent with the gender enrolment data over that period 2009–2014. Also consistent with enrolments was the ages of respondents with more than 60% being 30 years or younger at the time of the survey, that is, after they have graduated, with an average age of graduates of 31 years. Students of European descent accounted for 71% of the sample, with Maori (12.5%) and non-English speaking background New Zealand residents (6%) the next two largest ethnicities.

14.5.2. Employment Outcomes

Eighty per cent of respondents were currently employed and 20% were not employed. Graduates who identified as employed were asked whether their current employment was related to the Diploma in Business qualification: just over half said it was. This could imply that graduates are finding employment but not necessarily in the field of study they focused on. Graduates were also asked: 'Do you use the skills obtained during your NZ Diploma in Business?' Of the 104 students who responded to the question, 75% said yes and 25% no. They were then asked to identify which skills they use in their employment. Key word analysis identified the top 5 skills in order of frequency to be teamwork, reporting, communication, presentations, and research. Interestingly, a much higher number of female graduates (83%) than males (58%) were using the skills learned during diploma studies in their employment, so that a future inquiry might well be into the types of employment that male Diploma graduates are finding where they are not using the skills or content knowledge learned during their studies. There was also a significant difference between ethnicity and employment, with 89% of NZ European graduates being currently employed compared to 46% of Maori graduates, unfortunately a typical pattern for Maori representation in business occupations overall (Mintrom & True, 2005). This result raises the question of whether, and how this outcome can be influenced through programme or BoPP institutional changes.

14.5.3.   *Co-curricular Mentoring to Address Ethnic Achievement Gaps*

Raising outcomes for Maori students is a national challenge, and like employability, another of the Key Reporting Indicators required of education providers by government (MOE, 2014). One counter-measure to historical disadvantage which is gaining popularity, and has recently been trialled in our own organisation, is that of pairing Maori tertiary students with a Maori mentor drawn from the business area the student wishes to enter once graduated (Katu, 2015). Mentoring activities included a lot of co-curricular learning, with the mentee attending the mentor's workplace and meeting other business networks for the purpose of finding out more about the wider business industry, job functions, employment opportunities, study advice and cultural considerations. A key result was that the Maori tertiary students experienced a positive change in their personal development and expressed a greater motivation to complete their studies, confirming Buckley and Zimmerman's (2003) earlier study which found that mentoring can promote positive identity as well as the encouragement of employment ambitions. In the small study conducted to date, all mentors and mentees were satisfied with the mentoring activity they had completed together, and were pleased they were part of the process in deciding what they would do to prepare the Maori tertiary student for employment. A recommendation from this early trial is that mentees should be given a particular project to carry out, which would allow further depth and understanding of the business industry — in other words, a project similar to that undertaken as part of the Applied Management paper, although none of the mentee participants had selected this course option. All mentees agreed on the benefit of recording their mentoring goals alongside their study and employment plans — in other words, of providing evidence of learning outcomes from their out-of-class learning experience, as described by The Advisory Board Company (2011).

14.5.4.   *Degree Pathway*

Returning to the larger survey of Diploma graduates, results showed that of the 103 valid responses to a question about subsequent enrolment in a degree programme at UOW, 72 graduates or 69.9% had done so, and another 9 students had continued studies at other universities, both in New Zealand and overseas. Most students who had not continued on to higher qualifications had gained employment, or else cited financial constraints. The same group of students who did not continue with the degree pathway were asked 'What aspects of the Diploma in Business programme provided the most value?' and 'generic knowledge' was the primary response to this question. Once again, the biggest demographic difference noted in results was the lower number of Maori graduates (38%) who continued with their degree studies completed compared to 76% of NZ European. When this group was asked about the transition from a polytechnic to the university, the overwhelming majority (97%) of the students who responded to this question stated that the Diploma pathway assisted them in the transition to higher level study at UOW. Reasons for their rating ranked 'foundation knowledge' (43%) most prominently, followed by 'strong foundation of study/academic skills' (26%) and 'strong support' (11%). While this particular project did not seek to isolate individual courses within the Diploma for scrutiny, in a general sense it is possible to carry over the findings to the Applied Management paper and the co-curricular learning it offers through placing students in a commercial workplace and requiring them to research authentic organisational concerns. Students in the survey, whether they were in employment or pursuing higher qualifications, acknowledged the value of their Diploma experience in developing skills in teamwork, reporting, communication, presentations and research — all integral components of the semester-long external learning Applied Management experience.

14.6.   Concluding Remarks and Future Directions

Many of our Diploma students find the very term 'research' daunting and would happily avoid it, but we believe we would be remiss in our duty of providing a well-grounded and stable platform from which students can graduate into higher qualifications or employment if we shy away from the challenges of offering this type of academic work. As Brew (2007) emphatically puts it:

> For the students who are the professionals of the future, developing the ability to investigate problems, make judgements on the basis of sound evidence, [make] decisions on a rational basis, and understand what they are doing and why, is vital.
> Research and inquiry is not just for those who choose to pursue an academic career. It is central to professional life in the 21st Century. (p. 7)

This is not to dismiss the very real demands made on all stakeholders. The power to choose their own 'topic' and create their own 'knowledge' requires a paradigm shift in thinking for both students and teachers. In a simple model of traditional teaching, the teacher sets the topic (according to the course prescription), transmits the required information to the students via various means, and then tests them on how much they remember of the information they have been told. In a research-based setting, the students work in teams, decide what they need to know and the teacher facilitates the process: learning becomes a process of 'construction', rather than 'reception' (Barrett & Moore, 2011), and this requires a range of skills from the students that are not developed in traditional teaching settings (Bosworth & Hamilton, 1994). Developing new and transferable skills and graduate attributes through applied research projects is so similar to the rationale for promoting both co-curricular endeavours and group learning, that we were surprised not to find more written about how well these three learning pedagogies combine. We hope that this chapter provides a useful account of such a nexus, as well as some possible solutions to some of the challenges around evidencing and credentialing learning outcomes from engagement in the world beyond the lecture theatre. Today's world is complex: the graduate job market is highly competitive, knowledge is growing exponentially, economies and environments are in flux. If we want our students to be well-rounded, if we want our programmes to be transformative, and if we want institutes to be relevant, we need a wider curriculum. If we accept that our graduates will undertake many and varied roles in their future life, surely the learning experiences we provide should be equally diverse and multi-faceted. A one-semester, group learning, applied research project in a local business, is just the beginning!

References

Andrews, M. (2013). Why our students need co-curricular, not extra-curricular, activities. *The Guardian*, January 22. Retrieved from http://www.theguardian.com/higher-education-net-work/blog/2013/jan/22/student-development-university-curriculum-design

Appleblaum, E., & Blatt, R. (1994). *The new American workplace*. Ithaca, NY: Cornell University Press.

Baker, T., & Clark, J. (2011). *Cooperative learning lecturer training programme*. Wellington: Ako Aotearoa. Retrieved from https://akoaotearoa.ac.nz/download/ng/file/group-6/cooperative-learning-lecturer-training-programme.pdf

Barrett, T., & Moore, S. (2011). *New approaches to problem-based learning: Revitalising your practice in higher education*. New York, NY: Routledge.

Barrie, S. (2004). A research-based approach to generic graduate attributes policy. *Higher Education Research & Development, 23*(3), 261–275.

Belbin, M. (2010). *Management teams: Why they succeed or fail* (3rd ed.). Burlington, MA: Elsevier.

Biggs, J. (2003). *Teaching for quality learning at university — What the student does* (2nd ed.). Buckingham: Open University Press.

Bosworth, K., & Hamilton, S. J. (1994). *Collaborative learning: Underlying processes and effective techniques.* San Francisco, CA: Jossey-Bass.

Brew, A. (2007). Research and teaching from the students' perspective. Paper presented at the International Policies and Practices for Academic Enquiry: An International Colloquium, Winchester, UK, April. Retrieved from http://portal-live.solent.ac.uk/university/rtconference/2007/resources/angela_brew.pdf

Buckley, M., & Zimmerman, S. (2003). *Mentoring children and adolescents: A guide to the issues.* Connecticut, MA: Praeger Publishers.

Cicekli, E. (2013). Human resource needs of organizations in terms of the qualities they need and seek from new graduate employees. *International Journal of Business and Social Science, 4*(1), 49–58.

Ettington, D. R., & Camp, R. R. (2002). Facilitating transfer of skills between group projects and work teams. *Journal of Management Education, 26*(4), 356–379.

Gibbs, G., Rust, C., Jenkins, A., & Jaques, D. (1994). *Developing students' transferable skills.* Oxford: Oxford Centre for Staff Development.

Gutowski, J. (2006). Cocurricular transcripts: Documenting holistic higher education. *The Bulletin, 74*(5), 2.

Haar, J. M., & Brougham, D. (2012). *Testing a cultural inclusion dimension towards job outcomes: The mediating effects of perceived organizational support.* Unpublished presentation. *New Zealand Psychology Conference*, Wellington, New Zealand, 20–23 April.

Hamrick, F. A., Evans, N. J., & Schuh, J. H. (2002). *Foundations of student affairs practice: How philosophy, theory and research strengthen educational outcomes.* San Francisco, CA: Jossey-Bass.

Hansen, R. S. (2006). Benefits & problems with student teams: Suggestions for improving team projects. *Journal of Education for Business, 82*(1), 11–19.

Hernandez, S. (2002). Team learning in a marketing principles course: Cooperative structures that facilitate active learning and higher level thinking. *Journal of Marketing Education, 24*(1), 21–42.

Jackson, S. E. (1995). Consequences of diversity in multidisciplinary work teams. In M. A. West (Ed.), *Handbook of work group psychology* (pp. 53–75). Chichester: Wiley.

Katu, M. (2015). *The use of mentoring to prepare Maori tertiary students for employment.* Unpublished Master's thesis. Auckland University of Technology, Auckland, New Zealand.

Knight, J. K., & Wood, W. B. (2005). Teaching more by lecturing less. *The Journal of Cellular Biology Education, 4*(4), 298–310.

Kolb, D. A. (2014). *Experiential learning: Experience as the source of learning and development* (2nd ed). Upper Saddle River, NJ: Pearson Education.

Lee, C. H., & Bruvold, N. T. (2010). Creating value for employees: Investment in employee development. *The International Journal of Human Resource Management, 14*(6), 981–1000.

Leung, C. H., Ng, C. W. R., & Chan, P. O. E. (2011). Can co-curricular activities enhance the learning effectiveness of students? *International Journal of Teaching and Learning in Higher Education, 23*(3), 329–341.

Michaelsen, L. K., Bauman-Knight, A., & Fink, L. D. (2002). *Team-based learning: A transformative use of small groups in college teaching.* Westport, CT: Praeger.

Milton-Brkich, K. L., Shumbera, K., & Beran, B. (2010). Action research: How to create your own professional development experience. *Science & Children* (Summer ed.). Arlington, VA: National Science Teachers Association.

Ministry of Education. (2014). Tertiary education strategy 2014–2019. Priority 1: Delivering skills for industry. Wellington, New Zealand. Retrieved from http://www.education.govt. nz/ministry-of-education/overall-strategies-and-policies/tertiary-education-strategy

Mintrom, M., & True, J. (2005). *Framework for the future: Equal employment opportunities in New Zealand.* Wellington: Human Rights Commission.

New Zealand Qualifications Authority. (2011). *636 Applied management prescription, version 2.* [Course outline]. Retrieved from: http://www.nzqa.govt.nz/assets/qualifications-and-standards/qualifications/NZ-Diploma-in-Business/Prescriptions/636-applied-management-V2.pdf

New Zealand Qualifications Authority. (n.d.). *New Zealand diploma in business.* [Course outline]. Retrieved from http://www.nzqa.govt.nz/qualifications-standards/qualifications/business-qualifications/nz-diploma-in-business/

Penn State University. (2006). *Cocurricular learning outcomes.* Retrieved from http://edge. psu.edu/cocurr.shtml

Rotfield, H. (1998). Hello, bird, I'm learning ornithology. *Marketing Educator, 17*(4), 4–6.

Schaufeli, W., Bakker, A., & Salanova, M. (2006). The measurement of work engagement with a short questionnaire: A cross-national study. *Educational and Psychological Measurement, 66*(4), 701–716.

Spalding, H., Williams, D. R., & Wise, V. L. (2014, May). Designing and assessing learning outcomes: A framework for co-curricular sustainability programs. *Journal of Sustainability Education, 6*(May). Retrieved from http://www.jsedimensions.org

Storey, K. L. (2010). *Bridging the gap: Linking co-curricular activities to student learning outcomes in community college students.* Unpublished doctoral thesis. National Louis University, Chicago. Retrieved from http://digitalcommons.nl.edu/cgi/viewcontent.cgi?article=1030& context=diss

Tarricone, P., & Luca, J. (2002). Employees, teamwork & social independence – A formula for successful business? *Team Performance Management, 8*, 54–59.

The Advisory Board Company. (2011). Aligning co-curricular initiatives with learning outcomes: Key challenges facing student affairs leaders. Washington, DC. Retrieved from http://sa.utep.edu/assessment/files/2013/10/EAB-Report-Aligning-Co-Curricular-Initiatives-with-Learning-Outcomes.pdf

Tuckman, N. B. (1965). Developmental sequence in small groups. *Psychological Bulletin, 63*, 384–399.

Van der Vegt, G., & Bunderson, S. (2005). Learning & performance in multidisciplinary teams: The importance of collective team identification. *Academy of Management Journal, 48*(3), 532–547.

Verderber, K. S., & Serey, T. T. (1996). Managing in-class projects: Setting them up to succeed. *Journal of Management Education, 20*(1), 23–38.

Yamamoto, H. (2013). The relationship between employees' perceptions of human resource management and their retention: From the viewpoint of attitudes toward job-specialties. *The International Journal of Human Resource Management, 24*(4), 747–767.

Zakarian, A., & Kusian, A. (1999). Forming teams: An analytical approach. *IEE Transactions, 31*(1), 85–97.

APPENDIX: COURSE PRESCRIPTION FOR APPLIED MANAGEMENT

Source: http://www.nzqa.govt.nz/assets/qualifications-and-standards/qualifications/ NZ-Diploma-in-Business/Prescriptions/636-applied-management-V2.pdf; New Zealand Diploma in Business 636 version 2.

Prescription: 636 Applied Management
Elective prescription
Level 6
Credit 20
Version 2
Aim Students will identify a managerial problem, and research and apply management concepts and tools to find and recommend possible solutions to the problem.

Prerequisites 530 Organisations and Management or equivalent knowledge and skills.

Recommended Prior 560 *Business Communication* or equivalent knowledge and skills.

Table A.1: Assessment.

Learning outcomes	Assessment weighting (%)
1. Students will identify a managerial problem in an existing organisation and write a project proposal for the research of possible solutions.	15
2. Students will report (oral presentation and written report) on the team's research findings and the application of management concepts and tools in recommending solutions to an identified managerial problem.	60
3. Students individually will critically review the completed project process and outcomes.	25
Total	**100**

All learning outcomes must be evidenced; a 10% aggregate variance is allowed.

New Zealand diploma in business 636 version 2 Assessment notes

1. Assessment materials must reflect relevant and current legislation, standards, regulations and acknowledged industry/business practices.
2. *Organisation* refers to a specific entity which may be — in private, public, or community and volunteer sectors; a business unit, Maori, or other special-purpose body.

Table A.1: (*Continued*)

New Zealand diploma in business 636 version 2 Assessment notes

---

3. Students must work as part of a team of up to six students. In exceptional circumstances where students are unable to meet this requirement, they may work as part of an organisational team.
4. Individual contribution to the overall team effort must be verified and reflected in the individual's final grade (this may be achieved through Learning Outcome 3).
5. This prescription is not intended to allow for sociological issues to be researched and used as the managerial problem.
6. The managerial problem chosen must:
   (a) Be of a suitable size and scope to be effectively addressed within the timeframe of the course and within the parameters of the prescription.
   (b) Not have a simple or obvious solution and require research and analysis to devise an appropriate solution(s).
   (c) Require a solution which will improve efficiency or effectiveness.
   (d) Be capable of being the subject of primary research on a specific organisation.

Learning Outcome 1

Students will identify a managerial problem in an existing organisation and write a project proposal for the research of possible solutions.

Key elements:A problem in an existing organisation that will enable students to demonstrate key elements of Learning Outcome 2.
(a) The project proposal will include:
   problem identification with rationale
   project plan including scope, resources and time frame
   suitable problem solving model(s) and other management concepts and/or tools to be used
   research methodology to be used.

Learning Outcome 2

Students will report (oral presentation and written report) on the team's research findings and the application of management concepts and tools in recommending solutions to an identified managerial problem.
Key elements:
(a) The report will include:
   the problem
   secondary and primary research data
   analysis of data
   findings
   possible solutions

Table A.1: (*Continued*)

Learning Outcome 2
evaluation including consequences of possible solutions final recommendation/s with rationale the final project proposal (included in appendices) The report content will evidence the application of a range of management concepts and tools The oral presentation and the written report will be suitable for presentation to senior management of the organisation under study.
Learning Outcome 3

Students individually will critically review the completed project process and outcomes.
Key elements:
(a) Team evaluation:
   effectiveness of self and other team members in the project
   recommended improvements.
(b) Project evaluation:
   effectiveness of the processes used and solution(s) proposed
   recommended improvements.

PART V
LEVERAGING CO-CURRICULAR ENDEAVORS

Chapter 15

Assessing Competencies: Extending the Traditional Co-Curricular Transcript to Include Measures of Students' Skills and Abilities

Stan M. Dura

Abstract

Purpose — This chapter acknowledges the current dearth of direct evidence of student learning and discusses the limited value academic and co-curricular transcripts (CCTs) provided to students, educators, and employers.

Methodology/approach — This chapter studies the myriad outlets in which students acquire useful academic and non-academic skills outside of the grade point system. Disadvantages in the arbitration and secular nature of the common transcript are also addressed.

Findings — Exploring and responding to the concerns from a diverse chorus of higher education constituents and calls for increased accountability and improved student learning in higher education, this chapter proposes the development of an outcomes-based CCT, as an extension of the traditional CCT, to take advantage of the rich and numerous learning opportunities within the living laboratory of co-curricular experiences where students repeatedly demonstrate and hone their skills and competencies throughout their collegiate experience.

Originality/value — The chapter discusses a number of examples and models of what such a program might look like and provides insights and suggestions as to how it could be implemented thoughtfully and effectively. It also explores several of the benefits and challenges associated with implementing an outcomes-based CCT.

Keywords: Co-curricular; transcript; outcomes-based; accountability; improvement; assessment

Integrating Curricular and Co-Curricular Endeavors to Enhance Student Outcomes
Copyright © 2016 by Emerald Group Publishing Limited
All rights of reproduction in any form reserved
ISBN: 978-1-78635-064-0

15.1.   Where Is the Evidence?

15.1.1. Declining Confidence

Since at least the 1980s, various higher education stakeholders, including students, faculty, administrators, employers, parents, and lawmakers, had begun questioning whether higher education is effectively and efficiently educating its students. The 1980s saw several efforts to examine approaches to and assessment of teaching and learning, beginning with the establishment of the National Commission on Excellence in Education in 1981 (Ravitch, 1990), which resulted in the seminal and controversial report, "A Nation at Risk." There were numerous reforms at the national and state levels, and the National Board for Professional Teaching Standards was established to test credential new teachers (Ravitch, 1990). Arguably, the 1980s was when the term "educational reform" gained household recognition. In the 1990s, measures of productivity and institutional effectiveness were elevated in the discourse (Leveille, 2006). Government leaders began to set benchmark goals pertaining to grades, retention, college-readiness, literacy, etc. (Ravitch, 1990), and Congress established State Postsecondary Review Entities to review institutions with high default rates (Glidden, 1996). House Select Committee on Children, Youth, and Families released a report examining the negative correlation between tuition hikes and faculty teaching times; at schools where tuition went up the highest, teaching time decreased and class size increased (Schroeder, 1992).

Interestingly, these two decades served as a metaphorical fork in the road. In one direction lay the path of improvement embedded in the popular "learning-centered" and "student-centered" movements in the 1990s, where institutions focus on and measure what students learn, and in the other direction lay the path toward accountability, emphasizing inputs (test scores, faculty quality, endowments, etc.) and outputs (grades, graduation rates, satisfaction, etc.) as measures of institutional effectiveness (Leveille, 2006). Barr and Tagg (1995) best articulated the improvement perspective as the "Learning Paradigm," guided by the sentiment that institutions of higher education exist to produce learning (as compared to graduates, degrees, credit hours, research, etc.). The Learning Paradigm focused on the quality and effectiveness of teaching, asking the question "if learning did not occur, did teaching occur?" It concerned itself with a nuanced attention to students, their diverse needs, styles, backgrounds, etc. The accountability perspective was best exemplified by the rapid increase of performance indicators mandated by state legislatures and educational boards (Leveille, 2006), such as Astin's I-E-O model (1993), and the development of the National Survey of Student Engagement (NSSE) in 1998. The I-E-O model was an assessment structure focusing on inputs of actuarial, institutional, and student characteristics and outputs of grade point average (GPA), retention, etc., which are mediated by environmental variables, such as involvement, teaching quality, etc. The NSSE was the first comprehensive, high-level assessment tool designed to help discern the degree to which students reported behaviors and experiences that were positively or negatively correlated with student success. Thus, the accountability perspective concerned itself with quantitative, institutional-level indicators of institutional effectiveness and quality. Curiously, while these two paths are rather complementary, higher education sectors have tended to focus rather exclusively on one or the other; the "Learning Paradigm" is beginning to dominate in the classroom, and accrediting entities are beginning to emphasize direct evidence of student learning over inputs and outputs, yet administrators and governing boards, along with state and national lawmakers, focus heavily on inputs and outputs and tend to overlook or avoid actual learning.

Since the 1990s, and particularly following the economic recession of 2008, the inputs and outputs have been worrisome and stakeholder confidence in higher education has continued to suffer. College enrollment has increased 48% since 1990 according to the National Center for Education Statistics (2014), however there has not been a corresponding increase in degree attainment (Bound, Lovenheim, & Turner, 2010). The proportion of college students who receive degrees has actually been declining, while the length of time they take to graduate has been increasing, and this is almost entirely attributable to underprepared students at less selective colleges and universities (Bound, Lovenheim, & Turner, 2007).

Responding to these concerning inputs and outputs, diverse choruses of stakeholders have expressed their lack of confidence in higher education. With the average student loan debt at almost $30,000 (The Institute for College Access and Success, 2014), public concerns about student loan debt appear virtually weekly in the media. Public college and university presidents report a lack of confidence in their governing boards (Rivard, 2013), and the National Commission on College and University Board Governance (2014) criticized college and university boards for being out of touch with public sentiment, not working well with institutional leaders, and not paying enough attention to the educational qualifications of candidates in the recruitment of board members. College leaders believe employers are most interested in a graduate's major and academic achievement (Sternberg, 2013), while employers are criticizing higher education for producing graduates that cannot solve problems, communicate clearly, or think critically, arguing that these skills are more important to them than the student's major and field related knowledge (Hart Research Associates, 2013; Newman, Couturier, & Scurry, 2004).

15.2.   The Evidence We Have and the Evidence We Need

There are generally four sources of evidence colleges, and universities can use them to determine if they are achieving their educational mission, and institutions usually rely on just three of them, namely actuarial evidence, expert opinion, and the perceptions of students, alumni, and employees (Keeling & Hersh, 2012). Actuarial evidence consists of the financial and academic "bling": the inputs and outputs, that college and university leaders constantly reiterate, including endowments, research grants, scholarships, faculty expertise and publications, expenditures per student, average Scholastic Aptitude Test (SAT) of the incoming class, etc. Then, there are actuarial evidence leaders who tend to talk less openly about, including institutional debt, loan default rates, graduate employment rates and salaries, etc. They also enjoy bragging about presidential and media rankings when their institution places well within them, and they downplay them when the institution is ranked poorly. The most common form of evidence is student and alumni perceptions that usually take the form of surveys. These include the Chronicle's "Great Places to Work For" survey, various graduate student outcomes surveys, student and alumni testimonials, and student perceptions on several types of self-report surveys, such as benchmarking, satisfaction, and climate surveys. Many of the most common student surveys, such as the NSSE, Student Engagement at a Research University survey (SERU), the Multi-Institutional Study of Leadership survey (MSL), the Your First College Year survey, the Learning and Study Strategies Inventory (LASSI), the College Student Experiences Questionnaire (CSEQ), and the Global Perspectives Inventory (GPI), are virtually a part of our everyday vernacular. Colleges and universities select positive results from these data to showcase their success, and they can provide useful information about various facets of institutional performance, yet self-report measures have been found to be unreliable and often invalid across multiple disciplines (Del Boca & Noll, 2000; Donaldson & Grant-Vallone, 2002; Prince et al., 2008). Thus, they cannot provide the fourth and most critical type of evidence institutions need — *whether or not students are learning* (Ewell, 2008; Keeling & Hersh, 2012; Keeling, Wall, Underhile, & Dungy, 2008; U.S. Department of Education, 2006).

This important point often gets lost in the debates over academic preparedness, job readiness, and performance standards: *higher education has little evidence to show exactly if and what students learn.* With attention focused on the inputs and outputs, evidence of what students actually gain in terms of learning is scarce (Keeling et al., 2008). In 2000, the *Measuring Up* initiative of the National Center for Public Policy and Higher Education gave all states in the nation an "Incomplete" due to a complete lack of consistent evidence of student learning (Ewell, 2008). Between 2000 and 2008, several states participated in projects designed to look at student learning in a structured manner so as to be able to compare across institutions; however, participation in those projects has dwindled and attention to measuring student learning is widely uneven across states (Ewell, 2008). An increasing number of institutions are participating in the Voluntary System of Accountability (VSA), developed by the National Association of State Universities and Land Grant Colleges (NASULGC) and the American Association of State Colleges and Universities (AASCU), which is positive in many ways. Unfortunately, these efforts do not provide the evidence states and the nation need in terms of establishing policy, and the motivations behind them are mostly political in terms of avoiding the imposition of government standards and reporting requirements instead of improving student learning (Ewell, 2008).

15.3. What Are Students Learning?

While unfortunate, these political concerns are quite valid as initiatives to hold colleges and universities accountable for costs, graduation rates, loan default rates, and graduate employment outcomes are underway. It is not uncommon for state legislatures to consider bills that stipulate higher teaching loads for college and university faculty and educational funding models tied to superficial performance indicators. A recent task force of the U.S. Senate found that "many rules are unnecessarily voluminous and too often ambiguous, and that the cost of compliance is unreasonable" and many regulations were unrelated to education, student safety, or financial stewardship (Task Force on Federal Regulation of Higher Education, 2015, p. 1). Even the federal government has recently put higher education on notice (The White House, 2013) not long after the Spellings Report documented "disturbing signs that many students who do earn degrees have not actually mastered the reading, writing, and thinking skills" expected of college students, and noted that "literacy among college graduates has actually declined" (U.S. Department of Education, 2006, p. vi).

In a similarly grave tone, Keeling and Hersh (2012) write that "Too many of our college graduates are not prepared to think critically and creatively, speak and write cogently and clearly, solve problems, comprehend issues, accept responsibility and accountability, take the perspective of others, or meet the expectations of employers" (p. 1). Recent research generally supports this, indicating students, particularly those from structurally disadvantaged backgrounds, may not be learning or developing much in the areas of critical thinking, complex reasoning, and writing (Arum & Roksa, 2011) or leadership, well-being, diversity, and more (Blaich, 2007; Blaich & Wise, 2011); however, the implications and claims, as alarming as they are, are nonetheless debated (Benjamin, n.d.; Pascarella, Blaich, Martin, & Hanson, 2011). Arum and Roksa (2011) report that students demonstrated unimpressive gains in critical thinking, problem-solving, analytical reasoning, and written communication as measured by the Collegiate Learning Assessment (CLA): Where there were statistically significant gains, they were so small to be practically meaningless. However, Benjamin (n.d.) argued that effect sizes from national CLA data are meaningful and that the distribution of scores indicated several institutions where students are making very meaningful and statistically significant gains that would be excellent candidates to examine for the purpose of identifying best practices. Pascarella et al. (2011) argued that the two-year time frame specified by Arum and Roksa (2011) was too short and pointed to evidence from the Wabash National Study (WNS) that shows more meaningful gains after four years in some areas. Recent analyses from the WNS (Blaich & Wise, 2011) support this somewhat, but also show serious concerns. Over four years, percentages of students did show moderate to high growth in moral reasoning, critical thinking, leadership, and psychological well-being. However, *nearly half did not*, and less than half of the students demonstrated similar gains in other areas measured by the CLA, including diversity awareness, academic motivation, openness to diversity, and attitudes toward literacy, political, and social involvement. Even where more than half showed meaningful gains, there were still close to a third of the students who either showed no growth or declines in moral reasoning, critical thinking, leadership, and psychological well-being. So, while there is room for debate over a small but growing collection of evidence of student learning, the WNS data shows clear and worrisome concerns regarding just what and how well students are learning.

When it comes to evidence of student learning, institutions are not the only ones who are at a loss. Students can marshal even less evidence of what they have learned, and many cannot "extract these competencies ... and articulate them in the context of the world of work" when interviewing with employers (Chan & Gardner, 2013, p. 24). Chan and Gardner (2013) found that students could not effectively express their skills or link them to job responsibilities. This is not surprising. There is little in the way of frameworks or resources to help students identify the skills and knowledge they have learned in the context of work related or graduate school responsibilities. Students may have old syllabi, tests, notes, and textbooks, but those rarely articulate learning outcomes in the context of work related roles and tasks. Some students may have reference letters from staff or faculty with whom they were able to form relationships, and those letters may provide students with some connections between the two, but those are usually too short to provide much help. Some students may have copies of employment evaluations, which may provide some language and descriptions of demonstrated skills and, but too often the scales used are ambiguous and the qualitative comments cursory. One resource available to students at some schools is access to a list of their experiences beyond the classroom, often called a co-curricular transcript (CCT), which many schools market as being highly valuable to students and desired by employers and graduate schools.

15.4. Co-Curricular Transcripts

15.4.1. *History and Content of Co-Curricular Transcripts*

Generally speaking, the CCT essentially lists all or many of the out-of-class experiences an individual student had during their tenure at an institution. It is most often called a CCT, but other labels include co-curricular record, co-curricular learning certificate, involvement record or transcript, experiential transcript, and student activities record. They have been around for a long time and seem to have originated in the 1990s stemming from calls to bridge the divide between academic and student affairs (Kuh, 1996) and from efforts to tie student affairs work directly to the educational missions of institutions of higher education (Blimling & Whitt, 1998). Their use has proliferated somewhat following the release of Learning Reconsidered (Keeling, 2004), which specifically encouraged CCTs, and the release of Learning Reconsidered 2, which gave campuses a useful framework in which to link learning outcome domains and co-curricular experiences (Komives & Schoper, 2006). The advancement of educational technology has also aided the rapid adoption of CCTs across campuses as several software applications have been developed to facilitate the recording and documentation of co-curricular experiences, the most popular being Orgsync, CollegiateLink, Co-Curricular 180, Orbis Communications, and Check I'm Here.

Currently, CCTs are used at hundreds if not a thousand or more colleges and universities to varying degrees. Some, perhaps most, simply have it available to students where students enter all their information and there is no vetting or formal review of the content (e.g., http://www.vanderbilt.edu/anchorlink/student-user/my-involvement/co-curricular-resume/). Others have a mixture of validated experiences, such as employment or student organization membership and leadership roles, which the institution either validates the student entered information (which can create administrative bottlenecks) or uploads it from institutional records (e.g., http://www.bmcc.cuny.edu/cct/upload/sample_transcript.jpg). Increasingly, schools are implementing attendance taking systems, either through applications such as CollegiateLink, Orgsync, etc. or via homegrown systems, such as those at the University of Oregon or East Carolina University. CCTs virtually always contain a list of the student's experiences with differing levels of student control over what is displayed, and the opportunity for the student to enter their own experiences into it. Validation of these experiences is infrequent, but the practice appears to be increasing, particularly via attendance taking systems, leading some institutions to offer *official* CCTs (e.g., http://ndpnews.org/news/2014/10/17/co-curricular-transcript-in-works-for-next-semester/). They sometimes include some kind of written or graphic representations of the student's experience, leading CCT's to occasionally be confused with "learning portfolios" and "e-portfolios" (e.g., http://cms.cerritos.edu/ic/eportfolio/examples.htm); however, learning portfolios are often more formal and structured in the academic setting. These experiences are increasingly being *mapped* to learning domains (e.g., http://gold.geneseo.edu/index.php?pg=sampletranscript) that range from frameworks of lofty and broad aspirations or attitudes to more specific and measurable behavioral objectives. This is an important aspect covered later in this chapter.

15.5.   Are Co-Curricular Transcripts Really Useful?

These CCT programs tend to be relatively popular, but not necessarily useful, among students. They are freely available and usually require little effort on the part of students to obtain, and the list of experiences may help them in writing their résumé. That may be where their usefulness ends, though. Reuben Pressman, founder of Check I'm Here, believes that employers are unaware of CCTs, saying he has never heard of an employer asking to see one (R. Pressman, personal communication, April 29, 2015). Furthermore, student affairs supervisors do not ask for or look at the CCTs of the students they are hiring (R. Pressman, personal communication, April 29, 2015). One can understand that employers may not recognize value in them if they are not familiar with the nuances of those experiences, but student affairs professionals should be very familiar with CCTs; yet student affairs professionals do not appear to see much value in them either from an employment perspective.

A few schools, skeptical that the traditional CCTs offer much value, have stipulated more rigorous expectations that must be fulfilled in order for students to obtain their list of experiences. Slippery Rock University requires students to attend 144 workshops (across four years) within nine different domains in their "Co-Curricular Experience Program" (Slippery Rock University, n.d.). In a similar but more academically oriented manner, the University of Pittsburg requires students participating in its "Outside the Classroom Curriculum" (OCC) to attend and participate in 70 specific experiences, some required and some optional, across 10 learning domains (University of Pittsburgh, n.d.). These efforts are laudable; however, the completion rates of these programs are drastically lower than the participation rates in most of the programs that have no requirements, ostensibly because students do not perceive the value of that list of experiences is worth the extra effort.

In the end, the demonstrated value of CCTs is minimal. They provide no evidence of student learning, similar to the way academic transcripts provide no evidence of it, and they do not show *what students can actually do*. This is the Achilles heel of CCTs; the inferences required of employers and graduate schools in order to determine what students learned or demonstrated in those experiences is still large and unwarranted. The experiences by themselves offer no evidence of learning or competency. And even those that are mapped to a learning outcome offer no proof that the experience was implemented in a way that intentionally facilitated any learning or engaged the student in applying a particular skill in that area. For example, one student affairs unit at a large research institution mapped a particular student employment experience, Ticket Sales Clerk, to a multicultural competence outcome, reasoning that the student must interact with others from different backgrounds as they exchange currency and tickets. However, there was no training for the student in the area of multicultural competence, nor was the student evaluated on any behaviors or skills related to it. The supervisor did not intentionally observe related skills or behaviors and provided no coaching or feedback related to multicultural competence. In this case, the student may or may not experience a multicultural context, may or may not apply related competencies, and may or may not reflect on the experience or get feedback on it. This is where conceptual mapping falls apart without considerable rigor in place to ensure that the educational experiences are indeed designed to intentionally facilitate and evaluate learning or skill demonstration in any particular domain. Simply linking them because it is believed the student *may* employ or improve a skill is insufficient and requires an unreasonable inference to connect the experience to an outcome.

Employers recognize this and are finding academic transcripts and CCTs by extension rather meaningless. Carol Geary Schneider, president of the Association of American Colleges and Universities (AACU), commented on AACU employer studies saying that employers "basically find the transcript useless in evaluating job candidates" (as cited in Fain, 2013). Employers are seeking more clear evidence of what students can do (Fain, 2013; Pittinsky, 2014). In Britain, the Universities UK, the representative organization for universities in the United Kingdom, developed the Higher Education Achievement Record (HEAR) for precisely that reason (Burgess Implementation Steering Group, 2012). The HEAR extends the traditional academic transcript to include the identified learning outcomes associated with the student's academic program or major. Another European initiative, the European Credit System for Vocational Education and Training (ECVET) is also assessing and documenting specific skills to help learners validate learning that occurs across countries and contexts so that the evidence is accepted throughout Europe (European Commission, 2015). In a similar effort, one faculty member of Arizona State University is calling for the development of "Postsecondary Achievement Reports" that cover the collegiate experience more comprehensively and would be issued alongside or in lieu of the traditional academic transcripts (Pittinsky, 2014). Northern Arizona University has developed a Competency Report that will accompany the academic transcript and provide details on the quality of skills demonstrated by students (Fain, 2013), and 33 other institutions are engaging in similar direct assessment programs following the Department of Education's limited authorization for students attending approved programs to receive financial aid (Kelchen, 2015). Companies that provide CCTs see these trends and the limitations of the CCT and are vigorously trying to find ways to make them more meaningful and useful to both students and employers (R. Pressman, personal communication, April 29, 2015).

15.6. Enhancing the Co-Curricular Transcript

15.6.1. Outcomes-Based Co-Curricular Transcript

Given that students need to have a good understanding of their skills and abilities in order to be successful in graduate school and job applications and that employers need to know how well graduates can perform various skills in order to hire the best talent, perhaps the most mutually beneficial way to enhance CCTs is to make them *outcomes-based*. An outcomes-based CCT (OB-CCT) is one that provides documentation of both the nature and quality of skills students demonstrate in authentic contexts in addition to the list of experiences, and there is no better environment in which to obtain evidence of students demonstrating skills in real-world contexts than their experiences beyond the classroom. Students spend well over 2000 waking hours each academic year outside the classroom (four or five times the hours spent in the classroom), and much of that time is spent working on campus in roles of varied complexity and responsibility, creating, participating and/or leading student clubs and organizations, participating in or leading student government or athletic teams, and developing expertise in various transferable skills such as multicultural interactions, problem-solving, critical thinking, and motivating and influencing others, as well as important habits of life, including well-being, citizenship, community engagement, and more. The co-curricular environment offers remarkably rich opportunities for students to learn and develop important skills; it is a *living-laboratory* of experiential learning where both staff and faculty can deliberately design and facilitate experiences such that they engage students in intentionally selected behaviors that can be observed by staff and faculty and ultimately assessed so that students can improve and the institution can collect direct evidence of students' learning and competencies.

15.7. Demonstrating Skills within Common Co-Curricular Experiences

One of most common co-curricular experiences is that of student employment on campus. Virtually in every campus there are numerous roles that students fill, from peer leaders, to cashiers, to fitness instructors. Many of these positions are engaged as both a job *and a learning experience*, where supervisors not only manage but also coach and educate the student about professional expectations and skills, appropriate interpersonal interactions, problem-solving, etc. In most of these experiences, supervisors already engage in the evaluation of students' performance of various skills and behaviors. One such experience is that of a resident assistant (RA), a role where students in residence halls serve as peer leaders and are trained in a multitude of skills including helping skills, crisis and conflict management, administering policies and procedures, relationship and community building, and more. Figure 15.1 shows the first part of what a typical evaluation of an RA might look like.

The behaviors involved in achieving some of the objectives of the RA position involve various professional and transferable skills, including building trust, demonstrating compassion and empathy, initiating communication, etc. Identifying these more explicitly, such as one would in a rubric, can both help the student improve their understanding of expectations and assist in improving consistency across evaluations and evaluators (Jonsson & Svingby, 2007a; Stevens & Levi, 2005), and by including it in the OB-CCT, it can also provide evidence to the student and the institution regarding the quality of their performance. Rubrics are scoring tools that detail performance expectations for the qualitative evaluation and potential scoring of complex student work in authentic contexts (Jonsson & Svingby, 2007b; Stevens & Levi, 2005). Table 15.1 shows what the first two objectives in Figure 15.1 might look like if converted to a rubric.

The rubric version provides the student with a much clearer description of the behaviors expected and provides the supervisor with scoring benchmarks in order to help improve consistency. It also can provide an evaluative score in terms of how well the student performed the skill, which could be useful to both the student and the institution in terms of documentation of student learning and competencies in the OB-CCT, particularly if a common scale was used across rubrics allowing the scores to be aggregated over time at the student level.

This evaluation is a tool for RA's and their supervisors to compare and discuss expectations of meeting and exceeding performance standards. This evaluation process is designed to help RA's become aware of the degree to which they are meeting the expectations of the department and those of their supervisor. This process facilitates the sharing of honest feedback enabling staff to grow and continue in the process of self-development.

Scales:
1	Consistently does not meet expectations
2	Sometimes or partially meets expectations
3	Meets minimum expectations
4	Sometimes exceeds expectations
5	Consistently exceeds expectations

A. Overaching objectives of the Resident Assistant

	1	2	3	4	5
1. Develops a trusting and caring relationship with floor residents.	1	2	3	4	5
2. Demonstrates concern for the well-being of residents	1	2	3	4	5
3. Encourages and facilitates cooperation and collaboration among residents and staff	1	2	3	4	5
4. Establishes and maintains a floor atmosphere conducive to safety and academics.	1	2	3	4	5

Comments:

Figure 15.1: Resident Assistant Evaluation (Supervisor evaluation of RA).

Table 15.1: Resident assistant evaluation rubric.

Behavior	Explanation	1 Consistently does not meet expectations	2 Sometimes or partially meets expectations	3 Meets minimum expectations	4 Sometimes exceeds expectations	5 Consistently exceeds expectations
Develops a trusting and caring relationship with floor residents.	Ideally, RA's will actively try to develop trust and care with their residents, adapting their strategies to do so to meet individual styles.	Has to be asked consistently and directed to do so and/or focuses on a small group with whom the RA already has a good relationship with.	Has to be reminded sometimes to do so and reaches out to a few individuals outside those the RA feels comfortable with.	Rarely if ever needs to be asked or reminded to reach out to everyone on the floor and makes at least initial attempts to connect with almost all floor residents.	Never has to be reminded or asked to reach out to all residents, and makes some significant changes in personal style to connect with almost all floor residents.	Makes consistent changes in personal style to help connect with almost all or all floor residents.
Demonstrates concern for the well-being of residents.	As one aspect of creating a welcoming and inclusive community, RA's ensure that they are showing and communicating their empathy and concern for all residents, including those that may rarely be seen or	Shows concern and empathy for some select residents, but rarely others, and may show disdain for those that have violated policy or been disrespectful. Has to be reminded	May still show concern and empathy mostly for friends and those that are most accessible and receptive, but avoids showing disdain or dislike of any residents. Sometimes needs reminding address and respond to concerns of those	Shows concern and empathy for a the majority of residents as demonstrated by relaying concerns, intervening in problems, and often reaching out to those residents who	Shows concern and empathy for all residents as demonstrated by relaying concerns, intervening in problems, and often connecting with to those residents who are less	Shows concern and empathy for all residents, including those on other floors, as demonstrated by relaying concerns, intervening in problems, and consistently connecting with to those

Table 15.1: (*Continued*)

Behavior	Explanation	1 Consistently does not meet expectations	2 Sometimes or partially meets expectations	3 Meets minimum expectations	4 Sometimes exceeds expectations	5 Consistently exceeds expectations
	involved and those that may have violated a policy or were disrespectful in some way.	consistently about relaying concerns, reaching out to a larger portion of residents, intervening in problems, etc.	less accessible or receptive.	are less accessible or responsive to the RA.	accessible or responsive to the RA.	residents who are less accessible or responsive to the RA.

Another common example across institutions is that of student leaders, students who serve on student government boards, advisory boards, etc. In these experiences, students are usually advised by a faculty or staff member who has the responsibility of helping students perform their roles effectively by coaching their skills in leadership, teamwork, problem-solving, running meetings, event planning, and much more. Many of these experiences are developed and offered specifically as learning experiences for students, and some advisors may also be required to evaluate one or more of the student leaders similar to an employment context. For example, The National Association for Campus Activities (NACA) identified 10 core and 7 supplemental competencies of student leaders (National Association for Campus Activities, 2009), including:

- Leadership Development
- Assessment and Evaluation
- Event Management
- Meaningful Interpersonal Relationships
- Collaboration
- Social Responsibility
- Effective Communication
- Multicultural Competency
- Intellectual Growth
- Clarified Values.

It is unlikely that every student leadership experience will entail opportunity for faculty or staff to observe and evaluate students on everyone of these competencies, although some likely do. Observing and assessing students' demonstration of even a few of these can provide them and the institution with valuable data. For example, the University of Oregon adapted the AAC&U Teamwork VALUE Rubric (see https://www.aacu.org/value/rubrics for more details on the VALUE Rubric Development Project), and staff who advise student advisory boards across all of the Division of Student Life units use the rubric (Table 15.2) to observe and assess how well student leaders demonstrate the desired skills and behaviors.

One other experience that is common across nearly all campuses is that of the student internship. The student internship, due to the number of students who often participate in them, could provide the institution with considerable evidence of student competencies, and it can be a powerful opportunity for the student to reflect on and receive feedback on their performance in an authentic professional setting. Table 15.3 shows what a typical internship evaluation form might look like, and Table 15.4 shows what it might look like as a rubric.

Again, the rubric version allows for a much more nuanced understanding of what is expected on the part of the student and a good framework to improve consistency across evaluations. Although these are three examples that are likely shared across most campuses, there are hundreds of other co-curricular experiences, some common across campuses and some unique, that staff and faculty could leverage in

Table 15.2: University of Oregon student advisory board rubric.

Nurtures constructive team climate	Generally supports a constructive group climate by treating other members respectfully. May demonstrate some instances of unconstructive or unsupportive behavior or attitude.	Often supports a constructive group climate by treating other members respectfully and conveying a positive attitude about the group and its work. Sometimes makes an effort to motivate other members.	Consistently supports a constructive group climate by treating other members respectfully, conveying a positive attitude about the group and its work, and often motivates other group members.	Consistently supports a constructive group climate, treating other members respectfully, conveying a positive attitude about the group and its work, motivating other group members, and providing assistance when needed.
Negotiating conflict	Passively accepts alternate viewpoints, ideas, and opinions.	Sometimes redirects focus toward common ground, toward task at hand (away from conflict). But generally doesn't overtly call attention to there being any conflict.	Identifies and acknowledges conflict and stays engaged with it. Frequently redirects focus toward common ground, toward task at hand.	Consistently addresses conflict directly and helps to manage/resolve it in a way that strengthens overall group cohesiveness.

Table 15.3: Typical student internship evaluation.

Performance expectation	Poor	Fair	Good	Excellent
Dependability				
Volume and quality of work				
Applies academic knowledge				
Communication				

very similar ways by assessing how well students demonstrate desired skills and record those outcomes in an OB-CCT.

15.8.   Co-Curricular Experiences Where Students Demonstrate Skills

15.8.1.   Housing and Residence Life

In addition to the RA example mentioned earlier, RAs tend to experience significant training in various skills. For example, many schools have new RAs apply what they have learned in training by intervening in mock policy violations and crisis situations acted out by experienced RAs in scripted scenarios. The University of North Carolina — Chapel Hill (UNC — Chapel Hill) evaluates new RAs in their performance of helping skills, confrontation skills, and more using rubrics to structure staff members' observations (C. Heiser, personal communication, April 30, 2015). The new RAs receive useful feedback, and the housing staff get good data on the effectiveness of training. New RAs interpersonal skills and multicultural skills can be assessed in the same context.

New RA training also involves a significant amount of policy and procedural knowledge surrounding mandatory reporting, Title IX, codes of conduct, etc. Any and all of these can be assessed with knowledge-based exams examining the degree to which students can accurately respond to questions testing their recall or understanding of the policies and procedures. In a similar vein, many RA training curricula involve staff completing fictitious incident reports, duty logs, and other reports to their supervisor; each of these can be reviewed and assessed in terms of accuracy, thoroughness, etc.

At Muhlenberg College, RAs that want to reapply to be an RA the following year submit a portfolio intended to demonstrate what they have learned and achieved that year, and staff assess the content of the portfolio in terms of integrative learning and reflective thinking using a specific rubric (J. Schumacher, personal communication, March 3, 2015). Residence Life staff at Babson College also utilized RA portfolios and evaluated them. Portfolios like this can also be used to assess critical thinking, presentation and persuasive communication skills, as well as problem-solving and effective reasoning.

Table 15.4: Student internship rubric.

Performance expectation	Poor	Fair	Good	Excellent
Dependability	May tend to be unorganized, late, or absent from work frequently. Often doesn't take initiative; waits to be given direction and regularly needs reminding to follow through on tasks. Inconsistently demonstrates good judgment.	May tend to be unorganized, late, or absent from work occasionally. Sometimes takes initiative; once given direction, usually follows through. Usually demonstrates good judgment.	Usually appears organized, present and prompt at work, and often takes initiative and consistently follows through and demonstrates good judgment.	Consistently organized, present and prompt at work, and consistently takes initiative and follows through. Almost always demonstrates good judgment.
Volume and quality of work	May not produce the volume of work that is expected. Work is usually not thorough and lacks the expected level of quality.	Tends to produce the volume of work that is expected. Work is sometimes thorough and occasionally at desired level of quality.	Consistently produces the volume of work that is expected and it is often thorough and of the desired level of quality.	Consistently produces the volume of work that is expected and it is almost always thorough and of the desired level of quality.
Applies academic knowledge	May not apply theory and best practice to work without prompting. May not integrate knowledge and theory in novel situations.	Sometimes applies theory and best practice to work without prompting. Sometimes integrates knowledge and theory in novel situations.	Usually applies theory and best practice to work without prompting. Usually integrates knowledge and theory in novel situations.	Consistently applies theory and best practice to work without prompting. Consistently integrates knowledge and theory in novel situations.

| Communication (verbal, written, social media, etc.) | May not be consistently clear, concise, and professional in every form of communication (verbal, written, social media, etc.) | Is sometimes clear, concise, and professional across forms of communication (verbal, written, social media, etc.) | Is often clear, concise, and professional across forms of communication (verbal, written, social media, etc.) | Is consistently clear, concise, and professional across forms of communication (verbal, written, social media, etc.) |

In addition to student staff in Housing and Residence Life, residents also demonstrate skills that are frequently observed and evaluated and which could also be documented and included in their OB-CCTs in some way. For example, many housing programs require roommates to complete some form of "roommate agreement" which is intended to help them set and document expectations between them. Any campus housing professional could probably identify what distinguishes good roommate agreements from poor ones, and many campuses review at least some of the roommate agreements. These documents, like any other document, can be assessed, and since staff usually know what separates the good from the bad, it would not be difficult to develop a rubric to evaluate them.

Residence hall council members and leaders engage in a significant amount of event planning, teamwork, and leadership behaviors, all of which can be assessed and included in students' OB-CCTs. The Residence Life staff at the University of Oregon utilize a teamwork rubric to assess council members' behaviors related to negotiating conflict and nurturing a positive team dynamic as well as other factors, and those data are connected to students' OB-CCTs. Housing programs often have dining and catering programs which usually employ student staff. Those staff members frequently have to demonstrate knowledge of and adherence to food health and safety regulations, both of which can be assessed and included in their OB-CCTs.

15.9. Office Assistants and Desk Staff

Many academic and student affairs offices have student office workers who perform a host of tasks depending on the offices' needs. In many cases, students must frequently demonstrate knowledge of policies and procedures, interpersonal and multicultural skills, customer service, problem-solving, and communication. Taking advantage of this, UNC — Chapel Hill assesses several of their student office workers on their communication skills (C. Heiser, personal communication, April 30, 2015). Students' knowledge of policies and procedures can be assessed using a knowledge-based exam, and their interpersonal, multicultural and customer service skills could be observed and assessed as they engage them in their daily work. Their communication skills could be assessed by reviewing their e-mails, reports, logs, etc.

15.10. Physical Education and Recreation

Physical education and recreation units also employ many students in roles that vary greatly in nature and scope of responsibility they entail. As with the RA staff evaluations, these staff evaluations could also be converted to rubrics that allow departments to directly assess students' competencies, provide developmental feedback to them and student learning data to the institution, and added to their OB-CCTs so students have a record of how well they have demonstrated those skills. Staff at the University of Houston Central Campus use a rubric to evaluate their student recreation staff (P. Shefman, personal communication, March 5, 2015), as do staff at the University of Oregon, where those evaluations will also be connected to student's OB-CCTs. Additionally, fitness instructors constantly observe and evaluate the quality of the technique their fitness class participants demonstrate. These instructors could take a few participants at a time and document those observations and perhaps aggregate them over time and provide a direct measure of students' technical skills in a particular fitness routine, or instructors could observe and assess their ability to sustain motivation and engagement. Similarly, students who volunteer or are paid to referee intramural sports games demonstrate a variety of skills that can be observed and assessed, such as knowledge of rules and policies, negotiating conflict, etc. Intramural participants might also be assessed on their knowledge of rules and policies, as well as supportive team behaviors. Participants in outdoor sports activities could be assessed on their knowledge and practice of safety procedures, supportive behaviors. And because many programs involve journaling or reflection writing, student's reflective thinking might also be assessed.

15.11.   Career, Counseling, and Health Services

Career services offices conduct a lot of one-on-one counseling where staff observe students reflecting on their values, experiences, and goals; integrating knowledge of self with knowledge of the world of work; writing résumés; practicing interviews; developing career plans; etc. All of these are potential opportunities to assess students, provide feedback to them, and help them improve. At the University of Oregon and the University of California Merced (E. Langdon, personal communication, March 2, 2015), staff in the respective career services units use rubrics to observe staff on a variety of skills. As mentioned earlier, internship evaluations can be utilized as well, as can employers' evaluations of students who interview with them during career fairs or formal interview days.

Counseling and health centers also engage in a large number of one-on-one interactions. Where it does not interfere with the counseling or doctor/patient relationship, counselors and doctors can observe students perform the behaviors they desire in their patients. For example, medical practitioners at the University of Oregon's University Health Center are attempting to develop a means to assess students demonstrating their understanding of their diagnosis and treatment plan, what they understand about the consequences of not following their treatment plan, and what actions to take if there is a problem, all of which relate to individual skills in managing one's own health and healthcare needs. Mental health counselors might, again where it does not interfere with the counseling relationship, observe, and assess students' self-awareness, ability to advocate for themselves, interpersonal skills, and more. A considerable degree of privacy would have to be ensured if these sorts of evaluations were included in students' OB-CCTs, of course, but where they can be aggregated in a way that does not violate privacy policies and laws, those outcomes could be quite valuable to students and employers. Additionally, health centers and counseling centers often employ peer health educators, who must frequently demonstrate considerable health and prevention-related knowledge and presentation skills, and these units often have practicum students and interns who demonstrate a variety of health-based knowledge and interpersonal skills. Each of these could be assessed and connected to students' OB-CCTs.

15.12.   Leadership, Greek Life, and Service Learning

Students who participate in service learning programs and fraternity and sorority organizations engage in activities that allow them to demonstrate leadership, reflective thinking, knowledge of other cultures and social justice issues, empathy, conflict management, problem-solving, and much more. At the University of Oregon, Alternative Spring Break participants travel to various parts of the United States and other countries where there is the opportunity to engage in community development and learn about important cultural and social justice issues. Students write reflections regarding the social and cultural contexts which are assessed, and staff have considered having participants create concept maps to illustrate their conceptual understanding of the issues or context prior to and after their experiences as a means of helping students see how their experiences have changed their mental models. These are demonstrations of cognitive complexity and integration of knowledge that can be assessed in that context and connected to students' OB-CCTs. At the University of San Diego (USD), rubrics are being developed to assess various skills demonstrated by community service volunteers (M. Leary, personal communication, March 13, 2015). Students attending a variety of leadership workshops are assessed (via rubrics) on relevant leadership skills and knowledge at Texas A&M University (K. Cox, personal communication, March 23, 2015), UNC — Chapel Hill (C. Heiser, personal communication, April 30, 2015), and the University of Oregon, where several of those assessments are connected to students' OB-CCTs.

15.13.   Undergraduate Research Forums and Labs

Various academic and student affairs units sponsor programs related to showcasing undergraduate students' research and projects. Students who participate in these experiences often demonstrate presentation skills and data visualization skills. Inside related labs, students often engage in behaviors related to the knowledge of and adherence to health and safety regulations and a host of professional and academic behaviors. All of these can potentially be assessed and provided back to the student.

15.14.   Study Abroad

Students who study abroad often demonstrate many useful transferable skills in their experiences in other countries, some of which can be assessed and connected to their OB-CCTs. For example, students studying in different cultures usually demonstrate some degree of ability to adapt their behaviors and expectations to fit better with the local cultural norms, and to varying degrees, engage critical reflection on their own culture and values as well as those of the one they are visiting. Through coping with their challenges, resolving issues on their own, and reflecting on their adventures, students enhance their self-efficacy and agency through problem-solving and integrating their experiences; they often can demonstrate this in journal writing, blogs, online discussions, and interviews, all of which has the potential to be observed and assessed.

15.15. Athletic Advising and Conduct

At North Dakota State University, the Athletic Advising unit has developed an integrated set of rubrics which advisors use across all their formal and informal interactions with athletes to assess them in a holistic and authentic way (A. Voight, personal communication, April 22, 2015; J. Penn, personal communication, April 14, 2015). Advisors observe athletes' communication skills in the e-mails they send, the letters they write, messages they leave, etc., and they observe athletes' sense of responsibility in discussions around conduct and time management, and their willingness or reluctance to employ professional behaviors, etc. They also assess athletes' commitment and motivation in terms of their attendance at classes, meetings, practices, and willingness to understand others' points of view. All of these are important skills and could benefit students if there were documented in students' OB-CCTs.

In a similar manner, conduct offices at the University of California San Diego (M. Lowe, personal communication, March 3, 2015) and the University of Oregon either use or are considering using rubrics to evaluate reflection papers students write after participating in the conduct process regarding specific outcomes related to their context. Regardless of the context, reflection papers like that can at the very least be assessed as a demonstration of reflective thinking. Again, caution would need to be taken in order to ensure privacy in this case, but to the extent that can be done, these would be good outcomes for students to have recorded in their OB-CCTs.

15.16. Social Justice, Safety, and Other Campus Programming

Campuses across Europe and the United States often engage in various forms of programming around social justice, student safety, and other important cultural and community issues. Many of these can provide opportunities for students to demonstrate their skills and competencies, evidence of which would benefit them if included in their OB-CCT. For example, at Michigan State University, students engaged in a particular group project demonstrate skills in the field as they work on a reservation with a tribal population learning about and addressing local issues important to the tribe (B. Heinrich, personal communication, April 24, 2015). Advisors use rubrics to assess students' ability to integrate learning using students' reflections as evidence of how well students connect their academic and personal knowledge to what they are learning from their experiences and from those with whom they are interacting.

Recently, in the United States, sexual assault and interpersonal violence have been elevated significantly in the discourse on campuses, and institutions are looking for ways to assess students' knowledge and the impact of the programmatic efforts. One way to assess students' knowledge is to see just how well they know the definition of consent or the policy around sexual misconduct. Institutions can ask if students know the appropriate resources to go to or what the appropriate actions are to take if they witness something, etc. Students' responses to direct knowledge-based questions like this are direct measures of their knowledge and evidence of their knowledge and skills can be useful. At the University of Oregon, staff ask students what their definition of consent is and evaluate the qualitative evidence for critical components regardless of the exact words they use. Staff also ask students whether certain myths are true or not in order to demonstrate whether students retained the desired information.

15.17. Summary

Regarding all of these experiences, staff and faculty are already engaged in some form of observation and evaluation, although in most cases the evaluation is informal and never documented. When staff and faculty use rubrics, as in the many examples mentioned earlier, to collect and document evidence of students' skills and abilities, sometimes that information is shared with students in the way of feedback, and sometimes it is used for departmental reporting, but it is rarely collected and integrated in a systematic way such that individual students' data are aggregated across experiences, units, and divisions. It seems that many institutions are using rubrics and assessing students' skills in co-curricular context, but we have not yet recognized how we can leverage those data to benefit students, institutions, and employers. The Outcomes-Based CCT is one way to do this.

15.18. Designing and Implementing an Outcomes-Based Co-Curricular Transcript

15.18.1. *Traditional Components of Co-Curricular Transcripts*

Nearly all CCTs involve the following components: a means of documenting experiences, a system of tracking those experiences at the student level, and some kind of tangible product, such as a printout, an exportable file, a certificate, etc. First, there needs to be a means by which the student can self-enter experiences, particularly experiences that may not be associated with the campus or college but are important to the student nonetheless. All of the CCT software applications allow this in one form or another. There also needs to be a means for the administration to add experiences to a students' record, such as attendance data from a particular event, participation in alternative spring break, or working as a student employee. This can be done via attendance taking, which is supported by several of the CCT technologies, and it may be done by manually loading lists of students, which may also be supported by several of the CCT technologies. There must be ways for students to self-enter experiences and for administrators to add or validate experiences for inclusion in individual students' records. Second, there must be some kind of database system to store and organize the growing list of experiences and assessment data for each student, and all of the records must be connected to the individual student. While these may be done manually at first, such as recording on a spreadsheet, eventually the size of the data set will become so large, it will be necessary to utilize some kind of database. The CCT technologies noted earlier provide fairly robust database features, but some campuses prefer to develop "homegrown" solutions, in which case, technical experts on those campuses can better identify what would be needed, how it would be maintained, and how much it would cost. None of the current technologies offer the ability to incorporate and aggregate assessment data from co-curricular experiences and produce an OB-CCT, which is why the University of North Carolina — Chapel Hill (C. Heiser, personal communication, May 9, 2014) and the University of Oregon are in the process of developing their own platforms for tracking students' co-curricular experiences, assessing competencies within them, and producing individual student records of those competencies. This individual record is the last of the common elements of CCTs. It may take the form of a certificate or a printout of the students' list of experiences or some kind of digital file that the student can take with them. In the OB-CCT, this final product would emphasize a representation and explanation of a given student's aggregate scores across experiences and learning domains, but could still list the individual experiences in some way afterward. These components are currently standard, but if we are to expand the CCT to become an *outcomes-based CCT*, then there are several other components that are still needed.

15.19.   Overarching Framework

The vast and varied landscape of co-curricular experiences holds far too many possible experiences for us to connect student performance data from each one individually to students' OB-CCTs. Indeed, one of the problems of the traditional CCTs is that a list of 140 or more experiences over four to six years is a bit cumbersome. In order to make it useful and consumable, institutions must develop an overarching framework of learning domains or learning objectives within which experiences can be rigorously mapped and the measures aggregated within individual domains. Many institutions already have a formal set of learning goals and objectives often referred to as "general education outcomes," and many student affairs divisions already have a divisional framework of learning goals or objectives, which they may also refer to as "learning outcomes." It is important to note that outcomes tend to be much more specific and measurable than the objectives in these general education frameworks; thus referring to them as outcomes can be misleading. In some cases, student affairs divisions use the general education framework or align and map their framework to it, which can be quite beneficial if the general education framework is broad enough and encompasses the greater range of potential experiences that students engage in beyond the classroom.

Unfortunately, that is not often the case. Both academic and student affairs frameworks are often developed with a narrow perspective, either academically focused, values-based (as opposed to behavior-based), or otherwise limited. This can ultimately lead them to being inaccessible to employers and graduate schools and insufficient in serving as an overarching framework that can capture the diversity of co-curricular experiences across the campus. Indeed, capturing such experiences may be impossible without a broad, campus-wide effort to develop such a framework. In lieu of that, institutions can start wherever they are able and do their best to develop a framework that is as comprehensive as possible for their institution. Learning Reconsidered 2 provides a useful framework that is very comprehensive and may be accessible to employers and students (Komives & Schoper, 2006). The Council for the Advancement of Standards (CAS) also provides a useful, fairly comprehensive, and more succinct framework (Council for the Advancement of Standards in Higher Education and Dean, 2009).

Using the earlier-mentioned frameworks as blueprints, The Division of Student Life at the University of Oregon developed three learning domains (Think, Engage, Thrive) and 10 learning objectives within them, which they believe will cover all or virtually all co-curricular experiences.

- *Thinking and Reasoning Effectively* (*Think*) — Students will reason effectively, consider multiple perspectives, and demonstrate good judgment by making thoughtful, risk conscious decisions in their daily lives. They will think reflectively and evaluate the sources, assumptions, and structure of what they know. Students will know how to transfer and adapt their reasoning and problem-solving skills to ever-changing contexts.
  - *Effective Reasoning and Problem-Solving* — Knowledge and skills related to decision making, problem-solving and critical thinking and reasoning, including considering multiple perspectives, risk assessment, ethics, etc.
  - *Connecting Knowledge and Ideas* — Knowledge and skills related to transferring and adapting cognitive and behavioral skills from one context to another.
  - *Reflective Thinking* — Reflective analysis and evaluation of one's beliefs, experiences, actions, goals, motivations, decisions, mental models, etc.
- *Engaging Others and the Community* (*Engage*) — Students will develop meaningful relationships and engage others in effective ways and with a sense of responsibility and inclusiveness in a variety of interpersonal and intercultural contexts. They will understand relevant civic structures and engage in activities and opportunities at the campus, local and/or higher levels. They will understand multiple approaches to teamwork and leadership and know how to adapt their efforts to fit different situations.
  - *Intercultural and Interpersonal Knowledge and Skills* — Knowledge and skills related to interpersonal and intercultural competence, including knowledge of human differences, identity development models, as well as interacting effectively in multicultural environments.

- *Leadership and Civic Engagement* — Knowledge and skills related to leadership theory and civics, including group dynamics, teamwork, and participating in campus and community organizations and opportunities.
- *Social Engagement* — Knowledge of and participation in campus extracurricular activities and community related opportunities, developing meaningful relationships.
- *Responsibility to Others* — Knowledge and skills related to the concepts and practices pertaining to social responsibility, including social justice, human rights, community service, managing one's behavior, sustainability, and stewardship of resources.
- *Thriving Personally and Professionally* (*Thrive*) — Students will understand who they are and what they value in life, and they will communicate their ideas effectively. They will organize and execute their lives such that they are able to achieve their personal, academic, and professional goals successfully. Students will explore and develop effective routines regarding their physical, emotional, and mental health, engage the career development process and make appropriate choices in terms of their major and career choices.
  - *Personal Development* — Understanding of one's self, including motivation, strengths, and weaknesses, etc., and knowledge and skills related to organization, communication, planning, and goal setting. The ability to live and act in accordance with one's values, beliefs, and goals.
  - *Professional Success* — Knowledge and skills related to the world of work, major selection and career development, including professionalism, networking, job search, interviewing, etc.
  - *Health and Well-Being* — Knowledge of and engagement of university and community resources, as well as knowledge and skills pertaining to health and well-being, including developing personal routines and making decisions that enhance one's well-being.

The Division of Student Affairs at the University of North Carolina Chapel Hill has developed a framework they call, *Excellence in Action*, with four domains and 11 objective areas (UNC Student Affairs, n.d.).

- *Dynamic Learning* — The intellectual exploration of existing and emerging knowledge through the use of critical thinking, creativity, innovation, and communication skills that develops life-long learners with the capacity to address real-world problems.
  - *Critical Thinking*
  - *Creativity and Innovation*
  - *Communication*
- *Honor* — The fortitude, courage, and character to stand by personal and community principles. The willingness to sacrifice short term personal gain for the good of long term goals and the good of the community. Holding oneself to congruency between one's values and everyday actions and interactions. Exemplifies ethics, integrity, fairness, and respect for others.
  - *Ethics and Integrity*
  - *Fairness and Respect for Others*

- *Responsibility* — The ownership of one's actions and commitments through ongoing reflection and engagement with others, in order to develop self-awareness, interpersonal skills, wellness, and resiliency. This process allows one to achieve authenticity, balance, and a sense of purpose, which provides a path toward a congruent wholehearted life.
  - *Self-awareness*
  - *Interpersonal Development*
  - *Wellness and Resiliency*
- *Engagement* — The commitment of an individual to develop cross-cultural perspectives. To actively engage in local and global communities as a result of a sense of responsibility.
  - *Civic Involvement*
  - *Local and Global Citizenship*
  - *Cross-Cultural Perspectives*

  Both of these frameworks are situated within the divisions of student affairs, and while they are clearly intended to be broad and inclusive, they may not, despite their best efforts, capture all of the potential co-curricular experiences across their respective campuses. At the USD, academic faculty and administrators and student affairs staff are developing a campus-wide framework unique to USD and congruent with the Jesuit values of the institution. The current *draft* of that framework is below (M. Leary, personal communication, April 27, 2015).

- *Authentic Engagement*
  - *Advocacy/Using Voice*
  - *Social Change*
  - *Meaningful Dialogue*
- *Being, Belonging, and Becoming*
  - *Cultural self-awareness in the context of a diverse community*
  - *Engaging with difference and challenge*
  - *Empathy*
- *Courageous Living and Perseverance*
  - *Willingness to Risk*
  - *Resilience and Perseverance*
  - *Learning from Disappointment*
- *Self-Awareness and Purpose*
  - *Self-Identity*
  - *Impact*
  - *Uncertainty*
- *Self-Care and Healthy Relationships*
  - *Healthy Relationships*
  - *Self-care*

One noteworthy aspect of USD's model is that they have created rubrics for each of these domains and component skills, and those rubrics have four levels of competency. Instead of mapping experiences to the component skill alone, the experiences

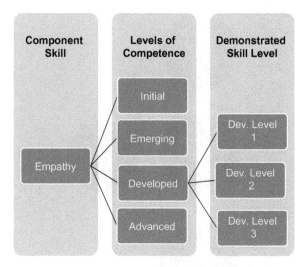

Figure 15.2: Assessing performance within the USD model.

are mapped to *a particular level* within that component skill, and then the quality of skills demonstrated would need to be determined within that level (see Figure 15.2).

As one can see, these frameworks have considerable differences in terms of whether language is more academic or not and whether their content is focused on concrete skills and abilities or loftier abstract aspirations. Their different structures impact how they are assessed. These aspects are important because developing learning outcomes from the objectives is much easier when dealing with skills and abilities than it is with less observable attitudes and concepts; the latter requires more of an inferential leap. They also differ in how accessible they may be to employers and students. This could lead institutions to look at framing learning outcomes strictly in terms of employability-related skills, such as those identified in the National Association of Colleges and Employers' reports on the skills and characteristics employers want in college graduates (National Association of Colleges and Employers, 2014). However, tempting and convenient this may be, defining our assessment of student learning strictly in terms of employability skills will ultimately limit students' and our own understanding of what students actually gain from their college experience. Thus, there is a delicate balance in developing these frameworks in terms of achieving something that speaks to the values and culture of an institution in a way that end users can relate to, such as students and employers, who may not be familiar with the institutional culture and academic vernacular.

15.20. Standardized Scoring System or Scale

Similar to the way academic grades are converted to a four-point scale, if we are to assess students' skills in co-curricular experiences and aggregate them under a framework of learning objectives, then we need to have a common scale or one to

Figure 15.3: Aggregating scores using a standard four-point scale.

which all evaluative scores could be converted. If one unit assesses a student's articulation of their leadership philosophy in the context of different leadership theories using a three-point scale, it would be hard to aggregate that with another unit's assessment of that student's demonstration of negotiating conflict using a five-point scale. Hence some standardization is helpful if not necessary in order to effectively aggregate assessment data from different units and experiences under a common learning objective or skill area (see Figure 15.3).

USD's model and the mapping of experiences to specific levels of performance is exceptional, although it could make the assessment more complex. If each experience is assigned to a particular level of competence, then the educators would need to discriminate between good and poor demonstrations within that level of competency. In other words, they would need to determine what a poor demonstration of Initial Empathy looked like compared to an exceptional demonstration of Initial Empathy. If they used a three-point scale, that would result in 12 possible levels of performance for a student (see Figure 15.4). That may be too complex of a system, and it may be better to assess them using only the four super-ordinate levels.

It may be also possible to allow units to use whatever scale they want and simply standardize the scores before aggregating them, such as converting raw scores to percentage of maximum possible scores(Cohen, Cohen, Aiken, & West, 1999). This has considerable advantages in terms of unit autonomy and flexibility, although it may simultaneously limit the development of shared rubrics or resources and frames of reference for staff and faculty. Whatever decision an institution makes, it will need to establish some way of standardizing the scoring so the individual scores can be aggregated across experiences. Doing so allows for an individual students' data

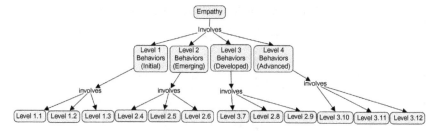

Figure 15.4: What empathy involves.

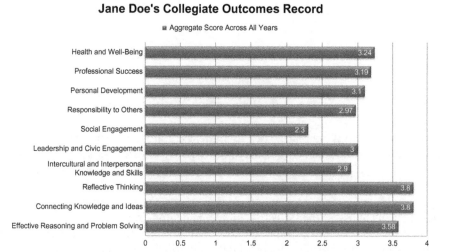

Figure 15.5: Standard bar graph representation.

to be represented in a useful way, condensing possibly hundreds of experiences into a more consumable format. Figures 15.5 and 15.6 show two potential ways of visualizing the aggregate data.

15.21. Identification and Mapping of Experiences and Outcomes

Next, an institution would need to identify their co-curricular experiences, distinguishing between those that involve the demonstration of a particular skill or ability that is or can be assessed and those that do not. One way to do this is to simply categorize them as "measurable" or "measured" and "non-measurable" or "non-measured," but institutions can determine what works best for their own context. It may also be useful to focus or emphasize *high-impact practices*, such as living and learning communities, common and extended intellectual experiences, collaborative projects, and team experiences (Kuh, 2008). Some of these experiences may already have some

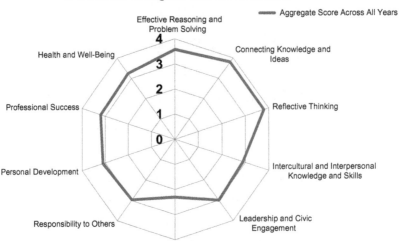

Jane Doe's Collegiate Outcomes Record

Figure 15.6: Radar graph representation.

kind of evaluation taking place, such as student employment experiences, leadership roles, training sessions, etc. Others may not currently have an assessment component, yet still involve students demonstrating skills that could be assessed relatively easily, such as role playing, articulating new knowledge in their own words, giving presentations, working on a team project, etc. In these cases, the facilitating educators could develop means to assess the skills that are being demonstrated.

It may be best for institutions to start small and identify those experiences that already involve some form of documented evaluation and perhaps those experiences where evaluations could be developed with ease. This would conveniently reduce the number of experiences to work with up front and allow the institution to get started more quickly. From there, the institution could map the specific items on which students are evaluated to their framework of learning objectives and determine how to standardize scores across the different evaluations. Recalling the "multicultural experience" noted earlier, mapping needs to be conducted with considerable rigor to ensure there is a direct link from the behavior to the objective so there are little-to-no inferential leaps required. The specific behavior being assessed should explicitly and directly relate to the objective it is mapped to. Of the four examples below, three directly involve the student actively engaging in a behavior, demonstrating their competency, and the fourth is a passive behavior that may or may not involve any use or demonstration of a skill at all.

✓ Leading a meeting → Leadership
✓ Values clarification → Personal Development
✓ Analyzing a budget proposal → Professional Success
✗ Watching a cultural movie → Multicultural Competence

Over time, institutions could expand the inclusion of experiences by identifying new experiences that involve some form of evaluation of students' skills and developing means of assessing students' skills in those that do not currently involve evaluation. It is important to develop means of assessment that naturally stem from the activity, that are valid and reliable, and that require little additional work on the part of the facilitator. The more comprehensive and valid the assessment is, the more useful they will be to students and employers. Invalid data will ultimately corrupt any confidence students, staff, or employers have in the OB-CCT.

15.22. Well Written Learning Outcomes

One of the most critical requirements of developing an OB-CCT is the use and development of well-developed learning outcomes. While learning goals and objectives articulate broad domains or areas of learning and related behaviors, outcomes are much more specific and measurable; they involve behaviors or products that are observable and measurable.

Essentially, learning outcomes articulate what the student will *demonstrate, produce,* or otherwise *represent* as evidence of their learning or competence. Well-developed learning outcomes meet the following criteria:

- They specify the conditions under which the behavior or product will occur or be produced, respectively.
- The behavior or product must be observable and directly measurable.
- The outcomes are pertinent to the learning goals/objectives and practical for the student.
- They articulate the cognitive or psychomotor activity in which the student will engage, such as those identified by Bloom's Taxonomy (e.g., *analyze, perceive, evaluate,* etc.).
  - Generally speaking, activity in the affective domain is not directly observable or measurable. They are usually inferred from cognitive behavior instead.
  - Another useful learning taxonomy is that proposed by Fink (2003) (application, integration, learning how to learn, etc.).
- Outcomes must be evaluated against standards or criteria; goals and objectives need not be.
- Good outcomes are difficult and challenging but realistic.

A very simple template for a learning outcome might look like this:

The student will [*behavior or item that is produced, demonstrated, or otherwise represented as evidence*].
The student will *write a paper and analyze and synthesize multiple perspectives on the use and misuse of alcohol among college students.*

While this may work, it leaves out several important components that educators often overlook, namely the context in which the student performs and is evaluated, what the student is provided to enable her to produce the behavior or item, how the student will be evaluated, and to what level the student is expected to perform. Thus a more advanced and useful template is presented below:

As a result of [*Activity*] in [*Specific learning experience*], and given [*Conditions or materials provided*], the student will [*The behavior the student will engage to demonstrate, produce, or otherwise represent as evidence of their learning*] as demonstrated in [*what is demonstrated or produced*] to a [*Minimum expected performance level*] as measured by [*Method of evaluation*].

As a result of *participating* in the *Alcohol Education Workshop* and given *handouts representing multiple and varied perspectives on college student alcohol use*, the student will *analyze and synthesize the multiple perspectives* as demonstrated in a *4 page reflection paper*, to a *level of 2* (*Intermediate*), as measured by the *Alcohol Workshop Reflection Rubric*.

This advanced version both specifies several aspects of the experience so that the learner and the educator understand what is going to happen. It also provides enough details so that another educator can more easily replicate the learning experience.

Note that neither template uses a phrase commonly found in learning outcomes, namely "will be able to ..." This is for a few subtle but important reasons. First, generally speaking, all students have some ability to do whatever is indicated in the learning outcome. All students are able to analyze, synthesize, etc. to varying degrees, which may range from very little to a great deal. In a subtle way, it can mislead educators to overlook the behavior the learner is actually performing or not recognize what needs to be assessed, but simply change "will be able to ..." to "will ..." and the behavior that needs to be assessed is much more obvious.

It is also important to note that these behaviors should be *rigorously* mapped to the learning objectives framework. Both faculty and staff can sometimes be somewhat uncritical of their assumptions and reasoning when they map experiences and outcomes to the framework. As noted earlier, however, if the method of evaluation does not yield reliable and valid results, then the meaning and value of the OB-CCT is diminished. Thus, it is important to employ methods to ensure rigor in this process. Having one or two colleagues and faculty critically examine your outcomes and your mapping is encouraged as one manner of achieving this. Another method is to have an expert review and provide feedback on the outcomes and mapping as a means of ensuring rigor and consistency.

15.23.   System and Tools for Evaluation

Another critical component needed to produce an OB-CCT is the system of evaluation and the tools used to facilitate it. In order to provide students evidence of their competence we must observe students performing the desired skills, and we must measure the degree to which they perform them. Sources of evidence for us to assess include, essays, reflection papers, role-plays, journals and blogs, on-the-job-observations, etc. There are many ways to achieve this, including, knowledge tests, rubrics, document reviews, interviews, etc.

Knowledge tests, while not often considered within co-curricular contexts can be remarkably useful in many ways. Testing students after training is an exceptional way to understand the effectiveness of training and what your students are leaving the training having learned (and not learned). It may be useful for workshops to attach program evaluations to the end of an activity for participants to provide quick feedback about what they understood, what they did not, etc. In fact, several classroom techniques identified in assessment and teaching texts can be transferred or adapted from the classroom and used in co-curricular workshops and trainings (Angelo & Cross, 1993; Fink, 2003; Suskie, 2009).

One of the most common tools educators use in co-curricular contexts is the *rubric*. As noted earlier, a rubric is a scoring tool that communicates performance expectations and allows educators to qualitatively evaluate and quantitatively score complex student work in authentic contexts (Jonsson & Svingby, 2007b; Stevens & Levi, 2005). Rubrics, *when designed well*, help improve the consistency of scoring, effective evaluation of complex competencies, and improved self-evaluation (Jonsson & Svingby, 2007a; Reddy & Andrade, 2010; Stevens & Levi, 2005; Tierney & Simon, 2004). Several rubrics have already been shown in this chapter, some of which are better than others. For detailed explanations of effective and ineffective rubrics see:

- Popham, J. (1997). What's wrong—and what's right—with rubrics. *Educational Leadership, 55*(2).
- Tierney, R., & Simon, M. (2004). What's still wrong with rubrics: Focusing on the consistency of performance criteria across scale levels. *Practical Assessment, Research & Evaluation, 9*(2).

According to Tierney and Simon (2004), the following questions can help educators evaluate and create rubrics.

1. *Are the performance indicators and criteria explicit in the rubric?* There should be nothing expected or considered in the evaluation that is not identified in the rubric.
2. *Are the attributes or component behaviors explicitly stated?* There should be no behaviors expected or considered in the evaluation that are not identified in the rubric.
3. *Are the identified attributes consistently listed and addressed from one level to the next along the progressive scale?* Each attribute should be addressed in each cell along the progression. When attributes are left out, such can lead the evaluator to not consider them.

These questions can help educators develop effective rubrics or evaluate the quality of rubrics they encounter or consider using. When developed well, rubrics can be a very useful tool to help evaluate the complex competencies students demonstrate in their co-curricular experiences.

15.24. Implementation

The previous components are those that would likely be needed in order to implement an OB-CCT. It is likely that any given institution will require some training regarding one or more of the components; how to write learning outcomes or how to create rubrics for example. One potential model for implementation is as follows:

1. Determine the technology needs and assign staff to develop the technology accordingly. The technology will likely need to be developed concurrently and in unison with the other components.
   a. If an institution wants an online interface for students to find potential experiences, interact with others, and build their own outcomes record, that requires different technology than wanting to simply collect the measurement data and have students request their OB-CCT from a particular office.
   b. A project manager skilled in managing technology projects that involve integrating multiple components, data sources, and constituents is critical, and their authority to manage all of the components to ensure they align is equally so.
   c. Attendance taking technology is not a requisite but may be helpful.
2. Determine how the final OB-CCT will be represented and what the final product look like.
   a. How an institution wishes the final product to be visually represented can impact many other aspects, but it is directly impacted by the data collected.
      i. If an institution wants to represent the skill levels in numeric form, then it will need scales of at least four points or more.
      ii. If an institution wants to represent skill levels in categorical form, it will need scales with enough range so that each category has a unique cut off.
3. Develop the overarching framework for the learning outcomes.
4. Identify learning experiences and rigorously map them to the framework. When mapping, be sure to distinguish between those that are assessed *indirectly* and those that are assessed *directly*.
   a. An OB-CCT requires direct measures, so only direct measures can be included in it.
5. Develop specific and measurable learning outcomes for each of the experiences involving direct measures.
6. Determine how outcomes in each experience will be directly assessed within the experience and develop appropriate instruments.
   a. A common scale can be helpful to make it easier to standardize measurement data across experiences and units.
   b. The assessment data will need to be connected to student identifiers so that all measurement data pertaining to a particular student can be aggregated for the final product.

7. Determine how data will be collected and integrated with the relevant technology.
   a. Not all experiences may be able to provide data in the same way. For example, in a service learning trip to Peru, the facilitator may not be able to access an online rubric when evaluating students in the field; however the online rubric may work well for a career services advisor conducting a 1-on-1 counseling session with a student.
8. Ensure these elements are integrated and are congruent with the technology.
   a. This is particularly important when different components are being developed independently and the project manager is not actively coordinating the components. When the project manager is aware of the details, she/he is ensuring congruency between the components in "real time."
9. Get feedback from users of the technology to determine improvements needed.
   a. Consider conducting usability and beta-testing on any technology interfaces, both at the student and staff levels.
10. Implement, evaluate the process and the outcomes, and apply improvements.
    a. Determine if any needs or contextual nuances were overlooked.
    b. Determine how well measurements performed and make improvements.

The final OB-CCT product would likely vary considerably between institutions; however, a few elements would probably be common among them. These include:

- General student information in terms of name, major, enrollment dates, etc.
- A visualization of the student's aggregate scores representing their level of mastery in each of the designated learning areas (see Figures 15.5 and 15.6).
- A summary or visualization of the total number of experiences a student has engaged in broken down in terms of the learning areas.
- Key roles and positions held, particularly those related to outcomes around leadership, teamwork, professionalism, etc.
- Key learning experiences outside of roles and positions, particularly those related to outcomes involving diversity, professionalism, etc.
- Selected examples of student work related to specific learning areas.
- Selected feedback from educators and student reflections.
- Full list of roles and experiences.

15.25. Benefits and Challenges

15.25.1. *Benefits*

There are both obvious and more subtle benefits of assessing students' competencies demonstrated in co-curricular experiences. First and foremost, by engaging students in discussions of the learning objective framework and the behaviors that are assessed in their co-curricular experiences, students are empowered with a framework with which to understand their co-curricular experiences in the context of learning and competencies and also articulate those experiences to others in interviews, on their résumé, etc. At the same time, faculty and staff can expand the range of evidence with which to understand an individual student's strengths and identify areas for further improvement. Additionally, employers and graduate schools can better identify the specific strengths of a student in relationship to the specific skills and knowledge for which they are looking.

It also provides students a powerful tool for feedback. Whether feedback is received from the educator, peers, or emerges from self-evaluation, the role of feedback in the process of learning is critical (Hattie & Timperley, 2007). By engaging students in self-evaluation or a discussion of feedback, we enlist them as an active rather than passive partner in their education and development, empowering them to take greater responsibility for their own learning. When students provide peer feedback, it requires them to develop a deeper understanding of the behavior and standards and to critically examine the other student's performance. Ideally, a student would transfer that deeper understanding and better evaluate their own performance.

There is also considerable advantage to the institution. With direct evidence of student learning from multiple contexts, such as student employment, health services, student recreation, student organizations, etc., the institution vastly increases its evidence for accreditation, strategic planning, marketing, and fundraising. Data showing that students engaged in leadership programs increase their competencies by a factor of three between their first year and final year would go a long way to securing grants and donations to support leadership programming. Data showing that students were not showing much improvement in their intercultural and multicultural competence could be very useful to institutional and divisional strategic planning efforts. With evidence such as this, the institution's ability to evaluate its effectiveness is substantially improved, better enabling it to fulfill its obligations to constituents in the areas of accountability and stewardship, not to mention improving student learning. Over time, this increases the value of the student's degree and the reputation of the institution.

One subtle benefit is that of equity and our ability to more fully support and facilitate students' learning. It is not equitable that all students pay for a majority of the co-curricular experiences, yet they get vastly different experiences within it. Some, just by chance or by privilege, get involved, get connected to a staff member, and start a journey of engagement, while others do not, sometimes due to the absence of privilege, even though they may be more than willing, even desperate, to do so. It is not ethically responsible that we engage students in co-curricular learning experiences, spend large sums of state funds and student fees on them, yet we do not attempt to ascertain whether they have indeed learned anything at all. How would we react if we paid $10,000 for a series of classes where the faculty said, "We know students learn a lot; they tell us they do! But we don't evaluate whether they learned anything or how well they learned it." We would be shocked and pull our young adults and our money out of there immediately. But that is what the co-curriculum is like. It is a rich, living classroom, where students potentially learn a lot, but we just do not know if it is what we intend for them to learn or how well they learn it. That is neither just nor equitable, and an OB-CCT would help enable institutions to better understand what students learn in their co-curricular experiences, identify who is not engaging or learning and why, and better improve access to and performance in those co-curricular learning experiences.

15.26. Challenges

As with most initiatives, there are challenges to implementing an effective OB-CCT, both structurally and culturally. In terms of structure, acquiring and implementing the technology can be challenging, and mapping experiences and adapting them to include direct measures can be time consuming, particularly when other large projects are also on-going. Perhaps the most important structural challenge, however, is the reliable and valid assessment of student learning and competence. As noted earlier, rubrics must be well-developed and effective; inaccurate assessment will ultimately devalue the experiences and the OB-CCT and eventually the institution's reputation. Thus it is critical that institutions ensure the application of rigor and assessment expertise in the development of evaluation tools, such as rubrics, tests, etc. It is likely that institutions will gravitate to the use of shared rubrics, which is definitely useful, however institutions will want to examine and improve inter-rater reliability to ensure rigor. Faculty use a host of rubrics in academic courses, and their quality runs the gambit, so institutions do not need to let this impede them from getting started and using rubrics, but they should utilize it as means of continuous improvement as the OB-CCT program gets settled.

Culturally, there are challenges as well. Perhaps most difficult is the cultural ideology surrounding the role of student affairs and faculty educators. While often described in dualistic terms, it is more nuanced. There is certainly the belief among some faculty educators that student affairs educators *are not* educators and thus have no business assessing any learning, and blunt territorial responses like this can intimidate student affairs educators. But underlying that is sometimes a concern or lack of awareness of how qualified student affairs educators really are to design learning experiences and assess student learning. There are many student affairs educators with doctorate and master's degrees in relevant fields, such as education, psychology, and educational psychology, who are perfectly qualified and capable of designing and assessing learning experiences. There are also student affairs educators who are far less skilled or knowledgeable of learning and measurement theory, just as there are some faculty educators who also lack expertise in those areas and are not as effective as a result. There are also student affairs staff members who refuse to see themselves as educators and operate from a framework of service provision and event planning, which is understandable because the knowledge and skills around service provision and event planning are much stronger across the field than are skills and expertise in learning and pedagogical theory, instructional design, and the assessment of learning. Even many student affairs educators, who fully see themselves as educators, have a difficult time accepting the responsibility of assessing learning, perhaps because of a sense of feeling under-skilled in that area.

Sometimes faculty educators can feel confined as well. They do not always feel, sometimes for good reason, that they have the license to design learning experiences that cross into areas that are more often associated with student affairs, particularly when it involves learning that is not directly related to their area of specialization. This is unfortunate, because there is a wealth of good ideas and motivation among faculty when it comes to engaging students in the act of asking questions and finding answers, and the living laboratory of the co-curriculum can be a remarkably ripe environment in that respect. Faculty educators are often not rewarded for this kind of work either. Faculty reward and incentive structures elevate research and publication over course-teaching, over service, and just about everything else. Given the increased reliance on adjunct faculty, it is hard for faculty to find the time and comfort to engage their interests in developing learning experiences beyond the classroom.

The development of an OB-CCT involves the collection and management of a large amount of data, and as a natural consequence, fears, assumptions, and such will inevitably arise. Yet there is a considerable evolution taking place in higher education around the use, sharing, and analysis of big data according to John Ittleson, Professor Emeritus, CSU Monterey Bay, and former Acting Executive Director of the Online Education Initiative for the California Community College Districts (as cited in Grush, 2014). Big data is beginning to be used in remarkable ways to improve admission decisions and student success and persistence, and as the field of student affairs has been increasing its expertise in the area of student learning and assessment, the use of big data is also coming up more and more. The old systems of data ownership and sharing, though, are often antiquated and governed by out-dated, traditionalist assumptions and a limited understanding of higher education assessment and evaluation. Traditional or risk-adverse registrars often fail to under-stand the role of assessment and evaluation outside of academic colleges and institutional research and subsequently block access to data that is essential for the units and the university to assess its impact and effectiveness. These can serve as barriers to the effective development of systems to collect and share co-curricular learning data in ways that benefit the institution as a whole. With that said, sometimes they have good reason to be concerned as student affairs educators can assume the right-eousness of their cause and idea, and sometimes being ignorant of laws and regulations regarding human subjects protections, data security, etc., and can access and use data in irresponsible ways. Student affairs professionals must improve and demonstrate their knowledge of and adherence to relevant laws and policies that are designed to protect students (among others) in order to earn the trust of data own-ers and gatekeepers; and registrars and gatekeepers need to recognize that assessing student learning and institutional effectiveness is a shared responsibility among all elements of the institution, including student affairs and faculty educators who engage students beyond the classroom.

Other cultural aspects can also erect barriers to effectively implementing initia-tives such as the OB-CCT. Some institutional cultures develop a preference for initiatives that look and sound innovative, inspiring, etc. and a corresponding disinterest for "looking under the hood." Whether due to recognition and reward systems, time and workload pressures, or personal preferences and styles, the process of normative influence (Etzioni, 1988; Rugs & Kaplan, 1993) makes it very easy to slip in to the practice of generating flashy programs and initiatives without effectively planning or critically evaluating them. Understanding the underlying culture and being overt in planning groups about the purpose and goals is critical to effective implementation, particularly being explicit in terms of whether value is placed on relationships, process, planning, quality, quantity, etc.

In addition to cultural challenges, technological challenges also deserve attention when implementing an OB-CCT. Most campuses have a "learning management system" (LMS) and a sophisticated database to manage academic courses, grades, assignments, files, syllabi, attendance, assessment, etc. Yet, there is no "co-curricular LMS" that facilitates the recording, administration, and tracking of co-curricular experiences and the evaluation of student performance within them. While some academic LMS platforms could be used for co-curricular efforts, not all institutions allow its use outside academic courses, and the language used and features offered are based on the academic context rather than the co-curricular context. The interfaces may refer to "Faculty" or "Instructor" and "Class" or "Course" as opposed to "Facilitator" and "Experience." Not all LMS systems allow for rubrics, and others don't allow the batch upload of scoring data when the facilitator is not able to use the system in the act of evaluation (e.g., service learning experience in a developing country).

Some current co-curricular tools, such as Orgsync and CollegiateLink, attempt to approximate a co-curricular LMS, but similar to how LMSs are designed based on an academic context, these co-curricular tools are built based on an organization/community management context that emphasize administration of organizational groups, such as administering forms, registration, attendance, mass communication, networking, etc. They may have retrofitted features and "work-around" steps that allow for reflections, evaluation, etc., but these are usually simplistic and sometimes cumbersome in the amount of work it takes for a user to engage them. Thus these systems essentially serve as administrative management tools more so than learning management tools.

Developing homegrown systems also has its challenges. Developing technology is a very detail oriented, structured, and iterative process, which are characteristics that may run counter to many administrative cultures, as noted earlier, that eschew details and deliberative processes in order to preserve relationships or time. It can also be disruptive to other projects and systems taking place, for when we pull a network engineer away from the campus network or mobile access needs to work on something else, it is likely some degree of performance degradation will occur in other areas as the engineer will have less time and be able to afford less attention to their other projects and responsibilities. In a similar manner, attempting to integrate assessment data from multiple units with insular individual systems, particularly when the data is not standardized, can also be time consuming and pull assessment and technology staff away from other efforts.

15.27. Conclusion

Outcomes-based CCTs are one of the richest and most salient opportunities available to respond to the increasing calls for accountability and improvement of student learning in higher education. Our outdated system of credit hours and uninformative transcripts are no longer sufficient in and of themselves, and students, educators, and employers are calling for more authentic and informative evidence of student learning and competencies. The co-curriculum is the perfect environment in which to collect that evidence; it is a living laboratory that is rich in high-impact experiences and educators diverse in their experience and expertise. It faces considerable challenges, though, in terms of cultural and technological barriers, but these can be overcome by leadership that acknowledges and takes ownership of the culture change, maintains a calm but urgent pace and an unwavering commitment to deliberate planning, implementation, and evaluation.

References

Angelo, T. A., & Cross, K. P. (1993). *Classroom assessment techniques: A handbook for college teachers* (2nd ed.). San Francisco, CA: Jossey-Bass.

Arum, R., & Roksa, J. (2011). *Academically adrift: Limited learning on college campuses.* Chicago, IL: University of Chicago Press.

Astin, A. W. (1993). *What matters in college? Four critical years revisited.* San Francisco, CA: Jossey-Bass.

Barr, R. B., & Tagg, J. (1995). From teaching to learning: A new paradigm for undergraduate education. *Change: The Magazine of Higher Learning, 27*(6), 12–26.

Benjamin, R. (n.d.). Three principle questions about critical-thinking tests. Council for Aid to Education. Retrieved from http://cae.org/images/uploads/pdf/Three_Principal_Questions_About_Critical_Thinking_Tests.pdf

Blaich, C. (2007). *Overview of findings from the first year of the Wabash National Study of liberal education.* Crawfordsville, IN: Center of Inquiry in the Liberal Arts at Wabash College. Retrieved from http://static1.1.sqspcdn.com/static/f/333946/3612649/1247854258370/Overview_of_Findings_from_the_First_Year_web_07.17.09.pdf?token=UudBT8bTyvjOR7OIHfkhl9SbP9I%3D

Blaich, C., & Wise, K. (2011). *From gathering to using assessment results: Lessons from the Wabash National Study.* National Institute for Learning Outcomes Assessment. Retrieved from http://www.learningoutcomeassessment.org/documents/Wabash_000.pdf

Blimling, G. S., & Whitt, E. J. (1998). Principles of good practice for student affairs. *About Campus, 3*(1), 10–15.

Bound, J., Lovenheim, M. F., & Turner, S. (2007). *Understanding the decrease in college completion rates and the increased time to the baccalaureate degree.* Retrieved from http://www.psc.isr.umich.edu/pubs/pdf/rr07-626.pdf

Bound, J., Lovenheim, M. F., & Turner, S. (2010). Why have college completion rates declined? An analysis of changing student preparation and collegiate resources. *American Economic Journal: Applied Economics, 2*(3), 129–157.

Burgess Implementation Steering Group. (2012). Bringing it all together: Introducing the HEAR. London. Retrieved from http://www.hear.ac.uk/assets/documents/hear/institution-resources/HEAR-Bringing-it-all-together.pdf

Chan, A., & Gardner, P. (2013). *An arts & science degree: Defining its value in the workplace.* East Lansing, MI: Collegiate Employment Research Institute.

Cohen, P., Cohen, J., Aiken, L. S., & West, S. G. (1999). The problem of units and the circumstance for POMP. *Multivariate Behavioral Research, 34*(3), 315–346. Retrieved from http://www.tandfonline.com/doi/pdf/10.1207/S15327906MBR3403_2

Council for the Advancement of Standards in Higher Education. (2009). CAS learning and development outcomes. In L. A. Dean (Ed.), *CAS professional standards for higher education* (7th ed.), Washington, DC: Council for the Advancement of Standards in Higher Education.

Del Boca, F. K., & Noll, J. A. (2000). Truth or consequences: The validity of self-report data in health services research on addictions. *Addiction, 95*(11s3), 347–360.

Donaldson, S. I., & Grant-Vallone, E. J. (2002). Understanding self-report bias in organizational behavior research. *Journal of Business and Psychology, 17*(2), 245–260.

Etzioni, A. (1988). Normative-affective Factors: Toward a new decision-making model. *Journal of Economic Psychology, 9*, 125–150. Retrieved from http://www.gwu.edu/~ccps/etzioni/A186.pdf

European Commission. (2015). *The European Credit System for Vocational Education and Training (ECVET).* Retrieved from http://ec.europa.eu/education/policy/vocational-policy/ecvet_en.htm

Ewell, P. T. (2008). *Stuck on student learning.* San Jose, CA. Retrieved from http://measuringup2008.highereducation.org/commentary/ewell.php

Fain, P. (2013, August 9). *Competency-based transcripts. Inside Higher Ed.* Retrieved from https://www.insidehighered.com/news/2013/08/09/northern-arizona-universitys-new-competency-based-degrees-and-transcripts

Fink, L. D. (2003). *Creating significant learning experiences: An integrated approach to designing college courses.* San Francisco, CA: Jossey-Bass.

Glidden, R. (1996). Accreditation at a crossroads. *Educational Record, 66*(4), 22–24.

Grush, M. (2014, May 28). *Big data: An evolution in higher education's technology landscape.* Campus Technology. Retrieved from http://campustechnology.com/Articles/2014/05/28/The-Big-Data-Evolution-in-Higher-Ed.aspx?Page=1

Hart Research Associates. (2013). *It takes more than a major: Employer priorities for college learning and student success.* Washington, DC. Retrieved from https://aacu.org/sites/default/files/files/LEAP/2013_EmployerSurvey.pdf

Hattie, J., & Timperley, H. (2007). The power of feedback. *Review of Educational Research, 77*(1), 81–112. Retrieved from http://doi.org/10.3102/003465430298487

Jonsson, A., & Svingby, G. (2007a). The use of scoring rubrics: Reliability, validity and educational consequences. *Educational Research Review, 2*(2), 130–144. Retrieved from http://doi.org/http://dx.doi.org/10.1016/j.edurev.2007.05.002

Jonsson, A., & Svingby, G. (2007b). The use of scoring rubrics: Reliability, validity and educational consequences. *Educational Research Review, 2*(2), 130–144. Retrieved from http://doi.org/http://dx.doi.org/10.1016/j.edurev.2007.05.002

Keeling, R. P. (Ed.). (2004). *Learning reconsidered: A campus-wide focus on the student experience.* Washington, DC: American College Personnel Association and National Association of School Personnel Administrators.

Keeling, R. P., & Hersh, R. H. (2012). *We're losing our minds: Rethinking American higher education.* New York, NY: Palgrave Macmillan.

Keeling, R. P., Wall, A. F., Underhile, R., & Dungy, G. J. (2008). Assessment reconsidered: Institutional effectiveness for student success. International Center for Student Success and Institutional Accountability.

Kelchen, R. (2015). The landscape of competency-based education: Enrollments, demographics, and affordability. American Enterprise Institute, Center on Higher Education Reform. Retrieved from http://www.luminafoundation.org/files/resources/competency-based-education-landscape.pdf

Komives, S., & Schoper, S. (2006). Developing learning outcomes. In R. P. Keeling (Ed.), *Learning reconsidered 2: Implementing a campus-wide focus on the student experience* (pp. 17–41). Washington, DC: ACPA, ACUHO-I, ACUI, NACA, NACADA, NASPA, and NIRSA. Retrieved from http://www.sa.ua.edu/documents/LearningReconsidered2_005.pdf

Kuh, G. D. (1996). Guiding principles for creating seamless learning environments for undergraduates. *Journal of College Student Development, 37*(2), 135–148.

Kuh, G. D. (2008). *High-impact educational practices: What they are, who has access to them, and why they matter.* Washington, DC: Association of American Colleges and Universities.

Leveille, D. E. (2006). *Accountability in higher education: A public agenda for trust and cultural change.* Berkeley, CA. Retrieved from https://escholarship.org/uc/item/38x683z5

National Association for Campus Activities. (2009). *Competency guide for college student leaders.* Retrieved from http://sbctc.edu/College/studentsvcs/naca_college_student_leader_competency_guide-facilitator_version.pdf

National Association of Colleges and Employers. (2014). *The skills/qualities employers want in new college graduate hires.* Retrieved from https://www.naceweb.org/about-us/press/class-2015-skills-qualities-employers-want.aspx

National Center for Education Statistics. (2014). Undergraduate enrollment. Retrieved from https://nces.ed.gov/fastfacts/display.asp?id=40

National Commission on College and University Board Governance. (2014). *Consequential boards: Adding value where it matters most.* Retrieved from http://agb.org/sites/default/files/legacy/2014_AGB_National_Commission.pdf

Newman, F., Couturier, L., & Scurry, J. (2004). *The future of higher education: Rhetoric, reality, and the risks of the market.* San Francisco, CA: Jossey-Bass.

Pascarella, E. T., Blaich, C., Martin, G. L., & Hanson, J. M. (2011). How robust are the findings of academically adrift? *Change, 43*(3), 20–24. doi: 10.1080/00091383.2011.568898

Pittinsky, M. (2014). *Extending the transcript.* Retrieved from https://www.insidehighered.com/views/2014/02/10/essay-calls-broader-concept-transcripts

Prince, S. A., Adamo, K. B., Hamel, M. E., Hardt, J., Gorber, S., & Tremblay, M. (2008). A comparison of direct versus self-report measures for assessing physical activity in adults: A systematic review. *International Journal of Behavioral Nutrition and Physical Activity, 5*(1), 56.

Ravitch, D. (1990). Education in the 1980's: A concern for "quality." *Education Week,* January 10. Retrieved from http://www.edweek.org/ew/articles/1990/01/10/09200009.h09.html?qs=education+in+the+1980

Reddy, Y. M., & Andrade, H. (2010). A review of rubric use in higher education. *Assessment & Evaluation in Higher Education, 35*(4), 435–448. Retrieved from http://class.web.nthu.edu.tw/ezfiles/669/1669/img/1381/6.Areviewofrubricuseinhighereducation.pdf

Rivard, R. (2013). Limited confidence in board. *InsideHigherEd.com,* September 4. Retrieved from https://www.insidehighered.com/news/2013/09/04/college-presidents-harbor-doubts-about-governing-boards

Rugs, D., & Kaplan, M. (1993). Effectiveness of informational and normative influences in group decision making depends on the group interactive goal. *British Journal of Social Psychology, 32*(2), 147–158.

Schroeder, P. (1992). *Report on the activities for the year 1992 of the select committee on children, youth, and families.* Washington, DC. Retrieved from https://ia802603.us.archive.org/30/items/reportonactiviti00unit_0/reportonactiviti00unit_0.pdf

Slippery Rock University. (n.d.). *Co-curricular experience program.* Retrieved from http://www.sru.edu/studentlife/studentleadership/Pages/CCE.aspx

Sternberg, R. J. (2013). Giving employers what they don't really want. *The Chronicle of Higher Education*, June 17. Retrieved from http://chronicle.com/article/Giving-Employers-What-They/139877/?cid=at&utm_source=at&utm_medium=en

Stevens, D. D., & Levi, A. J. (2005). *Introduction to rubrics: An assessment tool to save grading time, convey effective feedback and promote student learning.* Sterling, VA: Sterling.

Suskie, L. (2009). *Assessing student learning: A common sense guide* (2nd ed.), San Francisco, CA: Jossey-Bass.

Task Force on Federal Regulation of Higher Education. (2015). *Recalibrating regulations of colleges and universities.* Washington, DC. Retrieved from http://www.help.senate.gov/imo/media/Regulations_Task_Force_Report_2015_FINAL.pdf

The Institute for College Access and Success. (2014). *Student debt and the class of 2013.* Retrieved from http://ticas.org/sites/default/files/legacy/fckfiles/pub/classof2013.pdf

The White House. (2013). *The President's plan for a strong middle class and a strong America.* Washington, DC. Retrieved from https://www.whitehouse.gov/sites/default/files/uploads/sotu_2013_blueprint_embargo.pdf

Tierney, R., & Simon, M. (2004). What's still wrong with rubrics: Focusing on the consistency of performance criteria across scale levels. *Practical Assessment, Research & Evaluation*, 9(2). Retrieved from http://pareonline.net/getvn.asp?v=9&n=2

U.S. Department of Education. (2006). *A test of leadership: Charting the future of U.S. higher education.* Washington, DC. Retrieved from https://www2.ed.gov/about/bdscomm/list/hiedfuture/reports/pre-pub-report.pdf

UNC Student Affairs. (n.d.). *Excellence in action.* Retrieved from https://studentaffairs.unc.edu/excellence-action

University of Pittsburgh. (n.d.). *What is the OCC.* Retrieved from http://www.studentaffairs.pitt.edu/occwhatisit

Chapter 16

Promoting Student Engagement in the Classroom and Beyond

Richard L. Miller

Abstract

Purpose — This chapter aims to discuss methods for promoting student engagement to counteract declining academic motivation and achievement in the contemporary setting.

Methodology/approach — In this chapter, two studies are presented that describe ways to promote student engagement in and out of the classroom. The in-class study was conducted with psychology students at the University of Nebraska at Kearney (UNK). The Student Course Engagement Questionnaire (SCEQ) developed by Handelsman, Briggs, Sullivan, and Towler (2005) was used to measure student engagement. Study 2 examined the extent to which four high-impact educational practices promoted student engagement. Undergraduate UNK students who had participated in undergraduate research, learning communities, service learning, or internships were surveyed.

Findings — The results of the first study indicated that instructors can promote engagement by how the structure of the classroom (discussion classes), individuation (knowing student names and keeping class sizes small), and teacher support in the form of being responsive to student questions, encouraging students to seek assistance, and assigning effective aids to learning. The second study indicated that undergraduate research and internships were more engaging than service learning or learning communities.

Originality/value — These results suggest practical methods for meeting a variety of student needs, including their need for relatedness — by encouraging them to seek assistance and knowing their names, competence — by assigning effective learning aids and autonomy — by encouraging intrinsically motivating activities.

Keywords: Student engagement; intrinsic motivation; active learning; engaged learning; high-impact educational practice; positive classroom environments

16.1.   Research Background for Engaged Learning

Fredricks, Blumenfeld, and Paris (2004) suggest that there are historical, economic, theoretical, and practical reasons to focus on student engagement. From the historical perspective, educational institutions can no longer assume that those admitted to their ranks are motivated to take advantage of what is offered and student engagement has been touted as a possible solution to declining academic motivation and achievement. From an economic perspective, our global, rapidly evolving economy requires workers who can think critically, adapt to change, and solve problems. From a theoretical perspective, student engagement seems to improve intellectual achievement, critical thinking, and commitment to life-long learning. Practically speaking, student engagement has been shown to improve performance and reduce dropout rates (Miller, 2011). To insure that our educational institutions are meeting these challenges, colleges and universities are being asked to identify whether they are providing students with the type of educational experiences students expect, as well as the opportunities to attain the occupational and personal benefits students deserve (Involvement in Learning Study, 1984).

While students' reasons for attending college vary widely, researchers have identified a number of reasons that typically motivate students to devote the considerable personal and financial resources necessary to obtain a college degree (Astin, 1985; Kuh et al., 1991). Future financial well-being and ability to engage in leisure activities are often cited by traditional first-year students as their primary motivations for attending college (Astin, 1985).

Over time, students often identify additional motivators for continuing their education, including cognitive, emotional, and moral development; increased quality family life; and obtaining occupational competence (Astin, 1985; Kuh et al., 1991). As colleges and universities address ever-increasing demands for accountability, they are being called upon to quantifiably demonstrate that students are engaging in educational practices that prepare them for a changing workplace in an increasingly global economy (Fredricks et al., 2004; Pascarella, Edison, Nora, Hagedorn, & Terezini, 1996).

To address this need for accountability, educational research has focused on identifying factors related to students' personal and occupational success during the college years and on entry into the workforce after graduation (Astin, 1977; Astin, 1993; Kuh, 1995; Pascarella & Terezini, 1991). Some of the factors identified include increases in general knowledge and knowledge within their major (Astin, 1993), as well as increases in personal competence, verbal and quantitative skills, and cognitive complexity; all of which support success in one's occupational, personal, and social life (Astin, 1993; Kuh, 1995; Pascarella & Terezini, 1991).

In general, most college students in comparison with their non-college educated peers will experience increased autonomy, social maturation, estheticism, and awareness of interests, values, aspirations, and religious views, which are believed to foster opportunities for success in the occupational and personal realm (Astin, 1977, 1993). Finally, most students will experience decreases in characteristics such as irrational prejudices, political naiveté, and dogmatism (Pascarella & Terezini, 1991) as a result of their academic experiences.

The demand for accountability has led to a paradigm shift in what constitutes excellence in post-secondary education (Koljatic & Kuh, 2001). In the past, the quality of education provided by an institution was thought to be directly linked to the institution's status and reputation. However, the *Involvement in Learning Study* (The Study Group on the Conditions of Excellence in Higher Education, 1984), as well as more recent studies on student engagement and later success have challenged this view by asserting that the quality of education should be based on linking good educational practices and positive outcomes for students (Astin, 1993; Kuh, 1995; Kuh et al., 1991; Pascarella et al., 2006; Pascarella, Palmer, Moye, & Pierson, 2001) including job status and income (Avalos, 1996), growth in leadership and job-related skills (Astin, 1993), development of critical thinking skills (Pascarella et al., 2001), and openness to diversity and challenge (Pascarella et al., 2006).

In their article, *Seven Principles for Good Practice in Undergraduate Education*, Chickering and Gameson (1987) outline a set of good practices in education that are assumed to be valid and appropriate for the promotion of learning as well as student development at virtually all types of institutions (Gamson, 1991; Kuh, Pace, & Vesper, 1997). Thus, the most widely used measure of student engagement, The National Survey of Student Engagement, is designed to measure the degree to which students perceive that the following seven good educational practices are being implemented: (a) opportunities for active learning, (b) activities that promote cooperation among students, (c) a high level of student-faculty contact, (d) prompt feedback to students on performance, (e) the amount of time on task required by teacher's assignments, (f) high expectations for student performance by faculty, and (g) faculty respect for diversity (Koljatic & Kuh, 2001). Subsequent research has identified three more good educational practices, including (a) quality of teaching received (b) influential interactions with other students in non-course-related activities, and (c) a supportive campus environment (Astin, 1993; Pascarella et al., 1996).

16.2. Defining the Educational Practices That Promote Student Engagement

Active learning involves experiences that engage students in inquiry, action, imagination, invention, interaction, hypothesizing, and personal reflection (Cranton, 2012). Some active learning exercises are debate, case studies, role-playing, cooperative learning, simulations, games, and labs (Bonwell & Eison, 1991).

Cooperative learning puts the instructional emphasis on group activities and course related interactions among peers. It is structured and facilitated by the instructor and typically involves 3–6 students working on a common assignment. Some examples of cooperative learning are the jigsaw technique, group problem solving exercises, discussion groups, peer review assignments, and think pair share (Koljatic & Kuh, 2001). A typical survey item for measuring cooperative learning would ask about interactions such as having peers proofread a paper or assignment or attempting to explain course material to another student or friend.

Student-faculty contact refers to non-classroom interactions with faculty as well as students' perceptions of faculty interest in teaching and personal development (Tinto, 1997). A typical survey item designed to measure student-faculty contact might ask for information such as the number of times a student has visited informally with a faculty member after class or made an appointment to meet with a faculty member in his or her office (Koljatic & Kuh, 2001).

Prompt feedback to students is defined as the speed with which professors provide feedback about student performance (e.g., grading tests and quizzes) (Chickering & Gameson, 1987). Research suggests that feedback that is clear, specific, affirming, and corrective contributes to student learning and motivates students to improve (Walvoord & Anderson, 2010).

Time on task is a measure that refers to the degree to which students actively engage in activities related to the classroom experience (Chickering & Gameson, 1987). It is the time actually spent learning and may be the most important contributor to academic achievement (Slavin, 2003). Time on task includes measures such as time spent reading for class and number of drafts written for a paper.

High expectations are often reflected in the degree of difficulty of the course, the level of student effort expected, and whether the class has a scholarly/intellectual emphasis. Measures related to high expectations include factors such as student perceptions of expectations, number of textbooks, or readings assigned and the number of term papers (Tinto, 1997).

Respect for other students and diverse ways of knowing refers to students' willingness to be exposed to and tolerance of viewpoints that differ from their own. Factors used to measure respect for other students and diverse ways of knowing include frequency of discussions with people who have different viewpoints on particular subjects or are of a different racial or ethnic background (National Survey of Student Engagement, 2006).

Influential interactions with other students refer to the quality of interactions with students, non-course-related interactions with peers, and cultural and interpersonal involvement (Kuh, 1995). Such interactions could include amount of time spent socializing with peers and attendance at non-class-related institutionally sponsored events.

Supportive campus environment refers to students' perceptions of whether their particular institution places value on students' engaging in supportive interactions with others (Astin, 1993; Pascarella et al., 1996). Such factors include support for incoming freshmen as well as for students struggling with academic or personal issues.

When one considers the relevance of good educational practices, the question for accountability is whether involvement in these activities really matters? In other words, do students who engage in good educational practices stay in school, demonstrate greater cognitive, emotional, and personal development and have higher incomes and more personal fulfillment in their lives after college? The answer appears to be affirmative. Several studies have shown that students who are involved in good educational practices appear to get what they want and need out of college (Astin, 1984, 1993; Avalos, 1996; Fredricks et al., 2004; Johnson, Johnson, & Smith, 1998; Pascarella et al., 2006; Pascarella et al., 1996; Tinto, 1997). Included are cognitive skills, personal growth, psychosocial development, as well as improved employment opportunities (Miller & Butler, 2011).

16.3. Classroom Practices That Promote Student Engagement

Particular classroom practices have been shown to have a positive impact on educational outcomes (Handelsman, Briggs, Sullivan, & Towler, 2005; Pascarella et al., 1996). For example, cooperative learning in the classroom has been demonstrated to be more productive than the traditional lecture format in fostering greater individual learning. Collaboration has been shown to produce statistically significant increases in knowledge acquisition and problem solving skills as compared to individual learning (Johnson et al., 1998; Pascarella et al., 1996). Increased teacher clarity and organization has been demonstrated to increase student participation in the classroom, increase student knowledge acquisition and critical thinking skills, and have a significant influence on student plans to obtain a graduate degree (Pascarella et al., 1996).

Engagement in good educational practices prepares students for post-graduate success (Astin, 1993; Fredricks et al., 2004; Gurin, 1999). As the US workforce becomes increasingly more diverse in the current global economy, workers must be able to apply critical thinking skills in various environments with a vast array of diverse people (Fredricks et al., 2004). College students who engage in good educational practices report higher income levels and increased satisfaction with their careers as well as with the level of preparation given them by their institution of higher learning (Astin, 1993). Not surprisingly, students who engage in good educational practices, particularly racially, culturally, intellectually, and politically diverse activities, report that they are more successful in their occupations, are well prepared for their occupation, and have higher levels of community involvement than peers who do not engage in good educational practices (Gurin, 1999; Kuh et al., 1991).

A variety of factors exist that should strongly influence how and why colleges and universities identify the degree to which they are engaging students in good educational practices. Low academic achievement and high attrition rates persist for many students, and these factors appear to be substantially influenced by student engagement in good educational practices (Hsieh, Sullivan, & Guerra, 2007). As colleges and universities strive to obtain State and Federal funding and attract potential incoming students, it becomes increasingly important that these institutions demonstrate quantifiable evidence that they are providing the necessary interventions to prepare students for academic and personal success. The *Involvement in Learning Study* (1984) outlined a number of criteria that could be used to develop reliable and valid indices of student learning and development; these criteria have largely been adhered to by researchers responsible for developing nationally circulated research tools designed to measure practices in good undergraduate education (Kuh, 2001). The *Involvement in Learning Study* (1984) recommended that little emphasis should be placed on input characteristics (pre-college characteristics such as high school grade point average (GPA), and Scholastic Aptitude Test (SAT)/ American College Testing (ACT) scores) and that instead the focus should be on output characteristics (longitudinal data measuring the gains demonstrated in student knowledge, capacities, skills, and attitudes over the course of their college career). The study also asserted that these improvements needed to occur with established, clearly expressed, and publicly announced and maintained standards; these improvements also needed to be cost-effective in the use of student and institutional resources of time, money, and effort. Time has proven the wisdom of the Involvement in Learning Study's (1984) recommendations, as broad-based national surveys such as the National Survey of Student Engagement have demonstrated the positive effects of student engagement and the quality of education provided to students by various universities and colleges (Kuh, 2001; Pascarella et al., 2006).

The critical question seems to be how do colleges and universities foster student engagement, both in and outside of the classroom? Perhaps the most obvious route, one that is presently being utilized by hundreds of colleges and universities, is to utilize available research tools to identify areas in which they are currently engaging students in good educational practices and areas in which they are not (Koljatic & Kuh, 2001). Various researchers have made recommendations about how student engagement may be increased (see Guenther & Miller, 2011). Perhaps the clearest generalization that can be made is that a student's interpersonal environment (e.g., frequency and nature of contacts with faculty and peers) has the greatest impact on student increases in engagement (Pascarella et al., 1996). Providing opportunities and incentives for students to be involved in educationally diverse and purposeful activities (e.g., campus speakers, conversation tables with foreign students) are highly related to increased knowledge acquisition, openness to diversity and other associated cognitive and personal gains (Ewell & Jones, 1993; Koljatic & Kuh, 2001). Creating classroom environments that enhance increased self-efficacy and mastery goal orientation is related to high classroom achievement and increased student efforts directed toward academic assignments (Bandura, 1997; Hsieh et al., 2007). Engaging students in learning activities that are directly related to desired learning outcomes (e.g., utilizing information gleaned from class speaker as test material) promotes enhanced learning and retention of relevant classroom information (Guadalupe, 1996). Many universities have implemented entire learning communities and have developed quality programs designed to assist students who are struggling academically (Tinto, 1997). Given the recommendations, one might assume that the student engagement problems of the 1980s and 1990s would have been eradicated by now.

16.4. The Challenges in Promoting Student Engagement

Unfortunately, despite the vast amount of resources, time, and energy expended since the initial calls for reform began in the 1980s, student engagement does not appear to be increasing at a national level (Koljatic & Kuh, 2001). When evidence began to accumulate that engagement was not increasing, it was initially thought that, since a far higher percentage of Americans are pursuing a college education than there were in the 1980s, engagement was not increasing because far fewer people currently entering college were as prepared to be engaged students as were the students of the 1980s (Astin, 1977; Koljatic & Kuh, 2001). However, recent research on the influence of institutional selectivity indicates that student pre-college characteristics apparently have only a small mediating effect on whether students are engaged in good educational practices throughout their undergraduate careers (Pascarella et al., 2006). Thus, it appears that there remain barriers that prevent students and their institutions of higher learning from engaging in good practices in undergraduate education.

Change is often not easy to accommodate, and researchers have identified that resistance exists on many colleges and universities that inhibit institutional changes designed to promote increased engagement (Koljatic & Kuh, 2001). Indeed, it has been pointed out that the American university system, which has been ingrained with three centuries of ideas about what constitutes *higher education*, will not likely be revolutionized in 2–3 decades. Implementation of interventions such as learning communities, living learning centers, extra programs for struggling students, and other interventions are expensive and take time to implement (Pascarella et al., 2006). Various changes in the dynamics of United States' colleges and universities have created new challenges that inhibit engagement. Faculty participation in governance and expectations for high academic achievements such as publications serve to reduce the amount of teaching preparation time for faculty. The non-teaching duties have also been criticized by numerous researchers as reducing incentives faculty have to devote the time necessary to be high-quality teachers, because notoriety and tenure tend to be earned through academic achievement, not teaching (Involvement in Learning Study, 1984; Koljatic & Kuh, 2001; Pascarella et al., 2006). Technological interventions such as online classes may serve to reduce faculty-to-student and student-to-student contact. Many students also spend less time on campus and therefore reduce their opportunities for engagement in certain types of good educational practices (Pascarella et al., 2006). That said, many students who are not campus bound are actively engaged in the workforce and for many university majors, the service learning opportunities for such students are readily available.

Since increasing engagement on a macro-level can be extremely difficult, perhaps increasing engagement would best be addressed at the micro level. Interestingly, researchers have identified that the vast majority of American post-secondary colleges and universities have multiple sub-environments, departments, programs, majors, minors, co-curricular activities, and specialties like orchestra, or drama that have more immediate and powerful influences on student engagement within their sub-environment than any aggregate institutional characteristic (Pascarella et al., 2006). It is, therefore, reasonable to look to these sub-environments as both instigators and inhibitors of student engagement in good educational practices. Indeed, many departments within universities do an excellent job of engaging students in good educational practices (Kuh et al., 1991). All across the nation, students are engaging in the classroom, conducting research, collaborating with one another and faculty, and getting involved in their communities. However, many more students are not engaged. A number of barriers prevent individual professors and departments from engaging students (Involvement in Learning Study, 1984; Kuh et al., 1991; Pascarella et al., 1996). Professors and departments have little control over where students reside, whether students choose to have contact with diverse peers outside the classroom setting or how many racially diverse activities a university holds (Pascarella et al., 1996). Furthermore, many of the teachers who would best be able to facilitate engagement do not teach introductory level classes where engagement is perhaps most important because it aids in student success and retention (The Study Group on the Conditions of Excellence in Higher Education, 1984; Kuh et al., 1991). For professors in many departments, obtaining tenure may have little or nothing to do with the quality of teaching provided to students.

One may then ask, what may a single faculty member do to help foster engagement? Thirty years ago, the college classroom was the focal point of the educational structure of institutions of higher learning and thus served as the focal point for student experiences (Tinto, 1997). With the growth of online programs and the proliferation of online courses, the campus itself is perhaps no longer the focal point that it once was, particularly for an increasing number of non-traditional students. Given the relatively recent increases in the number of part-time students enrolled in colleges and universities, many of whom work many hours and have families, the college classroom remains, for many students, the only place where academic engagement regularly occurs. Many engagement researchers adhere to the principle that in order to most effectively promote engagement, faculty must embrace the principles underlying good educational practices that emphasize student learning, both in class and outside of class, and what learners do to integrate their learning from a variety of sources, instead of focusing on instruction and what teachers do (Koljatic & Kuh, 2001).

At the micro level, faculty have a great deal of control over the extent of engagement students have in their classrooms. Indeed, students' perceptions of the organization, clarity and expectations of their educational environment are strong predictors of their engagement levels (Koljatic & Kuh, 2001). Learning has often been thought to be a spectator sport in which faculty talk dominates the environment (Tinto, 1997). Some researchers report that faculty talk dominates 80–98% of the time in most college classrooms. Conventional wisdom would suggest that in such an environment collaborative learning and active learning are quite limited (Tinto, 1997).

Researchers have identified that students who engage in collaborative learning tend to invest more quality time in learning and enjoy these experiences more than the traditional lecture mode, which tends to favor assertive students who dominate the 10–20% of class time allotted for student feedback (Tinto, 1997). Given the fact that student engagement is a vitally important component of the learning process, it is reasonable to ask how faculty can measure and increase student engagement in their own classroom setting.

Research by Handelsman et al. has identified the presence of four distinct forms of engagement in the classroom setting: they are (a) skills engagement, (b) participation engagement, (c) emotional engagement, and (d) performance engagement (Handelsman et al., 2005). Skills engagement refers to the degree to which students practice skills that promote learning; examples include taking notes in class, studying regularly, and doing class readings. Participation, or interactive, engagement refers to engagement that occurs in relation to others.

Examples of participation engagement include asking questions in class, going to a professor's office to talk about class and participating in small group discussions. Emotional engagement refers to the degree to which students internalize class information and experiences. Examples of emotional engagement include students finding ways to make course materials relevant to their lives, thinking about course materials between class sessions and desiring to learn the material. Performance engagement refers to student engagement directed toward performance on graded materials and include factors such as importance students place on getting good grades and doing well on tests. To assess these four types of student engagement, Handelsman et al. (2005) developed the SCEQ, a 27-item instrument that measures skills engagement (e.g., taking notes in class), emotional engagement (e.g., applying course information to daily life), participation engagement (e.g., asking questions to understand), and performance engagement (e.g., doing well on tests). All student engagement factors show reasonable reliability that range from .76 to .82. Discriminant validity of the four factors was demonstrated by low inter-correlations ranging from .26 to .44. These four factors have been shown to be reliable indices of student engagement obtained through student self-report and are as reliable as student GPA and GRE scores (Guadalupe, 1996). Students are asked to respond to the 27 questions on five-point Likert scales ranging from *1 = not at all characteristic of me* to *5 = very characteristic of me*.

16.5. Promoting Student Engagement in the Classroom: Study 1

Researchers currently have little knowledge as to how faculty may increase students' participation in the four types of engagement. To address this gap in our knowledge, we conducted an empirical study to assess what instructional factors play a role in increasing classroom engagement. We were particularly interested in assessing the impact of the role of faculty-determined factors (e.g., class size, teaching style, responsiveness to questions) in influencing engagement. We were also interested in assessing the role of student motivation factors (e.g., intrinsic vs. extrinsic motivation) in mediating engagement and whether interactions exist between faculty-determined factors and student motivation factors. We hypothesized that factors related to the learning environment such as small class size and implementation of discussion-based classes would result in increased student engagement. We also hypothesized that instructors' activities, such as being responsive to students' questions and knowing the names of students in their classrooms would also be related to increased student engagement. Finally, based on the research by Skinner and Pitzer (2012), we hypothesized that intrinsically motivated students would be more engaged than extrinsically motivated students.

16.6.   Method

16.6.1.   Participants

The participants in the study were students enrolled in psychology classes at the University of Nebraska at Kearney (UNK) in Fall, 2006. We collected data from 665 undergraduate students (226 men, 439 women). Their ages ranged from 18 to 39 years of age, with a mean age of 20.16. Over 50% of the students enrolled in psychology classes did so to satisfy a General Education requirement and were not psychology majors or minors. We chose this group because we were able to obtain access to the student evaluations of the instructors from the faculty in our department.

16.6.2.   Materials and Procedure

We administered the 27-item Student Course Engagement Questionnaire (SCEQ) developed by Handelsman et al. (2005). The questionnaire measures the four types of course engagement previously identified by the authors, including skills engagement, emotional engagement, participation/interaction engagement, and performance engagement.

Each of the behavioral items on the SCEQ was accompanied by a Likert scale ranging from *1 = not at all characteristic of me* to *5 = very characteristic of me*. The overall course engagement score was the sum of the 27 items, and the sub-scale scores were the sum of those items measuring each particular type of course engagement. On this questionnaire, the reliability correlations for the student engagement factors ranged from .76 to .82. Discriminant validity of the four factors was demonstrated by low inter-correlations ranging from .26 to .44. We administered the SCEQ during a regular class meeting so that participants completed it when the specific course that they were evaluating was most salient.

To assess intrinsic versus extrinsic goal motivation, we asked: "If I had to choose between getting a good grade and being challenged in class, I would choose:___ . We also asked how important it was in the course to (a) get a good grade and (b) be challenged, on five-point scales ranging from 1 = *not important* to 5 = *very important*.

Faculty members provided information on course dynamics that could influence students' course engagement. We asked faculty members about the type of

Table 16.1: Questions on the faculty members' course evaluation form.

1. To what extent did the students in this course participate in classroom discussion?
2. To what extent were the students dependent on you for guidance/assistance in completing their coursework?
3. How intelligent and capable were the students in the class generally?
4. In general, to what extent did the students follow the rules and procedures required in this course?
5. How conducive was the classroom atmosphere to learning?

instructional style they employed (lecture only, lecture/discussion or discussion only). We also asked about heterogeneity of the students in terms of class standing (Freshman, Sophomores, Junior or Senior), indicated by whether the students were mostly from the same group, two contiguous groups, or widely distributed over three or four groups. We also asked faculty members to evaluate their course on several items that relate to the course dynamics that are dependent upon the students who register for the course. Table 16.1 contains those items.

Each of the five items on the course evaluation form was accompanied by a seven-point Likert scale ranging from 7 = *more than usual* to 1 = *less than usual*. Finally, we asked faculty members the percent of students' names they knew. Class size and target audience (service courses vs. courses for psychology majors) were obtained from the course record file. Information on instructional activities was obtained from the regular course evaluation form completed by all students at the end of the semester (see Table 16.2).

Each of the nine items on the course evaluation form was accompanied by a five-point Likert scale ranging from 1 = *strongly disagree* to 5 = *strongly agree*. Students' grades in the course they evaluated were obtained from university records.

16.7. Results

Does engagement matter? The results indicated that student engagement, as measured by the SCEQ was positively correlated with the grade the student received in the course, $r(665) = .62, p < .001$.

16.7.1. Course Characteristics

A small negative correlation was found between classroom engagement and class size, $r(665) = -.13, p < .05$. While significant, class size appeared to have less of an impact on student engagement than did the teaching style employed by faculty members. Students in discussion-based classes demonstrated higher levels of overall engagement as measured by the SCEQ ($M = 98.7$) than students in lecture

Table 16.2: Questions on the students' course evaluation form.

1. The faculty member stimulates thinking.
2. The faculty member is enthusiastic about the subject material.
3. The faculty member is responsive to student questions.
4. The faculty member is well prepared for class.
5. The faculty member explains and clarifies the subject material.
6. The faculty member grades fairly.
7. The faculty member assigns materials that are effective aids to learning.
8. The faculty member encourages students to seek assistance as needed and is available for assistance and consultation.
9. The faculty member is knowledgeable about the subject matter.

($M = 88.1$) or lecture/discussion classes ($M = 89.5$), $F(2, 597) = 8.73$, $p < .001$. The specific types of engagement that were responsive to teaching style included Emotional Engagement, $F(2, 597) = 3.45$, $p < .05$, Participation Engagement, $F(2, 597) = 15.48$, $p < .001$, and Performance Engagement, $F(2, 597) = 3.63$, $p < .05$. In each of these cases, discussion style classes led to greater student engagement. Teaching style did not have an effect on Skills Engagement, $F(2, 597) = 1.69$, $p > .10$.

We expected that students enrolled in courses in their major discipline would be more engaged than students taking courses as a part of the general education program. However, the results indicated that students in general education courses ($M = 87.9$) were as engaged as were students in courses designed for psychology majors/minors ($M = 89.3$), $F < 1$, $p = ns$.

There was a significant positive correlation between the instructor's rating of "How conducive was the classroom atmosphere to learning" and student engagement as measured by the SCEQ, $r(665) = .14$, $p < .01$, as well as a small positive correlation between the instructor's rating of participation in classroom discussion and student engagement, $r(665) = .08$, $p < .05$. and a small negative correlation between the instructor's rating of how dependent students were on guidance/assistance and student engagement, $r(665) = -.09$, $p < .05$.

16.7.2. Instructor Characteristics

For the instructor activities listed in Table 16.1, we found several activities that were positively correlated with student engagement as measured by the SCEQ. The rating of the item "The faculty member is responsive to student questions" was positively correlated with student engagement, $r(610) = .20$, $p < .01$. The rating of the item: "The faculty member assigns effective aids for learning" was positively correlated with student engagement, $r(610) = .19$, $p < .01$, as was the item "The faculty member encourages students to seek assistance," $r(610) = .19$, $p < .01$. Finally, there was a positive correlation between the percentage of names that the faculty member knew and student engagement $r(610) = .18$, $p < .01$. None of the other instructor activities identified in Table 16.1 were significantly correlated with student engagement.

16.7.3. Student Characteristics

Student motivation ratings were also significantly correlated with course engagement. A moderate positive correlation was found between the importance students placed on getting good grades and their engagement scores on the SCEQ, $r(665) = .27$, $p < .001$. An even stronger positive correlation was identified between student engagement and the importance students placed on being challenged in the classroom, $r(665) = .47, p < .001$.

We also analyzed whether differential engagement levels occurred between students who indicated that being challenged in the classroom (intrinsic motivation) was more important than grades (extrinsic motivation) or vice versa. A univariate analysis of variance was conducted with choice (grade or challenge) being the independent variable and overall engagement levels on the SCEQ being the dependent variable. Intrinsically motivated students were significantly more engaged ($M = 93.7$) than were extrinsically motivated students ($M = 88.2$), $F(1,597) = 16.53$, $p < .001$. Post-hoc analysis revealed that the types of engagement for which intrinsically motivated students scored higher were Emotional Engagement, $F(2, 597) = 27.69$, $p < .001$, and Participation Engagement, $F(2, 597) = 12.91, p < .001$, but not Skills Engagement, $F(2, 597) = 2.81, p > .09$, or Performance Engagement, $F < 1$. It should be noted that our measure of intrinsic motivation was limited and did not address the complexities identified by Skinner and Pitzer (2012) that they suggest promote intrinsic motivation, specifically the needs for competence, belonging, and autonomy.

16.8. Discussion

The results of this study indicate that there are many ways that instructors can promote course engagement including classroom structure (discussion classes), individuation (knowing student names and keeping class sizes small), and teacher support in the form of being responsive to student questions, encouraging students to seek assistance, and assigning effective aids to learning. These results suggest practical methods for meeting a variety of student needs that have previously been shown to increase engagement, including students' need for relatedness — by encouraging them to seek assistance and knowing their names (Furrer & Skinner, 2003), competence — by assigning effective learning aids (Connell, Spencer, & Aber, 1994), and autonomy — by encouraging activities that are intrinsically motivating (Patrick, Skinner, & Connell, 1993). In addition, small classes and discussion formats have been shown to promote engagement and enhance achievement because they build upon established cognitive learning strategies (Fisher, Frey, & Lapp, 2011; Mayer & Tucker, 2010).

While family, community, culture, and educational context have all been shown to influence student engagement (Fredricks et al., 2004), most of the research on student engagement among college students has focused on educational practices, student expectations, and peer influences. An additional area that needs examination is the role personality plays in student engagement. Measures of locus of control, openness to experience, conscientiousness, and extraversion may be important predictors of engagement.

16.9. Promoting Student Engagement Outside of the Classroom: Study 2

Another approach to promoting student engagement is the implementation of what Kuh (2008) has termed high-impact educational practices. These practices have been shown to increase rates of student retention and student engagement. Examples of high-impact practices listed by Kuh are First-Year Seminars and Experiences, Common Intellectual Experiences, Learning Communities, Writing-Intensive Courses, Collaborative Assignments and Projects, Undergraduate Research, Diversity/Global Learning, Service Learning, Community-Based Learning, Internships, and Capstone Courses and Projects.

16.10. High-Impact Educational Practices Defined

First-Year Seminars typically involve small groups of students working with faculty on a regular basis. In addition to providing students with basic academic skills, such as information literacy and writing, good experiences promote critical inquiry, quantitative analysis, collaborative learning, and other skills that develop students' intellectual and practical competencies. First-year seminars are often organized around a theme that can be related to cutting-edge research or global concerns (Keup et al., 2011).

Common Intellectual Experiences is an approach that has evolved from the traditional idea of a core curriculum. As currently implemented, these programs generally focus on broad themes such as global interdependence or the impact of technology on society. In place of the core curriculum, there are a series of courses and co-curricular events that contribute to an understanding of the broad theme.

Learning communities can be both curricular and residential. Typically, they include classes that are linked or clustered during an academic term, often around an interdisciplinary theme, and enroll a common cohort of students, based on common interests or career goals. An important goal for a learning community is the integration of what students are learning across a range of courses and the engagement of the students in the consideration of "big" questions that cut across disciplines and extend beyond the classroom (Laufgraben & Shapiro, 2004).

Writing-Intensive Courses provide students the opportunity to write and revise their writing. Most colleges and universities that require writing-intensive courses emphasize writing across the curriculum. Students are asked to write in different forms, within different disciplines, and for different audiences. This approach to writing instruction has proved effective and has been extended to similar efforts in teaching quantitative reasoning, oral communication, and information literacy.

Collaborative assignments and projects assist students in learning to work and solve problems in cooperation with others. In addition, students learn how to cope with group dynamics including social loafing and active listening (Barkley, Major, & Cross, 2014). Examples of collaborative activities include study groups, team-based projects and collaborative research.

Undergraduate research is a study or inquiry conducted by an undergraduate student and mentored by a faculty member that makes an original, intellectual or creative contribution to the discipline (Wenzel, 1997). Undergraduate research began in the scientific disciplines with strong support from the National Science Foundation. The goal is to involve students in addressing open questions through the use of empirical processes, to foster the excitement that comes from working to answer important questions (Miller, 2015).

Diversity/Global Learning allows students to explore human behavior, life experiences, and worldviews across different cultures. This approach often explores issues of diversity including race, ethnic, and gender differences as well human rights, power inequality, and freedom (Gadsby & Bullivant, 2010). Study abroad programs fall into this category.

Service learning is a teaching and learning strategy that integrates meaningful community service with instruction and reflection to enrich the learning experience, teach civic responsibility, and strengthen communities. Students are directly involved with issues that they are studying in class that provide opportunities for them to analyze and solve problems in the community. Service learning is based on the idea that an important outcome of the college experience is the desire to give something back to the community as a way of becoming a model citizen within a democratic society.

Community-based learning allows students to connect what they learn in class to what is happening in their community. Community-based learning can include history, literature, cultural heritage, and the natural environment. Community-based learning is based on the intrinsic educational assets and resources available in the community (Prast & Viegut, 2015).

Internships provide students with the opportunity for on-the-job training in a particular field. These experiences may be paid or unpaid and usually involve a significant amount of time invested in the experience. Students engaged in an internship are given the benefit of supervision and coaching from professionals in the field, in addition to that of the academic instructor/ supervisor (Rigsby, Addy Herring, & Polledo, 2013).

A capstone experience usually refers to a course or project that integrates or synthesizes the knowledge and experience learned during a student's academic career and concludes with a finishing experience that will allow them to think and act like an academic (Wadkins & Miller, 2011). In their survey of 500 college programs, Perlman and McCann (1999) found that 63% of psychology departments required that students complete a capstone course. The most common types of capstone courses reported were senior seminars, history and systems courses, field experiences, and research projects. The capstone experience can take the form of a research paper, a performance, a portfolio, or an exhibit. Capstones can be offered at both the departmental level and as a conclusion to a general education program.

To assess the extent to which four of these high-impact learning experiences contribute to the various forms of engagement, we examined service learning, undergraduate research, learning communities, and internships at the UNK. These were chosen because each of these four high-impact learning practices has long been established on our campus.

16.11.   Method

16.11.1.   *Participants*

The participants were 127 students (88 females, 39 males, *M* age = 21.1) from a public, mid-western American university. Participants were students who had participated in one of four engaged learning activities: Undergraduate research, internship, service learning, or learning community. Students from all four colleges at the University were represented including business/technology ($n=40$), education ($n=52$), fine arts/humanities ($n=17$), and natural/social sciences ($n=60$).

For analysis purposes, participants were assigned to an engaged learning activity group based upon their responses to the online survey through Qualtrics. There were 42 students in the undergraduate research group, 21 participants in the internship group, 27 participants in the service learning group, and 27 participants in the learning community group.

16.11.2.   *Materials*

16.11.2.1. Demographic information
All participants completed eight questions related to their age, gender, major, and academic standing/pursuits.

16.11.2.2. Student Course Engagement Questionnaire (SCEQ)
The SCEQ is a 27-item instrument that measures four types of engagement (Handelsman, et al., 2005). Specifically, the SCEQ measures the following engagement types: skills (e.g., taking notes in class), emotional (e.g., applying course information to daily life), participation (e.g., asking questions to understand), and performance (e.g., doing well on tests). All student engagement factors showed reasonable reliability that ranged from .76 to .82. The 27 questions were answered on

a five-point Likert scale ranging from *1 = not at all characteristic of me* to *5 = very characteristic of me.*

16.11.2.3. Student perceptions of engagement

This was an eight-item questionnaire created by these researchers to explore students' perceptions of their engagement in their learning activities. Students were asked questions such as *How engaged were you in the engaged learning activity?*; *In comparison to your other courses, how engaged were you in the engaged learning activity?*; and *How relevant was this activity in your life goals?* These questions were answered on five-point Likert scales.

16.11.2.4. Goal motivation information

Four questions were created to explore students' views on the importance of getting good grades and/or being challenged in their learning activities. Students also indicated whether they would recommend their learning activity to another student. These questions were answered on a 5-point Likert scale ranging from *1 = not important to 5 = very important.* Students were also asked to give a direct response of the letter grade the student received in the engaged learning activity.

16.11.3. Procedure

The researchers emailed and phoned the directors of academic departments who promote engaged learning activities to obtain the names and e-mails of students involved in undergraduate research, internships, service learning, or a learning community. e-mails containing the link to the Qualtrics on-line survey were sent to 520 students. The survey was available to students for three weeks and included an incentive of being included in a drawing for a gift card for participation. A response rate of 33% was obtained. Forty-four participants were eliminated from the analysis for failure to specify the form of engaged learning practice in which they had participated.

16.12. Results

In order to examine the impact of different types of engaged learning activities on the extent and type of student engagement, we performed several one-way ANOVAs. We compared the types of engaged learning activities (Undergraduate Research, Internships, Service Learning, & Learning Communities) on (a) the four types of student engagement (Skills, Emotional, Participation & Performance), (b) students' perceptions of engagement (Level of Engagement, Comparison with other Courses, Relevance to Life Goals, & Perceived Difficulty), and (c) student motivation (Intrinsic and Extrinsic).

Two questions in the survey addressed the issue of whether the four engaged learning activities differed in promoting student engagement. When asked how engaged the student was in this experience, there was a significant difference, $F(3,105) = 6.51$, $p < .001$, between the four activities. Undergraduate Research ($M = 4.79$) and Internships ($M = 4.65$) were significantly higher in perceived engagement than either Service Learning ($M = 4.29$) or Learning Communities ($M = 4.08$). A similar pattern was revealed when asked how engaging the activity was in comparison to other courses the students had taken, $F(3, 105) = 6.49$, $p < .001$. Again, Undergraduate Research ($M = 4.21$) and Internships ($M = 4.20$) were significantly higher in perceived engagement than either Service Learning ($M = 3.82$) or Learning Communities ($M = 3.29$).

Scores from the SCEQ were analyzed to determine whether the different engaged learning activities promoted different forms of engagement. For Skills Engagement, there was a significant difference, $F(3, 105) = 2.73$, $p < .05$, between the four activities. Undergraduate Research ($M = 4.46$) was significantly higher in skills engagement than Internships ($M = 4.14$), Service Learning ($M = 4.22$) or Learning Communities ($M = 4.19$). For Emotional Engagement, there was a significant difference, $F(3, 105) = 3.50$, $p < .05$, between the four learning activities. Undergraduate Research ($M = 4.16$) and Internships ($M = 4.05$) were both significantly higher in emotional engagement than either Service Learning ($M = 3.70$) or Learning Communities ($M = 3.75$). No significant differences between the four learning activities were found for either Participation Engagement, $F(3, 105) = 1.82$, $p > .05$, or Performance Engagement, $F(3, 105) = 0.89$, $p > .05$.

Three additional survey questions revealed further differences between engaged learning activities. When asked how hard they worked in the activity, there was a significant difference, $F(3, 105) = 6.55$, $p < .001$, between the four activities. Undergraduate Research ($M = 3.97$) and Internships ($M = 4.10$) were perceived as being significantly harder work than either Service Learning ($M = 3.50$) or Learning Communities ($M = 3.24$). When asked how relevant to life the activity was, there was a significant difference, $F(3, 105) = 6.35$, $p < .001$, between the four learning activities. Internships ($M = 4.47$) were perceived as the most relevant followed by Service Learning ($M = 3.89$) and Undergraduate Research ($M = 3.62$) with Learning Communities ($M = 3.33$) being perceived as the least relevant to life. When asked how actively they participated in the activity, there was a significant difference, $F(3, 105) = 5.18$, $p < .01$, between the four learning activities. Undergraduate Research ($M = 4.31$) and Internships ($M = 4.30$) were rated as having the highest levels of active participation followed by Service Learning ($M = 4.07$) with Learning Communities ($M = 3.60$) showing the lowest level of active participation.

Finally, differences in students' intrinsic and extrinsic motivation for the four activities were assessed. When asked to what extent being challenged was important to them in the engaged activity, there was a significant difference, $F(3, 105) = 3.13$, $p < .05$, between the four learning activities. The importance of being challenged was greatest for Internships ($M = 4.37$) followed by Undergraduate Research ($M = 4.15$) and Service Learning ($M = 3.93$) with Learning Communities ($M = 3.77$) showing the lowest level of importance. This suggests greater levels of intrinsic motivation for Internships and Undergraduate Research. There was no significant difference between the four learning activities, $F(3, 105) = 0.89$, $p > .05$, on Extrinsic motivation, as measured by the question on how important it was to get a good grade. However, all four learning activities did show high levels of grade importance; Undergraduate Research ($M = 4.55$), Internships ($M = 4.60$), Service Learning ($M = 4.71$), and Learning Communities ($M = 4.52$).

16.13.   Discussion

The results of this study indicated that undergraduate research and internships were generally more engaging than service learning or learning communities. There are several possible reasons for this finding that are based on the research, including the academic effort, active participation, collaborative learning, relevance, student-faculty interactions, and intrinsic interest that accompany both undergraduate research and internships.

Students responding to our survey indicated that they worked harder in undergraduate research activities and internships than they did in service learning activities or learning communities. Research by Astin (1993) found that academic effort contributes to student engagement. Students also indicated that they more actively participated in undergraduate research activities and internships than they did in service learning activities or learning communities. Kuh et al. (1997) found that active participation also contributes to student engagement.

Collaborative/shared learning and opportunities for dialogue are important factors in promoting student engagement (Wang & Holcombe, 2010). Undergraduate research activities tend to be highly collaborative as are many internships. It may also be the case that the engaged learning activities differ from one another in focus and intensity. Learning communities may involve taking classes together and perhaps a monthly get-together that is considerably less intense than an internship that involves on-the-job experiences and undergraduate research, which typically requires weekly meetings as well as hours in the lab or research site.

One advantage of the internship is that it was perceived as being directly relevant to the students' long-term career plans, a factor that Shernoff, Csikszentmihalyi, Schneider, and Shernoff (2003) have shown encourages student engagement. Another way that undergraduate research activities and internships may differ from service learning and learning communities is the extent of faculty/student contact. As shown by Tinto (1997) out-of-class contact can also promote student engagement.

Finally, it is worth noting that students in this study indicated that they were more intrinsically interested in the undergraduate research activities and internships than the service learning activities or learning communities. Intrinsic motivation is a powerful indicator of when individuals will work harder, persist longer, and maintain their interest in an activity longer. Thus, creating engaged learning experiences that are intrinsically interesting to students is a valuable means of promoting student engagement. Undergraduate research and internships would seem to naturally create intrinsic interest. To make service learning or learning communities more effective, they should be designed to appeal more to the intrinsic interests of the students.

16.14.   Conclusion

Student engagement can be defined as the "student's willingness, need, desire, and compulsion to participate in, and be successful in, the learning process promoting higher level thinking for enduring understanding" (Schlechty, 1994, p. 5). The value of student engagement has been demonstrated in studies that show engaged students do better on tests, report a greater sense of belonging, set and meet personal goals, persist longer on tasks, value educational outcomes, earn higher grades, and are less likely to drop out of school. Previous research has shown that instructors can enhance student engagement by implementing a variety of good educational practices, including encouraging active participation, collaborative learning, and promoting student autonomy.

In this chapter, two original studies provided empirical support for a number of activities that were shown to affect student engagement. At the level of the individual instructor/class, discussion formats, smaller classes, getting to know the students, responsiveness to student questions, and requests for assistance all have a positive effect on student engagement. Moreover, the utilization of effective pedagogical tools such as frequent quizzes and illustrative examples that go beyond textbook material can increase student engagement.

In terms of high-impact learning experiences, undergraduate research and internships seem most effective in promoting student engagement. In conducting research, students are transformed from passive to active learners. They are better able to think critically and creatively, and they become savvier information consumers. Ideally, undergraduate research experiences provide a number of benefits beyond research skill development. Some of the benefits of creating new knowledge include increased self-confidence and a sense of accomplishment in being the first person to know something, learning how to persevere at a task since many experiments will not work out as originally planned, development of self-discipline and leadership skills, the ability to solve technical and procedural problems, and for many, clarification of their career goals as they get a taste of what professionals in the field really do. For students who plan on continuing their education at the graduate level, undergraduate research is highly beneficial (Halonen, Brewer, Bell, & Miller, 2008).

Molseed, Alsup, and Voyles (2003) have suggested that in a typical internship program, the student works for an outside organization, which can be either a paid or unpaid position for an agreed upon number of hours and receives course credit. The student's work is overseen by a faculty member as well as a supervisor on the job. It is important to decide whether the focus of the internship will be on community service or academic understanding. Internships vary in their philosophical orientation. The ultimate goals of an internship should reflect what the department is hoping to accomplish and the structure of the internship will create different outcomes for the students, professors, university, partner organizations and the wider community. For students who intend to seek employment after receiving their bachelor's degree, internships can be quite useful in providing experiences that employers value.

In conclusion, what do undergraduate research and internships have in common that leads to greater student engagement? First, they both involve active learning — taking the initiative and going beyond that which is in the textbook. Second, both require that the student apply what they have learned to material outside of the classroom, in the case of undergraduate research the statistical and methodological skills are applied to answering questions of interest to the student. In the case of internships, communication skills needed for working with clients as well as specific job-related skills are applied. Both undergraduate research and internships require critical thinking in order make the leap between material as presented in a textbook and the demands required for the utilization of that material in situations that are seldom as straightforward as they sounded in a textbook. Both activities provide students with what Dunleavy and Milton (2009) found to be students' ideal learning environment. Undergraduate research and internships allow students to (1) learn from each other, (2) connect with experts in the field, and (3) provide opportunities for dialogue and conversation. Finally, it is worth noting that several of the educational practices discussed in Study 1, for example discussion classes, and frequent opportunities for assessment, also address these same three ideals.

Acknowledgments

I want to thank Martin Demoret, William Wozniak, Theresa Wadkins, Robert Rycek, and Krista Fritson who assisted in the process of data collection and contributed to earlier conference presentations of parts of this research.

References

Astin, A. (1977). *Four critical years: Effects of college on beliefs, attitudes and knowledge.* San Francisco, CA: Jossey-Bass.

Astin, A. (1985). *Achieving educational excellence.* San Francisco, CA: Jossey-Bass.

Astin, A. (1993). *What matters in college: Four critical years revisited.* San Francisco, CA: Jossey-Bass.

Avalos, J. (1996). *The effects of time-to-degree completion, stopping out, transferring, and reasons for leaving college on long-term retention, educational aspirations, occupational prestige, and income.* Doctoral dissertation. University of California, Los Angeles.

Bandura, A. (1997). *Self-efficacy: The exercise of control.* New York, NY: Freeman.

Barkley, E. F., Major, C. H., & Cross, K. P. (2014). *Collaborative learning techniques: A handbook for college faculty.* New York, NY: Wiley.

Bonwell, C., & Eison, J. (1991). *Active learning: Creating excitement in the classroom AEHE-ERIC higher education report no. 1*. San Francisco, CA: Jossey-Bass.

Chickering, A. W., & Gameson, Z. F. (1987). Seven principles for good practices in undergraduate education. *AAHE Bulletin, 39*, 3–7.

Connell, J. P., Spencer, M. B., & Aber, J. L. (1994). Educational risk and resilience in African-American youth: Context, self, action, and outcomes in school. *Child Development, 65*, 493–506.

Cranton, P. (2012). *Planning instruction for adult learners* (3rd ed.). Toronto: Wall & Emerson.

Dunleavy, J., & Milton, P. (2009). *What did you do in school today? Exploring the concept of student engagement and its implications for teaching and learning in Canada*. Toronto: Canadian Education Association (CEA).

Ewell, P. T., & Jones, D. P. (1993). Actions matter: The case for indirect measures in assessing higher education's progress on the national education goals. *Journal of General Education, 42*(2), 123–148.

Fisher, D., Frey, N., & Lapp, D. (2011). Focusing on the participation engagement gap: A case study on closing the achievement gap. *Journal of Education for Students Placed at Risk, 16*, 56–64.

Fredricks, J., Blumenfeld, P., & Paris, A. (2004). School engagement: Potential of the concept, state of the evidence. *Review of Educational Research, 74*(1), 59–109.

Furrer, C., & Skinner, E. (2003). Sense of relatedness as a factor in children's academic engagement and performance. *Journal of Educational Psychology, 95*(11), 148–161.

Gadsby, H., & Bullivant, A. (2010). *Global learning and sustainable development*. New York, NY: Routledge.

Gamson, Z. F. (1991). A brief history of the seven principles for good practices in undergraduate education. In A. W. Chickering & Z. F. Gamson (Eds.), *New directions for teaching and learning* (Vol. 47, pp. 5–12). San Francisco, CA: Jossey-Bass.

Guadalupe, A. (1996). College experiences and student learning: The influence of active learning, college environments, and cocurricular activities. *Journal of College Student Development, 37*(6), 611–622.

Guenther, C., & Miller, R. L. (2011). Factors that promote student engagement. In R. L. Miller, E. Amsel, B. M. Kowalewski, B. Beins, K. D. Keith, & B. Peden (Eds.), *Promoting student engagement, volume 1: Programs, techniques and opportunities* (pp. 10–17). Syracuse, NY: Society for the Teaching of Psychology. Retrieved from http://www.teachpsych.org/teachpsych/pnpp/

Gurin, P. (1999). *Expert report of patricia gurin*. Retrieved from http://www.vpcomm.umich.edu/admissions/legal/expert/gurintoc.html

Halonen, J., Brewer, C., Bell, P., & Miller, R. L. (2008). Why engage undergraduates in empirical research. In R. L. Miller, R. F. Rycek, E. Balcetis, S. Barney, B. Beins, S. Burns, R. Smith, & M. E. Ware (Eds.), *Developing, promoting and sustaining the undergraduate research experience in psychology* (pp. 17–28). Syracuse, NY: Society for the Teaching of Psychology. Retrieved from http://www.teachpsych.org/teachpsych/pnpp/

Handelsman, M. M., Briggs, W. L., Sullivan, N., & Towler, A. (2005). A measure of college student course engagement. *The Journal of Educational Research, 98*(3), 184–191.

Hsieh, P., Sullivan, J. R., & Guerra, N. S. (2007). A closer look at college students: Self-efficacy and goal orientation. *The Journal of Advanced Academics, 18*(3), 454–476.

Johnson, D., Johnson, R., & Smith, K. (1998). Cooperative learning returns to college. *Change, 30*(4), 26–35.

Keup, J. R., Hunter, M. S., Groccia, J. E., Garner, B., Latino, J. A., Aschcraft, M., ... Petschauer, J. W. (2011). *The first-year seminar: Designing, implementing, and assessing courses to support student learning & success*. National Resource Center, First-Year Experience and Students in Transition, Columbia, SC: University of South Carolina Press.

Koljatic, M., & Kuh, G. (2001). A longitudinal assessment of college student engagement in good practices in undergraduate education. *Higher Education, 42*(3), 351−371.

Kuh, G. (1995). The other curriculum: Out-of-class experiences associated with student learning and personal development. *Journal of Higher Education, 66*(2), 123−155.

Kuh, G. (2001). Assessing what really matters to student learning: Inside the national survey of student engagement. *Change, 33*, 10–17.

Kuh, G. (2008). *High-impact educational practices: What they are, who has access to them, and why they matter*. Washington, DC: American Association of Colleges and Universities.

Kuh, G., Pace, C., & Vesper, N. (1997). The development of process indicators to estimate student gains associated with good practices in undergraduate education. *Research in Higher Education, 38*(4), 435−454.

Kuh, G. D., Schuh, J. H., Whitt, E. J., Andreas, R. E., Lyons, J. W., Strange, C. C., ... MacKay, K. A. (1991). *Involving colleges: Successful approaches to fostering student learning and development outside the classroom*. San Francisco, CA: Jossey-Bass.

Laufgraben, J. L., & Shapiro, N. S. (2004). *Sustaining and improving learning communities*. New York, NY: Wiley.

Mayer, A. P., & Tucker, S. K. (2010). Cultivating students of color: Strategies for ensuring high academic achievement in middle and secondary schools. *Journal of School Leadership, 20*(4), 470−490.

Miller, R. L. (2011). An introduction to promoting student engagement. In R. L. Miller, E. Amsel, B. M. Kowalewski, B. Beins, K. D. Keith, & B. Peden (Eds.), *Promoting student engagement, volume 1: Programs, techniques and opportunities* (pp. 2−8). Syracuse, NY: Society for the Teaching of Psychology. Retrieved from http://www.teachpsych.org/teachpsych/pnpp/

Miller, R. L. (2015). Collaboration: Student-faculty research. In D. S. Dunn (Ed.), *The Oxford handbook of undergraduate psychology education* (pp. 225−240). New York, NY: Oxford University Press.

Miller, R. L., & Butler, J. M. (2011). Outcomes related to student engagement. In R. L. Miller, E. Amsel, B. M. Kowalewski, B. Beins, K. D. Keith, & B. Peden (Eds.), *Promoting student engagement, volume 1: Programs, techniques and opportunities* (pp. 18−23). Syracuse, NY: Society for the Teaching of Psychology. Retrieved from http://www.teach-psych.org/teachpsych/pnpp/

Molseed, T. R., Alsup, J., & Voyles, J. (2003). The role of the employer in shaping students' work related skills. *Journal of Employment Counseling, 40*(4), 161−171.

National Survey of Student Engagement. (2006). *Engaged learning: Fostering success for all students: Annual report 2006*. Retrieved from http://nsse.iub.edu/NSSE_2006_Annual_Report/docs/NSSE_2006_Annual_Report.pdf

Pascarella, E., Cruce, T., Umbach, P. D., Wolniak, G. C., Kuh, G. D., Carini, R. M., ... Zhao, G. C. (2006). Institutional selectivity and good practices in undergraduate education: How strong is the link? *The Journal of Higher Education, 77*(2), 251−285.

Pascarella, E., Edison, M., Nora, A., Hagedorn, L., & Terezini, P. (1996). Influences on students' openness to diversity and challenge in the first year of college. *The Journal of Higher Education, 67*(2), 174−195.

Pascarella, E. T., Palmer, B., Moye, M., & Pierson, C. T. (2001). Do diversity experiences influence the development of critical thinking? *Journal of College Student Development*, *42*(3), 257–271.

Pascarella, E. T., & Terezini, P. (1991). *How college affects students*. San Francisco, CA: Jossey-Bass.

Patrick, B. C., Skinner, E. A., & Connell, J. P. (1993). What motivates children's behavior and emotion? Joint effects of perceived control and autonomy in the academic domain. *Journal of Personality and Social Psychology*, *65*, 781–791.

Perlman, B., & McCann, L. I. (1999). The structure of the psychology undergraduate curriculum. *Teaching of Psychology*, *26*(3), 177–182.

Prast, H. A., & Viegut, D. J. (2015). *Community-based learning*. Thousand Oaks, CA: Sage.

Rigsby, J. T., Addy, N., Herring, C., & Polledo, D. (2013). An examination of internships and job opportunities. *Journal of Applied Business Research*, *29*(4), 1131–1144.

Schlechty, P. (1994). *Increasing student engagement*. St. Louis, MO: Missouri Leadership Academy.

Shernoff, D. J., Csikszentmihalyi, M., Schneider, B., & Shernoff, E. S. (2003). Student engagement in high school classrooms from the perspective of flow theory. *School Psychology Quarterly*, *18*, 158–176.

Skinner, E. A., & Pitzer, J. R. (2012). Developmental dynamics of student engagement, coping, and everyday resilience. In S. L. Christenson, A. L. Reschly, & C. Wylie (Eds.), *Handbook of research on student engagement*. New York, NY: Springer.

Slavin, R. (2003). *Educational psychology: Theory and practice*. Boston, MA: Pearson.

Study Group on the Conditions of Excellence in Higher Education. (1984). *Involvement in learning: Realizing the potential of American higher education*. Washington, DC: National Institute of Education.

Tinto, V. (1997). Classrooms as communities: Exploring the educational character of student persistence. *The Journal of Higher Education*, *68*(6), 599–623.

Wadkins, T. A., & Miller, R. L. (2011). Structuring the capstone experience in psychology. In R. L. Miller, E. Amsel, B. M. Kowalewski, B. Beins, K. D. Keith, & B. Peden (Eds.), *Promoting student engagement, volume 1: Programs, techniques and opportunities* (pp. 95–102). Syracuse, NY: Society for the Teaching of Psychology. Retrieved from http://www.teachpsych.org/teachpsych/pnpp/

Walvoord, B. E., & Anderson, V. J. (2010). *Effective grading* (2nd ed.). San Francisco, CA: Jossey-Bass.

Wang, M., & Holcombe, R. (2010). Adolescents' perceptions of school environment, engagement, and academic achievement in middle school. *American Educational Research Journal*, *47*(3), 633–662.

Wenzel, T. J. (1997). What is undergraduate research? *Council on Undergraduate Research Quarterly*, *17*(4), 163.

Chapter 17

Assessing Multiple Dimensions of Significant Learning

Jennifer E. Rivera and William F. Heinrich

Abstract

Purpose — This study aimed to match high-impact, experiential learning with equally powerful assessment practices.

Methodology/approach — We observed three examples of programs, analyzing individual student artifacts to identify multiple learning outcomes across domains through a novel approach to assessment.

Findings — Important outcomes from this effort were boundary-crossing qualities made visible through a multi perspective assessment process.

Research limitations/implications — Future research should focus on the nature of experiential learning and measurement thereof.

Practical implications — Learning design should consider experiences as a means to reflection, which complement content delivery. Instructors may restructure course credit loads to better reflect additional learning outcomes.

Social implications — Learners with this feedback may be able to better articulate sociocultural learning.

Originality/value — Describes learning in experiential and high-impact education; novel assessment of experiential learning in university setting.

Keywords: Authentic assessment; multiple outcomes; experiential; reflection; high-impact practice; embedded learning

Integrating Curricular and Co-Curricular Endeavors to Enhance Student Outcomes
Copyright © 2016 by Emerald Group Publishing Limited
All rights of reproduction in any form reserved
ISBN: 978-1-78635-064-0

17.1.   Introduction

High-impact educational practices in higher education have the capacity to affect multiple dimensions of student outcomes and help students integrate significant learning across courses, internships, collaborations, global experiences, and applied projects (Kuh & Schneider, 2008). High-impact practices include "institutional conditions ... linked with student success, such as supportive peers, faculty, and staff members who set high expectations for student performance, and academic programs and experience that actively engage students and foster academic and social integration" (Kuh, 2009, p. 68). Anchored in various cocurricular and curricular experiences, the value of high-impact practices have been broadly documented in the National Survey for Student Engagement (NSSE). According to NSSE, "Institutions use their data to identify aspects of the undergraduate experience inside and outside the classroom that can be improved through changes in policies and practices more consistent with good practices in undergraduate education" (NSSE, 2015, ¶. 5).

High-impact practices are usually only assessed at the institutional level, removing learners from the assessment and feedback cycle. Through the use of high-impact practices, many institutions claim the value of multiple dimensions of learning yet do not systematically assess for those learning outcomes known to contribute to myriad dimensions of learning. Traditional assessment for intended learning can identify deep disciplinary outcomes. It is less common for assessment of broader or embedded outcomes to take place once faculty or staff identifies intended gains. Because of the nature of high-impact educational practices including active, significant, or experiential inputs, multiple outcomes can be expected to emerge, often evidenced in institutional level aggregated assessments (Kuh & Schneider, 2008). High-impact educational practices can also be assessed at the time of the learning experience for a range of student development, socio-emotional, and affective outcomes in addition to intended outcomes. Broader assessment efforts may contribute to student learning in both deep systems coupled with boundary-crossing applications known to support college and career success (Gardner, 2014; Tinto, 1993).

The purpose of this chapter is to describe a robust assessment process spanning both curricular and cocurricular learning through which digital student artifacts such as video reflections, blogs, writing, and images, were assessed specifically to identify embedded — likely present, but not assessed — learning outcomes and give feedback to students. In this chapter, we identify and describe student learning in three high-impact educational experiences — an applied media service learning experience, a Professional Writing Study Abroad, and international community engagement program. Learners represented their authentic learning experiences through various media (Herrington & Kervin, 2007). Students created digital artifacts to document knowledge, ideas, emotions, actions, personal development, and integration thereof that took place in high-impact learning environments. These kinds of outcomes are often unassessed or undescribed during curricular and cocurricular assessment (Lambert, 2013). Our process to identify embedded outcomes is inclusive of multiple assessment perspectives and resulted in (a) student awareness of more outcomes and pathways, (b) feedback for instructors and institutions, and (c) discussion of additional credentials for learning. Outputs of this research informed course design, provided students feedback, and informed institutional policy about credentials, credit, and/or degree completion.

17.2.   Review of Relevant Literature

17.2.1.   *Experiential Learning*

Experiential learning is a versatile pedagogical approach that can contribute to a number of positive outcomes for college and adult learners (Sheckley & Bell, 2006; Dewey, 1938). This pedagogy uses a mixture of content and process (Kolb & Boyatzis, 2001) and places a value on a learner's relationship with the content (Estes, 2004). Experiential learning describes how learners move through a learning cycle beginning with concrete experiences, followed by reflective observation activity, followed by abstract conceptualization and development of new knowledge, followed by active experimentation with new knowledge and other scenarios (Kolb, 1984).

We adopt the view of experiential learning theory, that not every life event is an educational experience, but prior experience of the student and instructor play important roles in the nature of knowledge development and acquisition (Kolb & Boyatzis, 2001). We rely on one of the prevailing theories in the field, Kolb's (1984) experiential learning cycle, to frame our understanding and discussion of ways to foster curricular and cocurricular learning. Kolb's model of experiential learning is widely recognized and therefore accessible to many users. Kolb's experiential learning theory focuses heavily on the individual, perhaps leaving out inputs of time, context, and environment (Michelson, 1996) but creating opportunities for individual learners to link high-impact inputs and significant learning outcomes. In learning environments where experiential learning is linked with high-impact educational practices, outcomes include both deep levels of content knowledge and broad interdisciplinary sense-making (Gardner, 2014; Goralnik, Millenbah, Nelson, & Thorp, 2012).

17.2.1.1.   Experiential learning in higher education
The experiential learning cycle (Kolb, 1984) has potential to incorporate both high-impact educational practices, or inputs, and significant learning or outcomes. We operationalize experiential learning in the following cases as both an educational pathway chosen by instructors and a *significant learning* process for learners (Fink, 2013; Seaman, 2008). We describe the experiential learning cycle (Kolb, 1984) from the perspective of both the high-impact educational practices operationalized as input from instructors or facilitators and significant learning operationalized as activity and outcomes of students and other learners.

Kolb's model of experiential learning is also rooted in the pragmatic philosophy of Dewey (1938) who makes the case for deep learning, creating strong alignment between the research goals (identify embedded outcomes) and the use of Kolb's experiential learning framework. Assessing learning artifacts for *significant learning* is one way to inform how reflection contributes to the experiential learning cycle (Fink, 2013). We adopt the view that holistic, significant learning occurs as a result of a learner engaging in the full experiential learning cycle (Fink, 2013; Kolb, 1984).

17.2.1.2. High-impact educational practices

High-impact practices in higher education often make use of action and reflection cycles of experiential learning processes in planning and implementation (Kolb, 1984; Kuh & Schneider, 2008). These educational practices are developed at the program level and assessed at the institutional level, where they are known to have influence on students' persistence and degree attainment, as well as on intermediate sets of knowledge, skills, and abilities (Kuh & Schneider, 2008). The American Association of Colleges & Universities (AAC&U) identifies high-impact educational practices known to increase rates of student retention and student engagement. Experiences include:

- First-year seminars and experiences;
- Common intellectual experiences;
- Learning communities;
- Writing-intensive courses;
- Collaborative assignments and projects;
- Undergraduate research;
- Diversity/global learning;
- Service learning and community-based learning;
- Internships; and
- Capstone courses and projects.

Many college students plan to enter an increasingly globalized workplace with increased demands for applied professional skills. High-impact educational practices involve students in problem-solving, integrated learning, teamwork, and engagement in diversity associated with high rates of student success (Kuh & Schneider, 2008; Perez-Pena, 2012). Employers seek graduates who demonstrate both technical ability, and teamwork, interpersonal, and professional skills necessary to succeed in a global environment (Gardner, 2014). Little research is available linking experiential learning cycles with individuals engaged in high-impact practices in college. This research begins to connect rich learning associated with high-impact educational experiences to components of an experiential learning cycle and significant outcomes.

17.2.1.3. Significant learning

Significant learning goes further into Kolb's (1984) Experiential Learning Cycle by focusing on the integration of experience, reflection, and information and ideas (Figure 17.1). Focused at the program and instruction level inputs, significant

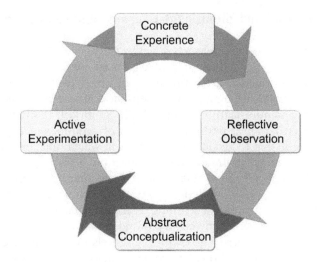

Figure 17.1: Kolb's (1984) Experiential Learning Cycle.

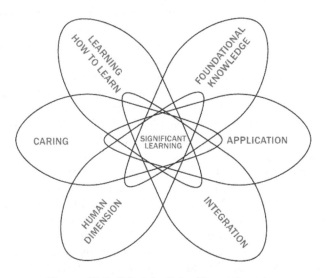

Figure 17.2: Model of significant learning.
Source: Reprinted from Fink (2003). Copyright [2003] by the Dee Fink and Associates. Reprinted with permission.

learning design encourages the use of regular feedback, including student self-assessment to improve the learning design and positively affect learner outcomes (Fink, 2003). As shown in Figure 17.2, good experience design principles integrate course curriculum with six domains to promote significant learning. In this model, responsibility of intentional planning and design falls to the instructor or facilitator while sense-making belongs to the learners, with feedback from instructors.

17.3.   Experiential and Significant Learning and Reflection

Significant learning takes the approach of active learning for integration and, much like high-impact practices can include problem based, place-based, service learning, internships, and other inputs. Educational experiences like these serve to help learners achieve significant learning and often form the concrete experience described in Kolb's (1984) experiential learning cycle. While Kolb (1984) situates experiential learning as a somewhat linear pathway, a number of variations on experiential pathways have been proffered to account for the ways in which time, physical space, and reflective practice interact in unique and idiosyncratic ways to produce meaningful learning for individuals (Seaman, 2008). Reflective practice is common in experiential education and many learning designs so can be valuable for integrated learning. Individuals engaged in significant learning experiences may utilize reflective practices to develop ideas and create ownership of individually gained knowledge.

Reflective practices are associated with high levels of student success indicators (Eynon, Gambino, & Török, 2014) and come in many shapes and sizes. For example, when an in-class lab experiment goes awry, the students and instructors likely make immediate observations (reflections) of the steps leading up to a mistake in order to learn and improve (significant learning). At the same time, a student returning from a six-month study abroad may make reflective observations about cross-cultural experiences for another six months as that person shares stories and/or encounters relatable cultural experiences at home.

However, reflection is an active learning process, and is only sometimes included in curricular planning. Too often reflection assignments are utilized as summative tools to assess learning and not as a practice of reflection-in-action, through which students might develop deeper meanings (Schön, 1987). While this type of summative assessment is valuable, students and facilitators have more to gain when reflective practices are integrated through all phases of an experiential learning cycle (Knapp, 1992) and across all dimensions of significant learning. Additionally, reflection is traditionally seen as a written sense-making tool based on a set of prompts developed by the instructor (Dyment & O'Connell, 2010). This practice stifles the organic nature of the students being able to make sense of the experience through more social forms such as discussion, portfolio artifacts, and artistic modalities (Shotter, 1996). The use of specific prompts is debated as some believe prompts confine critical thinking and transformational growth. As students respond to specific prompts they are inclined to be responding to implied expectations and not authentically reflecting upon experiences in relation to personal development and growth.

17.4.   Assessment for Significant and Experiential Learning

A limitation to the use of experiential learning and many high-impact practices in higher education is the lack of assessment by instructors for outcomes reflecting the significant or high-impact efforts of facilitators or instructors (Lattuca & Stark, 2009; Maki, 2010). Many learning assessments focus on intended, cognitive outcomes. Significant and high-impact outcomes are very often embedded learning outcomes at the individual learner level. Often, experiential education is implemented as an instructional tool without complementary assessments to capture, measure, and/or describe the depth and breadth of possible student learning gains. The individual instructor/facilitator unfamiliar with experiential learning often misunderstands the potential for embedded learning outcomes to contribute to student, program, and institutional gains (Hovland & Schneider, 2011). A combination of assessment tools enable instructors and learners to determine the relationship between programming and student learning outcomes (Scott, 2011).

Facilitators and instructors concerned with assessing planned or intended outcomes (Lattuca & Stark, 2009; Maki, 2010) generally lack the time and resources to assess transdisciplinary learning. In experiential learning activities (Kolb, 1984), reflection is a process in which multiple learning gains are developed, identified, and captured. Reflections are known to contribute to integration across experiences (Kolb & Boyatzis, 2001; Kuh & Schneider, 2008). Despite the importance of reflection, it does not enter into everyday teaching practices, and its use is a significant challenge for many instructors.

Using multiple styles of reflective activity throughout a learning experience (sketching, video, art) in conjunction with traditional activities (writing, discussion) can produce stronger student educational outcomes (Goralnik et al., 2012). For example, the use of video for reflections provides a sharable, multi-dimensional, reviewable artifact of learning domains (Robin, 2009). Video reflections allow for the visibility of embedded learning outcomes such as affective, emotional, and/or social learning (Lambert, 2013). Empirical evidence of the use of video reflection for assessing embedded learning outcomes in any educational context is still lacking (Robin, 2009).

Assessing a variety of pedagogical approaches to significant learning is important to success across disciplines, and influences the breadth of what is learned and understood by learners. Assessment is a central design element of both high-impact educational practices and significant learning and should take into account both the student learning gains on intended efforts and outcomes rooted in the experiences themselves, such as conflict management, problem-solving, and interpersonal communication skills. The institution can play a coordinating role in creating and supporting assessment for both planned and/or embedded learning outcomes (Ewell, 2009). A major factor to consider when assessing for multiple learning goals is that many goals are assessed and then transformed for different student, program, and institution audiences. Program and institutional assessments speak more to external stakeholders such as employers or funders, while student assessments focus on individuals' learning (Kuh & Schneider, 2008). New assessment perspectives are needed to engage both intended and embedded outcomes, known to contribute to student persistence in college and career success (Gardner, 2014; Tinto, 1993).

17.5.   A Method to Assess for Embedded Learning Outcomes

17.5.1.   *High-Impact and Experiential Learning Assessment (HELA)*

Three embedded case studies of student and instructor actions and reflections were used as the primary means of identifying and evaluating learning outcomes in this assessment process. The case studies are Case 1: media and communication students in the College of Communication and Arts and Sciences participating in a non-credit service learning program where they would have the opportunity to integrate and apply learned skills from their degree; Case 2: a College of Arts and Letters for-credit Professional Writing Study Abroad course focused on creative processes; and Case 3: a self-directed for-credit study abroad course in the College of Agriculture and Natural Resources focused on community engagement abroad. Both research-ers recruited the instructors of the planned learning experiences to participate with their students in this study. Recruitment of the cases was based on researcher famil-iarity with the planned experiences. Experiences were chosen because they met criteria of experiential learning in a high-impact educational practice and had potential for significant learning outcomes.

Analyses focused on reflective, rather than summative, artifacts in the form of video, writing, and multimedia experience reports. The analysis of each case varied based on the experiences of the students and the approach of the specific instructor. But in each case, researchers aimed to identify learning outcomes potentially embedded, but not specifically intended by instructors/facilitators.

17.5.1.1. Unit of analysis

The unit of analysis helps to bound and clarify the subject of the case studies. The units of analysis were three high-impact learning experiences, reflecting the research purpose to identify embedded learning outcomes (Yin, 2003). Sources of data included individual artifacts from students and information about the learning experiences from each instructor. Each case of high-impact learning included a defined experience, learners, instructors, and goals. This approach aligned with the project goals that aimed to explore embedded learning in high-impact educational practices.

Students across these learning experiences were undergraduates between 20 and 30 years of age comprised of 21 women and 7 men. The students self-selected into each learning experience as part of individual learning pathways. Instructors included two traditionally trained and experienced instructors (College of Agriculture and Natural Resources and College of Arts and Letters) and one instructor new to higher education with significant previous industry experience (Communication Arts and Sciences). For thematic analysis, the researchers reported on each group as a whole rather than individual students.

17.5.1.2. Coding

After meeting with instructors to review and becoming familiar with intended out-comes from each learning experience, two researchers engaged in an open thematic analysis to code student artifacts (Lichtman, 2013). Both researchers worked together to code all artifacts to identify embedded learning outcomes. Nvivo (v. 10) qualitative coding software was used for all coding. Individual codes emerged from interpretations of student artifacts with both researchers identifying and discussing possible instances of learning. Researchers then linked each learning instance to an existing code or created a new code. For each instance, intercoder agreement was reached through discussion focused on the presence or absence of learning. A single codebook was created for three cases. Initial efforts resulted in 75 unique codes across the three cases. Codes were then aggregated, sorted, and condensed to avoid overlapping concepts, reducing the number from 75 to 63 major codes. Each case description includes a list of all codes.

Secondary coding for rubric alignment took place using 63 major codes. Each code was aligned to all three different rubrics that were relevant to institutional, program, and student career development priorities. Each rubric is described in the discussion section. Rubric alignment characteristics were represented as attributes of each code, rather than new codes.

Descriptive reports of embedded learning outcomes and alignments to rubrics were developed for and distributed to instructors/facilitators at an aggregate level and students individually. Assessment method variations for specific cases will be discussed in each case. This study explored two questions that inform high-impact practices: (1) Can we know more about and describe the ways in which a single learning experience contributes to both intended and embedded learning outcomes? and (2) What are some factors in a high-impact experience that contribute to simultaneously broad and deep student learning?

17.5.1.3. Researcher positionality

Author 1 was trained in mixed methods education research and studies program development and assessment. She comes from higher education working with secondary and community educators and directs an undergraduate program in leadership in integrated learning. Author 2 was trained in qualitative education research methods and currently studies assessment policy and practice. He comes from higher education administration work experience and works part time in various outdoor and experiential leadership roles.

17.6. Case 1: Student-Directed, Cocurricular Applied Media Service Learning

17.6.1. *Project Overview*

The goal of the experience was to initiate a project through which students could apply media production knowledge, skills, and abilities to real-world settings. In this case, students initiated a non-credit, service-learning project. The students called themselves the MSU Media Sandbox, a program for integrated media and communications in the college.

In March 2014, the Media Sandbox implemented the South by Southwest (SxSW) media makeover road trip. The experience was a 10-day road-trip where seven students engaged with four non-profit organizations in three states to implement media makeovers. Students traveled from mid-Michigan to non-profit organizations in Indianapolis, IN, Nashville, TN, Dallas, TX, and ending in Austin, TX.

Students documented learning by reflecting on a regular basis during the trip. Reflections were filmed in a private space with no audience, only the student and the camera.

Students in this project were all between 20 and 24 years of age, two male, five female; all were from media and communications and had completed between 60 and 100 of 120 required credits at the time of the project. An iterative process of observing student reflections on video was the primary means of identifying embedded learning outcomes in this assessment process.

17.6.2.   Coding and Analysis

Coding, as described in the coding section above, took place from April to December 2014. Two researchers cleaned and uploaded the SxSW reflection videos from the seven students into Nvivo data analysis software. Each student submitted between 4 and 7 videos ranging in length from 3 minutes to 29 minutes each for a total of 4 hours and 42 minutes of analyzed film. Researchers applied an open thematic coding process of identifying behaviors, attitudes, emotions, skills, and lessons as evidence of learning throughout all seven sets of reflection videos. Saturation of codes was identified after the fifth student; however, coding continued in order to produce useful feedback reports for students as part of the larger project. Codes were aggregated and sorted for overlapping concepts resulting in 15 major codes and 43 sub-codes (Table 17.1).

Table 17.1: Media sandbox program outcomes identified.

1. Adaptation to challenge	32
Actively reframing problem	3
Dealing with ambiguity	7
Making the best of a situation	11
Role shifting	2
Troubleshooting	6
2. Applied technical skills	6
3. Emotions	23
Frustration	3
Loneliness	2
Neediness	6
Relief	3
Sad	1
Tension interpersonal	4
4. Engaged with community and process	9
Reflexive	1

Table 17.1: (*Continued*)

5. Expressed gratitude	20
MSU	4
Public supports	13
6. Feels optimistic	14
Career goals	3
Empowerment	6
7. Fundraising	2
8. Open to new experiences	7
Being inspired	4
9. Planning skills	21
Goal setting	10
Matching expectations to reality	10
Implementation	4
Recognition	6
10. Questioning	13
Authority	2
Education system	3
Value of experience	8
11. Resilience	3
12. Self-awareness	36
Integrity	1
Learning styles	7
Perception of others	1
Personality	10
Self-aware of presence in experience	9
Working styles	8
13. Teamwork	31
TDeveloping	6
Problem-solving	4
Sharing hardships	10
Successes	10
14. Use of metaphor	1
15. Working with others	50
Communication	6
Developing shared ethos	7
Identified feedback	2
Identify other's conflicts	6
Interdependence	6
Recognize value of other strengths	9
Role clarification	12
Persona-responsibilities	5
Skills	5

17.6.3. Data Description

Codes of knowledge, skills, and abilities that included 25 or more instances were considered high-instance (see Table 17.1). They include: adaptation to challenge (44); emotions (32), expressed gratitude (25); planning skills (31); self-awareness (52); teamwork (43); and working with others (68). These examples of working with others, adaptation to challenge and self-awareness were indicative of the analysis and thought given in video reflections.

17.6.3.1. Adaptation to challenge

Michelle (*Note: pseudonyms utilized throughout the chapter*) noted some personal challenges of engaging with non-profit organizations when volunteering in a home for elderly individuals, a population with whom she had not worked before.

> I asked if I could help out with something and one of the volunteers was asking me to go talk to the older people and see what colors they needed for their paintings. And I just had no idea how to do that, I didn't know how to approach it. One old man started yelling at me, and I didn't know what to do so it was kind of, it was honestly a bit uncomfortable but it was a really good experience. I love being able to actually go see what the nonprofit was doing because it just made me sort of connect with them on another level.

Another student, James, noted some of the challenges and the sense of success with planning and organizing an educational experience.

> This trip is a huge accomplishment for everyone who's been part of it because of a couple major things. We did this on our own, and for the most part. I mean we made this happen, students made this happen. And it took clawing and fighting to get university funding and we got it the last week .... It wasn't easy at all ... it was just ... such a huge impact on my life.

17.6.3.2. Working with others

A student, Anna, noted changes over the course of the trip in her role working with others. She was the appointed producer, so she spent time prior to the trip arranging and planning, so much so that not much was demanded of her early in the trip.

> It's weird for me going from the planning stages to going on the trip just because I had more responsibility when we were planning, taking on this producer role ... put me in charge of corralling the group and making sure that everything is in order and we are getting [things] done finished, and ... on track and things like that ... when we get to the nonprofit, everyone is really self-sufficient and that's great, it makes me really happy. [B]ut, I legitimately don't think that I

contributed anything towards the nonprofit [on the first day]. And that was really hard for me.

Later in the trip as ice storm delays and fatigue set in for the group, Anna was able to utilize both her planning skills to help the group adjust to schedule changes as well as her still-photography skills as roles shifted. These role changes seemed to increase her self-confidence later in the trip.

> I was still timid when I was working in the event taking photos. But I took photos and [non-profit staff member] really liked them, and they're on the new website. I felt needed at the [non-profit name] program as far as photos, which made me really happy because I hadn't been feeling that through most of our nonprofit visits.

17.6.3.3. Self-awareness

Students' self-awareness was present throughout the trip but focused on different aspects of the journey and depth of learning. On a pragmatic level, Michelle noted her own emotional response to an ice storm causing a missed opportunity for interpersonal interactions.

> And I think today was definitely a down … It just really sucked that we weren't able to actually go and help the nonprofit because that's one of my favorite parts is actually going and working with the people … and creating that relationship with them. I'm such an introvert, and I don't make friends very easily and I'm not very good … at people skills overall. So to be able to go and to help these nonprofit organizations and to meet the people who do such amazing work … we were all really bummed out that we couldn't actually go and help the [Organization Name] and meet the people behind the organization.

Later in the trip, Jasmine was able to step back and identify a potential future of these efforts by offering this reflection: "… And we're passionate about this project, and we think that it can impact a ton of people's lives, and if we do this right, it can grow, and it can become this moving, living thing." Students' sense of self-awareness was positively associated with time spent on the experience.

17.7.   Case 2: Faculty Designed, for Credit, Professional Writing Study Abroad

17.7.1.   *Project Overview*

The Professional Writing Study Abroad *experience report* asked students to describe the culmination of a study abroad experience intended and designed to have students explore creative spaces. The experience took place in London, UK, and the project was designed to encourage student reflection on "work, adventures, and experiences" (Grabill, personal communication, July 2014). For seven weeks, students were assigned to work with one of two creative media firms in London during the mornings, and to explore creative spaces in and around the city each afternoon.

Students in this project were all between 20 and 31 years of age, 5 male, 12 female; all from the Professional Writing major and mostly juniors and seniors. Students were enrolled in a course bearing between four and seven credits, as part of a degree program. The goal of the final project was an experience report that was intended to be both simple and complex. In the experience report, the instructor asked students to be able to account for work, to reflect on experience, and to render a story that others could understand. The audience for this report was described as two-fold, the instructor for evaluation and the student for reflection and growth.

17.7.2.   Coding and Analysis

The faculty member and two researchers each examined student work and reflections as the primary means of identifying and evaluating learning outcomes. The process took place in two efforts in the summer of 2014 (instructor) and the fall of 2014 (researchers). In summer, the faculty member identified major themes from analyzing 17 student final experience reports and reflections resulting in 17 categories of common codes. The instructor identified which of these codes were part of the intended outcomes of the course, but did not share that information with researchers.

Two researchers then conducted an independent analysis of the same artifacts. Researchers formatted and uploaded the Professional Writing experience report documents from 17 students into Nvivo data analysis software. Each student submitted one written artifact. One student submitted two short video syntheses in addition to the written artifact. Most written artifacts were in the form of blogs or websites containing pictures or illustrations. Researchers applied an open thematic coding process of identifying behaviors, attitudes, emotions, skills, lessons, and other evidence of learning throughout all 17 artifacts. Saturation of codes was identified after the third of 17 students in the process as students were guided by regularly occurring prompts. Coding continued in order to produce useful feedback reports for students as part of the larger project. As seen in Table 17.2, codes were aggregated and sorted resulting in 13 major code headings with 32 subcodes.

17.7.3.   Data Description

High Instance knowledge, skills, and abilities included codes with 25 or more instances. The categories that met this criteria were: adaptation to challenge (46); critical thinking (29); self-awareness (52); sense-making of experience (43); teamwork (50); and working with others (118).

Table 17.2: Professional Writing program outcomes identified.

1. Adaptation to challenge	46
Dealing with ambiguity	18
Making the best of a situation	14
Troubleshooting	14
2. Critical thinking	29
Compare and contrast experiences	17
Evaluating	10
3. Expressed gratitude	11
4. Feels optimistic	62
Accomplished more than expected	19
Career goals	16
Expectations meeting reality	27
5. Planning skills	14
Goal setting	1
Organizational skill	4
Time management	9
6. Questioning	17
Value of changes	4
Value of experience	13
7. Risk taking	14
8. Self-awareness	176
Cultural self-awareness	34
Learning styles	41
Meta learning	10
Self-aware of presence in experience	27
What do I value?	38
Who am I? (identity)	26
9. Sense-making of experiences	43
Learning transfer	25
10. Teamwork	50
Developing	17
Problem-solving	15
Sharing hardships	11
Successes	7
11. Tension of tourism	4
12. Working with others	118
Adaptation to individual differences	9
Adaptation to work environment	20
Building relationships	20
Communication	23
Developing shared ethos	8
Receiving feedback	18
Social learning	16
13. Interpersonal development	15
Perspective shift	11

17.7.3.1. Working with others

Even though students were working in a setting that closely aligned to their major of study, all students mentioned that there were challenges working with others in relation to the different cultural work environment. The ability to work with others that have different cultural norms and work ethos' was reported as challenging. In particular, Benjamin compared and contrasted the differences of working with others at his home institution to working with others at the agency abroad.

> However at school [MSU], working in groups lends to either dividing the work evenly and then covering for those that don't pull their wait *[sic]*, or taking responsibility for the entire group. Working with the groups I did at [firm] I had a new exposure to group work .... Once the third week rolled around and we got new groups I finally realized it would be easier to contribute what the other members would accept rather than introduce them to my ideas like I had previously tried .... Realizing that my group members process ideas and concepts differently was crucial to how I attempted to convey ideas to them.

All of the participants in this experience shared their perceptions of working with others — strengths, weaknesses, and lessons learned. However, London was an experience that spanned over seven weeks of time, allowing for the students to troubleshoot and improve their ability to work with others.

17.7.3.2. Teamwork

The students in this experience were placed in two different agencies. At each of the agencies the assignments and the tangible outcomes were different. However, at both sites the students were unable to accomplish the goals of the projects if they did not work together as a team. At some points a team could consist of two participants and at others, a team was the entire group including representatives from the local agency. In Lillian's situation, she was working in a team of two with a task to complete a writing project.

> Another difference is our writing. Somehow we cowrote *[sic]* a portion of our paper, and it turned out wonderfully. What happened was I would type a sentence that she said aloud then she would type something I said. We were on the same track and our ideas coincided to create flow. Our jargon varied dramatically though. One specific moment was when I was reading over a paragraph she wrote and it said "whilst." I turned to [classmate name] and said "whilst? Is that even a word?" She then explained how it is the British version of "while" and she thinks it sounds rather fancy. Another example of our differences is that she ends her paragraphs with quotes, and I would never dare to do that. I asked her about it and she laughed and said "I better get used to it" because she ends most paragraphs like that.

Many writing assignments in the *Professional Writing* program on campus are completed individually; however, this internship abroad required team-based writing, including the problem-solving inherent in writing and addressing new audiences. Teamwork became a common point of reflection for individuals on this project because of the style differences between individuals and the need of copywriting to send clear messages about a product.

17.7.3.3. Sensemaking of experience

Finding ways to make sense of challenging and novel experiences is a key factor to the success of experiential education and experiential learning. A student, Andrea, noted how observing the skills and presence of professional women helped her see herself in a future publishing role and gain confidence in her own abilities.

> As I got to know [female supervisor] and [female colleague] I really started to look up to them and they became great inspirations instead of people that I was terrified of. They were so smart and knowledgeable about so many things, and I know it's their job, but it really made me think about my future and how I can take all the things that I have learned with me into the publishing industry. They came across problems every day but ... they didn't freak out over them, they stayed calm and tried to find the best solution that would fix it. Being able to see them apply what they were teaching us to their real world problems made it so much clearer to understand what they meant and how to apply it. After finishing my work there I feel like there is nothing that I can't accomplish and I'm so happy that I have gained the confidence it takes to survive through tough situations.

A number of the students in both agencies noted feeling intimidated at various points by the pace of work, including creative demands, individual personalities, ways of knowing, and problem-solving tasks. The intentional design of learning experiences that led to significant outcomes in this case were not in any way protected from the realities of a demanding industry.

17.8. Case 3: Faculty and Student Co-Designed, for Credit, International Community Engagement

17.8.1. Project Overview

The goal of the experience, from the faculty perspective, was for students to engage in a community abroad and help build capacity with two non-for-profit organizations. In this case, students and alumni built relationships with community partners abroad and developed learning materials to assist with the agency needs. Students in this project were all between 20 and 23 years of age, one male, three female; all students were from different majors and colleges and all in a different level in their undergraduate degree. The students were members of the Bailey Scholars Program, a program in leadership in integrated learning in the College of Agriculture and Natural Resources.

The students worked with two different agencies (1) an elementary school where the local students were preparing to take their English and mathematics exam and (2) a woman's shelter where the women wanted to gain leadership skills in selling and marketing their homemade products. Four of the students participated in this experience for credit. These four students were asked by their instructors to develop a website based on their experiences abroad. The students were required to document their experience abroad through reflective journaling, pictures, and video clips. These artifacts were synthesized by the students and instructors to develop their website. The criteria for the website was co-developed by the instructors and the students. Before going public with their websites, the students were required to have their site analyzed by external reviewers to implement changes based on feedback. The final website (http://www.baileyconnect.org) was published.

17.8.2.   Coding and Analysis

Two researchers examined the website as the primary means of identifying and evaluating learning outcomes. Researchers formatted and uploaded the BSP website pages from four students into Nvivo data analysis software. Each student posted one story about their experiences in Belize and three digital artifacts for a total of 12 digital artifacts. Researchers applied an open thematic coding process of identifying behaviors, attitudes, emotions, skills, lessons, and other evidence of learning throughout all 12 artifacts. As seen in Table 17.3, codes were aggregated and sorted resulting in 16 major codes with 35 sub codes.

Table 17.3: International community engagement program outcomes identified.

1. Adaptation to challenge	1
Making the best of a situation	1
2. Applied technical skills	2
3. Critical thinking	4
Compare and contrast experiences	3
Evaluating	1
4. Emotions	4
Frustration	2
Neediness	1
Sad	1
5. Engaged with community and process	3
Reflexive	3

Table 17.3: (*Continued*)

6. Expressed gratitude	1
Public supports	1
7. Feels optimistic	7
Accomplished more than expected	2
Career goals	1
Expectations meeting reality	4
8. Open to new experiences	1
Being inspired	1
9. Planning skills	3
Goal setting	1
Implementation	1
10. Questioning	6
Authority	1
Education system	2
Value of experience	3
11. Self-awareness	20
Cultural self-awareness	3
Learning styles	1
Meta learning	1
Perception of others	1
Self-aware of presence in experience	2
What do I value?	6
Who am I? (identity)	5
Working styles	1
12. Sense-making of experiences	1
Learning transfer	1
13. Teamwork	5
Developing	2
Sharing hardships	1
Successes	2
14. Tension of tourism	2
15. Working with others	4
Building relationships	1
Recognize value of other strengths	1
Role clarification	1
Skills	1
Social Learning	1
16. Interpersonal development	1
Perspective shift	1

17.8.3. Data Description

Achievement of knowledge, skills, and abilities included codes with five or more instances. Four students resulted in fewer identified embedded outcomes. The categories that met this criteria were: feels optimistic (7); questioning (6); self-awareness (20); and teamwork (5).

17.8.3.1. Self-awareness
The strongest outcome was self-awareness, specifically awareness of values and identity. An example of this was shared by Hannah, who was unfamiliar with principles of community engagement and not experienced with international travel.

> Upon learning about the daily roles of women in Belize and their social status, I reflected on my "hopes" which I found were really, fears. Selfish. Petty. Miniscule …. I hoped to find service in something bigger than myself, while these women hope to enhance their skills to provide a hopeful future for their families.

Hannah was not the only person that expressed this sort of internal reflection. All four of the students in the experience had similar sentiments and related the change in their sense of self to the experience.

17.8.3.2. Feels optimistic
The second strongest outcome was a feeling of optimism. All of the students had indicated that the language barrier between themselves and the community hindered their ability to work together. In particular, Allison was one of the participants that had no familiarity with the Spanish language and felt as though this would be a weakness working in the school system.

> I felt as if I was unprepared for what I was about to partake in despite the weeks we spent preparing for this very moment … I pushed my discomforts aside and opened my eyes to the needs of classroom … As I began assisting the children with their worksheets I relied on other students to serve as interpreters between myself and students who spoke Spanish exclusively. In a way I felt that this was a disservice to the students who spoke Spanish exclusively because I was supposed to be preparing them for exams that would be in English. I later found out that some of the students knew both languages but weren't as comfortable with speaking in English. So, when one of the students who spoke primarily Spanish asked me a question in English, I felt that I had made a difference. It warmed my heart to see that in a matter of days the students trusted me enough to practice their English with me.

Allison demonstrated that she was able to troubleshoot her communication difficulties by working with bilingual youth. She felt more optimistic as the week progressed that the students were grasping the English language. This was very important to her since their exams would be in English, and so their ability to practice the English language without restriction was enlightening.

17.8.3.3. Questioning
The third strongest outcome was *questioning*, in particular questioning the value of the experience. Based on the experience design, questioning could be interpreted in two ways, questioning the value of the experience for the participants or questioning the value of the experience for the community partners. In Anton's case he grappled with both sides — questioning his value as a male contributing in a female safe-space environment and questioning whether the woman who he was working with would value his strengths and grow from this partnership.

> I honestly thought that the communication between the women and I would be hindered because I was not particularly familiar or comfortable with the social norms and customs in the country. It turns out, I was wrong. These women expressed what their needs were and this forged a partnership between them and us on the best way to assist them so that they would get what they needed out of that collaboration.

Most of the students expressed questioning the value of the experience as it related to the tangible outcomes that the women and the children in Belize would develop as a result of their partnership. There were some questions and concerns documented with the amount of Spanish spoken in schools since it was an English school and English is the country's native language. Additionally, MSU students questioned the modeling by leaders (i.e., teachers) since most of them spoke solely in Spanish, perpetuating the language gap.

17.9. Emergent Themes from Data Across Cases

This project analyzed three different high-impact practices to demonstrate that high-impact experience assessment is possible at the individual level. This method resulted in identifying evidence of embedded outcomes in multiple learning settings inclusive of different disciplines, with different goals, and levels of students. Furthermore, all three experiences yielded outcomes known to be associated with high-impact practices relative to the unique experience. The data from three cases are reported in Table 17.4.

Outcome similarities appeared across learning experiences in five major code clusters:

- *Self-awareness*: Presence in experience, What do I value? Cultural self-awareness, Learning styles

Table 17.4: Comparison of outcomes from three cases.

	(A) BSP ALL (4)	(B) SxSW ALL (7)	(C) WRAC ALL (16)
1. Adaptation to challenge	1	32	46
2. Applied technical skills	2	6	0
3. Critical thinking	4	0	29
4. Emotions	4	23	0
5. Engaged with community and process	3	9	0
6. Expressed gratitude	1	20	11
7. Feels optimistic	7	14	62
8. Fundraising	0	2	0
9. Open to new experiences	1	7	0
10. Planning skills	3	21	14
11. Questioning	6	13	17
12. Resilience	0	3	0
13. Risk taking	0	0	14
14. Self-awareness	20	36	176
15. Sense-making of experiences	1	0	43
16. Teamwork	5	31	50
17. Tension of tourism	2	0	4
18. Use of metaphor	0	1	0
19. Working with others	4	50	118
20. Interpersonal development	1	0	15

- *Teamwork and working with others*: Sharing hardships, Developing (teamwork)
- *Feels optimistic*: Expectations meeting reality
- *Questioning*: Questioning the value of an experience
- *Adaptation to challenge*: Making the best of a situation

In a second tier of outcomes we found communication, learning transfer, and problem-solving were demonstrated by learners in important ways. The commonly occurring outcomes led us to an exploration of experience design.

17.9.1.   Self-Awareness and Cultural Self-Awareness

Self-awareness appeared most for learners in the *Media Sandbox* experience, demonstrating high-levels across participants. However, cultural self-awareness outcomes occurred for learners in the *International Community Engagement* and *Professional Writing Study Abroad*. Cultural self-awareness is a central component in definitions of intercultural competence and reflect the realities of interacting with others as an outsider (Deardorff, 2006).

Self-awareness is a learning outcome that is difficult to describe as either intended or embedded, but is very often characterized as having a high-impact. By design of all three cases, instructors reported designing and planning for experiences that would encourage students to develop self-awareness, but did not actively assess for that particular outcome. The subcodes linked with self-awareness gave additional contextual meaning to this complex idea. Consisting of cognitive learning styles, affective values, identity, and behaviors in the experience, self-awareness occurred on many spectrums, perhaps simultaneously.

Upon discussing these findings with program leaders for *Community Development* (Belize) and *Professional Writing* (London), it was clear that learning designs were both intentional and fluid. As learners and outsiders, these students were uniquely positioned to develop self-awareness as instructors in both settings conducted pre-experience expectation setting meetings. Instructors holding an intention can allow space for authentic, and sometimes challenging, interpersonal interactions. Holding space for reflective work is an important planning tool to give attention to the learning dynamics of time spent in creative marketing or community development spaces.

17.9.2. Teamwork and Working with Others

The top *Media Sandbox* outcomes were working with others, inclusive of relationships, value of others, role clarification/skills, and social learning. The *Professional Writing Study Abroad* learners scored the second highest on this code. The key similarity in these two experiences was each required learners to interact with each other on creative projects with client needs placed at the center. The *Media Sandbox* project consisted of multiple short term design opportunities while the *Professional Writing* program placed teams of students on pre-existing marketing and design teams in two different firms in London.

While the *Professional Writing Study Abroad* program was a credit-bearing course and the *Media Sandbox* experience was student directed and non-credit, each endeavor had a similar amount of limited instructor intervention after the design of the experience. Each group of students formed teams and developed joint goals. Both instructors described their approach as advisory of student decisions rather than directive of student behavior and each provided regular mechanisms for reflection. The *Professional Writing* faculty member was in country with students and hosted daily meetings and workshops, which included reflection and debriefing. Much of the debriefing was framed around the work ethos and conversations as to how the day's events played out. Karla, a *Professional Writing* student reflected on her observations when it came to working with others and how to work better with others.

> High pressure seems to bring out everyone's true work ethic, making a very diverse situation. In these scenarios, I learned which type of people I work well with, which I don't, which people intimidate me,

which people really prohibit the group experience, and what my own creative process was. That's when I learned that sometimes others are afraid to speak up in group settings. In group scenarios, I need to look at body language, as well as audible language, to see what everyone really wants.

The *Media Sandbox* instructor, while not on the road-trip, required the use of daily video reflections for students. For *Professional Writing* and *Media Sandbox*, the sense of project success was closely tied to teamwork, perhaps more than a grade or program goals; ownership mattered to the students involved. Matthew, a *Professional Writing* student reflected on navigating the boundaries when working together as a team.

Most of our teamwork also occurred at [firm], and it was in these group projects that most of the navigation across boundaries had to be learned. While I initially assumed that this competency would involve mostly cultural boundaries between myself and native Londoners, I soon realized that these cultural boundaries were basically nonexistent (or, at the very least, insignificant) and that the boundaries across which I would be navigating would be those between myself and my teammates. Actually, the group I was in for the first project actually worked very well together — there were rough patches, of course, but we were initially open about our own creative processes, and sitting down and talking through all our thoughts and concerns every step of the way led to some very smooth sailing for the HR project.

In contrast, the *International Community Engagement* students were not asked to work as a team throughout the experiences and were provided with guided reflection time on a daily basis. They were given the opportunity and strongly advised to move around the agencies and so were not with the same group every day. By design the *International Community Engagement* program was an individualized learning experience.

17.9.3. Feels Optimistic

All three groups of students demonstrated outcomes in these task and career mindset categories: accomplished more than expected, career goals, and expectations meet reality. Students regularly and continually connected their program experiences to career and personal goals. Students demonstrated a continuum of thinking about their experience by demonstrating a readiness to apply lessons learned to career paths. These outcomes also reinforce the need to provide feedback to learners about the importance of reflections and applications of ideas to multiple academic and career environments. Feedback is what helps students develop a reliable narrative of experiences and skills necessary to secure a place in the workforce. Samantha from the *Media Sandbox* displayed optimism based on positive feedback from social media.

> I'm so proud ... our college, Michigan State University is following us on twitter and re-tweeting, telling us they love our story. And it's like, "Yeah, finally!" Seriously guys, we worked so hard and tried to get so much funding ... But I mean like, our university is following us, alumni are following us, everyone is trying to get in touch with us. Our followers are going through the roof on twitter and Facebook we're getting all these likes.

In both the *Professional Writing* and *Media Sandbox* experiences, learners noted feeling less stressed after accomplishing a project or a segment. In several cases, exuberance was present in the artifacts when students accomplished an especially difficult task. The feeling of success in an independent type of project is a marker of non-cognitive strength, an important variable in higher education success (Sedlacek, 2011).

17.9.4. *Questioning*

All three groups of learners demonstrated critical questioning in various ways, showing experiential engagement, comparative thinking, and independent ideas. Several learners in the *Media Sandbox* noted that the value of their MSU courses was limited in relationship to their current field experiences, immediately recognizing a paradox. The paradox was that they would like to have powerful experiences early in their academic career, but realized that they might not learn as much in the field without the benefit of multiple years of coursework. Students in *Professional Writing* questioned the value of group travel, commodified creative spaces, and the value of their education. A student, Jeanne, thoughtfully integrated experiential reflections, questioning her experiences in the context of assigned readings.

> What happened unexpectedly though, and despite my best attempts, was that we would begin our days as a group, travel as a group, experience London and Paris as a group; yet somewhere in this process, and rather frequently, I would get left behind. Separated from the group my experience quickly became at first, rather disheartening, and then my own, not shared. I found myself questioning the validity of my experience, the reality of what I saw and thought, because as Barbie Zelizer explains in *Reading the Past Against the Grain: The Shape of Memory Studies*, memory has been likened to social activity instead of an individual response. This insinuation that the memories I was making were invalid due to the fact that they were not shared with others disturbed me for some time; looking at some of the pictures from the trip, one would never know that I was even there.

Questioning is an important form of critical thinking that prepares students for complexities in future environments and workplaces. Karla, another *Professional Writing* student noted succinctly the nature of work she had experienced prior to the London experience. "The pressure has never been high enough at Michigan State for me to understand all of the different work ethics that everyone has, including myself." Students in the *International Community Engagement* experience noted discrepancies in the education and social service sectors between Belize and the United States, indicating ways they might contribute to closing the gaps. Each learning experience was designed to surface differences and encourage student exploration of these issues. Modes of reflection, including video and written artifacts, facilitated different levels of questioning shown by students.

17.9.5.   Adaptation to Challenge and Making the Best of a Situation

All three groups of students adapted to challenges during their experience. In particular they all demonstrated that they made the best of the situation when events did not go according to plan. In the *Professional Writing* and *Media Sandbox* experiences all students indicated that working with the agencies as planned prior to the experiences was challenging either for logistical reasons (i.e., acts of nature) or for personal reasons (i.e., work style conflicts). However, both groups included students that were able to adapt to said challenges by either changing the planned itinerary, setting new goals, or, through reflective practice. Anna from the *Media Sandbox* identified ways she found useful to engage with community members.

> Do your creative work for them, do what you can do and then do what they do, spend a day in their shoes, you know really figure it out. Talk to people, explore life from their perspective. I think we would learn so much more and I think we would've appreciated this so much more had we had the chance to really get to know and learn from these people. That being said, I do think the things we've done have been incredibly beneficial, and I do think we will stay in touch with the nonprofits.

The *International Community Engagement* students indicated making the best of a situation but at a low level. Guided daily reflections were held with these students as opportunities to express successes and challenges. During these reflections students had the opportunity to adjust practice through planning for the following day thereby avoiding repeating challenges.

The ability for undergraduate students to make the best of a situation is a skill set that is typically not demonstrated because instructors usually mediate the situation for students. Because of instructor mediation, students are not usually forced to adapt to challenging situations in an effort to facilitate content learning. The extent to which instructors intervene influences the way that challenges are mitigated by others and in the cases of *Professional Writing* and *Media Sandbox*, the instructors were much more hands off, while in *International Community Engagement* the instructors were more hands on. The ability for students to learn and apply flexibility in context is a valuable lifelong learning skill.

17.10.   Summary of Emergent Themes Across Cases

Important themes emerged supporting the research goal to surface embedded outcomes.

1. *Self-awareness*: Hold regular program space for reflective work.
2. *Teamwork*: Design experiences for students to work in variously configured teams, including other students and/or community partners.
3. *Feels optimistic*: Watch for learner changes from feeling nervous or anxious to feeling positive optimism.
4. *Questioning*: Design instruction with complementary modes of reflection to facilitate stretch learning.
5. *Adaptation to challenge*: Encourage flexibility in context to promote a lifelong learning skill.

17.11.   Discussion and Implications

17.11.1.   *Applying Institutional and Program Rubrics to Embedded Outcomes*

Institutions and programs place great value on the presence of embedded outcomes. Based on the themes that emerged from the three learning experiences, we aligned findings with three rubrics at the program and institutional level to link to a broader audience. Our reasons for selecting any rubrics were to translate various embedded learning outcomes into a common language that future instructors and learners might find useful. These rubrics were (1) Bailey Scholars Program 5-Questions, (2) MSU Undergraduate Institutional Learning Goals (UILG), and (3) T-shaped Professional. In essence, we asked which currently used learning frameworks might help individuals and the institution communicate the added values of high-impact practices beyond the reporting of course grades. Three learning frameworks are discussed in Table 17.5.

The first learning frame utilized was *The Bailey 5-Questions* (Bailey Scholars Program Faculty, 1999) The *5-Questions* are a learning reflection tool used within a self-directed, integrated learning curriculum at MSU. It focuses on students exploring their learning style by answering (1) Who am I? (2) What do I value? (3) What is my worldview? (4) How do I learn? and (5) How do these connect? Woven together, the *5-Questions* help to inform learners about the importance of lifelong learning and the importance of self-criticality.

Table 17.5: Rubrics alignment by program areas.

	BSP	**SxSW**	**WRAC**
T-Shaped	49	196	535
Bailey 5 Questions	42	168	420
MSU ULG	43	153	436

The second assessment rubric, MSU Undergraduate Institutional Learning Goals (UILG) is a university-level tool developed to assess undergraduate learning experiences (Undergraduate Learning Goals, n.d.). The MSU UILG's are intended to influence learning across the undergraduate experience. The MSU Undergraduate Institutional Learning Goals are

- *Analytical thinking*: The MSU graduate uses ways of knowing from mathematics, natural sciences, social sciences, humanities, and arts to access information and critically analyzes complex material in order to evaluate evidence, construct reasoned arguments, and communicate inferences and conclusions.
- *Cultural understanding*: The MSU graduate comprehends global and cultural diversity within historical, artistic, and societal contexts.
- *Effective citizenship*: The MSU graduate participates as a member of local, national, and global communities and has the capacity to lead in an increasingly interdependent world.
- *Effective communication*: The MSU graduate uses a variety of media to communicate effectively with diverse audiences.
- *Integrated reasoning*: The MSU graduate integrates discipline-based knowledge to make informed decisions that reflect humane, social, ethical, and aesthetic values.

Each learning goal is paired with a locally developed and vetted rubric to aid application across programs to link course learning with institutional values.

The third tool was the T-Shape Professional model (Figure 17.3), a career development tool (T-Shape Professional, 2015).

Grounded in career research (Gardner, 2014; Spohrer, Gregory, & Ren, 2010) the "T" model was developed by leaders from higher education, industry, government, foundations, and professional associations interested in innovative educational models that foster and develop integrated learning characteristics in high demand by employers today and in the future workforce. The vertical section has two parts, deep in one discipline and deep in one system. The horizontal section of the "T" represents the ability to collaborate across a variety of different disciplines. The "Me" in the middle is each student or learner. Engaging directly in the intersection of the "T" components gives individuals an ability to be fully engaged in a wide range of activities within a community that acknowledges their expertise in a particular craft or discipline. Further, the T-shaped professional is able to share information competently with those who are not experts.

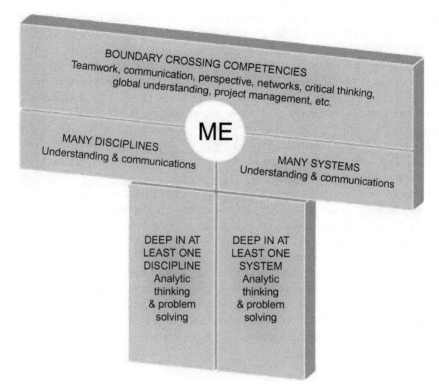

Figure 17.3: T-Shape professional.

17.12. Instructional Implications for HELA

While learning outcomes identified in this study had somewhat limited depth, these three groups of learners demonstrated broad development across learning domains. Unlike institutional surveys of student engagement, researchers observed embedded outcomes in this study, rather than relying on learner self-reports. Observation took place just after the instance of the high-impact educational practice, providing evidence of high-impact outcomes at the time of experience, rather than only in aggregate. By adding feedback reports to individuals, we informed learners how their learning has meaning for college credit, achievement, and career success. Institutional level surveys rarely give feedback to learners in these ways, but rather inform only the institutional leaders with access to the data.

17.12.1. Reflection Strategies

Reflection and any medium used to reflect both take time to develop as skills (Goralnik et al., 2012). The choice of written, video, and multimedia reflection artifacts demonstrated both advantages and drawbacks. A major advantage of video was clarity of affective outcomes. Drawbacks of video were related to technical skills of users such as recording without volume. Video can be a more fluid opportunity for processing reflections and serve to inform written synthesis and analysis as a part of later work (Lambert, 2013). Major advantages of written materials and multimedia with writing artifacts were in the clarity of cognitive outcomes. Drawbacks included artifacts that were not consistent in the quality of reflective material. As a writing style, reflection requires a specific set of behaviors. Stronger writers were able to adapt behaviors to the task, others were not. In written reflections, we had hoped to find evidence of affective and behavioral outcomes in addition to generally assessed cognitive gains.

Limitations to this assessment process centered on time and reflection prompts. Time was a major commitment for the researchers in assessing learning, developing codes, watching videos, reading transcripts, reading essays, and experience reports. Time was a major factor for the participants as well because experience schedules did not permit regular reflection times.

For video reflections, students had no prompts and intended to reflect daily, but could not. As a result, students reflected about three days or more of experience at one time, making video artifacts cumbersome and rambling. On the other hand, students with too narrow a prompt, identified in web artifacts, did not describe the breadth of experience and focused, perhaps too early in the learning process, on sensemaking and syntheses.

17.12.2.   *Provide Proximal Feedback*

Direct and proximal feedback to students on both intended and embedded outcomes provided a number of advantages. Identifying outcomes through a reflection-in-action iterative cycle could inform the program design as instructors modify and/or develop learning goals during experiences. Because significant learning stems from a combination of process and summative assessments of both curricular and cocurricular efforts, students gain more from instructor-generated summative assessment in addition to process-oriented reflective practices.

Through process-oriented assessment, students gain an additional viewpoint into their intended goals and learning, but also gain direct access to a multi-dimensional meta view of learning. At the same time, the use of formative assessments with program/institutional rubrics helps assessors and instructors see learning in the context of transdisciplinary learning goals. An individual student might see evidence of assessment across learning domains and become more aware of their own capabilities (Robin, 2009). This kind of meta-self-awareness is the foundation for lifelong learning (Tagg, 2003). In future research, we might guide formative reflections throughout the learning cycle and ask for multiple kinds of artifacts to capture broad and deep learning across multiple learning domains.

17.12.3. Inform Future Partnerships

Establishing a relationship among intended learning outcomes and embedded outcomes can clarify the interests held by program, institutional, and community stakeholders. HELA data can assist with developing future partnerships between the institution and the agencies based on boundary-crossing soft-skills. For example, service learning is a high-impact practice that has been scrutinized by researchers because students often lack the skill sets needed by an agency and could do harm for lack of awareness (Eby, 1998). Additional learning outcomes data could be used to coordinate a more authentic relationship with community partners.

Significant learning is built on experiences that encourage a learner to act, learn, reflect, and care for the people around them, through both planned experiences and in the course of life (Fink, 2013). HELA method supports pairing significant learning design with matched assessment practices to show all stakeholders the value of a planned experience. Instructors see a powerful pedagogy, community partners see valuable contributions that consider local needs, and learners see multiple ways that their contributions, efforts, and learning gains are valued.

17.12.4. Policy Implications

An assessment process that surfaces learning beyond what was intended may impact credentials, credit, and/or credibility. Instructors with additional feedback and information about student learning can impact the personal, institutional, and external value of a high-impact educational practice. By assessing embedded learning outcomes and reporting back to learners and instructors, we have effectively disaggregated teaching inputs and assessment in an institution that traditionally links these roles without much interruption. From the onset, the intention of this project was to benefit student learning with powerful assessment more aligned to experiential learning. However, asking instructors to accomplish more assessment was not in the range of possibility and given other expectations, may not occur anytime soon.

By collecting evidence of high-impact learning across single course offerings, an instructor could make the case that additional credit might be offered for that course because of known learning impacts. Making a three-credit, one semester experience into a four-credit, one semester experience across a curriculum full of high-impact practices could reduce time to degree for some students. Students might even seek out these kinds of courses in a planned effort to learn more and finish a degree more efficiently (same number of credits earned in less time).

Tuition from the additional credits would not increase teaching inputs because the existing teaching is already providing these outcomes. Additional institutional support from offering fewer courses could be used to hire assessment teams to evaluate high-impact student artifacts. Of course, myriad adjustments to financial aid and degree completion requirements would need consideration. However, shorter time-to-degree and evidence of integrated learning outcomes are attractive possibilities.

Short of additional credit, instructors could offer badges above and beyond the syllabus as an artifact of high-impact learning to support learner use for e-Portfolios, resumes, and other applications. Electronic badges are embedded with information about the activity and outcomes of a learning experience. Learners might cultivate badges to form a credential valued by employers. Minimally, a HELA feedback report provides individual students the opportunity to integrate feedback and lessons from the high-impact practice into their learning plans as well as career paths.

17.13. Summary and Conclusion

This research assessing high-impact practices for embedded learning outcomes utilized various forms of reflections to surface, describe, and compare embedded outcomes from three different high-impact learning experiences. Findings included noticeable levels of learner outcomes across self-awareness, teamwork/working with others, feeling optimistic, questioning, and adaptation to challenge indicating the presence of significant outcomes in experiential learning cycles. While these outcomes could be expected from high-impact educational practices in the course of a student's college career, we were able to identify evidence of outcomes at the time of the experience. Providing learners with this feedback proximal to the experience suggests the potential for utilization of this information for academic, career, and personal development.

The HELA method provides a mechanism to support academic leaders, instructors, and employers who are increasingly interested in self-reflective, emotionally intelligent, content knowledgeable individuals (Spohrer et al., 2010). In these three cases, existing institutional level rubrics were useful in articulating embedded outcomes. The HELA method helped point learners to broad, but contextual, learning goals. By assessing embedded outcomes at the time of the learning experience, students and instructors engaged real opportunities to identify institutional learning outcomes as well as course improvements, and importantly, student meta-learning, all contributing to future growth.

Acknowledgments

This research was made possible with support from Christine Geith, former Assistant Provost and Executive Director of MSU Global; David Wheeler, Director of the Media Sandbox within the College of Communication Arts and Sciences; Jeffery T. Grabill, Chairperson of the Department of Writing, Rhetoric & American Culture; Dale Elshoff, Founder of Spartans Without Borders at MSU. Authors contributed equally to this study.

References

Bailey Scholars Program Faculty. (1999). *ANR 110: New student seminar* [course syllabus]. Department of Agriculture and Natural Resources, Michigan State University, East Lansing, MI.

Deardorff, D. K. (2006). Identification and assessment of intercultural competence as a student outcome of internationalization. *Journal of Studies in International Education, 10*(3), 241–266.

Dewey, J. (1938). *Experience and education.* New York, NY: Collier Books.

Dyment, J. E., & O'Connell, T. S. (2010). The quality of reflection in student journals: A review of limiting and enabling factors. *Innovative Higher Education, 35*(4), 233–244.

Eby, J. (1998). Why service learning is bad. Villanova University. Retrieved from https://www1.villanova.edu/content/dam/villanova/artsci/servicelearning/WhyServiceLearningIsBad.pdf

Estes, C. (2004). Promoting student-centered learning in experiential education. *Journal of Experiential Education, 27*(2), 141–160.

Ewell, P. T. (2009). Assessment, accountability and improvement: Revisiting the tension. National Institute for Learning Outcomes Assessment. Retrieved from http://www.learningoutcomeassessment.org/documents/PeterEwell_005.pdf

Eynon, B., Gambino, L. M., & Török, J. (2014). What difference can ePortfolio make?: A field report from the connect to learning project. *International Journal of ePortfolio, 4*(1), 95–114.

Fink, L. D. (2003). *A self directed guide to designing courses for significant learning.* San Francisco, CA: Jossey-Bass.

Fink, L. D. (2013). *Creating significant learning experiences: An integrated approach to designing college courses.* San Francisco, CA: Jossey-Bass.

Gardner, P. (2014). *CERI research brief 2012-4: Liberally educated versus in-depth training.* Retrieved from http://www.ceri.msu.edu/home/attachment/ceri-research-brief-2012-4-liberally-educated-versus-in-depth-training/

Goralnik, L., Millenbah, K. F., Nelson, M. P., & Thorp, L. (2012). An environmental pedagogy of care: Emotion, relationships, and experience in higher education ethics learning. *Journal of Experiential Education, 35*(3), 412–428.

Herrington, J., & Kervin, L. (2007). Authentic learning supported by technology: 10 suggestions and cases of integration in the classrooms. *Educational Media International, 44*(3), 219–236.

Hovland, K., & Schneider, C. G. (2011). Deepening the connections: Liberal education and global learning in college. *About Campus, 16*(5), 2–8.

Knapp, C. (1992). *Lasting lessons: A teacher's guide to reflecting on experience.* Charleston, WV: ERIC Clearinghouse on Rural Education and Small Schools.

Kolb, D. A. (1984). *Experiential learning: Experience as the source of learning and development.* Upper Saddle River, NJ: Prentice-Hall.

Kolb, D., & Boyatzis, R. (2001). Experiential learning theory: Previous research and new directions. In R. Steinberg & L. Zhang (Eds.), *Perspectives on thinking, learning, and cognitive styles* (pp. 227–248). Mahwah, NJ: Lawrence Erlbaum Associates.

Kuh, G. D. (2009). Advising for student success. In V. N. Gordon, W. R. Habley, & T. J. Grites (Eds.), *Academic advising: A comprehensive handbook* (pp. 68–84). San Francisco, CA: Wiley.

Kuh, G. D., & Schneider, C. G. (2008). *High-impact educational practices: What they are, who has access to them, and why they matter*. Washington, DC: AAC&U.

Lambert, J. (2013). *Digital storytelling: Capturing lives, creating community*. New York, NY: Routledge.

Lattuca, L., & Stark, J. (2009). *Shaping the college curriculum: Academic plans in context* (pp. 145–181). San Francisco, CA: Jossey-Bass.

Lichtman, M. (2013). *Qualitative research in education: A user's guide* (3rd ed.). Thousand Oaks, CA: Sage.

Maki, P. (2010). *Assessing for learning: Building a sustainable commitment across the institution* (2nd ed.). Sterling, VA: Stylus.

Michelson, E. (1996). Usual suspects: Experience, reflection, and the (en)gendering of knowledge. *International Journal of Lifelong Education*, 15(6), 438–454.

National Survey of Student Engagement (NSSE). (2015). About NSSE. Retrieved from http://nsse.indiana.edu/html/about.cfm. Accessed on August 12, 2015.

Perez-Pena, R. (2012). The new community college try. *The New York Times*, July 20. Retrieved from http://www.nytimes.com/2012/07/20/education/edlife/the-new-community-college-cunys-multimillion-dollar-experiment-in-education.html. Accessed on August 18, 2014.

Robin, B. R. (2009). Digital storytelling: A powerful technology tool for the 21st century classroom. *Theory into Practice*, 47(3), 220–228.

Schön, D. A. (1987). *Teaching artistry through reflection-in-action educating the reflective practitioner*. San Francisco, CA: Jossey-Bass.

Scott, I. (2011). The learning outcome in higher education: Time to think again? *Worcester Journal of Learning and Teaching*, 5, 1–8.

Seaman, J. (2008). Experience, reflect, critique: The end of the "learning cycles" era. *Journal of Experiential Education*, 31(1), 3–18.

Sedlacek, W. E. (2011). Using noncognitive variables in assessing readiness for higher education. *Readings on Equal Education*, 25, 187–205.

Sheckley, B. G., & Bell, S. (2006). Experience, consciousness, and learning: Implications for instruction. *New Directions for Adult and Continuing Education*, 2006, 43–52. doi: 10.1002/ace.218

Shotter, J. (1996). Talk of saying, showing, gesturing and feeling in Wittgenstein and Vygotsky. *The Communication Review*, 1(4), 471–495.

Spohrer, J., Gregory, M., & Ren, G. (2010). The Cambridge-IBM SSME white paper revisited. In P. Maglio, J. Spohrer, & C. Kieliszewsk (Eds.), *Handbook of service science. Service science research and innovations in the service economy* (pp. 677–706). New York, NY: Springer.

T-Shape Professional. (2015). [Visual representation of a career development model]. *T-Summit*. Retrieved from http://tsummit.org/t

Tagg, J. (2003). *The learning paradigm college*. Bolton, MA: Anker Publishing Company, Inc.

Tinto, V. (1993). *Leaving college: Rethinking the causes and cures of student attrition*. Chicago, IL: University of Chicago Press.

Undergraduate Learning Goals. (n.d.). Retrieved from http://undergrad.msu.edu/programs/learninggoals

Yin, R. (2003). *Case study research: Design and methods* (3rd ed.). Thousand Oaks, CA: Sage.

Index